Oracle® Web Application Program for PL/SQL™ Developers

ISBN 0-13-047731-1

9 780130 477316

94499

THE PRENTICE HALL PTR ORACLE SERIES
The Independent Voice on Oracle

Oracle Web Application Programming for PL/SQL Developers

SUSAN BOARDMAN

MELANIE CAFFREY

SOLOMON MORSE

BENJAMIN ROSENZWEIG

PRENTICE HALL
Professional Technical Reference
Upper Saddle River, New Jersey 07458
www.phptr.com

Library of Congress Cataloging-in-Publication Data

Oracle Web application programming for PL/SQL developers / Susan
Boardman ... [et al.].
     p. cm. — (The Prentice Hall PTR Oracle series)
  ISBN 0-13-047731-1
  1. Internet programming. 2. Application software—Development. 3.
PL/SQL (Computer program language) 4. Oracle (Computer file) I.
Boardman, Susan. II. Series.
  QA76.625 .O73 2003
  005.2'76—dc21

                                                    2002153608

Editorial/production supervision: Jessica Balch (Pine Tree Composition, Inc.)
Cover design director: Jerry Votta
Cover designer: Nina Scuderi
Art director: Gail Cocker-Bogusz
Interior design: Meg Van Arsdale
Manufacturing manager: Alexis Heydt-Long
Publisher: Jeffrey Pepper
Marketing manager: Kate Hargett
Editorial assistant: Linda Ramagnano
Full-service production manager: Anne R. Garcia
Technical editor: Matthew Kirkpatrick

© 2003 by Pearson Education, Inc.
Publishing as Prentice Hall Professional Technical Reference
Upper Saddle River, NJ 07458

PRENTICE
HALL
PTR

Prentice Hall books are widely used by corporations and government agencies for training, marketing,
and resale.

For information regarding corporate and government bulk discounts, please contact: Corporate and
Government Sales (800) 382-3419 or corpsales@pearsontechgroup.com

10   9   8   7   6   5   4   3   2   1

ISBN 0-13-047731-1

Pearson Education Ltd., London
Pearson Education Australia Pty, Limited, Sydney
Pearson Education Singapore, Pte. Ltd.
Pearson Education North Asia Ltd., Hong Kong
Pearson Education Canada, Ltd., Toronto
Pearson Educaciòn de Mexico, S.A. de C.V.
Pearson Education-Japan, Tokyo
Pearson Education Malaysia, Pte. Ltd.

To Daniel Shultz, for his love, his faith in me, and his valuable insights.

Susan Boardman

To Lori, for her unwavering confidence and constant encouragement.

Melanie Caffrey

To my parents, Mr. and Mrs. Solomon Morse, Jr., for their love, support and guidance.

Solomon Morse

For my grandmother Anne Rosenzweig, who at the age of 93 continues to be a great inspiration.

Benjamin Rosenzweig

About Prentice Hall Professional Technical Reference

With origins reaching back to the industry's first computer science publishing program in the 1960s, Prentice Hall Professional Technical Reference (PH PTR) has developed into the leading provider of technical books in the world today. Formally launched as its own imprint in 1986, our editors now publish over 200 books annually, authored by leaders in the fields of computing, engineering, and business.

Our roots are firmly planted in the soil that gave rise to the technological revolution. Our bookshelf contains many of the industry's computing and engineering classics: Kernighan and Ritchie's *C Programming Language,* Nemeth's *UNIX System Administration Handbook,* Horstmann's *Core Java,* and Johnson's *High-Speed Digital Design.*

PH PTR acknowledges its auspicious beginnings while it looks to the future for inspiration. We continue to evolve and break new ground in publishing by providing today's professionals with tomorrow's solutions.

PRENTICE
HALL
PTR

CONTENTS

ACKNOWLEDGMENTS

This book would not have been possible without the invaluable contribution of several key people. We would like to thank our incomparable technical editor, Matthew Kirkpatrick, for his meticulous edits and painstaking attention to detail. Thanks to Victoria Jones and Jeff Pepper for their support of the book through the publishing process, and to Jessica Balch and her organized team of Mainers for their copyediting and proofreading. Thank you to Jack Smith and his student readers for providing helpful suggestions and comments, and to Douglas Scherer for contributing the Foreword. Special thanks to Dennis Green of Columbia University and Alice Rischert, for her advice, guidance, and encouragement. Most of all, we would all like to thank the students in Columbia University's Computing Technology and Applications (CTA) program. We have enjoyed working with you and wish you success in all your endeavors. Thanks to the staff at Cosi on 6th Ave and 13th St in New York City for patiently serving the four of us through those long 6-hour Friday night meetings.

ACKNOWLEDGMENTS FROM SUSAN BOARDMAN

I would like to thank my father, John Michael Boardman, and am very glad that he bought the Apple II all those years ago. Thank you to Alice Rigas for her encouragement, and to Ned Walsh for his computing expertise and patient willingness to share it. Thank you to Lia Kelerchian for her insight on the publishing process, and to Jim Brown for the privilege of working with a terrific architect and mentor. It has been an honor to write this book with a group of dedicated, generous, and admirable co-authors. I am very grateful for the experience of working with them.

Above all, thank you to my friends and family for their humor, love and understanding while this book took over my life for a little while.

ACKNOWLEDGMENTS FROM MELANIE CAFFREY

Though there were several people who were very instrumental in the writing of this book, the most instrumental were, of course, my co-authors, Susan Boardman, Sol Morse, and Ben Rosenzweig. Without their expertise, good humor, and hard work, this book (let alone the class at Columbia University that it is based upon) would never have come about. I am extremely proud to have partnered with them in this collaboration.

Thanks are also due to the support of my family and friends who understand when phone calls are not returned on time and I disappear into work for days on end. Their love and encouragement make all the effort worthwhile.

ACKNOWLEDGMENTS FROM SOLOMON MORSE

First I would like to thank my co-authors Susan Boardman, Melanie Caffrey, and Ben Rosenzweig. I have learned a great deal from working with them, both on writing this book and in developing the courses at Columbia University on which this book is based. I also value the friendships that I have developed with each of them.

I would like to thank Steven Harris for reading selected chapters and providing valuable feedback. Thanks also to my everyday working colleagues who unwittingly provided support and motivation: Seffi Bejarano, Ravi Urs, Rohit Anand, and Brad Lohnes.

Last, I would like to thank my family and friends for being supportive of me during the time of writing this book: my parents, my sisters Kaye Brewer and Kim Greiner, and my close friend Manoel Azevedo. And a special thanks to Manhattan Samba—the weekly drumming sessions helped to keep sane!

ACKNOWLEDGMENTS FROM BEN ROSENZWEIG

I would like to thank my co-authors Susan Boardman, Melanie Caffrey, and Sol Morse, who have been wonderful and extremely knowledgeable colleagues to work with. This book would not have been possible without them. Initially, the four of us put together the first course on this subject in the summer of 2001 at Columbia University, then we took that material as a basis of this book. This book is a team effort, and this has been a great group to work with.

Finally I would like to thank the many friends and family who saw much less of me than they would have liked during the year I wrote this book. This includes my parents Sandy and Rosie, my sisters Rebecca and Liz, my Grandmother Anne Rosenzweig, and especially Edward Clarin and Edward Knopping for helping me through the long process of putting this book together.

ABOUT THE AUTHORS

Susan Boardman is an Applications Architect for Intrasphere Technologies, Inc. She specializes in the design and development of database applications to meet business objectives. She has supplied and supported intranet Web applications, data marts, retail systems, and university applications. She teaches Oracle Design and Oracle Development lab courses in Columbia University's Computer Technology and Applications program.

Melanie Caffrey is a lead consultant for Proximo Consulting Services, Inc., in New York City, providing front-end and back-end Oracle solutions for the business needs of various clients. She is co-author of several technical publications, including *The Oracle DBA Interactive Workbook* and *Oracle Database Administration: The Complete Video Course,* both published by Prentice Hall. Additionally, she instructs students in Columbia University's Computer Technology and Applications program, teaching courses in advanced Oracle database administration, as well as the class that is the foundation for this book, an introduction to PL/SQL development tools.

Solomon Morse works as a Consultant for Net Quotient Consulting Group in New York City, where he develops e-business Web applications integrated with databases. He has a B.A. in philosophy from the College of Charleston, a J.D. from the University of South Carolina Law School (admitted in New York and South Carolina), and a certificate in database development and design from Columbia University. He teaches Oracle Development lab and Intro to Oracle SQL courses in Columbia University's Computer Technology and Applications program.

Benjamin Rosenzweig is an Integration Specialist at IQ Financial Systems. Prior to that he was a principal consultant for more than three years at Oracle Corporation in the Custom Development Department. His computer experience ranges from creating an electronic Tibetan–English Dictionary in Kathmandu, Nepal, to supporting presentation centers at Goldman Sachs and managing a trading system at TIAA-CREF. Benjamin has been an instructor at the Columbia University Computer Technology and Application (CTA) program in New York City since 1998. In 2002 he was awarded the "Outstanding Teaching Award" from the Chair and Director of the CTA program. He holds a B.A. from Reed College and a certificate in database development and design from Columbia University. His previous titles with Prentice Hall are *Oracle PL/SQL Interactive Workbook, Oracle PL/SQL: The Complete Video Course,* and *Oracle Forms Developer: The Complete Video Course.*

FOREWORD

In Bamenda, Cameroon, an e-mail system "helps the search for global initiatives to improve the living standards of rural communities. It is an invaluable tool for researching issues related to the environment, agriculture and livestock raising."[1] In Bhutan, Internet access is setup in 1998.[2] Meanwhile, the United Nations Development Programme (UNDP), which participates in many of these types of activities, maintains a "Knowledge Connection" site for itself that is used for "linking all the country offices to help share and disseminate [their] best practices on policy and programme issues."[3]

In the business world, executives and other decision makers are armed with sophisticated technology that too often does not provide the information they need. The vast databases in their organizations contain transactional and warehouse data, but end up coupled with only static and marginally useful means for basing strategic and managerial decisions. The mere existence of high technology on a desk, in a server room, or in a village is just one step towards making that technology useful. Rather, successful projects are driven by intelligent and valuable goals.

Focusing too much on technology leads us to forget that we build systems to help businesses, the environment, and people. If we focus on the strategy we're supporting, rather than the technology we're providing, we will not only be more likely to provide the correct technology, but we will additionally make use of non-technological means that allow information to flow through groups of people. UNDP's Knowledge Connection is simply a technological enhancement of the knowledge-sharing culture they had already nourished.

The concept of a Portal emerged as something different than a home page. A home page is "the main page on a Web site. Usually this page will point to all other pages on the site and will be the page people come to first."[4] A Portal is

---

[1]Ghandi, Tamfu Hanson. "Information Empowers Women" Internet (June, 2000) Available: wwwx.undp.org/dpa/choices/2000/june/p20-21.htm, October 2002.
[2]Osborn, Derek. "Prospects for a New Global Deal for Sustainable Development." *Choices*, (March 2002): 26.
[3]Brown, Mark Malloch. "The Internet And Development." Internet (June, 2000) Available: www.undp.org/dpa/choices/2000/june/p4.htm, October 2002.
[4]"Home Page." Internet Available: personalweb.about.com/library/glossary/bldef-homepage.htm?terms=Home+page, October 2002.

"one type of Web site, that aggregates multiple different types of content through uniform navigation."[5] This is an important distinction; the Portal concept more strongly supports an environment for information and knowledge sharing.

Oracle Portal (Oracle's portal development environment and toolset) makes extensive use of the PL/SQL Web Toolkit. So, when Oracle Portal needs extensions that are data driven, PL/SQL makes a great language choice. Entire transactional applications, Matrix reports, and Oracle Portal extensions can be built with the PL/SQL Web Toolkit, then used as either stand-alone applications or portlets.

I was recently asked if PL/SQL is a dying language. The answer, as shown by the techniques and teachings in this book is "no." True, it is a language proprietary to the Oracle database environment, limiting its reach. But PL/SQL has a long life ahead. First, PL/SQL runs quickly because of Oracle 9i improvements. Second, there is a huge existing code base using PL/SQL that would have to be converted to eliminate it completely. Finally, PL/SQL can be used by Oracle database programmers to provide data driven front-ends in a thin-client architecture.

All of the authors are instructors in the Computer Technologies and Applications (CTA) program at Columbia University. CTA is not just a menu choice of classes, but it is a set of four focus areas, each with a strategic and rigorous curriculum culminating in a final project. This book is borne out of the original syllabus the authors developed for the Introduction to PL/SQL Development Tools course. Their students create their final, working projects using the technical skills demonstrated in this book. Now, we can all be their students, and use these same essential techniques in our own PL/SQL Web application development.

Douglas Scherer
Founder and CEO
Core Paradigm, LLC

---

[5]"Enterprise Information / Corporate Portals" Internet Available: compnetworking.about. com/cs/portalscorporate/index.htm?terms=Definition+Of+Web+Portal, October 2002.

PREFACE

Oracle Web Application Programming for PL/SQL Developers gives PL/SQL programmers the knowledge necessary to build powerful applications on the Web.

PL/SQL, together with the Oracle Internet Application Server (iAS), provides a programmer with the ability to truly develop an entire application, from control over complex data processing on the back end, to the creation of a standardized, professional look-and-feel on the front end.

A programmer familiar with PL/SQL, but not necessarily familiar with the Web, can make the leap to building dynamic Web applications using this book. This book brings together the core pieces of the puzzle of PL/SQL Web development in one volume. In addition to reviewing a few basic PL/SQL concepts with examples, the practicalities of building a Web site are covered, including HTML and JavaScript. The essentials of how a computer connects to the Internet are explained, along with how a Web server handles requests for Web pages, Web browsers, image handling, FTP, and some of the basic UNIX commands you need to get started developing PL/SQL Web applications.

As you read and complete the exercises, you apply what you learn by building an application of your own. You create Web pages, connect them to an Oracle database, and use the power of PL/SQL to create a dynamic, database-driven, Web front-end application. The application presented in this book includes PL/SQL procedures developed using both PL/SQL Web Toolkit and PSP approaches, so that you learn and evaluate different development strategies. This hands-on approach gives you the opportunity to address many of the day-to-day challenges that a PL/SQL Web developer faces. Once you create the application, you should find you are ready to apply your knowledge to other projects.

Throughout the book you will analyze code in detail and are offered practical advice on writing—and debugging—complex code. Anyone that has struggled with the realities of JavaScript validation when it is embedded in HTML and PL/SQL, or dealt with similar situations, can refer to this book for tips and examples.

So many different elements work together to create a Web page that coordinating them can easily become the greatest challenge faced by the PL/SQL Web developer. This book focuses, in particular, on clarifying these issues. Many of the questions that a Web developer would ask are answered in this book. For example: There are references available on PL/SQL, HTML, and JavaScript individually, but how do these elements interact? In cases where they can accomplish the same task, how do they compare? What are the limits of each?

Putting all these various elements together to make an Oracle Web Application is much like preparing tapas, a Spanish meal comprised of many different appetizer-sized dishes. The beauty of tapas is the way individual elements work together to create a complex and delicious meal. That complexity is also a characteristic of Web programming. To achieve the results you desire, you must combine your knowledge of many different areas, and how they interact. This can be a tricky and frustrating process, but ultimately very powerful, and ideally very satisfying as well.

WHO THIS BOOK IS FOR

This book is intended for anyone who needs an introduction to Web application programming with Oracle's PL/SQL language.

Readers are expected to be familiar with Oracle's SQL and PL/SQL languages. This book assumes you have the Oracle knowledge that can be obtained from the companion books in this series: *Oracle SQL Interactive Workbook* by Alice Rischert (Prentice Hall), and *Oracle PL/SQL Interactive Workbook* by Ben Rosenzweig and Elena Silvestrova (Prentice Hall). The ideal readers are those with some experience with Oracle relational databases. This book reviews basic PL/SQL concepts, particularly those that are helpful in building the Web application you create by completing the exercises in this book.

Readers of this book are not required to know HTML or JavaScript. When the fundamentals of how to create a Web page are covered, basic HTML and some of the JavaScript used most frequently in Web applications are introduced. We let you know where you can find details on the more advanced HTML and JavaScript features.

The content of this book is based on the material taught in the Database Application Development and Design concentration of Columbia University's Computer Technology and Applications (CTA) program in New York City. The student body is rather diverse, in that there are some students who have years of experience with Information Technology (IT) and programming, but no experience with building a Web application and then there are those with absolutely no experience in either IT or programming. The content of the book, like the class, is balanced to meet the needs of both extremes. The exercises in this book can be used as a lab and homework to accompany the lectures in such a course on Web application development.

HOW THIS BOOK IS ORGANIZED

The intent of this workbook is to teach you about Oracle Web applications by presenting you with a series of exercises that builds towards a complete application. The book consists of three sections. The first section is an introduction to the Web, as well as key concepts and skills required to develop a Web application.

The second section is called "Building the Application." In this section, each chapter walks you through the construction of procedures and Web pages that ultimately comprise a complete application by providing you with all the coding skills required. Chapters in this section cover HTML, JavaScript, PL/SQL, the PL/SQL Web Toolkit and PL/SQL Server Pages (PSP). The complete application specification and source code can be found on the book's companion Web site: http://www.phptr.com/boardman/. The last section is called "Tapas." This section goes a step beyond and introduces the reader to a number of other tools and utilities available to a developer creating a Web site based on PL/SQL code.

ABOUT THE COMPANION WEB SITE

The companion Web site is located at http://www.phptr.com/boardman/. Here you will find three very important items:

1. Files you will need *before* you begin completing the exercises in the workbook.
2. Specification for the application developed in Section II.
3. Complete source code for the application developed in Section II.

All of the exercises and questions are based on a sample database schema called STUDENT. The files required to create and install this STUDENT schema are downloadable from the Web site.

In addition to required files and application source code, the Web site will have other features like additional review questions, a message board and periodically updated information about and errata for the book.

 You should visit the companion Web site to this book, located at www.phptr.com/boardman, to download the STUDENT schema and install it in your database.

WHAT YOU WILL NEED

There are software programs, as well as knowledge requirements, necessary to complete the exercises in this book.

SOFTWARE

Oracle 9i or higher

Oracle 9iAS

SQL*Plus 8.1.7 or higher

Internet Access to the World Wide Web

Oracle 9i Enterprise Edition and Oracle 9i Personal Edition include the Oracle 9i database and SQL*Plus, as well as a core version of the Oracle 9iAS. Further information about installing and configuring the 9i Application Server is provided in Chapter 2, "Oracle 9iAS."

There are various ways to obtain Oracle software. The educational version of this book comes with CDs containing the Oracle software for educational purposes. Oracle also offers trial versions of Oracle 9i for evaluation purposes. These CDs can be purchased at the Oracle Store http://oraclestore.oracle.com.

 Readers are encouraged to join the Oracle Technology Network, or Technet, at http://technet.oracle.com, Oracle's free community for sharing technical information. There is no fee to register with TechNet and some software is available for free download from TechNet for registered users. All Oracle documentation can also be found at Oracle's document site http://docs.oracle.com.

USING SQL*PLUS

You should be familiar with using SQL*Plus to execute SQL statements (refer to the other book in the Prentice Hall Interactive Workbook series on this topic, Alice Rischert's *Oracle SQL Interactive Workbook*). You should also be familiar with compiling PL/SQL programs (refer to Rosenzweig/Silvestrova's *Oracle PL/SQL Interactive Workbook*).

BUILD AN APPLICATION

As you progress through the exercises in this book, you will build your own Oracle Web application. It serves as a helpful, real-world example and a context for the material covered. Employing a hands-on approach is an excellent way to truly learn new material. To gain the maximum benefit this book has to offer, readers are strongly urged to follow along with the exercises. Once you create the application, you should find you are ready to apply your knowledge to other projects.

STUDENT SCHEMA

The STUDENT schema (Appendix A) contains tables and other objects meant to keep information about a registration and enrollment system for a fictitious university. There are tables in the system that store data about students, courses, instructors, and so on. In addition to storing contact information (addresses and telephone numbers) for students and instructors, and descriptive information about courses (costs and prerequisites), the schema also keeps track of the sections for particular courses, as well as the sections in which students have enrolled.

The section and enrollment tables are two of the most important tables in the schema. The section table stores data about the individual sections that have been created for each course. Each section record also stores information about where and when the section will meet, and which instructor will teach the section. The section table is related to the course table and the instructor table.

The enrollment table is equally important, because it keeps track of which students have enrolled in which sections. Each enrollment record also stores information about the student's grade and enrollment date. The enrollment table is related to the student table and the section table.

Furthermore, the schema contains a number of other tables that manage grading for each student in each section.

CONVENTIONS USED IN THIS BOOK

There are several conventions used in this book to make your learning experience easier. These are explained here.

This icon is used to convey notes or advice from the authors to you, the reader. For instance, if there is a particular topic or concept that you really need to understand for the exercises, or if there is something that you need to keep in mind while working, you will find it set off from the main text and accompanying this icon.

This icon is used to flag tips or especially helpful tricks that will save you time or trouble. For instance, if there is a shortcut for performing a particular task or a method that the authors have found useful, you will find it set off from the main text and accompanying this icon.

Web application programming, which combines different technologies to work as an integrated whole, can have many pitfalls. This icon is used to flag information and precautions that will save you headaches in the long run.

This icon is used to flag passages in which there is a reference to the book's companion Web site, located at http://www.phptr.com/boardman.

S E C T I O N   I

INTRODUCTION

C H A P T E R 1

INTRODUCTION TO ORACLE WEB APPLICATIONS

The Web is a powerful front-end for an application, particularly an application built with Oracle PL/SQL.

To build applications on the Web, it is vital to understand what makes the Web work. This chapter reviews the basics of the Internet, the Web, and how a browser works to retrieve a page that you request. The concept of a Web application is explained, both for intranets and for the Internet. Finally, the advantages of using PL/SQL for Web applications are discussed.

U N I T   1 . 1

INTERNET AND WEB BASICS

THE INTERNET

Ask the next person who says *Internet* what they mean by the term, and you may get a surprisingly vague reply. Simply put, the Internet is a decentralized, world-wide network of interconnected computers that communicate with each other in a standardized way. The computers are connected using modems and phone lines, cable lines, ISDN lines, Ethernet cards, and fiber-optic cables. To provide convenient wireless communication, infrared and radio waves are being used increasingly as well.

Physical connectivity is not enough to define the Internet. Communication would not be possible if these interconnected computers did not use a shared protocol for transmitting information. A protocol is a set of common standards and software for communication. You can think of it as a common language utilized for communication between all of the different types of computers and operating systems across the Internet. If an English-speaking person in London calls a French-speaking person in Paris, the telephone network connects the two parties, but that does not guarantee that they understand each other. To send information such as an email from one computer to another, both computers, as well as any intermediate computers the message must travel through, must be able to read instructions about the type of message, its source and destination, and how it should be handled, so that it can be successfully transmitted to and read by the intended recipient.

The protocol of the Internet is TCP/IP, which stands for Transmission Control Protocol/Internet Protocol. TCP/IP actually consists of two protocols working together, TCP and IP, though they are commonly referred to as a single protocol, TCP/IP. Messages sent according to this protocol contain a header—beginning lines of text that are separate from the information being sent. This header provides instructions for transmitting the data. In ground mail, letters are enclosed in envelopes that contain addresses in a standard format, as well as conventional phrases for special handling such as "Air Mail," "Poste Restante," or in less fortunate cases, "Return to Sender." Similarly, when information is sent across the Internet, it is sent with a TCP/IP "envelope" that indicates who originated the transmission, who should receive it, and other instructions to ensure the information is sent and received correctly.

To make it possible to find a machine on the Internet, each Internet location has been assigned its own address, called an IP address, or Internet Protocol address. The IP address is used in TCP/IP when specifying the source and destination for the transmission. An IP address is a 32-bit number. Rather than using a cumbersome 32-digit procession of ones and zeros, an IP address is expressed as four numbers separated by decimal points. An example of an IP is 192.239.92.40. Each number can range from 0 to 255, resulting in 256 possibilities, or 8 bits (2 to the power of 8), so each number can be referred to as an "octet."

Sometimes information being transmitted via TCP/IP has its own internal protocol as well. For example, Web pages are transmitted via TCP/IP, but because they are Web pages, they are also sent with an additional header that is compliant with the protocol HTTP, or Hypertext Transfer Protocol. This protocol, HTTP, is a familiar beginning, or prefix, for Web page addresses.

WHAT IS THE WEB?

The World Wide Web, the Web, or the W3, was started by scientists working at CERN, the European Organization for Nuclear Research, in Bern, Switzerland. They needed a convenient way to collaborate and share technical information with their colleagues. By publishing documents on the Internet, they could access colleagues' technical papers and related information easily. Tim Berners-Lee is credited with being the "Father of the Web" for his vision on how to accomplish this. Standards for the Web are maintained currently by the W3C, or World Wide Web Consortium, an international organization. Its Web site is http://www.w3.org.

As explained earlier in this chapter, there is a separate protocol, HTTP, designed specifically for handling Web pages. Web pages themselves are constructed primarily in HTML. HTML, or Hypertext Markup Language, started as a way to add formatting commands, or "markup" in publishing terms, to a technical paper. The "hypertext" part of the name refers to text that can be selected to provide a link to another document. This makes information retrieval easy, and it is one of the hallmarks of the Web; for example, a technical paper that refers to previously published results can include a link to that previous paper, and the user can click back and forth between documents. HTML is covered in further detail in Chapter 5, "Introduction to HTML: Basic Tags, Tables, and Frames," and Chapter 6, "Advanced HTML: Forms, Nested Tables, and Nested Frames."

 For a preview of what HTML looks like, go to a Web page, right-click in the browser window, and choose "View Source." This text is what your browser is reading and displaying in the browser window.

Usage of the Web quickly spread beyond the scientific community. With the advent of browsers such as Netscape and Internet Explorer, many users could easily enjoy the ease of publishing and accessing material on the Internet. The Web was born from a need to exchange ideas freely, and that spirit is a large part of the success of the Web.

HOW DO WEB BROWSERS WORK?

The Web browser's basic role is to take a request for a Web page from a user, and then display that page to the user. This is referred to as "rendering" a Web page.

Typing the address of a Web page into a browser to retrieve a Web page is an increasingly familiar activity. What happens behind the scenes?

When a user requests a Web page, the browser locates the Web page on the Internet, retrieves it, and displays it in the browser's window.

Someone who is enthused about U.S. tax returns might enter the following address:

```
http://www.irs.gov/search/srchelp.html
```

This address is also known as a URL. A URL, or Uniform Resource Locator, is the complete address for locating a specific page, or "resource," on the Internet. Each Web page has a unique URL, and to view a Web page, you must know its URL. You can also use the term URI, Uniform Resource Identifier, though this is really synonymous with URL.

The first step for the browser is to identify who has the file being requested by the user, using the URL. The browser divides a URL such as the one displayed above into three parts. The first part of the URL is the protocol. In this case, the protocol is "http://", which indicates that the file should be retrieved using HTTP, or Hypertext Transfer Protocol. Another protocol you may see often, particularly if you conduct any business on the Web, is HTTPS. This indicates that a Secure Socket Layer, or SSL, is layered on top of the HTTP protocol for additional security. Despite the HTTP or HTTPS, realize that communication also still takes place using the protocol TCP/IP. TCP/IP governs the connection and transmission of the information, whereas HTTP is concerned with the Web page itself. Because the protocol is identified as HTTP in the URL, the browser knows how to structure its request for the Web page.

The second part of the URL is the domain. In this example, it is "www.irs.gov". The domain identifies a specific server machine on the Internet. A domain ends with characters that give a general indication of the site's purpose, such as .com, .org, .net, .gov, .mil, and .edu, as well as many country suffixes such as .uk for United Kingdom, .de for Germany (Deutschland), and .fi for Finland. The middle portion of the domain provides specific information on the site being accessed. In "www.irs.gov", it is "irs", which happens to be the United States Internal Revenue Service, or IRS. For name recognition, most organizations use their own name, or a familiar abbreviation of it, for this part of a URL, unless the preferred URL is already claimed by another organization.

The leftmost part of the domain is the actual machine name, or hostname. Many organizations use "www" as a convention, instead of a specific machine on their network. When a request arrives for a page on the "www" machine, the company's network has configuration files that redirect such requests to an appropriate machine. Using "www" instead of a specific machine name makes it easier for a company to move pages from one machine to another, or to use multiple machines to handle requests, because the user is not specifying a machine name.

As discussed earlier in this chapter, machines on the Internet are identified by an IP address—four numbers divided by decimal points, such as 192.239.92.40. Yet the domain listed above, "www.irs.gov", is alphanumeric. Which is the correct syntax to identify a machine on the Internet? In fact, both methods of identifying a machine on the Internet are correct. One advantage of using a name like "www.irs.gov" is that it is easier to remember than a numeric IP address, to the relief of U.S. taxpayers on April 14. Another advantage is that the systems administrator can associate an alphanumeric domain with another IP address if need be. If you use the IP address for a site that has been moved to a new location on the Internet, you may have problems getting to the site.

If you know the IP address of the site you wish to visit, then you can use that IP address in place of the domain name, and a browser can understand the request. In fact, you eliminate an extra step for the browser. When an alphanumeric domain is used, the browser has to translate that domain name into a numeric IP address before it can request the Web page. To resolve domains, the browser contacts a specific type of server known as a Domain Name System server, or DNS server. The browser may need to contact several DNS servers to translate the domain into an IP address. Companies may also have an internal DNS server, which must be contacted to provide further translation of domains within a company. Eventually, the browser resolves the domain name into a valid IP address, or returns an error.

The third part of the URL, to the right of the domain, is optional. It may be a file name, perhaps with a path. This part refers to the specific resource being requested. In this example, it is "/search/srchelp.html". The user is requesting the resource called "srchelp.html", which is located in a directory called "search." If the URL does not contain this third part, then a default page is displayed. Most Web sites have an initial page with an address that contains only the domain name, for ease in remembering the URL.

Once the browser reads the URL and knows the protocol to use, the IP address of the machine to contact, and the specific path and file being requested, if any, it initiates a request. It connects to the IP address using a specific point of connection on the target server called a port. Ports are numbered, and by convention, the overwhelming majority of systems administrators configure their machines to use port 80 as the default for HTTP Web documents. For this reason, the port number is not usually included in a URL, but the port can be included after the domain if needed. The syntax is a colon followed by the port number. The IRS example could also have been written:

```
http://www.irs.gov:80/search/srchelp.html
```

to retrieve the same Web page as:

```
http://www.irs.gov/search/srchelp.html
```

Through the connection it has established, the browser sends a request, called a GET request, for the Web page. The server processes the request by looking for the directory and file requested. Sometimes the request is for a page that exists on the server already; this type of page is a static page, and the server can transmit the page to the browser that requested it. In other cases, the page has to be generated. The URL invokes scripts that produce the page dynamically, and then transmit the page. This is how you create the application in this book—using PL/SQL to dynamically generate Web pages that contain database content.

If the request is successful, the server returns the requested page to the browser. If it cannot find the resource being requested, it returns an error message to the browser.

Although a user apparently requests a single file to view a Web page, that page may in turn spark additional requests for files to complete the Web page. When rendering a Web page, the browser may find that the page contains several images, which need to be retrieved in turn. Images on a Web page are themselves separate files, as are audio and video files. If you request a Web page with six separate images, the browser will need to retrieve seven documents to display the full page. Thankfully, the browser figures out which additional files are needed, requests them one by one, and assembles them for you, which would be a tedious task otherwise.

This transparent operation allows users to think of visiting a single Web page, even though that one page may be a combination of several files, or the result of a script that created the page upon request.

UNIT 1.1 EXERCISES

a) What is the protocol of the Internet?

b) What is the main protocol of the Web?

c) Will the two addresses below retrieve different pages? Why or why not?

```
http://www.bbc.co.uk:80
http://www.bbc.co.uk
```

UNIT 1.1 EXERCISE ANSWERS

a) What is the protocol of the Internet?

Answer: TCP/IP, which contains instructions for how to handle a message being transmitted from one location to another across the Internet.

b) What is the main protocol of the Web?

Answer: HTTP. If a message contained within a TCP/IP transmission has an HTTP header, this indicates that the message happens to be a Web transmission; for example, a Web page or a request for a Web page.

c) Will the two addresses below retrieve different pages? Why or why not?
```
http://www.bbc.co.uk:80
http://www.bbc.co.uk
```

Answer: They retrieve the same page. The default port for HTTP is 80, so including the port number 80 in the URL is not necessary.

UNIT 1.2

WHAT ARE WEB APPLICATIONS?

ADVANTAGES OF WEB APPLICATIONS

Applications are software designed to meet a specified need. Word processing software, spreadsheet programs, and data entry tools are some examples of applications.

A Web application is just an application that is deployed on the Web. It is a Web page, or series of Web pages, allowing users to accomplish a task like obtaining information and forms, shopping, applying for a job, listening to Internet radio, or any of the many activities possible on the Web. To use a Web application, a user needs to know a URL for the application, and possibly a name and password. Another way to think of a Web application is a Web site offering a great deal of functionality.

Web pages are truly powerful when they are connected to a database. Such pages are referred to as database-driven pages. Pages are generated dynamically, and include up-to-the-minute information, without requiring someone to manually update the content of the Web page. Pages can provide current news, stock quote information, product availability data, or shipping information by retrieving information from a database at the time pages are requested. Users in turn conduct transactions directly with the database in real time. Connecting a Web page to a database truly makes for a powerful Web site. It is said that Web site programmers eventually find that they need to connect their site to a database, while database developers find that sooner or later their database needs to be accessible through the Web.

Businesses with a Web presence tend to be viewed as more competitive in the marketplace, and some conduct business entirely on the Web. Deploying an application on the Web gives an organization a way to extend their reach beyond the borders of the organization to the public directly. A Web site can be made publicly accessible to anyone with an Internet connection. Interactions with customers that were previously handled by phone, by mail, or in person can be handled via the Web. For example, consumers are familiar with the concept of an online retail store that lets users shop for goods and services, fill up a shopping cart, and "check out" their purchases by paying with a credit card.

INTERNET VS. INTRANET

Organizations can set up an internal network, known as an intranet. An intranet protects the organization from having its internal files and confidential information accessed by someone outside the company. Intranets are often used to facilitate file sharing and email among members of an organization, while blocking access to outsiders.

Web applications can be deployed on an intranet, rather than the Internet. This simply means they are accessible to a smaller group of individuals. Web applications for internal use can be restricted to specific users, and in some cases, specific IP addresses.

When companies create custom applications tailored to meet their internal needs, they make a decision about what type of "front-end" to create, or what interface the users will work with when they use the application. Internal Web applications, restricted to specific users or computers, are increasingly popular within companies. Enterprise applications, which are larger applications used by every area of a company with the aim of every employee conducting business on the same, integrated system, are also being designed (or redesigned) for the Web.

Consider the advantages of using the Web from the company's perspective. An application that is not deployed on the Web typically requires employees to have some type of system software installed on their machines. Installation can be a time-consuming process that grows more burdensome as new versions of the software are released and must be installed on each computer. For example, an annoying screen problem is fixed in Version 1.3.5.2 of the software, but you only have Version 1.3.5.1, so you need to install the update to fix the problem.

Monitoring is needed as people leave and join the company and as computers are reused. This is in sharp contrast to an internal Web site, which only requires a Web browser and an Internet connection. Web browsers come preinstalled on the majority of office computers, and many companies connect computers to networks as a matter of course. In Web architecture, which is discussed further in Chapter 2, application code is housed on server machines instead of on each computer. New versions of Web applications can be made available immediately to all users at the same time by making changes on the servers, instead of going to each individual user's machine.

Perhaps the main advantage of choosing a Web interface is that many employees are already familiar with it. The conventions of browsing the Web—clicking on links, navigating pages, entering data on forms—are fairly consistent. More people are using the Web for shopping or to retrieve information. Colleges and universities are producing more graduates accustomed to having sophisticated on-line services to register for classes, check their accounts, request transcripts, and update their personal information. When new applications require less training because they have a familiar look and feel, then a company can save a consider-able amount of money in training.

Employees may also more readily accept a new application if the interface is a fa-miliar and intuitive one, ensuring that a company's investment in software is a worthwhile one. An elegant and powerful system is neither if it is never used.

The ease of providing information to their employees on the Web has made com-panies increasingly think of ways to computerize and Web-enable their internal op-erations. Many organizations have an internal Web "home" site, restricted to employees only, for publishing relevant information and links. Internal sites are more than a way to communicate information. As a company computerizes more of its operations, an employee can conduct day-to-day business quickly and easily on the Web: request meeting rooms, fill out timesheets, request travel reimburse-ments, apply for internal job postings, and access up-to-date employee directories, to name a few possibilities. The relative ease of developing for the Web means that more and more business functions can be automated on-line. Although the "pa-perless office" is more of a dream than a reality, paperwork or processing time often can be minimized or eliminated by moving to a Web-based application.

ADVANTAGES OF PL/SQL FOR WEB DEVELOPMENT

SQL is the industry-standard language for reading, inserting, updating, and delet-ing data in a database, so it is an essential part of creating dynamic Web pages. PL/SQL, or Procedural Language/Structured Query Language, is Oracle's exten-sion to SQL. PL/SQL adds the sophisticated control structures of a procedural lan-guage, such as loops, if-then-else statements, variable declaration, and exception handling. It was first introduced by Oracle in 1988 and has continued to mature since its introduction. Oracle is committed to supporting PL/SQL, and regularly produces enhancements and refinements to the language.

Because PL/SQL is compiled and stored directly in the database, it has the distinct advantage of being fast. It does not require compilation or interpretation at run-time, and it interacts with the database quickly. Other existing technologies that generate Web content by making use of a database require many trips to and from the database. A JSP, ASP, or Perl script run on the server might go back and forth to the database while generating the HTML page. PL/SQL has the advantage of being in the database, so none of these back-and-forth trips are required.

The advantages in speed are particularly apparent as the volume of data being handled increases. The code is also reliable and secure. Backup and recovery processes for the database also save the PL/SQL code stored in the database. The security and access controls put in place for Oracle database objects, such as ta-bles, also protect PL/SQL packages, procedures, and functions, which are them-selves database objects.

As the title of this book promises, the PL/SQL language that is so effective at handling back-end processing can also generate the front-end application that the user sees. Oracle's 9i Application Server, previously known as the Oracle Application Server (OAS), is the middleware that enables the PL/SQL stored in the database to generate Web pages displayed in a browser. System architecture, middleware, and the Oracle 9iAS are described in more detail in Chapter 2.

Companies using the Oracle 9i database already have PL/SQL, since it is included with the database and does not require separate licensing. Companies using Oracle are also likely to have PL/SQL expertise in-house; there is a large knowledge base of PL/SQL programmers.

UNIT 1.2 EXERCISES

a) What is the main factor that determines whether an application will be deployed on an intranet or the Internet?

b) Why is a Web interface becoming the accepted standard for applications?

c) Does a PL/SQL programmer work on an application's front-end or back-end?

d) Describe some advantages of using PL/SQL for Web applications.

UNIT 1.2 EXERCISE ANSWERS

a) What is the main factor that determines whether an application will be deployed on an intranet or the Internet?

Answer: The audience for the application determines where it will be deployed. If you want to limit access to users within an organization, use an intranet.

b) Why is a Web interface becoming the accepted standard for applications?

Answer: Web applications are relatively easy to build and deploy through leveraging existing skill sets within the business. Users are familiar with the interface, and only need a browser, which is installed on most computers already.

c) Does a PL/SQL programmer work on an application's front-end or back-end?

Answer: Both. A PL/SQL programmer can write programs that manipulate data within the database, behind the scenes. A PL/SQL programmer can also write programs that generate dynamic Web pages for the user.

d) Describe some advantages of using PL/SQL for Web applications.

Answer:

Speed—PL/SQL is stored in the database, so multiple back-and-forth trips to the database are avoided.

Security—PL/SQL programs are database objects and are protected by Oracle's database security.

Integration—You can use Oracle for the entire application, from front-end to back-end.

Flexibility—You can apply existing PL/SQL skills to front-end work or back-end data processing.

C H A P T E R   2

ORACLE 9iAS

CHAPTER OBJECTIVES

After reading this chapter you will learn about:

- ✔ Oracle 9iAS Architecture   Page 16
- ✔ Oracle 9iAS Configuration   Page 32

Oracle 9iAS integrates many technologies required to build and deliver an e-business Web site. The emphasis of this chapter will be to explain how Oracle 9iAS generates dynamic Web content from PL/SQL procedures. We also review the required steps to install and configure 9iAS in order to run these applications. And while Oracle 9iAS has many components, only the core modules of Oracle 9iAS are discussed here.

Oracle 9iAS provides the middleware component of the Oracle Internet Platform and delivers and manages applications and data requested by client browsers. The two other components of the Oracle Internet Platform are the Oracle9i Database and the Oracle Internet Developer Suite. The Internet Developer Suite contains Oracle Tools to build applications, such as Developer, Designer, Oracle Warehouse Builder, and Discoverer. The Application Server is supplied in four versions: Core, Minimal, Standard, and Enterprise. We look at these in more detail later on in the chapter.

UNIT 2.1

ORACLE 9iAS ARCHITECTURE

THE HISTORY OF ORACLE 9iAS

In June 2000, Oracle released a revamped version of their Application Server called Oracle 9iAS (Internet Application Server). The earlier version had fewer features and was called the Oracle (Web) Application Server (OAS). The first release of the OAS came out in 1995. The last production version of the OAS was released as version 4.0.8.2 in 1999. The OAS was desupported by Oracle in October 2002 because the new Oracle 9iAS has become the standard. The basic functionality of the OAS and Oracle 9iAS are similar but the back-end architecture and configuration are considerably different. Oracle 9iAS has a much larger array of technologies and languages it can support. You can generate Web pages using the PL/SQL Web Toolkit with the OAS but you cannot make use of PL/SQL Server Pages (PSPs). In order to fully utilize this book, you need to have the Oracle 9iAS and version 8.1.7 of the Oracle database or higher installed as your Database Server. The reasons for this are explained later in this chapter.

Oracle 9iAS primarily competes with application servers from IBM, Sun Microsystems, BEA Systems, and Microsoft. Other application servers in the market are Borland AppServer, ColdFusion, Delano e-Business Interaction Suite, Galileo, Ganjo, HahtSite, Intertop, JRun, Lotus Domino, NetDynamics, Netscape, Orion Server, PowerTier for EJB, SilverStream, Sybase Enterprise Server, Tango 2000, Total-e-Server, Versata Business Logic Server, Vision Business Logic Server, WebApp Server, and WebObjects. Before deciding which application server you will use, it is good to evaluate the features of the application server you are going to use. In this book we make use of the Oracle 9iAS; this way all components that are being used are also from Oracle Corporation.

TWO-TIER ARCHITECTURE

You must take a look at the basics of system architecture in order to understand the role played by the 9iAS. A very straightforward architecture is to store an application on a single machine with enough processing power to handle it. This is only sufficient for a single user. When an application is shared by many users, the architecture is split into different parts, or "tiers." Two-tier architecture is composed of two parts, client and server, and these two tiers must communicate with each other. The "client," or *front-end,* is what the user sees; it is the user's point of entry into the system. The client tier consists of what programs are required by the client computer to access the application on the server. What the client accesses is the "server," or *back-end,* which houses the database and handles requests for information. In this Client–Server model, many clients can access the same server tier, and receive consistent information.

The two-tier model has several disadvantages. The clients in a two-tier model are "fat" clients, meaning that a considerable portion of the processing power and application logic resides on the client. A client–server application requires a full installation of the client components of the application on the client PC. This involves an executable and supporting DLL files. DLL stands for Dynamic Link Library and refers to a file that is used by a number of applications to perform a common task. It saves applications from having to write repeat program code for common tasks such as printing a file. DLLs are constantly being updated and are available in many versions. These DLL files may conflict with other applications on the client. This becomes difficult to resolve since each user in a company may have a different set of applications on their PC. For this reason, maintaining client PCs in a two-tier application is very costly. An additional problem may be that clients can be operating on different platforms (such as flavors of Windows, Unix, and Mac operating systems), necessitating the deployment of platform-specific versions of applications. Administration and distribution of applications can be a nightmare for the computer support team.

MULTI-TIER ARCHITECTURE

The multi-tier model evolved to address the problems of the two-tier model. In a multi-tier model, a middle tier exists between clients and the database server. This middle tier often consists of an application server that contains the bulk of the application logic. Clients in this model are "thin" clients, meaning very little processing of application logic occurs on the client. Instead, the client requests information from the middle tier, and the middle tier facilitates retrieval of the information from the server, relieving the client of some of the processing load. In this architecture, application logic resides in a single tier and can be maintained easily at one location. In the two-tier model there was one set of application logic on the server and another set on the client. The architectural design of the middle tier is optimized for server functions including access to a database, so it can speed processing. The middle tier can also manage further tasks such as user authentication, caching, as address in Chapter 20, "Web Application Architecture, and balancing the requests it receives, depending on the software.

When an application is deployed on the Web, a web server must be part of the middle tier. The Web server listens for requests for Web pages from clients, which are usually Web browsers. The Web server routes a request to the application server for processing. Once the request is processed, the Web server sends the

Web page to the browser that requested it. Web servers and application servers may be sold individually or as an integrated product.

ORACLE'S MIDDLE TIER

In Oracle's multi-tier architecture, the Oracle 9iAS is the middleware, or software residing on the middle tier. It incorporates both a Web server and an application server. The Oracle 9iAS resides between the client and the back-end database and in this way moves application logic from the client; it is the central, middle tier in shared enterprise applications, providing such services as security, message brokering, database connectivity, transaction management, and process isolation.

Oracle 9iAS enables users to deploy applications on the Web. Web browsers are "thin" clients that do not need any additional software installation since they are accessing the middle tier via HTTP protocol. The only thing the user needs is a URL (Uniform Resource Locator, explained later in the chapter) to launch the application. A server tier houses the original database so that transaction processing can be optimized on the database. This multitiered model offers great savings in administration and maintenance costs when deploying applications.

The HTTP entry point to Oracle 9iAS is the Oracle HTTP Server powered by the Apache Web server. Oracle 9iAS functions both as a simple Web server and as an application server. The function of a Web server is to translate a uniform resource location (URL) into a filename on the server and send that file back to the client's Web browser over the Internet or an intranet. The function of an application server is to run a program or a component and to generate dynamic content. This dynamic content results in an HTML file being sent back to the client's browser. The output is the result of running a program or a script.

The Oracle HTTP Server functions as an HTTP listener and request dispatcher. Based on the Apache Server, the Oracle HTTP Server is mostly C code that runs on top of the operating system. The Oracle HTTP Server receives HTTP requests from clients and is able to serve static files from the file system. It routes those requests that are not static to other services through modules (for example, mod_plsql). These modules, often referred to as simply *mods*, are plug-ins to the HTTP Server. A plug-in is a program that extends the functionality of another program, and could be considered a subprogram. The mods are plug-ins that offer native services (e.g., mod_ssl, which handles a secure socket layer) or serve as a dispatcher for requests requiring external processes (e.g., mod_jserv, which dispatches requests to the Apache JServ). In addition to the compiled Apache mods provided with Oracle HTTP server, Oracle has enhanced several of the standard mods and has added Oracle-specific mods such as mod_plsql.

The middleware is able to determine to which module to hand the request based on the URL. The first section of the URL is the name of the server and the next section is the name of the module. For example, a request for mod_plsql will have a URL beginning as follows: http://ServerName:PortNumber/pls/. . . . The

PLS portion indicates to the Oracle HTTP server that this is a request for the module mod_plsql.

Oracle 9iAS Communication Services are responsible for handling requests from the different clients. The Oracle HTTP Server may directly process a portion of the client requests while other requests may be routed to other components of Oracle 9iAS for processing. Oracle 9iAS can be used to support wireless technologies as well, although this book focuses predominantly on the HTTP services of Oracle 9iAS.

Oracle 9iAS provides multiple features and capabilities that are commonly supplied via separate products. An example of a recent impressive addition to the array of components is Oracle 9iAS Unified Messaging, which gives access to email, voice mail, and fax messages from any device, including computers, telephones, personal digital assistants, and pages. Oracle 9iAS is still under constant development and you will see many additional services being added and modified in the coming years.

THE CLIENT TIER

Clients access PL/SQL Web applications through a browser using the Web protocol HTTP. Oracle 9iAS application components generate HTML, which is returned to the browser and displayed as Web pages. Since Web browsers behave in a similar manner across platforms and they all read HTML and JavaScript, it does not matter what type of operating system a client Web browser is operating on.

THE DATABASE TIER

PL/SQL Web applications are developed as PL/SQL packages and procedures and stored in an Oracle database. You can access database tables through these packages and present the data as dynamic information in your generated Web pages. First introduced with the Oracle Application Server available with Oracle8i, the Oracle 9iAS provides a collection of PL/SQL packages called the PL/SQL Web Toolkit. These packages are also stored in the database and are used in Web-based application packages to generate Web page components and other related functionalities.

THE APPLICATION SERVER TIER: THE PL/SQL GATEWAY

The PL/SQL Gateway enables you to call PL/SQL programs from a Web browser. The PL/SQL programs run on the server and return HTML to the browser. The 9iAS acts as the intermediary between the database and the browser.

STATIC VS. DYNAMIC

A static file is the simplest type of resource the Oracle 9iAS can deliver. A static resource is just a file that resides in the directory of the file system. To make the file accessible from the Web, the Oracle 9iAS maintains a list of mappings (in a configuration file) between physical directories and symbolic aliases called virtual directories.

A dynamic Web page is where the content is selected from the database and assembled into HTML to create an html file. For example, the number of students enrolled in a class may constantly change as students sign up and later drop out. An administrator may need to see a list of students officially enrolled in a course at any given time. This information is available in the database. A dynamic Web page will show this information by querying the database. The HTML is written and then sent to the client browser of the administrator. The Web server delivers this to the client. Oracle 9iAS can deliver content for the Internet or for internal and external intranets in the form of static and dynamic Web pages.

STATE

When a user logs into a database, all of their activities are tracked as being part of that user's session. One challenge for Web application developers is to maintain information from one Web page to the next in the same way that a user connected to a database has a series of transactions that can be rolled back or committed. Web browsing does not inherently preserve state. A browser requests a page, and the page is returned to the browser, end of story. The IAS can process two types of transactions, stateless and stateful transactions.

- Stateless transactions (the most common Web transactions) do not carry "state" from one Web page to another. They consist of a request from the client and then a response from the server. Once the response has been delivered the transaction is complete. The next transaction will have no relation to the prior transaction or the following transaction. Generally, user and session information is not captured by the application server.

- Stateful transactions do carry "state" from one transaction to another. They are similar to a database session. In a database session, a user may perform a number of inserts or updates before committing or rolling back the information. A stateful transaction operates in a similar manner.

In a stateless environment, each HTTP request from a client maps to a new database session. Application state is typically maintained in HTTP cookies or database tables. Transaction state cannot span across requests. If a PL/SQL procedure executes successfully, an implicit commit is performed. If it executes with an error, an implicit rollback is performed. Cookies will be covered in more detail in Chapter 15, "Maintaining State with Cookies and Tables."

In a stateful environment, each HTTP request from a client maps to the same database session. Application state is preserved in PL/SQL package variables. A transaction can span across requests because no implicit commits or rollbacks are performed.

- Oracle 9iAS with mod_plsql supports running in stateless mode only. This is the recommended configuration for users who want to develop stateless PL/SQL-based Web applications. In stateless mode, mod_plsql has a connection that keeps the database sessions open between HTTP requests, preventing the need for the user to log in with each Web page.

- Oracle 9iAS with mod_ose supports running in both stateless and stateful mode. When using mod_ose, the stateful mode is preferable because a new database session does not have to be created and destroyed for every HTTP request.

ORACLE HTTP SERVER MODULES (MODS)

In addition to the compiled Apache modules (referred to here as simply *mods*) provided with the Oracle HTTP Server, which support current Internet application technologies to deliver dynamic Web pages, Oracle has enhanced several of the standard Apache mods and has added Oracle-specific mods. For more information, refer to http://www.apache.org/docs/mod/index.html. main mods to consider are:

> MOD_PLSQL: This module is an HTTP Server plug-in that dispatches requests for PL/SQL and Java stored procedures to an Oracle database. Mod_PLSQL is the most efficient SQL interface for generating HTML. The HTTP Server identifies the request as belonging to this module, based on the URL from the client. HTTP requests that are identified are handed from the HTTP Server to mod_plsql. These requests are then mapped to database stored procedures. The module maintains database connections specified by database access descriptors (DAD). The application that is built in this book is designed to run using this module. This module is installed in all versions of the Oracle 9iAS.

> MOD_OSE: This module delegates URLs to stateful Java and PL/SQL servlets in the Oracle Servlet Engine (OSE) contained in an Oracle database. It keeps session IDs in cookies, or redirected URLs, and routes requests to the appropriate OSE sessions over NS (Net8, referred to as Oracle Net in Oracle9i.)

The other mods that are commonly used are the mod_perl for Perl; mod_jserv, a servlet engine; and mod_ssl for secure socket layer connections. Oracle 9iAS has many other exciting features, but there are far too many to discuss them all in detail here. They range from Oracle Forms, Reports, and Discoverer Queries being deployed over the Web as well as innovations such as the Oracle Internet File System, which is a service that stores files in an Oracle database. The range also includes Oracle products such as Oracle Portal, an application that can quickly build a Web portal. Refer to the Oracle 9iAS installation guide for details on installation and configuration.

IMPORTANT ORACLE 9iAS COMPONENTS

The Oracle 9iAS consists of numerous components. These are constantly evolving and more components are being added. The components that are addressed in this book are:

- *Oracle PL/SQL Server Pages (Oracle PSP)*—These are very similar to Oracle JSP. Oracle's LoadPSP will translate a PSP file and create a database stored procedure. This stored procedure is then accessed by Web requests through mod_plsql. This will be addressed in detail in Chapter 12, "Working with PL/SQL Server Pages (PSPs)."
- *PL/SQL Web Toolkit* provides support for building and deploying PL/SQL-based applications on the Web. PL/SQL stored procedures can retrieve data from database tables and generate HTTP responses containing data and code to display in a Web browser. This will be discussed in more detail starting with Chapter 10, "Web Toolkit I: HTML and JavaScript with PL/SQL."
- *Servlets* are often Java applications (though Oracle now offers PL/SQL servlets) that run in a server-side environment and service requests from the clients.
- *Database and Web Cache* stores frequently accessed data and applications on the middle tier. This setup routes queries transparently to the cache or back-end database.
- *Load Balancing* maximizes scalability and uses hardware efficiently through balancing the client load among various servers.
- *iSQL*Plus* is a Web-based SQL*Plus client tool. Figure 2.1 is a sample of the logon screen and Figure 2.2 is a sample of working within the SQL*Plus application.

If the Oracle 9iAS server had the name MyServer, then the iSQL*Plus application could be run by the URL http://MyServer/isqlplus. If the Oracle 9iAS server and the Database were installed on the same server and in the same Oracle Home, then a connect string would not be needed. In any other situation you will need to use the proper service name from the tnsnames.ora file in the network/admin directory of the Oracle 9iAS Oracle Home.

PL/SQL WEB TOOLKIT PACKAGES

The PL/SQL Web toolkit consists of a number of Oracle-supplied packages. You have worked with Oracle-supplied packages such as DBMS_OUTPUT when you were learning PL/SQL. In the former version of the application server the OAS installed the PL/SQL Web Toolkit packages in an OWA (Oracle Web Application) user such as OAS_PUBLIC. Starting with Oracle 8.1.7 and Oracle 9iAS, a number of new packages have been added to the Toolkit. These packages are installed in

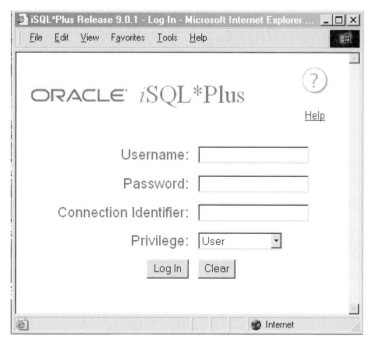

Figure 2.1 ■ The iSQL*Plus Logon screen.

the SYS user's schema. Oracle 9iAS installs the following packages: OWA_CUSTOM, OWA_GLOBAL, HTF, HTP, OWA_COOKIE, OWA_IMAGE, OWA_OPT_LOCK, OWA_PATTERN, OWA_SEC, OWA_TEXT, OWA_UTIL, OWA_INIT, OWA_CACHE, and WPG_DOCLOAD. Note that Oracle Portal 3.0 depends on the new PL/SQL Web Toolkit packages.

- In earlier versions of Oracle iAS, users of mod_plsql were required to manually install these packages into the SYS schema. These packages are located under the $IAS_HOME/Apache/modplsql/owa directory.
- In an 8.1.7 installation and above, the new PL/SQL Web Toolkit packages are located under the $ORACLE_HOME/rdbms/admin directory and are installed into the SYS schema.

THE PROCESS OF RUNNING A WEB PAGE VIA MOD_PLSQL

When entering a URL that launches a Web page generated by an Oracle procedure, follow this format:

```
Http://Host_Name:Port_Number/pls/DAD_Name/Procedure_Name
```

The default port for the Oracle HTTP server is 80, so if you are using this default port you do not need to specify the port number in the URL. Different versions of the Oracle iAS install on different default ports. It can be 80 and is also often Port 7778.

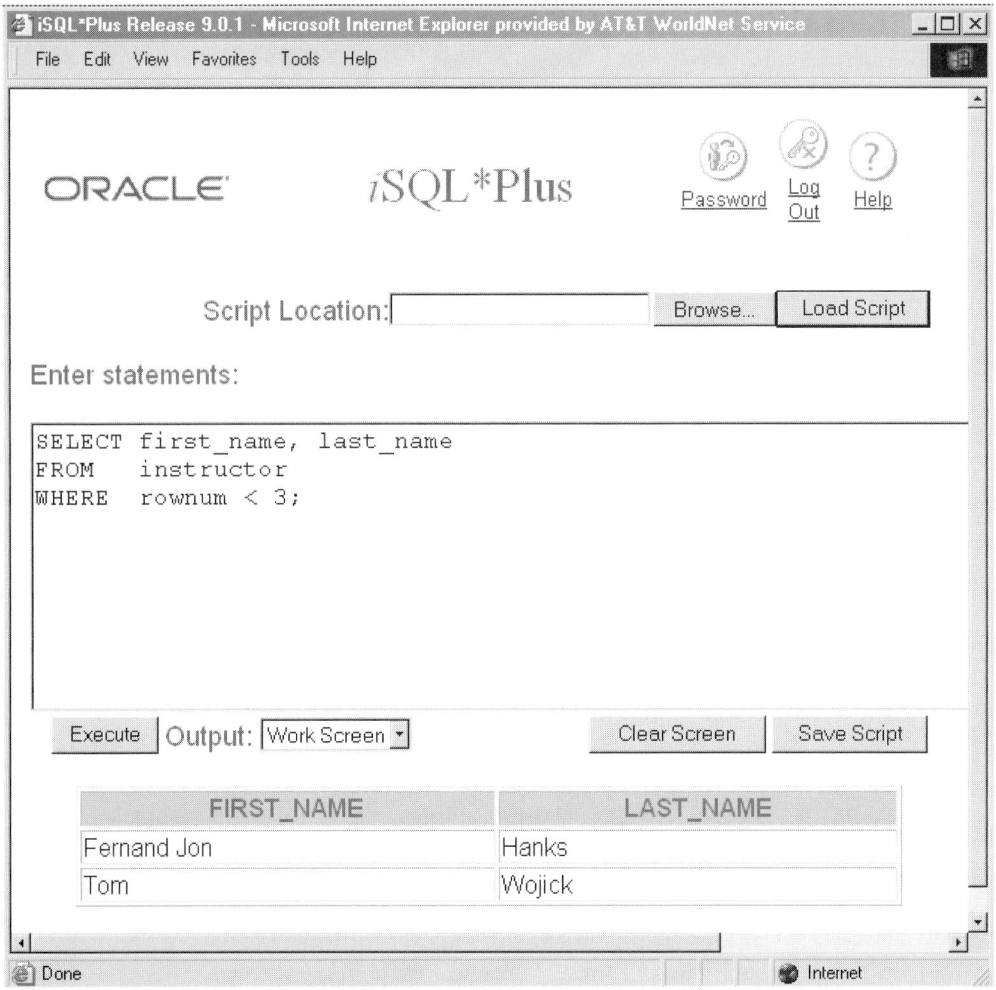

Figure 2.2 ■ The iSQL*Plus application.

Each PC or server on a network has a unique IP address. This IP address has virtual divisions and these divisions are known as ports. Certain ports are set aside for certain processes. For example, Port 1521 is generally reserved for the Oracle Database listener. Port 80 is used for a Web server.

COMMUNICATION FLOW: THE PATH OF HTTP REQUESTS

1. The browser sends a URL to the HTTP listener. The listener examines the URL and determines that the request is for the PL/SQL Gateway (a URL beginning with the format http://servername:PortNumber/pls gives this indication.)

2. The mod_plsql uses the Database Access Descriptor's (DAD) configuration values to determine how to connect to the database.

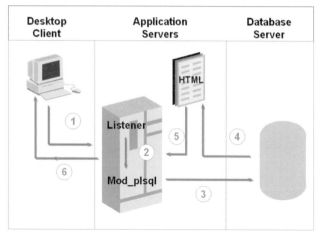

Figure 2.3 ■ mod_plsql communication flow.

3. The mod_plsql connects to the database, prepares the call parameters, and invokes the named PL/SQL procedure.

4. The PL/SQL procedure generates an HTML page, which can include dynamic data accessed from tables in the database, as well as static data.

5. The output from the procedure is returned by way of the response buffer to the PL/SQL Gateway.

6. The Oracle HTTP Server sends the response back to the client.

CONNECTING TO A REMOTE DATABASE SERVER

A full discussion of Oracle networking is beyond the scope of this book; however, since you are learning to build Web applications that access an Oracle database, some discussion in how to get started in connecting your applications to an Oracle database is necessary.

Oracle's networking solutions involve many different components, as well as many different implementations. This chapter focuses on the basic networking components that a Web developer would be concerned with. All other types of networking configurations are usually set up and maintained by a database administrator or systems administrator.

Oracle Net (a set of networking components, known as Net8 for Oracle8 and Oracle8i and SQL*Net prior to Oracle8) makes database communication with an Oracle database possible. These components can support connections from the same machine that the database is on, or from remote machines.

The Oracle *listener* is one of the important components of Oracle networking. It is the process responsible for receiving database connection requests and redirecting them to another process, which then becomes the main point of contact between the client and the database. The information needed to establish connections with an Oracle database is stored in several configuration files. Two such files are the listener.ora file and the tnsnames.ora file.

Your database administrator should maintain the listener.ora file. A typical Web developer is not responsible for maintaining this file since it resides only on the database server. Therefore, this discussion will focus on the one of these two files that a Web developer will most often be working with—tnsnames.ora, which resides on both the client and the server.

Both of these files can be found in a location referred to as the TNS_ADMIN directory. The TNS_ADMIN directory location depends on the version of the Oracle Server that is installed. For versions 7.x, 8.1.x, and beyond (for instance, in an NT environment), the TNS_ADMIN directory is usually <ORACLE_HOME>\ network\admin; for version 8.0.x, it is usually found at ORACLE_HOME\net80\ admin. In UNIX, the default location for these files would be written as $ORACLE_HOME/network/admin.

The listener.ora file simply contains configuration information for the Oracle listener. The tnsnames.ora file is used in defining *TNS net service names*. "TNS" stands for Transparent Network Substrate, and it serves as a single, common interface to most industry-standard networking protocols. TNS service names are resolved in the tnsnames.ora file, which contains information on where to locate particular databases.

For example, you might define a TNS service name called WEB_DEV. In your tnsnames.ora file, the configuration information for WEB_DEV may indicate that the listener for this database is located at port 1521 (the default port location if you don't specify otherwise) on IP address 111.222.333.444 (or the name of the machine at that address) and listens for connection requests to a database called "web_dev." Oracle Net's location transparency is largely made possible due to the tnsnames.ora file. If you move a database from one machine to another, you need only update the tnsnames.ora files on the clients that connect to this database to reflect the new address for the existing service name (which, as you read later, is often the same as the database or instance name).

If your environment uses TNSNames (as opposed to one of the other Oracle networking solutions, like the Oracle Names Server), a tnsnames.ora file is configured and maintained on both the database server and the client. Therefore, to effectively support connections to the database, service name listings in both files (the file residing on the server and the file residing on the client) must be identical.

■ *FOR EXAMPLE*

The following is a sample tnsnames.ora file (lines beginning with # are comments):

```
# TNSNAMES.ORA Network Configuration File:
#C:\ORACLE\ORA817\network\admin\tnsnames.ora
# Generated by Oracle configuration tools.
WEB_DEV =
  (DESCRIPTION =
   (ADDRESS_LIST =
    (ADDRESS = (PROTOCOL = TCP)
               (HOST = web_development)
               (PORT = 1521)
    )
   )
   (CONNECT_DATA =
    (SERVICE_NAME = web_dev)
   )
  )
```

Most of this listing—from the keyword, DESCRIPTION, to the last parentheses—is known as a *connect descriptor*. It contains the definition of a protocol address and the service name to which to connect. The ADDRESS section specifies the protocol address of a listener. With the ADDRESS_LIST keyword present, multiple ADDRESS sections may be defined, with multiple protocols and protocol addresses, for a single net service name. Multiple addresses are simply listed after the ADDRESS_LIST parameter. The CONNECT_DATA keyword is always followed by the name of the service to which you'd like to connect. Typical types of services used with CONNECT_DATA are:

- SID, which identifies the database instance by the Oracle System Identifier (SID)
- SERVICE_NAME, which identifies the global database name, a name comprised of the database name and domain name, created during installation or database creation
- INSTANCE_NAME, which identifies the database instance to access

You can make changes to your tnsnames.ora file using the following steps:

1. If there is an existing tnsnames.ora file in your TNS_ADMIN directory, back it up. (If you have problems with the tnsnames.ora file after making the edits in this chapter, you can restore the original from the backup.) You should name this backup file tnsnames.ora.01. If you do not already have a file called tnsnames.ora in your TNS_ADMIN directory, then you can create a new one with a text editor (like Notepad). If you choose to create this file manually, then create it as shown in the above template. If you already have a tnsnames.ora file, then append it with the text from the template above.

2. You can change "WEB_DEV" to "*<SID>*", where *<SID>* is the SID (System Identifier) of the database Instance on the remote machine. Note that since this is a logical name, you can name it anything you like; it does not have to be the same as the name of the database (however, for purposes of simplification, it is often the same as the database name). You could, for example, leave the name as "WEB_DEV" and still use it to locate a database called "db_instance_01".

3. Change "Host = web_development" to "Host = <name of the machine or network name for the machine where the database is located>". You can either use the name or the IP address. It is recommended that you use the name if you know what it is.

4. Change "Port = 1521" to "Port = *<the port number of the listener>*". Note that 1521 is the default port for an Oracle listener and should not be changed unless another service is already using that port or you are instructed to do so in the Oracle documentation.

5. Change "db_instance_01" to "*<SID>*". <SID> should be the name of the database Instance to which you will be connecting.

6. Save the file and close your text editor.

SID is most commonly used with Oracle8. Oracle recommends that, with Oracle8i and 9i, you use SERVICE_NAME as opposed to SID.

Once you have entered configuration information for your TNS service name in your tnsnames.ora file, you can open SQL*Plus and attempt to connect to the database it represents using the following syntax:

```
CONNECT <username>/<password>@<TNSservicename>
```

ORACLE NET MANAGER

You can accomplish the task of creating your networking configuration files by using Oracle Net Manager. This GUI (graphical user interface) utility was previously named Net8 Assistant in Oracle8. As you can see from the example above, Oracle Net configuration files have a very specific syntax with multiple levels of nested brackets. You can avoid the errors sometimes common to hand-typed configuration files by using the Oracle Net Manager.

You can access the Oracle Net Manager by going to your Start menu, then going to Programs, your Oracle 9i program listing, Network Administration, then Oracle Net Manager. Once there, follow the wizard prompts to set up your net service names. If you need further reference on what each prompt is asking for, refer to the list of steps laid out earlier for those brave enough to hand-code their tnsnames.ora file.

If you're having a problem with your network, back up the current configuration files and use the Oracle Net Manager to regenerate them.

TNSPING

Oracle Net provides a utility, tnsping, which can be used to validate both the name resolution to, and the existence of, an Oracle Listener service. Oracle Net interfaces with a variety of Network and Transport layer protocols, one of which is TCP/IP (Transmission Control Protocol/Internet Protocol). If TCP is the protocol being used, then the utility tnsping uses TCP for its communication. TCP is an OSI (Open Systems Interconnection) Transport layer protocol that is connection-oriented. This connection-oriented protocol requires an exchange of sequencing numbers in the initial connection setup. This exchange is commonly called the "three-way handshake." When tnsping is issued from the command line, a lookup on the Oracle Net Alias (or Service Name) is performed. This can occur using your local tnsnames.ora file. The purpose is to get the host name and port number the target Listener is listening on. Once this information is acquired, a TCP connection is opened to the target host and port the Oracle Listener is on. To open this TCP connection, the host name must be resolved to the IP address of the target host. TCP/IP then performs the three-way handshake to complete the connection. tnsping sends an Oracle TNS Connect packet (the "ping") to the Oracle Listener. The Listener responds with a TNS Refuse packet (the "pong"). The TCP/IP connection between the two hosts is then terminated. The total time from Oracle Net Alias lookup to TCP/IP connection termination is then reported back to the command line. Here is an example of the output after invoking the tnsping utility:

```
C:\>tnsping web_dev
WEB_DEV 4 TNS Ping Utility for 32-bit Windows: Version
8.1.7.0.0 -
Production on 04-FEB-2002 21:25:57 c) Copyright 1997 Oracle
Corporation.
All rights reserved.
Attempting to contact ADDRESS=(PROTOCOL=TCP)
(HOST=web_development)(PORT=1521))
OK (15100 msec)
OK (10 msec)
OK (0 msec)
OK (10 msec)
```

This example shows a 15100-millisecond period for the first "ping." This time period is comprised of the lookup of the alias WEB_DEV in a local tnsnames.ora file, a DNS resolution of the destination host web_development and port 1521, the TCP/IP three-way handshake, the actual transport of the TNS Connect and Refuse packets, and the tearing down of the TCP/IP connection. The second time only took 10 milliseconds because all the connection information, the alias WEB_DEV, and IP address had already been cached. Tnsping still does the connection setup and teardown for TCP/IP for each invocation of tnsping, however.

PING

TCP/IP uses its own utility called "ping," named after the sound SONAR makes underwater. It is the command-line interface to the TCP/IP protocol ICMP (Internet Control Message Protocol). One of ping's primary responsibilities is to gather information about general roundtrip times for a variety of IP packet sizes. This measurement can be used to estimate the overall performance and response time of an application on a network. Ping uses IP, which does not require the three-way handshake. When ping operates, it only sends one IP packet and receives only one. This is fewer packets, by quite a bit, than Oracle's tnsping issues. It is typical for ping to show an initial response time being longer than the average. This is usually due to the time it takes to perform a host name to IP address lookup (or *resolve*). This lookup can be performed with either a local hosts file or by using a DNS server. An example output for a ping looks like the following:

```
Pinging web_development [111.22.333.444] with 32 bytes of
data:
Reply from 555.66.777.888: bytes=32 time<50ms TTL=315
Reply from 555.66.777.888: bytes=32 time<10ms TTL=315
Reply from 555.66.777.888: bytes=32 time<10ms TTL=315
Reply from 555.66.777.888: bytes=32 time<10ms TTL=315
```

This example shows a 50-millisecond ping time for the first attempt. This time included a DNS resolve for the target host.

UNIT 2.1 EXERCISES

a) Explain where Oracle's Internet Application Server (iAS) fits into an *n*-tier architecture.

b) Explain how a dynamic Web differs from a static Web.

c) Explain what the mods in the Oracle 9iAS are.

UNIT 2.1 EXERCISE ANSWERS

a) Explain where Oracle's Internet Application Server (iAS) fits into an *n*-tier architecture.

Answer: The 9iAS is the middle tier in a multi-tier environment. The client and the database are the other tiers.

b) Explain how a dynamic Web differs from a static Web.

Answer: A static page is a page that does not change and is server as is to the client. A dynamic Web page is generated at the time the client makes a request to the server. A dynamic Web page can display the current date and time. A static page cannot do this.

c) Explain what the mods in the Oracle 9iAS are.

Answer: The mods in the Oracle 9iAS are modules, extensions to the IAS to handle different programming languages. A mod can be an additional application that is called by the IAS to handle certain requests.

ORACLE 9iAS CONFIGURATION

INSTALLATION OF ORACLE 9iAS

There are three types of the Oracle9i Database (Enterprise, Standard, and Personal) and each includes an installation of the Oracle HTTP server in the same Oracle Home directory as the database. The Oracle HTTP server is automatically installed with whatever type of installation you choose (unless you choose the "custom" installation where you choose each component). The Oracle-supplied packages for the PL/SQL Web toolkit will be installed in the SYS schema. The application in this book is developed using the simplest type of the Oracle 9iAS installation, the Personal installation. In Windows NT/2000/XP the default installation will set this up as an automatic service rather than a manual service. This means that the Oracle HTTP server starts every time the server or PC is powered on regardless of whether a user is logged on to the operating system or database. Your setup of the Oracle9iAS using this functionality is sufficient to build the application developed in this book. You need to configure a Database Access Descriptor (DAD) to view Web pages for the application you create in this book. Refer to the section "Configuring a Database Access Descriptor (DAD)" later in this unit.

The Oracle 9iAS also can be installed on its own in a separate Oracle Home or on a separate server. This is necessary if you will be using any of the other features of the Oracle 9iAS, such as Oracle Portal or Oracle Portal to Go. It is also necessary to install the 9iAS separately if you are using an Oracle 8i database, which does not contain the built-in HTTP server. This would be version 8.1.5 and below.

In order to perform the separate 9iAS installation, you need the Oracle CD Pack for the Oracle 9iAS. Remember, if you are installing Oracle 9iAS separately, as opposed to using the 9iAS included with the 9i database, then the 9iAS must be installed in a different Oracle Home. Otherwise, shared components could be overwritten, which might cause problems later on.

An "Oracle Home" is part of the Optimal Flexible Architecture (OFA) standard designed by Oracle to assist users in laying out their databases to support high performance and ease of maintenance. The Oracle Home portion of this standard is simply an Oracle version/product-specific directory. In this way, since Oracle Homes are product- and version-specific, a database server can potentially have multiple Oracle Homes. For example, in NT, an Oracle Home for Oracle9i typically looks like:

```
C:\ORACLE\ORA91
```

and in UNIX, an Oracle Home for Oracle9i might be written as:

```
/u01/app/oracle/product/9.0.1
```

If you must install Oracle 9iAS separate from the server, you still have some choices to make. After specifying a new Oracle Home to install the Application server, you are given a prompt to choose which type of installation you are performing, as shown in Figure 2.4.

The following is a list of what will be installed with each choice:

> *Oracle 9iAS Core Edition:* Installs Oracle9iAS Containers for J2EE (OC4J), Oracle9iAS Web Cache, and Oracle HTTP Server
>
> *Oracle 9iAS Minimal Edition:* Installs a subset of the Oracle9iAS Standard Edition components: Oracle9iAS Portal, Oracle9iAS Wireless, Oracle Enterprise Manager Client, and Oracle HTTP Server
>
> *Oracle 9iAS Standard Edition (SE):* Installs Oracle9iAS Portal, Oracle9iAS Wireless, Oracle Enterprise Java Engine, Oracle Enterprise Manager Client, Oracle HTTP Server, and Oracle Internet File System

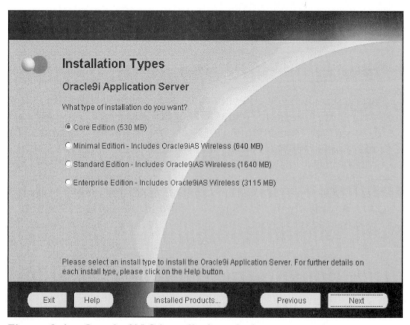

Figure 2.4 ■ Oracle 9iAS installation choices.

Oracle 9iAS Enterprise Edition (EE): Installs Oracle9iAS Database Cache, Oracle9iAS Discoverer, Oracle9iAS Forms Services, Oracle9iAS Portal, Oracle9iAS Reports Services, Oracle9iAS Web Cache, Oracle9iAS Wireless, Oracle Enterprise Java Engine, Oracle Enterprise Manager Client, Oracle HTTP Server, Oracle Internet File System, and Oracle Management Server

If you wish to make use of the additional features available with these four installation types of 9iAS, it is important that you follow the installation instructions very carefully. The CD pack for this installation comes with a full CD of documentation. One of these documents is the complete installation manual.

CONFIGURING A DATABASE ACCESS DESCRIPTOR (DAD)

The *database access descriptor* (DAD) is a mechanism defined through the 9iAS configuration that maps the URL to the correct database schema. Once connected to the database, your PL/SQL code can run and access database information and call PL/SQL subprograms in the PL/SQL Web Toolkit.

In order to create the application developed in this book, it is advised that you install the Oracle 9iAS included as part of the Oracle9i database installation. In this case, the only configuration you need to perform in order to develop and run your application is a correct net service name entry in your tnsnames.ora file and configuring a DAD on the Oracle HTTP Server.

A DAD is a named set of configuration values used for database access. It specifies information such as a database alias, a connect string if the database is remote, and a procedure for uploading and downloading documents.

NAVIGATE TO THE DAD CONFIGURATION PAGE

1. The first step is to go to the main setup page for the Oracle HTTP Server. In the HTDOCS root directory exists a file named index.htm. This is the file you see when you enter the URL for the computer that is running the Oracle 9iAS. If the name of the server is MyServer and you enter http://MyServer:port#/index.html, you will see the main HTTP Server Components page. The literal http://localhost/ will also work when you are viewing these pages from the server terminal (if default port 80 is used, you do not have to enter a port number; in more recent versions, Oracle uses port 7778—check the Oracle documention of your version to verify the port.) You will see the configuration page shown in Figure 2.5. You will not be required to provide any userID or password to access this page. In a production environment, you should add a layer of security to this page.

Go to the companion Web site for this book (www.phptr.com/boardman) for information on how to add additional security to this configuration page.

Figure 2.5 ■ **Oracle HTTP server components Web page.**

2. Click on the mod_plsql link in order to configure a DAD. The next page you see is shown in Figure 2.6.

3. The next step is to click on the lower link "Gateway Database Access Descriptor Settings," and you will Figure 2.7. (NOTE: At this point, there are two DADs that have been set up already during the initial installation. One is the SIMPLEDAD and the other is the SSODAD. These are just samples; they have not yet been configured for you to make use of.) This page can also be found by going directly to the page: `http://<hostname>:<port>/pls/admin_/gateway.htm`

4. In order to add a new DAD, click on the link "Add Default," and you will see the page shown in Figure 2.7 (this is the page where you enter information about the DAD that you are creating).

CREATING AN ANY DAD

The first DAD that you will create is one that does not have any details regarding Oracle User Name, Password, or Schema. The user is prompted to enter a user-name and password when the URL is invoked. This setup is ideal in a development or class environment where there will be many developers using various

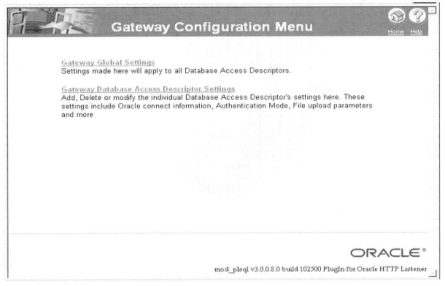

Figure 2.6 ■ Gateway configuration menu.

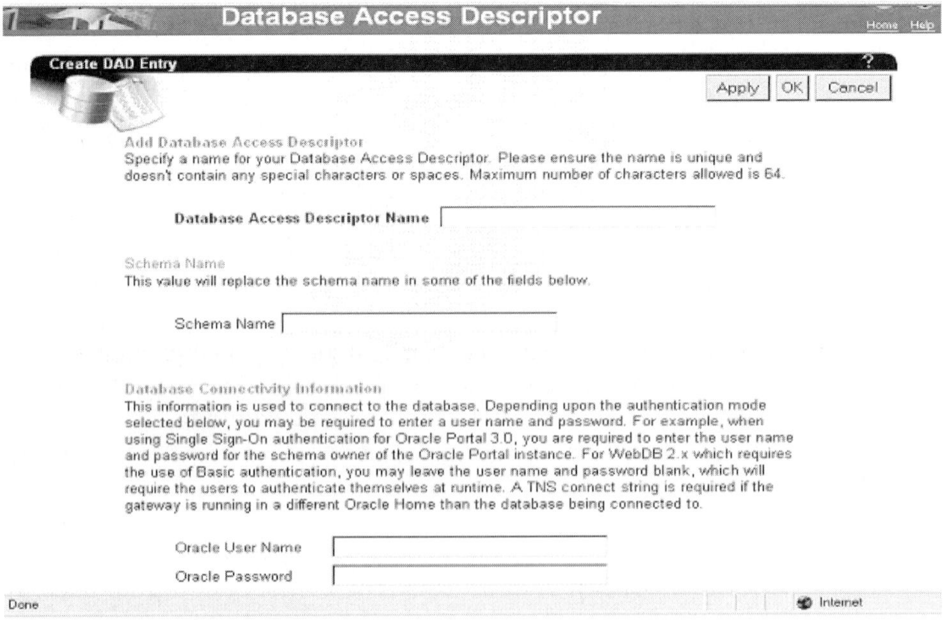

Figure 2.7 ■ Database Access Descriptor setup page.

schemas to test procedures. You will name this DAD "ANY" because it can be used for any user.

The name ANY has no particular meaning here; you could name your DAD after your own father, for instance, and call it the "BOB" DAD, as-suming, of course, that your father is named Bob.

1. Go the companion Web site for this book http://www.phptr.com/ boardman. Follow the directions to install the student schema. This sample schema includes a procedure, Hello_World, that you will use to test the DAD installation.

2. In order to configure the DAD you will need to know the Service Name entry in the tnsnames.ora file on the server. This will be explained in more detail later on in this chapter. You can also get by if you know the Oracle SID and the name or IP address of the server where your Database is located. There are numerous ways to find this out if you do not know it. The easiest is to ask the database administration or the system administrator. If this happens to be you, and you still do not know the name of the server, there are a few things you can do. It would be a good idea to get yourself a number of qualified resources to manage an Oracle Database. This would be knowledgeable friends as well as manuals on the database and the operating system of the server that hosts the database.

If you do not know the name of your computer, here are a few things that you can try. If your server has a Windows operating system you can open a Command Prompt session (directly or from a telnet session). If you cannot find the icon for the Command Prompt (it is in different places on different versions of Windows) on your menu you can go to the start menu. Then go to "Run" and type **cmd.** *In the DOS session type* **hostname** *and the name will be returned. You can also find out the IP address by typing the DOS command* **ipconfig** *and the address will be returned.*

On UNIX you can also type **hostname** *at a shell prompt and the name of the server will be returned.*

Connect to the Oracle Database as System and run the following select statement:

```
SELECT instance_name, host_name
FROM  sys.v_$instance;
```

You will see the SID and host name of the Database in the result set.

**UNIT
2.2**

3. There are only two entries that you have to make in order to configure an ANY DAD. One is the name of the DAD and the other is the CONNECT STRING. The Connect string will be an entry in the tnsnames.ora file. As an alternative you can also create an entry in the format <HOST>:<PORT>:<SID>. For example, if the server was named MyServer, you were using the standard port of 1521 and the name of the database instance was ORCL, then you could enter MyServer:1521:ORCL.

4. Test this DAD by using the Hello_World procedure that was installed with the sample student schema. Assuming your server's name is MyServer, enter the following URL: http://MyServer/pls/any/Hello_World

This Web page does not end with any extension. Don't worry—it doesn't need an HTM or HTML extension.

5. You will be prompted for a Username and Password; use the username *Student* and the password *Learn*. You will see a simple Web page that says Hello_World.

   A method to log off the database (also known as deauthentication) is to add **/logmeoff** after the DAD in the URL, for example, **http://MyServer/pls/myDad/logmeoff**. The browser then displays a page that reads: **You have been successfully deauthenticated**.

6. Log off using the logmeoff deauthentication method.

CREATING A SCHEMA-SPECIFIC DAD

If your application does not involve each user logging on to a separate schema, then you may wish to create a DAD that has the Oracle user name and password specified by the DAD. This would be an easier setup if you were developing an application on a standalone computer with only one user at a time. In this case you need to fill in the next three properties:

1. Oracle Schema Name
2. Oracle User Name
3. Oracle Password

This is the same username and password combination you would use to connect to SQL*Plus. The schema name refers to the schema whose objects you will be accessing and the connect string indicates the Service Entry from the tnsnames.ora file. To proceed, follow these four steps:

1. Create, a DAD named Student that will not ask the user to log in.
2. Start by naming the DAD Student, enter Student for the schema and username. Enter Learn for the password and the same connect string that you just created.

3. Test the Student DAD. Assuming your server is named MyServer, enter the URL: `http://MyServer/pls/student/hello_world`

   You will not be asked to login and you will see the same page that you did in the previous exercise.

4. Log off with the logmeoff deauthentication method.

There are a number of other properties of the DAD you may wish to configure. The most useful will be the Default Home Page. The entry here is the procedure that will run if you do not indicate a procedure. If you specify a default home page of MyHomeProcedure for the DAD named MyDad, then an end user would simply enter the following URL in a browser: *http://MyServer/pls/MyDad/* to invoke the procedure MyHomeProcedure, which generates an HTML page to display.

There are two other types of entries here and they will be addressed in later chapters. The properties such as Document Path and Document Procedure relate to storing and retrieving documents from the Database. This will be covered in Chapter 13, "Images."

The PL/SQL Gateway allows users to log off (clear HTTP authentication information) programmatically through a PL/SQL procedure without having to exit all instances of the browser. Because of the use of cookies, this feature is supported on Netscape 3.0 or higher and Internet Explorer. On other browsers, the user may have to exit the browser to deauthenticate. Cookies are discussed more in Chapter 15, "Maintaining State with Cookies and Tables."

STARTING AND STOPPING THE ORACLE 9iAS

In a Windows NT/2000/XP installation the Oracle HTTP Server will be installed so that it is configured as an automatic service that is started when the computer is turned on. You can also start the service manually by going into the Windows Control Panel and running the service setup (under Administrative tools in Windows 2000 and XP), selecting the service, and clicking on the start icon. When you start Oracle HTTP Server, you are starting just the parent process. It loops through the configured modules and initializes them before reading the rest of the configuration files. The parent process then takes care of starting the other (child) processes. This is extremely important because modules implement most of the configuration directives in Oracle HTTP Server configuration files. The main configuration file is **httpd.conf**.

Note that if you are using a test PC, you can also make a batch file to start and stop the Oracle services. This will make it easier for you to turn on and off the Oracle services when you are performing other tests. You first need to open a DOS session when the services are on. Query the services with NET START. This will give you a list of the services that are running. The service that starts the database will be named "Oracle<OracleHome name><SID Name>", and the Oracle 9iAS will have the name "Oracle<Oracle Home name>HTTPServer". To save on typing you can enter these into a text file. To proceed, follow these steps:

1. Open a command session and type "Net Start |more". This will give you the names of the services that are running.

2. Create a batch file called StopIAS.bat and enter one line based on the names you found in step 1:

   ```
   Net Stop Oracle<Oracle Home name>HTTPServer
   ```

3. Save this file to your desktop and then double click on it.

4. You will see: "The Oracle<Oracle Home name>HTTPServer service is stopping" and then "The Oracle<Oracle Home name>HTTPServer service was stopped successfully". You may see the message "The Oracle<Oracle Home name>HTTPServer service is not started". You can't stop a service that is not active.

5. Create a second batch file called StartIAS.bat and enter one line based on the name you found in step 1 "Net Start Oracle<Oracle Home name>HTTPServer".

6. Save this file on your desktop and double click on it.

7. The service will start and you will see the message "The Oracle<Oracle Home name>HTTPServer service is starting" and then "The Oracle <Oracle Home name>HTTPServer service was started successfully". You can also make a similar file to stop and start your Oracle Listener and database instance.

Go the companion Web site for some tips on troubleshooting the Apache Server. The Web site for this book is http://www.phptr.com/ boardman.

You can also start and stop the Apache Server by going into the Windows NT or 2000 services. Click on the **Oracle<OracleHome>HTTPServer service.** Right-click and select **stop** or **start**.

STARTING THE ORACLE HTTP SERVER ON UNIX

In order to start the iAS on UNIX you must first check that the executable is in the PATH. To do this, type echo $PATH at the command line.

To start iAS on UNIX from the command line, enter the following:

```
Apachectl start
```

or

```
httpd
```

To have iAS start automatically when the server is turned on, edit:

```
/etc/rc.d/rc.local
```

by adding:

```
$ORACLE_HOME/Apache/Apache/bin/httpd
```

STOPPING THE ORACLE HTTP SERVER ON UNIX

To shut down the iAS in Unix, enter

```
apachectl shutdown
```

or

```
kill -9 'cat $ORACLE_HOME/Apache/Apache/logs/httpd.pid'
```

LOOKING AT THE LOG FILES FOR ORACLE 9iAS

CONFIGURATION FOR ORACLE HTTP SERVER

Once the 9iAS is installed, it must be configured for the machine it resides on, and then configured to handle each new application that is created. Making changes to the configuration files known as *conf files* configures the Oracle HTTP server. There is one directory on the server identified by the 9iAS as the root directory. All files in this root directory and in child directories are served as static Web pages by the Web server component of the Oracle HTTP server. The default root directory is

```
<OracleHome>\Apache\Apache\Htdocs\
```

For example, imagine your Oracle Home is C:\oracle\oracle9\, the computer (PC or Server) is named MyServer, and you had a file named HelloWorld.htm. You then place the file in the root directory so the local address on the server ends up being C:\oracle\oracle9\Apache\Apache\Htdocs\HelloWorld.htm.

In order to view the file in a Web browser you use the following URL: http://MyServer/HelloWorld.htm.

In Chapter 3, "Remote Server Access," you will learn how to transfer files using the File Transfer Protocol (FTP), so it is important to know where in the directory tree files should be transferred in order to be accessible to the 9iAS. It is also important to note that an FTP account may have its own virtual root directory. For more details, see the section on FTP in Chapter 3.

DIRECTORY STRUCTURE

By default, these directories are placed in the Oracle Home in which Oracle 9iAS was installed. Remember, if you installed the simple version of the Oracle 9iAS as part of an Oracle 9i database installation then the Home of the Oracle database and the Home of the Oracle 9iAS will be the same. If you used the separate database CD Pack from Oracle, then the Oracle Home for the Oracle 9iAS will be different. You are prompted for this at the beginning of the installation. All the directories listed here are subdirectories of the Apache directory in the Oracle Home where the Oracle 9iAS was installed (<Oracle Home>/Apache/Apache/):

htdocs—This is the default root directory. This directory contains static HTML pages. This directory and those below it are accessible to anyone on the Web and therefore pose a severe security risk if used for anything other than public data.

conf—Contains the configuration files. These are text files that are read when the Oracle HTTP Server is started.

log—Contains the log data, both of accesses and errors.

cgi-bin—Contains the CGI scripts. These are programs or shell scripts that can be executed by the Oracle HTTP Server on behalf of its clients.

Now take a look at your log files to see how the exercises that you have performed in this chapter have been logged. To access your log files, follow these steps:

1. Go to your Windows explorer if you are on Windows or whatever file explorer application you use on UNIX.

2. Navigate yourself to the directory $ORACLE_HOME/Apache/Apache/ log and view the files with Windows explorer. You can also view the files in the DOS command window by typing *dir* on Windows or *ls* on UNIX.

3. You will see a file named access_log.

4. Open the file in Textpad and have a look. You will see an entry for every page that you have viewed.

   Here is an example from the access_log:

   ```
   169.254.104.206 - - [06/Jan/2002:23:56:12 -0500]
   "GET /pls/student/hello_world HTTP/1.1" 401 511
   ```

5. Try to break down the line and figure out what it means.

CONFIGURING SECURITY FOR ORACLE 9iAS

There are numerous configuration files in the Apache subdirectories that deal with many different settings such as security issues. In this exercise you will change the security settings to allow Oracle-supplied packages to be run via the Oracle 9iAS.

To begin:

1. Open an Internet Explorer Window and view your page HelloWorld with the Oracle-supplied package OWA_UTIL.SHOWSOURCE, as follows:

```
http://MyServer/pls/student/owa_util.showsource?cname=
hello_world
```

2. Note that you might see the following:

   "You don't have permission to access /pls/dadname/owa_util.show-source on this server." In the Oracle 9iAS, prior to Oracle 9iAS version 1.0.2.2, and in all versions of the OAS you could view the source code of a procedure by using the owa_util.showsource in the URL This will not work by default in Oracle 9iAS version 1.0.2.2. Oracle developers made the decision that packages under the SYS schema should be secured from Web viewing unless the decision was made by the administrator to open them up. You are going to need these in later chapters, so now is a good time to make the required changes:

3. Shut down the service Oracle<OracleHome>HTTPServer on your server running the Oracle 9iAS.

4. Make a backup copy of the configuration file $ORACLE_HOME\Apache \modplsql\cfg\wdbsvr.app (note the $ORACLE_HOME refers to the directory on which you installed your Oracle server).

5. Edit the file $ORACLE_HOME\Apache\modplsql\cfg\wdbsvr.app as follows in the section that starts with:

   ```
   [DAD_any]
   ;exclusion_list
   ```

6. Change the line so it no longer starts with ';' and is as follows:

   ```
   exclusion_list  = sys.*, dbms_*, utl_*
   ```

7. Start the service Oracle<OracleHome>HTTPServer.

8. Open an Internet Explorer window and enter the URL: http://MyServer/pls/student/owa_util.showsource?cname=hello_world.

   You will see the PL/SQL source for this Web page.

Go the companion Web site for additional tips on methods to secure your Web site. The Web site for this book is http://www.phptr.com/boardman/.

You can change the default Web server port for the Oracle HTTP server by changing the configuration file found at: <OracleHome>\Apache\Apache\conf\http.conf. There will be a line:

```
Port 7778
```

(or another port depending on your version) that should be changed to the desired port. It is recommeneded to change this to port 80. Port 80 is the default port that a browser is calling; if you use port 80 on the server side, the clients do not have to put a port number in their URL. The line would then read:

```
Port 80
```

Changes to a configuration file are not dynamic. You need to stop and restart the server for the changes to take effect.

UNIT 2.2 EXERCISES

In order to test your progress, you should be able to answer the following questions.

a) What is the purpose of a DAD and what is the minimal amount of information needed to configure a DAD?

b) This chapter details the steps to create an ANY DAD. What is the significance of the word ANY?

c) In which directory on the Application server should you put an HTML document that you wish to be visible by a URL with the name of the server followed by a backslash and the name of the file? How is this different from a stored procedure that is written to called by a URL? What would that URL be?

UNIT 2.2 EXERCISE ANSWERS

a) What is the purpose of a DAD and what is the minimal amount of information needed to configure a DAD?

Answer: The Database Access Description (DAD) defines the method the Oracle IAS will use to connect to a database. The minimal information required is the name of a Service Name from the tnsnames.ora file on the application server. If you do not provide a username and password you will be prompted for one when the DAD is being used. If you provide a username and password in the configuration, that is what will be used when the procedure is called and the user will not be prompted for one.

b) This chapter details the steps to create an ANY DAD. What is the significance of the word ANY?

Answer: The word ANY is an arbitrary name that is used in the creation of a DAD. It was named ANY because the DAD configuration did not include a username and pass-

word and thus could be used by any user. If the DAD had been named BOB, it would have worked in the same manner.

c) In which directory on the Application server should you put an HTML document that you wish be visible by a URL with the name of the server followed by a backslash and the name of the file? How is this different from a stored procedure that is written to called by a URL? What would that URL be?

Answer: The directory would be under Oracle Home as follows: <Oracle_Home>/apache/ apache/htdocs/ and a file in this directory would be seen from a Web browser as fol-lows: http://Server_Name/file_name.htm. This is a static page and it is very different from a dynamic page that is generated from an Oracle stored procedure. In order to view the stored procedure, the URL must contain an indication that it is using the mod_plsql module with the /pls/ and the name of the DAD to be user. The URL would be as follows: http://Server_Name/pls/any/procedure_name.

SUMMARY

In this chapter, you learned many concepts that you should keep in mind when you read the subsequent chapter. These concepts include:

- Multi-tier architecture in general and with the Oracle 9iAS
- Static versus dynamic Web pages
- Oracle HTTP server modules
- The PL/SQL module in Oracle 9iAS Mod_plsql
- The URL used for PL/SQL pages in Oracle 9iAS

In the chapters of this book you will create an application for maintaining stu-dents and teachers in a school database. In the exercises of this chapter you set up your Oracle 9iAS server to perform the exercises in the rest of the book. This consisted of the following:

- Downloading and installing the student schema
- Finding the DAD configuration page
- Creating an "any" DAD and a schema-specific DAD to run PL/SQL procedures via a URL
- Stopping and starting the Oracle 9iAS
- Viewing the log files for the Oracle 9iAS
- Configuring security for Oracle-supplied packages on the Oracle 9iAS

At this point your server is ready to serve both static Web pages and dynamic Web pages generated from an Oracle database. Enjoy the next chapter.

C H A P T E R   3

REMOTE SERVER
ACCESS

UNIT 3.1

WORKING WITH THE SERVER

REMOTE VS. LOCAL

For this book's purpose, there are two possible installation configurations: remote and local. A remote configuration uses your computer to access a remote server machine. A local configuration first determines whether you need to access a remote server machine.

You could be working locally, on a computer that has the Oracle database, application server, and client software all installed on the same machine, or you could be working remotely, using your computer to access a remote server machine. If you have installed Oracle9i Personal Edition on your computer, then you have a local installation.

Understand that most real-world databases are housed on a server machine, which is accessed remotely by client machines. If you have a remote configuration, like that often found in a corporate training environment or an educational setting, then you should find the information in this chapter immediately applicable to your work. You may have been granted access to a remote server machine on which you can complete the exercises in this book. In this case, check with the system administrator to see if you have access privileges needed to complete the exercises in this chapter. It is also possible that your company may have a development configuration where the client, Web server, and database server are on one machine, isolated from the rest of the network. This type of configuration is illustrated as you work through the exercises in this book.

The same holds true for Web sites; the majority of Web sites are also housed on server machines (commonly referred to as simply *servers*), with a connection to the Internet. Web applications, such as the one you build in this book, have many Web pages that are dynamically generated from database procedures, so there is not a great need to store static HTML files on a server. Yet image files can be stored inside the database or they can be stored on a Web server, as can any static HTML pages you wish to use in your application. It depends on how your database is configured. Documents that require a plug-in to view, and any files of other types other than HTML or image that are used in the application, such as Adobe Acrobat files or Word documents that are intended to be downloaded, can be stored on the Web server or in the database. Chapter 13, "Images," illustrates the method for storing and retrieving documents from an Oracle 9i database.

If you do not have access to a remote server machine, then refer to Chapter 2, "Oracle 9iAS," in which you learn that your local machine can be used as the server, the client, and the middleware necessary to complete the exercises in this book. Remember that if you install an Oracle9i database on your own machine, the installation includes a basic Oracle 9iAS. You can store static HTML pages or images in your own computer's file directory, and configure the Oracle HTTP Server component of the Oracle 9iAS to find the files you want. This is done by identifying the directory where your images and HTML files are stored in the Oracle 9iAS, and giving that directory a virtual name, as explained in Chapter 2, "Oracle 9iAS."

THE SERVER

The server is a large file directory that you need to access in order to complete the exercises in this book. You store files there, such as HTML files or image files, that you wish to make accessible to users on the Internet. You must map specific directories on the server machine to virtual directories in the 9iAS so that the correct directories can be accessed, depending on the URL (Uniform Resource Locator) the user supplies.

About 80% of databases are stored on machines that run the UNIX operating system, and are familiarly known as "UNIX boxes." Since databases are also stored on machines running NT, many NT commands, where they differ from UNIX commands, are noted throughout this chapter.

TELNET

Telnet is software that provides a user or developer a way to connect to a server machine. It is a terminal emulator, which means it gives users the ability to log in to a server machine and work on it remotely. When a developer connects to a server via Telnet, the developer begins a Telnet "session" on the server. Telnet allows you to cross platforms, meaning that if you are on a Windows PC, you can Telnet to a UNIX server and vice versa.

Most computers running Windows come with a basic version of Telnet software installed. The quickest way to begin a Telnet session is to go to the Start menu and choose "Run...." You are asked to "Type the name of a program, folder, or document, and Windows opens it for you." Type the word "telnet" and click OK. A window should pop up that has the word "Telnet" in the title bar.

Once you have successfully invoked a Telnet session, the next step is to connect to a server. No matter what version of Telnet software you use, you must know three things ahead of time in order to be able to successfully connect to a remote server—the name of the server, a login ID, and a password. If you are going to be connecting to a server and working there, chances are the system administrator knows that you are going to be doing this, and has provided you with the name of the machine and a login ID and password. A sample server name might be server4.virgil.com, where server4 is the name of the machine on the virgil network. Some people prefer to call a machine by its numeric IP address, such as 111.22.33.44.

The method you use to connect to the server depends on the kind of Telnet software installed on your machine. If your Telnet window has a prompt, you can enter the words "open server4.virgil.com" to open a connection. If your version of Telnet does not have a prompt, then look on the menu bar for an item called "Connect." This is probably the first item on the menu bar. Click on Connect and you are provided with a place to enter the server name. The *host* name is another term for server name—the server you are connecting to hosts your guest connection.

You are then prompted for a login name (ID) and password. Enter the login name and password provided by your system administrator. Once you are connected, you should see a $ prompt, or possibly a % or # prompt. This is somewhat anticlimactic. However, be assured that you are connected. You may also see a list of environment or user settings, or a short message of greeting that was configured by the system administrator.

The main security flaw with Telnet is that it does not encrypt passwords. If security is one of your main concerns, you may want to use more secure communications software, like ssh (Secure Shell). You can find out more about ssh by checking out ssh's Web site:http://www.ssh.com/products/ssh/.

BASIC UNIX COMMANDS

Once you have connected to the server, you need to know how to navigate around the directory structure of the server and handle your files. You accomplish this using basic UNIX commands.

The first step in navigation is to know where you are. When a user logs in, the user will always begin from the same initial directory, called the *home directory*. This home directory is determined when a user account is created by the system administrator, and is included in the configuration for each user who will be accessing the server. Different users are usually assigned different home directories. In order to find out which directory you are presently in, type the UNIX command pwd. This will *print* your present *working directory*. You see different values for pwd as you travel through the file system. In NT, your prompt is always inclusive of the present working directory.

To see a list of all of the contents of the present directory, type `ls` and enter. The names of all of the files and subdirectories in the current directory will be *listed*. To obtain a list with more details, type `ls  -l` and press the Enter key. The `-l` after the `ls` is called an *argument*. Supplying arguments after UNIX commands is a way to supply more specifics about what you want the UNIX command to accomplish. Arguments are listed after the command, and the syntax is a minus sign followed by one or more letters that indicate what options you'd like. The `-l` is a valid argument for the `ls` command, which tells the server to display a longer description of each file and subdirectory.

As you navigate through directories, `pwd` and `ls  -l` (or simply reading the prompt itself and typing `dir` in NT) will probably be the commands you use most often, to find out where you are and what is in the directory where you are.

If the `ls  -l` command returns more file and directory names than fit on the screen, enter `ls  -l  |  more` instead. The screen fills one page, so to speak, with data, and then UNIX waits for you to press a key before displaying another screen page of data. The same is accomplished in NT by including `/p` after the command, to indicate that the computer should *pause* and wait for a key to be pressed before displaying more information.

Take a look at the results from `ls  -l` in more detail. Here is some sample output from running the `ls  -l` command in UNIX:

```
-rw-r--r-- 1 bobo devel   118253 Jul 17 12:05 1stlog1.wav
drwxr-xr-x 2 bobo devel     4096 Nov 14 18:30 gfx
-rw-r--r-- 1 bobo devel     1036 Nov 14 19:04 index.html
-rw-r--r-- 1 bobo devel      973 Nov 14 18:32 index_old.html
-rw-r--r-- 1 bobo devel    17451 Sep  5 00:35 syllabus.html
-rw-r----- 1 bobo devel        0 May 24  2001 test.htm
```

The first column shows the file permissions, which are discussed in more detail later. Note that the first character is either a "d" or a dash. You could also see an "l" here (indicating a symbolic link). A "d" in the first spot indicates a directory. The second column (denoted here by a list of numbers) shows the number of links to a file. The third column shows the owner of this file or directory; in this case, the owner is *bobo*. The owner is the user who has control over the file. The fourth column shows the group that the user bobo belongs to; in this case, *devel*. The fifth column shows the size of the file in bytes. The sixth column shows the date and time the file was created or last changed. Finally, the name of the file is displayed in the seventh column.

One of the most important columns to pay attention to when developing Web applications or documents is the first column. It indicates what permissions its owner has granted on the file. These permissions are powerful; they determine how much access users can have to each file, and what users can do with each file. Through permissions, files are made accessible on the Internet, or blocked from being accessible on the Internet, so it is important to understand and check file permissions, and to apply them carefully.

Table 3.1 ■ File Permissions

Permission	Character	Number Equivalent
read	r	4
write	w	2
execute	x	1
none	-	0

(Note that a hyphen symbol, "-", is the character displayed when none of the other three permissions is granted for a file.)

There are three types of file permissions that can be granted on a file or directory. Table 3.1 outlines these three types. Though "none" is listed in Table 3.1 in the "Permission" column, it is not a permission type, per se. Rather, it is the option available to you if you do not choose to enter one of the other three.

There are four levels of *users* when granting permissions, however. These four levels are outlined in Table 3.2.

Listed in Table 3.3 are some examples of different types of granted permissions. Take a look at the permissions listings in the left column. After the first character, which indicates whether the current file is actually a directory or just a file, the other nine characters indicate the permissions for each type of user. The second, third, and fourth characters show permissions at the **user** level. The next three characters show permissions at the **group** level, and the last three characters denote permissions for everyone else, the **other** level. These last three characters govern whether the public can read, write, or execute a file. These permissions examples provide a description of what each set of permissions permits, and to whom.

Table 3.2 ■ Levels of Users

Level	Letter	Who is This
user	u	The owner of the file, not just any user
group	g	A group of users—users can be associated with groups by the system administrator
other	o	Anyone who is not already included in either of the first two levels
all	a	All users

Table 3.3 ■ Examples of File Permissions

Sample Permissions	Access
`-rwxrwxrwx`	The user, group, and everyone else can read, write, and execute
`-rwxr-xr-x`	Only the owner can read, write, and execute. Everyone else can only read and execute.
`-rwxrwx---`	Only the owner and group can read and execute.

Remember that file permissions determine whether a file is accessible to the public on the Web. In the examples above, the public would be able to access files with the first two permission sets, but not the third set of permissions. The first file would also be writeable, that is, updateable, by the public.

Always check file permissions to make sure that they are correct for each file. Files that are not intended for public access on the Web should not be made accessible to the public. When it is time to "publish" a file, the permissions for all users must be changed to allow others to view the file.

Each set of permissions has a three-digit numeric equivalent. For example, the permissions `-rwxr-xr-x` are also known as `755`. How is this determined? Each digit corresponds to one of the three levels of permissions; the three digits indicate the permissions for the user, group, and other levels, respectively. The number for each level is arrived at by adding the numeric equivalents for each level. As listed above, each permission—read, write, and execute—has a numeric equivalent. These numbers are added to arrive at each digit. In 755, the 7 in the user slot means the user can read (4), write (2), and execute (1) the file; 4 + 2 + 1 = 7 and 7 is used. The second slot has the value 5, meaning that at the group level, only read (4) and execute (1) permissions have been granted; 4 + 1 = 5, so 5 is used. The third digit is also 5, meaning that the permissions at the "other" level are the same as they are at the group level; everyone else has the ability to read (4) and execute (1), and 4 + 1 = 5, so 5 is used again.

The UNIX command to change a file's permissions, or "change mode," is chmod.

■ FOR EXAMPLE

```
chmod 755 myfile
```

The 755 indicates what the file permissions should be for the file "myfile". A 755 is a popular choice for a file that is intended to be accessed by the public, since it prevents anyone but the owner from updating the file, while allowing everyone else to access it.

Be extremely careful not to make files accessible that should not be. To remove access from a level, use a zero (0) for the corresponding digit. This example gives full rights on the file to the owner, but revokes access from everyone else:

```
chmod 700 myfile
```

NT users, note that you may change permissions on your files using basic Windows Explorer functionality.

BASIC NAVIGATION

Now that you know how to determine which directory you are in and what its contents are, how can you navigate? The cd command lets you change directories in both UNIX and NT. Table 3.4 lists some basic navigation commands you can use for moving up and down in a directory tree.

 Be sure to pay attention to the space between the command and the action of that command; for example, cd<space>directoryname.

Table 3.5 lists some additional commands you can use in a Telnet session on the server to manage your files.

The cp, or *copy,* command is particularly useful for making backup copies of documents before changing them or creating new versions of them. The convention

Table 3.4 ■ **Basic Navigation Commands**

Command	Description
cd directoryname	Navigates downward in the directory tree to the subdirectory "directoryname." If you are unable to move to that directory, use ls -l to see if you are using a valid subdirectory name.
cd ..	Navigates upward one level in the directory tree.
cd	cd without anything after it takes you to your own *home* directory (*NOTE:* In NT, entering this command by itself will simply print your current working directory onto the screen.)
cd /mydirectory	The forward slash means you want to skip to the highest level in the directory tree, start from there, and go to the subdirectory "mydirectory." This is the equivalent of typing cd .. repeatedly until you are at the topmost directory, and then typing cd mydirectory.

Table 3.5 ■ Additional Commands for File Management and Manipulation

Command Example	Description
rm myfile	Deletes or removes the file called "myfile."
rm –i	Prompts the user before the system deletes the file (as a safety measure).
mkdir mydirectory	Creates a directory called "mydirectory."
rmdir mydirectory	Deletes or removes the directory called "mydirectory."
cp myfile mynewfile	Copies the file "myfile"; the copy is called "mynewfile" and is located in the same directory as the original "myfile" file.
cp myfile /home/app/mynewfile	Copies the file "myfile"; the copy is called "mynewfile" and is located in the /home/app/ directory. The cp command can copy files to another directory.
mv myfile mynewfile	Moves the file, or renames it. In this example, the file will be moved from its present location under the name "myfile" to the same directory under the name "mynewfile." This effectively renames the file. This is the way to rename a file in UNIX.
mv myfile /home/app/	Moves the file "myfile" to the directory /home/app/. In moving the file, it is not also renamed, because no new name was specified.

is to keep the same name for the file, but append to the name the date that you are changing the file. If you are creating a backup file for myfile on March 1, 2002, you might create a copy called `myfile20020301`.

ABSOLUTE VS. RELATIVE PATH AND FILENAMES

A full pathname, a pathname starting at the root or topmost directory, is also known as the *absolute pathname*. The pathname starting from where you are currently, wherever that may be, is known as the *relative pathname*. Consider the following directory structure as an example. *classnotes* is the topmost directory. *homework* is a subdirectory of *classnotes*, and *homework_one* is a subdirectory of *homework*.

```
Docroot>
classnotes
    homework
        homework_one
```

 For this section, the term "file" refers to a Web page, inline image, or other file that can be hyperlinked or referenced on a Web page.

ABSOLUTE PATHS

An absolute path contains the complete URL (Uniform Resource Locator) for a file. A URL typically consists of four parts: the protocol, the server/domain, the path directory, any subdirectories, and finally, the actual file name itself. An example of an absolute path listing is http://www.server4.virgil.edu/classnotes/ homework/homework_one/hw1Answers.htm.

An absolute path is the same as the path in the address window of a browser (this address window is also referred to as a *location*). Absolute paths are fine for linking to files outside of your Web site. However, using the absolute path to link to other files within your Web site has disadvantages.

Say that a Web site uses absolute paths for all of its links and images. This prevents the Web site from being portable. The result is the site's files cannot be moved to another server without having to change each and every file path to reflect the new address. This really becomes an issue if there are different environments. A typical network infrastructure has multiple environments, each on its own server machine. These include:

- a development environment where the coding is done
- a testing environment where user-acceptance testing, among other tests, is done
- a production environment where the Web site will "go live" (be made available for its intended users)

Using absolute paths requires that the links be changed each time the site is moved to the next environment on the next machine. How can you avoid this and at the same time make a Web site portable? The answer is to use relative paths.

RELATIVE PATHS

It's preferable to use relative pathnames when linking to documents within your own Web site. There are two types of relative paths: root-relative paths and document-relative paths.

A relative path uses as its starting point either (1) the Web site's docroot, or (2) the location of the page that holds the relative path. Using this starting point, the browser is able to find a file.

ROOT-RELATIVE PATHS   A root-relative path always starts with '/' (a forward slash) and does not include the protocol and domain names. The starting point is the Web server's docroot based on the current document.

■ *FOR EXAMPLE*

/classnotes/homework/homework_one/hw1Answers.htm

In this example the search begins in the docroot of the Web server on which the current page resides, or www.server4.virgil.edu. To reference the file, hw1Answers.htm, simply start at the topmost directory and drill down to the directory where the file resides.

DOCUMENT-RELATIVE PATHS   A document-relative path does not begin with '/' (a forward slash) and, like a root-relative path, does not include the protocol and domain. The starting point is the current document displayed in the browser. Thus, these paths are relative to the document.

To reference a file in the same directory as the current browser document, just reference the name of the file:

Hw1Answers.htm

To reference a file located in a directory below the current page, reference the subdirectory and file:

subdirectory/file.htm

To reference a file located in a directory above the current page, type in two sequential periods, "..". If the current document is located in the directory "homework_one" and you want to reference a document in "homework", then the path would be written like this:

../file.htm

Add an extra set of ".." for each directory that you need to go up. For example, to reference a file located two directories up from the current document, you could write the following:

../../file.gif

In this case, navigating two directories up from the "homework_one" directory puts you in the "classnotes" directory.

ROOT-RELATIVE VERSUS DOCUMENT-RELATIVE PATHS   Now that you understand that a relative path is preferable to an absolute path for linking to files within your Web site, which type of relative path should you use: root-relative or document-relative paths?

It depends. Both give you the desired portability. If a site has an *images* directory that will not be moved, then a root-relative path is preferable for such a directory since the path to the images contained in it will always be valid regardless if the Web document (that references this directory) itself is moved to another directory. Document-relative paths, however, tend to be shorter, and may be preferable for that reason alone. Both types of relative paths can become invalid if a file is moved. So, the choice of whether to use root-relative or document-relative paths depends on the particular Web site and Web developer.

TRANSFERRING FILES VIA FTP

There are two options for delivering static files with Oracle 9iAS. You can store the files in the database or you can deliver them using the Apache Web server component. In the latter case, you are delivering, or *serving,* files from the file system of the server. When you have files that you want to make accessible on the Web, you must place them on the server. Files can be transferred to a remote server using FTP. FTP stands for File Transfer Protocol, which is an apt description of what it does.

You also use FTP to retrieve files for editing. This book does not discuss how to edit files directly on the server, since the editing tools available within the UNIX and NT environments (save for the book's discussion concerning Notepad) are outside the scope of this book. However, it is just as effective to transfer files from a server to a local machine, edit the files locally using Notepad or another plain text editor, and then transfer the edited file back to the server; in fact, there are developers who prefer to work this way.

To use FTP, you need the same three pieces of information you need when connecting to the server: the server name, a login ID, and a password for that machine.

You also need to know what type of transfer you want to accomplish. There are two modes for transferring files: binary and ASCII. The type of the file being transferred determines which mode should be used. ASCII is used strictly for plain text files only, such as files you open and read in Notepad without affecting the content. All other files, including word processing documents, images, and .pdf files, must be transferred in binary mode. If you are not certain what type of file you have, try opening it in Notepad and see if the content is displayed correctly. If not, use binary mode.

You use text commands to transfer files via FTP. Be aware that products exist that offer a graphical interface for using FTP, such as WS_FTP and Hummingbird. These can be easier to use if you find yourself transferring large numbers of files often.

Do not overwrite files if you have not made a backup copy of them! Use Telnet to connect to the server and the basic commands outlined in Table 3.5 to create a backup copy first.

To transfer files, you must first access a "command-line prompt" in MS-DOS. Go to the Start menu and choose "Run..." off the menu popup. Type cmd or command in the space provided and click OK. A window should pop up with a prompt such as C:\WINDOWS>.

The FTP utility can connect a Windows PC to a UNIX server, or a Windows PC to a Windows server. The example used here illustrates a Windows PC connection to a UNIX server. At the prompt, type ftp followed by the name of the server you wish to access.

■ FOR EXAMPLE

```
C:\WINDOWS>  ftp server4.virgil.edu
```

You will be prompted to supply your user name and password. If successful, you see an ftp> prompt. To view a list of ftp commands available at this prompt, type help followed by the Enter key. To view help for a specific command, such as put, type help followed by the command, such as help put.

The pwd, ls, and cd commands introduced earlier in this chapter are also available at the ftp> prompt, so use them to navigate to the directory where the file should be placed. Be sure you are in the directory where you want to place the document before you proceed.

Set the transfer mode that you want, using either of the two commands, binary or ascii. Below is an example of switching to binary, and then to ASCII mode.

■ FOR EXAMPLE

```
ftp> binary
200 Type set to I.
ftp> ascii
200 Type set to A.
ftp>
```

To transfer the file, use the put command and the path and filename for the file you are transferring. If you stored a file in C:\TEMP\DOCUMENTS called NEW-PAGE.HTM, and you want to transfer it, you enter the following:

```
ftp> put c:\temp\documents\newpage.htm
```

Following are sample messages received after issuing the put command:

```
200 PORT command successful.
150 Opening ASCII mode data connection for NEWPAGE.HTM.
226 Transfer complete.
ftp: 83 bytes sent in 0.6Seconds 1.38Kbytes/sec.
ftp>
```

You can also retrieve a file from the server to work with locally. To accomplish this you use the get command:

```
ftp> get myserverfile.htm
```

The myserverfile.htm file is retrieved, and placed in the directory on your file system that you started from when you issued the ftp command.

If you wish to transfer many files at once, you can use different versions of the get and put commands: mget and mput. Since these are commands for many files, instead of specifying one file, use the asterisk (*) as a "wildcard" character. Using *.* indicates that all files should be transferred. Here is an example of mput that will put all files with the extension .htm on the server:

```
ftp>mput c:\temp\documents\*.htm
```

Here is the command with sample output. Note that there are two files, apple.htm and orange.htm, and that the ftp program prompts the user to supply a "y" or an "n" for each file before transferring it. The first file is confirmed for transfer while the second is not:

```
ftp>mput c:\temp\documents\*.htm
mput c:\temp\documents\apple.htm? y
200 PORT command successful.
150 Opening ASCII mode data connection for orange.htm
226 Transfer complete.
ftp: 7330 bytes sent in 0.6Seconds 1.38Kbytes/sec.
mput c:\temp\documents\orange.htm? n
ftp>
```

The mget command makes similar use of the asterisk as a wildcard character. Here is a sample of the mget command that retrieves all types of files from the server that begin with an "a":

```
ftp>mget a*.*
200 Type set to A.
mget apple.htm? y
200 PORT command successful.
150 Opening ASCII mode data connection for apple.htm(11
bytes).
226 Transfer complete.
ftp: 7330 bytes sent in 0.6Seconds 1.38Kbytes/sec.
mget artichoke.pdf? n
ftp>
```

Keep in mind whether the current transfer type is binary or ASCII. In the `mget` example, the transfer type was set to A or ASCII. The second file to be transferred was artichoke.pdf, which is not a plain text file. If the file had been retrieved from the server in ASCII mode, the resulting local file would have been unreadable. It would have to be transferred a second time, with the transfer mode set to binary. Be mindful of the transfer mode whenever you are transferring files. It is particularly easy to overlook the transfer type when working with multiple files, so the way the ftp program prompts the user to confirm transfer of each individual file is extremely helpful here.

Finally, to end the FTP session, type `quit` or `bye` and press the `Enter` key.

Once your files are transferred to the server, remember to connect to the server using Telnet, and check the permissions on the files, changing the permissions as necessary.

UNIT 3.1 EXERCISES

For this first exercise, the current browser document location is http://www.server4.virgil.edu/classnotes. The file you wish to access is located at http://www.server4.virgil.edu/classnotes/homework/menu.htm.

> **a)** Write the document-relative path to the file you wish to access.

> **b)** Write the root-relative path.

For this second exercise, the current browser document location is http://www.server4.virgil.edu/classnotes/homework/homework_one/HW1.htm. The file you wish to access is located at http://www.server4.virgil.edu/classnotes/notes_one.htm.

> **c)** Write the document-relative path you'd need to access the notes_one.htm file.

An image file rests on another server at this path: http://www.anotherserver.com/mydirectory/myfile.gif.

> **d)** Write the path you would use to link to the "myfile.gif" image.
> Assume that you'd like to change access permissions for the notes_one.htm file once you've accessed it.

e) Write the command you would use to grant the following permissions to the following levels of users:

- **user/owner**   All permissions
- **group**   Read and execute only
- **other**   No permissions granted yet

UNIT 3.1 EXERCISE ANSWERS

a) Write the document-relative path to the file you wish to access.

Answer: The document-relative path to the file you wish to access, menu.htm, is written as:

```
homework/menu.htm
```

Since your current directory is the classnotes directory, you must navigate downward though the directory tree to the subdirectory, homework, in order to access the menu.htm file.

b) Write the root-relative path.

Answer: Conversely, the root-relative path to the file you wish to access, menu.htm, is written as:

```
/classnotes/homework/menu.htm
```

c) Write the document-relative path you'd need to access the notes_one.htm file.

Answer: The document-relative path you'd need to access the notes_one.htm file is written as:

```
../../notes_one.htm
```

Since your starting point is the homework_one directory, note that it is necessary for you to navigate upward a total of two directories in the directory tree. Hence the notation, "../../".

d) Write the path you would use to link to the "myfile.gif" image.

Answer: The path you would use to link to the "myfile.gif" image would be written as:

```
http://www.anotherserver.com/mydirectory/myfile.gif
```

Since the file is located on another server, and not in the Web site's docroot, an absolute path must be used.

e) Write the command you would use to grant the following permissions to the following levels of users:

user/owner	All permissions
group	Read and execute only
other	No permissions granted yet

Answer: The command you would use to grant these permissions accordingly would be written as:

```
chmod 750 notes_one.htm
```

In order to set permissions for files in UNIX, you use the "change mode," or chmod, command. The "7" in the first position of the three-digit number outlining permissions to be granted denotes that all permissions have been granted to the "user/owner" level, (4(read) + 2(write) + 1(execute) = 7(all three permissions). The "5" in the second position of this three-digit number denotes that only two of the possible three permissions have been granted to the "group" level (4(read) + 1(execute) = 5(read and execute permissions only)). Lastly, the "0" in the third position of this three-digit number denotes that no permissions whatsoever have been granted to the "other" level. Therefore, in this example, this file has not yet been made publicly available.

UNIT
3.1

CHAPTER 4

WEB APPLICATION DESIGN

Before building an application, a Web developer must have a clear map of the system being built. There are proven strategies and methodologies for designing applications and designing Web pages. No code should be written until these steps are taken.

There is no right answer when it comes to how an application should look and how its screens should be designed. What everyone can agree on, however, is that design is a necessary step before building an application, and there are tools and methodologies that help make design easier and more effective. Moreover, everyone should also agree that the application should be straightforward and easy for the user to understand and use.

The steps outlined in this chapter must be undertaken before you start coding. If a design team provides you with a prototype, storyboard, and detailed design document, you have the information you need to start building the application, and you are well on your way. If the application has not been clearly outlined, however, or if you find yourself acting in the role of both designer and developer, then take the steps outlined in this chapter to be sure your project does not derail.

UNIT 4.1

WHAT IS WEB DESIGN?

WEB DESIGN VERSUS APPLICATION DESIGN

Web application design is really a fusion of two areas: Web design and application design. These areas have overlapped as applications have been created for the Web.

Application design refers to mapping out how an application will look and how users can accomplish tasks with it. The unit of a computer application is a screen. Designing an application means identifying each screen that is needed, the elements that comprise each screen, and the functionality of each screen. Another important part of application design is deciding how users will navigate the application. The architecture of moving from one screen to the next must be worked out in advance of building the application. Clearly, these decisions must be made for any application, regardless of whether it will be deployed on the Web or not.

Until recently, Web design specifically referred to making creative decisions about how to arrange a Web page. A Web designer is ideally a graphic artist. Web designers do not work with the back-end database. Web designers focus on the front-end—the look and feel of the screens. These designers are responsible for the effect that a page creates. They create a sample for each screen needed in an application. They may employ HTML and JavaScript to create a model, or they may create model pages using graphics software, and then hand that model page off to a programmer to create. Clearly, a sample page developed in HTML and JavaScript is more helpful for the programmer later on, since the HTML and JavaScript used to create the model can be reused when coding the actual application.

When an application is designed for the Web, the artistic skills of a Web designer transfer over quite easily to Web application design. Web designers have expertise in how a person interacts with a screen, how people respond to color schemes and artwork, and how to effectively present information. They have a grasp of how people navigate between screens, and how to create a consistent look and feel across an application. They understand the conventions of the Web, and they may have researched how users interact with a screen using the mouse versus the keyboard, how download times affect users, and other issues unique to the Web. In fact, more Web designers are styling themselves as experts on "usability," which means that they know how to focus on the user's experience when creating a design, instead of creating pages that are artistically interesting, yet may not be very easy to work with.

A programming project can benefit greatly from the input of a Web designer, who can make the application more effective.

DESIGN IN THE SYSTEM DEVELOPMENT LIFE CYCLE

Since programming projects can involve big budgets and a large cast of characters, a popular model has evolved to give a shape to the process, called the System Development Life Cycle (SDLC), shown below.

- Analysis
- Design
- Build
- Test
- User acceptance
- Migration
- Maintenance

The SDLC breaks down the work of a project into many phases, and each phase involves people with the specific skills necessary for dealing with that area. While there are slight differences in how the SDLC is envisioned, it is generally agreed upon that the first three phases are analysis, design, and build/develop. In the analysis phase, business analysts collect the business requirements and identify the data that the application must handle. In the design phase, the designers envision how the application itself will work. The requirements collected earlier, during the analysis phase, are translated into sample screens and descriptions of functionality. With a clear guide for what to create, the build phase can begin, in which programmers develop the application.

The end result of the design phase is a detailed design specification that a programmer can use to build an application. A specification should be clear and unambiguous. As stated earlier, the specifications are ideally created with the input of a Web designer. A specification that consists of a prototype of sample screens, and a design document, provides a solid specification for the programmers, as outlined further on in this chapter.

OBTAIN USER SIGNOFF

Users should approve the design before the developers start working on implementing the specifications. At each point in the design phase, it is important to verify assumptions with the users. The typical user is not a computer programmer or Web designer, and what is intuitive to a programmer or designer may not be intuitive to a user. If users do not approve the design, then it can be revisited and reworked multiple times until it meets with the users' approval. Obtaining approval at each phase is the way to ensure that the project being built will meet the users' needs. Specifications that everyone can point to when a project is complete avoid misunderstandings and increase the chances that the client will pay for the work.

The key is to resolve screen design issues and obtain approval for a final design before the developers start developing.

WHY TAKE TIME FOR DESIGN?

Good design forces decisions to be made ahead of time, before the application is actually built. The more thought that is put into design, the greater the chance of success for the project, and the happier everyone will be. If it seems easy to envision how the application will flow, then take a few minutes to write it down—and don't be surprised if it takes longer than you anticipated.

Good designers will seek out the gray areas and resolve them—amazingly enough these ambiguities will go away if addressed. If it is uncertain whether two departments—auditing and accounting, for instance—will both be using the system, that is not a way to proceed. Make a decision one way or the other, and provide a clear specification to the programmers. Or, focus on an area of the system that has no ambiguities, design that area of the system, and hold off on designing and building the part that is undetermined. Any design decisions not made in the design phase are left to the programmers, who tend not to appreciate this.

There is a great temptation to jump straight into the build or development phase without proper design. When time is short, spending valuable time on design seems like a waste when a programmer can start developing a screen right away. But the benefits of designing the application first are enormous. The more time spent on the design phase, the less time wasted reworking screens that do not meet the users' needs. Trying to ascertain what a user needs without clear guidelines takes time and energy away from programming the application. In fact, it is shown again and again that extra time spent in the design phase saves time on the programming side.

Another challenge comes in a smaller project where the same person is both designing and building an application. If you are doing both design and development, put aside development concerns and focus on good design first. As you design the application, if you find yourself thinking about how to make a screen work using PL/SQL or JavaScript or HTML, you are being distracted from your main job—effective design of the application. Concentrate on meeting the requirements of the users first. How the specification will be implemented is the programmer's job, so you do not need to worry about that while you are designing the application.

UNIT 4.2

HOW TO DESIGN A WEB APPLICATION

WHO IS THE USER?

The first and most important step in design is to identify the user of the application. If an application is built for a group of people, but no one can use it, then it is not a good application, no matter how flawlessly it works or how brilliantly it was coded. Remember, too, that the user is often paying for the application, which is another good reason to make the user your first consideration.

There might be several types of users. If this is the case, identify each distinct group of users and check that the design meets each group's needs. Suppose that the accounting department and the auditing department of a large corporation both need the application that you are building for them. Determine what each department will need from the application. Make sure there are not other groups of users whose needs are not being addressed. Then create a design that you think both departments can use. Finally, be sure to verify the design with each group.

Nothing will focus an application's design like identifying the user, and making sure the application meets the user's needs. If you cannot identify the user, you are in trouble.

STORYBOARD

The next step in design is to create a "storyboard." The idea of a storyboard has been borrowed from film and television, where a storyboard is used to map out successive scenes to help chart an entire film or show. It is a useful tool for communicating what something will look like before it exists. Once a storyboard is approved, the production schedule can be set up, and the film or show can be made.

In the Web application world, storyboards depict each successive application screen in detail. They serve as a blueprint for an application. They are more effective in most cases than a verbal description; programmers and users and designers can look at the same sample screen and understand it, even if the programmer is wondering how to build it, and the user is wondering if the screen will help in day-to-day work. In any design meeting, it will not be long before words fail and someone seeks out a whiteboard or piece of paper and starts drawing screens. These early scribbles can take on the status of hallowed historical documents once the application is built.

A good test of a storyboard is to show it to someone else, even someone unfamiliar with the application. If that person has trouble following the screens, ask yourself why and reexamine your choices. Designers like to use the word "intuitive" when describing a good design. This means it is fairly easy for someone who is new to the design to understand it.

Create a storyboard either by hand or through a software tool. Many kinds of software—flowchart software, presentation software, and graphics software—let users draw boxes, text, buttons, or drop-down menus on a page. This is all that is needed to give an idea of the page layout. Note that these tools do not generate HTML. That type of tool is discussed in the next section, "Build a Prototype."

BUILD A PROTOTYPE

A prototype is a model of the application. Prototypes are built to give users an even clearer idea of how an application will work. The prototype is built for display on a computer screen, so that a user can see what the application looks like.

For a Web application, prototypes should be built in HTML and JavaScript. Developers can reuse the HTML and JavaScript code when building the application.

What is the difference between building a prototype and building an application? A prototype is not fully functional. Buttons do not have to work; a prototype may be presented to the user with an explanation such as, "When the user clicks on this button here, they will see the following screen," as the designer manually opens the next HTML page in the sequence. A prototype is not connected with a database. Instead, "dummy data" is shown on each screen, to give users an idea of what a screen will look like when it is filled in with data. The HTML Web pages that you create in Chapter 5, "Introduction to HTML: Basic Tags, Tables, and Frames," and Chapter 6, "Advanced HTML: Forms, Nested Tables, and Nested Frames," are examples of prototype Web pages. Later in this book, you take these HTML pages and make them fully functional using PL/SQL and the Oracle 9iAS.

Again, the question must be raised: Why spend time on building a prototype? Why not build a fully functional application instead of a prototype? The question should really be phrased: Why build a fully-functional application and then have to change it numerous times at great expense, when it is much easier to build prototypes and change them until a design can be settled upon? It is a fact that users often change their minds once they see a prototype. A user might say, "I realize that is exactly what I asked for. But now that I see it, I need to change it."

TOOLS FOR BUILDING A PROTOTYPE

Building prototypes is simplified by the many tools available on the market, classified as HTML editors or Web development tools, such as Dreamweaver™ or HomeSite™. These types of tools offer a graphical interface to help write HTML code. Often they will utilize color-coding for different types of tags, which helps avoid typos and HTML coding errors. They can also let the user switch between the HTML view of a page, and the page as rendered in a browser, making it easy to track your progress. Tasks like creating a table can be accomplished via menu items and buttons and clicks, instead of writing out the HTML opening and closing tags for tables. Web designers refer to "painting" a button or a drop-down menu on a screen, and "painting" a screen. A Web designer has learned to work with at least one of these tools, and can build an HTML prototype for the programmer to use.

It is also a good idea for programmers to learn one of these HTML tools. Not every programmer on every project is handed an HTML prototype as a starting point for developing code. If a programmer is given a picture of a screen to build, instead of HTML code, the programmer has to start coding from scratch. The programmer can put the HTML elements of a page together more quickly if they can use a Web design tool, instead of writing the HTML code "by hand." Another time to use a Web design tool is when a legacy application is being moved to the Web. The screen design is clear from the old application, but it must be recreated in HTML code. Again, knowing a Web design tool gives the programmer an edge. The programmer can use the tool to concentrate on creating the look and feel that the users want. After all, these tools are created for just that purpose. Once the programmer has an HTML prototype, the programmer can switch gears and start making that page functional using programming expertise.

When using commercially available software, beware of extra tags that clutter up the code. The HTML will be reused later, so use a program like Dreamweaver™ that does not add many extra unneeded tags. Also watch for HTML tools that offer "styles" to the designer. Supporting these styles later may mean importing many directories of images and stylesheets, and chances are you will need to create your own look and feel rather than use a template provided by a software tool.

DESIGN DOCUMENT

A storyboard or prototype needs to be accompanied by a design document. Storyboards and prototypes provide the visuals. The design document provides text that explains the visuals in more detail. For a screen that lets users update information about a student, this document lists each field on the screen and explains where the data is stored in the database.

The design document also describes the actions that can be taken on the screen, and the possible results. Buttons on the screen should be listed one by one in the design document, with a full description of what will happen when the user clicks them. The design document provides the additional detail needed by the programmer.

UNIT 4.3

TIPS FOR WEB DESIGN

WORKING ON THE WEB

This unit contains some general tips for designing Web pages in your storyboard and prototype. There are no right answers, and there are pros and cons for every design choice you might make. However, there are general rules and conventions that most Web developers have adopted. Below are some tips and advice that might prove helpful, and some pitfalls that you can avoid.

SEARCH SCREENS

Consider whether you need to offer the user a search screen. The primary function of most applications is to retrieve information for the user. Whether this is referred to as reporting, records retrieval, display, inquiries, queries, or viewing records, it is the same task of quickly accessing and showing a user the information that is needed. The majority of the time, people go to an application for information.

For this reason, many applications begin with a "search screen." A search screen is used to find a particular record so that the record can be viewed or updated, or even deleted. Sometimes the search confirms that the record does not exist in the system. At other times, multiple records may be returned that all meet the criteria for the search.

Starting from the data entry screen is akin to thinking like a developer. Developers often focus on the need for screens that interact with the database, such as data entry screens and screens to update data. For example, a developer might know that an application needs to add a record to the STUDENT table, so the developer designs a screen that lets users enter a first name, last name, and so on. That will not make sense as a starting point for a user. It is true that database applications require data entry screens. However, that cannot be the first screen that a user sees. A user may want to check what data is in the system before entering a new record. How does a user find the record that they need to change? If you start with a search screen, you can include a button called "Add a New Record." If you want to present a data entry screen to the user first, make sure to include a button that reads "Search." Otherwise, from the user's perspective, all he or she can ever do is enter records.

For search screens, think about which identifiers are meaningful to a business user. For a database with student records, are users required to know a student ID number to look up a student? Can first name and/or last name be used to look up students?

Also imagine each of the following cases, and envision the screens that you would need in each case:

- Multiple records are returned from a search
- One record is returned from a search
- No records are returned from a search

REUSING SCREENS

In many cases, the same screen can be used for multiple purposes. This is common for screens that both add and update records.

Draw a screen that allows a user to add a student to the system. The user needs to add the student's first and last name, address information, employer, and a phone number. For an example, refer to Figure 4.1, which you build later in this book as part of the sample application.

Now draw a screen for updating a student's record, as shown in Figure 4.2.

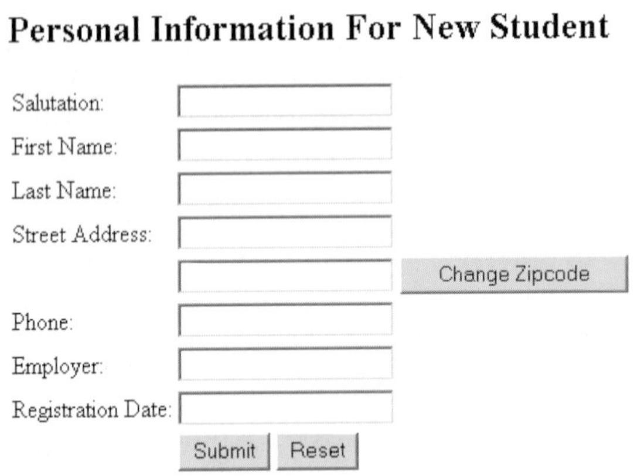

Personal Information For New Student

Salutation:
First Name:
Last Name:
Street Address:
                                        Change Zipcode
Phone:
Employer:
Registration Date:
                        Submit   Reset

Figure 4.1 ■ Screen to add a student's personal information.

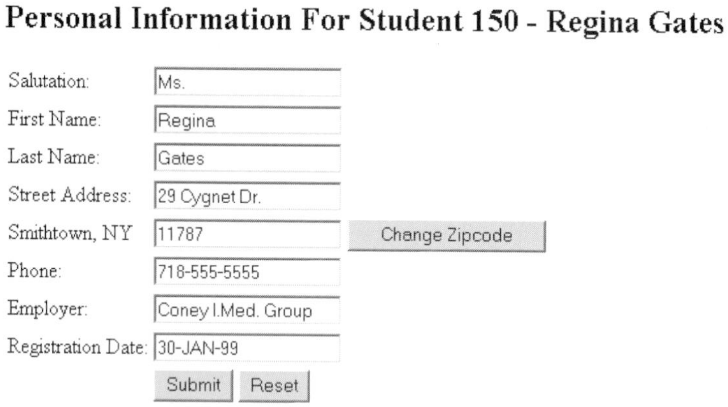

Personal Information For Student 150 - Regina Gates

Salutation:	Ms.	
First Name:	Regina	
Last Name:	Gates	
Street Address:	29 Cygnet Dr.	
Smithtown, NY	11787	Change Zipcode
Phone:	718-555-5555	
Employer:	Coney I.Med. Group	
Registration Date:	30-JAN-99	
	Submit Reset	

Figure 4.2 ■ Screen to update a student's personal information.

In Figure 4.2, the user can enter information about the student's first and last name, address information, employer, and a phone number, as in Figure 4.1. However, since this screen updates an existing student, the student has been assigned a student ID number by the system, and the student's ID number and current name are displayed.

Compare these two screens. Except for the heading, the screen layout is identical. Often, screens to add records and update records can often be combined into a single screen. Since the screens in this application will be generated dynamically, using PL/SQL, the appropriate title can be given to the page at the time it is put together.

Combining screens appropriately has many benefits. If two separate screens are designed, one for updating and one for inserting, then the screens might be given to two different programmers to develop. Not only would the programmers be duplicating each other's efforts needlessly, but also it is likely that differences will crop up between the screens, and this is confusing for everyone. For example, screens should include some kind of error checking on what the user has entered, as is covered in Chapter 14, "JavaScript Form Validation." If this validation is not handled identically, then the screens will function differently, in ways the user does not expect. The add-new-record screen may allow a dash to be entered in the middle of a zipcode, whereas the update screen requires the zipcode to be five or nine numbers only, without a dash. Data that is accepted by the add-new-record screen will be rejected by the update screen as invalid. Small differences in layout and appearance are also likely. Rather than requesting two screens, design this as one screen. One programmer would then create a screen that either displays a student ID and database information in the case of an update, or does not if the user is adding a record. Moreover, the customer will be paying for one screen instead of two.

Keep this in mind when creating a storyboard or prototype. Identifying screens that can be reused for multiple purposes can simplify the design and reduce the number of screens you are working with, and it makes sense from a programming perspective, too.

NAVIGATION DESIGN

Navigation is an important consideration. It is vital to plan for how users will move through an application. Part of creating a storyboard is deciding the order in which users can navigate to pages. Make sure that no page is a dead end, or "orphan" page, that does not provide a menu or some other means to get to another page in the application.

On the Web, navigation is most often accomplished by clicking on buttons or links. For more on buttons that submit forms, see Chapter 6, "Advanced HTML: Forms, Nested Tables, and Nested Frames." For more on JavaScript events like clicking on buttons, see Chapter 7, "Introduction to JavaScript." A few other JavaScript events can trigger loading a new page, such as changing a value in a drop-down list or changing a radio button selection, but for the most part, buttons and links are the connections holding an application together.

This is where knowing the users comes in. What are the day-to-day tasks that users will need to accomplish? As stated earlier in this chapter, users may need to access very different areas of the system, such as areas for updating data or viewing cumulative reports that reflect the most current data. Avoid forcing users to navigate through five screens to get to the one they want every day. Identify each task the user needs to accomplish, and create a link for each area. Then create the screens the user needs.

Links can be grouped into menus. Menus make navigation more flexible. If users have a menu or a consistent list of links available to them at all times, they can move easily from one area to another as needed.

Also consider what will happen when users save changes. In most cases they should be returned to the same screen to see that their changes have taken effect. Then they may make more changes and click the "Save" button again, or use a different button to take them to another area of the application entirely.

TIPS FOR PAGE LAYOUT

If you are responsible for designing a Web application, it is important to adhere to some of the principles of Web design. These are some guidelines for Web page design, from the perspective of a Web designer. Not everyone will agree with even these general rules of Web design, but it is good to know the rules before deciding to break them.

CONSISTENT LOOK AND FEEL

As a user clicks through pages in a Web site or application, they should have the impression that they are moving about within the same world. Every page must be identified with the application. This can be achieved by using consistent color schemes, fonts, graphics, and backgrounds on all screens in an application. Some of the real estate on each page may be devoted to a logo or company name.

Positioning a logo in the upper-left corner of a screen is extremely effective. The upper-left corner is the first place the eye travels to on a page, so it is considered "prime real estate," and placing a logo there will have maximum impact. Creating an association based on a certain logo or look and feel is known as *branding*. Branding is important for Internet sites, because organizations want to establish their presence on the Web. Even within a company, different applications may have to compete for attention or funds, so branding may be helpful to promote an application, and the new logo may appear on t-shirts or pens to attract attention for the application.

**UNIT
4.3**

TEXT

Hold up this book to a computer screen, and compare the page width with the screen width. Chances are that the computer screen is wider than your book. If text is printed from one side of a screen to the other, it is a tiring trip for the eye. Use narrow columns for large blocks of text. Visit some news Web sites and you will see that most, if not all, use narrow columns of text in their articles, even when doing so means having blank space to the sides of the column, or making the article stretch further down on the screen.

Blank space on a page is better than too much clutter. In the world of print media, blank space, or "whitespace," is a waste of increasingly expensive paper. On Web sites, designers strive for a clean look and feel, and too much clutter on a page is considered distracting. Try using more empty space when possible.

The original HTML specification did not allow developers to use more than one font. However, for some time Web pages have been able to handle multiple fonts. That does not mean a developer should strive to use as many as possible on a page. Mixing font faces, font sizes, and font colors on a page can distract from the information you are trying to convey. Unless you are commissioned to create a Web page for Times Square, be very careful when you are mixing different fonts.

Although the Web is a familiar interface, there are application screens where the user might benefit from instructions about what the screen does. On the other hand, remember that instructions will be seen every time the user navigates to a page, long after the user's first visit. On later visits, once users have mastered the application, perhaps from performing the same tasks upon it daily, lengthy instructions may become an annoyance, and instructions take up space, or "real estate," on the page. One solution is to remove instructions from a page, but provide a link that the user can click on to receive instructions for that page. Instructions can appear in a separate pop-up window, which can be done using JavaScript, as shown in Chapter 7, "Introduction to JavaScript."

Writing for the Web is also different from writing for print media. A print publication may have an opening "Welcome" page, with grandiloquent text that serves as an introduction. Some of this text can seem bloated or inappropriate on the Web. Most Web pages exist to effectively communicate information.

 Don't underline text for emphasis. Underlined text will be confused with a hyperlink on the Web.

FRAMES

Some design disputes are over whether to use frames or not to use frames. Frames have many helpful uses. To show how frames can be implemented, the sample application included in this book makes use of frames. First, let's consider some of the benefits of using frames.

Frames can serve as an excellent tool for navigation. A frameset divides a screen up into separate regions, or frames, as described in Chapter 5, "Introduction to HTML: Basic Tags, Tables, and Frames." One or more of the frames can be devoted to menus for navigation. This makes the application more "user-friendly." No matter which part of the application a user is in, the user knows where on the screen to look to move to another screen.

Frames are also a good tool for promoting a consistent look and feel. One frame can be devoted to displaying a company logo, application name, or artwork, and remain fixed in place while other parts of the page change or are scrolled through. For example, the top frame in a page displays a logo, while the bottom frame contains a large report that the user can scroll through downwards. Having the logo consistently at the top of the screen creates the impression of being in the same place, despite other frames that change.

Frames are absolutely necessary when one part of a page must remain stationary, while another part of the page can be scrolled through.

Frames have their detractors. Frames can look messy when each frame is displayed with a scrollbar. If a user wants to bookmark a page that uses frames, the original frameset is bookmarked, not the specific combination of frames that the user is seeing. That can be an acceptable result for an application, as opposed to a Web site.

BUTTONS AND LINKS

Buttons and links allow users to move through an application. A user will come to depend on them and expect to find them easily.

Buttons should be placed in the same part of the page on every screen. There is no reason to have a "Save" button on the bottom of one screen, a "Save" button on the top of another screen, and a "Save" button mischievously off to the side of a third screen. The Web offers many outlets for creativity without this kind of innovation. Users do not wish to hunt for the "Save" button, nor do they appreciate clicking on the wrong button by mistake because it appears in a different place than they have come to expect.

One easy trap to fall into is to give buttons inconsistent labels. The label is the text that appears on the button itself. If this label reads "Save" on one screen and "Store" on another, that is unnecessarily confusing. "Next" and "Continue" are often used within the same application to accomplish the same task of moving the user to the next screen in a sequence. Choose one label or the other for a more professional application.

Cryptic links will not be clicked on. Newspaper headlines will sometimes have teaser headlines to draw the readers' attention. Once the reader is looking at the headline, they can drop their eye downward to view the article. On the Web, the reader cannot simply glance over to the article to get an idea of the content. The user must click on a link to find out what the text in the link means. If a user is presented with a page full of links, they are not likely to explore every link simply to decipher each one's meaning. A title such as "Discount Books" is much more effective, and more easily remembered, than a link that reads, "A Penny Saved is a Penny Earned."

HORIZONTAL AND VERTICAL MENUS

Consider horizontal and vertical menus to help users navigate through the application. A horizontal menu is a collection of links listed across the top of a page. A vertical menu is a list of links positioned to the left or right side of the screen, usually underneath the horizontal menu. These menus, or navigation bars, are a staple of the Web, and are known familiarly as "nav bars."

Typically, the horizontal navigation bar has links to general areas of the application. This navigation bar does not change while the user moves through one area or another. If an application has several general areas that each have different functionality, then a horizontal menu may be appropriate.

Vertical menus, on the other hand, change depending on which section of the application the user is in. The options listed in the vertical menu are specific to the area that the user is currently visiting. When a new area is clicked on the horizontal menu bar, the vertical menu bar changes to reflect what is available in the new area.

ACCESSIBILITY

The Web is largely a visual medium, and users with vision impairments should be kept in mind. Moreover, it is a legal requirement to do so in the United States.

The Americans with Disabilities Act (ADA), enacted in 1992, establishes requirements for businesses of all sizes to offer equal opportunities to their workers.

A screen reader, or text-to-voice speech synthesis program, reads the text in an HTML document, but needs information about any images it encounters. It is easy to provide an image label by including an ALT attribute in each image tag. The ALT attribute specifies alternate text that can be displayed or read in place of the image. A screen reader can read the value in the ALT attribute when it encounters an image. Including an ALT attribute is good practice in any case, since users may set their browsers not to display images because of the longer download times required for images. You may also have seen alternate text appear in a yellow box when the mouse is positioned over an image. Sample HTML is shown below.

Unit 4.3

■ *FOR EXAMPLE*

```
<IMG SRC= "inst.gif" ALT= "Instructor Information"
HEIGHT=50 WIDTH=50>
```

A common error is to neglect to include an ALT attribute for images used as buttons and menu item images. Every image on a page should have an ALT attribute.

In addition, each page should also be assigned a title, using the <TITLE> tag. A screen reader will often start with the title of a page, so an informative title is extremely helpful.

Approximately 10 percent of people have some form of colorblindness. The majority of people who are colorblind experience red and green hues as shades of gray. The other .01 percent experience a much rarer form of blue and yellow colorblindness. An application that uses red and green to demarcate text from backgrounds could confuse a significant portion of the audience. Experienced designers account for colorblindness when choosing a color palette.

REVIEWING THE DESIGN

To test the validity of your design, walk through the application the way each type of user would. Imagine having to perform tasks, such as going to the new system for information, and see if the design meets your needs.

Compare the design against the CRUD matrix. "CRUD" stands for Create–Read–Update–Delete. For each table of information in the database, how will these four operations be handled? For operations in which the application is responsible for providing this function, does it do so?

Keep notes about the tasks that the system is designed to handle. These imaginary walk-throughs that you conduct will provide the basis for testing later on in the SDLC. To test an application thoroughly, testers must attempt to use the application the way the users will, and they need scripts with specific tasks to attempt. Your notes are a valuable head start for the testing process.

UNIT 4.3 EXERCISES

CREATE A STORYBOARD FOR THE SAMPLE APPLICATION

Below are the requirements for the sample application in this book. Create a storyboard of screens that meet the requirements. Then compare your storyboard with the specifications on the companion Web site provided for this book.

- Users will be the administrators of a technical program.
- Administrators need to perform the following tasks:
  - Look up student information and change it and add students
  - Enter grade information for students
  - Look up instructor information and change it and add instructors
  - Assign classes to classrooms
  - Calculate a final grade

As with all design, there is more than one right answer.

SECTION II

CREATING
THE APPLICATION

C H A P T E R   5

INTRODUCTION TO HTML: BASIC TAGS, TABLES, AND FRAMES

CHAPTER OBJECTIVES

After reading this chapter, you will be able to understand:

Creating a Web site is next to impossible without some use of Hypertext Markup Language (HTML). HTML is the text markup language currently used on the World Wide Web to indicate the structure and formatting of most Web pages. Web developers use this language to tell Web browsers how to display Web pages. HTML is a relatively simple Web development language to learn and you can quickly and easily build a very professional-looking set of Web pages immediately by implementing a few common HTML tags.

An HTML document is a plain text file (often referred to as an *ASCII file*) with codes (referred to as *tags*) inserted in the text to define elements in the document. These tags generally have two parts, a beginning tag (sometimes called an *on-code*) and an ending tag (sometimes called an *off-code*), that contain the text to be defined. A few tags don't require ending tags. These tags will be noted as they are covered. You can represent a tag in the following manner, where the ellipsis (...) denotes the text you want to define:

```
<TAGNAME> ... </TAGNAME>
```

For example, the following HTML code represents a line of text to be bolded within an HTML document:

```
<B>This line of text will be displayed by your Web browser
in boldface.</B>
```

In this chapter you learn to create a few simple Web pages using common HTML tags. Later in this chapter you are given an opportunity to further refine the look and feel of your pages by adding basic HTML tables and basic HTML frames. You learn that tables and frames can be used to logically separate parts of a Web application, as well as to provide a cleaner presentation due to their ability to assist in areas such as aligning the various elements of your Web pages.

UNIT 5.1

BASIC HTML CONCEPTS

THE DIFFERENCE BETWEEN A WEB PAGE AND A WEB SITE

WHAT IS A WEB PAGE?

A *Web page* is a hypertext (HTML) document contained in a single file. It is simply a plain text document that can be any length, although display of most Web pages usually extends to no more than two or three screens. All codes (HTML tags) are entered into the document as ordinary text.

Text editors such as word processors use binary-level formatting and embed this formatting in their text documents. When you mark some text as boldface in a word processing document, you don't see the actual computer code that causes the text to appear or print in boldface; instead, the formatting instructions are stored at the binary level. This is not the case with HTML documents. You have to do it all yourself. There is no underlying program code to translate what you type as you go. You type in **<B>** where you want the browser to turn boldfacing on and **</B>** where you want it to turn boldfacing off. This cuts down on the computer overhead when sending an HTML file to a browser.

WHAT IS A WEB SITE?

A *Web site* often has a couple of different meanings. Servers are often referred to as Web sites (since they are sites/locations on the Web), but any grouping of related and linked Web pages sharing a common theme or subject matter may also be called a Web site. It is simply a collection of related Web pages, similar to the chapters in a book, tied and linked together, usually through a *home page* (sometimes referred to as an *index page* or a *default page*). This home page serves as the navigational starting point and directory to the rest of the Web site. Web pages only comprise a Web site if they are interlinked and related to each other as parts of a whole. If Web pages are not related and linked to one another they do not form a Web site, even if they're stored in the same directory on the same server.

WHAT IS A HOME PAGE?

The term *home page* has a number of different meanings. The page that is loaded automatically when you first start your browser is sometimes referred to as the browser's home page, or *start page*. This Web page can be located on either the Internet or your own hard drive. The HOME button, located in the toolbar of most browsers, takes you to the page designated as the browser's home page. You can specify which page you want as your browser's home page.

The home page is the entry point to all of the other pages that comprise a Web site. The entry point is usually a small Web page, serving as a menu or directory to the Web pages that comprise the rest of the Web site. A user of such a Web site needs only to type in the URL of the Web site's home page to then decide what else to view in the remainder of the Web site.

WHAT IS HTML?

As stated in the chapter overview, an HTML document is simply a plain ASCII text file containing text and HTML markup tags that define the composition of a Web page—the body of the text, headings, paragraphs, line breaks, text elements, images, and so on.

A markup language like HTML is merely a collection of codes—*tags* or *elements* in this case—that are used to indicate the structure and format of a document. The codes are interpreted by a formatting program, such as a Web browser, that renders the document. Elements in HTML consist of alphanumeric tags within angle brackets. They are usually grouped into pairs, but there are some exceptions. Table 5.1 displays a few common HTML elements.

The tags themselves are not case-sensitive. As far as Web browsers are concerned, **<p>** is interpreted the same as **<P>**, and **
** is equivalent to **
**. In the interest of using good programming style, however, case should be kept consistent.

Notice that some of the above beginning tags require ending tags and some do not. Tags that consist of both beginning and ending tags that bracket text or

Table 5.1 ▪ A Few HTML Elements

Begin Tag	End Tag	Description
<H1>	</H1>	The largest page heading available
<I>	</I>	Italicized text
<BODY>	</BODY>	Encloses most viewable page content
<P>	</P> (optional)	Denotes a paragraph of text
 	None	A line break

other tag elements are sometimes referred to as *container tags*, for example, **<I></I>**. Tags that stand alone, like the **
** tag, may be called *empty tags*. And some tags may look like empty tags, but they are actually container tags with implied end tags, for example, **<P>**.

To make it easier to distinguish markup text from regular document content, write all HTML tags in uppercase. There are many HTML editing tools available that provide tag-coloring features to make reading and writing HTML easier.

HTML elements often have attributes that affect how the content of a particular element(s) will be rendered. For example, attributes are very common with complex elements such as **<FONT>**, which specifies how a line or lines of text should be rendered. Attributes in the **<FONT>** tag specify the font's face, size, color, and so on. Consider the following line of HTML code:

```
<FONT FACE="Arial" SIZE="+1" COLOR="Blue">
```

Attribute values should be enclosed within double quotes. Many browsers allow you to use single quotes or no quotes at all, especially for values that consist of just one word. There are some situations in which single quotes may be used within attribute values. This usually occurs when JavaScript is used, or when the value of the attribute includes special characters like spaces or punctuation.

While HTML elements are not case-sensitive, the contents of attributes usually are. As someone who is familiar with coding SQL statements using an Oracle database, you remember that the SQL keywords are case-insensitive while everything enclosed in single quotes or double quotes is case-sensitive. Similarly, the HTML line of code **<IMG SRC="myImage.gif">** is not necessarily equivalent to **<IMG SRC="MYIMAGE.gif">**. The IMG tag and its SRC attribute are explained later in this chapter.

HTML files are also not generally sensitive to spacing. Most browsers collapse multiple spaces or tabs into a single space, and ignore line breaks that are not specified with the **
** tag. For instance, this HTML code:

```
<B>Once rendered by the browser, this text will display as
a bold line of text.</B>
```

and this HTML code:

```
<B>Once rendered by the browser,     this
text will display
as a bold line of text.</B>
```

are both displayed the same way in a browser:

```
Once rendered by the browser, this text will display as a
bold line of text.
```

Spaces, tabs, and returns collapse when HTML files are displayed in a browser, unless they are included within elements such as the **<PRE>** preformatted element. This element, if surrounding the second line of text, displays the text exactly as is.

Since HTML allows for judicious use of spacing and line breaks, utilize spaces and line breaks in your source code for readability, particularly for separating markup from content. Remember, unless your text is included within the <PRE> element, additional spacing does not affect how the browser renders your document.

How can tags be used together? One more aspect of HTML elements is that they may be *nested*. In other words, they can surround each other. For example, if you'd like to both bold and italicize a line of text, you may write the following:

```
<B><I>Once rendered by the browser, this text will display
as a bold and italicized line of text.</I></B>
```

It is quite easy to cross tags. In other words, to write something like the following:

```
<B></I>Once rendered by the browser, this text will dis-
play as a bold line of text.</B></I>
```

However, doing so does not comply with the formal definition of HTML and may be misinterpreted by the browser. Always close tags in the reverse order in which you opened them:

```
<B><I></I></B>, NOT   <B><I></B></I>.
```

You may need to nest a tag within itself, because each occurrence of the tag has different attribute values. The following example shows a **<FONT>** tag nested within another **<FONT>** tag, but with different values for the color attribute.

```
<FONT FACE="Arial" COLOR="black">Nesting tags is an
<FONT COLOR="red"> important concept.</FONT></FONT>
```

Note that there are two **</FONT>** closing tags, because there are two opening **<FONT>** tags. Even though the same **<FONT>** tag is used, one closing **</FONT>** tag will not suffice. Remember to include a closing tag for each opening tag.

WHAT HTML IS NOT

HTML is not a programming language. It does not specify logic. It specifies merely the layout and structure of a document. You use HTML to define the composition of a Web page. The display of its appearance is rendered and controlled by how the browser you use interprets your HTML code.

For instance, you may write a line of HTML code that uses the <H1>...</H1> tags. The browser translates these codes into a first-level heading. One browser may show H1 as Times New Roman 20-point text, whereas another browser might show this same set of tags in a completely different font face and size.

At this time, it is worth taking a moment to explain how HTML-coded Web pages and Web browsers work together. To display a Web page on your computer, a Web browser must first download it and any graphics you'd like included on the page to your computer. If the Web page document were to specify the formatting and appearance details the way a word processing document does, it would increase the amount of data to be transmitted, not to mention the size of the file, thereby increasing the amount of time it takes to transfer. Leaving these formatting details to the Web browser means that the size of HTML documents sent over the Web can remain relatively small, since they're just simple ASCII text files.

However, the result is that every Web browser often has its own idea about how best to display a particular Web page. Your Web page may look different in Internet Explorer than it does in Netscape Navigator. Your Web page may also look different in different versions of each browser, or at different resolutions on different monitors, or when rendered on a Mac or PC machine. To be thorough, you'll need to test your completed page on more than just one version of a browser and on more than one computer.

UNIT 5.2

COMMON HTML TAGS

 This unit is, by no means, intended to be an exhaustive introduction to the HTML language. For more information on any of the HTML tags introduced in this chapter or subsequent chapters, please consult a text solely devoted to the discussion of HTML.

CREATING AND VIEWING HTML FILES

Since HTML files are simple ASCII text files, you don't need anything special to create them. Any ordinary text editor will do. When starting out, you can use something as simple as Windows Notepad. In contrast, using a word processing program to write HTML can be problematic. You cannot keep the same file open in both your word processor and your Web browser, which means you won't be able to dynamically debug your HTML files, and you will have to save the document as a plain text file instead of the word processor's own default format. Use either Notepad or an HTML editor similar to Notepad.

The preferred browser to be used when completing this book's exercises is Microsoft Internet Explorer (IE), version 5.5 and higher.

Browsers can display HTML documents stored locally on a computer, as well as documents stored remotely and accessed via the Internet. You can edit and preview local HTML files by performing the following steps:

1. Start Microsoft Internet Explorer.
2. If your dialer begins to dial your ISP's access phone number, click the Cancel button.
3. If you receive the message "Unable to retrieve Web page in offline mode," click the OK button.
4. To open and display a local HTML file (Web page) from your hard drive (please don't ever load files from your floppy drive; it is far more time-consuming than loading from your hard drive, not to mention

the fact that your hard drive contains much more available space), select File, Open, Browse. Navigate to the folder where the local HTML file you want to view is stored, and then double-click it to open it. Click the OK button to finally load the page into your browser.

BEGIN TO CODE HTML: THE DOCUMENT TAGS

All HTML files should include at least the following tags:

- <HTML></HTML>
- <HEAD></HEAD>
- <TITLE></TITLE>
- <BODY></BODY>

The HTML tag defines the topmost element in an HTML document. It has both a start tag and an end tag. All other text and tags are nested within it. For example:

```
<HTML>
All HTML text and other element tags should be placed
here.
</HTML>
```

 Remember that the HTML start tag, <HTML>, must always be the very first HTML tag in your file, while the HTML end tag, </HTML>, must always be the very last HTML tag in your file.

The HEAD tag contains information about your HTML file, such as its title. It can also contain other tags that provide identification and supplementary information about the document. Browsers do not display this information. Regardless of how the HEAD tag is used, it should always be included in an HTML file for purposes of style and legibility. Adding to the example already begun in this chapter, the latest version of this HTML Web page looks like the following:

```
<HTML>
<HEAD>
</HEAD>
Other HTML text and other element tags should be placed
here.
</HTML>
```

The only element required in the head of a document is the **<TITLE>** tag element. It identifies your page to the rest of the world. Other browsers and indexing robots use the text included in the TITLE tag as a link to the page, and as the document title while the Web page is being viewed. The text within this tag appears on your browser's title bar, but it doesn't display as part of the page. The title should be descriptive, but short. Someone else should be able to determine what your page is about merely by reading the title. Including the TITLE tag in this chapter's example results in the following:

```
<HTML>
<HEAD>
<TITLE>This is your title: with a short description</TITLE>
</HEAD>
Other HTML text and other element tags should be placed here.
</HTML>
```

The **<BODY>** tag is the complement of the **<HEAD>** tag. It contains all the tags, text, and other elements that a browser actually displays as the body of an HTML document. Both the HEAD tag and the BODY tag, as well as all other tags, are nested inside the HTML tag. It is important to note, however, that the BODY tag comes after the HEAD tag. They each denote distinct, separate parts of an HTML document. In other words, the **<BODY>** tag (the beginning tag for the BODY container element) is placed only after the **</HEAD>** tag (the ending tag for the HEAD container element) appears, not before. This code is acceptable:

```
<HEAD></HEAD><BODY></BODY>.
```

This code is not:

```
<HEAD><BODY></HEAD></BODY>.
```

Nor is this code acceptable:

```
<HEAD><BODY></BODY></HEAD>.
```

 The HEAD and BODY tags are the only tags that are nested directly in-side the HTML tag. All other text and tags are contained within the <HEAD> or <BODY> tags. The </BODY> and </HTML> ending tags should always be the last two tags in your HTML file.

Include the BODY tag inside the HTML tag, but after the HEAD tag, by typing the following:

```
<HTML>
<HEAD>
<TITLE>This is your title: with a short description</TITLE>
</HEAD>
<BODY>
Other text, elements and tags to be included in your HTML
Web page should be placed here.
</BODY>
</HTML>
```

You've probably noticed that Web pages you view on the Web can have either an .HTM or an .HTML extension. The .HTML extension is the most conventional extension for HTML files on a UNIX Web server. However, some operating systems only recognize a three-letter file extension. You'll be safe with most, if not all, operating systems if you simply stick to using .HTM extensions for any HTML files you create.

With some operating systems (like Windows NT, for instance), you may notice that, when using Notepad as your HTML editor, you occasionally run into the problem where your action of saving your file results in Notepad's default .TXT extension being appended to your HTML filename. For example, you mean to save your file as Test.htm, however, it is actually saved as Test.htm.txt, even though you specify Test.htm as the file name and set the File Type to All Files (*.*). To get around this problem, enclose your filename with double quotes when assigning a filename to your HTML file. In other words, when saving your HTML file in Notepad, you can simply type "Test.htm" (be sure to include the double quotes) in the File Name text box of the Save As dialog pop-up.

Save your file as C:\Guest\Test.htm and view it through your browser using the instructions listed at the beginning of this unit. Your file should resemble the example file shown in Figure 5.1.

In Internet Explorer, you can press the Refresh button each time you want to view the latest version of your HTML files. Therefore, each time you make a change to your HTML file, after saving it, you should immediately check your work by hopping over to your browser, then loading the page (if you haven't already done so) or reloading it to get the latest version by pressing Refresh. Alternatively, you can refresh your page by typing Ctrl+R.

Figure 5.1 ■ **Your first Web page.**

HEADING LEVELS

Headings are used to organize your Web page into levels of hierarchy. The top-level heading (the H1 tag) should be the title that you'd like displayed at the top of your Web page. (Don't confuse this with the title that appears in the browser's title bar, which you create with the TITLE tag.) Since the H1 tag is used to create the title of your Web page, you should only have one H1 tag per Web page. This is the typical stylistic convention for most Web pages on the Web.

A second-level heading (created with the H2 tag) should be used to define a major division within your page, and a third-level heading (H3 tag) delineates a subdivision within a major division. Most browsers support up to six different heading levels.

Within the BODY element of your Test.htm file, type the following:

```
<HTML>
<HEAD>
<TITLE>This is your title: with a short
description</TITLE>
</HEAD>
<BODY>
<H1>The title of your web page should be placed here.</H1>
<H2>This H2 heading level denotes a major division within
this document.</H2>
<H3>This H3 heading level denotes a sub-division within a
major division.</H3>
Other text, elements and tags to be included in your HTML
Web page should be placed here.
</BODY>
</HTML>
```

Each time you add something to your Test.htm file, make sure you save your changes, then reload the file into your browser to check the result of your work. Your file should resemble the example file shown in Figure 5.2.

As you can see, when displayed in a browser, different level headings appear as different size fonts, from largest (the H1 tag) to smallest (the H6 tag). However, each browser decides which fonts and font sizes to use.

CREATING PARAGRAPHS

The **<P>** tag (Paragraph) allows you to insert paragraphs and lines of text onto your page. Though it is clear that you can, depending on your browser, occasionally get away with simply writing plain, untagged text in the body of an HTML document, it is always best to include it in some other HTML element such as a heading, list, or paragraph. The most common way to tag plain text is to include it in the Paragraph element.

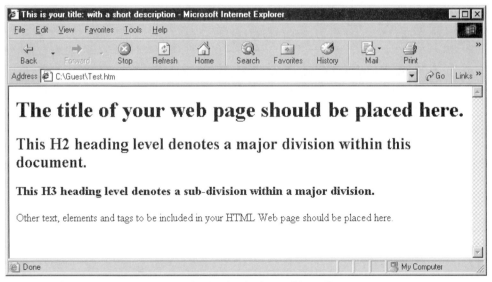

Figure 5.2 ■ Your Web page with the inclusion of headings.

The **<P>** tag is a container element with an implied ending, so technically you don't have to include the **</P>** tag. To be on the safe side, however, you should always add a **</P>** tag at the end of a paragraph. For example, some versions of XML (Extensible Markup Language) require this tag.

 A Web browser automatically wraps text in an HTML file to fit inside its window. Therefore, it is not necessary for you to insert returns at the ends of your lines of code to get them to display neatly inside a browser window. The effort would be futile in any event because Web browsers ignore hard returns that aren't specified with <BR> or typed within the <PRE> tag.

Paragraphs are placed inside the BODY tag. Any paragraph text that you type after the **<P>** tag should show up in a browser with at least one blank line after it. A **<P>** tag that contains no text has no effect. Therefore, the **<P>** tag cannot be relied upon as a tag to be used simply for inserting blank lines into a document. If you'd like to insert a line break in your HTML document, you should use the **
** (Line Break) tag.

INSERTING LINE BREAKS

The **
** tag is a standalone tag (meaning there is no need to code a corresponding **</BR>** tag) that merely inserts a line break into your document.

Change your Test.htm file to reflect the following lines of code:

```
<HTML>
<HEAD>
<TITLE>This is your title: with a short
description</TITLE>
</HEAD>
<BODY>
<H1>The title of your web page should be placed here.</H1>
<P>Here is a paragraph with multiple lines of text. The
point in displaying this paragraph is to demonstrate that
when this paragraph ends and another begins, a line break
should occur after the first paragraph, and a blank line
should separate the first paragraph from the second para-
graph. No Line Break tag is used here.</P>
<P>Here is the second paragraph. This one is slightly dif-
ferent from the first paragraph, for it uses BR (Line
Break) tags, here <BR>
and here <BR>
and here, again, <BR>
inside the second paragraph.</P>
</BODY>
</HTML>
```

Reload this file into your browser to check the result of your work. Your file should resemble the example file shown in Figure 5.3.

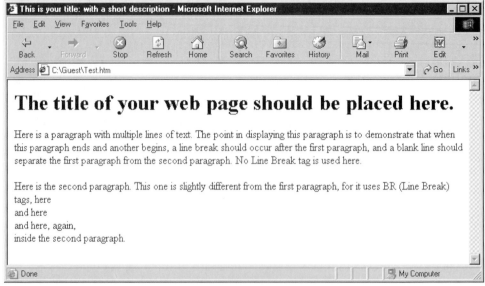

Figure 5.3 ■ **Your Web page with the inclusion of paragraphs and line breaks.**

You can use the <BR> tag almost anywhere you have text. For instance, it can be placed inside an <H1> or <H2> tag to force a heading to show up on two or more lines.

In terms of not just inserting line breaks but inserting blank lines, it is important to note that, though most browsers will let you get away with using the <BR> tag to insert blank lines into your document, doing so does not constitute standard HTML. To quote from the draft specification for HTML 4.0, "a sequence of contiguous whitespace characters, such as spaces, horizontal tabs, form feeds, and line breaks, should be replaced by a single word space."

The tag you should use for inserting blank lines into an HTML document is the <PRE> (Preformatted Text) tag. Using this tag works for all browsers. You can simply type regular hard returns inside the <PRE> tag like this:

```
<P>The PRE tag is used here to add extra space between
paragraphs. All one has to do is type hard returns within
the PRE tag.</P>
<PRE>

</PRE>
<P>There should be three blank lines separating the first
paragraph from this paragraph.</P>
```

A FEW WORDS ABOUT SPACING

In HTML, only the tags are used for all of your page's formatting. Therefore, unless they're inside a **<PRE>** tag, a browser ignores more than one space inserted into the text. Whether you've typed two, six, or twelve spaces, when the HTML document is displayed, only one space will appear. This same circumstance holds true for all tabs and hard returns as well. Therefore, the only reason to insert extra space (again, without the use of HTML tags or HTML special characters) into your HTML files is to make your raw HTML files (your source code) more readable as you work.

SPECIAL CHARACTERS

Since HTML documents are plain text ASCII files, they cannot easily display a graphical copyright symbol such as © and they may misinterpret characters that have a function within HTML such as < and >. To use characters or symbols such as these in an HTML document, make use of *special characters*. This name is given to codes that generate a character to the screen. Special characters always begin with an ampersand, &, and end with a semicolon, ;. Between the ampersand and semicolon go either a standard set of characters or a number. Table 5.2 lists some of the most commonly used special characters.

Table 5.2 ■ Special Characters

HTML Code	Special Character	Description
		non-breaking space
&copy;	©	copyright symbol
&lt;	<	less-than symbol
&gt;	>	greater-than symbol
&amp;	&	ampersand

The last of these is interesting: there needs to be a special character to render the ampersand because the ampersand has a special use in HTML, indicating the start of a special character.

If you want three consecutive horizontal spaces in your document, similar to what a paragraph tab needs, you can type the following, and it will work in almost all Web browsers:

```
     
```

CREATING COMMENTS

You should annotate your HTML documents with comments. Any text placed inside an HTML comment will not be displayed in a Web browser. The comment tag has no name, per se, included in the tag. It begins with this tag, <!--, and ends with this tag, -->.

Any text inserted between these tags is completely ignored by a browser. For example:

```
<!-- Your comment should be placed here. -->
```

You can place a comment virtually anywhere in your HTML document as long as it is typed inside an HTML comment tag. For instance, you can place a comment between two lines of text by typing something similar to the following:

```
<P>Type your text first, then type your comment.</P>
<!-- This comment will not be displayed by the browser. -->
<P> This line is preceded by an HTML comment.</P>
```

These two paragraphs appear in a Web browser as if they were originally typed as one paragraph line of text after another, with no additional vertical space between them.

The comment tags can also be used to "comment out" HTML tags. This is useful if you want to take out some HTML code, but might want to put it back later. Simply add and remove the comment marks to comment out or restore the text.

ITALICIZING AND BOLDFACING YOUR TEXT

There are two ways to include italic or bold text in your HTML document. The first way is to use *literal tags:* I (italic) and B (bold) tags. The second way involves using *logical tags:* EM (emphasis) and STRONG (strong emphasis) tags. Most browsers should display the <I> and <EM> tags identically. They should also display the <B> and <STRONG> tags identically.

The philosophy behind the difference between these tags is that the browser should be left to interpret the logical elements of a page and display them as it chooses. Therefore, to be true to this philosophy one should always use logical tags and avoid using literal tags. However, the <B> and <I> tags are obviously quicker to code. So if you want to be true to the basic philosophy of how a browser should interpret such highlighted text, use the <EM> and <STRONG> tags to italicize or boldface your text. On the other hand, if you'd like to save some keystrokes, substitute the literal <I> tag for the <EM> tag and the literal <B> tag for the <STRONG> tag. The literal tags also give a Web developer more control over how the page is displayed.

To see an example of using these tags, change your Test.htm file to reflect the following lines of code:

```
<HTML>
<HEAD>
<TITLE>This is your title: with a short
description</TITLE>
</HEAD>
<BODY>
<H1>The title of your web page should be placed here.</H1>
<P><B>This is literally boldfaced text.</B></P>
<P><STRONG>This text is logically boldfaced using the
STRONG tag.</STRONG></P>
<P><I>This is literally italicized text.</I></P>
<P><EM>And this text is logically italicized using the EM
tag.</EM></P>
</BODY>
</HTML>
```

Reload this file into your browser to check the result of your work. Your file should resemble the example file shown in Figure 5.4.

You can also nest these tags inside one another to get both italicized and boldfaced text. Just remember that you should not overlap them.

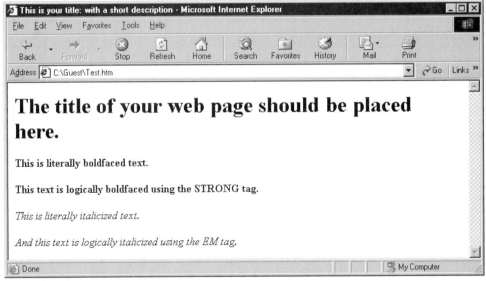

Figure 5.4 ■ **Your Web page with the inclusion of bold and italicized text using mixed tags.**

CREATING HYPERTEXT LINKS

One of the primary reasons to create a Web document is to create links to other pages. The word *hypertext* refers to any text that is linked to somewhere else, usually another page. To create a link, you can use the A (Anchor) tag. Hypertext links can be used to perform tasks such as the following:

- Jump to and view another Web page
- Jump to a specific place in either the same or another Web page
- Read a PDF (Portable Document File)
- Display an image
- Download a program
- Send an email message
- Play an audio or video clip
- Run a script
- Access a database
- Telnet to a server

Hypertext links can be used to have a user of your Web site jump to anything that has an address on the Internet (not just on the Web), as long as a password is not necessary.

A hypertext link contains the following three parts:

> 1. Start and end tags that enclose the link
> 2. The link target
> 3. The link text

Here is an example of a hypertext link using the <A> tag:

```
<A HREF="Test_two.htm"> This link, when clicked, should
direct a user to an HTML page called Test_two.htm</A>
```

The Anchor tag's HREF (Hypertext Reference) attribute is used to specify the URL of the object of the link. In most cases, this is simply another Web page. Note that, in the example above, the full URL (absolute path) is not provided, only the file name. This link makes use of a relative path, as explained in Chapter 3, "Remote Server Access." For this link to work, Test_two.htm must be located in the same directory as the Web page from which the link is being made. When you want to create a link with a Web page somewhere else on the Web, you must include the full URL, for instance, http://www.another_server.com/test_two.htm.

You should always nest the Anchor tag inside a document element, such as the Paragraph tag, not just within the BODY tag.

CREATING INLINE IMAGES

The IMG (Image) tag allows you to display inline images on your Web page. *Inline* refers to the fact that an image is inserted at a particular location within a Web page. The most commonly used file types for inline images are JPG (Joint Photographic Experts Group, or JPEG) and GIF (Graphic Interchange Format). Most, if not all, Web browsers can display JPG and GIF files as inline images.

These two types of graphic files tend to serve different purposes. GIF images are limited to 256 colors, but they can have a color set to transparent. GIF images also have the added advantage of being interlaced. This means that a GIF image can be progressively displayed while its file is being downloaded to the browser. GIF images can also be animated. JPG images can choose from up to 16.7 million colors, but they cannot be animated or transparent. It is best to include JPG files when you want to include a photographic image. If your image will be nonphotographic, such as a logo, then you should use a GIF, because it is less likely to require more than 256 colors to display properly. It can also display more sharply than a JPG file because of the compression method used for JPG files.

The Image tag uses the following format:

```
<IMG SRC="imagefile">
```

The SRC (Source) attribute is required. It specifies the address of the image to be displayed. This address can, like the HREF attribute of the Anchor tag, be either a full or partial URL, or just its file name.

To link to an image file that is neither in the same directory as the Web document it is being inserted into, or even on the same server as the current Web document, you could type something similar to the following:

```
<P>The image that is to be displayed will be inserted
directly into this line of text because it is an
<I>inline</I> image.
<IMG SRC="http://www.another_server.com/imagefile.gif">
If you want the image to be displayed on its own line of
text, you would need to precede the IMG tag with another
P tag.</P>
```

However, linking to someone else's graphic on the Web is not considered good Web authorship. You should always ask permission to use someone else's graphic file before you include it in your own Web page. As an alternative, plenty of repositories of public domain graphics exist on the Web. To be on the safe side, so you don't have to worry about violating someone's copyright, you can start out by using graphics downloaded from any of these public repositories.

USING THE ALT ATTRIBUTE

You can include the ALT attribute in an IMG tag to help textually identify the image. In many browsers, if you pass the mouse cursor over an image, the text of an included ALT attribute will be displayed. For Web users that use text-based browsers (which don't display images) or those Web users that may be using a graphical browser with the display of images turned off (a practice that sometimes speeds up the process of Web surfing), using the ALT attribute provides a text description of what an image contains.

An example of using the ALT attribute with an IMG tag is:

```
<IMG SRC="imagefile.gif" ALT="A sample image file">
```

In a text-based browser, the message "A sample image file" would be displayed to the user, rather than the alternative message "[Image]" (which is displayed if an ALT attribute is not included). In a graphical Web browser with the display of images turned off, the message "A sample image file" appears alongside a dummy graphic file icon, as shown in Figure 5.5.

A sample image file

Figure 5.5 ■ A Web page with the display of images turned off.

A browser will also display the dummy graphic file icon if the SRC of your IMG tag has not specified the location of your image file properly in relation to the Web document the image is being inserted into. In other words, if the browser cannot properly locate the image file, it will simply display the dummy graphic file icon.

RELATIVE URLs VERSUS ABSOLUTE URLs

As mentioned in Chapter 3, "Remote Server Access," you don't always have to specify a full, or *absolute,* URL when creating a hypertext link or inserting an in-line image. If a Web page or other file to which you are linking, or a graphic file you are inserting into your Web document, is either in the same folder, directory, or even the same server (domain), you can exclude those parts of the URL that are common to both. A URL created in this manner is referred to as a *partial* URL.

Apart from being a shorter name, an advantage to using this type of URL is that you can move a Web page and its locally linked files from one directory to another, or from one server to another, without having to recreate the links accordingly. The link hierarchy remains essentially intact. You want to create and test your Web pages in your development environment (which may be your own computer), then FTP them up to your Web site on your production server without having to redo any of the links.

CREATING HORIZONTAL RULES

The HR (Horizontal Rule) tag is a standalone element that allows you to add horizontal rules to your Web pages.

To see an example of how the <HR> tag may be used, change your Test.htm file to reflect the following lines of code:

```
<HTML>
<HEAD>
<TITLE>This is your title: with a short
description</TITLE>
</HEAD>
<BODY>
<H1>The title of your web page should be placed here.</H1>
<P><B>This is literally boldfaced text.</B></P>
<HR>
```

```
<P><STRONG>This text is logically boldfaced using the
STRONG tag.<STRONG></P>
<HR>

<P><I>This is literally italicized text.</I></P>
<HR>

<P><EM>And this text is logically italicized using the EM
tag.</EM></P>
<HR>
</BODY>
</HTML>
```

This updated bit of code demonstrates two interesting points. First, it shows that portions of HTML code can be separated by white space, yet that white space is not interpreted by the browser as such. Second, it illustrates how horizontal rules are often used in Web pages as separators. They can separate distinct, logical parts of a Web document. Reload this file into your browser to check the result of your work. Your file should resemble the example file shown in Figure 5.6.

Remember that the blank lines of text you see displayed between each horizontal rule and its subsequent paragraph in Figure 5.6 have to do with the fact that each time a paragraph ends and another begins, a blank line is inserted between the two. The blank lines displayed by the browser have nothing to do with the blank lines inserted into the source code you just typed. To test this theory, feel free to take out the blank lines you just inserted into your source code, save your changes, and refresh your file in your browser. The result should be the same as that displayed in Figure 5.6.

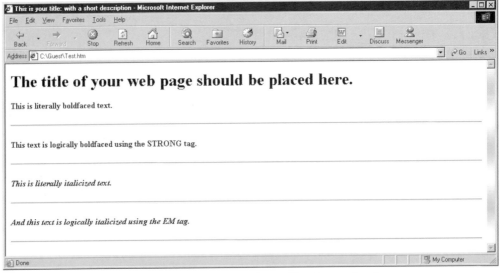

Figure 5.6 ■ **Your Web page with the inclusion of horizontal rules.**

USING FONTS

The font tag is used to change font faces, sizes, and colors.

 The FONT tag has been "deprecated" in HTML 4.0. The reason for this is to encourage the use of style sheets in place of the FONT tag. Usually, a deprecated HTML tag is one that may be obsolete in future versions of HTML. However, it is a much easier tag for a novice HTML user to learn and code with (than style sheets). Furthermore, many pages have already been created using this tag, so for backward-compatibility purposes, future versions of HTML will continue to support it.

WORKING WITH FONT SIZES

The FONT tag uses its SIZE attribute to change the size of a font. You can set font sizes using either absolute or relative size values.

You can set seven absolute (*fixed*) sizes. These fixed sizes are numbered from 1 to 7. The default is 3, which is the same as regular paragraph text. 1 is the smallest and 7 is the largest. Therefore, you can set two absolute font sizes that are smaller than normal paragraph text, and four sizes that are larger. Each Web browser determines the sizes of these fonts as it sees fit.

To see an example of what these different font sizes look like in your Web browser, change your Test.htm file to reflect the following lines of code. Your file should resemble the example file shown in Figure 5.7.

```
<HTML>
<HEAD>
<TITLE>This is your title: with a short description</TITLE>
</HEAD>
<BODY>
<H1>The title of your web page should be placed here.</H1>

<P><FONT SIZE="1">This line of text uses Font Size 1.</FONT><BR>
   <FONT SIZE="2">This line of text uses Font Size 2.</FONT><BR>
   <FONT SIZE="3">This line of text uses Font Size 3.</FONT><BR>
   <FONT SIZE="4">This line of text uses Font Size 4.</FONT><BR>
   <FONT SIZE="5">This line of text uses Font Size 5.</FONT><BR>
   <FONT SIZE="6">This line of text uses Font Size 6.</FONT><BR>
   <FONT SIZE="7">This line of text uses Font Size 7.</FONT>
</P>
</BODY>
</HTML>
```

UNIT
5.2

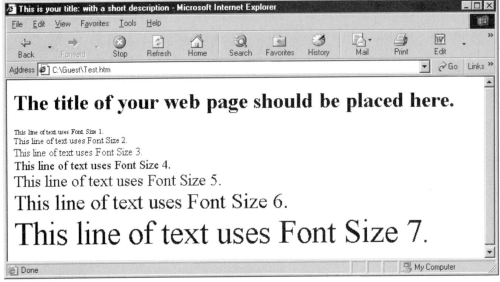

Figure 5.7 ■ **Your Web page with the inclusion of different absolute font sizes.**

You can set relative font sizes by indicating either a plus (+) or minus (–) sign preceding the font size number. For example, FONT SIZE="+2" indicates a font size that is two sizes larger than the base font size. The default base font size is identical to the Size 3 absolute font. Therefore, a SIZE="+2" relative font size is equivalent to a Size 5 absolute font (3 + 2 = 5).

For an example of using relative font size changes to indicate the seven possible font sizes, change your Test.htm file to reflect the following lines of code:

```
<HTML>
<HEAD>
<TITLE>This is your title: with a short description</TITLE>
</HEAD>
<BODY>
<H1>The title of your web page should be placed here.</H1>

<P><FONT SIZE="-2">This line of text uses Font Size -2.</FONT><BR>
   <FONT SIZE=-"1">This line of text uses Font Size -1.</FONT><BR>
   This line of text uses the Default Font Size.<BR>
   <FONT SIZE="+1">This line of text uses Font Size +1.</FONT><BR>
   <FONT SIZE="+2">This line of text uses Font Size +2.</FONT><BR>
   <FONT SIZE="+3">This line of text uses Font Size +3.</FONT><BR>
   <FONT SIZE="+4">This line of text uses Font Size +4.</FONT>
</P>

</BODY>
</HTML>
```

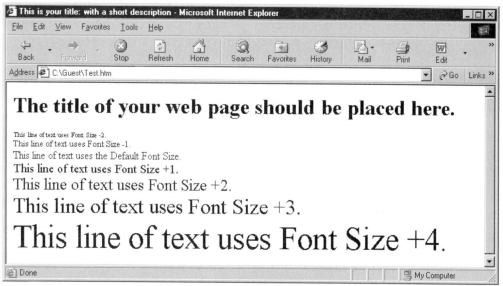

Figure 5.8 ■ Your Web page with the inclusion of different relative font sizes.

Reload this file into your browser to check the result of your work. Your file should resemble the example file shown in Figure 5.8.

You should notice by looking at Figure 5.8 that relative –2 is the same as absolute 1, relative –1 is the same as absolute 2, relative +1 is the same as absolute 4, and so on. Absolute 3, which is the default font size, requires no font size change.

USING THE BASEFONT TAG

The BASEFONT tag allows you to change the size of the *base font*—the default font or the font used in paragraph text. You can set it using any of the absolute font sizes, 1 through 7 (again, 3 is the default). The BASEFONT tag is a standalone tag that is set the same way you set an absolute font size.

It is important to note that the BASEFONT tag is another deprecated tag; however, it is still just as much in use as the FONT tag.

The BASEFONT tag may only be used to increase the size of the base font. For example, you can increase the base font size by one to an absolute font size of 4:

```
<BASEFONT SIZE="4">
```

When you change the base font size using the BASEFONT tag, all following relative font sizes will change relative to the new base font. For example, if you change the base font size to 4, then a following relative font size of +1 has the same effect as setting an absolute font size of 5 (4 + 1 = 5).

You can insert the BASEFONT tag anywhere within a Web page. It stays in effect until another BASEFONT tag changes the base font size. It affects all text sized with relative font sizes. However, any headings or text set with absolute font sizes are not affected.

WORKING WITH FONT COLORS

The FONT tag uses its COLOR attribute to change the color of a font. To specify a font color, you can either use one of 16 color names that match the Windows 16-color palette, or you can use RGB (Red Green Blue, indicative of the color spectrum) hexadecimal codes. Using the RGB hex codes is more difficult, but gives you greater access to a much wider range of colors.

The 16 Windows color names are black, white, aqua, blue, fuchsia, gray, green, lime, maroon, navy, olive, purple, red, silver, teal, and yellow.

For an example of specifying font colors using color names, change your Test.htm file to reflect the following lines of code (this bit of code excludes the font colors black and white):

```
<HTML>
<HEAD>
<TITLE>This is your title: with a short description</TITLE>
</HEAD>
<BODY>
<H1>The title of your web page should be placed here.</H1>

<P><FONT SIZE="6">
    <FONT COLOR="maroon">Maroon </FONT>
    <FONT COLOR="teal">Teal </FONT>
    <FONT COLOR="green">Green </FONT>
    <FONT COLOR="red">Red </FONT>
    <FONT COLOR="fuchsia">Fuchsia </FONT>
    <FONT COLOR="olive">Olive </FONT>
    <FONT COLOR="aqua">Aqua </FONT>
    <FONT COLOR="lime">Lime </FONT>
    <FONT COLOR="purple">Purple </FONT>
    <FONT COLOR="yellow">Yellow </FONT>
    <FONT COLOR="gray">Gray </FONT>
    <FONT COLOR="navy">Navy </FONT>
    <FONT COLOR="silver">Silver </FONT>
    <FONT COLOR="blue">Blue </FONT>
</P>
```

```
</BODY>
</HTML>
```

Reload this file into your browser to gain an idea of how your browser displays these colors.

Using RGB hex codes to set your font colors is much more difficult than setting font colors using color names, but it gives you access to a much broader range of colors. It allows you to specify values from 0 to 255 (00 to FF, in hexadecimal), for the red, green, and blue components of a color, providing you with up to 16.7 million different colors to choose from.

You can set the RGB hex code for a color in the FONT tag by using the following general form:

```
<FONT COLOR="#RRGGBB">This text is the color of whatever
RGB hexadecimal color value belongs to the surrounding
FONT tag's COLOR attribute.</FONT>
```

In the example above, RR stands for red, GG stands for green, and BB stands for blue. FF is the highest hexadecimal number, equaling 255, whereas 00 is the lowest, equaling 0. Therefore, to specify red, green, and blue, you would type the RGB hexadecimal codes, FF0000, 00FF00, and 0000FF, respectively.

To practice assigning font colors using RGB hex codes, feel free to change the red, green, and blue font color values in your Test.htm file to the corresponding RGB hex codes. Don't forget to include the # sign in front of the hex code:

```
<FONT COLOR="#FF0000">.
```

Then reload the file into your browser to check out how it looks.

Historically, instead of the 16.7 million possible colors mathematically available with hexadecimal notation, developers have been limited to a palette of 216 colors deemed Web-safe, or compatible with machines that can only support 8-bit, 256-color resolution. For Web-safe colors, each RGB color value can only be set to values like 00, 33, 66, 99, CC, or FF, for a maximum of 216 color possibilities. Since the majority of computers can support a higher color depth, there is not the necessity there once was to support 8-bit users. If you find that you need to utilize Web-safe colors for your audience, browse the Web for a listing of Web-safe colors and their corresponding hexadecimal codes.

One of the quickest ways to get started using RGB hex color codes in your HTML document is to use some kind of color chart or wheel that allows you to choose the color you want and obtain the corresponding hex code. There are many charts and utilities available on the Web for obtaining the hex codes for colors. Additionally, many HTML editors, like EditPlus and TextPad, have built-in color charts that allow you to select a color, then insert the corresponding hex code into your Web page.

WORKING WITH FONT FACES

The FACE attribute of the FONT tag allows you to specify a font, or list of fonts, in which you would like your text to be displayed. A browser that supports this attribute will search the local computer to see if any of the fonts specified are present. If so, it will display the text in the first available font from the font list. If none of the fonts are found, it will display the text in the local computer's default font.

Your goal in using this attribute should be to specify a list of fonts that will be present on as many computers as possible. A good method is to specify a list of fonts that fit into the same *family*, or category, such as serif, sans serif, or monospaced fonts. For instance, if you'd like a line of text to be displayed in a sans serif font, your best bet would be to provide a list in order to maximize your chances. Consider the following example:

```
<P><FONT SIZE="4" COLOR="teal" FACE="Arial, Helvetica,
Verdana">You have maximized your chances for displaying
this text in a sans serif font, since you have listed a
family of fonts after your FACE attribute, rather than
specifying just one font face value. Which font face is
ultimately selected depends on which fonts are installed
on a local system.</FONT></P>
```

You should not use the FONT tag as a substitute for any of the heading level tags (H1, H2, and so forth). The reason for this is that text-based browsers and Braille browsers, for instance, need the heading level tags in order to determine the structure and order of precedence within a document. You can, however, combine the two by either nesting a FONT tag inside a heading level tag or vice versa.

CREATING BACKGROUND COLORS AND IMAGES

You can set your background, text, and links colors for your entire Web page by specifying values for the following attributes in the BODY tag, as outlined in Table 5.3.

Go to the top of your Test.htm file and add the following code to the BODY tag for an example of setting these attributes:

```
<BODY BGCOLOR="#99CCFF" TEXT="yellow" LINK="#99CCCC"
VLINK="salmon" ALINK="#FF0000">
```

This sets the background color to pale blue, the text to yellow, the links to light teal, the visited links to salmon pink, and the activated links to bright red.

Be sure to reload the file into your browser to then see how your changes affect your HTML document.

Be careful when specifying colors. Avoid color combinations that render any part of your page less readable. You should develop and organize your content first, then hone the appearance of your Web page.

The BACKGROUND attribute of the BODY tag allows you to specify a background image. The general format for specifying a value for this attribute is:

```
<BODY BACKGROUND="imagefile.gif">
```

Alternatively, keeping in line with the circumstance that an image file may not be in the same folder, directory, or server, the following syntax may also be used:

```
<BODY BACKGROUND="http://www.another_server/imagefile.gif">
```

Please see the sections titled "Creating Inline Images" and "Relative URLs versus Absolute URLs" earlier in this unit for a discussion on specifying file locations for images. When using background images, avoid busy or high-contrast images. When using dark background images, set the color of your text and links to light colors.

Table 5.3 ▪ Attributes for Setting Background, Text, and Links Colors

<BODY> Attribute	Description
BGCOLOR	Sets the background color
TEXT	Sets the text (or foreground) color
LINK	Sets the color of unvisited links
VLINK	Sets the color of visited links
ALINK	Sets the color of activated links (the link your mouse button is currently selecting, or clicking on)

If you specify a dark background image (using the BACKGROUND attribute) with light text and link colors, your text and links may not be readable in a browser that has the display of images turned off. To ensure that your page will be readable against the default white background of such browsers, specify a value for the BGCOLOR attribute to set a background color against which the text will still be readable.

U N I T   5 . 3

BASIC TABLES

FORMATTING WITH HTML TABLES

A convenient way to display information or data in a nicely aligned tabular format is to place it inside an HTML table. To do so, you must use the TABLE tag. The TABLE tag brackets your table. All other text or tags to be included in your table should be nested inside the TABLE tag.

Copy your Test.htm file and save it with a new name, Table.htm. Create a table inside your new Table.htm file with the following example code:

```
<HTML>
<HEAD>
<TITLE>This is your title: with a short
description</TITLE>
</HEAD>
<BODY>
<H1>The title of your web page should be placed here.</H1>

<P><TABLE></TABLE></P>

</BODY>
</HTML>
```

 Since the table element is not a block element (like the P tag), but instead an inline element (like the IMG tag), you should insert a P tag in front of the TABLE tag to ensure sufficient space is added above the table.

The TR (Table Row) and TD (Table Data) tags should be used to create a grid of rows and columns. For example:

```
<P><TABLE>
<TR><TD>Row 1 - Col 1</TD><TD>Row 1 - Col 2</TD><TD>Row 1
- Col 3</TD></TR>
<TR><TD>Row 2 - Col 1</TD><TD>Row 2 - Col 2</TD><TD>Row 2
- Col 3</TD></TR>
</TABLE></P>
```

**UNIT
5.3**

Note that the **<TR>** begin tag and **</TR>** end tag bracket each row.

Add these new lines of code to your Table.htm file (between the **<TABLE>** and **</TABLE>** tags), and load the page into your browser to see the effect. Your file should resemble the example file shown in Figure 5.9.

A table won't look like a table without a border. In this case, you can include the table BORDER attribute inside the TABLE tag. For instance, you can type the following:

```
<P><TABLE BORDER="1">
<TR><TD>Row 1 - Col 1</TD><TD>Row 1 - Col 2</TD><TD>Row 1
- Col 3</TD></TR>
<TR><TD>Row 2 - Col 1</TD><TD>Row 2 - Col 2</TD><TD>Row 2
- Col 3</TD></TR>
</TABLE></P>
```

Add this BORDER attribute to Table.htm, then refresh your page to view your changed table. Your file should resemble the example file shown in Figure 5.10.

Increasing the value of the BORDER attribute increases the thickness of the outer border of the table, causing the outer border to display in 3-D relief.

Change the value of the BORDER attribute in Table.htm from 1 pixel to 7 pixels, then view your changes. Your file should resemble the example file shown in Figure 5.11.

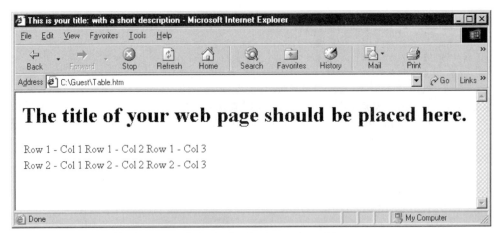

Figure 5.9 ■ Your Web page with the inclusion of a table.

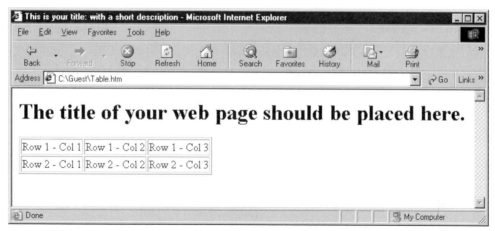

Figure 5.10 ■ Your Web page with the inclusion of a border for your table.

To further define the appearance of table borders, you can also utilize the BOR-DERCOLOR attribute. Use BORDERCOLOR to set the color of the border equal to a hexadecimal color or one of the 16 named colors in HTML described earlier in this chapter.

The CELLSPACING attribute adds space between cells, while the CELLPADDING attribute adds space within each cell.

Add 5 pixels of spacing and padding to your table in Table.htm like the following additional code:

```
<P><TABLE BORDER="7" CELLSPACING="5" CELLPADDING="5">
<TR><TD>Row 1 - Col 1</TD><TD>Row 1 - Col 2</TD><TD>Row 1
- Col 3</TD></TR>
```

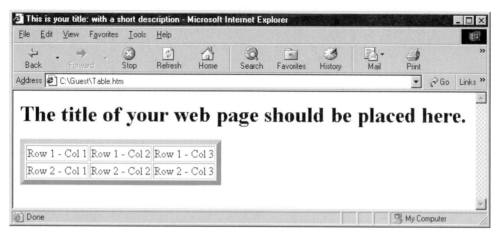

Figure 5.11 ■ Your Web page with an increased table border.

```
<TR><TD>Row 2 - Col 1</TD><TD>Row 2 - Col 2</TD><TD>Row 2
- Col 3</TD></TR>
</TABLE></P>
```

Your changed table should resemble the example file shown in Figure 5.12.

The TH (Table Heading) tag is very similar to the TD (Table Data) tag, except that it defines a particular cell as a heading cell rather than as a simple data cell. Any text entered into a TH tag will be rendered as centered, boldfaced type.

Add a row of column headings to your table in Table.htm with the following additional code:

```
<P><TABLE BORDER="7" CELLSPACING="5" CELLPADDING="5">
<TR><TH>First</TH><TH>Second</TH><TH>Third</TH></TR>
<TR><TD>Row 1 - Col 1</TD><TD>Row 1 - Col 2</TD><TD>Row 1
- Col 3</TD></TR>
<TR><TD>Row 2 - Col 1</TD><TD>Row 2 - Col 2</TD><TD>Row 2
- Col 3</TD></TR>
</TABLE></P>
```

You should notice that your headings are displayed similarly to those displayed in the example file shown in Figure 5.13.

To center the table, just insert an ALIGN="center" attribute value in the TABLE tag.

Add this attribute to the TABLE tag in Table.htm like this:

```
<P><TABLE ALIGN="center" BORDER="7" CELLSPACING="5"
CELLPADDING="5">
<TR><TH>First</TH><TH>Second</TH><TH>Third</TH></TR>
```

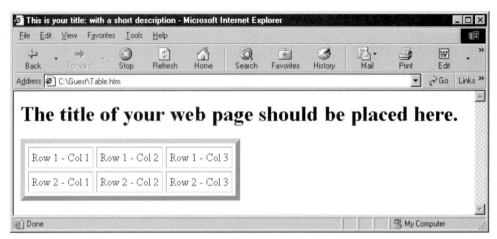

Figure 5.12 ■ **Your Web page's table with extra spacing and padding.**

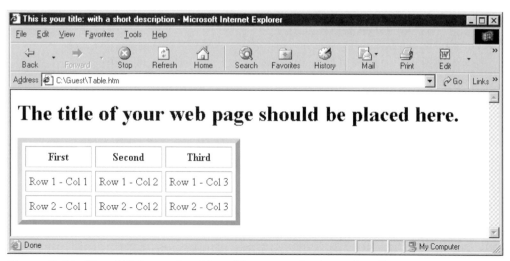

Figure 5.13 ■ Your Web page's table with a row of column headings.

```
<TR><TD>Row 1 - Col 1</TD><TD>Row 1 - Col 2</TD><TD>Row 1
- Col 3</TD></TR>
<TR><TD>Row 2 - Col 1</TD><TD>Row 2 - Col 2</TD><TD>Row 2
- Col 3</TD></TR>
</TABLE></P>
```

When you view your centered table, it should resemble the newly centered table displayed in the example file shown in Figure 5.14.

Alternatively, you can see the same effect by putting your table inside a CENTER tag or by placing it inside a center-aligned paragraph.

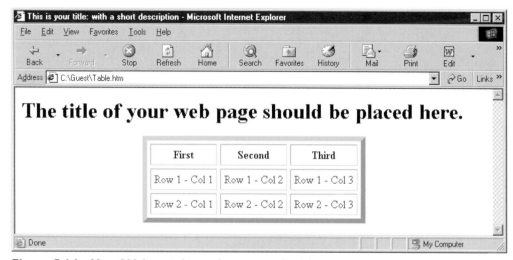

Figure 5.14 ■ Your Web page's newly centered table.

You can specify the size of your table by including WIDTH and HEIGHT attributes. You can use either absolute values (pixels) or relative values (percentages).

Specify a table width of 80% for your table in Table.htm like this:

```
<P><TABLE ALIGN="center" BORDER="7" CELLSPACING="5"
CELLPADDING="5" WIDTH="80%">
<TR><TH>First</TH><TH>Second</TH><TH>Third</TH></TR>
<TR><TD>Row 1 - Col 1</TD><TD>Row 1 - Col 2</TD><TD>Row 1
- Col 3</TD></TR>
<TR><TD>Row 2 - Col 1</TD><TD>Row 2 - Col 2</TD><TD>Row 2
- Col 3</TD></TR>
</TABLE></P>
```

When you view your newly changed table, you should notice that it now occupies 80% of the browser window's width, like that of the example file shown in Figure 5.15.

You can horizontally align your cell contents by placing an ALIGN attribute value in either the TR tag (which will align the entire row), or in a TD tag individually. The setting placed in a TD tag will override a similar setting placed in its containing row's TR tag. For instance, if a table row has been set as left-aligned, however, one of the table data items within it has been set as right-aligned, that table data item will remain right-aligned, even if all the other table data items in that row are left-aligned due to the row alignment setting.

The default alignment for table rows (that do not contain TH tags) and table data items is left-aligned.

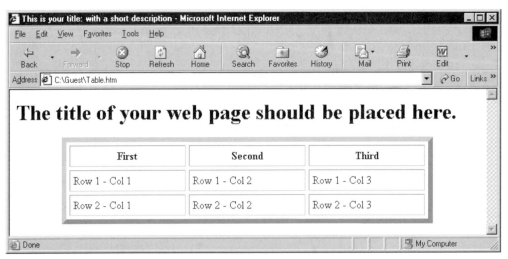

Figure 5.15 ■ Your Web page's table with its new table width.

Use the ALIGN attribute to right-align the first row of your table in Table.htm by adding the following code:

```
<P><TABLE ALIGN="center" BORDER="1" CELLSPACING="5"
CELLPADDING="5" WIDTH="80%">
<TR><TH>First</TH><TH>Second</TH><TH>Third</TH></TR>
<TR ALIGN="right"><TD>Row 1 - Col 1</TD><TD>Row 1 - Col
2</TD><TD>Row 1 - Col 3</TD></TR>
<TR><TD>Row 2 - Col 1</TD><TD>Row 2 - Col 2</TD><TD>Row 2
- Col 3</TD></TR>
</TABLE></P>
```

UNIT
5.3

When you view your newly changed table, you should notice that the first row values are right-aligned while the second row values are left-aligned. Your table should resemble that of the example file shown in Figure 5.16.

Use the ALIGN attribute to horizontally align the values of table rows (TR), table headings (TH), and table data cells (TD). The possible values are "left," "center," and "right." Recall that center alignment is the default for table heading cells and left alignment is the default for table data cells.

By inserting a WIDTH attribute in the top cell of a column, you can specify the width of the entire column. Like table widths, column widths can be specified in either percentages or pixels. The columns of your table start out being fairly equal in width. A browser will expand or contract the columns of a table depending on their contents. Column widths set in percentages will expand or contract depending on the width of the browser window. Column widths set in pixels will remain the same width, irrespective of the width of the browser window. If you set all the columns of a table to a fixed width using pixels, you should not set a percentage width in the TABLE tag.

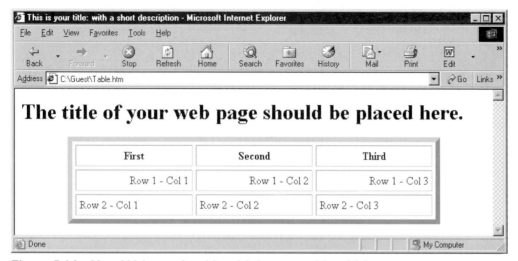

Figure 5.16 ■ Your Web page's table with its new table width.

You can vertically align your TH, TR, or TD cell contents by using the VALIGN attribute. The possible values are "top," "middle," and "bottom." The default is middle alignment.

Set the bottom row to top alignment in your table in Table.htm by adding the following code:

```
<P><TABLE ALIGN="center" BORDER="1" CELLSPACING="5"
CELLPADDING="5" WIDTH="80%">
<TR><TH>First</TH><TH>Second</TH><TH>Third</TH></TR>
<TR ALIGN="right"><TD>Row 1 - Col 1</TD><TD>Row 1 - Col
2</TD><TD>Row 1 - Col 3</TD></TR>
<TR VALIGN="top"><TD>Row 2 - Col 1</TD><TD>Row 2 - Col
2</TD><TD>Row 2 - Col 3</TD></TR>
</TABLE></P>
```

When you view your newly changed table, you should notice that the first row values are middle-aligned while the second row values are top-aligned.

UNIT 5.4

BASIC FRAMES

FRAMES AND FRAMESETS

A frame document is used to set up separate spaces on a page for separate HTML documents. Every frame document begins with a FRAMESET tag. This tag replaces the BODY tag you find in regular HTML documents. The frameset defines how the page will be divided up, and it can be described in terms of either horizontal units (rows) or vertical units (columns), but not both (you can obtain this latter effect by nesting a frameset inside another frameset, which is covered in Chapter 6, "Advanced HTML: Forms, Nested Tables, and Nested Frames.")

To define a frameset in terms of rows, for example, you must first decide how big you'd like each row to be. The rows can be sized relatively (using the percentage of the screen width), or by absolute value (in pixels).

Copy your Table.htm file to a new file called Main_Frame.htm. This file should consist of the following example HTML code:

```
<HTML>
<HEAD>
<TITLE>Main Frameset for the University Maintenance Website
for Administrators</TITLE>
</HEAD>
<FRAMESET ROWS="25%, 75%">
</FRAMESET>
</HTML>
```

So here you can see that there are two rows. The top row will take up 25% of the screen width and the bottom row will take up 75% of the screen width. Note that values are separated by a comma.

A frameset always divides up all of the available space in a browser window. A frameset can never take up more or less than the available screen space. If the percentages provided in the <FRAMESET> tag add up to more or less than 100%, the browser will attempt to recalculate percentages, and divide up all of the available screen space according to its recalculations, often with unpredictable results. Similar recalculations are made when numeric pixel values provided do not add up to the available area of the browser window.

You can also use an asterisk (*) to indicate that all remaining space should be used. To create two columns, one that has a fixed width of 110 pixels, and a second column that fills up the rest of the screen, however wide that is, use this notation for the <FRAMESET> tag:

```
<FRAMESET COLS="110,*">
```

After you've defined the frameset, you can then describe the frames within it. Each frame (region) in a document is described by a single frame tag. The FRAME tag has several attributes, the two most common being the SRC (Source) and the NAME attributes. The SRC tag tells the browser which document to pull into the frame. The NAME attribute becomes important when you want to link between frames.

Frames are always described from left to right, and top to bottom.

Add the following FRAME tags to your Main_Frame.htm document.

```
<HTML>
<HEAD>
<TITLE>Main Frameset for the University Maintenance Web-
site for Administrators</TITLE>
</HEAD>
<FRAMESET ROWS="25%, 75%">
<FRAME SRC="Top_Nav.htm" NAME="top">
<FRAME SRC="Splash.htm" NAME="main">
</FRAMESET>
</HTML>
```

So again, SRC (Source) indicates the HTML document to be pulled into this frame. And NAME is simply the name assigned to the frame (which doesn't necessarily have to correspond to the name of the HTML document).

CHAPTER 5

BUILDING THE APP

Create the first Web page of your Web-based University Application for Administrators (which you will be enhancing throughout the rest of this book) with the following instructions:

1) Create an HTML file with the name Splash.htm.
2) Create an appropriate heading (title) for your application.
3) Be sure to provide a title to appear in the browser window when this page is displayed.
4) Add some introductory text explaining that this page is the introductory page to the rest of the University Application for Administrators Web site.
5) Feel free to experiment with different font sizes, colors, faces, and emphasis (boldfacing and italicizing).
6) Experiment with adding inline images and BODY tag attributes.
7) Experiment with any of the other tags introduced in this lab (like annotating this page with comments).

Create your top navigational bar by following these directions:

1) Create an HTML file called Top_Nav.htm.
2) Display the heading "University Maintenance Application for Administrators".

Create 3 hypertext links (inside a table so that they will be spaced horizontally evenly) called "Students", "Instructors", and "Classes". For now, the HREF attributes for all 3 links will hold no value.

After you FTP these files to a Web server, everyone who has a frames-capable browser should be able to invoke your Main_Frame.htm file by typing its URL in a browser. When they do so, they should be able to see that your Top_Nav.htm file is loaded into the top navigational bar, while your Splash.htm file is loaded into the lower half (the main portion) of the screen. However, the way this page is currently coded, anyone using a browser that does not support frames will be greeted with an empty page.

To account for this possibility you can include the NOFRAMES tag. This tag and everything that follows it is read by browsers that cannot interpret frames, and ignored by those that can. For an example of how the NOFRAMES tag is used, include the following code in your Main_Frame.htm document:

```
<HTML>
<HEAD>
<TITLE>Main Frameset for the University Maintenance Web-
site for Administrators</TITLE>
</HEAD>
<FRAMESET ROWS="25%, 75%">
<FRAME SRC="Top_Nav.htm" NAME="top">
<FRAME SRC="Splash.htm" NAME="main">
</FRAMESET>
<NOFRAMES>
    <BODY><H2>
    Sorry.  This document uses frames.  But your
    browser does not support them.
    </H2></BODY>
</NOFRAMES>
</HTML>
```

Note that while the FRAMESET tag does not include a BODY tag, the NOFRAMES tag does.

In the preceding example, people using frames-savvy browsers will see your intended page, and those who cannot see frames will instead see the message written in the NOFRAMES section. Though the user will receive a message (better than nothing at all), it is actually better to create a page that delivers the same content, if not the same functionality, for non-frames viewers. This means you'll have to put some thought into delivering another solution. Without frames, you might have to be a little more creative; you might have to work out a solution using tables, for instance.

After you've created your Top_Nav.htm file and Main_Frame.htm file, load your Main_Frame.htm file into your browser to ensure that your Top_Nav.htm and Splash.htm files are being loaded properly into the page painted by Main_Frame.htm. An example of what you should be working towards can be seen in the companion Web site for this book, located at http://www.phptr.com/boardman. Visit the Web site periodically to share and discuss your answers with other readers.

ADVANCED HTML: FORMS, NESTED TABLES, AND NESTED FRAMES

In the last chapter you learned the basics of HTML. In this chapter you expand on that knowledge. First, forms are discussed. Forms are essential for developing Web sites with Oracle's PSP or PL/SQL Web Toolkit technology. They give the developer an important means for passing parameters from one Web page to another.

Next, tables are further discussed as to how they can be used for formatting a Web page and also elements within a Web page, such as a form.

Last, two methods for nesting frames are discussed.

U N I T   6 . 1

AN INTRODUCTION TO FORMS

Forms allow a Web site to interact with the user. The user can enter information or make choices. This data can be collected and processed. Processing form data usually involves inserting to or updating a database. Traditionally, the file with the processing instructions was a script file in a CGI/Bin. In our case the processing file is a PL/SQL procedure or PSP page.

WHAT EVERY FORM NEEDS

For a procedure to be able to process information submitted in a form, the following elements must be in place:

- Form fields (where users enter data or make a choice). Each form field must have a name to enable the script to match the name with the value the user enters into the form field. It is recommended that these names be unique.
- A way for the user to initiate the submittal process. Often this is a submit button.
- A form handler (a set of instructions that tells the server how to process the information the user submits).

<FORM> TAGS

OPENING/CLOSING <FORM> TAGS

First, begin with the outer form tags:

```
<FORM ACTION="main.html" METHOD="post" NAME="myform">
</FORM>
```

Everything in the form should be written between these opening and closing tags. These two tags define the boundaries of the form's "container." Every form element that is to be a part of the form must be placed within these tags. If a form element is not located between these tags, then it will not be considered a part of the form when the form is submitted for processing.

Three important attributes of the <FORM> tag are ACTION, METHOD, and NAME.

ACTION   This attribute specifies the file to which the information will be passed. The purpose of a form is to gather information, bundle it up, and send it to some place to be processed. This is known as submitting a form.

When a form is submitted the gathered information is sent to the file specified in the ACTION attribute. In our case the file will usually be a PL/SQL procedure, which will insert or update the data in a database.

METHOD   This attribute refers to the method of passing the information. There are two options here: GET or POST. If the METHOD is not specified, the default method is GET.

GET adds the information as a query string to the URL. A query string is attached to the end of a URL and begins with a question mark. The data is passed as name/value pairs. When there is more than one name/value pair, they are separated by ampersand (&) characters. An example is:

```
http://myhost/pls/any/procedurename?fname=Bill&lname=Smith
```

POST passes the information inside the HTTP header so the user cannot view the query string information as they can with a GET.

Initially you may choose the METHOD to be GET so that you can see all the parameters that are being submitted. This will help while you are developing the Web page and need to debug it. When you release a form in a production environment you may choose the METHOD to be POST so as to hide all parameters from the user.

NAME   This attribute specifies the name of the form. It is important when using JavaScript. It is not necessary unless the page is using JavaScript. This is covered in detail in Chapter 14, "JavaScript Form Validation." For now it is good practice to include a NAME for each form.

Some <FORM> tag attributes:

> ACTION="URLPath"
> ENCTYPE="encodingType"
> METHOD="GET"|"POST"
> NAME="NameOfForm"
> TARGET="NameOfWindow"

THE DATA HOLDERS

The data holders allow a form to collect data from the user through such elements as text boxes, radio buttons, or checkboxes. The majority of the form elements, though not all, use the <INPUT> tag, so all form elements may be referred to loosely as form inputs because of this. Again, these data holders must be placed within opening and closing <FORM> tags. Except in a few cases, each form element should have a unique name. This allows you to be able to refer to it with no problems in the form handler when processing the form's data.

The TYPE attribute of the <INPUT> tag must be set as shown below in order to create the specified form element.

TEXT BOX

```
<INPUT TYPE="text" VALUE="Default Content" NAME="p_txtBox"
MAXLENGTH="25" SIZE="40">
```

Figure 6.1 shows a text box as rendered in the browser:

```
Default Content
```

Figure 6.1 ■ Text box as rendered in the browser.

Some text box attributes:

> INPUT TYPE="TEXT"
> MAXLENGTH="25"
> NAME="name"
> SIZE="25"
> VALUE="initialValue"

A text box allows the user to input free-form data via the keyboard, such as first name or last name. The size of the field is controlled with the SIZE attribute. You can allow more or less data than what is displayed on screen by adding the MAXLENGTH attribute. The VALUE attribute is displayed initially in the text box. If the contents of the text box are changed by the user, then the changed value is passed when the form is submitted.

TEXT AREA

```
<TEXTAREA COLS="25" ROWS="6" NAME="p_txtArea" WRAP="soft">
Default Content of TextArea </TEXTAREA>
```

Figure 6.2 shows a text area as rendered in the browser:

Figure 6.2 ■ **Text area as rendered in the browser.**

Some text area attributes:

> COLS="5"
> NAME="name"
> ROWS="3"
> WRAP="OFF"|"HARD"|"SOFT"

A text area is similar to a text box. It allows for a larger display space and has a scrollbar. Note that text areas are created not with the <INPUT> tag but with their own <TEXTAREA> tag. Like the text box, the VALUE attribute is displayed in the text area. And just like a text box, the data inside of the text area is passed when the form is submitted. You can indicate the size of the text area through the attributes COLS and ROWS.

The WRAP attribute controls what happens to the text if a line is longer than the text area. OFF disables word wrapping. If a line of text is longer than the text area, then the user will have to scroll horizontally to view the rest of the line. This is the default with Netscape browsers. SOFT wraps the text if a line is longer than the Text Area but the soft line breaks are not included when the form is submitted; the text will be submitted as originally input. This is the default for Internet Explorer browsers. HARD also causes the text to wrap but the line breaks are included when the form is submitted.

CHECKBOXES

```
Choice One <INPUT TYPE="checkbox" NAME="p_check1" VALUE="value one"
CHECKED>
Choice Two <INPUT TYPE="checkbox" NAME="p_check2" VALUE="value two">
```

Figure 6.3 shows a check box as rendered in the browser:

Choice One ☑ Choice Two ☐

Figure 6.3 ■ **Checkboxes as rendered in the browser.**

Some check boxes attributes:

> TYPE="CHECKBOX"
> CHECKED
> NAME="name"
> VALUE="initialValue"

Checkboxes allow the user to select one or more predefined options. Checkboxes are typically used when the user can check "all that apply," for example, in response to the question, "How did you hear about our site?" To precheck a checkbox, add the attribute CHECKED. Note that only the word "CHECKED" is required.

The VALUE attribute is passed when the form is submitted and is not what is displayed alongside the checkbox. The display text beside the checkbox is not passed. In the example above, "value one" is passed and not "Choice One" when the form is submitted. Since "Choice Two" is not checked, "value two" is not passed during submission of the form.

Multiple checkboxes can have the same name. Be sure to give each checkbox a different value, however. If more than one checkbox is checked, then multiple name/value pairs are passed. For example, p_check1=Hi&p_check1=Bye.

RADIO BUTTONS

```
Radio One <INPUT TYPE="radio" NAME="p_radio1" VALUE="value one"
CHECKED>
Radio Two <INPUT TYPE="radio" NAME="p_radio1" VALUE="value two">
```

Figure 6.4 shows radio buttons as rendered in the browser:

Radio One ⦿ Radio Two ○

Figure 6.4 ■ Radio buttons as rendered in the browser.

Some radio button attributes:

> TYPE="RADIO"
>
> CHECKED
>
> NAME="name"
>
> VALUE="initialValue"

Radio buttons are an either/or, mutually exclusive option. They are usually part of a group where only one button may be selected.

What links radio buttons together in a group, and forces the user to select only one of the choices, is that each radio button is given the same name. This is an exception to the rule of unique names for each form element. The browser treats all radio buttons with the same name as a radio button group. As with checkboxes, the VALUE attribute of the checked radio button is passed when the form is submitted. The text beside the radio button is only for display purposes.

SELECT LISTS/DROP-DOWN LISTS

```
<SELECT NAME="p_dropdown">
<OPTION VALUE="1">DropDown Item 1</OPTION>
<OPTION VALUE="2">DropDown Item 2</OPTION>
</SELECT>
```

Figure 6.5a shows a select list as rendered in the browser. Figure 6.5b shows a select list after the user clicks the button.

Figure 6.5a ■ Drop-down list as rendered in the browser.

Figure 6.5b ■ Drop-down list contents when the button is clicked.

Some select list attributes:

> <SELECT> tag:
>> NAME="selectName"
>> MULTIPLE
>> SIZE="number"
> <OPTION> tag:
>> VALUE="optionValue"
>> SELECTED

Select lists are preferable to free-form data entry fields when the input information is already known. For example, instead of providing a text box for the user to input the type of credit card, use a select list. The list of credit cards that a company accepts is already known. This eliminates potential errors due to user input, because you control the values to be passed. The user can only choose from the list of values that you have created.

A select list is created with the opening and closing <SELECT> tags. Every list item must be placed between these opening and closing tags. To name a select list, place the NAME attribute in the opening Select tag. Do not place it in the OPTION tag.

The list items are created with the <OPTION> tag. Two attributes of the <OPTION> tag are:

VALUE=valuehere

SELECTED

The VALUE attribute specifies the data that is passed when the form is submitted. The text between the opening and closing <OPTION> tags are for display purposes only.

The SELECTED attribute tells the browser which list item to preselect. If this attribute is not used, then the first option in the Select List is usually displayed.

The example above has only two <OPTION> tag elements but a select list can contain many more. For example, a common use of select lists is for zipcodes that may contain hundreds of <OPTION> elements.

The most common use of select lists is to display only one element at a time and allow only one element to be selected. If needed, the number of elements displayed can be increased, and a scrollbar appears. Multiple elements can be selected by adding two attributes to the <SELECT> tag:

SIZE=n

MULTIPLE

Figure 6.6 shows a multiple select list as rendered in the browser:

Figure 6.6 ■ **A select list that displays more than one option and allows multiple options to be selected. In this case, "10016" is preselected due to the "SELECTED" attribute in its <OPTION> tag. "10015" has additionally been selected by the user.**

■ FOR EXAMPLE

```
<SELECT NAME="p_zip" SIZE="3" MULTIPLE>
<OPTION VALUE="0">Please Select a Zipcode</OPTION>
<OPTION VALUE="10015">10015</OPTION>
<OPTION VALUE="10016" SELECTED>10016</OPTION>
<OPTION VALUE="10017">10017</OPTION>
<OPTION VALUE="10018">10018</OPTION>
</SELECT>
```

HIDDEN VALUES

```
<INPUT TYPE="hidden" VALUE="My Hidden Value" NAME="p_hidden1">
```

Some hidden attributes:

> INPUT TYPE="HIDDEN"
> NAME="name"
> VALUE="initialValue"

Hidden values are not rendered in the browser. They are used to store values that do not need to be displayed to the user, but are necessary for the processing of the form. For example, hidden values are often used to pass a customer id from page to page. The display of the customer id is an internal number that should not be shown to the user but is necessary for the selection of the correct data from the database.

Be mindful of the values stored in a hidden value. Web hackers can manipulate them to breach security.

The HTML code for a Web page is viewable through View > Source. The code for Hidden Values is visible in the HTML source code. Hidden in this case simply means that there is nothing displayed for this tag when the page is rendered by the browser.

FILE INPUT

```
File name:<INPUT TYPE="file" NAME="p_file" VALUE="PathOfFile">
```

Figure 6.7 shows a file input as rendered in the browser:

File name: [   ] Browse...

Figure 6.7 ■ File input and browse button.

This form element allows a user to input a file. The browser adds a "Browse" button, allowing the user to navigate to the file and input the path of the file in the file-input area. If you use this element in one of your forms, then the ENCTYPE attribute of the <FORM> tag should be set to "multipart/form data," Also, the METHOD attribute must be set to "post."

The form attribute ENCTYPE controls how the form data is encoded before being submitted. You most likely will never need to set ENCTYPE unless you use the File Input. The default is "application/x-www-form-urlencode." If using File Input, ENCTYPE must be set to "multipart/form-data." The <FORM> tag should look like this:

```
<FORM METHOD=POST ENCTYPE="multipart/form-data"
ACTION="myProcessingFile.html">
```

File Input is relatively new and not supported by all browsers. Use sparingly.

BUTTONS

Buttons do not hold or receive data. Buttons are a way for the user to interact with a Web page. They initiate an action upon the form and can cause different results, depending on the type of button used.

SUBMIT BUTTON

```
<INPUT TYPE="submit" VALUE="Submit">
```

Figure 6.8 shows a submit button as rendered in the browser:

Submit

Figure 6.8 ▪ A SUBMIT button as rendered in the browser.

Some submit button attributes:

INPUT TYPE="SUBMIT"
NAME="name"
VALUE="text"

The Submit button is a special button. When clicked, it initiates the submit process. The submit process gathers all of the data contained within the form and sends it to the file specified in the ACTION attribute of the <FORM> tag.

The VALUE attribute applied to a Submit button is for display purposes only and does not have to be "Submit." Often the more familiar and user-friendly text "Save" is used instead. Note that the TYPE attribute of "submit" indicates that this is a Submit button.

If the Submit button is outside of the opening and closing <FORM> tags, or if the ACTION attribute of the <FORM> tag is empty, then clicking the Submit button will have no effect.

RESET BUTTON

```
<INPUT TYPE="reset" VALUE="Reset">
```

Figure 6.9 shows a reset button as rendered in the browser:

Reset

Figure 6.9 ■ A RESET button as rendered in the browser.

Some reset button attributes:

> INPUT TYPE= "RESET"
> NAME="name"
> VALUE="text"

The Reset button returns the form to its original state since it last loaded into the browser. Any changes made to the form elements, such as text fields, radio buttons, and select lists, are reversed when the Reset button is clicked. Think of this button as an "undo" button. Again, the TYPE attribute determines that this is a Reset button. The VALUE can be any word or words you wish to see displayed on the button, though "Reset" is the convention.

JAVASCRIPT BUTTON

```
<INPUT TYPE="button" VALUE="Button">
```

Figure 6.10 shows an image submit button as rendered in the browser:

Button

Figure 6.10 ■ A button as rendered in the browser.

Some button attributes:

> TYPE="BUTTON"
> NAME="buttonName"
> VALUE="text"

A button can also have a TYPE of "button." Unlike buttons of TYPE "submit" or "reset," these buttons have no predefined functionality. This type of button is used in conjunction with JavaScript. In the example below, clicking this button will not do anything, because no JavaScript has been added to it.

Note that the use of JavaScript with buttons is explained more completely in Chapter 14, "JavaScript Form Validation."

IMAGE IN PLACE OF SUBMIT BUTTON

```
<INPUT TYPE="image" ALT="Click to Submit" SRC="beijaflor.gif">
```

Figure 6.11 shows an image submit button as rendered in the browser:

Click to Submit

Figure 6.11 ■ An image as a Submit button.

Some image button attributes:

> INPUT TYPE="IMAGE"
> ALT="text"
> SRC="imagePath"

An image can be displayed that acts as a Submit button. The ALT attribute for an image displays the text when the mouse hovers over the image. The SRC attribute contains the path for the image (relative paths are discussed in Chapter 3, "Remote Server Access," in Unit "Absolute versus Relative Paths").

Naming a button causes the form submission process to pass it as a parameter to the called PL/SQL procedure named in the ACTION attribute of the form. To avoid generating an error, this parameter must be declared in the called Web Toolkit procedure. To avoid this, do not name form buttons unless necessary.

EXTRA: DISABLED ATTRIBUTE

```
<INPUT TYPE="text" DISABLED NAME="p_state" VALUE="NY">
```

If you ever have a form element that you want to disable for user input, then use the DISABLED attribute. A disabled form element:

- Will not receive focus
- Will be skipped in tabbing navigation
- Will not be able to receive user input
- Will not be included upon form submission

The form elements that support the disabled attribute are:

- Buttons
- Input data holders (text, checkbox, radio button, hidden, file)

- Option tags
- Select lists
- Text areas

The browser determines how it will render a disabled form element. In some browsers the disabled form element will appear "grayed out" and in others not.

A FIRST FORM

Create the form Student_Personal_Info. This form is used for inputting a new student record or editing an existing student record. When a user submits the form, it should be submitted to "update_student." In Chapter 18, "Web Tips and Techniques," you learn how to create update_student as a PSP file. The form should contain form fields for name, address, telephone, and employer.

First, start with the opening and closing <FORM> tags:

```
<FORM ACTION="update_student" METHOD="post" NAME="student_
personal_form">
</FORM>
```

This creates the form's container within which all of the data is to be placed.

Next, add the form elements for the data to be displayed/collected. Use the structure of your database to help guide you. In this case first name, last name, address, city, state, zipcode, telephone, and employer are all separate columns in the database. So, a separate form element should be created for each of them. Also, do not create a form field that is larger than the correlating table column. Let the length of the database column dictate the length of each field.

■ FOR EXAMPLE

```
<FORM ACTION="update_student" METHOD="post" NAME="student_personal_
form">
Salutation: <INPUT TYPE="text" NAME="p_salutation" VALUE="Salutation"
SIZE="5"><BR>
First Name: <INPUT TYPE="text" NAME="p_fname" VALUE="FirstName"
SIZE="25"><BR>
Last Name: <INPUT TYPE="text" NAME="p_lname" VALUE="LastName"
SIZE="25"><BR>
Address: <TEXTAREA COLS="21" ROWS="6" NAME="p_street_address"
VALUE="100 Main Street"WRAP="soft"></TEXTAREA><BR>
Zipcode: <SELECT NAME="p_zip">
<OPTION VALUE="0">Please Select a
Zipcode</OPTION>
<OPTION VALUE="10015">10015</OPTION>
<OPTION VALUE="10016" SELECTED>10016</OPTION>
```

```
<OPTION VALUE="10017">10017</OPTION>
<OPTION VALUE="10018">10018</OPTION>
</SELECT><BR>
Phone Number:<INPUT TYPE="text" VALUE="555-555-5555" NAME="p_phone"
MAXLENGTH="15" SIZE="15"><BR>
Employer:<INPUT TYPE="text" VALUE="MyEmployer" NAME="p_employer"
MAXLENGTH="50" SIZE="25"><BR>
<INPUT TYPE="hidden" VALUE="111" NAME="p_id">
</FORM>
```

Text fields are used for first name, last name, phone number, and employer. A text area is used for the address since it allows more than one line. A drop-down list is used for zipcodes. This is a good example of when to use a drop-down list. Most databases with address records have a "lookup" zipcode or postal code table. Using a drop-down list enables the programmer to control the input since the user must choose from the list.

A rule of thumb is to offer the user predefined choices whenever possible, using checkboxes, radio buttons, or select lists. Not only does it mean less typing for the user, it also helps ensure that a user will only submit acceptable data to the database. A good front-end will prevent users from entering "bad data" that will be rejected by the database.

Notice that the above form code has <BR> tags. These line breaks are added to provide a minimum amount of formatting. If these were not added, then the fields would align on one line and wrap, appearing jumbled. To see for yourself, copy the form code into a Notepad file, and save it with an .html extension. Go to your browser and choose File > Open. Input the path of the file in the dialog window.

Now that a form is displaying correctly it must be made functional. For a form to function it needs a way to send the data it has collected to be processed. In short, it needs buttons. The file to receive the data is already defined in the ACTION attribute in the opening <FORM> tag. To enable the user to send the data to this file a <SUBMIT> button is needed. A <RESET> button is standard and allows a user to undo any changes prior to submitting the form.

There are other ways to submit a form other than with buttons. These are rarely used and do not accomplish anything that cannot be accomplished using a button. For example, JavaScript can be used in the HREF tag of a hyperlink to call a function that submits the form. This is not recommended, however.

The following example shows the complete form code.

■ *FOR EXAMPLE*

```
<FORM ACTION="update_student" METHOD="post" NAME="student_personal_
form">
Salutation: <INPUT TYPE="text" NAME="p_salutation" VALUE="Mr."
SIZE="5"><BR>
First Name: <INPUT TYPE="text" NAME="p_fname" VALUE="FirstName"
SIZE="25"><BR>
Last Name: <INPUT TYPE="text" NAME="p_lname" VALUE="LastName"
SIZE="25"><BR>
Address: <TEXTAREA COLS="21" ROWS="6" NAME="p_street_address"
WRAP="soft">100 Main Street</TEXTAREA><BR>
Zipcode: <SELECT NAME="p_zip">
<OPTION VALUE="0">Please Select a
Zipcode</OPTION>
<OPTION VALUE="10015">10015</OPTION>
<OPTION VALUE="10016" SELECTED>10016</OPTION>
<OPTION VALUE="10017">10017</OPTION>
<OPTION VALUE="10018">10018</OPTION>
</SELECT><BR>
Phone Number:<INPUT TYPE="text" VALUE="555-555-5555" NAME="p_phone"
MAXLENGTH="15" SIZE="15"><BR>
Employer:<INPUT TYPE="text" VALUE="MyEmployer" NAME="p_employer"
MAXLENGTH="50" SIZE="25"><BR>
<INPUT TYPE="hidden" VALUE="111" NAME="p_id">
<INPUT TYPE="reset" VALUE="Reset">
<INPUT TYPE="submit" VALUE="Submit">
</FORM>
```

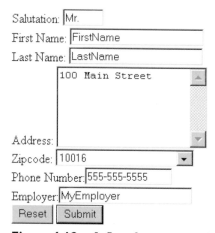

Figure 6.12 ■ **A first form as rendered in the browser.**

This form is not neatly formatted. Formatting a form is covered later in this chapter in "Formatting a Form Using Tables."

Here the form values are "hard coded." When you begin building dynamic Web pages with PSP/Toolkit technology, the "hard-coded" values are substituted with variables. This is discussed in detail in Chapter 10, "Web Toolkit I: HTML and JavaScript with PL/SQL"; Chapter 11, "Web Toolkit II: Frames, Forms, and Parameters"; and Chapter 12, "Working with PL/SQL Server Pages (PSPs)."

Notice that the select list has "Please Select a Zipcode" as one of its options. This is there for when the form is being used to add new data. All the fields should be blank and no zipcode should be presented. Since this option is the first option in the select list, then the browser will display it when no option has the "SELECTED" attribute. This provides a more professional-looking and user-friendly Web page. And as you will see in Chapter 14, "JavaScript Form Validation," having this option allows you to check if a user has indeed selected a zipcode.

UNIT 6.1 EXERCISE

CREATE THE FORM F_CUSTINFO

Write the HTML code for a form called f_custInfo with the following requirements. The form should be submitted to "processingFile." You decide which form element to use for each requirement.

- Input for a credit card number
- Input for a credit card type:
  - Master Card
  - Visa
  - Diner's Club
  - Discover
- A form element to hold the user's ID
- Input for an expiration date
- A large area in which to write a paragraph for "Feedback"

- A Submit button with the text "Save" displayed on it
- A Reset button with the text "Undo" displayed on it, and
- Format as best you can using <BR> tags.

EXERCISE 6.1 ANSWER

```
<FORM ACTION="processingFile" METHOD="post" NAME="f_custInfo">
Card Number:  <INPUT TYPE="text" NAME="p_cardNumber" VALUE=""
SIZE="25"><BR>
Card Type:  <SELECT NAME="p_cardType">
<OPTION VALUE="0">Please Select One</OPTION>
<OPTION VALUE="mc">Master Card</OPTION>
<OPTION VALUE="vs">Visa</OPTION>
<OPTION VALUE="dc">Diner's Club</OPTION>
<OPTION VALUE="ds">Discover</OPTION>
</SELECT><BR>
Expiration Date:  <INPUT TYPE="text" NAME="p_cardDate" VALUE=""
SIZE="25"><BR>
Feedback:  <TEXTAREA COLS="25" ROWS="6" NAME="p_cardFeedbck">
</TEXTAREA><BR>
<INPUT TYPE="hidden" VALUE="" NAME="p_id">
<INPUT TYPE="submit" VALUE="Save"> <INPUT TYPE="reset"
VALUE="Undo">
</FORM>
```

UNIT 6.2

ADVANCED TABLES

In Chapter 5, "Introduction to HTML: Basic Tags, Tables, and Frames," you learned how to create a basic table and insert text into it. Tables are very flexible. Forms and even other tables can be inserted into tables. For this reason, tables are good for formatting.

FORMATTING A FORM USING TABLES

As you saw in Figure 6.12, a form can be fully functional yet look sloppy when rendered in the browser. This form has <BR> tags added to each text field so that they will not appear on the same line. To make this form look nice the text fields and text field descriptors should be aligned. A standard way to format a form is to right-align the text labels next to each field, and left-align the text fields. Tables can achieve this for you along with alignment attributes.

Think of a table as a grid. Within that grid there are ways to align the contents of each square or cell within that grid. As you learn in Chapter 5, "Introduction to HTML: Basic Tags, Tables, and Frames," horizontal alignment can be set for the <TABLE>, <TR>, and <TD> tags. Values are LEFT, RIGHT, and CENTER. Vertical alignment can be set within <TD> tags. Values are TOP, BOTTOM, and CENTER.

To format the form in Figure 6.12, a table with two columns and five rows is needed. The text field descriptors should be placed in column one. The text fields should be placed in column two. For each <TD> tag that holds a display text, the attribute ALIGN is set to "right." Since the default alignment is "left," there is no need to align the <TD> tags for those cells that hold the form input fields. Figure 6.13 shows a formatted form as rendered in the browser.

■ FOR EXAMPLE

```
<FORM ACTION="update_student" METHOD="post" NAME="student_personal_
form">
<TABLE ALIGN="center"><INPUT TYPE="hidden" NAME="p_id" VALUE="">
```

```
<TR>
    <TD ALIGN="right">Salutation:</TD>
    <TD><INPUT TYPE="text" NAME="p_salutation" VALUE=""
    SIZE="5"></TD>
  </TR>

  <TR>
    <TD ALIGN="right">First Name:</TD>
    <TD><INPUT TYPE="text" VALUE="" NAME="p_first_name"
    MAXLENGTH="25" SIZE="25"></TD>
  </TR>

  <TR>
    <TD ALIGN="right">Last Name:</TD>
    <TD><INPUT TYPE="text" VALUE="" NAME="p_last_name"
    MAXLENGTH="25" SIZE="25"></TD>
  </TR>
  <TR>
    <TD ALIGN="right" VALIGN="upper">Street Address:</TD>
    <TD><TEXTAREA COLS=21 ROWS=6 NAME="p_street_address"
    WRAP="soft"></TEXTAREA>
</TD>
  </TR>
  <TR>
    <TD ALIGN="right">City:</TD>
    <TD><INPUT TYPE="text" VALUE="" NAME="p_city" MAXLENGTH="25"
    SIZE="25"></TD>
  </TR>
  <TR>
    <TD ALIGN="right">State:</TD>
    <TD><INPUT TYPE="text" VALUE="" NAME="p_state" MAXLENGTH="2"
    SIZE="25"></TD>
  </TR>
  <TR>
    <TD ALIGN="right">Zip:</TD>
    <TD><INPUT TYPE="text" VALUE="" NAME="p_student_zip"
    MAXLENGTH="5" SIZE="25">
    </TD>
  </TR>
  <TR>
    <TD ALIGN="right">Phone Number:</TD>
    <TD><INPUT TYPE="text" VALUE="" NAME="p_phone" MAXLENGTH="15"
    SIZE="25"></TD>
  </TR>
  <TR>
    <TD ALIGN="right">Employer:</TD>
    <TD><INPUT TYPE="text" VALUE="" NAME="p_employer"
    MAXLENGTH="50" SIZE="25"></TD>
  </TR>
```

Salutation:	
First Name:	
Last Name:	
Street Address:	
City:	
State:	
Zip:	
Phone Number:	
Employer:	

Reset | Save

Figure 6.13 ■ A neatly formatted form using tables.

```
<TR>
  <TD ALIGN="center" COLSPAN=2><INPUT TYPE="reset" VALUE="Reset">
  <INPUT TYPE="submit" VALUE="Save"></TD>
</TR>

</TABLE>

</FORM>
```

Be careful not to overlap the form and table tags. If the opening <FORM> tag is within the opening <TABLE> tag, then the closing </FORM> tag should be placed before the closing </TABLE> tag.

Notice that the last <TD> tag that contains the buttons uses a new attribute: COLSPAN.

ROWSPAN AND COLSPAN ATTRIBUTES

Sometimes it is necessary to have a cell span more than one row or one column. Take the form in Figure 6.13—in order to center the buttons beneath the form, it is necessary to use COLSPAN. COLSPAN makes the cell span the number of columns specified. Likewise, ROWSPAN makes a cell to span the number of rows specified.

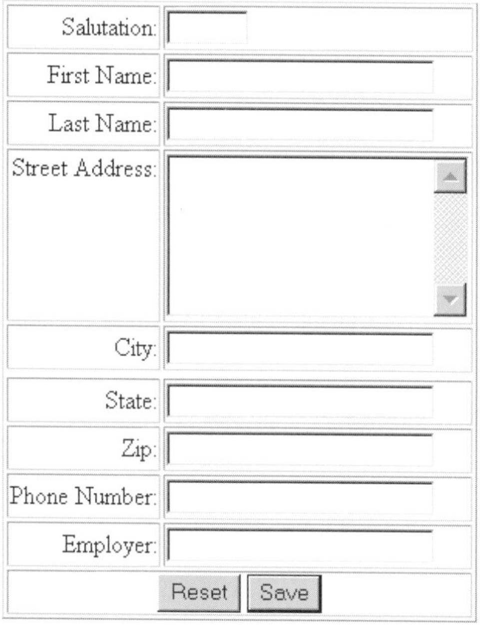

Figure 6.14 ■ A border on the table showing the effects of the COLSPAN attribute.

By adding a border to the table, you can see more clearly the effects of COLSPAN (Figure 6.14).

NESTING TABLES

As you learned in the previous Unit, "Advanced Tables," tables are useful for aligning things on a Web page. For a simple Web page layout, a single table is adequate. If the Web page is more complex, then more control is needed. Suppose that you need additional formatting within one cell of a table. Nesting tables within cells of other tables allows you the control you need to create such a complex Web page. The page can be divided into segments via a table's rows and columns. If more control is needed in a segment, insert a table between the opening and closing <TD> tags of that segment.

First, an example of nesting tables.

■ FOR EXAMPLE

```
<TABLE BORDER="1">
    <TR>
        <TD WIDTH="150">
            Row 1, Col 1 of Table 1
        </TD>
        <TD ALIGN="center">
```

```
<TABLE BORDER="1">
    <TR>
        <TD>Inner Table 2
        </TD>
    </TR>
    <TR>
        <TD>
            <TABLE BORDER="1">
                <TR>
                    <TD>
                        Inner Table 3
                    </TD>
                </TR>
            </TABLE>
        </TD>
    </TR>
</TABLE>
                    </TD>
                </TR>
            </TABLE>
        </TD>
    </TR>
    <TR>
        <TD WIDTH="150">
            Row 2, Col 1 of Table 1
        </TD>
        <TD>
            Row 2, Col 2 of Table 1
        </TD>
    </TR>
</TABLE>
```

Figure 6.15 displays the nested tables with shading in the browser.

Create the layout for your application using nested tables (later on you will recreate the same layout using frames). The application has three areas: Top Navigation Bar (Top), Left Navigation Bar (Left), and Main Area (Main). Figure 6.16 desplays the three layout areas in the browser.

Start with the outer table. In this case, the outer table has two rows and two columns. The second column of the first row should be your Top area, the first column of the second row your Left area, and the second column of the second row should be the Main area.

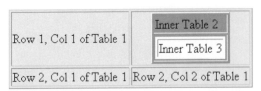

Figure 6.15 ■ **Light gray (1) is outer table, dark gray (2) is nested within light gray (1), and white (3) is nested within dark gray (2).**

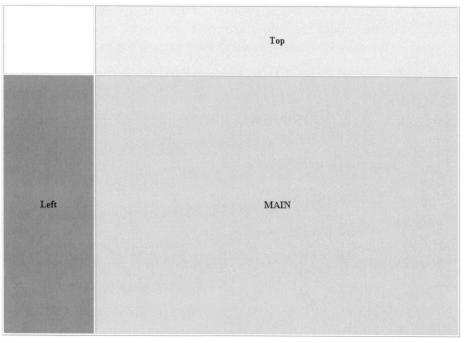

Figure 6.16 ■ **The three areas for the page layout.**

UNIT 6.2 EXERCISE

BEGIN BUILDING THE LAYOUT FOR THIS BOOK'S APPLICATION

- Create the HTML code according to the above specification.

- Add the name of the Application to the second column of the first row.

- Nest a table within the second column of the first row. This new table should have one row and three columns. Center the text in the columns.

- Nest a table in the first column of the second row. This new table should have one column and two rows. Center the text in the columns. Make the nested table align to the top.

EXERCISE 6.2 ANSWER

Your page should now look like Figure 6.17a.

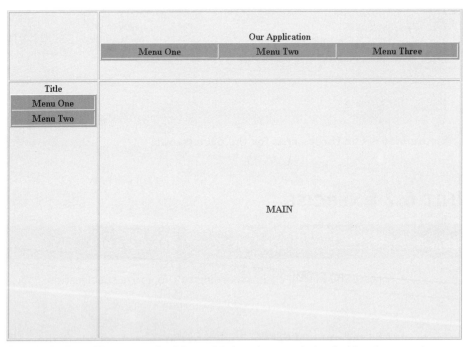

Figure 6.17a ■ **The nested tables with borders and shaded background: outer table in light gray and nested tables in dark gray.**

Figure 6.17b shows the nested table without shading.

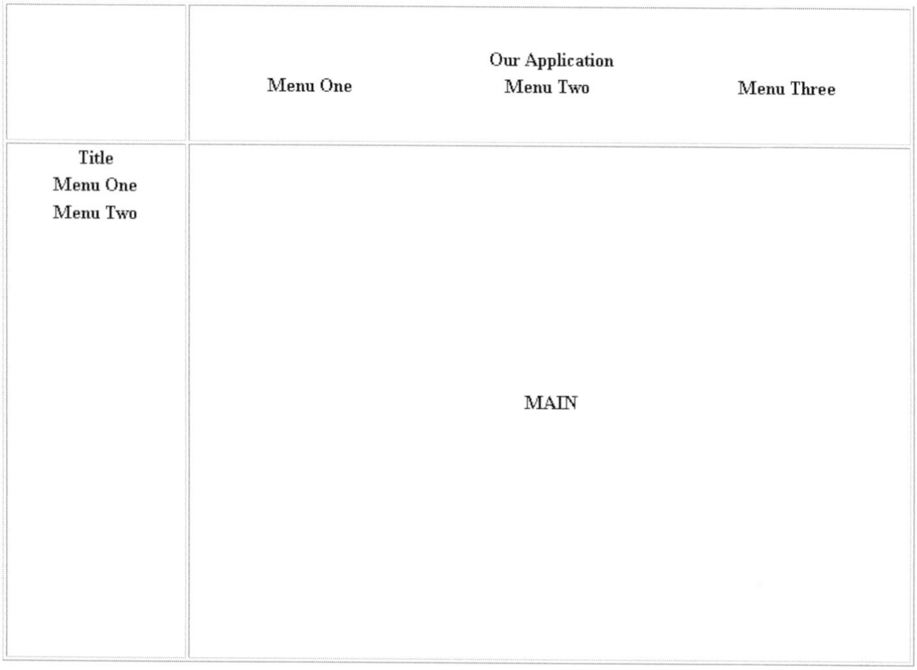

	Our Application		
	Menu One	Menu Two	Menu Three
Title Menu One Menu Two	MAIN		

Figure 6.17b ■ The same nested table code without background color or borders on nested tables.

Below is the code for Figure 6.17b:

■ FOR EXAMPLE

```
<TABLE BORDER="1" WIDTH="100%" HEIGHT="542">
  <TR>
    <TD WIDTH="20%" ALIGN="center" HEIGHT="53"> </TD>
    <TD WIDTH="80%" ALIGN="center" HEIGHT="53"><B>Our
Application</B> <TABLE
    BORDER="0" WIDTH="100%">
      <TR>
        <TD WIDTH="33%" ALIGN="center"><B>Menu One</B></TD>
        <TD WIDTH="33%" ALIGN="center"><B>Menu Two</B></TD>
        <TD WIDTH="34%" ALIGN="center"><B>Menu Three</B></TD>
      </TR>
    </TABLE>
    </TD>
  </TR>
  <TR>
```

```
    <TD WIDTH="20%" ALIGN="center" HEIGHT="277"
    VALIGN="top"><B>Title</B>
    <TABLE BORDER="0" WIDTH="100%">
      <TR>
        <TD ALIGN="center"><B>Menu One</B></TD>
      </TR>
      <TR>
        <TD ALIGN="center"><B>Menu Two</B></TD>
      </TR>
    </TABLE>
    </TD>
    <TD ALIGN="center"><B>MAIN</B></TD>
  </TR>
</TABLE>
```

The story or main page will be displayed in the Main area. This area can contain any number of things, including text within <P> tags or a form within <TABLE> tags.

U N I T 6 . 3

ADVANCED FRAMESETS

In Chapter 5, "Introduction to HTML: Basic Tags, Tables, and Frames," you created a two-frame frameset. This frameset is sufficient for the splash page since it does not require a left navigation bar. The Student section, however, requires a left navigation. A nested frame is needed to incorporate this section into our already existing frameset.

NESTING FRAMESETS

First, let's look at how to nest frames using one frameset.

■ *FOR EXAMPLE*

```
<FRAMESET ROWS="20%,*">
  <FRAME SRC="topnav.htm" NAME="top">
  <FRAMESET COLS="30%,*">
      <FRAME SRC="students_left_nav.htm" NAME="students_left">
      <FRAME SRC="student_search.htm" NAME="students_main">
  </FRAMESET>
  <NOFRAMES>
  <BODY>
  <P>
  You must use a browser that can display frames to see this page
  </P>
  </BODY>
  </NOFRAMES>
</FRAMESET>
```

The main frameset specifies two frames. The first frame is defined by the following:

```
    <FRAME SRC="topnav.htm" NAME="top">
```

Define the second frame with a frameset instead of another <FRAME> tag as you did in Chapter 5. This nested frameset is bold in the example above.

This method is fine if the application will always have a left navigation bar. In your application, however, the Splash Page has no left navigation bar. How do you set up the framesets so that when a user clicks on Student Info the Splash Page is replaced with a left navigation bar frame and a main frame?

First, create a two-frame frameset with a top frame and main frame.

■ FOR EXAMPLE

```
<FRAMESET ROWS="64,*">
  <FRAME NAME="top" SCROLLING="no" NORESIZE SRC="topnav.htm">
  <FRAME NAME="main" SRC="splash.htm">
  <NOFRAMES>
  <BODY>
  <P>THIS PAGE USES FRAMES, BUT YOUR BROWSER DOESN'T SUPPORT
  THEM.</P>
  </BODY>
  </NOFRAMES>
</FRAMESET>
```

The links in the top navigation bar will link to a frameset and target the main frame:

```
<A HREF="student_main_frame.htm" TARGET="main">Student Information</A>
```

So, instead of loading a regular HTML document into the frame 'Main' you are loading a frameset into it. The code for 'students_main_frame.htm' looks like this:

■ FOR EXAMPLE

```
<FRAMESET COLS="30%,*">
  <FRAME SRC="students_left_nav.htm" NAME="students_left">
  <FRAME SRC="student_search.htm" NAME="students_main">
  <NOFRAMES>
  <BODY>
  <P>THIS PAGE USES FRAMES, BUT YOUR BROWSER DOESN'T SUPPORT
  THEM.</P>
  </BODY>
  </NOFRAMES>
</FRAMESET>
```

Now, create the files to be loaded into the frames students_left and students_main. The student left navigation bar contains two menu items: Search Student and Add/Edit Student. Name the file 'students_left_nav.htm.' For the Search Student menu item, create a simple HTML page with the text 'Student Search' and name it 'search_student.htm.'

Below is sample HTML code for 'students_left_nav.htm':

■ *FOR EXAMPLE*

```
<HTML>
<HEAD>
<TITLE>Student Left Nav</TITLE>
</HEAD>
<BODY>
<TABLE BORDER="0" WIDTH="100%">
  <TR>
    <TD ALIGN="center"><A HREF="search_student.htm" TARGET="students_
    main"><SMALL><FONT
FACE="Arial">Search Student</FONT></SMALL></A>
    </TD>
  </TR>
  <TR>
    <TD ALIGN="center"><A HREF="student_personal_info" TARGET=
    "students_main"><SMALL><FONT
FACE="Arial">Add/Edit Student</FONT></SMALL></A>
    </TD>
  </TR>
</TABLE>
</BODY>
</HTML>
```

MORE FRAMESET ATTRIBUTES

NORESIZE AND SCROLLING ATTRIBUTES

The <FRAME> tag has two attributes that give you further control over the look and feel of the frames:

```
NORESIZE
SCROLLING="YES" | "NO" | "AUTO"
```

NORESIZE   This attribute prevents users from resizing the frame. All of the edges of a frame cannot be resized even if an adjacent frame is resizable.

SCROLLING   Determines whether scrollbars are available for a frame. "AUTO" will apply scrollbars to a frame only if needed as determined by the browser. "YES" will apply a scrollbar whether needed or not. And "NO" prevents a scrollbar from being applied to a frame if needed or not. If the SCROLLING attribute is not specified the default is "AUTO".

BORDER AND FRAMEBORDER ATTRIBUTES

You can also control whether frames appear with or without a border. If you choose to apply a border to the frames, the width of the border can also be set:

```
BORDER="width in pixels"
FRAMEBORDER="YES"|"NO"
```

BORDER

The BORDER attribute is an attribute of the <FRAMESET> tag and can only be used in the outermost frameset. It controls the thickness of the border. The thickness is specified in pixels. If no BORDER attribute is present, the default is 5 pixels.

```
<FRAMESET BORDER="2" ...>
```

FRAMEBORDER

The FRAMEBORDER is an attribute of both the <FRAMESET> and <FRAME> tags. It determines whether a border is applied to a frame or not. The default is to apply a border.

```
<FRAME ... FRAMEBORDER="NO"...>
```

or

```
<FRAMESET ...FRAMEBORDER="NO" ...>
```

FRAMES VS. TABLES

TABLES

Table 6.1 ■ Benefits and Negatives of Using Tables

Benefits	Negatives
Most Web designers favor tables over frames for page layouts. The designer has more control over how the page is rendered in the browser.	Tables can be difficult to work with or slow to load if there are too many nested tables.
Frames can cut off part of a document if there is no scrollbar, and scrollbars on the frames are not aesthetically pleasing.	

FRAMES

Table 6.2 ▪ Benefits and Negatives of Using Frames

Benefits	Negatives
Frames allow for better performance because the entire page does not have to be reloaded every time. If a user clicks on a link in the left nav bar, then only the document in the main frame has to be loaded and not the top nav bar, left nav bar, and main area.	Web pages using frames cannot be bookmarked. Only the frameset is bookmarked. Frames can be difficult when trying to access a page through JavaScript.

UNIT 6.3 EXERCISES

6.3.1 CREATE A CLASSES FRAMESET

Create a frameset for the Classes menu item. Name it classes_frame.htm. It will have a left nav bar and a main frame. Name them classes_left and classes_main, respectively. Set the frame classes_left to 150 and the frame classes_main to fill up the rest of the window.

6.3.2 LOAD TOP NAVIGATION BAR LINKS IN TO MAIN FRAME

In the top navigation bar, make the link Classes load classes_frame.htm into the main frame.

6.3.3 CREATE THE INSTRUCTOR FRAMESET

Using the skills you have learned in this chapter create the instructor frameset, instructor left navigation bar, and instructor personal info form. Refer to the Application Specifications located on this book's Web site for the requirements.

EXERCISE ANSWERS

6.3.1 ANSWER

Create a frameset for the Classes menu item. Name it classes_frame.htm. It will have a left nav bar and a main frame. Name them classes_left and classes_main, respectively. Set the frame classes_left to 150 and the frame classes_main to fill up the rest of the window.

UNIT 6.3

```
<HTML>
<HEAD>Student Details</HEAD>
<FRAMESET COLS="150,*">
  <FRAME NAME="classes_left" SRC="classes_left_nav.htm">
  <FRAME NAME="classes_main" SRC="classes_list.htm" SCROLLING="auto">
  <NOFRAMES>
  <BODY>
  <P>This page uses frames, but your browser doesn't support them. </P>
  </BODY>
  </NOFRAMES>
</FRAMESET>
</HTML>
```

6.3.2 ANSWER

In the top navigation bar, make the link Classes load classes_frame.htm into the main frame.

```
<A HREF="classes_frame.htm" TARGET="main">Student Details</a>
```

CHAPTER 6

BUILDING THE APP

The answers to these projects can be found at the companion Web site to this book, located at http://www.phptr.com/boardman. Visit the Web site periodically to share and discuss your answers with other readers.

Forms, nested tables, and nested frames allow a Web developer to create more sophisticated and interactive Web sites. Forms allow information to be collected from a user and processed. Nested tables and frames give a Web developer more options in designing the layout of a Web page.

You should have the following parts of the application after this chapter:

- Student Frameset
- Instructors Frameset
- Classes Frameset
- Student_Personal_Info Form
- Instructor_Personal_Info Form
- Student Left Navigation Bar
- Instructor Left Navigation Bar

C H A P T E R   7

INTRODUCTION TO JAVASCRIPT

JavaScript allows a Web developer to create Web pages that are more interactive and more interesting. Using the Document Object Model, the Web developer has vast access to the browser and elements of the HTML document. JavaScript is an indispensable part of Web site development.

JavaScript is an interpreted, object-based scripting language. As with any programming language it comes replete with:

- control statements
    - for...each
    - if-then-else
    - while
    - switch

- values, variables, and string literals
- operators (such as =, >, ==)
- the ability to create and call functions
- string pattern matching using Regular Expressions
- predefined functions for handling math, dates, and arrays (called math, date, and array)

This set of basic statements and language elements is known as Core JavaScript. Core JavaScript is extended by Client-side JavaScript and Server-side JavaScript. Server-side JavaScript executes on the server and only the results are returned to the browser; the code cannot be viewed. Server-side JavaScript is rarely used in Web development. When the term "JavaScript" is used in this book it is referring to Client-side JavaScript.

Client-side JavaScript extends Core JavaScript with objects that allow access to and control over the Web browser and the Document Object Model (DOM). You learn about the DOM in detail later in this chapter in Unit 7.3, "The Document Object Model." For now, you only need to know that the DOM is a hierarchical structure that allows you to access and control the Web browser and HTML document.

JavaScript and Java are two different languages and one should not be mistaken for the other. Java is a compiled, class-based programming language. It is not integrated into the Web browser and HTML document as JavaScript is. Java code, such as applets, are compiled and stored on a server. It is downloaded to a Web browser to be executed, but the Java applet is completely separate from the HTML document. JavaScript, on the other hand, is an interpreted language that is run and executed by the Web browser and is intimately a part of the HTML document. The two languages are different and serve different purposes. They should not be confused.

JavaScript was created by Netscape in 1995 out of a need to make Web pages more dynamic. It was initially called LiveScript but the name was changed to JavaScript. It was first supported by the beta version of Netscape 2.0 in 1995. Microsoft subsequently added support for JavaScript to its Internet Explorer browser as well. JavaScript is fully integrated with HTML and Web browsers. As a result, a Web developer has almost complete access to and control over a Web browser and the HTML document. For example, using JavaScript, a Web developer can, among other things:

1. Respond to user events such as clicking a button or changing a value in a form field.
2. Control Web browser features such as the URL window, status bar, the back/forward buttons, and the opening/closing of browser windows.
3. Read and change the values in form fields.
4. Change document properties such as background color.

5. Swap images as the user passes the cursor over a certain area of a Web page.

6. Send messages to the user.

7. Set and read cookies (explained in further detail in Chapter 15, "Maintaining State with Cookies and Tables").

JavaScript code and HTML code are served by the Web server to the client and loaded into the browser. Thus, JavaScript code runs completely on the client. This can be used to your advantage in a number of ways. One example is with form validation. You can validate the data in the form on the client before sending it to the back-end to be processed. If you do not validate the data on the client and the user has entered invalid data, the following is a typical scenario of what happens when the "Submit" button is clicked by the user:

1. The data is sent via the network to the back-end process named in the ACTION attribute of the FORM tag.

2. An insert/update statement to the data in the database causes processes in the database to be initiated, rows locked for update, roll-back memory allocated, and so on.

3. Since the data is invalid, constraints on allowable data cause a halt to the insert/update process.

4. An error message is generated upon attempting to insert/update the data.

5. This error message is captured and code is then executed to handle it.

6. An error message HTML page is generated.

7. This HTML page is served by the Web server to the client via the network.

Compare this to what happens when there is JavaScript validation in place. When the "Submit" button is clicked by the user:

1. A JavaScript function, already loaded in the browser, is called.

2. The data in the form is validated by the function. Depending on how the function has been written, validation can simply mean checking that data is entered in all required fields, that no illegal characters have been entered, and that the datatype is correct for each field, among other possible checks.

3. If the data is invalid, then a JavaScript message, in the form of a pop-up window, is displayed to the user. The user clicks "OK" on the message and corrects the data. There are no trips to the back-end database and no processes are initiated on the Web server or database server. Since everything takes place on the client, the response time is very fast.

You learn about form validation using JavaScript in detail in Chapter 14, "JavaScript Form Validation."

UNIT 7.1

EMBEDDING JAVASCRIPT IN HTML

A FIRST EXAMPLE

JavaScript can be embedded within HTML. The <SCRIPT> tag allows you to do this.

■ *FOR EXAMPLE*

```
<HTML>
<HEAD>
<SCRIPT language="JavaScript">
<!--Begin hiding content from old browsers.
alert("This is an Alert!");
document.write("I'm being written by JavaScript!");
//End hiding here-->
</SCRIPT>
</HEAD>
<BODY>
<H2>A First JavaScript Script</H2>
<P>This is text within paragraph tags.</P>
</BODY>
</HTML>
```

The example above is a very simple JavaScript script embedded within an HTML page. It does two things:

1. It creates a pop-up message, called an alert, with the text "This is an Alert!" (Figure 7.1a)
2. It writes to the HTML document the text "I'm being written by JavaScript!" (Figure 7.1b)

To see this for yourself, do the following:

1. Type the entire code into a Notepad file, or other similar text editor, and Save As firstJS.htm. Include text from the opening <HTML> tag to the closing </HTML> tag.
2. Select File > Open in your browser, browse to the directory where this file resides, and select "OK". You may have to select "OK" or "Open" if there is another dialog box.
3. The file should open in the browser causing the JavaScript to run.

As the document and JavaScript load into the browser, the JavaScript code runs. Figure 7.1 is what you should see.

<SCRIPT> TAGS

To embed JavaScript within HTML, use the opening and closing <SCRIPT> tags and place all of your JavaScript code in between them. JavaScript-enabled browsers will not display in the browser any of the text in between the opening <SCRIPT> tag and the closing </SCRIPT> tag.

What happens if a non-JavaScript–enabled browser encounters the opening and closing <SCRIPT> tags? It will ignore them and display the text in between them. This is why the HTML comment tags are used right after the opening <SCRIPT> tag and immediately before the closing </SCRIPT> tag.

■ *FOR EXAMPLE*

```
<SCRIPT language="JavaScript1.3">
<!--
...
//-->
</SCRIPT>
```

Figure 7.1a ■ The Alert pops up first. After "OK" is clicked, the document continues to load into the browser and Figure 7.1b should appear.

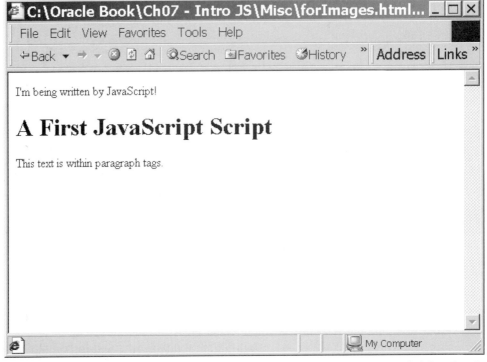

Figure 7.1b ■ **After the Alert shown in Figure 7.1a, the HTML page finishes loading into the browser.**

The HTML comment tags are not required. However, it is good practice to include them in the case that someone calling your page is using a non-JavaScript–enabled browser. If you do use them, be sure to also include the JavaScript comment tag before the closing HTML comment tag:

```
//-->
```

Notice that the closing HTML comment tag is preceded by the single-line JavaScript comment tag. This hides the HTML comment tag from the JavaScript code for browsers that are JavaScript-enabled.

 If this all seems a little confusing, don't spend too much time trying to make sense of it. There are many more important concepts in JavaScript to spend time learning. Simply adopt these practices as your standard when writing JavaScript.

LANGUAGE ATTRIBUTE

```
<SCRIPT LANGUAGE="JavaScript1.3">
```

This attribute specifies the script language and version being used. JavaScript is the most widely used scripting language today, but tomorrow there may be another one. By specifying the LANGUAGE attribute you avoid any situation where JavaScript is not the default language and this attribute would be required. As of now, the LANGUAGE attribute is not required since most browsers assume that the default scripting language is JavaScript. However, it's good practice to include it in the case that other scripting languages become more widely used.

Specify the version only if you are using functionality that exists in later versions. For example, if the JavaScript code works in older versions as well as the latest version of JavaScript, then do not specify the latest version, that is, LANGUAGE= Javascript1.3. Browsers that do not support JavaScript 1.3 will ignore the JavaScript code if it comes across a LANGUAGE attribute specifying version 1.3.

On the other hand, what happens when a browser encounters a version of JavaScript that it doesn't support, that is, a browser supports only up to version 1.1 of JavaScript and your code uses version 1.3 but you have not specified a version in the LANGUAGE attribute? The browser will try to run JavaScript, ignoring any of the newer features of the code not already part of version 1.1.

SRC ATTRIBUTE

As an alternative to including the JavaScript code within HTML you can place the JavaScript code in a .js file and "source" it like this:

```
<SCRIPT SRC="myScripts.js"></SCRIPT>
```

Using the SRC attribute is a good way to include the same JavaScript code in many HTML pages. Changes then only need to be made in one place instead of in every HTML page that uses it. Think of it as a PL/SQL library. It also helps to "hide" your JavaScript code since it is not viewable as part of the HTML code through View > Source. But don't rely on this if you want to keep your JavaScript code private. A determined user can usually find a way to download and view a .js file.

Below is an example of a .js file.

■ *FOR EXAMPLE*

```
function myJS() {
    alert("Stop");
}
document.write("<SCR" + "IPT
            SRC='includeMe.js'></SCR"+"IPT>");
document.write("<H1>Welcome to My Web Page</H1 >");
```

The .js file example above contains the function myJS();. This function is now accessible by any function calls in the document. This .js file also contains

JavaScript that writes to the main document another <SCRIPT> tag that references another .js file. The plus sign is JavaScript's way of concatenating two strings. HTML tags and text can also be written to a document using this same technique. The heading "Welcome to My Web Page" will be written to the main document.

 Since the HTML parser is reading the generated text as it is being written, split up the <SCRIPT> tags using concatenation. This will avoid confusing the parser since technically you are already inside of a <SCRIPT> tag. If the parser finds another opening <SCRIPT> tag before it finds a closing <SCRIPT> tag, then this will confuse the parser and most likely generate an error message.

There are a few things to keep in mind when using the SRC attribute:

- <SCRIPT> tags with the SRC attribute cannot contain text or code between the opening and closing <SCRIPT> tags.
- The .js file can contain only pure JavaScript code. No HTML tags are allowed. If you need to include HTML code or another .js file within a .js file, use document.write(), as shown above.
- As with any file reference, the correct path for that file must be cited. Please refer to Chapter 3, "Remote Server Access," Unit "Absolute versus Relative Path and Filenames," for more detailed information.
- The external file must have the file extension ".js."
- If you are not using local files, then the server must map the .js suffix to the MIME type application/x-javascript. The server returns this MIME type in the HTTP header. To map the suffix to the MIME type, the mime.types file in the server's config directory must be modified and the server restarted.

COMMENTS

It is good coding practice to add comments to your code. JavaScript provides for single-line and multiline comments. The JavaScript interpreter ignores comments.

Single-line comments use '//':

```
// A single-line comment.
```

Multiline comments use '/*' and '*/':

```
/* A multi-line
comment */
```

Comment tags can also be used to "comment out" code while develop-ing and testing.

<NOSCRIPT> TAGS

As with the <NOFRAMES> tags for frames, the <NOSCRIPT> tags present a friendly message to the user when using a non-JavaScript–enabled browser. If a user has disabled scripting functionality in the browser, the <NOSCRIPT> message will be displayed. Use this tag only if you want to display a message to the user. It is not required.

■ FOR EXAMPLE

```
<NOSCRIPT>
<P>Your browser is not enabled to run JavaScript, and this
page will not display properly</P>
</NOSCRIPT>
```

Web browsers that do not support script languages must render the text in the <NOSCRIPT> tag. There is no requirement as to where it should be placed in the document; however, it is good coding practice to place it immediately after the closing <SCRIPT> tag.

Some users may choose to turn off scripting functionality in their browsers for security reasons. There are well-known security holes in JavaScript that can exploit vulnerabilities in a user's browser. To disable JavaScript in Internet Explorer 5.50, for example, go to Tools > Internet Options. Click on the Security tab. Click on the button "Custom Level..." and scroll down to "Scripting." Select "disable" for "Active Scripting."

OTHER IMPORTANT THINGS TO KEEP IN MIND

LOCATION OF JAVASCRIPT WITHIN AN HTML DOCUMENT

It's good coding practice to place JavaScript in the <HEAD> tags because it will be loaded first into the page. HTML pages load from top to bottom, and JavaScript runs as it is loaded into the browser (unless, of course, it's a function that needs to be called or requires an event). By placing your JavaScript in a location to en-sure that it is loaded first and fully, you decrease the possibility that part of your code is not loaded into the browser by the time that it is needed.

ENDING A JAVASCRIPT STATEMENT

Semicolons are usually used to end a JavaScript statement, though they are optional as long as each statement begins on a new line. A good coder will use semicolons anyway. It's safer and it helps in reading the code. In the example below there are two separate JavaScript statements:

```
alert("This is an Alert!");
document.write("I'm being written by JavaScript!");
```

Since semicolons are being used, these two statements can be placed on the same line:

```
alert("This is an Alert!");document.write("I'm being
written by JavaScript!");
```

Or on separate lines with no semicolons:

```
alert("This is an Alert!")
document.write("I'm being written by JavaScript!")
```

The code is easier to read if you place each statement on a separate line and end it with a semicolon.

VIEWING RUNTIME ERROR MESSAGES

An error message is generated when a runtime error occurs in JavaScript. In Internet Explorer the error message can be viewed by clicking the Warning icon in the bottom left-hand corner of the browser, as shown in Figure 7.2.

This will bring up the dialog box in Figure 7.3a.

Click on the "Show Details" button to view the error message in Figure 7.3b.

If there is more than one error message, the "Previous" and "Next" buttons will be enabled.

In Netscape, there are two ways to see JavaScript runtime error messages: Go to Tasks > Tools > JavaScript Console or type "javascript:" in the URL window and hit Enter.

The JavaScript Console will open and display all JavaScript error messages, as shown in Figure 7.4.

Figure 7.2 ■ Warning icon in Internet Explorer.

Figure 7.3a ■ Double-clicking on the Warning icon results in this dialog box.

WAYS TO EXECUTE JAVASCRIPT CODE

There are several ways for JavaScript to execute:

1. JavaScript statements can be executed as they load into the browser. These types of JavaScript statements need to be within <SCRIPT> tags, or within a .js file that is referenced in an HTML document.

■ *FOR EXAMPLE*

```
<SCRIPT LANGUAGE="JavaScript1.3">
alert("JavaScript that runs as it's loaded into the
browser");
</SCRIPT>
```

In this example, the alert statement would be executed at the point that it is loaded into the browser. Remember that the browser loads documents from top to bottom. If this JavaScript were placed at the

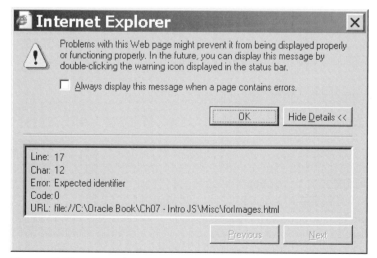

Figure 7.3b ■ Details of the dialog box in Figure 7.3a.

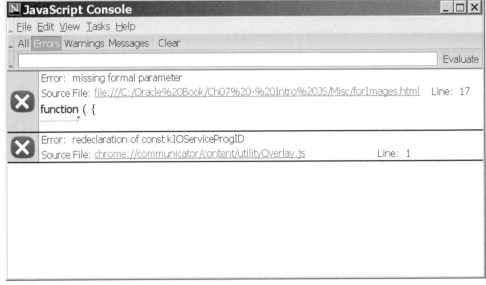

Figure 7.4 ■ Netscape's JavaScript console.

very bottom of the document, then the entire page would be loaded and then code would be executed.

2. JavaScript statements that are part of a function are not executed unless that function is called. The call can either be upon some event initiated by the user or a call that executes as it is loaded into the browser. If the alert in the example above is now placed in a function, then that function must be called in order for the alert statement to execute.

■ *FOR EXAMPLE*

```
<SCRIPT LANGUAGE="JavaScript1.3">
    function myAlert() {
alert("JavaScript that runs as a result of a function call.");
}
//Here is a call to the function.
myAlert();
</SCRIPT>
```

In this example, the alert statement is executed as a result of the function call being executed as it is loaded into the browser. This function call also could have been associated with an event handler, discussed later in this chapter in Unit 7.4, "JavaScript Events."

3. JavaScript statements or function calls associated with an event handler are executed only upon the occurrence of an event initiated by the user. Below is an example of a JavaScript function being called using an event handler.

■ *FOR EXAMPLE*

```
<SCRIPT LANGUAGE="JavaScript1.3">
    function myAlert() {
alert("JavaScript that runs as a result of a function call.");
}
</SCRIPT>
...
<INPUT TYPE="button" VALUE="Save" onClick="myAlert();">
```

In this example, when the user clicks on the button created by the <INPUT> tag, the function is called and executed.

 JavaScript statements and function calls can be placed in a <A HREF=...> tag, which are executed when the user clicks on the associated hyperlink. Instead of a using a URL in the HREF attribute, specify JavaScript as the protocol with "javascript:". Then place the JavaScript statements after the colon.

```
<A HREF="javascript:myAlert();">Click Here</A>
```

The function myAlert(); is called and the alert statement is executed upon a user clicking on the hyperlink. This can be used instead of associating an event with a button. You learn about associating events with document components later in this Chapter in Unit 7.4, "JavaScript Events."

UNIT 7.1 EXERCISES

a) Embed the following JavaScript code in an HTML page. Be sure to hide the JavaScript code from older browsers that do not support JavaScript. The code to embed is:

```
alert("Embed me in HTML");
```

b) JavaScript code can be added directly into an HTML page by placing the code in between the <SCRIPT> tags. How else can JavaScript code be loaded with a document into a browser?

c) True or False: Client-side JavaScript is executed on the application server and returns the output to the client.

d) Take the following two JavaScript statements and place them correctly within the <SCRIPT> tags:

```
Statement 1: alert("Number 1")
Statement 2: alert("Number 2")
```

UNIT 7.1 EXERCISE ANSWERS

a) Embed the following JavaScript code in an HTML page. Be sure to hide the JavaScript code from older browsers that do not support JavaScript. The code to embed is:

```
alert("Embed me in HTML");
```

Answer:

```
<HTML>
<HEAD>
<SCRIPT LANGUAGE="JavaScript1.3">
alert("Embed me in HTML");
</SCRIPT>
<NOSCRIPT>
<P>Your browser is not enabled to run JavaScript, and this
page will not display properly</P>
</NOSCRIPT>
</HEAD>
<BODY>
<P>Document Text Here.</P>
</BODY>
</HTML>
```

b) JavaScript code can be added directly into an HTML page by placing the code in between the <SCRIPT> tags. How else can JavaScript code be loaded with a document into a browser?

Answer: By using the SRC attribute of the <SCRIPT> tag:

```
<SCRIPT SRC="myScripts.js"></SCRIPT>
```

The .js file can contain only pure JavaScript code. Use the method document. write(); if HTML or another .js file needs to be included.

c) True or False: Client-side JavaScript is executed on the application server and returns the output to the client.

Answer: False. Client-side JavaScipt is loaded into the browser along with the HTML document and is executed on the client.

d) Take the following two JavaScript statements and place them correctly within the <SCRIPT> tags:

```
Statement 1: alert("Number 1")
Statement 2: alert("Number 2")
```

Answer: There are several correct answers to this question. The suggested answer is:

```
<SCRIPT>
alert("Number 1");
alert("Number 2");
</SCRIPT>
```

A semicolon or a new line indicates the end of a JavaScript statement. When you place the statements on separate lines and end them with semi-colons, you make the code easier to read. However, either one of the following is acceptable:

```
<SCRIPT>
alert("Number 1");alert("Number 2");
</SCRIPT>
```

or

```
<SCRIPT>
alert("Number 1")
alert("Number 2")
</SCRIPT>
```

U N I T   7 . 2

JAVASCRIPT SYNTAX

VARIABLES, LITERALS, AND VALUE TYPES

VALUE (DATA) TYPES

The value types in JavaScript are:

- Numbers
- Boolean—"true" or "false"
- Strings
- Null—keyword
- Undefined—the value of an unassigned variable

JavaScript is a loosely typed language. The word "typed" here refers to the data type and not the keyboard habits of coders. Unlike languages such as PL/SQL, there is no need to declare a variable's data type in JavaScript. Furthermore, the same variable can be used to store different data types. JavaScript automatically does the data conversion for you. In PL/SQL, a variable declared to be of data type Number can only hold a value of the data type Number. Not so in JavaScript. A variable can be assigned a Number data type value and then later be assigned a String data type value.

 In Oracle, it's datatype; in JavaScript, it's data type.

VARIABLES

Variables have the same use in JavaScript as in other languages. They hold values that you assign to them. This value can vary (thus the term "variable") but the name of the variable remains the same. You can name your variables anything you desire, but variable names are subject to the following JavaScript rules:

VARIABLE NAMES MUST BEGIN WITH "_" OR A LETTER. A variable name can contain numbers as long as a number is not the first character in the variable name.

Examples of legal variable names are:

- _myVar
- myVar
- my567
- My_Var1

An example of an illegal variable name is:

- 1myVar

VARIABLE NAMES ARE CASE-SENSITIVE. Thus, "myVar" is different from "MyVar." A common mistake for beginning JavaScript coders is to try and reference a variable using the wrong case. Doing so will generate an error.

It is also good coding practice to establish a variable naming standard and apply that standard throughout your application. For example, try prefixing the variable name with an appropriate abbreviation. To create variables to hold the values of a form's elements, prefix the variable names with "frm." Thus, "frmName" for the name of the form, "frmSelectListVal" for the select list form element, and so on. It's common among JavaScript developers to combine abbreviated words where the first word is written in all lowercase and the second abbreviated word is written in initial caps.

Try to resist the temptation to use the same variable name over and over again as you code. Some coders will use "x", for example, as a variable name, because it is short, easy to type, and doesn't require any thought. This is bad practice. The variable name "x" is not indicative of the value it is to hold, and if you are not careful with the scope of a variable (explained shortly) you may inadvertently overwrite a global variable.

DECLARING A VARIABLE   Variables in JavaScript are declared in one of two ways, with or without the keyword var:

```
myVar = "Some Value Here";
var myVar = "Some Value Here";
```

Note that the "=" symbol is used to assign the value on the right to the variable identifier on the left. This is known as assigning a value to a variable. Declaration and assignment of a variable is accomplished in this one JavaScript statement. In PL/SQL, := is the assignment operator.

Declaring a variable with or without var affects two things: scope and evaluation.

SCOPE. The scope of a variable refers to which parts of your code are able to access that variable. A global variable is accessible from anywhere in the code on that page, as well as accessible by other frames or windows as long as the window or frame name is known where the global variable is set. Local variables are accessible only within the functions in which they are set.

Global variables are set outside of a function. It does not matter if you use the "var" keyword or not when setting global variables.

Local variables are set within functions and the keyword "var" must be used.

To see this for yourself, type the following JavaScript into the <HEAD> tags of an HTML page. Go to File > Open and view it in a browser.

■ *FOR EXAMPLE*

```
<SCRIPT>
noVarGlobal = "Global no var";
var withVarGlobal = "Global with var"
//Create a function which accesses the two global and one local
variable
function f_testVar () {
    var localVariable = "Local within function";
    alert(noVarGlobal);
    alert(withVarGlobal);
    alert(localVariable);
}
//Call the function to test scope of variables
f_testVar();
//Now try to access the local variable from outside the function
alert(localVariable);
</SCRIPT>
```

Remember that HTML documents load from top to bottom. The script is executed as it is loaded. The sequence of events for this script is:

1. The global variables are declared and set.
2. The function f_testVar() is loaded.
3. The call to that function loads and f_testVar() is executed.
4. The execution of f_testVar() first declares and sets the local variable, localVariable, and then the three alerts are executed in order. Each of these alerts is successful in accessing the two global and one local variable from within the function.
5. Finally, an alert outside of the function attempts to access the function's local variable and fails. It is out of scope. View the error message

generated (the procedure to view a JavaScript error message is different depending on the browser you are using).

EVALUATION. A variable that has been declared but that has not been assigned a value is equal to "undefined." If the variable has been declared using "var", then evaluating that variable does not result in a runtime error and instead the variable evaluates to "undefined" (Figure 7.5).

■ FOR EXAMPLE

```
<SCRIPT>
var myUndefinedVariable
alert(myUndefinedVariable);
</SCRIPT>
```

On the other hand, declaring a variable without "var" and not assigning a value to it results in a runtime error when that variable is evaluated (Figure 7.6).

■ FOR EXAMPLE

```
<SCRIPT>
noVar =
alert(noVar);
</SCRIPT>
```

This characteristic of variables declared with "var" can be advantageous to you. First, no runtime errors are generated when attempting to reference such a variable. Second, you can test the variable to see if it has been assigned a value or not.

■ FOR EXAMPLE

```
if {myVar == "undefined"} {
  do this
} else {
  do this with a value
}
```

Figure 7.5 ■ The result of evaluating a declared but unassigned variable using "var."

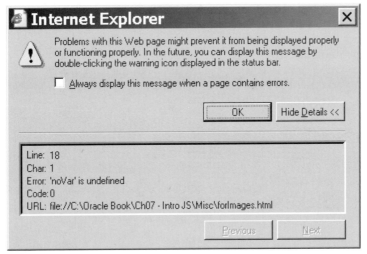

Figure 7.6 ■ A runtime error message generated during evaluation of a variable declared without "var" and not assigned a value.

STRING LITERALS: QUOTES, ESCAPING CHARACTERS, AND SPECIAL CHARACTERS

In the above script example, the variable "withVarGlobal" is set using a string literal:

```
var withVarGlobal = "Global with var"
```

A string literal is any number of characters enclosed with double (") or single (') quotes. The same beginning and ending delimiter must be used. These are both legal string literals:

- "Some string text 111"
- 'Some string text 111'

However, this is an illegal string literal:

- "Some string text 111'

Upon encountering the start of a string literal, the JavaScript interpreter notes whether a single or double quote is used as the beginning delimiter. It looks for this to end the string literal. If it encounters the other type of delimiter, the interpreter does not interpret it as the ending delimiter and includes it as part of the string literal. Look at this example below:

"I'm being written by JavaScript."

The beginning and ending delimiters are double quotes. Single quotes can be used within this string literal without the interpreter ending the string prematurely. The single quote is interpreted as another nonspecial character. The inverse is also true:

> 'This is a "quote" as an example.'

Since the beginning and ending delimiters are single quotes, then double quotes are not interpreted as special characters.

The ability to use either single or double quotes as string delimiters is very useful when coding. You can also escape characters with the backslash character "\". For example:

> "This is a \"quote\" as an example."

This is also true if the quotes are inversed:

> 'This is a \"quote\" as an example.'

In addition to the ordinary characters permissible within string literals, JavaScript allows the following special characters:

\b	Backspace
\f	Form feed
\n	New line
\r	Carriage return
\t	Tab
\\	Backslash character

These are especially useful when composing an alert message. The "\n" special character creates a new line. To display a backslash you must use two backslashes in succession, that is, "The file is located at c:\\home." This will display "The file is located at c:\home."

OTHER LITERALS

Boolean literals—either true or false

Integer literals—can be decimal (35), hexadecimal (0x144), or octal (0455)

OPERATORS

EXPRESSIONS

An expression is two or more literals or variables that use operators and evaluate to a single value. The most familiar expression to you may be the mathematic operator:

100 + 5

The '+' symbol is the sum symbol when used with numbers. When used with non-numbers the '+' symbol is the concatenation symbol.

Listed below are some of the more commonly used operators. For a complete list of JavaScript operators, refer to http://developer.netscape.com.

ASSIGNMENT OPERATORS

Assignment operators assign the value on the right of the operator to the variable on the left of the operator (Table 7.1).

COMPARISON OPERATORS

Comparison operators return a value of true or false based on the comparison of the left-hand values to the right-hand values of an operation (Table 7.2). Comparison operators are most often used in Control Statements such as If-Then-Else. Note that comparison operators may be used on numbers or strings. If used to compare two strings, standard character ordering is employed.

In JavaScript, = is an assignment operator and = = is an evaluator. In PL/SQL, := is an assignment operator and = is an evaluator.

Table 7.1 ■ Assignment Operators

Operator	Definition	Example
=	Assigns the value on the right-hand side to the variable on the left-hand side.	myVariable = "myLiteral"
+=	Appends the value of var2 to the end of the value of myVar and assigns the new value to myVar.	myVar = "string1";var2 = "end of string";myVar += var2 returns:"string1 end of string"

Table 7.2 ■ Comparison Operators

Operator	Definition	Example
==	Equal	myVar == 55777
===	Compares two expressions to determine if they are equal in value and if their values have the same data type.	myVar === 55777
!==	Compares two expressions to determine that they are not equal in value or of the same data type.	myVar !== 55777
!=	Not equal	myVarString != "a string"
>	Is greater than	myVar > 55777
<	Is less than	myVar < 55777
>=	Is greater than or equal to	myVar >= 55777
<=	Is less than or equal to myVar	<= 55777

LOGICAL OPERATORS

Logical operators take a Boolean value as an operand and return a Boolean value (Table 7.3).

MATHEMATICAL OPERATORS

Mathematical operators take numeric values as operands and return a numerical value (Table 7.4).

OTHER OPERATORS

Other operators perform operations that do not fall into the other categories but enhance the functionality of JavaScript (Table 7.5).

Table 7.3 ■ Logical Operators

Operator	Definition	Example
&&	And	exprA && exprB
||	Or	exprA || exprB
!	Not	!exprA

Table 7.4 ■ Mathematical Operators

Operator	Definition	Example
+	Sum	5 + 9
-	Subtract	10 – 3
*	Multiply	4 * 7
/	Divide	100 / 2
++	Increment	i++

FUNCTIONS

CREATING AND CALLING A FUNCTION

A JavaScript function requires:

- The keyword "function" followed by the name of the function.
- List of arguments enclosed in parentheses and separated by commas. If the function does not require arguments, the parentheses are still essential.
- The body of the function enclosed in curly braces.

Table 7.5 ■ Other Operators

Operator	Definition	Example
,	Causes two expressions to be executed sequentially.	5+7, 12/6
new	Creates a new object.	new Array();
void	Prevents an expression from returning a value.	<A HREF="javascript:void(window.open('home.htm','','scrollbars=no'))">Home</A>
typeof	Returns a string that identifies the data type of an expression.	var color = "blue";typeof(color) returns stringvar howMany = 7;typeof(howMany) returns numberFor a variable, noValue, that is not defined:typeof(noValue) returnsundefinednewObj = new Array();typeof(newObj) returns object

■ *FOR EXAMPLE*

```
<SCRIPT LANGUAGE="JavaScript1.3">
function nameFunction () {
    set variables
    if-then-else/loops
    alerts
    calls to other functions
}
</SCRIPT>
```

**UNIT
7.2**

In the example above, the name of the function is "nameFunction" and it receives no arguments. To create a function that receives arguments, simply list the arguments in the parentheses separated by a comma.

■ *FOR EXAMPLE*

```
<SCRIPT LANGUAGE="JavaScript1.3">
function nameFunction (arg1, arg2) {
    alert(arg1);
    alert(arg2);
}
</SCRIPT>
```

The body of the function, can consist of a variety of things, everything from a simple alert to logic statements (such as if-then-else statements). The body of a function can even include a call to another function defined within the scope of the calling function.

To create a function that returns some result to the calling statement, use the "return" keyword plus the output to be returned.

■ *FOR EXAMPLE*

```
<SCRIPT LANGUAGE="JavaScript1.3">
function myFunction (arg1, arg2) {
    var vSum = arg1 + arg2;
    return vSum;
}
document.write(myFunction(1,2));
</SCRIPT>
```

In the example above, "myFunction" is passed two arguments that are added together, assigned to a variable, vSum, and returned to the calling statement. Without a calling statement the function would load into the browser along with the HTML page but it would not execute. A function must be called for it to execute. To call a function simply use the name of the function and pass it any required arguments:

```
myFunction(5, 8);
```

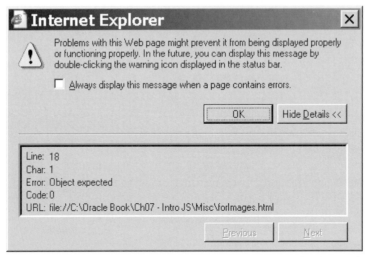

Figure 7.7 ■ The runtime error message displayed when a function is called before it has been loaded into the browser.

Remember that JavaScript is loaded into the browser along with the HTML page. The HTML page is loaded from top to bottom, and JavaScript runs as it is loaded. If a function call is loaded into the browser and executed before the function itself is loaded, then the function will not be found and a runtime error will be generated. This can occur by placing a function call before the called function in the HTML page itself. Placement in the HTML page is significant. Figure 7.7 is an example of a runtime error caused by placing a call to a function that has not yet loaded into the browser.

PREDEFINED JAVASCRIPT FUNCTIONS

Just like there are predefined packages in PL/SQL, JavaScript has predefined functions. These functions are case-sensitive:

EVAL. Evaluates a string without reference to an Object: eval(5+5) returns 10

ISFINITE. Evaluates a number and determines if it is finite: isFinite(1000) returns true

ISNAN. Evaluates a number and determines if it is NaN (Not a Number): isNaN(1000) returns false

NUMBER AND STRING. Converts an object reference to a number or string:

- string(objReference)
- number(objReference)

ESCAPE AND UNESCAPE. Escape makes a string safe for use in a URL:

```
escape("name=Manoel Azevedo&location=Niteroi Brazil")
```

returns

```
name%3DManoel%20Azevedo%26location%3DNiteroi%20Brazil.
```

Unescape returns an escaped string to its original format:

```
unescape("name%3DManoel%20Azevedo%26location%3DNiteroi%20Brazil")
```

returns

```
name=Manoel Azevedo&location=Niteroi Brazil.
```

CONTROL STATEMENTS

Control statements allow you to write code logic that makes your Web page more interactive and dynamic. Brackets are used in the syntax examples below to indicate the parts of the syntax that are optional and not required.

CONDITIONAL STATEMENTS

IF...ELSE STATEMENTS　Conditionally executes a group of statements, depending on the value of an expression.

Syntax:

```
if (condition) {
   statements1
}[else if (condition) {
statements2
} else {
statements3
}
```

There is no required "end if" like there is in PL/SQL.

■ *FOR EXAMPLE*

```
color = "blue";
if (color == "red") {
  document.bgColor = color;
```

```
    } else if (color == "green") {
      document.write(color + " is the color of grass");
    } else {
      alert("The sky is " + color);
    }
```

UNIT
7.2

SWITCH STATEMENTS   Enables the execution of one or more statements when a specified expression's value matches a label.

Syntax:

```
switch (expression){
    case label :
        statement;
        break;
    case label :
        statement;
        break;
    . . .
default : statement;
}
```

■ *FOR EXAMPLE*

```
color = "blue";
switch (color) {
  case "red":
    document.bgColor = color;
    break;
  case "green":
    document.write("Green is the color of grass");
    break;
  default:
    alert("The sky is " + color);
    break;
}
```

Notice that the above example performs the same logic as the earlier If...Else example.

LOOP STATEMENTS

FOR STATEMENTS   Executes a block of statements for as long as a specified condition is true (and therefore, may never even execute at all).

Syntax:

```
for ([set initial-expression]; [condition]; [increment-expression]) {
    statements
}
```

■ *FOR EXAMPLE*

```
function countI() {
lgth = 5
  for (var i = 0; i < lgth; i++) {
    alert('The value i is:\n' + i);
  }
}
```

■ *FOR EXAMPLE*

```
function getRdio() {
lgth = document.formOne.rdioB.length;
  for (var i = 0; i < lgth; i++) {
   var checkedButton = ""
    if (document.formOne.rdioB[i].checked) {
        checkedButton=document.formOne.rdioB[i].value
        alert('The checked button is:\n' + checkedButton);
        break;
    }
  }
}
```

DO...WHILE STATEMENTS   Executes a statement block once, and then repeats execution of the loop until a condition expression evaluates to false.

Syntax:

```
do {
   statement
} while (condition)
```

■ *FOR EXAMPLE*

```
i=""
do {
  i++;
  alert(i);
}
while (i<5);
```

WHILE STATEMENTS   Executes a statement until a specified condition is false (and may even never execute at all).

Syntax:

```
while (condition) {
statements
}
```

■ *FOR EXAMPLE*

```
function whileLoop() {
frmLgth = 5
z=0;
  while(z < frmLgth) {
    alert('The value of z is:\n' + z);
  z++
  }
}
```

■ *FOR EXAMPLE*

```
function ckFrm() {
frmLgth = document.forms[0].elements.length;
z=0;
  while(z < frmLgth) {
     propty=document.forms[0].elements[z].type;
     if(propty == "text" && document.forms[0].elements[z].value ==
     "") {
        alert("You must enter data into this field.");
     }
  z++
  }
}
```

OTHER STATEMENTS AND OPERATORS

RETURN RETURN exits from the current function and returns a result from the function.

```
return funcResult;
```

THIS THIS refers to the current object:

```
this.objectProperty
```

UNIT 7.2 EXERCISES

a) JavaScript is a loosely typed language. Explain loosely typed.

b) What is the syntax for a JavaScript function?

c) If a JavaScript function is called before it is loaded in an HTML page, what potential problems, if any, might occur?

d) If you declare a variable with the keyword var, but do not explicitly assign it a value, what result can you expect when attempting to reference this variable?

e) If, within a function, you declare a variable with the keyword var and assign it a value, what are the scope issues, if any?

UNIT 7.2 EXERCISE ANSWERS

a) JavaScript is a loosely typed language. Explain loosely typed.

Answer: Loosely typed refers to the data type of variables. In programming languages such as PL/SQL, the data (or value) type of a variable must be declared when declaring a variable. When assigning a value to that variable, the value must be of the same data type as the variable. This is not the case in JavaScript. The data type of a variable does not need to be declared when declaring a JavaScript variable. Furthermore, values of different data types can be assigned to the same variable; JavaScript performs an automatic conversion for you.

For example, the value "This is a test" is assigned to the variable myVar. You can then assign the value 123 to the same variable and not generate an error message.

b) What is the syntax for a JavaScript function?

Answer: A JavaScript function requires:

- *The keyword "function" followed by the name of the function.*

- *List of arguments enclosed in parentheses and separated by commas (or, at the very minimum, the parentheses).*

- *The body of the function enclosed in curly braces.*

```
<SCRIPT LANGUAGE="JavaScript1.3">
function nameOfFunction (arg1,arg2) {
JavaScript statements here
}
</SCRIPT>
```

c) If a JavaScript function is called before it is loaded in an HTML page, what potential problems, if any, might occur?

Answer: The call will fail. Placement is significant with JavaScript in an HTML page while the page is loading. JavaScript, as discussed in this chapter, resides and executes totally on the client and is loaded into the client browser with the HTML page. If a function call cannot find the function because it does not yet exist on the client, then it will fail.

d) If you declare a variable with the keyword var, but do not explicitly assign it a value, what result can you expect when attempting to reference this variable?

Answer: Referencing a variable declared with the keyword var and not assigned a value will not result in a runtime error. It is equal to undefined. It can also be checked for whether a value has been assigned to it yet:

```
if (myVariable == "undefined") {
      myVariable = "Set it now!"
}
```

A variable declared without the var keyword will generate a runtime error if no value has been assigned to it. Plus, it cannot be tested as to whether it is defined or undefined.

e) If, within a function, you declare a variable with the keyword var and assign it a value, what are the scope issues, if any?

Answer: You have just created a local variable that is accessible from within that function. Any attempt to reference this variable from outside of the function will fail.

UNIT 7.3

THE DOCUMENT OBJECT MODEL

THE DOM

The Document Object Model, or DOM, is the hierarchical structure that allows you to access the different parts of a browser and the components of a document using a scripting language. The DOM itself is actually a part of the browser and not of JavaScript. JavaScript uses a browser's DOM to navigate around the browser and document. Furthermore, any other scripting language can access the browser's DOM. JavaScript just happens to be one of the most widely used scripting languages at this time.

The DOM is object-based. When a document is loaded into a browser, the browser creates objects corresponding to each component of the document. JavaScript is then able to access these DOM objects to get information about a component or to change it. If an additional window is opened by a session, you can also access document components of the other window via the DOM.

Since the DOM is built by the browser, this opens up the possibility of different browsers creating different versions of the DOM. In fact, this has happened— while Internet Explorer and Netscape have a similar DOM, they do differ in some details. Fortunately, the World Wide Web Consortium (W3C) has in 2001 approved a specification for a standardized DOM. The W3C is the international standards body, and it sets the standards for HTML and XML, among other Web development standards. This is significant for the Web developer since a standard will greatly facilitate cross-browser Web development.

DOCUMENT OBJECT MODEL HIERARCHICAL STRUCTURE

Imagine that you were given the job of designing the hierarchy of the DOM. You were told to design a hierarchy that would allow a Web developer to navigate to the different components of a window and document. What would you name as the highest object in this hierarchy? Would it be a form? A document (an HTML page)? A frame? Or (browser) window?

The window makes the most sense as the highest object since it contains everything else. What would you define as the next level of objects underneath the Window object? A logical choice would be the document. The document contains subcomponents such as links, layers, and forms. Wouldn't it make sense to make each of these a subobject of the Document object?

In fact, this is the structure of the DOM. Without knowing anything about the DOM structure you could almost guess the entire hierarchy. Figure 7.8 shows a typical Document Object Model hierarchy. Only the most important objects are shown.

Each object has properties and methods. Properties are characteristics of an object. A document has properties like bgcolor for background color. Likewise, a document has methods like alert(). The DOM is used to navigate to an object in order to access that object's properties and methods. Thus, knowing how to navigate the DOM is important.

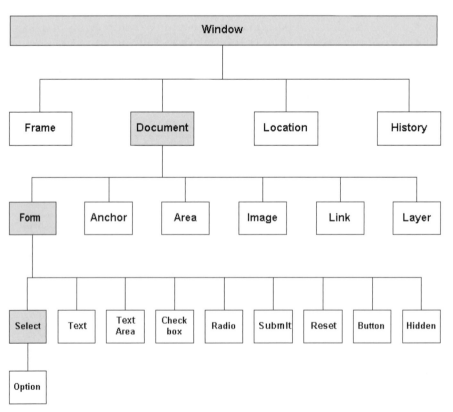

Figure 7.8 ■ Generic Document Object Model hierarchy.

NAVIGATING THE DOM

Knowing how to navigate the DOM in order to access and update Document object components is essential in learning JavaScript. The format for referencing an object and its properties is to "drill down" the hierarchy, listing the objects from highest to lowest until you reach the desired property. These are separated by a period.

REFERENCING A DOCUMENT AND ITS COMPONENTS

To change the background color of an HTML page you could reference it like this:

```
document.bgColor
```

Note that the window is assumed to be the same window in which the JavaScript code resides. Otherwise, you would have to refer to the other window specifically.

In this example bgColor is a property of the Document object. To read the value of bgColor you simply refer to it as in the example above. To change the value of bgColor, use the assignment statement. The following example first reads and then changes the background color property of the document. Alerts are used in order to show you the results.

 #0000FF is blue and #FF0000 is red. These are known as hexadecimal color codes. Browsers read colors using these codes. There are a handful of colors that can be referenced by name such as red, blue, black, white, and green. These are limiting, however. There are 216 colors that all browsers can recognize. To refer to all of these you must use the hexadecimal color code.

■ *FOR EXAMPLE*

```
<HTML>
<BODY bgColor="#0000FF">
<SCRIPT LANGUAGE="JavaScript1.3">

//First, read the current background color
alert(document.bgColor);

//Second, change the background color to red
document.bgColor = "#FF0000"

//Now, read the background color to confirm the change
alert(document.bgColor);

</SCRIPT>
</BODY>
</HTML>
```

You can view the results yourself by typing the above code into a text editor and saving with a file extension of .htm. Then go to File > Open and open the file in your browser. The first alert will display the current background color as set in the <BODY> tag, or #0000FF. According to your assignment statement, the background color will change and the second alert will reflect the change, or #FF0000.

As noted in the previous unit, a document is loaded from top to bottom and JavaScript executes as it is loaded. If you were to move the JavaScript code in this example above the opening <BODY> tag, then the first alert would display a different value from the background color set in the <BODY> tag. This is because the <BODY> tag has not yet loaded, and so JavaScript cannot yet read it. It therefore displays the default background of the browser. Also, note that the background never displays as blue. That's because the <BODY> tag is not loaded before the bgColor attribute is changed to red. Always be mindful of where you place JavaScript code within a document in order to achieve the desired result.

Now, take a look at how to access the different elements of a form. You can use the Student Information form you created in Chapter 6, "Advanced HTML: Forms, Nested Tables, and Nested Frames." Added to this is a JavaScript function that is called by clicking the "Submit" button. Function syntax and how to call a function is covered in detail in Unit 7.2, "JavaScript Syntax." For now, just concentrate on the syntax for accessing the DOM.

■ FOR EXAMPLE

```
<HTML>
<SCRIPT LANGUAGE="JavaScript1.3">
function readFrm() {
    alert(document.f_studInfo.p_fname.value);
}
</SCRIPT>
<BODY>
<FORM ACTION="save_student_info.htm" METHOD="post"
NAME="f_studInfo">
First Name: <INPUT TYPE="text" NAME="p_fname" VALUE="FirstName"
size="25"><BR>
Last Name: <INPUT TYPE="text" NAME="p_lname" VALUE="LastName"
size="25"><BR>
Address: <TEXTAREA COLS="21" ROWS="6" NAME="p_street_address"
WRAP="soft">100 Main Street</TEXTAREA><BR>
Zipcode: <SELECT NAME="p_zip">
<OPTION VALUE="0">Please Select a Zipcode</OPTION>
<OPTION VALUE="10015">10015</OPTION>
```

```
<OPTION VALUE="10016" SELECTED>10016</OPTION>
<OPTION VALUE="10017">10017</OPTION>
<OPTION VALUE="10018">10018</OPTION>
</SELECT><BR>
Phone Number:<INPUT TYPE="text" VALUE="555-555-5555" NAME="p_phone"
MAXLENGTH="15" SIZE="15"><BR>
Employer:<INPUT TYPE="text" VALUE="MyEmployer" NAME="p_employer"
MAXLENGTH="50" SIZE="50"><BR>
<INPUT TYPE="hidden" VALUE="111" NAME="p_id">
<INPUT TYPE="reset" VALUE="Reset">
<INPUT TYPE="button" VALUE="Submit" onClick="readFrm();">
</FORM>
</BODY>
</HTML>
```

Clicking on the "Submit" button will pop up an alert with the initial value of the VALUE attribute of the first name text field, shown in Figure 7.9.

If any changes are made to the form fields, JavaScript can read those changes. To see this, click into the First Name text field and replace "FirstName" with your first name. Click the "Submit" button. The alert should now display the value that you typed into the First Name text field.

How did JavaScript access this information? By navigating the DOM and "drilling down" to the desired object property.

Begin at the top and work your way down the DOM hierarchy. Since you are not trying to access another window, the window object is assumed. So the first object you must list is the document object. The next level down is the form object. You can refer to the form by name since you specified a name as an attribute in the <FORM> tag.

```
document.f_studInfo
```

Now you need to access the First Name text field. This form, however, contains many elements. There are the two buttons, the hidden field, the drop-down list, and all of the text fields. Just as you accessed the form by name, you can also ac-

Figure 7.9 ■ **Accessing the value of the p_fname text field.**

cess a form element by name. This is why it is good practice to name your forms and form elements. The name you have given to the First Name text field is p_fname.

```
document.f_studInfo.p_fname
```

Finally, you need to specify which attribute of the <INPUT> tag for the First Name text field you want. For example, this <INPUT> tag has the attributes, size, type, and value, among others. To access the value, simply add it to the DOM statement you have created so far:

```
document.f_studInfo.p_fname.value
```

If you replace value with type or size, then you will see how you can access other form elements.

Don't forget to add the value element when trying to access the value for a form element. A common mistake of beginning JavaScript coders is to code document.f_studInfo.p_fname instead of document.f_studInfo.p_fname.value

A form can also be referenced by its array number. As the document is loaded into the browser, objects are created for the document and each component within the document. An array object is also created that references the forms in a document. Thus, forms can be tracked by name, if names are assigned to them, or by their array numbers. Arrays start at an index value of "0." In the example above you could access the form like this:

```
document.forms[0].p_fname.value
```

The second form in the document would be referenced as forms[1], and so on.

PASSING OBJECTS TO JAVASCRIPT FUNCTIONS   A DOM object can be passed as a parameter. Passing an object is a way to make JavaScript functions reusable. Suppose you want to create a JavaScript function, verifySave, which verifies whether a user wants to continue before the function submits the form. You realize that your page will involve three frames, and this functionality is helpful for all of them. Instead of writing three functions that are identical except for the name of the form being submitted, the function can find out which form to submit from a parameter, and then perform actions on whichever form is passed in.

The syntax for passing objects is similar to passing literal values. To pass an object to a JavaScript function, send it within parentheses after the function name, as you would a literal value. However, the difference is that quotes are not needed around object names within the parentheses. When the quotes are not present, JavaScript sees the text being passed as a description of something in the DOM, instead of a literal value.

The object being passed must reflect its place in the DOM hierarchy. The example below passes a form object called "instructor_personal_form," which is in the document of the current window.

■ *FOR EXAMPLE*

```
<TD><INPUT TYPE="button"  VALUE="Save"
onClick="javascript:verifySave(window.document.instructor_
personal_form);"></TD>
```

The function receiving this object must have a name to identify this parameter. Again, datatypes are not used in JavaScript, so a natural-language name is sufficient to identify an expected parameter. As an example, the verifySave JavaScript function below expects a parameter called "theform." Because a form is being passed, the submit() method will work; submit() is a valid method for a form object.

■ *FOR EXAMPLE*

```
function verifySave(theform){
    if (prompt("Are you sure you want to continue?")){
      theform.submit();
    }
}
```

UNIT 7.3 EXERCISES

a) What is the DOM and what can you do with it?

b) Indicate the level in the DOM hierarchy for each of the objects listed below. One indicates the highest level, 2 the next highest, and so on.

_____ document
_____ form
_____ hyperlink
_____ browser window
_____ text field in a form
_____ frame

UNIT 7.3 EXERCISE ANSWERS

a) What is the DOM and what can you do with it?

Answer: The DOM, or Document Object Model, is a hierarchical structure for a document and browser window. It allows you to read and/or change the different components of a browser and a document. A DOM structure is constructed for each HTML document that is loaded into the browser window.

b) Indicate the level in the DOM hierarchy for each of the objects listed below. One indicates the highest level, 2 the next highest, and so on.

Answer:

2	document
3	form
3	hyperlink
1	browser window
4	text field in a form
2	frame

U N I T   7 . 4

JAVASCRIPT EVENTS

EVENTS

JavaScript enables a Web page to be interactive with the user instead of the Web page merely displaying content to the user. It does this by recognizing when a user performs an action. The action initiates the execution of JavaScript code. These actions are known as events, and the methods that recognize them are known as event handlers. Most JavaScript code runs as a result of the occurrence of some event caused by the user. An exception to this would be JavaScript code embedded in HTML that runs as the document is loaded into the browser.

Almost any action that can occur in regard to a Web site is an event with a corresponding event handler. Some events and their handlers are:

- Completing the download of an HTML document into the browser (onLoad).
- Giving focus to a form field, that is, clicking into a text box (onFocus).
- Clicking the "Save" button of a form (onClick).
- Changing the selected option in a drop-down list (onChange).
- Moving the cursor over a hyperlink (onMouseOver).
- Submitting a form (onSubmit).

These are just a few examples of events and event handlers. This functionality is very important in Web site development. In fact, some of this functionality is now taken for granted, and JavaScript is the only way to accomplish effects that are now considered commonplace. These events allow you, among other things, to validate form field data before submitting it across the network (onSubmit); to swap images as the cursor passes over a hyperlink, giving emphasis to that hyperlink (onMouseOver); or to detect if a user attempts to resize a window (onResize).

Table 7.6 lists the most common JavaScript Events and their Event Handlers. As you read this list, consider how much power JavaScript has to respond to events on a Web page, and what you might wish to do with these events.

Table 7.6 ■ Common JavaScript Events and Handlers

Event	Applies to	Occurs upon	Event handler
Abort	Images	User aborts the loading of an image (by clicking a link or clicking the Stop button).	onAbort
Blur	Windows and all form elements	User removes input focus from window or form element.	onBlur
Change	Text fields, text areas, select lists	User changes value of element.	onChange
Click	Buttons, radio buttons, checkboxes, submit buttons, reset buttons, links	User clicks form element or link.	onClick
Error	Images, windows	The loading of a document or image causes an error.	onError
Focus	Windows and all form elements	User gives input focus to window or form element.	onFocus
KeyDown	Documents, images, links, text areas	User depresses a key.	onKeyDown
KeyPress	Documents, images, links, text areas	User presses or holds down a key.	onKeyPress
KeyUp	Documents, images, links, text areas	User releases a key.	onKeyUp
Load	Document body	User loads the page in the browser.	onLoad
MouseDown	Documents, buttons, links	User depresses a mouse button.	onMouseDown
MouseMove	Nothing by default	User moves the cursor.	onMouseMove
MouseOut	Areas, links	User moves cursor out of a client-side image map or link.	onMouseOut
MouseOver	Links	User moves cursor over a link.	onMouseOver
MouseUp	Documents, buttons, links	User releases a mouse button.	onMouseUp

**UNIT
7.4**

Table 7.6 ■ *(continued)*

Event	Applies to	Occurs upon	Event handler
Move	Windows	User or script moves a window.	onMove
Reset	Forms	User resets a form (clicks a Reset button).	onReset
Resize	Windows	User or script resizes a window.	onResize
Select	Text fields, text areas	User selects (highlights text) from element's input field.	OnSelect
Submit	Forms	User submits a form.	onSubmit
Unload	Document body	User exits the page.	onUnload

It is important to note that events are actually part of and defined by the DOM. As explained in the earlier Unit, "The Document Object Model," the DOM is a part of the browser and accessed by JavaScript. Netscape and Internet Explorer have slightly different DOMs and event models. For the most part they are the same, except that Internet Explorer's DOM includes more events and allows more document components to respond to events.

USING EVENT HANDLERS

To execute JavaScript code upon the occurrence of an event, you must create an event handler. An event handler is created by associating an event with a document component. This is done by including event instructions inside of the appropriate HTML tag. The syntax is:

```
<HTMLTAG eventHandler="JavaScript code">
```

Say you want to execute a JavaScript function named "myFunc()" when the user changes the value of a particular text field in a form. To do this, place the event handler within the HTML tag for that form field. The same HTML rules regarding quotes apply.

```
<INPUT TYPE="text" VALUE="The sky is blue." NAME="myText"
onChange="myFunc();">
```

JavaScript statements can be placed directly in the event handler:

```
<INPUT TYPE="text" VALUE="The sky is blue" NAME="myText"
onChange="alert('Hi');">
```

It is good coding practice, however, to create a function and call that function in the event handler. Place the function as close to the top of the document as possible, preferably within the <HEAD> tags. This makes your code more modular, easier to read, and ensures that the JavaScript is fully loaded into the browser.

 Notice that prefixing the name of the event with "on" creates an event handler. It is standard practice to use lowercase except for the first letter of the event. However, in JavaScript1.1 and earlier, the event handler names are case-sensitive and must be in lowercase, for example, on-change.

UNIT 7.4 EXERCISES

**UNIT
7.4**

a) Write the code that will pop up an alert when a user passes the cursor over a hyperlink.

b) Write the code that will pop up an alert when the document finishes loading into the browser.

c) Write the code that will pop up an alert when the user exits from the current document.

d) Write the code to pop up an alert when the user places the cursor into a form text field.

e) Write the code to load another page in the browser window when the user chooses an option in a select list.

UNIT 7.4 EXERCISE ANSWERS

a) Write the code that will pop up an alert when a user passes the cursor over a hyperlink.

Answer:

```
<A HREF="" onMouseOver='alert("Hi")'>Pass the cursor over me.</A>
```

b) Write the code that will pop up an alert when the document finishes loading into the browser.

Answer:

```
<BODY onLoad="alert('onload');">
```

c) Write the code that will pop up an alert when the user exits from the current document.

Answer:

```
<BODY onUnLoad="alert('unload');">
```

d) Write the code to pop up an alert when the user places the cursor into a form text field.

Answer:

```
<FORM>
<INPUT TYPE="text" onFocus="alert('You have given focus to
this field.');">
</FORM >
```

e) Write the code to load another page in the browser window when the user chooses an option in a select list.

Answer:

```
<SCRIPT LANGUAGE="JavaScript1.3">
function goTo(frm) {
  opt = frm.p_website.selectedIndex
  val = frm.p_website.options[opt].value;
  window.location.href   = val;
}
</SCRIPT>

<FORM>
<SELECT NAME="p_website" onChange="goTo(this.form);">
  <OPTION VALUE="http://www.Prentice-Hall.com">Prentice Hall</OPTION>
  <OPTION VALUE="http://www.phptr.com/morrison">SQL Interactive
  Site</OPTION>
  <OPTION VALUE="http://www.phptr.com/rosenzweig/">PL/SQL Interactive
  Site</OPTION>
  <OPTION VALUE="http://www.phptr.com/boardman/">Oracle Web APP
  Programming Site Site</OPTION>
</SELECT>
</FORM>
```

UNIT 7.5

WINDOW AND DOCUMENT OBJECTS

WINDOW OBJECT

The window object is the topmost object in the Document Object Model hierarchy. A window object can represent either a browser window or a frame. Table 7.7 lists most of the properties of the window object.

Table 7.8 lists most of the methods of the window object.

Table 7.7 ■ **Window Object Properties**

Property	Description
document	Contains information about the current document and provides methods for displaying HTML output to the user.
frames	An array reflecting all the frames in a window.
history	Contains information on the URLs that the user has visited within a window.
innerHeight	Specifies the vertical dimension, in pixels, of the window's content area.
innerWidth	Specifies the horizontal dimension, in pixels, of the window's content area.
location	Contains information on the current URL.
locationbar	Represents the browser window's location bar.
menubar	Represents the browser window's menu bar.
name	A unique name used to refer to this window.
opener	Specifies the window name of the calling document when a window is opened using the open method.
parent	A synonym for a window or frame whose frameset contains the current frame.
scrollbars	Represents the browser window's scroll bars.
self	A synonym for the current window.
status	Specifies a priority or transient message in the window's status bar.
statusbar	Represents the browser window's status bar.
toolbar	Represents the browser window's toolbar.
top	A synonym for the topmost browser window.
window	A synonym for the current window.

**UNIT
7.5**

Table 7.8 ▪ Window Object Methods

Method	Description
alert	Displays an Alert dialog box with a message and an OK button.
back	Undoes the last history step in any frame within the top-level window.
blur	Removes focus from the specified object.
captureEvents	Sets the window or document to capture all events of the specified type.
close	Closes the specified window.
confirm	Displays a Confirm dialog box with the specified message and OK and Cancel buttons.
focus	Gives focus to the specified object.
forward	Loads the next URL in the history list.
handleEvent	Invokes the handler for the specified event.
moveBy	Moves the window by the specified amounts.
moveTo	Moves the top-left corner of the window to the specified screen co-ordinates.
open	Opens a new Web browser window.
print	Prints the contents of the window or frame.
prompt	Displays a Prompt dialog box with a message and an input field.
resizeTo	Resizes an entire window to the specified outer height and width.
setResizable	Specifies whether a user is permitted to resize a window.

OPENING A WINDOW USING JAVASCRIPT

A new window can be opened using HTML by setting the TARGET attribute of a link to "_blank." You have no control, however, over the new window as far as size, position, and so on. With JavaScript, you can open a new window and control the size and position of the new window. You can also specify whether the new window should have scrollbars or toolbars, among other things.

First, let's look at the basic syntax for opening a new window. The code in this example runs a JavaScript statement in the URL extension:

```
<A HREF = "javascript:void(window.open('http://myURL/window.htm',
'myNewWin','width=640,height=480, scrollbars=yes,
resizable=yes'));">No Function Call</A>
```

Table 7.9 shows JavaScript in more detail.

Table 7.9 ■ **Breakdown of window.open Syntax**

Syntax Element	Required/ Optional	Notes
"	Required	Note that the entire JavaScript statement is enclosed by opening and closing double quotes.
javascript:	Required	Indicates the protocol of the HREF. The usual protocol is http, but here it is JavaScript.
void	Required	The "window.open" method returns an object. "Void" tells it not to return anything. If you use "window.open" in a function, then you would assign the object to a variable:winVar = window.open(…).
window.open	Required	This is a reference to the DOM. A call is made to the method "open" that is part of the "window" object.
(	Required	Within parentheses, pass to the window.open method 3 parameters, enclosed in single quotes and separated by commas.
'http://myURL/window.htm'	Optional (a blank window is opened if no file is specified); first parameter	The path of the file to be loaded into the new window.
'myNewWin' able	Optional; second parameter	The name of the new window. Required if you want to be to refer to it from another window.
'width=640, height=480, scrollbars=yes, resizable=yes'	Optional; third parameter	Properties of the new window.
)	Required	End of parameter list.
;		End of JavaScript statement.
"	Required	Closing double quote.

OPENING A WINDOW BY CALLING A JAVASCRIPT FUNCTION   First, create the JavaScript function. Create the pop-up Zipcode window:

■ *FOR EXAMPLE*

```
<SCRIPT Language="JavaScript1.3">
<!--Begin to hide script contents from old browsers.
function openWin() {
openW = window.open('zip_window.htm','zipPopUp','width=640,
height=480, scrollbars=yes,resizable=yes');
}
// End the hiding here. -->
</SCRIPT>
```

Here is the syntax for calling this function:

```
<INPUT TYPE="button" VALUE="Zipcodes" onClick="openWin();">
```

Be careful with cutting and pasting JavaScript. For example, the script above would not work if you were able to cut and paste into an HTML document because of the line break after 'height=480.' The JavaScript statement has not ended but a new line character is an end of statement indicator for JavaScript. To make it work, simply delete the newline character and place the complete statement on one line.

REFERRING TO THE PARENT WINDOW FROM A CHILD WINDOW

When you open a new window using JavaScript, an object is created for the new window. One of the properties of this new window object is the "opener" property. It specifies the name of the window from which the new window was opened. This makes referring back to the opener window easy.

In the Zipcode pop-up window, a user selects a zipcode and clicks the "OK" button. To copy the selected zipcode into the zipcode text field of the original window, the code looks like this:

```
window.opener.personal_form.p_zip.value=window.zip_form.
p_newzip.value;
```

This JavaScript statement takes the value of the selected zipcode in the pop-up window (window.zip_form.p_newzip.value) and assigns it to the zipcode text field in the opener window (window.opener.personal_form.p_zip.value).

Look at the left side of the assignment statement:

```
window.opener.personal_form.p_zip.value
```

This refers to the value of the p_zip text field in the form personal_form in the opener window. As you learn in the Unit, "The Document Object Model," of this chapter, you are able to access the value of a form's elements by navigating the DOM's hierarchy.

- window.opener is the name of the window that opened the Zipcode pop-up window.
- personal_form is the name of the form in the opener window.
- p_zip.value is the name and value of the zipcode text field in the form personal_form.

Without the opener property you would have to know the name of the opening window in order to refer back to it. Using window.opener makes it easier to open multiple windows and be able to refer back without keeping track of window names.

CLOSING A WINDOW

JavaScript also allows you to programmatically close a window. A requirement for the Zipcode pop-up window in this book's sample application is to close it after writing the selected zipcode to the opener window. The code for this is:

```
window.close();
```

 Only windows that have been opened programmatically can be closed programmatically, that is, using window.close();, without the browser security first alerting and receiving the user's permission to close the window. If you try to close a window that was opened by the user, then a confirm box will be presented to the user with a warning that a program is trying to close the window and asking whether this is ok.

ALERTS, CONFIRMS, AND PROMPTS

ALERTS Alerts simply pop up a message with an OK button (Figure 7.10). Focus stays on the Alert until OK is selected.

The JavaScript for an Alert is:

```
alert("Alert Text Here.");
```

CONFIRMS Confirms ask the user to answer yes (OK) or no (CANCEL) (Figure 7.11). OK returns true and Cancel returns false.

The JavaScript for a Confirm box is:

```
confirm("Are you sure you want to do this?");
```

Figure 7.10 ■ Alert pop-up message box.

The confirm() method returns a Boolean true or false. To handle the return, you must assign the return value to a variable.

■ *FOR EXAMPLE*

```
function confFunc() {
  var confVar = confirm("Are you sure you want to do this?")
  if (confVar) {
    alert("You selected 'OK'");
  } else {
    alert("You selected 'Cancel'");
  }
}
```

PROMPTS   Prompts display a message from you and allow the user to input data (Figure 7.12).

The JavaScript for a Prompt is:

```
prompt("Type in something and click OK.", "Type Here");
```

If "OK" is selected, then the value of the input field is returned. Otherwise, nothing is returned.

Figure 7.11 ■ Confirm pop-up message box.

Figure 7.12 ■ Prompt pop-up message box.

■ *FOR EXAMPLE*

```
function promptFunc() {
  var promptAns = prompt("Type in something and click OK.", "Type
  Here");
  if (promptAns != null) {
    window.document.frmName.textNm.value = promptAns;
  }
}
```

DOCUMENT OBJECT

Table 7.10 lists most of the properties of the document object.

Table 7.11 lists most of the methods of the document object.

WRITING TO A DOCUMENT AS IT LOADS

The write(); method of the Document object is perhaps the most widely used JavaScript method. It allows you to write HTML and JavaScript to a document while it is loading. Most often the write(); method is used in a conditional statement. For example, you might test for the browser being used and write different HTML for Netscape and Internet Explorer. Web designers often develop different style sheets for Netscape and Internet Explorer browsers. Using this method, a developer can test for the browser and write the appropriate stylesheet to the document. The page will then display properly for that browser.

Look again at the script in the Unit, "A First JavaScript Script":

■ *FOR EXAMPLE*

```
<SCRIPT language="JavaScript1.3">
<!--Begin hiding content from old browsers.
alert("This is an Alert!");
document.write("I'm being written by JavaScript!");
//End hiding here-->
</SCRIPT>
```

Table 7.10 ▪ Document Object Properties

Property	Description
alinkColor	A string that specifies the ALINK attribute.
anchors	An array containing an entry for each anchor in the document.
bgColor	A string that specifies the BGCOLOR attribute.
classes	Creates a Style object that can specify the styles of HTML tags with a specific CLASS attribute.
cookie	Specifies a cookie.
domain	Specifies the domain name of the server that served a document.
fgColor	A string that specifies the TEXT attribute.
formName	A separate property for each named form in the document.
forms	An array containing an entry for each form in the document.
height	The height of the document, in pixels.
ids	Creates a Style object that can specify the style of individual HTML tags.
images	An array containing an entry for each image in the document.
lastModified	A string that specifies the date the document was last modified.
layers	Array containing an entry for each layer within the document.
linkColor	A string that specifies the LINK attribute.
links	An array containing an entry for each link in the document.
referrer	A string that specifies the URL of the calling document.
tags	Creates a Style object that can specify the styles of HTML tags.
title	A string that specifies the contents of the TITLE tag.
URL	A string that specifies the complete URL of a document.
vlinkColor	A string that specifies the VLINK attribute.
width	The width of the document, in pixels.

Table 7.11 ■ Document Object Methods

Method	Description
captureEvents	Sets the document to capture all events of the specified type.
close	Closes an output stream and forces data to display.
handleEvent	Invokes the handler for the specified event.
open	Opens a stream to collect the output of write or writeln methods.
write	Writes one or more HTML expressions to a document in the specified window.
writeln	Writes one or more HTML expressions to a document in the specified window and follows them with a newline character.

```
</HEAD>
<BODY>
<H2>A First JavaScript Script</H2>
<P>This is text within paragraph tags.</P>
</BODY>
</HTML>
```

UNIT 7.5

As the document is loaded into the browser, this script first pops up an alert and then writes, "I'm being written by JavaScript." Then the document finishes loading. Modify this script to include a conditional statement. Use Confirm, introduced earlier in this chapter, and modify it to write a message to the document instead of popping up an alert.

■ FOR EXAMPLE

```
<SCRIPT Language="JavaScript1.3">
function confFunc() {
  var confVar = confirm("Are you sure you want to do this?")
  if (confVar) {
    document.write("Hey, you're OK!");
  } else {
    document.write("Why not?");
  }
}
confFunc();
</SCRIPT>
```

Always keep in mind that document.write can only write to a document as it is loading into the browser. Once the document has fully loaded into the browser, then you cannot write to that document without reloading it. To see this more clearly, modify the script above to include a button with a call to the function upon clicking the button. Delete the function call in the <SCRIPT> tags.

■ *FOR EXAMPLE*

```
<HTML>
<HEAD>
<SCRIPT LANGUAGE="JavaScript1.3">
function confFunc() {
var confVar = confirm("Are you sure you want to do this?")
  if (confVar) {
    document.write("Hey, you're OK!");
  } else {
    document.write("Why not?");
  }
}
</SCRIPT>
</HEAD>
<BODY><P>Original Document</P>
  <FORM>
    <INPUT TYPE="button" VALUE="Click Me" onClick="confFunc();">
  </FORM>
</BODY>
</HTML>
```

**UNIT
7.5**

If you type this code into a text editor and save it with an .htm extension and then load it into a browser, you should see a result similar to Figure 7.13.

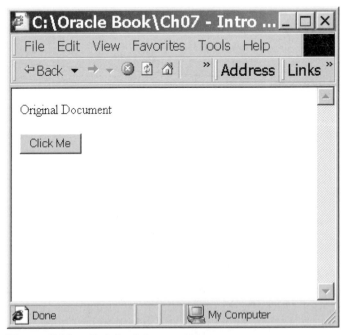

Figure 7.13 ■ **Original document.**

Now click the button to call the function. A Confirm dialog box will pop up. The conditional statement determines which button was selected and executes the appropriate code. If "OK" is selected, a new document is loaded into the browser with the message shown in Figure 7.14.

Notice that this is not the original document and that a new document has been loaded into the browser. Once a document has fully loaded into the browser it cannot be written to using document.write();. A new document will be created as happens here.

The write method is also used in conjunction with window.open. Instead of loading a preexisting document into the new window, a new document can be written into it.

■ FOR EXAMPLE

```
<HTML>
<HEAD>
<SCRIPT LANGUAGE="JavaScript1.3">
function winOpener() {
//first set a variable with a handle to the new window's object
newWindow=window.open("","popUpWindow","menubar=yes");
//using the variable set with the new window object, use the document
//object's write method to write to it
newWindow.document.write("<HTML>");
```

Figure 7.14 ■ Newly loaded document with the document.write message.

```
newWindow.document.write("<HEAD><TITLE>My New Window</TITLE></HEAD>");
newWindow.document.write("<BODY>");
newWindow.document.write("<CENTER><H1>A new document using document.
write.</H1></CENTER>");
newWindow.document.write("</BODY>");
newWindow.document.write("</HTML>");
}
</SCRIPT>
</HEAD>
<BODY><P>Click on the button below to open a new window.</P>
<FORM>
<INPUT TYPE="button" onClick="winOpener();" VALUE="Click Me">
</FORM>
</BODY>
</HTML>
```

COOKIE PROPERTY OF THE DOCUMENT OBJECT

A *cookie* is a text string that is stored in the file system of a user's machine by the user's browser or in the session memory of a browser. You learn about cookies and how to read/write a cookie with the PL/SQL Web Toolkit in greater detail in Chapter 15, "Maintaining State with Cookies and Tables." This Unit will not cover cookies in detail since they are covered later on in this book. However, it is important to be aware of how you can read and write cookies using JavaScript. Even if the cookie has been set using the PL/SQL Web Toolkit, you can still use JavaScript to read that cookie. This is especially useful when debugging code that sets a cookie.

SETTING A COOKIE   Cookie syntax is:

```
cookieName = cookieValue
```

You can set a cookie using the following code.

■ FOR EXAMPLE

```
<SCRIPT LANGUAGE="JavaScript1.3">
document.cookie = "testCookie=" + escape("hi");
</SCRIPT>
```

The name of this cookie is testCookie and its value is hi. The built-in JavaScript function escape is used to escape the value string. Remember, escape substitutes special characters such as question marks, ?, with their url-safe code number. The value attribute is the only attribute set for this cookie. Other attributes that can be set for a cookie are expiration date, domain, and path. No expiration has been set for this cookie so it is automatically created as a session cookie. That means that the cookie is stored in the browser's session memory and is deleted upon closing the browser. If an expiration date is specified, then the cookie is stored on the computer's hard drive and will expire on the date set.

If no domain is set, the default is the domain of the document. If no path is set, the default is '/', or the docroot.

Note that using document.cookie in an assignment expression results in setting a cookie. However, invoking document.cookie with no assignment simply reads the cookie.

READING A COOKIE   You can read all of the cookies associated with an HTML document using document.cookie. A cookie is associated with an HTML document if it matches the path and domain of the document. This is part of the security paradigm for cookies. This is explained in further detail in Chapter 15, "Maintaining State with Cookies and Tables." The following JavaScript code sets a variable with all of the cookies associated with that page and displays them in an alert.

■ *FOR EXAMPLE*

```
<SCRIPT LANGUAGE="JavaScript1.3">
var myCookie = document.cookie;
alert(myCookie);
</SCRIPT>
```

The alert will be blank if no cookie is set for the document.

This is especially useful where you are debugging code that sets and/or reads a cookie. There is a quicker way to view all of the cookies associated with a document. Once the document has fully loaded into the browser, type the following into the URL location window of the browser:

```
javascript:document.cookie
```

Hit Enter. All of the cookies associated with that document will be displayed in the browser. To return to the document, hit the "Back" button. This can be used to view a document's cookies for any page on the Web.

UNIT 7.5 EXERCISES

a) True or False: A window object represents only the browser window.

b) What are the advantages, if any, of opening a new window through JavaScript instead of using the HTML TARGET=_blank in a hyperlink tag?

c) What does window.opener refer to?

d) An HTML page has fully loaded into the browser. An event handler attached to a button calls a function that contains the following JavaScript code:

```
document.write('You must follow the instructions.');
```

The user clicks on that button. Describe what occurs, if anything.

UNIT 7.5 EXERCISE ANSWERS

a) True or False: A window object represents only the browser window.

Answer: False. The window object can also represent a frame.

b) What are the advantages, if any, of opening a new window through JavaScript instead of using the HTML TARGET=_blank in a hyperlink tag?

Answer: Opening a new window through JavaScript allows you to control the position and size of the new window. You can also indicate whether the new window should have, among others, scrollbars or a toolbar. A name can also be given to the new window, allowing you to reference the DOM of that window. Last, a window opened through JavaScript can be closed through JavaScript without prompting the user. A window opened through HTML does not have any of these options.

c) What does window.opener refer to?

Answer: When a new window is opened through JavaScript an object is created in the new window that contains information on the window that opened it. In the new win-

dow the code window.opener refers back to the parent window. In this way a JavaScript coder does not need to know that name of the parent window.

d) An HTML page has fully loaded into the browser. An event handler attached to a button calls a function that contains the following JavaScript code:

```
document.write('You must follow the instructions.');
```

The user clicks on that button. Describe what occurs, if anything.

Answer: A new document will load into the browser with the text "You must follow the instructions."

Remember that document.write() can only write to the current document if it is still loading into the browser. Once a document has finished loading into the browser, then document.write() cannot be used to write to it. There are ways around this, however. An Iframe could be used. This is an in-line frame embedded within the document and document.write() could write to the Iframe without reloading the page. Iframes, however, are not supported by all browsers.

UNIT 7.5

CHAPTER 7

BUILDING THE APP

The answers to these projects can be found at the companion Web site to this book, located at http://www.phptr.com/boardman/.

Visit the Web site periodically to share and discuss your answers with other readers.

In this Chapter you learned many concepts that you keep in mind when you read the subsequent chapters, especially Chapter 14, "JavaScript Form Validation." These concepts include:

- Embedding JavaScript in HTML
- JavaScript Syntax
- Document Object Model
- JavaScript Events
- Properties and Methods of the Window and Document Objects

In the chapters of this book you create an Application for maintaining students and teachers in a school database. The concepts learned in the chapter allow you to implement JavaScript form validation; create a pop-up Zipcode window and to write the selected value back to the main window; and to integrate JavaScript messages in the application, such as Alerts and Confirms, among others.

C H A P T E R 8

SQL REMINDERS AND TIPS

Knowledge of SQL is essential for any Web developer. It's rare to see a Web site comprised solely of static HTML pages. Most Web sites select data from a data source to be assembled into an HTML page and delivered to the browser. The data source in many cases is a relational database, as is the case with this book's application.

It is assumed that users of this book already have a strong understanding of SQL and relational databases. This chapter is meant for those who need a quick reference to Oracle's SQL. Some advanced tips are also provided. These tips can be directly used in coding this book's application. Only the SELECT statement is covered; Data Manipulation Language (DML) and Data Definition Language (DDL) are not discussed in this chapter. For more detailed information on SQL, please refer to another book in this series, *The Oracle SQL Interactive Workbook*, by Alice Rischert.

UNIT 8.1

SQL BASICS

CLAUSES OF THE SELECT STATEMENT

Table 8.1 shows the clauses and keywords of a SELECT statement. The clauses are listed in the recommended order for an actual SELECT statement.

The most basic SELECT statement is one with only a SELECT and FROM clause. The SELECT clause lists the columns to be included in the result set. The FROM clause lists the tables from which to select the data.

■ FOR EXAMPLE

```
SELECT first_name, last_name
   FROM student;
```

This will select the first name and last name columns for all of the rows in the student table. To limit the number of rows returned, the WHERE clause is needed. The WHERE clause has two functions: to filter out data and to join tables.

To select all students whose first name begins with 'A':

■ FOR EXAMPLE

```
SELECT first_name, last_name
   FROM student
  WHERE f_name LIKE 'A%';
```

LIKE in the above example is a comparison operator that is explained later in this unit. Only those students whose first name begins with *A* will be returned. All other rows will be filtered out.

The second function of a WHERE clause is to join two tables together. In a relational database, tables relate to each other through foreign keys. In the student

Table 8.1 ■ SELECT Statement Clauses

Clause	Definition	Required
SELECT	Specifies the data items to be retrieved from the database. The items to be selected (select list) are separated by commas. Select item can be: a) A column name from the table named in the from clause b) A constant c) A SQL expression	Y
FROM	Defines the source table(s)	Y
WHERE	Filters the rows you want to retrieve. The keyword WHERE is followed by the search condition. Search condition can produce one of three results (3 value logic): a) IS TRUE b) IS FALSE c) IS NULL (unknown)	N
GROUP BY	Groups together selected rows that return a single row of summary information. If an aggregate function column and a nonaggregate column are used in the SELECT clause, then the GROUP BY clause must be used and the result set must be grouped by the nonaggregate column(s).	N
HAVING	Restricts which groups of rows defined by the GROUP BY clause are returned.	N
ORDER BY	Determines the order of the rows of a SELECT statement result set.	N

UNIT 8.1

schema, the table's course and section are related. Course_no is the primary key in course and course_no is the foreign key in section. These tables can be joined using these columns.

■ *FOR EXAMPLE*

```
SELECT c.course_no, section_no, location
  FROM course c, section s
 WHERE c.course_no = s.course_no
ORDER BY c.course_no;
```

This will select all of the data in the two tables where there is a match in the WHERE clause.

ORACLE'S DUAL TABLE

When installing Oracle, the Dual table is automatically created. It is owned by SYS and accessible by all users. The Dual table has one row and one column. The Dual table can be used as a "scratchpad" for testing the results of Oracle functions. It can also be used to retrieve the user and sysdate, or to SELECT the nextval from a sequence.

■ FOR EXAMPLE

```
SELECT UPPER('hello')
   FROM dual;
SELECT user, sysdate
   FROM dual;
SELECT mysequence.nextval
   FROM dual;
```

The column in the dual table is DUMMY and defined as VARCHAR2(1). The row has a value of *X*.

COMPARISON AND BOOLEAN OPERATORS

Comparison operators are used to compare columns, string literals, numbers, functions, or mathematical computations. Boolean operators are used to group expressions of a WHERE clause. Tables 8.2 and 8.3 list and define the comparison and Boolean operators available in Oracle.

SQL FUNCTIONS

Once the desired rows have been selected using the SELECT...FROM...WHERE clauses, the display of these rows can be manipulated using SQL functions.

AGGREGATE FUNCTIONS

These functions take the returned data set and group the rows together in some fashion. Table 8.4 lists the Aggregate functions.

If a nonaggregate and an aggregate column exist in the SELECT clause, then the GROUP BY clause must be used to group by the nonaggregate column. If not, an error message will be generated. The GROUP BY clause is discussed later in this unit.

STRING FUNCTIONS

SQL string functions manipulate the data for display purposes or for comparison tests. Table 8.5 lists the string functions.

Table 8.2 ■ Comparison Operators

Operator	Definition	Example
BETWEEN	Tests for a range of values, including both values that define the range.	SELECT course_no, cost FROM course WHERE cost BETWEEN 1000 and 1100; result includes courses that cost $1,000 and $1,100 and all in between.
IN	Tests against a list of values.	SELECT course_no, cost FROM course WHERE cost IN (1095, 1595); Result set includes only those courses that cost either $1,095 or $1,595.
LIKE	Tests using pattern matching. The percent (%) is a wildcard for multiple characters. The underscore (_) is a wildcard for a single character.	SELECT city, state, zip FROM zipcode WHERE city LIKE 'N%'; Result set includes all cities that begin with an uppercase N.
=	Equal to	SELECT course_no, cost FROM course WHERE cost = 1095;
!=	Is not equal to	SELECT course_no, cost FROM course WHERE cost != 1095;
<>	Is not equal to	SELECT course_no, cost FROM course WHERE cost <> 1095;
<	Is less than	SELECT course_no, cost FROM course WHERE cost < 1095;
>	Is greater than	SELECT course_no, cost FROM course WHERE cost > 1095;
<=	Is less than or equal to	SELECT course_no, cost FROM course WHERE cost <= 1095;
>=	Is greater than or equal to	SELECT course_no, cost FROM course WHERE cost >= 1095;

Table 8.3 ■ Boolean Operators

Operator	Definition	Example
AND	Returns true if both expressions are true. Returns false if one or both expressions are false.	SELECT first_name, last_name FROM instructor WHERE last_name LIKE 'M%' AND ZIP = '11215';
OR	Returns true if either expression is true. Returns false if both expressions are false.	SELECT course_no, description FROM course WHERE cost = 1095 OR cost = 1595;
NOT	Returns true if expression is false. Returns false if expression is true.	SELECT course_no, description FROM course WHERE NOT (cost BETWEEN 1095 AND 1595);

Table 8.4 ■ Aggregate Functions

Aggregate Function	Definition	Example
COUNT	Returns the number of rows for that column. If the parameter in parentheses is a column, then NULLS are not counted. If an asterisk, for example, COUNT(*), then all rows, including NULLS, are counted.	SELECT COUNT(cost) FROM course; SELECT COUNT(*) FROM course;
SUM	Returns the sum of the column values of a group of rows.	SELECT SUM(cost) FROM course;
MAX	Returns the maximum within a group of rows	SELECT MAX(cost) FROM course;
MIN	Returns the minimum within a group of rows	SELECT MIN(cost) FROM course;
AVG	Returns the average within a group of rows	SELECT AVG(cost) FROM course;

Table 8.5 ▪ SQL String Functions

String Function	Definition	Example
LENGTH	Tells you how long a string is, that is, the number of characters, letters, spaces in a string.	LENGTH(string) Ex.: SELECT description, LENGTH (description) "How Long?" FROM course;
INSTR	Returns a number, which tells you where a set of characters is located in a string.	INSTR(string, set [,start[, occurrence]]) Ex.: SELECT INSTR ('CORPORATE FLOOR', 'OR', 3, 2) FROM dual; Returns 14
SUBSTR	Clips out a section: tell it where to start and how many characters to include (count, which is optional). If count not included, goes to end of string. If 'start' is a negative number, then Oracle counts backwards from string.	SUBSTR(string, start [,count]) Ex.: SELECT substr ('1234567890',4, 3) FROM dual; Returns 456 Ex.: SELECT substr ('1234567890',-4, 3) FROM dual; Returns 789
UPPER	Takes any string and converts it to all uppercase.	UPPER(string) Ex.: SELECT last_name, UPPER(last_name) FROM student;
LOWER	Takes any string and converts it to all lowercase.	LOWER(string) Ex.: SELECT last_name, LOWER(last_name) FROM student;
INITCAP	Takes any string and converts the first letter of every word to uppercase.	INTICAP(string) Ex.: SELECT last_name, INITCAP(last_name) FROM student;
RPAD	Adds to, or pads, the right side of the string spaces or the character specified in set.	RPAD(string, length [,'set']) Ex.: SELECT RPAD(last_name, 20, '.') from student;
LPAD	Adds to, or pads, the left side of the string spaces or the character specified in set.	LPAD(string, length [,'set']) Ex.: SELECT LPAD(student_id, 5, '*') from student;

(continued)

Table 8.5 ■ continued

String Function	Definition	Example
RTRIM	Trims off characters from the right; removes characters from the right with set characters up to first character not in set.	RTRIM(string [,'set']) Ex.: SELECT RTRIM ('xyxXxyLASTxyXxyx', 'xy') FROM dual; Returns xyxXxyLASTxyX
LTRIM	Trims off characters from the left; removes characters from left with set characters up to first character not in set.	LTRIM(string [,'set']) Ex.: SELECT LTRIM ('xyxXxyLASTxyXxyx', 'xy') FROM dual; Returns XxyLASTxyXxyx
TRIM	Trims off a specified character from the left when LEADING is specified; removes character from the right when TRAILING is specified; removes character from the left and right when neither is specified. If no character is specified, spaces are trimmed.	TRIM([LEADING|TRAILING] [character FROM] string) Ex.: SELECT TRIM (' x ') FROM dual; Returns x SELECT TRIM ('x' FROM 'xyxXxyLASTxyXxyx') FROM dual; Returns yxXxyLASTxyXxy
REPLACE	Replaces one string for another string when the if condition is true.	REPLACE(string, if, then) Ex.: SELECT REPLACE(phone, 212, 718) FROM instructor;

Functions are often used together. Functions can be nested as needed. Before the TRIM function became available, the only way to trim spaces from the right and left of a string was to combine the RTRIM and LTRIM functions, as shown below:

■ FOR EXAMPLE

```
SELECT RTRIM(LTRIM(first_name))
  FROM student;
```

The functions UPPER and TRIM are helpful for performing a case-insensitive comparison of strings, and trimming off any spaces from either end. The functions SUBSTR and INSTR are often used together, because the INSTR function provides the position numbers needed by the SUBSTR function.

CONVERSION FUNCTIONS

Conversion functions convert columns or literals from one datatype to another. Conversion functions can be used in comparison tests, for formatting purposes, or when inserting/updating data into the database. Although Oracle performs some implicit datatype conversions, it is a good practice to always explicitly perform the conversion yourself.

Refer to Oracle's online documentation for the format masks for each of the conversion functions in Table 8.6.

NUMBER FUNCTIONS

Number functions perform various mathematical operations on numbers. Table 8.7 lists some of the Oracle number functions.

DATE FUNCTIONS

Date functions allow you to perform arithmetic on dates. For instance, you can get the system date and add month(s) to that date. Table 8.8 lists some Oracle date functions.

Table 8.6 ■ SQL Conversion Functions

Conversion Function	Definition	Example
TO_CHAR	Converts numbers to character or date to character. The format mask determines how the value will be displayed.	TO_CHAR (date/number, 'fmt') Ex.: SELECT TO_CHAR(sysdate, 'dd MON YYYY HH24:MI' FROM dual;
TO_NUMBER	Converts characters to number.	TO_NUMBER (char [,'fmt']) SELECT TO_NUMBER(cost, '999') FROM course;
TO_DATE	Converts characters to date. A format mask is required when the standard Oracle date format is not used.	TO_DATE (char[,'fmt']) SELECT course_no, section_no FROM section WHERE start_date_time > TO_DATE('01/02/2002', 'MM/DD/YYYY');

Table 8.7 ■ SQL Number Functions

Number Function	Definition	Example
ABS	Returns the absolute value.	ABS(value) Ex.: SELECT ABS(-43) FROM DUAL; Returns 43.
CEIL	Returns smallest integer larger than or equal to value.	CEIL(value) Ex.: SELECT CEIL(3.3) FROM DUAL; Returns 4.
FLOOR	Returns largest integer smaller than or equal to value.	FLOOR(value) Ex.: SELECT FLOOR(2.6) FROM DUAL; Returns 2.
MOD	Returns remainder after dividing value by divisor.	MOD(value, divisor) Ex.: SELECT course_no, section_no FROM section WHERE MOD(section_no, 2) = 0; Returns the even numbered sections from the section table.
ROUND	Rounds the column, expression, or value, to n decimal places, or if n is omitted, no decimal places. If n is negative, numbers to the left of the decimal point are rounded.	ROUND(value/expression, n) Ex.: SELECT ROUND (45.923, 2), ROUND (45.923, 0), ROUND (45.923, -1) FROM dual; Returns 45.92, 46, 50
TRUNC	Truncates the column, expression or value to n decimal places, or if n is omitted, no decimal places. If n is negative, numbers left of the decimal point are truncated.	TRUNC(column/expression, n) Ex.: SELECT TRUNC (45.923, 2), TRUNC (45.923, 0), TRUNC (45.923, -1) FROM dual; Returns 45.92, 45, 40

Table 8.8 ■ SQL Date Functions

Date Function	Definition	Example
ADD_MONTHS	Add calendar months to date. Returns the date *d* plus *n* months.	ADD_MONTHS (d , n) Ex.: SELECT start_date_time, TO_CHAR (ADD_MONTHS (start_date_time, 4), 'DD-MON-YYYY') NEXT FROM section;
LAST_DAY	Returns the last day of the month.	LAST _DAY (d) Ex.: SELECT SYSDATE, LAST_DAY (SYSDATE) last, LAST_DAY(SYSDATE)- SYSDATE days_left FROM dual; Returns the number of days left in the current month.
NEXT_DAY	Returns the date of the next weekday named by char that is later than the date *d*.	NEXT_DAY (d, char) Ex.: SELECT TO_CHAR (NEXT_DAY('31-DEC-99', 'MONDAY'), 'DD-MON-YYYY') FIRST_MON FROM dual; Returns the date of the first Monday in the year 2000.
MONTHS_BETWEEN	Returns number of months between dates d1 and d2. If days in month are the same in d1 and d2, return value is an integer. If d1 and d2 are both last days in month, return value is integer. Else: fractional portion of return value is based on a 31-day month.	MONTHS_BETWEEN (d1, d2) Ex.: SELECT course_no, section_no, MONTHS_ BETWEEN(sysdate, start_date_time) 'Months until class begins' FROM section WHERE start_date_time > sysdate;

GROUPING: DISTINCT, GROUP BY, HAVING

DISTINCT

In the SELECT clause of your SQL statement you make use of the key word DISTINCT (or UNIQUE) if you want Oracle to return only one row of each set of duplicate rows selected. Duplicate rows are those with matching values for each expression in the select list. Take a look at this example with and without the use of the DISTINCT keyword.

■ *FOR EXAMPLE*

```
SQL> SELECT zip FROM instructor;
ZIP
-----
10015
10025
10025
10035
10015
10025
10005
10025
10015
SQL> SELECT DISTINCT zip FROM instructor;
ZIP
-----
10005
10015
10025
10035
SQL> SELECT COUNT(section_id),
            COUNT(DISTINCT section_id), COUNT(*)
      FROM enrollment;
COUNT(SECTION_ID) COUNT(DISTINCTSECTION_ID)   COUNT(*)
----------------- ------------------------- ----------
              226                        64        226
```

DISTINCT works on the entire row and not individual columns or expressions. Also, DISTINCT is placed immediately after the SELECT keyword.

GROUP BY CLAUSE

You use the GROUP BY clause to group selected rows and return a single row of summary information. If you use the GROUP BY clause in a SELECT statement, the rows of the queried table are divided into the groups specified by the group by clause.

■ *FOR EXAMPLE*

```
SELECT prerequisite, COUNT (*)
   FROM course
GROUP BY prerequisite;
```

Every column that you select that is not used in an aggregate function must be used in the GROUP BY clause. The following example is a SELECT statement that determines if any sections meet at the same time and location.

■ *FOR EXAMPLE*

```
SELECT start_date_time, location, COUNT(*)
   FROM section
GROUP BY start_date_time, location;
```

If the GROUP BY clause is used with a SELECT clause consisting of all nonaggregate columns, then this produces the same result as using Distinct—only unique rows will be returned.

HAVING CLAUSE

The HAVING clause is used to restrict which groups of rows defined by the GROUP BY clause are returned. In the next example, the SELECT statement will list the courses for which the total number of students enrolled exceeds the average capacity over all sections.

■ *FOR EXAMPLE*

```
SELECT course_no, COUNT (*)
   FROM section s, enrollment e
  WHERE s.section_id = e.section_id
  GROUP BY course_no
HAVING COUNT (*) > (SELECT AVG (capacity)
                       FROM section);
```

WHERE, GROUP BY, HAVING CLAUSES

Oracle executes these clauses in the following order: the WHERE clause is evaluated first, any rows that do not satisfy the criteria in the WHERE clause get eliminated first and are not included in the groups formed by the GROUP BY clause. The groups are then formed and the group by function is performed; then any groups that do not satisfy the condition in the HAVING clause are eliminated.

ANSI SQL STANDARDS

The American National Standards Institute (http://www.ansi.org) first published a standard SQL specification in 1989. The ANSI SQL standard was later revised in 1992, often referred to as SQL-92 or SQL-2. This was revised again giving rise to the latest standard known as SQL-99. Sometimes it is called SQL-3. Database vendors and third-party software companies have varying levels of adherence to this standard. At a minimum, most major database vendors support the SQL-92 standard. Generally, what you find is that most vendors have their own extensions to the SQL language. Oracle is no exception in this matter. Many functions you see in Oracle SQL, such as DECODE, are not supported by other database vendors. You also find that many ANSI SQL standards such as JOIN syntax have not been used in Oracle SQL until recently. Nonetheless, Oracle has made efforts to maintain the ANSI standard. The reason for this is to provide an easier migration to and from third-party applications without a need to modify the SQL code. In Oracle 8i, and again in Oracle 9i, Oracle has introduced a number of enhancements to conform to the SQL-99 standard, which is more widely used by other vendors. You will now be able to take SQL code from an application such as MS Access and run it on Oracle. The SQL-99 standard is still relatively new in the Oracle world, so it is important that you are able to write your SQL using the old and new SQL standards.

JOINS

Many queries depend on data in more than one table. The basic operation in a Join is a process of forming pairs of rows by matching the data values of related columns from the tables. The SELECT statement for a multitable query must contain a join condition in the WHERE clause that specifies the column that will be matched. It is important to make sure the columns being joined are of compatible datatypes.

SIMPLE JOINS (TWO TABLES)

A simple join is when a result set requires data from two tables. Usually these two tables have a parent/child relationship. The join condition would match the foreign key constraint between the two tables.

■ FOR EXAMPLE

```
SELECT student.last_name, zipcode.city, zipcode.state, zipcode.zip
  FROM student, zipcode
 WHERE student.zip = zipcode.zip;
```

Look closely at this example and you will notice that in the WHERE clause the search condition matches the corresponding columns for each table (the zip column in each table). You will also notice that the FROM clause lists more than one source table for the data. It is the primary keys and foreign keys that create the parent/child relationship. Search condition joins the primary key of one table to the foreign key of the other table.

You can make use of table aliases so that your code is easier to read. If the join columns have the same name, then they must be qualified by the table name or the alias for the table. If the join columns have unique names, you do not have to qualify the column. The previous example can be qualified by making use of an alias 's' for the student table and 'z' for the zipcode table. The columns last_name, city, and state do not need aliases because they only exist in one table.

```
SELECT last_name, city, state, s.zip
   FROM student s, zipcode z
  WHERE s.zip = z.zip;
```

Note that WHERE clauses serve multiple purposes in SQL. As shown earlier in this chapter, WHERE clauses are used for filtering a result set against specific conditions. The WHERE clause can also be used to join tables together, as in the example above.

JOINING THREE OR MORE TABLES

The general rule for joining three or more tables is that the number of join conditions in the WHERE clause should be one less than the number of tables in the FROM clause. So, if you have three tables in the FROM clause, then you need two joins.

■ *FOR EXAMPLE*

```
SELECT s.course_no, s.section_no,
       c.description, i.last_name
  FROM section s, course c, instructor i
 WHERE s.course_no = c.course_no
   AND s.instructor_id = i.instructor_id
```

In this example, the desired result set is a list of the course number, section number, course description, and the name of the instructor for each section. You can include supplementary conditions to the WHERE clause so as to only include courses with a cost of over $1,000 and courses that have an instructor living in New York. The additional WHERE clause conditions below make use of a subquery to determine the zipcodes for the state of New York.

```
AND c.cost > 1000
AND i.zip IN (SELECT zip
                FROM zipcode
               WHERE state = 'NY')
```

SQL-99 JOINS

The 1999 ANSI Standard introduced complete JOIN syntax in the FROM clause instead of the WHERE clause. The SQL-92 method was to list the tables needed in the query in the FROM clause, and then to define the joins between these tables in the WHERE clause. Using WHERE clauses both to define joins and to filter data can be confusing. With SQL-99, the division of labor is clear; the join is defined entirely in the FROM clause, and the WHERE clause is used only for conditions.

The 1999 ANSI join syntax includes cross joins, equi joins, full outer joins, and natural joins.

SQL-99 EQUI JOINS

The EQUI JOIN syntax indicates the columns that comprise the JOINS between two tables. Prior to Oracle 9i you would indicate a join condition in the WHERE clause by stating which two columns were part of the foreign key. For example, prior to Oracle 9i, you would join the Student table to the Zipcode table as follows:

■ *FOR EXAMPLE*

```
SELECT   s.first_name, s.last_name,
         z.zip, z.city, z.state
  FROM   student s, zipcode z
 WHERE   s.zip = z.zip
```

The new syntax is as follows:

```
SELECT s.first_name, s.last_name,
       zip, z.city, z.state
  FROM student s JOIN
       zipcode z USING (zip)
```

The reason for this syntax is so that the join condition between the two tables is immediately obvious when looking at the tables listed in the FROM clause. This example is very short but generally your SQL statements are very long and when the join condition is in the WHERE clause it can be difficult to find them.

Notice that the ZIP column in the SELECT list did not have an alias. It is necessary in the new JOIN syntax that the column that is referenced in the JOIN does not have a qualifier. In the old syntax if you did not use an alias for ZIP as in this example:

```
SELECT   s.first_name, s.last_name,
         zip, z.city, z.state
  FROM   student s, zipcode z
 WHERE   s.zip = z.zip
```

the result is the following Oracle error:

```
ORA-00918: column ambiguously defined
```

In the new JOIN Syntax if you use a qualifier as in this example:

```
SELECT s.first_name, s.last_name,
       z.zip, z.city, z.state
  FROM STUDENT s JOIN
       zipcode z USING (zip)
```

the result is the following Oracle error:

```
ORA-25154: column part of USING clause cannot have qualifier
```

The new JOIN syntax also allows you to define the join condition using both sides of the join. This is done with the ON syntax. When using the ON syntax for a JOIN you must use the qualifier. This is also useful when the two sides of the join do not have the same name.

The ON syntax can also be used for three-way joins (or more).

■ *FOR EXAMPLE*

```
SELECT s.section_no, c.course_no,
       c.description, i.first_name, i.last_name
  FROM course c
  JOIN section s ON
       (s.course_no = c.course_no)
  JOIN instructor i ON
       (i.instructor_id = s.instructor_id)
```

The syntax for a multiple table join becomes more complex. Notice that one table is mentioned at a time. In the first JOIN, only columns in tables from the first two tables can be used in the ON section. Once the third table has been indicated in the second JOIN, then it can be used in the ON clause of the following condition.

SQL-99 NATURAL JOINS

The NATURAL JOIN is another part of the ANSI 1999 syntax that can be used when joining two tables based on columns with the same name and datatype. In a NATURAL JOIN, all of the columns with the same name in both tables comprise the join condition. You cannot use this syntax when the columns have the same name but a different datatype. Another benefit of this is that if you use the SELECT * syntax the columns that appear in both tables will only appear once in the result set.

Because a NATURAL JOIN assumes that all columns with the same name and datatype can be joined, there can be undesirable consequences. Consider the columns used by the NATURAL JOIN in the following statement:

■ FOR EXAMPLE

```
SELECT   *
    FROM  instructor NATURAL JOIN
          zipcode
```

The join that will be used here is not only the ZIP column in both tables, but also the CREATE_BY, CREATED_DATE, MODIFIED_BY, and MODIFIED_DATE columns. The student schema does not lend itself to using the NATURAL JOIN, since we have created audit columns that have the same name in each table, but are not used in the foreign keys between the two tables. If you have installed the sample Scott schema with the EMP and DEPT tables, you will be able to test the NATURAL JOIN condition. These two tables are defined as follows:

```
SQL> desc dept
 Name                 Type
 ----------------------------
 DEPTNO               NUMBER(2)
 DNAME                VARCHAR2(14)
 LOC                  VARCHAR2(13)
SQL> desc emp
 Name                 Type
 ----------------------------
 EMPNO                NUMBER(4)
 ENAME                VARCHAR2(10)
 JOB                  VARCHAR2(9)
 MGR                  NUMBER(4)
 HIREDATE             DATE
 SAL                  NUMBER(7,2)
 COMM                 NUMBER(7,2)
 DEPTNO               NUMBER(2)
```

A result set of the join of these two tables can be made with the following SQL, which makes use of the only column that shares the same name and datatype, DEPTNO:

```
SELECT   *
    FROM  dept NATURAL JOIN emp
```

CARTESIAN PRODUCT

Whichever syntax you use for joins, be sure that you join all of the tables used in the FROM clause of your query, so that you do not inadvertently generate a Cartesian product. A Cartesian product is a table (the product table) that is produced as a set of all possible pairs of rows from two tables (source tables). The columns of the product table are all the columns of the first source table followed by the columns of the second source table. If you specify a two-table query without a WHERE clause, SQL produces the product of the two tables as the query result.

■ FOR EXAMPLE

```
SELECT first_name, last_name, zip
   FROM student, zipcode;
61908 rows selected.
```

This is a result of every row combination of the 268 rows in the Student table and the 231 rows in the Zipcode table. The result is 268 × 231 or 61,908. As you might imagine, this can take a considerable toll on performance.

 It is an easy mistake to cite two or more tables in the FROM clause and forget to join them in the WHERE clause. This is a common mistake of students new to Oracle's SQL.

ANSI 99 CROSS JOINS

The result set from a Cartesian product is usually meaningless, but it can be used to generate a lot of rows if you need to do some performance testing. In the unusual case where you wish to create a Cartesian product from two tables, always use the CROSS JOIN syntax. The advantage of this new syntax is that the words CROSS JOIN immediately show that the user did not make a mistake, but rather intended to create a Cartesian product.

■ FOR EXAMPLE

```
SELECT count(*)
   FROM instructor i
        CROSS JOIN
        course c
```

The result set from this is 300. This is because the course table has 30 rows and the instructor table has 10 rows. The CROSS JOIN will count all possible combinations resulting in the 300 rows.

OUTER JOIN

Inner join or equi join is the result of joining two tables that contain rows only where a match occurred on the join condition. It is possible to lose information through an inner join, because only those rows that match on the join condition will appear in the final result set. An outer join can help circumvent this problem. The result set of an outer join will contain the same rows as the inner join plus rows corresponding to the rows from the source tables where there is no match. The outer join has been supported by a number of versions of the Oracle SQL language. The Oracle syntax for an outer join is to place a (+) by the columns in the WHERE clause where you may generate nulls for this item once it is joined to another table. It is important that you make use of the (+) syntax in every condition in the WHERE clause or you may lose your outer join. Also note that prior to Oracle 9i you could only make one outer join on each table.

■ FOR EXAMPLE

```
SELECT c.description, c.course_no ,s.section_no
  FROM   section s, course c
 WHERE   s.course_no(+) = c.course_no;
(80 rows)
```

This example will create a result set that will show courses and sections. It will include all courses, whether or not they have sections.

■ FOR EXAMPLE

If you want to list all the zipcodes not listed in the Student table, you would do the following steps. First you would select all the zipcodes that are used in the Student table as follows:

```
SELECT z.zip, s.zip
  FROM zipcode z, student s
 WHERE z.zip = s.zip;
```

Next you would select all the zipcodes used in both Student and Zipcode tables but emphasizing which are used in the Student table and which are not as follows:

```
SELECT z.zip, s.zip
  FROM zipcode z, student s
 WHERE z.zip = s.zip (+);
```

Finally, put these together so that you can show only the zipcodes in the Zipcode table that are not in the Student table as follows:

```
SELECT z.zip
  FROM zipcode z, student s
 WHERE z.zip = s.zip (+)
   AND s.zip is null
ORDER BY z.zip;
```

Using an outer join in this way is usually faster than using NOT IN.

SQL-99 OUTER JOINS

The new method of outer joins adopted in Oracle 9i allows the case of an outer join on either side or both at the same time. For example, suppose you wanted to see all the instructors and their states, plus all the states whether or not an instructor lives in that state. In other words, you wanted to see all the instructors and all the states in both these tables. This could be done using the new Outer Join syntax. This requires the JOIN syntax stated above but the outer join attributes are added. The choice is LEFT/RIGHT/FULL OUTER JOIN. The same OUTER JOIN can now be stated as:

```
SELECT i.first_name, z.state
   FROM    instructor i
     RIGHT OUTER JOIN
     zipcode z
     ON (i.zip = z.zip)
  GROUP BY  i.first_name, z.state
```

The RIGHT indicates that the values on the right side of the JOIN may not exist in the table on the LEFT side of the join. This can be replaced by the word FULL if there are some instructors who do not have a zipcode, or zipcodes that are not in the ZIPCODE table.

SELF JOIN

A self join is what happens when a table has a recursive relationship with itself and can thus be joined to itself. The best example would be the course table, which holds both courses and the names of other courses that are the courses' prerequisites.

■ FOR EXAMPLE

```
SELECT c.course_no, c.description, c.prerequisite, p.description
  FROM course c, course p
 WHERE c.prerequisite = p.course_no
```

SQL-99 CASE

The CASE expression is a wonderful enhancement. It allows you to extend what was generally handled by a DECODE. CASE has an IF THEN ELSE type structure, like DECODE. However, while DECODE can only compare to a literal value, CASE can also evaluate conditions. In a basic CASE expression, each WHEN clause is followed by a literal value. In the more complex CASE expression, also known as "Searched CASE," a condition is indicated for each WHEN clause. This condition or predicate can be any SQL logical operator. Note that in the complex CASE expression, the CASE keyword is not followed by a column, but in the simple CASE it is. A simple CASE expression evaluates only one column, whereas a complex CASE expression can evaluate a number of columns to determine the result set.

■ *FOR EXAMPLE*

```
SELECT first_name, last_name,
       (CASE
        WHEN created_date
            BETWEEN '01-JAN-1999' AND '21-JAN-1999'
                THEN 'First 3 Weeks'
        WHEN created_date
            BETWEEN '22-JAN-1999' AND '10-FEB-1999'
                THEN 'Next 3 Weeks'
        WHEN created_date
            BETWEEN '11-FEB-1999' AND '01-MAR-1999'
                THEN 'Last 3 Weeks'
        ELSE 'beyond'
        END) AS "Date Entered"
FROM student
```

CASE can also be used in a manner very similar to DECODE.

```
SELECT  i.first_name, i.last_name,
        (CASE z.state
        WHEN 'NY' THEN 'New York'
        WHEN 'NJ' THEN 'New Jersey'
        WHEN 'CT' THEN 'Connecticut'
        ELSE 'Not in the Northeast'
        END) State
  FROM  instructor i
  JOIN  zipcode z
    ON (i.zip = z.zip)
```

It is important to note that CASE can also be used in PL/SQL. You will see an example of this in the next chapter.

SQL 99 NULLIF AND COALESCE

The NULLIF and COALESCE functions are defined by the ANSI 1999 standard to be "CASE abbreviations." You can achieve the same results using DECODE and NVL, but these new functions are more compact, and show off your ANSI-99 knowledge.

The NULLIF function is the opposite of an NVL function. This function returns a NULL value if a column is a certain value. The next two statements return the same result set.

■ *FOR EXAMPLE*

```
SELECT NULLIF(STATE, 'NY'), state, count(*)
   FROM  zipcode
GROUP BY  state
```

```
SELECT DECODE(STATE, 'NY', null, STATE), state, count(*)
   FROM zipcode
GROUP BY state
```

The COALESCE function is like a nested NVL. You can have an infinite number of expressions. Each expression is tested to see if it is NULL. If it is NULL, then the next expression is tested, and so on. The last value is the default.

■ FOR EXAMPLE

```
SELECT  e.student_id,
        COALESCE(e.final_grade, g.numeric_grade, 0)
   FROM enrollment e
   JOIN grade g
     ON (g.student_id = g.student_ID
    AND e.section_id = g.section_id)
  WHERE g.grade_type_code = 'FI'
```

The line COALESCE(e.final_grade, g.numeric_grade, 0) has the same meaning as a nested NVL NVL(e.final_grade, NVL(g.numeric_grade, 0)).

SUBQUERIES

A subquery is a query in which the WHERE clause criteria is constructed from another table or tables. Pay close attention to the use of aliases in subqueries. The following example will show the use of a subquery by building the query in stages. The result set that you are looking for is a list of courses and section numbers for courses that Anita Morris is teaching. In the first SQL statement you get a list of course_no and section_no.

```
SELECT  course_no, section_no
   FROM section
```

The second SQL statement looks for the instructor_id of Anita Morris as follows:

```
SELECT instructor_id
   FROM instructor
  WHERE first_name = 'Anita'
    AND   last_name = 'Morris'
```

Now combine the two as follows:

```
SELECT course_no, section_no
   FROM section
  WHERE instructor_id = (SELECT instructor_id
                           FROM instructor
                          WHERE first_name = 'Anita'
                            AND   last_name = 'Morris')
```

Another example is used to produce a list of the instructors teaching sections with a capacity greater than 20.

```
SELECT first_name, last_name
  FROM instructor
 WHERE instructor_id IN (SELECT instructor_id
                           FROM section
                          WHERE capacity > 20);
```

ORACLE 9I SCALAR SUBQUERY

A scalar row subquery is a subquery that returns a single row. If the scalcar subquery returns more than one row, an error will be the result. Oracle 9i increases the support of scalar subqueries beyond what was available in Oracle 8i.

■ FOR EXAMPLE

```
SELECT city, state,
       (SELECT count(*)
          FROM student s
         WHERE s.zip = z.zip) as student_count
  FROM zipcode z
 WHERE state = 'CT'
```

IN-LINE VIEWS

An in-line view is an entire SELECT statement within the FROM clause. This is a way to create a virtual table or view.

■ FOR EXAMPLE

```
SELECT s.first_name, s.last_Name, a.type,
       a.avg_grade section_avg,
       AVG(g.numeric_grade) student_avg
  FROM student s, enrollment e, grade g,
     (SELECT AVG(numeric_grade) avg_grade,
             grade_type_code type, section_id
        FROM   grade
     GROUP BY grade_type_code, section_id) a
 WHERE s.student_id = e.student_id
 AND   e.section_id = a.section_id
 AND   e.section_id = g.section_id
 AND   e.student_id = g.student_id
 AND   e.section_id = 101
 AND   g.grade_type_code = a.type
 GROUP BY s.first_name, s.last_Name, a.type,
       a.avg_grade
 ORDER BY 1, 2, 3
```

In the previous example you see the in-line view with an alias of 'g'. This view is created so that there is a view of the average numeric grade for each grade type code for the section ID 101. This is then joined to another instance of the grade table to show the average grade for just one student.

UNIT 8.1 EXERCISES

In order to test your progress, you should be able to answer the following questions.

a) True or False: It was not possible to use the CASE syntax in Oracle prior to Oracle 9i.

b) True or False: An aggregate function can be performed on a single row.

c) Complete the sentence: Oracle adopted the ANSI 99 SQL standard so that (select all that are true)

1) Oracle could introduce a new type of SQL for all database vendors.
2) Full outer joins would be available.
3) SQL syntax that had been in use by various other database vendors could now be used in Oracle as well.
4) The same SQL code could not be run on any database.
5) Oracle could contain some SQL syntax not available by other vendors.

d) True or False: The TO_CHAR conversion functions allows you to format the data of a row with the datatype of VarChar2.

e) Which of the following clauses does a SQL Select statement need in order to be valid:

1) SELECT clause
2) FROM clause
3) WHERE clause

4) GROUP BY clause
5) HAVING clause
6) ORDER BY clause

f) True or False: Oracle's Dual table is accessible only by a DBA.

UNIT 8.1 EXERCISES ANSWERS

a) True or False: It was not possible to use the CASE syntax in Oracle prior to Oracle 9i.

Answer: True.

b) True or False: An aggregate function can be performed on a single row.

Answer: False.

c) Complete the sentence: Oracle adopted the ANSI 99 SQL standard so that (select all that are true)

1) Oracle could introduce a new type of SQL for all database vendors.
2) Full outer joins would be available.
3) SQL syntax that had been in use by various other database vendors could now be used in Oracle as well
4) The same SQL code could not be run on any database.
5) Oracle could contain some SQL syntax not available by other vendors.

Answer: 1 and 3.

d) True or False: The TO_CHAR conversion function allows you to format the data of a column defined as VarChar2.

Answer: False. The TO_CHAR function converts numbers or dates to a string.

e) Which of the following clauses does SQL Select statement need in order to be valid:

1) SELECT clause
2) FROM clause
3) WHERE clause
4) GROUP BY clause

5) HAVING clause
6) ORDER BY clause

Answer: I and 2. A valid SQL Select statement needs only the SELECT and FROM clause.

f) True or False: Oracle's Dual table is accessible only by the DBA.

Answer: False. Oracle's Dual table is owned by SYS and available to all users.

UNIT 8.2

ADVANCED USES OF SQL'S NVL AND DECODE FUNCTIONS

Dynamic Web applications often require users to input values in a form, such as when users perform data entry or request a search based on their input. If you do not restrict the kind of input entered into your Web interface, then it is possible for many different values to be passed to your underlying Oracle PL/SQL procedure. Moreover, it is possible that your user may choose to not enter any value(s) at all before submitting the form, and NULL values could be passed to the application procedure. If DEFAULT values are not defined for your input parameters, then it is necessary for you to be able to handle NULL values in your server-side code.

Less-experienced PL/SQL programmers may respond to the challenge of handling NULL values by coding a plethora of explicit IF-THEN-ELSE statements. For example:

```
IF parameter_1 IS NULL THEN ...  ELSE ... END IF;
```

Though this type of logic seems plausible for one parameter, it can easily become cumbersome when you consider the possibility of there being *many* input parameters with NULL values in your procedure. Using this technique might require you to code a separate IF-THEN-ELSE statement for each parameter. An easier solution is to consider similar functionality already provided by Oracle SQL's NVL and DECODE functions.

NVL—REPLACING NULL VALUES WITH DEFAULT VALUES

It is easy to account for possible NULL values in your procedural input parameters by using a few of the functions implicit in Oracle SQL. One of these functions is the NVL function. NVL is a substitution function that allows you to substitute a known value for one that is unknown. It requires two parameters: an input expression (i.e., a literal, computation, or column), and the expression to be used as a substitute if the input expression is NULL (unknown). If the input parameter contains a NULL value, then the substitution parameter is used instead. Otherwise, the input expression is used. The syntax is:

■ *FOR EXAMPLE*

```
SELECT  NVL(input_expression, substitute_value)
   FROM  tablename;
```

The input expression can be any Oracle datatype. The alternate value must be the same datatype as the input expression. It can be a literal, another column, or an expression.

The NVL function is really useful only in cases where the data is unknown, not where it is irrelevant.

Consider the following example:

```
SELECT employee_name, NVL(salary_raise, salary * .10)
FROM employee;
```

In this example, two columns are selected from a fictitious *employee* table: employee_name and salary_raise. Where the value for the salary_raise column is NULL, the value for the salary column multiplied by 10% (.10) is substituted instead.

The NVL function can also allow records to be included that would otherwise be excluded due to NULL values. Consider an example where the NVL function is used in the WHERE clause of a SELECT statement.

■ *FOR EXAMPLE*

```
SELECT employee_name, salary, salary_raise
  FROM employee a, company_records b
 WHERE NVL(a.mid_year_review, 'Z') =
       NVL(b.mid_year_review, 'Z');
```

Equality tests with NULLs are different from other equality tests. Recall that the syntax to test for a NULL value is done with the phrases IS NULL or IS NOT NULL, rather than the equals sign. If the WHERE clause of this statement is written like this:

```
WHERE a.mid_year_review = b.mid_year_review
```

then any mid_year_review column value that is NULL, in *either* the employee table or the company_records table, is excluded. To also include those employees for whom you do not yet have a mid_year_review value, you can use the NVL function. The substitute used in this example is 'Z'; it could be anything as long as the same substitute is used in both NVL functions. AND, of course, as long as the datatype of the substitute is the same as that of the mid_year_review column. In this example, the datatype of the mid_year_review column is VARCHAR2. This is why a substituted value of 'Z' (or any other value enclosed in single quotes), is an acceptable substitution.

In the above example, the value for mid_year_review can be NULL in both tables. But suppose that in one of the tables this value is actually required. Consider the following alternate statement:

■ FOR EXAMPLE

```
SELECT employee_name, salary, salary_raise
  FROM employee a, company_records b
 WHERE a.mid_year_review =
       NVL(b.mid_year_review, a.mid_year_review);
```

This example provides an interesting twist on what can be accomplished with the NVL function. In the employee table, the mid_year_review column is required (*non-nullable*), and therefore the check for a possible NULL value is unnecessary. However, the mid_year_review column in the company_records table is not required (*nullable*) and a check for a possible NULL value is still necessary. There is one crucial difference between this example and the example shown earlier. The substitution value for b.mid_year_review (a nullable value) is a.mid_year_review (a non-nullable value).

This statement takes any possible NULL value from the mid_year_review column of the company_records table and substitutes it with an actual value from the mid_year_review column of the employee table. In order to be able to write such a statement, you must know your data rather well. It is important to know as much as possible about the tables you are going to be working with in your application. Running a simple DESCRIBE statement on the tables involved in your application will tell you immediately about the datatype and nullability (which columns have been defined as NOT NULL) of your table columns.

Notice that this statement has only one filter:

```
WHERE a.mid_year_review =
      NVL(b.mid_year_review, a.mid_year_review);
```

However, suppose that this statement is placed in a PL/SQL procedure, for example, and a parameter value for the mid_year_review column is passed in. Suppose also that only one table, EMPLOYEE, is being queried. Then this WHERE clause might possibly be rewritten as:

```
WHERE mid_year_review =
      NVL(p_mid_year_review, mid_year_review);
```

Additionally, it is possible that more than one parameter may be passed into this procedure, resulting in the following addition to the WHERE clause:

```
WHERE mid_year_review =
      NVL(p_mid_year_review, mid_year_review)
  AND salary = NVL(p_salary, salary);
```

As more parameters with possible NULL values are passed to this procedure, more code for handling these NULL values is required. As you can see, the above statement with two filters in a WHERE clause requires less coding than a separate IF-THEN-ELSE statement for each parameter. There is also less chance that you will forget to account for a possible NULL value in one of your parameters if the handling is done, as much as possible, within available SQL functionality using the NVL function.

DECODE—A POWERFUL IF-THEN-ELSE FUNCTION

DECODE provides you with an alternative Oracle SQL method for value substitution. It substitutes values based on a condition using IF-THEN-ELSE logic. It has the following syntax:

```
DECODE(test_value, if_equals_cond1, then_use_value1,
[elsif_equals_cond2, then_use_value2, ... else_use_default_value])
```

A value (which can be a column, variable, literal, or expression) is passed as the first parameter to the DECODE function as the condition to be tested. It is compared against the second parameter, which is a test condition. If they are equal, then the third parameter is returned or used as a result. Otherwise, a comparison is made against a fourth parameter, which is either an *elsif* condition, or an *else* value to be returned or used. If the fourth parameter is an ELSIF condition, then another comparison of this next test condition to the original input value is made. These comparisons can continue for as many IF-THEN pairs as you'd like to construct. Otherwise, the default ELSE value is returned or used. Consider the following example:

■ *FOR EXAMPLE*

```
SELECT last_name, first_name,
       DECODE(salutation, 'Miss', 'Female',
                          'Ms.', 'Female',
                          'Mrs.', 'Female',
                          'Mr.', 'Male',
                          'Unknown') gender
  FROM student
 ORDER BY last_name, first_name, gender;
```

This statement returns the last name, first name, and gender values for students listed in the STUDENT table. There is no actual column for gender in the STU-

DENT table. Each student's gender is inferred by looking at the salutation for each student. This is a common technique for determining gender when it is not stored in the database. A substitution, of sorts, is performed using the DECODE function on the SALUTATION column. By examining the above DECODE statement, you can see that, based on the value of the salutation column for each row that is returned in the SELECT statement, anyone whose salutation value is 'Miss,' 'Ms.,' or 'Mrs.' is defined in this query as 'Female.' Similarly, anyone whose salutation value is 'Mr.,' is defined as 'Male.' All others are defined as 'Unknown,' since both male and female students may have salutation values of 'Dr.,' 'Rev.,' 'Hon.,' and the like, or even NULL.

Since DECODE is a substitution function, like its NVL counterpart, it generally requires that the datatypes of the substitution values match that of the tested input value. However, simply by placing single quotes around substitution values, you can get around this restriction for input values that are of type NUMBER. Contrast this with the exercise from Unit 8.2.A, Question B.

■ FOR EXAMPLE

```
SELECT course_no, NVL(TO_CHAR(prerequisite), 'None')
  FROM course;
```

Using the NVL function, you are required to explicitly cast the PREREQUISITE column, defined as a number, to a VARCHAR2 datatype, in order to display the character string substitution value and avoid the *ORA-01722: invalid number* error message. However, this same SELECT statement can be rewritten using the DECODE function on the PREREQUISITE column and no explicit data conversion is necessary as long as the substitution value is enclosed in single quotes. The following code illustrates this:

■ FOR EXAMPLE

```
SELECT course_no, DECODE(prerequisite, NULL, 'None',
                         prerequisite)
  FROM course;
```

As you can see from this code, if the PREREQUISITE column value is NULL, then the word "None" is displayed. Otherwise, the PREREQUISITE column value is displayed. Feel free to run this statement in SQL*Plus, logged on as the STUDENT user, to ensure that the result is the same as that received when running the query from Unit 8.2.A, Question B.

UNIT 8.2 EXERCISES

8.2.1 SUBSTITUTING NULL VALUES USING NVL

To begin the exercises, you need to import the data for the STUDENT schema and create the STUDENT user if you have not done so already. Navigate to the Web site for this book (accessible through http://phptr.com/boardman/) and download the files required to create and install the STUDENT schema. Read the instructions supplied in the README.TXT file and carefully follow the directions. Within this book and on the accompanying Web site, you will find an ERD (Entity Relational Diagram), as well as a brief description of each of the tables in the STUDENT schema. Once all the scripts have completed successfully and you have loaded all the STUDENT schema objects into your database, you can begin the exercises in this chapter.

a) Create a query to select course numbers and their prerequisites from the COURSE table. If a value for a prerequisite is NULL, display five numeral ones, 11111. Be sure to use the NVL function in the SELECT clause of your SELECT statement.

b) Recreate the same query as above, but instead of displaying five numeral ones, display the word "None". Here again, be sure to use the NVL function in the SELECT clause of your SELECT statement.

c) Now write a query that displays instructor first names, last names and zipcode values. Include those instructors for whom there is no zipcode value by using the NVL function in the WHERE clause of your SELECT statement. If there is no zipcode value for a particular instructor, display the words, "No Zip Code."

8.2.2 SUBSTITUTING VALUES , NULL OR OTHERWISE, USING DECODE

a) Create a query to select grade values from the grade table. Convert the numeric grade to a letter grade using the following criteria.

- For this example, you are most interested in the number of "A" grades currently in the grade table.
- Select only those numeric grades where the result of the numeric grade subtracted from 100 is less than or equal to 10.
- If the numeric grade subtracted from 100 is between 0 and 3, then display a letter grade of "A+" for that numeric grade. If this result is between 4 and 6, then display a letter grade of "A" for that numeric grade. For all others, display the words, "A- or below."

b) Now create a statement that uses one DECODE statement nested inside another DECODE statement. For each course in the COURSE table, display each section's start date/time and location information. Use the following criteria.

- To display all courses, regardless of whether a course currently has any sections, try using an outer join.
- Your SELECT clause should include the course number, the section number (NOT the section ID number), and a column that concatenates the start date and time with location information. Use the following criteria to obtain the start date/time and location information:
  1. If the location is not NULL, then display the start date/time concatenated with the location, and separated by a space. For example: `'29-APR-99 L507'`
  2. If the location is NULL, then check the value for start date/time. If the value for start date/time is NULL, then display the words "To Be Determined." Otherwise, display the words, "January 21 - 9:00 A.M. - Newton Hall."
  3. Since this selected column holding the start date/time and location uses a couple of DECODE statements, give it a more meaningful title by providing it the alias, "Day 1."
  4. Also, again due to the nested DECODE statements, this column can be quite long. So, use the Oracle SQL string

function, SUBSTR, to display only the first **36** characters of the result.

• Sort your result set by course number and section number.

UNIT 8.2 EXERCISE ANSWERS

8.2.1 ANSWERS

a) Create a query to select course numbers and their prerequisites from the COURSE table. If a value for a prerequisite is NULL, display five numeral ones, 11111. Be sure to use the NVL function in the SELECT clause of your SELECT statement.

Answer: You could write a query like the following:

```
SELECT course_no, NVL(prerequisite, 11111)
  FROM course;
```

And the result of running this query should look similar to:

```
SQL>  SELECT course_no, NVL(prerequisite, 11111)
  2      FROM course;
 COURSE_NO NVL(PREREQUISITE,11111)
---------- ----------------------
        10                  11111
        20                  11111
        25                    140
        80                    204
       100                     20
       120                     80
       122                    120
       124                    122
       125                    122
       130                    310
       132                    130
       134                    132
       135                    134
       140                     20
       142                     20
       144                    420
       145                    310
       146                  11111
       147                     20
       204                     20
       210                    220
```

220	80
230	10
240	25
310	11111
330	130
350	125
420	25
430	350
450	350

```
30 rows selected.
```

While the substituted value in this result set is of the correct datatype, it isn't very informative. This is where a statement like the one created in Question B, next, comes in handy.

b) Recreate the same query as above, but instead of displaying five numeral ones, display the word "None." Here again, be sure to use the NVL function in the SE-LECT clause of your SELECT statement.

Answer: This query could be rewritten as follows:

```
SELECT course_no, NVL(TO_CHAR(prerequisite), 'None')
  FROM course;
```

And the result of running this newer version of the query should look similar to:

```
SQL> SELECT course_no, NVL(TO_CHAR(prerequisite), 'None')
  2    FROM course;
COURSE_NO NVL(TO_CHAR(PREREQUISITE),'NONE')
---------- -------------------------------------
       10 None
       20 None
       25 140
       80 204
      100 20
      120 80
      122 120
      124 122
      125 122
      130 310
      132 130
      134 132
      135 134
      140 20
      142 20
      144 420
      145 310
      146 None
      147 20
```

```
204 20
210 220
220 80
230 10
240 25
310 None
330 130
350 125
420 25
430 350
450 350
```
30 rows selected.

The numeric prerequisite value in the latest version of this query is explicitly cast to a character datatype with the TO_CHAR function. This datatype conversion allows the substituted value of "None" to take place when NULLs are present in the prerequisite column. If a datatype conversion had not been used in the SELECT statement then the resulting Oracle error message, ORA-01722: invalid number, would have been returned.

c) Now write a query that displays instructor first names and last names. Include those instructors for whom there is no zipcode value by using the NVL function in the WHERE clause of your SELECT statement.

Answer: You could construct a query like the following:

```
SELECT DISTINCT first_name, last_name
  FROM instructor i, zipcode z
WHERE z.zip = NVL(i.zip, z.zip);
```

And the result of running this query should look similar to:

```
SQL> SELECT DISTINCT first_name, last_name, NVL(i.zip, 'No
  2            Zip Code') zipcode
  3      FROM instructor i, zipcode z
  4     WHERE z.zip = NVL(i.zip, z.zip);
```

FIRST_NAME	LAST_NAME	ZIPCODE
Anita	Morris	10015
Charles	Lowry	10025
Fernand	Hanks	10015
Gary	Pertez	10035
Irene	Willig	No Zip Code
Marilyn	Frantzen	06905
Nina	Schorin	10025
Rick	Chow	10015
Todd	Smythe	10025
Tom	Wojick	10025

```
10 rows selected.
```

The instructor, Irene Willig, has no zipcode value in the INSTRUCTOR table. However, her name appears in this list anyway. The reason for this is that whenever the NVL function in the above query's WHERE clause came across a NULL value for the ZIP column in the INSTRUCTOR table, it simply replaced it with an actual value from the Zipcode table. Since the ZIP column in the ZIPCODE table is a primary key, it is never NULL. This is why it is possible to use a value from this column as the substitution in the NVL clause for this query. It is also the reason why no NVL function is necessary on the left-side operand (that of the ZIP column from the ZIPCODE table).

Note that it is necessary to include the DISTINCT keyword. This is due to the fact that the record is now being matched against every zipcode value. To avoid returning every possible combination of Irene Willig's NULL zipcode value with every existing zipcode value in the ZIPCODE table, the DISTINCT keyword must be employed.

If you change the WHERE clause of this statement to employ an outer join (a join between two tables that returns all the records that satisfy an equijoin condition, plus the records from one of the tables with no matching records in the other table), as opposed to using the NVL function, your result set will be different. Consider the following statement:

```
SELECT DISTINCT first_name, last_name, NVL(i.zip, 'No Zip
      Code') zipcode
  FROM instructor i, zipcode z
   WHERE z.zip = i.zip(+);
```

The result of executing this changed statement produces the following output:

```
SQL> SELECT DISTINCT first_name, last_name, NVL(i.zip, 'No
  2          Zip Code') zipcode
  3      FROM instructor i, zipcode z
  4       WHERE z.zip = i.zip(+);

FIRST_NAME                LAST_NAME           ZIPCODE
------------------------- ------------------- -------
Anita                     Morris              10015
Charles                   Lowry               10025
Fernand                   Hanks               10015
Gary                      Pertez              10035
Marilyn                   Frantzen            06905
Nina                      Schorin             10025
Rick                      Chow                10015
Todd                      Smythe              10025
Tom                       Wojick              10025
                                              No Zip Code
```

```
10 rows selected.
```

Note that the same number of rows, 10, is returned here as is returned in the result set for the answer to Question C. However, the values for first name and last name for that instructor who has no zipcode value, "Irene Willig," are not returned. Instead, only the substitution for the missing zipcode value, "No Zip Code," is returned. Notice also that the outer join places the record with a zipcode value of NULL last in the result set.

8.2.2 ANSWERS

a) Create a query to select grade values from the grade table. Convert the numeric grade to a letter grade using the following criteria.

- For this example, you are most interested in the number of "A" grades currently in the grade table.
- Select only those numeric grades where the result of the numeric grade subtracted from 100 is less than or equal to 10.
- If the numeric grade subtracted from 100 is between 0 and 3, then display a letter grade of "A+" for that numeric grade. If this result is between 4 and 6, then display a letter grade of "A" for that numeric grade. For all others, display the words, "A- or below."

Answer: You could write a query like the following:

```
SELECT DISTINCT DECODE((100 - numeric_grade), 0, 'A+',
                         1, 'A+', 2, 'A+', 3, 'A+', 4,
                         'A', 5, 'A', 6, 'A', 'A- or
                         Below') letter_grade,
               numeric_grade
  FROM grade
 WHERE (100 - numeric_grade) BETWEEN 0 AND 10
 ORDER BY numeric_grade DESC;
```

And the result of running this query should look similar to:

```
SQL> SELECT DISTINCT DECODE((100 - numeric_grade), 0,
                         'A+', 1, 'A+', 2, 'A+', 3,
                         'A+', 4, 'A', 5, 'A', 6,
                         'A', 'A- or Below')
                         letter_grade,
               numeric_grade
  3    FROM grade
  4   WHERE (100 - numeric_grade) BETWEEN 0 AND 10
  5   ORDER BY numeric_grade DESC;

LETTER_GRAD NUMERIC_GRADE
----------- -------------
A+                     99
A+                     98
```

```
A+                         97
A                          96
A                          95
A                          94
A- or Below                93
A- or Below                92
A- or Below                91
A- or Below                90

10 rows selected.
```

This query illustrates how the displayed value does not necessarily have to match either the original value or the datatype of the original value in the database table's column it is performed upon. The drawback to using DECODE is that it does not allow for greater than or less than comparisons. A separate IF-THEN-ELSE statement could be used for each anticipated condition you'd like to account for, even for those values that may fall within a range. As explained in Unit 8.1 of this chapter, a less cumbersome syntax to use is the CASE statement, available with the 9i version of the Oracle database. The CASE statement does allow for range comparisons. So, in the example above, the CASE statement could be used to simplify and reduce the number of checked conditions.

b) Now create a statement that uses one DECODE statement nested inside another DECODE statement. Display the start date and time and location information for every section of every course, regardless of whether each course is currently being offered this semester, using the following criteria.

- HINT: To display all section information for all courses, regardless of whether a course is currently being taught, try using an outer join.
- Your SELECT clause should include the course number, the section number, (NOT the section ID number), and the start date and time, and location information. Use the following criteria to obtain the start date and time and location information:
    1. If the location is NULL, then check the start date and time value. If it is NULL, then display the words "To Be Determined," otherwise, display the words "January 21 - 9:00 A.M. - Newton Hall."
    2. If the location is not NULL, then display the start date and time concatenated with the location, and separated by a space.
    3. Since this selected column uses a couple of DECODE statements, give it a more meaningful name by providing it the alias, "Day 1."
    4. Also, again due to the nested DECODE statements, this column can be quite long. So, use the Oracle SQL substring function, SUBSTR, to display only the first 32 characters of the result.
- Sort your result set by course number and section number.

Answer: You could construct this statement as follows:

```
SELECT c.course_no, section_no,
       SUBSTR(
```

```
DECODE(location, NULL,
       DECODE(start_date_time, NULL,
       'To Be Determined',
       'January 21 - 9:00 A.M. - Newton Hall'),
start_date_time||' '||location),
1, 36) "Day 1"
FROM section s, course c
WHERE c.course_no = s.course_no (+)
ORDER BY course_no, section_no;
```

And the result of running this query should look similar to:

```
SQL> SELECT c.course_no, section_no,
     SUBSTR(DECODE(location, NULL, DECODE(start_date_time,
NULL, 'To Be Determined', 'January 21 - 9:00 A.M. -
Newton Hall'),
start_date_time||' '||location), 1, 36) "Day 1"
     FROM section s, course c
     WHERE c.course_no = s.course_no (+)
  ORDER BY course_no, section_no;
COURSE_NO SECTION_NO Day 1
---------- ---------- ---------------------------------
        10          2 24-APR-99 L214
        20          2 24-JUL-99 L210
        20          4 03-MAY-99 L214
        20          7 11-JUN-99 L509
        20          8 11-JUN-99 L210
        25          1 14-JUL-99 M311
        25          2 10-JUN-99 L210
        25          3 14-APR-99 L507
        25          4 04-MAY-99 L214
        25          5 15-MAY-99 L509
        25          6 12-JUN-99 L509
        25          7 12-JUN-99 L210
        25          8 13-JUN-99 L509
        25          9 13-JUN-99 L507
        80            To Be Determined
       100          1 14-APR-99 L214
       100          2 24-JUL-99 L500
       100          3 03-JUN-99 L509
       100          4 04-MAY-99 L507
       100          5 15-MAY-99 L214
       120          1 16-MAY-99 L507
       120          2 24-JUL-99 L206
       120          3 24-MAY-99 L509
       120          4 04-MAY-99 L509
       120          5 15-MAY-99 L210
       120          7 12-JUN-99 L507
       122          1 29-APR-99 M311
       122          2 24-JUL-99 L211
```

```
122        3 21-MAY-99 L507
122        4 04-MAY-99 L210
122        5 15-MAY-99 L507
124        1 14-JUL-99 M500
124        2 24-JUL-99 H310
124        3 09-APR-99 L214
124        4 07-MAY-99 L210
125        1 22-MAY-99 L509
125        2 24-JUL-99 L509
125        3 09-APR-99 L214
125        4 03-MAY-99 L211
125        6 11-JUN-99 L507
130        1 14-JUL-99 L507
130        2 15-APR-99 L214
130        3 24-APR-99 L509
130        4 03-MAY-99 L509
132        1 21-MAY-99 L509
132        3 09-JUN-99 L509
134        1 16-APR-99 L509
134        2 10-JUN-99 L509
134        3 08-APR-00 L509
135        1 16-MAY-99 L509
135        2 02-JUN-99 L214
135        3 15-APR-99 L509
135        4 07-MAY-99 M200
140        1 14-JUL-99 L509
140        2 02-JUN-99 L210
140        3 09-MAY-99 L507
142        1 14-JUL-99 L211
142        2 10-JUN-99 L214
142        3 09-APR-99 L507
144        2 15-APR-99 L214
145        1 14-JUL-99 L214
145        3 09-MAY-99 L210
146        1 29-APR-99 L509
146        2 24-JUL-99 L507
147        1 14-APR-99 L509
204        1 14-APR-99 L210
210        1 07-MAY-99 L507
220        1 15-APR-99 L509
230        1 07-MAY-99 L500
230        2 09-JUN-99 L214
240        1 16-APR-99 L509
240        2 24-MAY-99 L214
310        1 29-APR-99 L507
330        1 14-JUL-99 L511
350        1 09-MAY-99 L509
350        2 03-JUN-99 L214
350        3 14-APR-99 L509
```

```
420           1 07-MAY-99 M311
430             To Be Determined
450           1 14-APR-99 L507
```

80 rows selected.

As you can see, only two courses are not currently being taught (in boldface), and for those courses, no start date/time values are currently stored. Hence, the phrase "To Be Determined" is returned from your nested DECODE statement.

CHAPTER 8

BUILDING THE APP

The answers to these projects can be found at the companion Web site to this book, located at http://www.phptr.com/boardman/.

Visit the Web site periodically to share and discuss your answers with other readers.

In the following chapter, "PL/SQL Review," and subsequent chapters, like Chapter 12, "Working With PL/SQL Server Pages: PSPs," you apply your knowledge of working with the NVL and DECODE substitution functions. The next chapter discusses the CASE statement. You may wish to substitute the CASE statement for functionality you would otherwise obtain with NVL and DECODE.

C H A P T E R   9

PL/SQL REVIEW

CHAPTER OBJECTIVES

In this chapter, you will review:

This book assumes that you have mastered the basic concepts of Oracle SQL and PL/SQL. If you need further review, then it is recommended that you read the two companion books in this series: *Oracle SQL Interactive Workbook,* by Alice Rischert, and *Oracle PL/SQL Interactive Workbook,* by Ben Rosenzweig and Elena Silvestrova.

The application that you build for this book is done using PL/SQL. For this reason, this chapter presents a brief review of PL/SQL. At the end of this chapter, you create a PL/SQL procedure to calculate the final grade for a student. Then you put this procedure into a package, and add a package variable and package PL/SQL table to be used by procedures in the subsequent chapters.

U N I T 9 . 1

BASIC CONCEPTS OF PL/SQL

INTRODUCTION TO PL/SQL

When Oracle applications are built using multitiered architecture, the Oracle database resides on a database server. The program that makes requests against this database resides on a client machine. This program can be written in C, Java, or PL/SQL. PL/SQL is closely integrated with Oracle SQL, but it adds constructs that are not native to Oracle SQL. PL/SQL is a procedural language that allows you to code a series of steps or procedures. It allows you to control the flow of logic by such constructs as IF-THEN-ELSE statements, loops, and so on. PL/SQL, like any other programming language, has syntax and rules that determine how programming statements work together.

PL/SQL allows you to send an entire block of statements to the server for processing rather than just one SQL statement at a time. Stored procedures are compiled once and stored in executable form in the database, so the calls are quick and efficient. Network traffic is reduced, as there is only one call to the stored procedure. With stored procedures, you can split up logic between the client and the server.

It is important for you to realize that PL/SQL is not a standalone programming language. PL/SQL is a part of the Oracle Relational Database Management System (RDBMS). The RDBMS server contains a PL/SQL processing engine. Many of the components of the Oracle 9iAS, housed on the middle tier, also have their own PL/SQL engine. This means that PL/SQL processing can occur on either the application server or the database server. The application that you build in this book uses only the PL/SQL engine on the database server. The PL/SQL engine processes and executes any PL/SQL statements and sends any SQL statements to the SQL statement processor. The SQL statement processor is always located on the Oracle database server.

PL/SQL BLOCK STRUCTURE

A block is the most basic unit in PL/SQL. All PL/SQL statements are combined into blocks. These blocks can also be nested, one within the other. Usually, PL/SQL blocks combine statements that represent a single logical task. Therefore, different tasks within a single program can be separated into blocks. As a result, it is easier to understand and maintain the logic of the program. PL/SQL blocks can be divided into two groups: named and anonymous. Named blocks are used when creating subroutines. These subroutines are procedures, functions, and packages. The subroutines can then be stored in the database and referenced by their names later on. Anonymous blocks are also used for subroutines such as procedures and functions. However, these subroutines exist for only as long as they are executing, and therefore cannot be referenced outside of their block scope. Anonymous PL/SQL blocks, you have probably guessed, do not have names. As a result, they cannot be stored in the database and referenced later. You can use an anonymous block as a means to test pieces of your code, or to test calling stored subroutines.

PL/SQL blocks contain three sections: a *declaration* section, an *executable* section, and an *exception-handling* section, followed by the "END" keyword. The executable section is the only mandatory section of the block. Both the declaration and exception-handling sections are optional. As a result, a PL/SQL block has the following structure:

```
DECLARE
    Declaration statements
BEGIN
    Executable statements
EXCEPTION
    Exception-handling statements
END;
```

Blocks can be nested within each other. For example, an exception handler can have a complete block just to handle one exception.

ANONYMOUS BLOCK

Anonymous blocks are very much the same as modules, which will be explained at the end of this chapter, except anonymous blocks do not have headers. However, there are other important distinctions. As the name implies, anonymous blocks have no name and, thus, cannot be called by another block. They are not stored in the database and must be compiled, then run each time the script is loaded.

DECLARATION SECTION

The declaration section is the first section of a PL/SQL block. It contains definitions of PL/SQL identifiers such as variables, constants, cursors, and so on.

■ *FOR EXAMPLE*

```
DECLARE
    v_last_name VARCHAR2(25);
    v_first_name student.first_name%TYPE;
    v_counter NUMBER := 0;
    v_discount CONSTANT NUMBER := 0.95;
    CURSOR c_zipcodes is
            SELECT city, state, zip
            FROM zipcode;
BEGIN
```

This example illustrates a declaration section of an anonymous PL/SQL block. It begins with the keyword DECLARE and contains three variable declarations, one constant declaration, and one cursor declaration. The names of the variables are followed by their datatype and size. The variable v_first_name has an anchored datatype, meaning that its datatype is defined by referencing an object in the database. The name of the constant, v_discount, is followed by its datatype and a value assigned to it. Notice that a semicolon terminates each declaration. The cursor declaration is the SELECT statement for the cursor ending with a semicolon.

The datatype that you assign to a variable can be based on a database object. This is called an anchored (or strong-typed) declaration since the variable's datatype is dependent on that of the underlying object. It is wise to make use of this when possible so that you do not have to update your PL/SQL procedures if the datatypes of base objects change.

```
Syntax:   <variable_name> <type attribute>%TYPE
v_first_name student.first_name%TYPE;
```

The type is a direct reference to a database column. In the example above the variable v_first_name is assigned the same data type as the first_name column in the student table.

In PL/SQL, variables must be declared in order to be referenced. This is done in the initial declarative section of a PL/SQL block. Remember that each declaration must be terminated with a semicolon. Variables can be assigned using the assignment operator ':=', a colon followed by an equals sign. If you declare a numeric constant, it will retain the same value throughout the block; in order to do this, you must give it a value at declaration.

```
gc_student_id  CONSTANT  varchar2(8)  := 125;
```

A variable that has been declared in the declaration section of a PL/SQL block can later, in the executable section, be given a value with a SELECT statement. The correct syntax is as follows:

```
SELECT item_name
   INTO variable_name
   FROM table_name;
```

It is important to note that any single-row SQL function can be performed on the item to give the variable a calculated value. SELECT statements that return no rows or multiple rows will cause an error to occur, which can be trapped by using an exception.

EXECUTABLE SECTION

The executable section is the next section of a PL/SQL block. This section contains executable statements that allow you to manipulate the variables that have been declared in the declaration section.

■ FOR EXAMPLE

```
BEGIN
   SELECT last_name, first_name
     INTO v_last_name, v_first_name
     FROM student
    WHERE student_id = 123;
   DBMS_OUTPUT.PUT_LINE
       ('Student name: '|| v_last_name
       ||', '||v_first_name);
END;
```

This example illustrates the executable section of a PL/SQL block. It begins with the keyword BEGIN and contains a SELECT statement from the STUDENT table. Students' first and last names for student ID 123 are selected into two variables: v_first_name and v_last_name. Then the values of the variables, v_first_name and v_last_name, are displayed on the screen with the help of the DBMS_OUTPUT.PUT_LINE function. The end of the executable section of this block is marked by the keyword END. The executable section of any PL/SQL block always begins with the keywords BEGIN and END (END always comes at the end of the block, not necessarily at the end of the executable section).

In every program you write, you need to make decisions. For example, suppose that at the beginning of a new school year, the cost for courses will increase. The administration may have decided to increase only certain classes and keep the intro classes at the same cost. In order to accomplish this the program will need conditional control. Conditional control allows you to control the flow of execution of the program based on a condition. In programming terms, it means that the statements in the program are not executed sequentially. Rather, one group of statements, or another will be executed depending on how the condition is evaluated.

In PL/SQL, there are two types of conditional controls: IF statement and ELSIF statement. You now explore both types of conditional controls and how these types can be nested one inside of another.

An IF statement has two forms: IF-THEN and IF-THEN-ELSE. An IF-THEN statement allows you to specify only one group of actions to take. In other words, this group of actions is taken only when a condition evaluates to TRUE. An IF-THEN-ELSE statement allows you to specify two groups of actions, and the second group of actions is taken when a condition evaluates to FALSE.

IF-THEN STATEMENT

An IF-THEN statement is the most basic kind of conditional control and has the following structure:

```
IF CONDITION
THEN
    STATEMENT 1;
    ...
    STATEMENT N;
END IF;
```

The reserved word IF marks the beginning of the IF statement. Statements 1 through N are a sequence of executable statements that consist of one or more of the standard programming structures. In this example the word *CONDITION* between keywords IF and THEN determines whether these statements are executed. END IF is a reserved phrase that indicates the end of the IF-THEN construct.

When an IF-THEN statement is executed, a condition is evaluated to either TRUE or FALSE. If the condition evaluates to TRUE, control is passed to the first executable statement of the IF-THEN construct. If the condition evaluates to FALSE, the control is passed to the first executable statement after the END IF statement.

IF-THEN-ELSE STATEMENT

An IF-THEN statement specifies the sequence of statements to execute only if the condition evaluates to TRUE. When this condition evaluates to FALSE, there is no special action to take except to proceed with execution of the program after the end of the IF-THEN statement.

An IF-THEN-ELSE statement enables you to specify two groups of statements. One group of statements is executed when the condition evaluates to TRUE. Another group of statements is executed when the condition evaluates to FALSE. This is indicated as follows:

```
IF CONDITION
THEN
    STATEMENT 1;
ELSE
    STATEMENT 2;
END IF;
STATEMENT 3;
```

When *CONDITION* evaluates to TRUE, control is passed to STATEMENT 1, and when *CONDITION* evaluates to FALSE, control is passed to STATEMENT 2. After the IF-THEN-ELSE construct has completed, STATEMENT 3 is executed.

An ELSIF statement has the following structure:

```
IF CONDITION 1
THEN
    STATEMENT 1;
ELSIF CONDITION 2
THEN
    STATEMENT 2;
ELSIF CONDITION 3
THEN
    STATEMENT 3;
ELSE
    STATEMENT N;
END IF;
```

The reserved word IF marks the beginning of an ELSIF construct. In this example the words *CONDITION 1* through *CONDITION 3 (there is no CONDITION N)* are a sequence of the conditions that evaluate to TRUE or FALSE. These conditions are mutually exclusive. In other words, if *CONDITION 1* evaluates to TRUE, STATEMENT 1 is executed, and control is passed to the first executable statement after the reserved phrase END IF. The rest of the ELSIF construct is ignored. When *CONDITION 1* evaluates to FALSE, the control is passed to the ELSIF part, *CONDITION 2* is evaluated, and so forth. If none of the specified conditions yield TRUE, the control is passed to the ELSE part of the ELSIF construct. An ELSIF statement can contain any number of ELSIF clauses.

You have encountered different types of conditional controls: IF-THEN statement, IF-THEN-ELSE statement, and ELSIF statement. These types of conditional controls can be nested inside of one another, for example, an IF statement can be nested inside an ELSIF statement and vice versa.

CASE STATEMENTS

CASE statements are another type of conditional control. Though they are not new programming constructs, they are new features to the PL/SQL programming language, and they are not supported by PL/SQL in versions of the Oracle database prior to Oracle 9i.

A CASE statement has the following structure:

```
CASE selector
    WHEN EXPRESSION 1 THEN STATEMENT 1;
    WHEN EXPRESSION 2 THEN STATEMENT 2;
    ...
    WHEN EXPRESSION N THEN STATEMENT N;
    ELSE STATEMENT N+1;
END CASE;
```

The reserved word CASE marks the beginning of the CASE statement. A *selector* is a value. Based on the selector, the program determines which WHEN clause should be executed. Each WHEN clause contains an EXPRESSION that is evaluated against the selector, as well as one or more executable statements that are executed if the comparison of the expression with the selector evaluates to TRUE. The ELSE clause is optional and works similar to the ELSE clause used in an IF-THEN-ELSE statement. END CASE is a reserved phrase that indicates the end of the CASE statement. The selector is evaluated only once. The WHEN clauses are evaluated sequentially. The value of an expression is compared to the value of the selector. If they are equal, the statement associated with a particular WHEN clause is executed, and subsequent WHEN clauses are not evaluated. If no expression matches the value of the selector, the ELSE clause is executed.

Here is an example of an IF-THEN-ELSE statement that is later converted into a CASE statement:

■ FOR EXAMPLE

```
DECLARE
    v_num NUMBER := &sv_user_num;
BEGIN
    -- test if the number provided by the user is even
    IF MOD(v_num,2) = 0  THEN
        DBMS_OUTPUT.PUT_LINE (v_num||' is even number');
    ELSE
        DBMS_OUTPUT.PUT_LINE (v_num||' is odd number');
    END IF;
    DBMS_OUTPUT.PUT_LINE ('Done');
END;
```

This anonymous block makes use of a substitution variable. This is done by initializing the variable to a value with an ampersand (&) symbol and a variable name. In SQL*Plus the user will be prompted for the value of the variable name given after the ampersand. The user will be prompted to enter the value and once it is given the initial variable will be given the value the user entered.

The use of substitution variables is covered in Oracle SQL Interactive Workbook by Alice Rishert and Oracle PL/SQL Interactive Workbook by Benjamin Rosenzweig and Elena Silvestrova. If this topic or any topic in this chapter is not clear to you, refer to these books for more detailed information.

Consider the new version of the same example with the CASE statement instead of the IF-THEN-ELSE statement:

■ FOR EXAMPLE

```
DECLARE
    v_num NUMBER := &sv_user_num;
    v_num_flag NUMBER;
BEGIN
    v_num_flag := MOD(v_num,2);
    -- test if the number provided by the user is even
    CASE v_num_flag
        WHEN 0 THEN
            DBMS_OUTPUT.PUT_LINE
                (v_num||' is even number');
        ELSE
            DBMS_OUTPUT.PUT_LINE (v_num||' is odd number');
    END CASE;
    DBMS_OUTPUT.PUT_LINE ('Done');
END;
```

In this example, the variable v_num_flag is used as a selector for the CASE statement. If the MOD function returns a value of zero, then the value of v_num is an even number, otherwise it is an odd number.

SEARCHED CASE STATEMENTS   A searched CASE statement has search conditions that yield Boolean values: TRUE, FALSE, or NULL. When a particular search condition evaluates to TRUE, the group of statements associated with this condition is executed. This is indicated as follows:

```
CASE
    WHEN SEARCH CONDITION 1 THEN STATEMENT 1;
    WHEN SEARCH CONDITION 2 THEN STATEMENT 2;
    ...
    WHEN SEARCH CONDITION N THEN STATEMENT N;
    ELSE STATEMENT N+1;
END CASE;
```

When a search condition evaluates to TRUE, the control is passed to the statement associated with it. If no search condition yields TRUE, then statements associated with the ELSE clause are executed. Consider a modified version of the example shown earlier in this chapter.

■ *FOR EXAMPLE*

```
DECLARE
    v_num NUMBER := &sv_user_num;
BEGIN
    -- test if the number provided by the user is even
    CASE
        WHEN MOD(v_num,2) = 0 THEN
            DBMS_OUTPUT.PUT_LINE
                (v_num||' is even number');
        ELSE
            DBMS_OUTPUT.PUT_LINE (v_num||' is odd number');
    END CASE;
    DBMS_OUTPUT.PUT_LINE ('Done');
END;
```

In the earlier example, an additional variable, v_num_flag, was used as a selector, and the result of the MOD function (performed upon the v_num variable) was assigned to it. The value of the selector was then compared to the value of the expression. In this example, you are using a searched CASE statement, so there is no selector present. The variable v_num is used as part of the search condition, so there is no need to declare the extra variable, v_num_flag. This example produces the same output as that of the example shown earlier when the same value is assigned to v_num.

LOOPS

In PL/SQL, there are four types of loops: simple loops, WHILE loops, numeric FOR loops, and cursor FOR loops. A simple loop, as you can see from its name, is the most basic kind of loop and has the following structure:

The reserved word LOOP marks the beginning of the simple loop. Statements 1 through N are a sequence of statements that is executed repeatedly. These statements consist of one or more of the standard programming structures. END LOOP is a reserved phrase that indicates the end of the loop construct.

Every time the loop is iterated, a sequence of statements is executed, then control is passed back to the top of the loop. The sequence of statements will be executed an infinite number of times because there is no statement specifying when the loop must terminate. Hence, a simple loop is called an *infinite loop* because there is no means to exit the loop.

As a result, a properly constructed loop needs to have an exit condition that determines when the loop is complete. This exit condition has two forms: *EXIT* and *EXIT WHEN*.

It is important that every LOOP contain a means to exit. If there is no EXIT or counter, your LOOP will go on forever.

EXIT

The EXIT statement causes a loop to terminate when the *EXIT condition* evaluates to TRUE. The EXIT condition is evaluated with the help of an IF statement. When the EXIT condition is evaluated to TRUE, control is passed to the first executable statement after the END LOOP statement. This is shown by the following:

```
LOOP
    STATEMENT 1;
    STATEMENT 2;
    IF CONDITION
    THEN
        EXIT;
    END IF;
END LOOP;
STATEMENT 3;
```

In this example, you can see that after the EXIT condition evaluates to TRUE, control is passed to STATEMENT 3, which is the first executable statement after the END LOOP statement.

The EXIT statement is valid only when placed inside of a loop. When placed outside of a loop, with the intention of exiting the PL/SQL block entirely, EXIT will cause a syntax error. Use the RETURN statement to terminate a PL/SQL block before its normal end is reached, and use EXIT specifically to exit a LOOP.

EXIT WHEN

The EXIT WHEN statement causes a loop to terminate only if the *EXIT WHEN condition* evaluates to TRUE. Control is then passed to the first executable statement after the END LOOP statement. The structure of a loop using an EXIT WHEN clause is as follows:

```
LOOP
    STATEMENT 1;
    STATEMENT 2;
    EXIT WHEN CONDITION;
END LOOP;
STATEMENT 3;
```

During each iteration, the loop executes a sequence of statements. Control is then passed to the EXIT condition of the loop. If the EXIT condition evaluates to FALSE, control is passed to the top of the loop. The sequence of statements will be executed repeatedly until the EXIT condition evaluates to TRUE. When the EXIT condition evaluates to TRUE, the loop is terminated, and control is passed to the next executable statement following the loop. The EXIT condition is included in the body of the loop, between LOOP and END LOOP. Therefore, the decision about loop termination is made inside the body of the loop. *As a result, the body of the loop or a part of it will always be executed at least once. However, the number of iterations of the loop depends on the evaluation of the EXIT condition and is not known until the loop completes.* It is important to note that when the EXIT statement is used without an EXIT condition, the simple loop will execute only once. Consider the following example. The flow of logic for the structure of EXIT and EXIT WHEN statements is the same even though two different forms of EXIT conditions are used. In other words,

```
IF CONDITION
THEN
    EXIT;
END IF;
```

is equivalent to

```
EXIT WHEN CONDITION;
```

WHILE LOOPS

A WHILE loop has the following structure:

```
WHILE CONDITION
LOOP
    STATEMENT 1;
    STATEMENT 2;
    ...
    STATEMENT N;
END LOOP;
```

The reserved word WHILE marks the beginning of a while loop construct. In this example the word *CONDITION* is the *test condition* of the loop that evaluates to TRUE or FALSE. The result of this evaluation determines whether the loop is executed or not. Statements 1 through N are a sequence of statements that is executed repeatedly. The END LOOP is a reserved phrase that indicates the end of the loop construct. The test condition in a while loop is evaluated prior to each iteration of the loop. If the test condition evaluates to TRUE, the sequence of statements is executed, and the control is passed to the top of the loop for the next evaluation of the test condition. If the test condition evaluates to FALSE the loop is terminated and the control is passed to the next executable statement following the loop.

As mentioned earlier, before the body of the loop can be executed, the test condition must be evaluated. Therefore, the decision whether to execute the statements in the body of the loop is made prior to entering the loop. As a result, the loop will not be executed at all if the first evaluation of the test condition yields FALSE.

While the test condition of the loop must evaluate to TRUE at least once for the statements in the loop to execute, it is important to ensure that the test condition will eventually evaluate to FALSE as well. Otherwise, the WHILE loop will execute continually.

Check that loops will always end!

To test and troubleshoot loops, figure out what will happen on the first iteration, the last iteration, the second-to-last iteration—and what will occur if there are no trips through the loop.

■ *FOR EXAMPLE*

```
DECLARE
    v_counter NUMBER := 1;
BEGIN
    WHILE v_counter < 5
    LOOP
        DBMS_OUTPUT.PUT_LINE('v_counter = '||v_counter);
        -- decrement the value of v_counter by one
        v_counter := v_counter - 1;
    END LOOP;
END;
```

This is an example of what you should not create: the infinite WHILE loop. The test condition always evaluates to TRUE because the value of v_counter is decremented by one, and is therefore always less than five. It is important to note that Boolean expressions can be used to determine when the loop should terminate as well. When using a Boolean expression as a test condition for a loop, you must make sure that a different value is eventually assigned to the Boolean variable in order to exit the loop. Otherwise, the loop is infinite.

NUMERIC FOR LOOPS

A numeric FOR loop is called numeric because it requires an integer as its terminating value. Its structure is as follows:

```
FOR loop_counter IN[REVERSE] lower_limit..upper_limit
LOOP
    STATEMENT 1;
    STATEMENT 2;
    ...
    STATEMENT N;
END LOOP;
```

The reserved word FOR marks the beginning of a FOR loop construct. The variable loop_counter is an implicitly defined index variable. So, there is no need to define loop_counter in the declaration section of a PL/SQL block. This variable is defined by the loop construct. *Lower_limit* and *upper_limit* are two integer numbers that define the number of iterations for the loop. The values of the lower_limit and upper_limit are evaluated once, for the first iteration of the loop. At this point, it is determined how many times the loop will iterate. Statements 1 through N are a sequence of statements that is executed repeatedly. END LOOP is a reserved phrase that marks the end of the loop construct.

The reserved word IN or IN REVERSE must be present when defining the loop. If the REVERSE keyword is used, the loop counter will iterate from upper limit to lower limit. However, the syntax for the limit specification does not change. The lower limit is always referenced first.

CURSORS

Cursors are memory areas that allow you to allocate an area of memory and access the information retrieved from a SQL statement. For example, you use a cursor to operate on a set of rows from the STUDENT table for those students taking a particular course (having associated entries in the ENROLLMENT table).

The process of working with an explicit cursor consists of the following steps:

1. DECLARING the cursor. This initializes the cursor into memory.
2. OPENING the cursor. The previously declared cursor can now be opened and memory is allotted.
3. FETCHING the cursor. Previously declared and opened cursor can now retrieve data; this is the process of fetching the cursor.
4. CLOSING the cursor. Previously declared, the opened and fetched cursor must now be closed to release memory allocation.

DECLARING A CURSOR

Declaring a cursor defines the name of the cursor and associates it with a SELECT statement. The first step is to declare the cursor with the following syntax:

```
CURSOR c_cursor_name IS select statement;
```

■ *FOR EXAMPLE*

This is a PL/SQL anonymous block that demonstrates the full use of a cursor. The cursor c_course is declared as a SELECT statement of the first five rows in the course table. In the executable section of the block the cursor is opened, fetched, and finally closed.

```
SET SERVEROUTPUT ON
DECLARE
   CURSOR c_course IS
      SELECT course_no, description
         FROM course
        WHERE rownum <= 5;
   vr_course c_course%ROWTYPE;
BEGIN
   OPEN c_course;
   LOOP
      FETCH c_course INTO vr_course;
      EXIT WHEN c_course%NOTFOUND;
      DBMS_OUTPUT.PUT_LINE(
         vr_course.course_no||
         ' '||vr_course.description);
   END LOOP;
   CLOSE c_course;
END;
```

RECORD TYPES

A record is a composite data structure, which means that it is composed of more than one element. Records are very much like a row of a database table, but each element of the record does not stand on its own. PL/SQL supports three kinds of records: (1) table-based, (2) cursor-based, and (3) programmer-defined.

A table-based record is one whose structure is drawn from the list of columns in the table. A cursor-based record is one whose structure matches the elements of a predefined cursor. To create a table-based or cursor-based record use the %ROW-TYPE attribute. For example:

```
<record_name>    <table_name or cursor_name>%ROWTYPE
```

CURSOR FOR LOOPS

There is an alternative method for handling cursors. It is an additional type of LOOP, called the Cursor FOR LOOP because of the simplified syntax that is used. When using the Cursor FOR LOOP, the processes of opening, fetching, and closing are implicitly handled. This makes the blocks much simpler to code and easier to maintain. The Cursor FOR LOOP specifies a sequence of statements to be repeated once for each row returned by the Cursor. Use the cursor FOR LOOP if you need to

FETCH and PROCESS each and every record from a cursor. You will not have to explicitly OPEN, FETCH, and CLOSE a Cursor FOR LOOP. Also, you will not have to declare a record type for the cursor; this is done implicitly in a Cursor FOR LOOP. For these reasons, Cursor FOR LOOPS are more common since the code is tighter.

If no records are retrieved by the cursor, then the loop in a cursor for loop will not be executed at all. This means that you cannot use cursor attributes. Account for this possibility in your code.

■ FOR EXAMPLE

In this example you will first create a table to be used in the next PL/SQL block.

```
create table table_log (description VARCHAR2(250));
```

Now that you have created the table table_log you can run the following code:

```
DECLARE
   CURSOR c_student IS
      SELECT student_id, last_name, first_name
        FROM student
       WHERE student_id < 110;
BEGIN
   FOR r_student IN c_student
   LOOP
      INSERT INTO table_log
         VALUES(r_student.last_name);
   END LOOP;
END;
```

USING PARAMETERS IN CURSORS

A cursor can be declared with parameters. This enables a cursor to generate a specific result set, which is on the one hand narrow but on the other hand, reusable. A cursor of all the data from the ZIPCODE table may be very useful, but it would be more useful for certain data processing if it could retrieve information for a specific U.S. state. Up to now, you know how to create such a cursor. But, wouldn't it be more useful if you could create a cursor that could accept a parameter for a state, and then retrieve only that state's records?

■ FOR EXAMPLE

```
CURSOR c_zip (p_state IN zipcode.state%TYPE) IS
   SELECT zip, city, state
     FROM zipcode
    WHERE state = p_state;
```

The main points to keep in mind for parameters in cursors are as follows:

- Cursor parameters make the cursor more reusable.
- Cursor parameters can be assigned default values.
- The scope of the cursor parameters is local to the cursor.
- The mode of the parameters can only be IN.

When a cursor has been declared as taking a parameter, it must be called with a value for that parameter. The c_zip cursor that was just declared is called as follows:

```
OPEN c_zip (parameter_value)
```

The same cursor could be opened with a Cursor FOR loop as follows:

```
FOR r_zip IN c_zip('NY')
LOOP  ...
```

Cursor loops can be nested inside each other. Although this may sound complex, it is really just a loop inside a loop. If you have one parent cursor and two child cursors, then each time the parent cursor makes a single loop, it will loop through each child cursor as many times as necessary, and then begin a second round. In the following two examples, you encounter a nested cursor with a single child cursor. The child cursor takes an IN parameter from one of the values in the parent cursor.

■ FOR EXAMPLE

```
SET SERVEROUTPUT ON SIZE 1000000
  1   DECLARE
  2      v_course_flag CHAR;
  3      CURSOR c_instructor IS
  4         SELECT instructor_id, first_name, last_name
  5           FROM instructor;
  6      CURSOR c_course
  7         (i_instructor_id IN instructor.instructor_id%TYPE) IS
  8         SELECT c.course_no course_no,
  9                c.description  description
 10           FROM course c, section s
 11          WHERE c.course_no = s.course_no
 12          AND   s.instructor_id = i_instructor_id;
 13   BEGIN
 14     FOR r_instructor IN c_instructor
 15     LOOP
 16        v_course_flag := 'N';
 17        DBMS_OUTPUT.PUT_LINE(CHR(10));
 18 DBMS_OUTPUT.PUT_LINE(r_instructor.first_name||'  '||
 19            r_instructor.last_name);
```

UNIT
9.1

```
20      FOR r_course in c_course
21           (r_instructor.instructor_id)
22      LOOP
23         DBMS_OUTPUT.PUT_LINE(
24             r_course.course_no||
25             ' '||r_course.description);
26         v_course_flag := 'Y';
27      END LOOP;
28      IF v_course_flag = 'N'
29         THEN
30         DBMS_OUTPUT.PUT_LINE('There are no courses taught by '||
31         'this instructor'||chr(10));
32      END IF;
33   END LOOP;
34  END;
```

There are two cursors in the previous example. The first is a cursor of instructors and the second cursor is a list of courses that each instructor teaches. The c_instructor cursor is declared in lines 3–5, and it is opened in line 14. First it prints the instructor's name using DBMS_OUTPUT.PUT_LINE in lines 17–19. It then opens the c_course cursor in line 20. The instructor_id is passed as an IN parameter so that the c_course cursor is acquiring only the courses that are taught by the particular instructor in the parent cursor. The DBMS_OUTPUT.PUT_LINE in lines 23–25 is executed once for each iteration of the child loop, producing a line of output for each course. The DBMS_OUTPUT.PUT_LINE statement in lines 30–31 only executes if the inner loop does not execute. This is accomplished by using a variable, v_course_flag. The reason that cursor attributes cannot be used here is because the cursors are opened and closed with a FOR loop. When the child cursor is passed a parameter that will result in no rows returned, the cursor never opens. This means the cursor attributes cannot be used. The v_course_flag variable is set to "N" in the beginning of the parent loop. If the child loop executes at least once, the variable is set to "Y." After the child loop has closed, a check is made, with an IF statement, to determine the value of the variable. If it is still "N," then it can be safely concluded that the inner loop did not process. This then allows the last DBMS_OUTPUT.PUT_LINE statement to execute.

 Sometimes when DBMS_OUTPUT.PUT_LINE is about to generate a lot of output, your SQL*Plus session will generate the dreaded error ORA-20000: ORU-10027: buffer overflow, limit of 2000 bytes. *You need to increase the buffer in one of the following ways:*

- *At the SQL*PLUS prompt, type* SET SERVEROUTPUT ON SIZE n *where n is an integer between 2,000 and 1,000,000.*
- *Inside the PL/SQL block, type DBMS_OUTPUT.ENABLE(n) where n is an integer between 2,000 and 1,000,000.*

EXCEPTION-HANDLING SECTION

The exception-handling section is the last section of a PL/SQL block. This section contains statements that are executed when a runtime error occurs within the block. Runtime errors occur while the program is running and cannot be detected by the PL/SQL compiler. Once a runtime error occurs, the control is passed to the exception-handling section of the block. The error is then evaluated, and a specific exception is raised or executed. This is best illustrated by the example below.

■ *FOR EXAMPLE*

```
SET SERVEROUTPUT ON
DECLARE
    v_first_name student.first_name%TYPE;
    v_last_name  student.last_name%TYPE;
 BEGIN
    SELECT first_name, last_name
      INTO v_first_name, v_last_name
      FROM student
     WHERE student_id = 999;
    DBMS_OUTPUT.PUT_LINE
       ('Student name: '||v_first_name||' '||
         v_last_name);
EXCEPTION
    WHEN NO_DATA_FOUND THEN
        DBMS_OUTPUT.PUT_LINE
('There is no student with a student ID value of 999.');
END;
```

This shows the exception-handling section of the PL/SQL block. It begins with the keyword EXCEPTION. The WHEN clause evaluates which exception must be raised. In this example, there is only one exception called NO_DATA_FOUND, and it is raised when the SELECT statement executed in the executable section does not return any rows. NO_DATA_FOUND is a "built-in" exception supplied by Oracle as part of PL/SQL. If there is no record for student ID 999 in the STUDENT table, the control is passed to the exception-handling section, the exception is recognized to be a NO_DATA_FOUND exception, and the DBMS_OUTPUT.PUT_LINE function (or whatever code has been written to handle this exception) is executed.

You have seen examples of the declaration section, the executable section, and the exception-handling section, and an overview of how these can be combined into a single PL/SQL block. The declaration section holds definitions of PL/SQL identifiers such as variables, constants, cursors, and so on. The declaration section starts with the keyword DECLARE. This declaration section:

```
DECLARE
    v_name VARCHAR2(50);
    v_total NUMBER;
```

contains definitions of two variables, v_name and v_total.

The executable section holds executable statements. It starts with the keyword BEGIN and ends with the keyword END (the block, not the executable section, ends with END).

An exception-handling section allows a program to execute to completion, instead of terminating prematurely. Another advantage offered by the exception-handling section is isolation of error-handling routines. In other words, all error-processing code for a specific block is located in the single section. As a result, the logic of the program becomes easier to follow and understand. Finally, adding an exception-handling section enables event-driven processing of errors. In case of a specific exception event, the exception-handling section is executed.

When a built-in exception occurs, it is said to be raised implicitly. In other words, if a program breaks an Oracle rule, the control is passed to the exception-handling section of the block. At this point, the error-processing statements are executed. After the exception-handling section of the block has executed, the block terminates. Control will not return back to the executable section of the block.

You have probably noticed that, while every Oracle runtime error has a number associated with it, it must be recognized by its name in the exception-handling section. One error that you will get if your code has a statement where a number is divided by zero is:

```
ORA-01476: divisor is equal to zero
```

The "ORA-01476" part of this error message is an Oracle error number. You can find more details about the error by reading your Oracle software documentation. This error number refers to the error named ZERO_DIVIDE. So, some common Oracle runtime errors are predefined in the PL/SQL language as exceptions.

You can get more information about the error message you receive by going to one of two Oracle Web sites. The first one is http://technet. oracle.com. It is a free site. It requires a registration but there is no charge for the registration. The other site is the main Oracle Support site, http://metalink.oracle.com. This site is only available to users with valid Oracle licenses. You are required to provide your CSI number in order to use the Metalink site.

PREDEFINED EXCEPTIONS   The list shown below explains some commonly used predefined exceptions and how they are raised:

NO_DATA_FOUND. This exception is raised when a SELECT INTO statement, which makes no calls to group functions, such as SUM or COUNT, does not return any rows. For example, you issue a SELECT INTO statement against the STUDENT table where a student ID value equals 101. If there is no record in the STUDENT table that meets this criteria (student ID equals 101), the NO_DATA_FOUND exception is raised.

When a SELECT INTO statement calls a group function, such as COUNT, the result set is never empty. It is always some value, or NULL. When used in the SELECT INTO statement against the STUDENT table for the value of student ID, 999, the function COUNT will return zero. Hence, any SELECT statement that calls any group function will never raise the NO_DATA_FOUND exception.

TOO_MANY_ROWS. This exception is raised when a SELECT INTO statement returns more than one row. By definition, a SELECT INTO statement can return only a single row. If a SELECT INTO statement returns more than one row, the definition of the SELECT INTO statement is violated. This causes the TOO_MANY_ROWS exception to be raised.

For example, you issue a SELECT INTO statement against the STUDENT table for a specific zipcode. There is a big chance that this SELECT statement will return more than one row because many students may live in the same zipcode area.

ZERO_DIVIDE. This exception is raised when a division operation is performed in the program, and a divisor is equal to zero.

LOGIN_DENIED. This exception is raised when a user is trying to login to Oracle with an invalid username or password.

PROGRAM_ERROR. This exception is raised when a PL/SQL program has an internal problem.

VALUE_ERROR. This exception is raised when a conversion or size mismatch error occurs. For example, you select a student's last name into a variable that has been defined as VARCHAR2(5). If the selected student's last name contains more than five characters, the VALUE_ERROR exception is raised.

DUP_VAL_ON_INDEX. This exception is raised when a program tries to store a duplicate value in the column or columns that have a unique index defined on them. For example, you are trying to insert a record into the SECTION table for the course number "QC2203," section number "1." If a record for the given course and section number already exists in the SECTION table, the DUP_VAL_ON_INDEX exception is raised because these columns have a unique index defined on them.

OTHERS. This is a catch-all exception. It will be raised for any Oracle error where you are not using the specific error handler for that Oracle error.

USE USER-DEFINED EXCEPTIONS   Often in your programs you may need to handle problems that are specific to the program you write. For example, your program asks a user to enter a value for student ID. This value is then assigned to the variable v_student_id that is used later in the program. Generally, you want a positive number for an ID. By mistake, the user enters a negative number. However, no error has occurred because student ID has been defined as a number, and the user has supplied a legitimate numeric value. Therefore, you may want to implement your own exception to handle this situation. The steps involved in using your user-defined exceptions are as follows:

Step 1: Declare in Declaration section

Step 2: State the condition in Executable section

Step 3: Specify/raise in the Exception section

This type of an exception is called a user-defined exception because it is defined by the programmer. As a result, before the exception can be used, it must be declared. A user-defined exception is declared in the declarative part of a PL/SQL block, as shown below:

```
DECLARE
  exception_name EXCEPTION;
```

Notice this declaration looks similar to the variable declaration. You specify an exception name followed by the keyword EXCEPTION. Consider the following code fragment.

■ FOR EXAMPLE

```
DECLARE
    e_invalid_id EXCEPTION;
```

In the example, the name of the exception is prefixed by the letter *e*. This is not a required syntax; rather, it is a naming convention. Such conventions help you to differentiate among variable names and exception names.

Once an exception has been declared, the executable statements associated with this exception are specified in the exception-handling section of the block. The format of the exception-handling section is the same as it is for built-in exceptions. Consider the example shown below.

■ FOR EXAMPLE

```
DECLARE
    e_invalid_id EXCEPTION;
BEGIN
    ...
EXCEPTION
    WHEN e_invalid_id
    THEN
        DBMS_OUTPUT.PUT_LINE
            ('An id cannot be negative');
END;
```

You already know that built-in exceptions are raised implicitly. In other words, when a certain error occurs, a built-in exception associated with this error is raised. Of course, you are assuming that you have included this exception in the exception-handling section of your program. For example, the TOO_MANY_ ROWS exception is raised when a SELECT INTO statement returns multiple rows. A user-defined exception must be raised explicitly with the keyword RAISE. In other words, you need to specify in your program under which circumstances an exception must be raised, as shown below:

```
DECLARE
    exception_name EXCEPTION;
BEGIN
    IF CONDITION
    THEN
        RAISE exception_name;
    ELSE
    END IF;
EXCEPTION
    WHEN exception_name
    THEN
        ERROR-PROCESSING STATEMENTS;
END;
```

In the structure shown above, the circumstances under which a user-defined exception must be raised are determined with the help of the IF-THEN-ELSE statement. If *CONDITION* evaluates to TRUE, a user-defined exception is raised. If *CONDITION* evaluates to FALSE, the program proceeds with its normal execution. In other words, the statements associated with the ELSE part of the IF-THEN-ELSE statement are executed. Any form of the IF statement can be used to check when a user-defined exception must be raised.

UNIT 9.2

STORED PROCEDURES

MODULAR CODE

Modular code is a methodology to build a program from distinct parts (modules), each of which performs a specific function or task toward the final objective of the program. Once a program, or code module, is stored on the database server, it becomes a database object, or subprogram, that is available to other program units for repeated execution. In order to save code into the database, the source code needs to be sent to the server so that it can be compiled and stored in the database.

BENEFITS OF MODULAR CODE

A PL/SQL module is any complete logical unit of work. There are four types of PL/SQL modules: 1) anonymous blocks that are run with a text script (this is the type this chapter has illustrated thus far), 2) procedures, 3) functions, and 4) packages.

There are several main benefits to using modular code: 1) it is more reusable, 2) it is more manageable, and 3) it is easier to maintain.

You create a procedure either in SQL*Plus or in one of the many tools for creating and debugging stored PL/SQL code. If you are using SQL*Plus you will need to write your code in a text editor and then run it at the SQL*Plus prompt.

BLOCK STRUCTURE

The block structure is common for all the module types. The block begins with a <u>Header</u> (for named blocks only), which consists of 1) the name of the module, and 2) a Parameter list (if used).

The *Declaration* section consists of variables, cursors, and subblocks that are needed in the following *Executable and (optional) Exception* sections.

The main part of the module is the *Execution* section where all the calculations and processing are performed. This section contains executable code such as IF – THEN – ELSE, LOOPS, calls to other PL/SQL modules, and so on.

The last section of the module is an optional exception handler, which is where the code to handle exceptions is placed.

PROCEDURES

A procedure is a module performing one or more actions; it does not need to return any values. The syntax for creating a procedure is as follows:

```
CREATE OR REPLACE PROCEDURE name
   [(parameter[, parameter, ...])]
AS
   [local declarations]
BEGIN
    executable statements
[EXCEPTION
    exception handlers]
END [name];
```

■ FOR EXAMPLE

```
SET SERVEROUTPUT ON SIZE 1000000
create or replace
procedure show_zipcode
(p_count  NUMBER)
IS
   v_count NUMBER;
   CURSOR c_zipcode (v_count NUMBER) IS
      SELECT city, state, zip
        FROM zipcode
       WHERE rownum <= v_count;
BEGIN
   FOR rec in c_zipcode(p_count) LOOP
      DBMS_OUTPUT.PUT_LINE
         (rec.city||' '||rec.state||'  '||rec.zip);
   END LOOP;
END;
```

This example could be executed as follows:

```
SET SERVEROUTPUT ON
EXECUTE show_zipcode(5);
```

A procedure may have zero to many parameters. This is covered in the next lab. Every procedure has two parts: 1) the header portion, which comes before the keyword AS (sometimes you will see IS—they are interchangeable) (this contains the procedure name and the parameter list.), 2) the body, which is everything after the AS (or IS) keyword. The words "OR REPLACE" are optional. When the words OR REPLACE are not used in the header of the procedure, in order to change the code in the procedure, it must be dropped first and then recreated. Since it is very common to change the code of the procedure, especially when it is under development, it is strongly recommended that you use the OR REPLACE option.

PARAMETERS

Parameters are the means to pass values to and from the client to the server. These are the values that will be processed or returned via the execution of the procedure. There are three types, or modes, of parameters (Table 9.1): IN, OUT, and IN OUT.

FORMAL AND ACTUAL PARAMETERS

Formal parameters are the names specified within parentheses as part of the header of a module. Actual parameters are the values, expressions specified within parentheses as a parameter list, when a call is made to the module. The formal parameter and the related actual parameter must be of the same or compatible datatypes.

DATATYPES FOR FORMAL PARAMETERS   Formal parameters leave out constraints in datatype. For example, you do not specify a constraint such as VARCHAR2(60). You just say VARCHAR2 against the parameter name in the formal parameter list. The constraint is passed with the value when a call is made.

MATCHING ACTUAL AND FORMAL PARAMETERS   Two methods can be used: positional notation and named notation.

Table 9.1 ■ Parameter Modes

Mode	Description	Usage
IN	Pass a value into the program.	Read-only value Constants, literals, expressions Cannot be changed within program Default mode
OUT	Pass a value back from the program.	Write-only value Cannot assign default values
IN OUT	Pass a value in and also send a value back.	Has to be a variable Value will be read and then written

Positional notation is simply association by position. The order of the parameters used when executing the procedure must match the order in the procedure header exactly.

Named notation is explicit association using the symbol =>

```
Syntax: formal_parameter_name => argument_value
```

In named notation, the order does not matter. If you mix notation, list positional notation before named notation. Note that it makes no difference which style is used; they will both function similarly.

Default values can be used if a call to the program does not include a value in the parameter list.

FUNCTION BASICS

Functions are another type of stored code that is very similar to procedures. The significant difference is that a function is a PL/SQL block that *returns* a single value. Functions can accept one, many, or no parameters, but a function must have a return clause in the executable section of the function. The datatype of the return value must be declared in the header of the function. A function is not a standalone executable in the way that a procedure is. A function must be used in some context; you can think of it as a sentence fragment. A function has output, which needs to be assigned to a variable, or it can be used in a SELECT statement.

FUNCTION SYNTAX

The syntax for creating a function is as follows:

```
CREATE [OR REPLACE] FUNCTION function_name
  (parameter list)
    RETURN datatype
IS
BEGIN
   <body>
   RETURN (return_value);
END;
```

■ *FOR EXAMPLE*

```
CREATE OR REPLACE FUNCTION what_day
(p_day DATE DEFAULT SYSDATE)
RETURN varchar2
is
  v_return varchar2(10);
BEGIN
  SELECT  to_char(p_day, 'DAY')
```

```
       INTO    v_return
       FROM    DUAL;
       RETURN  v_return;
    END;
```

This function can be executed within a SQL statement as follows:

```
    SET SERVEROUTPUT ON
    SELECT first_name,
           last_name,
           what_day(registration_date)
    FROM   student
    WHERE  rownum < 5;
```

The function does not necessarily have any parameters, but it must have a RETURN value declared in the header, and it must return a value for all the varying possible execution streams. The RETURN statement does not have to appear as the last line of the main execution section and there may be more than one RETURN statement (there should be a RETURN statement for each exception).

A function may have IN, OUT, or IN OUT parameters, but you rarely see any type of parameter other than IN, since it is bad programming practice to do otherwise.

UNIT 9.2 EXERCISES

a) Create a procedure named Grade_Calc. This procedure will calculate the final grade for a student making use of the grades that have been entered in the Grade table.

The procedure should take in two parameters; the student_id and the section_id. Additionally, there should be two out parameters. One is the final_Grade and the second is the exit_code. The reason there is an exit code is because this procedure is utilized in Web pages in later chapters. The procedure that generates the Web page needs to know the various errors that can occur and should display different messages depending on what exit code it receives.

This exercise is a good review of data relationships among tables. Even before you begin this exercise, review Appendix B, "The Student Schema," which has an ERD of the Student schema and descriptions of the tables and their columns. When calculating the final grade there are many things that you must keep in mind:

- Each student is enrolled in a course and this information is captured in the enrollment table.

- The table holds the final grade only for each student's enrollment in one section.
- Each section has its own set of elements that are evaluated to make the final grade.
- All grades for these elements (which have been entered, i.e., not NULL) are in the Grade table.
- Every grade has a grade type code. These codes represent the grade type. For example, the grade type QZ stands for quiz. The description for each GRADE_TYPE comes from the GRADE_TYPE table.
- The GRADE_TYPE_WEIGHT table holds key information for this calculation. There is one entry in this table for each grade type that is utilized in a given section (not all grade types exist for each section).
- In the grade_type_weight table the NUMBER_PER_SECTION column lists how many times a grade type should be entered to compute the final grade for a particular student in a particular section of a particular course. This helps you determine if all grades for a given grade type have been entered, or even if too many grades for a given grade type have been entered.
- Also realize that you have to take into consideration the drop_lowest flag. The drop_lowest flag can hold a value of Y, N, or NULL. If the drop_lowest flag is Y [Y=yes, N=no, consider null as N], then you must drop the lowest grade from the grade type when calculating the final grade. The PERCENT_OF_FINAL_GRADE column refers to all the grades for a given grade type. If the homework is 20% and there are five homeworks and a drop_lowest flag, then each remaining homework is worth 5%. When calculating the final grade you should divide the PERCENT_OF_FINAL_GRADE by the NUMBER_PER_SECTION (note that would be NUMBER_PER_SECTION - I if DROP_LOWEST = Y).

Exit codes should be defined as follows:

S = Success, the final grade has been computed. If the grade cannot be computed then the final grade will be NULL and the exit code will be one of the following.

I = Incomplete, not all the required grades have been entered for this student in this section.

T = Too many grades exist for this student. For example, there should only be four homework grades, but instead there are six.

N = No grades have been entered for this student in this section.

E = There was a general computation error (WHEN_OTHERS).

There are many ways that you can handle this. Most likely you will have numerous cursors, loops, and IF/THEN statements to handle all the factors. The exit codes (other than S) could be handled using user-defined exceptions. This way as soon as you reach one of the conditions you can raise an exception and exit with the required code.

b) Write an Anonymous block to test your grade_calc procedure. The block should ask for a STUDENT_ID and SECTION_ID in order to test the procedure. Test your procedure with a number of different STUDENT_ID and SECTION_ID values.

UNIT 9.2 EXERCISE ANSWERS

a) Create a procedure named Grade_Calc. This procedure will calculate the final grade for a student making use of the grades that have been entered in the Grade table.

Answer: Your script should look similar to the script below. The script contains comments and these will be further explained.

```
-- ch09_1a.sql
 1    CREATE OR REPLACE
 2    PROCEDURE grade_calc
 3       (P_student_id    IN student.student_id%type,
 4        P_section_id    IN section.section_id%TYPE,
 5        P_final_grade   OUT enrollment.final_grade%TYPE,
 6        P_exit_code     OUT CHAR)
 7    AS
 8       v_student_id            student.student_id%TYPE;
 9       v_section_id            section.section_id%TYPE;
10       v_grade_type_code       grade_type_weight.grade_type_
                                 code%TYPE;
11       v_grade_percent         NUMBER;
12       v_final_grade           NUMBER;
13       v_grade_count           NUMBER;
14       v_lowest_grade          NUMBER;
15       v_exit_code             CHAR(1) := 'S';
```

```
16   --   Next two variables are used to calculate whether a cursor
17   --   has no result set.
18     v_no_rows1              CHAR(1) := 'N';
19     v_no_rows2              CHAR(1) := 'N';
20     e_no_grade              EXCEPTION;
21   -- Cursor to loop through all grade types for a given section.
22     CURSOR   c_grade_type
23              (pc_section_id   section.section_id%TYPE)
24              IS
25     SELECT GRADE_TYPE_CODE,
26            NUMBER_PER_SECTION,
27            PERCENT_OF_FINAL_GRADE,
28            NVL(DROP_LOWEST, 'N') DROP_LOWEST
29       FROM   grade_Type_weight
30   WHERE   section_id = pc_section_id
31        AND section_id IN (SELECT section_id
32              FROM grade WHERE student_id = p_student_id);
33   -- Cursor to loop through all grades for a given student
34   -- in a given section.
35    CURSOR   c_grades
36              (p_grade_type_code
37                   grade_Type_weight.grade_type_code%TYPE,
38              pc_student_id   student.student_id%TYPE,
39              pc_section_id   section.section_id%TYPE) IS
40      SELECT grade_type_code,grade_code_occurrence,
41             numeric_grade
42      FROM    grade
43      WHERE   student_id = pc_student_id
44      AND     section_id = pc_section_id
45      AND     grade_type_code = p_grade_type_code;
46   BEGIN
47   v_section_id := p_section_id;
48   v_student_id := p_student_id;
49   -- Start loop of grade types for the section.
50      FOR r_grade in c_grade_type(v_section_id)
51      LOOP
52   -- Since cursor is open it has a result
53   -- set, change indicator.
54          v_no_rows1 := 'Y';
55   -- To hold the number of grades per section,
56   -- reset to 0 before detailed cursor loops
57          v_grade_count := 0;
58          v_grade_type_code := r_grade.GRADE_TYPE_CODE;
59   -- Variable to hold the lowest grade.
60   -- 500 will not be the lowest grade.
61          v_lowest_grade := 500;
62   -- Determine what to multiply a grade by to
63   -- compute final grade, must take into consideration
64   -- if the drop lowest grade indicator is Y
```

```
65      SELECT (r_grade.percent_of_final_grade /
66             DECODE(r_grade.drop_lowest, 'Y',
67                     (r_grade.number_per_section - 1),
68                      r_grade.number_per_section
69             ))* 0.01
70      INTO  v_grade_percent
71      FROM dual;
72  -- Open cursor of detailed grade for a student in a
73  -- given section.
74      FOR r_detail in c_grades(v_grade_type_code,
75                     v_student_id, v_section_id) LOOP
76  -- Since cursor is open it has a result
77  -- set, change indicator.
78      v_no_rows2 := 'Y';
79      v_grade_count  := v_grade_count + 1;
80  -- Handle the situation where there are more
81  -- entries for grades of a given grade type
82  -- than there should be for that section.
83      If v_grade_count > r_grade.number_per_section THEN
84          v_exit_code := 'T';
85          raise e_no_grade;
86      END IF;
87  -- If drop lowest flag is Y determine which is lowest
88  -- grade to drop
89      IF  r_grade.drop_lowest = 'Y' THEN
90          IF nvl(v_lowest_grade, 0) >=
91                  r_detail.numeric_grade
92        THEN
93                  v_lowest_grade := r_detail.numeric_grade;
94          END IF;
95      END IF;
96  -- Increment the final grade with percentage of current
97  -- grade in the detail loop.
98      v_final_grade := nvl(v_final_grade, 0) +
99              (r_detail.numeric_grade * v_grade_percent);
100     END LOOP;
101  -- Once detailed loop is finished, if the number of grades
102  -- for a given student for a given grade type and section
103  -- is less than the required amount, raise an exception.
104     IF  v_grade_count < r_grade.NUMBER_PER_SECTION THEN
105         v_exit_code := 'I';
106         raise e_no_grade;
107     END IF;
108  -- If the drop lowest flag was Y then you need to take
109  -- the lowest grade out of the final grade, it was not
110  -- known when it was added which was the lowest grade
111  -- to drop until all grades were examined.
112     IF  r_grade.drop_lowest = 'Y' THEN
113         v_final_grade := nvl(v_final_grade, 0) -
```

```
114                          (v_lowest_grade *  v_grade_percent);
115             END IF;
116       END LOOP;
117    -- If either cursor had no rows then there is an error.
118    IF v_no_rows1 = 'N' OR v_no_rows2 = 'N'    THEN
119          v_exit_code := 'N';
120          raise e_no_grade;
121    END IF;
122    P_final_grade   := v_final_grade;
123    P_exit_code     := v_exit_code;
124    EXCEPTION
125       WHEN e_no_grade THEN
126          P_final_grade := null;
127          P_exit_code   := v_exit_code;
128       WHEN OTHERS THEN
129          P_final_grade := null;
130          P_exit_code   := 'E';
131 END grade_calc;
```

This is a long procedure; it is best to look at it in sections. First of all, you should review the elements of the code that contribute to the calculation of the final grade, and then you should consider how different types of errors are trapped.

- The method used here is to determine the percent that each grade element contributed to the final grade.
- There are two cursors, and as each cursor is executed, it runs through each grade, multiplies it by the percentage related to the particular grade, and then adds it to the running total.
- The drop_lowest flag is handled by evaluating each grade in one category to the prior grade to determine if it is the lower grade. In the end, the lowest grade is subtracted out of the running total.
- Take a look at the two cursors and review how they are being used. The first cursor is c_grade_type. This is declared in lines 22–29. This cursor takes in a section_id as a parameter. It generates a result set of one row for each grade type that is used in the given section. It also generates the other pertinent information for determining the calculation. This includes the percent of that grade type for the final grade, the number per section, and whether the drop_lowest flag is used.
- There is a child cursor named c_grades. This is declared in lines 35–45. This cursor takes the student_id and the section_id as IN parameters. It generates the grades for that student, in the given section, and only for the particular grade type of the parent cursor.
- The parent cursor is opened in a FOR loop in line 50. The percentage for each grade element (Quiz One, for example) is determined by the SELECT statement in lines 65–71.
- The percentage is held in the variable, v_grade_precent, so that it can be used while the child cursor is processed.

- The child cursor is opened in line 74. After checking for a number of possible errors and determining whether the drop_lowest flag is being used, it increments the running total of the final grade. This is done in lines 98–99 where the running total is contained in the variable, v_final_grade.

- The child loop is then closed in line 101. If the drop_lowest flag is Y, then the lowest grade of the given grade type needs to be reversed out of the running total. The IF statement in lines 112 to 115 performs this action. There is no ELSE in this IF statement. It simply evaluates the drop_lowest flag, and only performs the calculation IF the flag is Y.

- There are many errors that can occur.
  - Errors that are not standard PL/SQL errors can be trapped explicitly with user-defined exceptions that are specific to this program. When writing a long procedure, it is best to add one type of error trap at a time and test that you have implemented it correctly.
  - In this example, the different types of errors are all handled by one user-defined exception.
  - The exception, e_no_grade, is explicitly raised when an error condition is determined to exist. A variable called v_exit_code is given a value just before the exception is raised. The value of v_exit_code is assigned to the out parameter P_exit_code. This way, one exception can be used for many possible errors.
  - The possible error of having more instances of a grade type then are allowed for that section is evaluated in the IF statement in lines 83–86. A test of the opposite error, not enough instances of a grade type, is evaluated in the IF statement in lines 104–107.

- The two cursors are opened using the FOR loop structure. This means that if the parameter that is passed in creates a result set of no rows then the cursor will never open, fetch, and execute. This also means that cursor attributes cannot be used to determine if a cursor was processed or not. The procedure must check for no trips through the loop. The test of a cursor being processed or not is thus taken care of by a variable that is first initialized to N in the declaration section on lines 18 and 19. If the cursors are opened, then it is assigned a value of Y in lines 57 and 80. The test is made in lines 119–122. If the test fails, then the exception is raised and the exit code is assigned a value of N, for no rows. After the loop executes, the value of the variable can be checked to see if it is Y or N.

- The test for using the lowest_grade flag is done by keeping a running tally of the lowest grade. The running grade is held in the variable, v_lowest_grade. It is first assigned a value of 500 in the child cursor. The first grade that is encountered in the child cursor will be lower than this value of 500, therefore, v_lowest_grade is reassigned this new lowest grade value. This is done in lines 89–95.

Now that you have read this detailed explanation, you should read through the entire code with comments to get an understanding of how all the elements are being used.

b) Write an Anonymous block to test your grade_calc prodedure. The Block should ask for a student_id and section_id in order to test the procedure. Test your procedure with a number of different students.

Answer: It is often good practice to run the DESCRIBE command on the procedure you are about to test to ensure that you have the correct parameters and their datatypes. Here is the result of describing the grade_calc procedure you create in this exercise.

```
SQL> desc grade_calc
PROCEDURE grade_calc
 Argument Name                  Type                 In/Out Default?
 ----------------------------   ------------------   ------ ----
 P_STUDENT_ID                   NUMBER(8)            IN
 P_SECTION_ID                   NUMBER(8)            IN
 P_FINAL_GRADE                  NUMBER(3)            OUT
 P_EXIT_CODE                    CHAR                 OUT
```

The following anonymous block is an example of one method you can use to test this procedure:

```
SET SERVEROUTPUT ON
DECLARE
   v_STUDENT_ID   student.student_id%TYPE   := &sv_student_id;
   v_SECTION_ID   section.section_id%TYPE   := &sv_section_id;
   v_FINAL_GRADE  enrollment.final_grade%TYPE;
   v_EXIT_CODE    CHAR;
BEGIN
   grade_calc(v_STUDENT_ID,v_SECTION_ID,
              v_FINAL_GRADE, v_EXIT_CODE);
   DBMS_OUTPUT.PUT_LINE('For student ID '||v_STUDENT_ID||
      ' enrolled in section ID '||v_SECTION_ID);
   DBMS_OUTPUT.PUT_LINE('The Final Grade is '||v_FINAL_GRADE );
   DBMS_OUTPUT.PUT_LINE('The Exit Code is '||v_EXIT_CODE);
END;
```

If you run this procedure for student_ID 102 in section_id 86, you will see the following output in SQL*Plus.

```
Enter value for sv_student_id: 102
old   2:   v_STUDENT_ID   student.student_id%TYPE   := &sv_student_id;
new   2:   v_STUDENT_ID   student.student_id%TYPE   := 102;
Enter value for sv_section_id: 86
old   3:   v_SECTION_ID   section.section_id%TYPE   := &sv_section_id;
new   3:   v_SECTION_ID   section.section_id%TYPE   := 86;
For student ID 102 enrolled in section ID 86
The Final Grade is 89
The Exit Code is S
PL/SQL procedure successfully completed.
```

It is important to note that this value has not been entered into the final grade column of the enrollment table. The insert will be done in a procedure that will be part of the final application.

Details on the final application can be found on the companion Web site: http://www.phptr.com/boardman/. The complete code for the application will also be found on this Web site.

UNIT 9.3

PACKAGES

USING PACKAGES

A package is a collection of PL/SQL objects grouped together under one package name. Packages include procedures, functions, cursors, declarations, types, and variables.

THE BENEFITS OF USING PACKAGES

There are numerous benefits of using packages as a way to bundle your functions and procedures. A well-designed package is a logical grouping of objects such as functions, procedures, global variables, and cursors. All of the code is loaded on the first call of the package. In a stateful transaction this means that the first call to the package is very expensive (this does not mean it will cost you a lot of money, the expense is in processing of CPU, memory, etc.), but all subsequent calls will result in an improved performance. Packages are therefore often used in applications where procedures and functions are used repeatedly. There is an additional level of security using packages. When a user executes a procedure in a package (or stored procedures and functions), the procedure operates with the same permissions of its owner. Packages also allow the creation of private functions and procedures, which can only be called from other functions and procedures in the package. This enforces information hiding.

THE PACKAGE SPECIFICATION

The package specification contains information about the contents of the package, but not the code for the procedures and functions. It also contains declarations of global/public variables. Anything placed in the declarative section of a PL/SQL block may be coded in a package specification. All objects placed in the package specification are called public objects. Any function or procedure not in the package specification, but coded in a package body, is called a private function or procedure.

THE PACKAGE BODY

The package body contains the actual executable code for the objects described in the package specification. The package body contains code for all procedures and functions described in the specification, and may additionally contain code for objects not declared in the specification; the latter type of packaged object is invisible outside the package and is referred to as being hidden or private. When creating stored packages, the package specification and body can be compiled separately.

RULES FOR THE PACKAGE BODY

There are a number of rules that must be followed in package body code:

1. There must be an exact match between the cursor and module headers and their definition in the package specification.
2. Do not repeat declaration of variables, exceptions, TYPEs, and/or constants in the specification, again in the body.
3. Any element **declared** in the specification can be **referenced** in the body.

REFERENCING PACKAGE ELEMENTS

Use the following notation when calling packaged elements from outside of the package: **Package_name.element**

You do not need to qualify elements when declared and referenced inside the body of the package. You do not need to qualify elements when declared in a specification and referenced inside the body of the same package.

PUBLIC AND PRIVATE PACKAGE ELEMENTS

Public elements are elements defined in the package specification. If an object is defined only in the package body, then it is private.

Private elements cannot be accessed directly by any programs outside of the package.

You can think of the package specification as being a "menu'" of packaged items that are available to users; there may be other objects working behind the scenes, but they aren't accessible.

The first time a package is called within a user session, the code in the initialization section of the package will be executed, if it exists. This is only done once if other procedures or functions for that package are called by the user.

Variables, cursors, and user-defined data types used by numerous procedures and functions can be declared once at the beginning of the package and can then be used by the functions and procedures within the package without having to declare them again.

UNIT 9.3 EXERCISE

a) Create a package specification for a package named Instruct. Include the specification for the grade_calc procedure as a part of the Instruct package. In the following exercises and chapters you continue to add new elements to this procedure.

UNIT 9.3 EXERCISE ANSWER

a) Create a package specification for a package named Instruct. Include the specification for the grade_calc procedure as a part of the Instruct package. In the following exercises and chapters you continue to add new elements to this procedure.

Answer: Your script should look similar to the script below. The script contains comments and these are further explained later in this chapter.

```
-- ch09_2a.sql
CREATE OR REPLACE PACKAGE Instruct
AS
   PROCEDURE grade_calc
             (i_student_id   IN student.student_id%type,
              i_section_id   IN section.section_id%TYPE,
              o_final_grade  OUT enrollment.final_grade%TYPE,
              o_exit_code    OUT CHAR);
end Instruct;
```

UNIT 9.4

PL/SQL TABLES

PL/SQL tables are Oracle's version of an array. You can think of an array as a list, similar to an Excel worksheet with only two columns. In the same way you refer to a cell in the Excel worksheet by its column letter and row number, each element of a PL/SQL table is referenced by its index number. In this chapter, you review how to make use of PL/SQL tables.

PL/SQL TABLE BASICS

PL/SQL tables are PL/SQL's way of providing arrays. Arrays are like temporary tables in memory and thus are processed very quickly. It is important for you to realize they are not database tables, and DML statements cannot be issued against a PL/SQL table. This type of table is indexed by a binary integer counter (it cannot be indexed by another type of number), whose value can be referenced using the number of the index. Remember that PL/SQL tables exist in memory only, and, therefore don't exist in any persistent way, disappearing after the session ends.

A PL/SQL TABLE DECLARATION

There are two steps in the declaration of a PL/SQL table. First, you must define the table structure using the TYPE statement. Second, once a table type is created, you declare the actual table.

■ *FOR EXAMPLE*

```
DECLARE
   TYPE LnameType IS TABLE OF
   -- Table structure definition
   student.last_name%TYPE
   INDEX BY BINARY_INTEGER;
-- Create the actual table
   SlnameTab LnameType;
   IlnameTab LnameType;
```

```
BEGIN
   NULL; -- ...
END;
```

REFERENCING AND MODIFYING PL/SQL TABLE ROWS

In order to specify a particular row in a PL/SQL table, you must name the table and the index.

```
Syntax:          <table_name> (<index_value>)
```

The datatype of the index value must be compatible with the BINARY_INTEGER datatype. You assign values to a row using the standard assignment operator.

PL/SQL TABLE ATTRIBUTES   Here are seven PL/SQL table attributes you can use to gain information about a PL/SQL table or to modify a row in a PL/SQL table:

- **DELETE**—Deletes rows in a table.
- **EXISTS**—Returns TRUE if the specified entry exists in the table.
- **COUNT**—Returns the number of rows in the table.
- **FIRST**—Returns the index of the first row in the table.
- **LAST**—Returns the index of the last row in the table.
- **NEXT**—Returns the index of the next row in the table after the specified row.
- **PRIOR**—Returns the index of the previous row in the table before the specified row.

PL/SQL table attributes are used with the following syntax:

```
<table_name>.<attribute>
tab_student.COUNT
```

If you declare a PL/SQL table named t_student, then you can get a rowcount for the table as follows:

```
v_count := t_student.count;
```

The DELETE and the EXISTS attributes function differently from the other attributes. These two generally operate on one row at a time, so you must add the following syntax:

```
<TableName>.<attribute>(<IndexNumber> [,<IndexNumber>])
```

t.student.delete deletes all rows from the t_student table, whereas t_student.delete(15) deletes the 15th row of the t_student table. Likewise, t_student.exists(100) returns a value of true if there is a 100th row and a value of false if there is not.

The EXISTS attribute can be used to determine if a particular index value exists in a PL/SQL table or not.

PACKAGE INITIALIZATION, VARIABLES, AND CURSORS

The first time a package is called within a user session, the code in the initialization section of the package is executed if it exists. This is only done once, and not repeated if the user calls other procedures or functions for that package. The initialization section begins with the BEGIN keyword and ends with the END keyword.

Variables, cursors, and user-defined datatypes used by numerous procedures and functions can be declared once at the beginning of the package, and can then be used by the functions and procedures within the package without having to declare them again.

**UNIT
9.4**

UNIT 9.4 EXERCISES

a) Alter the package specification so that it contains a package variable to hold the Font data used in the Web procedures that are used in future chapters. Also create a package PL/SQL table to hold instructor information (ID, first name, and last name). You will need a package cursor in order to load data into the PL/SQL table.

b) Write an initialization section for this package that will load the PL/SQL table with data from the cursor.

UNIT 9.4 EXERCISE ANSWERS

a) Alter the package specification so that it contains a package variable to hold the Font data used in the Web procedures that are used in future chapters. Also create a package PL/SQL table to hold instructor information (ID, first name, and last name). You will need to create a package cursor in order to do this.

Answer: Your script should look similar to the script below.

```
-- ch09_3a.sql
1   CREATE OR REPLACE PACKAGE Instruct
2   AS
3     V_FONT   VARCHAR2(150);
4     CURSOR   c_instruct_list IS
```

```
5      SELECT   first_name, last_name, instructor_id
6        FROM   instructor;
7      TYPE Inst_Tbl_Type IS TABLE OF c_instruct_list%ROWTYPE
8           INDEX BY BINARY_INTEGER;
9      Instruct_Table              inst_tbl_type;
10      i                   NUMBER := 1;
11     PROCEDURE grade_calc
12               (i_student_id    IN student.student_id%type,
13                i_section_id    IN section.section_id%TYPE,
14                o_final_grade   OUT enrollment.final_grade%TYPE,
15                o_exit_code     OUT CHAR);
16   end Instruct;
```

The package variable V_FONT is declared in line 3. The package cursor c_instruct_list is declared in lines 4–6, and will be used in the initialization section of the package. A package TYPE inst_tbl_type is declared as a TABLE in lines 7–8. The Instruct_table is then declared to be an element of the type inst_tbl_type, meaning it is a table with the elements of the cursor c_instruct_list indexed by a binary integer. The package variable i is declared in line 10, and will also be needed in the initialization section.

b) Write an initialization section for this package that will load the PL/SQL table with data from the cursor.

Answer: Your script should look similar to the script below.

```
-- ch09_3b.sql
-- add the following code to the end of the package body:
BEGIN     /* One time Code */
   FOR rec IN c_instruct_list LOOP
      Instruct_Table( i ).first_name      := rec.first_name;
      Instruct_Table( i ).last_name       := rec.last_name;
      Instruct_Table( i ).instructor_id   := rec.instructor_id;
      i := i + 1;
   END LOOP;
```

The code between the BEGIN and END keywords should be placed at the end of the package and will be executed only the first time the package is called. The cursor c_instruct_list is opened, for each line in the cursor a new line is created in the instruct_ table, and values from the cursor are added to the values in the table. The data in the table can now be used in all procedures and functions in the INSTRUCT package.

C H A P T E R 9

BUILDING THE APP

The full text of this procedure can be found on the companion Web site at http://www.phptr.com/boardman/.

Visit the Web site periodically to share and discuss your answers with other readers.

In order to test this package it is necessary to write some scripts and run them in SQL*Plus. You can find some samples on the Web page. You should have the following parts of the application after this chapter:

- Instructor package with the following:
  - V_FONT variable
  - C_Instruct_list cursor
  - Inst_Tbl_Type Type
  - Instruct_Table PL/SQL Table
  - Grade Calculation Procedure (grade_calc)

Once you learn the PL/SQL Web Toolkit you will create a Web page that makes use of the grade calculation procedure that you made in this chapter. The full specifications for these procedures as well as a possible solution will also be found on the companion Web site.

C H A P T E R   1 0

WEB TOOLKIT I:
HTML AND JAVASCRIPT
WITH PL/SQL

CHAPTER OBJECTIVES

After this lab, you will know how to:

- ✔ Web-enable Databases   Page 313
- ✔ Create Web Pages in PL/SQL   Page 316

The Web Toolkit is introduced in this chapter and further explained in Chapter 11, "Web Toolkit II: Frames, Forms, and Parameters." The Web Toolkit allows a Web developer to create dynamic Web pages from an Oracle database. It allows for inserting into or updating a database with user input or displaying database data in a Web browser.

This chapter begins with an explanation of what the Web Toolkit is and a short description of its built-in packages. Then you learn how to decipher the URL that calls a Web Toolkit procedure. Finally, you learn to create Web pages with the Toolkit and view them immediately in your browser.

In previous chapters you learned HTML and JavaScript, and review PL/SQL. This chapter introduces not only new PL/SQL built-in packages but also the concept of combining HTML, JavaScript, and PL/SQL in one file. Programmers new to Web development often find this the most difficult aspect of Web development to grasp. HTML or JavaScript or PL/SQL by itself is easily mastered. But, making them work together as an integrated whole is the difficult part.

Beginning with this chapter you begin building the dynamic portions of the application for this book. The requirements and complete source code for this book's application is located on the accompanying Web site for this book, http://www.phptr.com/boardman. This chapter and the following chapters use examples from this book's application to demonstrate different concepts. You build most of the application in the chapters, but some parts of the application are left as exercises for you to do. The answers to these exercises are available in the source code.

UNIT 10.1

WEB-ENABLE DATABASES

WHAT THE WEB TOOLKIT IS

The Web Toolkit is a collection of built-in packages provided by Oracle to allow a Web developer to Web-enable a database. The packages are written in PL/SQL and stored in the database. They are owned by SYS by default.

By using Web Toolkit packages in your PL/SQL procedures, you can make them generate HTML code that a browser can understand. A user can type a URL into a browser that calls a PL/SQL procedure. Then the PL/SQL procedure is executed on the server. If the procedure contains Web Toolkit code, then an HTML page is generated and sent back to the Web browser. The browser then displays the Web page. The Web page that is built by the PL/SQL procedure and served to the browser can include HTML, embedded JavaScript, and data from the database.

WEB TOOLKIT PACKAGES

Table 10.1 lists all the Web Toolkit packages and a brief description of each.

This chapter and Chapter 11, "Web Toolkit II: Frames, Forms, and Parameters," covers the HTP and HTF packages. Chapter 15, "Maintaining State with Cookies and Tables," covers the OWA_COOKIE package. Chapter 13, "Images," covers the OWA_IMAGE package. Chapter 16, "The Owa_Util Package: Dynamic SQL, HTML, DATE Utilities, and More," covers the OWA_UTIL package.

HTP VERSUS HTF   For every HTP procedure that generates HTML tags, there is a corresponding HTF function with identical parameters. The function versions do not directly generate output in your Web page. Instead, they pass their output as return values to the statements that invoked them. Use these functions when you need to nest calls. To learn more about HTF functions just look up the corresponding HTP procedures in your Oracle software documentation. They respond in similar ways.

UNIT 10.1

Table 10.1 ■ Web Toolkit Packages

Package Name	Description
HTP	Generates HTML through procedures
HTF	Generates HTML through functions
OWA_CACHE	Caches Web pages for improved performance using the PL/SQL Gateway cache
OWA_COOKIE	Sends cookies, retrieves cookies
OWA_IMAGE	Creates an image map
OWA_OPT_LOCK	Handles optimistic locking of data
OWA_PATTERN	Searches for/replaces values in text strings, "pattern matching"
OWA_SEC	Security subprograms
OWA_TEXT	Other types of string manipulation
OWA_UTIL	Retrieves environment variables; redirects users to another site; other utilities like printing query results directly in a table

■ FOR EXAMPLE

```
htp.tableData (htf.formOpen('pr_update_class')||
                    htf.formSubmit()||htf.formClose);
```

will generate:

```
<TD><FORM ACTION="pr_update_class" METHOD="POST">
<INPUT TYPE="submit" VALUE="Submit"></FORM></TD>
```

ANATOMY OF A URL CALLING A PL/SQL PROCEDURE

Creating PL/SQL procedures using the Web Toolkit enables you to view the results of those procedures (HTML pages generated on the server side) in a Web browser. To do this requires being able to properly construct the URL. Below is the format for such a URL:

```
protocol://server:port/pls/dad/name_of_procedure
```

An example would look like this:

```
http://www.server4.virgil.edu/pls/any/my_procedure
```

The above example is calling a procedure that is not part of a package. To call a procedure that is part of a package, simply prefix the procedure name with the

Table 10.2 ■ Anatomy of a Web Toolkit URL

Parts of a URL	Description
Protocol	*http*—the protocol of the Web
Server	www.server4.virgil.edu—the name of the server
Port	Often this is not specified, and the default for the Web, port 80, is used. Note that the default port of the Oracle http server in 9.2.0 is 7778. If a port is specified, then it is appended to the server using a colon. For example, to indicate the port as 7778: http://www.server4.virgil.edu:**7778**/...
PL/SQL Gateway	*pls*—tells the server to dispatch the request to the PL/SQL module, mod_plsql.
DAD	*any*—the Database Access Descriptor or Application being accessed. This DAD was set up when you configured the Oracle 9iAS.
Package/Procedure	*my_procedure*—the procedure name. Notice that no file extension is used.

package name, and separate them with a period. For example, to call *my_proce-dure* in the package named *my_package,* the URL would look like this:

```
http://www.server4.virgil.edu/pls/any/my_package.my_procedure
```

The normal Oracle security rules still apply to Web Toolkit procedures. If you are the owner of a procedure, then you can call it with a URL. If you are not the owner of the procedure, then the owner must grant you access to execute it before you will be able to call it in a URL:

```
grant execute on my_procedure to floyd;
```

Functions are not called in the URL, only procedures.

UNIT 10.2

CREATE WEB PAGES IN PL/SQL

A FIRST WEB TOOLKIT WEB PAGE

The HTP package contains procedures that generate HTML tags. For every HTML tag there is an HTP procedure that produces that tag. The most commonly used procedure in the HTP package, however, is the print, or *htp.print('parameter')* procedure. This procedure simply prints whatever is passed to it as a parameter and adds a new line to the end of the parameter.

■ FOR EXAMPLE

```
htp.print('This is an example.');
htp.print('This is the second line.');
```

produces this on a Web browser:

```
This is an example.
This is the second line.
```

The alias for htp.print(); *is* htp.p();.

The htp.p procedure is perhaps the easiest way to generate a first Web Toolkit Web page. To create your first Web Toolkit Web page, convert the following HTML code into a PL/SQL Procedure using htp.p. Name the procedure my_first_page and provide error handling:

```
<HTML>
<HEAD>
<TITLE>My First Page</TITLE>
</HEAD>
<BODY>
Hello world<BR>
</BODY>
</HTML>
```

There are a few ways to create this HTML with the Web Toolkit. Below is the HTML code generated using htp.p.

■ FOR EXAMPLE

```
CREATE OR REPLACE PROCEDURE my_first_page
  AS
BEGIN
   htp.p('<HTML>');
   htp.p('<HEAD>');
   htp.p('<TITLE>My First Page</TITLE>');
   htp.p('</HEAD>');
   htp.p('<BODY>');
   htp.p('Hello world.<BR>');
   htp.p('</BODY>');
   htp.p('</HTML>');
EXCEPTION
   WHEN OTHERS THEN
   htp.p('An error occurred on this page.
          Please try again later.');
END;
```

Sometimes it is easier to put multiple lines inside the htp.p procedure like this:

■ FOR EXAMPLE

```
CREATE OR REPLACE PROCEDURE my_first_page
  AS
BEGIN
   htp.p('
      <HTML>
        <HEAD>
          <TITLE>My First Page</TITLE>
        </HEAD>
        <BODY>
          Hello world.<BR>
        </BODY>
      </HTML>
   ');
```

```
EXCEPTION
   WHEN OTHERS THEN
      htp.p('An error occurred on this page.
            Please try again later.');
END;
```

**UNIT
10.2**

The same HTML code is converted to a PL/SQL procedure using the HTML tag-specific HTP procedures in place of htp.p.

■ FOR EXAMPLE

```
CREATE OR REPLACE PROCEDURE my_first_page
  AS
BEGIN
   htp.htmlOpen;
   htp.headOpen;
   htp.title('My First Page');
   htp.headClose;
   htp.bodyOpen;
   htp.p('Hello world.<BR>');
   htp.bodyClose;
   htp.htmlClose;
EXCEPTION
   WHEN OTHERS THEN
      htp.p('An error occurred on this page.
            Please try again later.');
END;
```

Once you have successfully compiled the procedure, call it via the URL:

```
http://[your_server]/pls/any/my_first_page
```

The name of the procedure as it appears in the PL/SQL code, and not as it appears with a .sql file extension, is used in the URL to call the procedure.

Once you have successfully called the procedure with the URL, view the source. To view the source of a Web page, right-click the mouse in the part of the page that you want to see, and choose "View Source." Notice that there is only HTML code in the source and no PL/SQL code. The PL/SQL and SQL code is executed on the server, and only the results are displayed in the browser page.

At compile time, the PL/SQL compiler checks the PL/SQL code, not the HTML code. You could have improper HTML syntax, but no exception will be raised as long as it is part of a string inside the htp.p procedure. Be sure to test your procedure by viewing the HTML code it is meant to generate in a browser.

OVERVIEW OF ADDITIONAL HTP PROCEDURES

Table 10.3 is a list of some of the commonly used HTP procedures and output. For a comprehensive list of HTP procedures, please check Oracle's online documentation.

With regard to the Web Toolkit, Web developers find themselves using either http.p or the HTML tag-specific procedures. Which should you use? You may find yourself on a project where the standard is already set. In that case you have to follow the coding standards. Apart from that situation there are pros and cons of using the tag-specific Web Toolkit packages that you should consider.

On the one hand...

- Makes it easy to avoid HTML syntax errors.
- Lets Oracle keep up with new versions of HTML so you don't have to.
- May set useful default values for tag attributes so you don't have to.
- Saves typing.
- Saves you from having lots of quotes inside your htp.p();, which can get confusing.

Table 10.3 ■ Additional HTP Procedures

HTP Procedure	Output
htp.htmlOpen;	<HTML>
htp.headOpen;	<HEAD>
htp.title('My Title');	<TITLE> My Title<TITLE>
htp.headClose;	</HEAD>
htp.bodyOpen;	<BODY>
htp.header(1, 'My Heading');	<H1> My Heading</H1>
htp.anchor('url''Anchor Name') 'Click Here';	<A HREF="url" NAME="Anchor Name"> Click Here</A>
htp.line;	<HR>
htp.bold;	<B></B>
htp.paragraph;	<P>
htp.tableOpen;	<TABLE>
htp.tableCaption;	<CAPTION></CAPTION>
htp.tableRowOpen;	<TR>
htp.tableHeader('Emp ID');	<TH>Emp ID</TH>
htp.tableData('data');	<TD>data</TD>
htp.tableRowClose;	</TR>
htp.tableClose;	</TABLE>
htp.bodyClose;	</BODY>
htp.htmlClose;	</HTML>
htp.script('alert("This is an alert!");','JavaScript');	<SCRIPT LANGUAGE="JavaScript"> alert("This is an alert!"); </SCRIPT>

On the other hand...

- What are the parameters for each procedure? May have to look this up.
- And what is the parameter order? May still need to look this up.
- HTML shows attribute = value. HTP procedure call does not show attribute names, just values being passed in, which may not be as informative to look at.
- You just learned HTML—now you need to learn a body of processes that performs the same tasks?

ADD DATABASE INFORMATION

Now you are ready to add database data and information to your procedure. To add the system date to your page, concatenate *sysdate* to a message string in htp.p. Experiment with adding the following htp.p procedure to the procedure you just created, *my_first_page*.

```
htp.p('Current date and time is:' ||
to_char(sysdate,'MM/DD/YYYY HH:MI'));
```

You can also display a more informative error message by concatenating PL/SQL's SQLERRM to your exception-handling message. Below is an example of this:

```
htp.p('An error occurred on this page. Please contact Tech
Support with the following message:' || SQLERRM ||'.');
```

DISPLAYING DATABASE DATA

The Instructor Personal Info page of this book's application requires a form with fields to display Instructor personal information. This information must be selected from the database using an instructor ID that has been passed in to the procedure. For now, set the IN parameter with a default ID. Call it *p_instructor_id*. You learn about parameter passing and the Web Toolkit in Chapter 11, "Web Toolkit II: Frames, Forms, and Parameters." Name the procedure *instruct_personal_info*.

Begin by naming the procedure and declaring any parameters. In this case, the instructor ID is passed in as a parameter by the procedure call. Set the default value to 101.

■ *FOR EXAMPLE*

```
CREATE OR REPLACE PROCEDURE instruct_personal_info
(p_instructor_id IN instructor.instructor_id%TYPE DEFAULT 101)

AS
```

Now declare all of the variables to be used for holding and displaying the instructor information selected from the database. In the Instructor Personal Info form there are text fields for salutation, first name, last name, address, city, state, zipcode, and telephone number. So, a variable must be declared for each form field. Following a naming standard, begin each name with a *v_*.

```
v_instructor_id    instructor.instructor_id%TYPE;
v_salutation       instructor.salutation%TYPE;
v_first_name       instructor.first_name%TYPE;
v_last_name        instructor.last_name%TYPE;
v_street_address   instructor.street_address%TYPE;
v_city             zipcode.city%TYPE;
v_state            zipcode.state%TYPE;
v_zip              instructor.zip%TYPE;
v_phone            instructor.phone%TYPE;
```

This form displays the information for one instructor. The IN parameter is the instructor ID, or primary key of the INSTRUCTOR table. This means that your SQL SELECT statement will return one row, and there is no need for a cursor. Instead, use the *Select...Into* syntax to select the values from the database into the variables declared above.

```
BEGIN
    SELECT instructor_id,
           salutation,
           first_name,
           last_name,
           street_address,
           city,
           state,
           i.zip,
           phone
      INTO v_instructor_id,
           v_salutation,
           v_first_name,
           v_last_name,
           v_street_address,
           v_city,
           v_state,
           v_zip,
           v_phone
      FROM instructor i, zipcode z
     WHERE i.zip = z.zip
       AND instructor_id = p_instructor_id;
```

Up to this point, the procedure is a regular PL/SQL procedure. You declare all the variables, select the data from the database, and assign that data to an appropriate variable. Now you are ready to paint the Web page with this data and build an HTML Web page. To do this you can use the Web Toolkit procedures.

Using htp.p, begin to paint the page with the opening HTML tags.

```
htp.p('<HTML>');
htp.p('<HEAD>');
htp.p('<TITLE>Instructor Personal Info</TITLE>');
htp.p('</HEAD>');
htp.p('<BODY bgColor="#99CCCC">');
htp.p('<CENTER>');
```

Using the concatenation symbols, concatenate the variables *v_first_name* and *v_last_name* to the header message. The same rules apply here as when concatenating a column name to a string in a SQL SELECT statement. Be sure to open and close all string segments with a pair of single quotes.

```
htp.p('<H1>Personal Info For '||v_first_name||' '
||v_last_name||'</H1>');
htp.p('<H2>This Is The Current Information On Record.</H2>');
```

Also as in SQL SELECT statements, to escape a single quote within a string, use two single quotes. For example, the word *Save*, in the example shown below, displays in the browser with single quotes around it. But, if you try to use only single quotes, then the htp.p procedure will interpret that as the end of the string; then it will expect a closing parenthesis and semi-colon. It won't find these and an error message will be generated. To prevent generating an error message, escape the single quote by using two single quotes when you want to print single quotes within an htp.p string.

Now create a form for updating this instructor's information. For a cleaner display, use tables to format the page. Where each input needs a value, concatenate the value you retrieved from the database into the HTML you are generating.

```
htp.p('<H3>To Make Changes, Edit The Information And
Select ''Save''.</H3>');
htp.p('<FORM ACTION="" METHOD="post" NAME="instructor_
personal_form">');
htp.p('<INPUT TYPE="hidden" NAME="p_instructor_id"
VALUE="'||v_instructor_id||'">');
htp.p('<TABLE >');
htp.p('<TR>');
htp.p('<TD>Salutation:</TD>');
htp.p('<TD><INPUT TYPE="text" NAME="p_salutation"
VALUE="'||v_salutation||'" SIZE="5"></TD>');
htp.p('</TR>');
htp.p('<TR>');
htp.p('<TD>First Name:</TD>');
htp.p('<TD><INPUT TYPE="text" NAME="p_first_name"
VALUE="'||v_first_name||'" SIZE="25"></TD>');
htp.p('</TR>');
htp.p('<TR>');
htp.p('<TD>Last Name:</TD>');
```

```
htp.p('<TD><INPUT TYPE="text" NAME="p_last_name"
VALUE="'||v_last_name||'" SIZE="25"></TD>');
htp.p('</TR>');
htp.p('<TR>');
htp.p('<TD>Street Address:</TD>');
htp.p('<TD><INPUT TYPE="text" NAME="p_street_address"
VALUE="'||v_street_address||'"></TD>');
htp.p('</TR>');
htp.p('<TR>');
htp.p('<TD>City:</TD>');
htp.p('<TD>'||v_city||'</TD>');
htp.p('</TR>');
htp.p('<TR>');
htp.p('<TD>State:</TD>');
htp.p('<TD>'||v_state||'</TD>');
htp.p('</TR>');
htp.p('<TR>');
htp.p('<TD>Zipcode:</TD>');
htp.p('<TD><INPUT TYPE="text" NAME="p_zip"
VALUE="'||v_zip||'"></TD>');
```

Put a button labeled "Change Zipcode" next to the zipcode field. For now, the button Change Zipcode," described below, will do nothing. You learn how to use JavaScript with Web Toolkit later in this chapter in the Unit, "Incorporating JavaScript with Web Toolkit." Also add buttons for processing the form and add the closing tags for the document.

```
htp.p('<TD><INPUT TYPE="button" VALUE="Change Zipcode"></TD>');
htp.p('</TR>');
htp.p('<TR>');
htp.p('<TD>Telephone:</TD>');
htp.p('<TD><INPUT TYPE="text" VALUE="'||v_phone||'" NAME="p_phone"
MAXLENGTH="15" SIZE="15"></TD>');
htp.p('</TR>');
htp.p('<TR>');
htp.p('<TD></TD>');
htp.p('<TD ALIGN=left>');
htp.p('<INPUT TYPE="submit" VALUE="Save">');
htp.p('<INPUT TYPE="reset" VALUE="Reset">');
htp.p('</TD>');
htp.p('</TR>');
htp.p('</TABLE>');
htp.p('</FORM>');
htp.p('</CENTER>');
htp.p('</BODY>');
htp.p('</HTML>');
```

Once you finish painting the Web page, finish the procedure by providing exception handling. Do not neglect the exception section in your procedures. Although this procedure paints an HTML page, which does not have any sort of exception handling, it is a PL/SQL procedure. If an error is raised in a PL/SQL procedure, you can handle it gracefully by displaying a message in the browser.

```
EXCEPTION
WHEN OTHERS
THEN
   htp.p('An error occurred:  '||SQLERRM||'.  Please try
again later.');
END instruct_personal_info;
```

Figure 10.1 shows how the page looks when viewed in a browser.

LOOPING THROUGH A CURSOR

You can also add conditional control to your procedure to refine what and how data is displayed on the Web page. The sample application in this book calls for a Web page that lists all of the instructor names. Each instructor name is to be a hyperlink to another page. For now, simply list each instructor listed in the database in its own table row. Name the procedure *instructor_list_info*.

Begin by creating and naming the procedure. Then open a cursor to hold the names and IDs of all of the instructors in the database.

Personal Info For Fernand Hanks

This Is The Current Information On Record.

To Make Changes, Edit The Information And Select "Save".

Salutation:	Mr
First Name:	Fernand
Last Name:	Hanks
Street Address:	100 East 87th
City:	New York
State:	NY
Zipcode:	10015
Telephone:	2125551212

Change Zipcode

Save   Reset

Figure 10.1 ■ Output of procedure instruct_personal_info as viewed in a Web browser.

■ *FOR EXAMPLE*

```
CREATE OR REPLACE PROCEDURE instructor_list_info
AS
        CURSOR get_instructor IS
            SELECT first_name, last_name, instructor_id
            FROM instructor
            ORDER BY last_name, first_name;
```

Unlike the example in the previous section, this procedure does not need to declare any variables and it has no IN parameters. Begin painting the Web page:

```
   BEGIN
http.p('<HTML>');
http.p('<HEAD>');
http.p('<TITLE>Instructor Maintenance Web Site</TITLE>');
http.p('</HEAD>');
http.p('<BODY BgColor="#99CCCC">');
http.p('<CENTER>');
http.p('<H2>List of Instructors</H2>');
http.p('<TABLE ALIGN="center" BORDER="3" BORDERCOLOR="midnight blue"
CELLPADDING="5" WIDTH="100%">');
http.p('<TR>');
http.p('<TH ALIGN="center">Instructor Names</TH>');
http.p('</TR>');
```

Now you are ready to list the instructors selected into the cursor. To write the name of each instructor inside of a table row, the Loop statement can be used. The code listed below loops through each instructor name in the cursor. For each record in the cursor the name is written to the Web page. It is also placed within its own table row. As before, simply concatenate the cursor information with the HTML code and text:

```
   FOR rec IN get_instructor
   LOOP
http.p('<TR>');
http.p('<TD><FONT FACE="Arial">'||rec.last_name||','||rec.first_name
||'</FONT></TD>');
http.p('</TR>');
   END LOOP;
```

End the procedure by closing the table tag as well as any other tags that need closing. Again, an exception handling section is provided for:

```
        http.p('</TABLE>');
        http.p('</CENTER>');
        http.p('</BODY>');
        http.p('</HTML>');
```

```
EXCEPTION
WHEN OTHERS
THEN
   htp.p('An error occurred:  '||SQLERRM||'.  Please try
again later.');
END instructor_list_info;
```

Take a look at the Loop statement code. This code:

```
FOR rec IN get_instructor
  LOOP
  htp.p('<TR>');
  htp.p('<TD><FONT FACE="Arial">'||rec.last_name||',
  '||rec.first_name||'</FONT></TD>');
  htp.p('</TR>');
  END LOOP;
```

generates this as the final output in the browser:

```
<TR>
  <TD><FONT FACE="Arial">Chow, Rick</FONT></TD>
</TR>
<TR>
  <TD><FONT FACE="Arial">Frantzen, Marilyn</FONT></TD>
</TR>
<TR>
  <TD><FONT FACE="Arial">Hanks, Fernand</FONT></TD>
</TR>
<TR>
  <TD><FONT FACE="Arial">Lowry, Charles</FONT></TD>
</TR>
<TR>
  <TD><FONT FACE="Arial">Morris, Anita</FONT></TD>
</TR>
<TR>
  <TD><FONT FACE="Arial">Pertez, Gary</FONT></TD>
</TR>
<TR>
  <TD><FONT FACE="Arial">Schorin, Nina</FONT></TD>
</TR>
<TR>
  <TD><FONT FACE="Arial">Smythe, Todd</FONT></TD>
</TR>
<TR>
  <TD><FONT FACE="Arial">Willig, Irene</FONT></TD>
</TR>
<TR>
  <TD><FONT FACE="Arial">Wojick, Tom</FONT></TD>
</TR>
```

You do not need to know in advance how many rows the table will have. The number of rows in the table will be determined by the number of records retrieved by the cursor. If you paint a new table row each trip through the loop, you will have as many rows as you need.

INCORPORATING JAVASCRIPT WITH WEB TOOLKIT

Look at the requirements for *instruct_personal_info* in the Appendix. The requirements call for a zipcode button that pops up a window for the user to select a new zipcode from a Select List. The user can then click the "Select Zipcode" button to write the new zipcode into the form in *instruct_personal_info*. This requires JavaScript. JavaScript code can be added to the final output in the Web page the same way that HTML and text appear as final output. Place the HTML and JavaScript code in between the single quotes of the htp.p procedure. This will print it out to the Web page. In the example below, the Web Toolkit code is bolded.

■ *FOR EXAMPLE*

```
htp.p('<TD><INPUT TYPE="BUTTON" VALUE="Change Zipcode"
onClick="javascript:window.open(''showzip'', ''instructor_zip'',
''TOOLBAR=no, STATUS=yes, MENUBAR=no, SCROLLBARS=auto,
RESIZABLE=yes, WIDTH=640, HEIGHT=480'');"></TD>');
```

The JavaScript in this code opens a new window. Parameter passing is covered in detail in Chapter 11, "Web Toolkit II: Frames, Forms, and Parameters."

You create the showzip procedure at the end of this chapter. If you execute the above code and showzip does not exist, then the window will open but no page will be displayed.

Be careful with the single quotes in the JavaScript code. As already discussed, it is necessary to escape the single quotes when using them within a Web Toolkit procedure. You may find it easier to define your JavaScript Functions in a separate .js file on the server. Later in Chapter 12, "Working with PL/SQL Server Pages (PSPs)," you learn to create PSP pages. These pages allow you to write HTML and JavaScript in an Oracle Web Toolkit procedure without having to escape the quotes.

HTP.SCRIPT PROCEDURE FOR JAVASCRIPT

The htp.script procedure generates the <SCRIPT> opening and closing tags around any string fed to it. For example:

```
htp.script('alert("This is an alert!");','JavaScript');
```

which generates:

```
<SCRIPT LANGUAGE="JavaScript">
alert("This is an alert!");
</SCRIPT>
```

This is especially helpful for short JavaScript code blocks, such as the alert shown above. The drawback is that it does not include tags to make the JavaScript invisible to early versions of browsers that do not support JavaScript. If you must make an application compatible with older versions of browsers, then htp.script may not be a good choice.

UNIT 10.2 EXERCISE

10.2.1 BEGIN BUILDING THE SHOWZIP PROCEDURE

a) Begin building the *showzip* procedure. You finish building this procedure in Chapter 11, "Web Toolkit II: Frames, Forms, and Parameters." Create a Web Toolkit procedure that produces the following:

- A multi-line select list that displays all of the zipcodes in the database. Do not preselect any value.
- Include two buttons:
  - Select Zipcode—for now this button will not do anything.
  - Cancel—closes the window with JavaScript when clicked.
- Provide for exception handling

10.2.2 BEGIN BUILDING THE INSTRUCT_PERSONAL_INFO PROCEDURE

a) Incorporate the code for instruct_personal_info into a Web Toolkit procedure and compile it. Be sure to add the JavaScript code to the Change Zipcode button. Once it is compiled, view it in a Web browser.

UNIT 10.2 EXERCISE ANSWERS

10.2.1 ANSWER

a) Begin building the *showzip* procedure. You finish building this procedure in Chapter 11, "Web Toolkit II: Frames, Forms, and Parameters." Create a Web Toolkit procedure that produces the following:

- A multiline select list that displays all of the zipcodes in the database. Do not preselect any value.
- Include two buttons:
  - Select Zipcode—for now this button will not do anything.
  - Cancel—closes the window with JavaScript when clicked.
- Provide for exception handling

```
1   CREATE OR REPLACE PROCEDURE showzip
2   IS
3      CURSOR c_zip IS
4         SELECT city, state, zip
5         FROM zipcode
6         ORDER BY state, city, zip;
7   BEGIN
8   htp.htmlOpen;
9   htp.headOpen;
10  htp.title('Instructor Zipcode');
11  htp.headClose;
12  htp.bodyOpen(cattributes => 'BGCOLOR="#99CCCC"');
13  htp.centerOpen;
14  htp.p('<FORM NAME="zipcode_form" ACTION="" METHOD="post">');
15
16  htp.p('<SELECT NAME="p_new_zip" SIZE="15">');
17
18     FOR rec IN c_zip
19     LOOP
20         htp.p('<OPTION VALUE="'||rec.zip||'">'
21                ||rec.city||', '||rec.state||'  '||rec.zip||
22             '</OPTION>');
23     END LOOP;
24  htp.p('</SELECT>');
25  htp.p('<BR>');
26  htp.p('<BR>');
27
28  htp.p('<INPUT TYPE="button" VALUE="Select Zipcode">');
29  htp.p('<INPUT TYPE="button" VALUE="Cancel"
    onClick="window.close();">');
30  htp.formClose;
31  htp.centerClose;
32  htp.bodyClose;
```

```
33   htp.htmlClose;
34
35   EXCEPTION
36   WHEN OTHERS
37   THEN
38       htp.p('An error occurred:  '||SQLERRM||'.  Please try again
         later.');
39   END;
```

10.2.2 ANSWER

a) Incorporate the code for instruct_personal_info into a Web Toolkit procedure and compile it. Once it is compiled, view it in a Web browser.

```
1   CREATE OR REPLACE PROCEDURE instruct_personal_info
2   (p_instructor_id IN instructor.instructor_id%TYPE DEFAULT 101)
3
4   AS
5     v_instructor_id     instructor.instructor_id%TYPE;
6     v_salutation        instructor.salutation%TYPE;
7     v_first_name        instructor.first_name%TYPE;
8     v_last_name         instructor.last_name%TYPE;
9     v_street_address    instructor.street_address%TYPE;
10    v_city              zipcode.city%TYPE;
11    v_state             zipcode.state%TYPE;
12    v_zip               instructor.zip%TYPE;
13    v_phone             instructor.phone%TYPE;
14  BEGIN
15      SELECT instructor_id,
16             salutation,
17             first_name,
18             last_name,
19             street_address,
20             city,
21             state,
22             i.zip,
23             phone
24        INTO v_instructor_id,
25             v_salutation,
26             v_first_name,
27             v_last_name,
28             v_street_address,
29             v_city,
30             v_state,
31             v_zip,
32             v_phone
33        FROM instructor i, zipcode z
34       WHERE i.zip = z.zip
```

```
35          AND  instructor_id = p_instructor_id;
36   htp.p('<HTML>');
37   htp.p('<HEAD>');
38   htp.p('<TITLE>Instructor Personal Info</TITLE>');
39   htp.p('</HEAD>');
40   htp.p('<BODY bgColor="#99CCCC">');
41   htp.p('<CENTER>');
42   htp.p('<H1>Personal Info For '||v_first_name||' '
     ||v_last_name||'</H1>');
43   htp.p('<H2>This Is The Current Information On Record.</H2>');
44   htp.p('<H3>To Make Changes, Edit The Information And Select
     ''Save''.</H3>');
45   htp.p('<FORM ACTION="" METHOD="post" NAME="instructor_personal_
     form">');
46   htp.p('<INPUT TYPE="hidden" NAME="p_instructor_id" VALUE="'||
     v_instructor_id||'">');
47   htp.p('<TABLE >');
48   htp.p('<TR>');
49   htp.p('<TD>Salutation:</TD>');
50   htp.p('<TD><INPUT TYPE="text" NAME="p_salutation" VALUE="'||
     v_salutation||'" SIZE="5"></TD>');
51   htp.p('</TR>');
52   htp.p('<TR>');
53   htp.p('<TD>First Name:</TD>');
54   htp.p('<TD><INPUT TYPE="text" NAME="p_first_name" VALUE="'||
     v_first_name||'" SIZE="25"></TD>');
55   htp.p('</TR>');
56   htp.p('<TR>');
57   htp.p('<TD>Last Name:</TD>');
58   htp.p('<TD><INPUT TYPE="text" NAME="p_last_name" VALUE="'||
     v_last_name||'" SIZE="25"></TD>');
59   htp.p('</TR>');
60   htp.p('<TR>');
61   htp.p('<TD>Street Address:</TD>');
62   htp.p('<TD><INPUT TYPE="text" NAME="p_street_address" VALUE="'||
     v_street_address||'"></TD>');
63   htp.p('</TR>');
64   htp.p('<TR>');
65   htp.p('<TD>City:</TD>');
66   htp.p('<TD>'||v_city||'</TD>');
67   htp.p('</TR>');
68   htp.p('<TR>');
69   htp.p('<TD>State:</TD>');
70   htp.p('<TD>'||v_state||'</TD>');
71   htp.p('</TR>');
72   htp.p('<TR>');
73   htp.p('<TD>Zipcode:</TD>');
74   htp.p('<TD><INPUT TYPE="text" NAME="p_zip"
     VALUE="'||v_zip||'"></TD>');
```

```
75   htp.p('<TD><INPUT TYPE="BUTTON" VALUE="Change Zipcode"
     onClick="javascript:window.open(''showzip'',
     ''instructor_zip'', ''TOOLBAR=no, STATUS=yes, MENUBAR=no,
     SCROLLBARS=auto, RESIZABLE=yes, WIDTH=640,
     HEIGHT=480'');"></TD>');
76   htp.p('</TR>');
77   htp.p('<TR>');
78   htp.p('<TD>Telephone:</TD>');
79   htp.p('<TD><INPUT TYPE="text" VALUE="'||v_phone||'"
     NAME="p_phone" MAXLENGTH="15" SIZE="15"></TD>');
80   htp.p('</TR>');
81   htp.p('<TR>');
82   htp.p('<TD></TD>');
83   htp.p('<TD ALIGN=left>');
84   htp.p('<INPUT TYPE="submit" VALUE="Save">');
85   htp.p('<INPUT TYPE="reset" VALUE="Reset">');
86   htp.p('</TD>');
87   htp.p('</TR>');
88   htp.p('</TABLE>');
89   htp.p('</FORM>');
90   htp.p('</CENTER>');
91   htp.p('</BODY>');
92   htp.p('</HTML>');
93   EXCEPTION
94   WHEN OTHERS
95   THEN
96      htp.p('An error occurred:  '||SQLERRM||'.  Please try again
        later.');
97   END;
```

C H A P T E R   1 0

BUILDING THE APP

The answers to these projects can be found at the companion Web site to this book, located at http://www.phptr.com/boardman.

Visit the Web site periodically to share and discuss your answers with other readers.

The Web Toolkit is a set of PL/SQL packages that, when used with the 9iAS server, allows a Web developer to Web-enable a database. Procedures written with Web Toolkit packages are viewable in a browser. Static HTML pages can be created, or dynamic pages can be created that incorporate data from the database at runtime. JavaScript can also be incorporated into the final HTML page served to the client.

You should have the following parts of the application after this chapter:

- instruct_personal_info
- instructor_list_info
- showzip

Note: You implement parameter passing for each of these procedures in the Chapter 11, "Web Toolkit II: Frames, Forms, and Parameters."

C H A P T E R   1 1

WEB TOOLKIT II: FRAMES, FORMS, AND PARAMETERS

CHAPTER OBJECTIVES

After this chapter, you will be able to work with:

- ✔ Frames   Page 336
- ✔ Forms and Form Handlers   Page 343
- ✔ Passing Parameters without Submitting Forms   Page 369

A Web application is not a series of standalone pages, but rather a set of pages that must communicate and relay information to one another. A programmer must know many ways to pass data from one page to another, using HTML forms, JavaScript, querystrings, and PL/SQL with the Web Toolkit.

Passing parameters can be a tricky topic to grasp, because these parameters can be passed according to HTML or JavaScript syntax within PL/SQL, and even by using PL/SQL itself. Understanding how to share information between procedures and pages is the key to creating a cohesive and robust application.

This chapter further explores Oracle's Web Toolkit, which was introduced in Chapter 10, "Web Toolkit I: HTML and JavaScript with PL/SQL." First it looks at related frames and how they are grouped in framesets using the Web Toolkit. Then it covers HTML forms, showing how they use a variety of parameter passing. On the Web, forms are a common way to collect and then pass data from one procedure to another. Finally, it reviews how parameters are passed in PL/SQL, and explores other methods of parameter passing within HTML name/value pairs and JavaScript.

UNIT 11.1

FRAMES

FRAMES AND FRAMESETS

HTML to create frames can be embedded in PL/SQL like any other type of HTML. Frames require multiple HTML documents. One document dictates the layout and contents of the overall frameset. The other documents are called by the frameset to serve as the source for each individual frame's content. Similarly, to create a frameset using the Web Toolkit requires multiple PL/SQL procedures: one that creates the HTML frameset document, and additional procedures that populate each frame.

HTML FRAMESET

What links multiple frames together is the frameset document. As described in Chapter 6, "Advanced HTML: Forms, Nested Tables, and Nested Frames," the frameset document divides the screen into frames, and identifies the source (SRC) for each frame. The source is always a URL, though it may be a relative URL rather than a full URL that begins with http://.

Here is HTML that creates a sample frameset composed of two frames named instructors_left and instructors_main. The procedures identified as the source for the two frames are *instructor_left_nav* and *instructor_list_info*:

```
<HTML>
<HEAD>
  <TITLE>Instructors Frame</TITLE>
</HEAD>
<FRAMESET COLS="150,*">
  <FRAME NAME="instructors_left" SRC="instructor_left_nav" NORESIZE>
  <FRAME NAME="instructors_main" SRC="instructor_list_info"
  SCROLLING="AUTO">
<NOFRAMES>
  <BODY>
    <P>This page uses frames, but your browser doesn't support them. </P>
```

```
  </BODY>
</NOFRAMES>
</FRAMESET>
</HTML>
```

Recall that a frameset document does not contain a <BODY> tag, though a <BODY> tag is necessary in the <NOFRAMES> tag when you elect to include one.

As shown above, the frameset should assign each frame a name. This makes frames easier to work with in JavaScript and HTML, particularly when links in one frame are supposed to change content in a different frame. To make a link in the instructors_left frame, load content into the other frame, "instructors_main"; include the frame's name as a TARGET attribute for the hyperlink:

```
<A HREF="nextpage" TARGET="instructors_main">
This will load "nextpage" into the instructors_main frame.
</A>
```

HTML FRAMESET CREATED BY PL/SQL

You can embed the HTML above in PL/SQL simply by using the htp.p procedure. Create the procedure called instructor_frame by adding the PL/SQL code, shown in bold, to the HTML above, as shown here:

```
1   CREATE OR REPLACE PROCEDURE instructors_frame  AS
2   BEGIN
3   htp.p('
4   <HTML>
5   <HEAD>
6     <TITLE>Instructors Frame</TITLE>
7   </HEAD>
8
9   <FRAMESET COLS="150,*">
10    <FRAME NAME="instructors_left" SRC="instructors_left_nav"
      NORESIZE>
11    <FRAME NAME="instructors_main" SRC="instructor_list_info"
      SCROLLING="AUTO">
12
13  <NOFRAMES>
14    <BODY>
15      <P>This page uses frames, but your browser doesn''t support
        them. </P>
16    </BODY>
17  </NOFRAMES>
18
19  </FRAMESET>
20  </HTML>
21  ');
22    END;
```

Remember to escape single quotes when using them in a Web Toolkit procedure. The single quote in "doesn't," above, is escaped with a second quote.

WEB TOOLKIT FRAMESET PROCEDURES

Oracle provides procedures specifically for generating framesets in the HTP package.

Table 11.1 is a list of some of the commonly used frame-related procedures and output. For a comprehensive list of HTP procedures, please check Oracle's online documentation.

These frame-related Web Toolkit procedures and the HTP procedures covered in Chapter 10, "Web Toolkit I: HTML and JavaScript with PL/SQL," can be used to rewrite the above procedure, instructors_frame:

```
1   CREATE OR REPLACE PROCEDURE instructors_frame   AS
2   BEGIN
3   htp.htmlOpen;
4   htp.headOpen;
5   htp.title('Instructors Frame');
6   htp.headClose;
7
8   htp.framesetOpen(NULL,'150,*');
9   htp.frame('instructors_left_nav','instructors_left',
    null,null,null,'Y');
```

Table 11.1 ■ Additional HTP Procedures for Frames and Framesets

HTP Procedure	HTML Output
htp.frame('instructors_left_nav', 'instructors_left');	<FRAME SRC="instructors_left_nav" NAME="instructors_left">
htp.frame('instructors_left_nav', 'instructors_left', '0', '0', 'AUTO', 'Y');	<FRAME SRC="instructors_left_nav" NAME="instructors_left" MARGINWIDTH="0" MARGINHEIGHT="0" SCROLLING="AUTO" NORESIZE>
htp.framesetOpen(NULL, '125,*');	<FRAMESET COLS="125, *">
htp.framesetOpen('*,65%', NULL);	<FRAMESET ROWS="*,65%">
htp.framesetOpen('*,65%');	<FRAMESET ROWS="*,65%">
htp.framesetClose;	</FRAMESET>
htp.noframesOpen;	<NOFRAMES>
htp.noframesClose;	</NOFRAMES>

```
10  htp.frame('instructor_list_info','instructors_main',
    null,null,'AUTO');
11
12  htp.noframesOpen;
13   htp.p('<BODY>
14        <P>This page uses frames, but your browser doesn''t
          support them.</P>
15        </BODY>');
16  htp.noframesClose;
17
18  htp.framesetClose;
19   htp.htmlClose;
20   END;
```

UNIT 11.1 EXERCISES

a) Recreate the procedure *instructors_frame*. There are two versions shown in this unit. The first uses the htp.p procedure. The second version makes use of additional htp procedures specifically for frames and framesets. Use either version.

b) Create a procedure called *instructors_left_nav* that will paint two navigation links: "Edit Instructor" and "View Classes." The link for "Edit Instructor" will call the procedure *instructor_list_ info* and load it into the instructors_main frame. The link for "View Classes" will call the procedure *instructor_list_class* and load it into the instructors_main frame. You will create *instructor_list_class* in the exercises for Unit 11.2 of this chapter.

c) View *instructors_frame*. Test that *instructors_left_nav* is displayed properly in the left frame, and *instructor_list_info* appears in the right frame. When "Edit Instructors" is clicked in the left frame, the right frame should be calling *instructor_list_classes*. When "View Classes" is clicked, the right frame will display an error, until the *instructor_list_classes* procedure is created later in Unit 11.2 of this chapter.

UNIT 11.1 EXERCISE ANSWERS

a) Recreate the procedure *instructors_frame*. There are two versions shown in this unit. The first uses the htp.p procedure. The second version makes use of additional htp procedures specifically for frames and framesets. Use either version.

Answer: Using htp.p:

```
1   CREATE OR REPLACE PROCEDURE instructors_frame   AS
2   BEGIN
3   htp.p('
4   <HTML>
5   <HEAD>
6     <TITLE>Instructors Frame</TITLE>
7   </HEAD>
8
9   <FRAMESET COLS="150,*">
10    <FRAME NAME="instructors_left" SRC="instructors_left_nav"
      NORESIZE>
11    <FRAME NAME="instructors_main" SRC="instructor_list_info"
      SCROLLING="AUTO">
12
13  <NOFRAMES>
14    <BODY>
15      <P>This page uses frames, but your browser doesn''t support
        them. </P>
16    </BODY>
17  </NOFRAMES>
18
19  </FRAMESET>
20  </HTML>
21  ');
22    END;
```

Using HTP procedures for frames and framesets:

```
1   CREATE OR REPLACE PROCEDURE instructors_frame   AS
2   BEGIN
3   htp.htmlOpen;
4   htp.headOpen;
5   htp.title('Instructors Frame');
6   htp.headClose;
7
8   htp.framesetOpen(NULL,'150,*');
9   htp.frame('instructors_left_nav','instructors_left',
    null,null,null,'Y');
10  htp.frame('instructor_list_info','instructors_main',
    null,null,'AUTO');
```

```
11
12  htp.noframesOpen;
13   htp.p('<BODY>
14        <P>This page uses frames, but your browser doesn''t
             support them.</P>
15        </BODY>');
16  htp.noframesClose;
17
18  htp.framesetClose;
19  htp.htmlClose;
20  END;
```

b) Create a procedure called *instructors_left_nav* that will paint two navigation links: "Edit Instructor" and "View Classes." The link for "Edit Instructor" will call the procedure *instructor_list_info* and load it into the instructors_main frame. The link for "View Classes" will call the procedure *instructor_list_class* and load it into the instructors_main frame. You will create *instructor_list_classes* in the exercises for Unit 11.2.

Answer:

```
1   CREATE OR REPLACE PROCEDURE instructors_left_nav  AS
2   BEGIN
3   htp.p('
4   <HTML>
5   <HEAD>
6     <TITLE>Instructors Left Nav</TITLE>
7   </HEAD>
8   <BODY BGCOLOR="#99CCCC">
9
10  <TABLE BORDER="0" WIDTH="100%">
11    <TR>
12      <TD ALIGN="center">
13        <A HREF="instructor_list_info"
14        TARGET="instructors_main">
15        <FONT FACE="Arial"><SMALL>Edit Instructor</SMALL>
          </FONT></A>
16      </TD>
17    </TR>
18    <TR>
19      <TD ALIGN="center">
20        <A HREF="instructor_list_class"
21        TARGET="instructors_main">
22        <FONT FACE="Arial"><SMALL>View Classes</SMALL></FONT></A>
23      </TD>
24    </TR>
25  </TABLE>
26
```

```
27   </BODY>
28   </HTML>
29   ');
30   END;
```

c) View *instructors_frame*. Test that *instructors_left_nav* is displayed properly in the left frame, and *instructor_list_info* appears in the right frame. When "Edit Instructors" is clicked in the left frame, the right frame should be calling *instructor_list_classes*. When "View Classes" is clicked, the right frame will display an error, until the *instructor_list_classes* procedure is created later in Unit 11.2.

Answer: View instructors_frame in a browser. The instructors_frame frameset should appear as described.

UNIT 11.2

FORMS AND FORM HANDLERS

FORMS AS A CONTAINER FOR SENDING DATA

Forms are containers for collecting data. The most common tag used in forms, <INPUT>, points to the purpose of form elements: to collect user input and send it off for processing. As described in Chapter 5, "Introduction to HTML: Basic Tags, Tables, and Frames," the form's ACTION attribute indicates where the form data will be sent, and therefore how it will be acted upon. Without a value for the ACTION attribute, a form will do nothing. Similarly, a completed paper job application for an employment agency will accomplish nothing sitting on one's own desk; it must be sent to the agency, who can act upon the data collected in the form. The data collected in an HTML form needs a destination in order for meaningful action to take place.

It is important to consider where form data should be sent, and what the consequences will be. If a job application intended for an employment agency is sent instead to the local public library, the sender will not hear back from the agency as expected, though the library might unexpectedly call to request an interview.

The values that are collected in form elements must be passed to a program that can handle them. This could be a CGI (*Common Gateway Interface*) script, Perl script, ASP, or JSP. In this book's case, it is a PL/SQL procedure that is the ACTION of the form and receives the form's data. PL/SQL can read these incoming values and use them to update a database or to help build the next screen the user sees.

The ACTION of a form cannot be a static HTML page. A static HTML page will not be able to process the information sent to it. Depending on the form's METHOD attribute, one of two things will happen. If the "POST" method is used, the browser will report an error. If the "GET" method is used, the form elements will be included at the end of the URL as name/value pairs. However, they are merely along for the ride. Data is not handled by a static HTML page. When you request an HTML document directly, an HTML page is returned to the browser. When you call PL/SQL procedures from a URL, you are not calling HTML pages directly; you are calling PL/SQL procedures that build HTML pages dynamically and return them to the browser.

> *When you see a form on the Web, this indicates that there must be something at work other than HTML.*

INSTRUCT_PERSONAL_INFO PROCEDURE

In Chapter 10, "Web Toolkit I: HTML and JavaScript with PL/SQL," you build a procedure called instruct_personal_info that contains a form for instructor's personal information. The procedure has an IN parameter of p_instructor_id that determines whose information will be displayed. A default of "101" is used to ensure that someone's information will be displayed even if no instructor id is passed to the procedure. However, this default is purely for development purposes; in this chapter you will call instruct_personal_info with different id numbers to display information for different instructors. You will also build a proper form handler for instruct_personal_info, and specify it as the ACTION attribute; currently, because the FORM tag in this procedure has no value for the ACTION attribute, nothing happens when you click the "Submit" button to submit the form.

Here is the instruct_personal_info procedure from Chapter 10 for easy reference:

```
1   CREATE OR REPLACE PROCEDURE instruct_personal_info
2   (p_instructor_id IN instructor.instructor_id%TYPE DEFAULT 101)
3
4   AS
5     v_instructor_id    instructor.instructor_id%TYPE;
6     v_salutation       instructor.salutation%TYPE;
7     v_first_name       instructor.first_name%TYPE;
8     v_last_name        instructor.last_name%TYPE;
9     v_street_address   instructor.street_address%TYPE;
10    v_city             zipcode.city%TYPE;
11    v_state            zipcode.state%TYPE;
12    v_zip              instructor.zip%TYPE;
13    v_phone            instructor.phone%TYPE;
14  BEGIN
15      SELECT instructor_id,
16             salutation,
17             first_name,
18             last_name,
19             street_address,
20             city,
21             state,
22             i.zip,
23             phone
```

```
24          INTO v_instructor_id,
25               v_salutation,
26               v_first_name,
27               v_last_name,
28               v_street_address,
29               v_city,
30               v_state,
31               v_zip,
32               v_phone
33          FROM instructor i, zipcode z
34        WHERE i.zip = z.zip
35          AND  instructor_id = p_instructor_id;
36  htp.p('<HTML>');
37  htp.p('<HEAD>');
38  htp.p('<TITLE>Instructor Personal Info</TITLE>');
39  htp.p('</HEAD>');
40  htp.p('<BODY bgColor="#99CCCC">');
41  htp.p('<CENTER>');
42  htp.p('<H1>Personal Info For '||v_first_name||' '
    ||v_last_name||'</H1>');
43  htp.p('<H2>This Is The Current Information On Record.</H2>');
44  htp.p('<H3>To Make Changes, Edit The Information And Select
    ''Save''.</H3>');
45  htp.p('<FORM ACTION="" METHOD="post" NAME="instructor_personal_
    form">');
46  htp.p('<INPUT TYPE="hidden" NAME="p_instructor_id"
    VALUE="'||v_instructor_id||'">');
47  htp.p('<TABLE >');
48  htp.p('<TR>');
49  htp.p('<TD>Salutation:</TD>');
50  htp.p('<TD><INPUT TYPE="text" NAME="p_salutation"
    VALUE="'||v_salutation||'" SIZE="5"></TD>');
51  htp.p('</TR>');
52  htp.p('<TR>');
53  htp.p('<TD>First Name:</TD>');
54  htp.p('<TD><INPUT TYPE="text" NAME="p_first_name"
    VALUE="'||v_first_name||'" SIZE="25"></TD>');
55  htp.p('</TR>');
56  htp.p('<TR>');
57  htp.p('<TD>Last Name:</TD>');
58  htp.p('<TD><INPUT TYPE="text" NAME="p_last_name"
    VALUE="'||v_last_name||'" SIZE="25"></TD>');
59  htp.p('</TR>');
60  htp.p('<TR>');
61  htp.p('<TD>Street Address:</TD>');
62  htp.p('<TD><INPUT TYPE="text" NAME="p_street_address"
    VALUE="'||v_street_address||'"></TD>');
63  htp.p('</TR>');
64  htp.p('<TR>');
```

```
65  htp.p('<TD>City:</TD>');
66  htp.p('<TD>'||v_city||'</TD>');
67  htp.p('</TR>');
68  htp.p('<TR>');
69  htp.p('<TD>State:</TD>');
70  htp.p('<TD>'||v_state||'</TD>');
71  htp.p('</TR>');
72  htp.p('<TR>');
73  htp.p('<TD>Zipcode:</TD>');
74  htp.p('<TD><INPUT TYPE="text" NAME="p_zip"
    VALUE="'||v_zip||'"></TD>');
75  htp.p('<TD><INPUT TYPE="BUTTON" VALUE="Change Zipcode"
    onClick="javascript:window.open(''showzip'',
    ''instructor_zip'', ''TOOLBAR=no, STATUS=yes, MENUBAR=no,
    SCROLLBARS=auto, RESIZABLE=yes, WIDTH=640,
    HEIGHT=480'');"></TD>');
76  htp.p('</TR>');
77  htp.p('<TR>');
78  htp.p('<TD>Telephone:</TD>');
79  htp.p('<TD><INPUT TYPE="text" VALUE="'||v_phone||'"
    NAME="p_phone" MAXLENGTH="15" SIZE="15"></TD>');
80  htp.p('</TR>');
81  htp.p('<TR>');
82  htp.p('<TD></TD>');
83  htp.p('<TD ALIGN=left>');
84  htp.p('<INPUT TYPE="submit" VALUE="Save">');
85  htp.p('<INPUT TYPE="reset" VALUE="Reset">');
86  htp.p('</TD>');
87  htp.p('</TR>');
88  htp.p('</TABLE>');
89  htp.p('</FORM>');
90  htp.p('</CENTER>');
91  htp.p('</BODY>');
92  htp.p('</HTML>');
93  EXCEPTION
94  WHEN OTHERS
95  THEN
96    htp.p('An error occurred:  '||SQLERRM||'.  Please try again
      later.');
97  END instruct_personal_info;
```

WEB TOOLKIT FORM PROCEDURES

Oracle has supplied a number of procedures for creating form elements. You can use htp.p with the HTML as you see in the above example or you can use the HTP procedures shown in Table 11.2. The resulting HTML will be the same and the performance will not be affected by which one you choose. As with the frameset procedures listed in Unit 11.1, it is a matter of style which you use.

Table 11.2 ■ Additional HTP Procedures for Forms and Form Elements

HTP Procedure	Output
htp.formOpen('show_zipcode');	<FORM ACTION="show_zipcode" METHOD="POST">
htp.formOpen('show_zipcode','GET', "main_window",null,'NAME="my_form"');	<FORM ACTION="show_zipcode" METHOD="GET" TARGET= "main_window" NAME="my_form">
htp.formText('p_name','20');	<INPUT TYPE="text" NAME="p_name" SIZE="20">
htp.formHidden('p_id','101');	<INPUT TYPE="hidden" NAME="p_id" VALUE="101">
htp.formCheckbox('cname', 'cvalue');	<INPUT TYPE="checkbox" NAME= "cname" VALUE="cvalue">
htp.formCheckbox('cname', 'cvalue', 'CHECKED');	<INPUT TYPE="checkbox" NAME="cname" VALUE="cvalue" CHECKED>
htp.formRadio('p_salutation','Mr.'); htp.p('Mr.');	<INPUT TYPE="radio" NAME= "p_salutation" VALUE="Mr."> Mr.
htp.formRadio('p_salutation','Mrs.', 'CHECKED'); htp.p('Mrs.');	<INPUT TYPE="radio" NAME= "p_salutation" VALUE="Mrs." CHECKED>
htp.formSelectOpen('p_salary', 'Select a Salutation:','1');	Select a Salutation:<SELECT NAME= "p_salary" SIZE="1">
htp.formSelectOption('Less than 5000', cattributes => 'VALUE="low"');	<OPTION VALUE="low">Less than 5000
htp.formSelectOption('5001 to 20000', cattributes => 'VALUE="medium" SELECTED');	<OPTION VALUE="medium" SELECTED>5001 to 20000
htp.FormSelectOption("Greater than 20000', cattributes => 'VALUE="high"');	<OPTION VALUE="high">Greater than 20000
htp.formSelectClose;	</SELECT>
htp.FormSubmit(null, 'Save', 'cattributes');	<INPUT TYPE="submit" VALUE="Save" cattributes>
htp.formReset('Reset the Form', 'cattributes'); htp.FormClose;	<INPUT TYPE="reset" VALUE="Reset the Form" cattributes> </FORM>

FORM HANDLER PROCEDURE

Procedures tend to come in pairs: one procedure that paints a form and one procedure that processes the form data. The procedure that handles processing the form data is known as a "form handler." The form handler is the procedure identified in the ACTION attribute of the FORM tag.

The form handler's job is to take action on the form data it is sent. Accordingly, form handlers tend to contain more PL/SQL and SQL than Web Toolkit commands. They may be concerned entirely with back-end processing, such as inserting or updating records in the database, and they may not use the Web Toolkit to paint any information to the screen. Instead they may call different form-painting procedures when they have finished processing the data, depending on the results.

 Remember to use COMMIT after you have completed processing in the database to save the user's changes.

Whenever a form's purpose is to allow a user to change data, the form should contain an element that uniquely identifies which record is being changed. Usually this identifier is placed in the form as an input of the type "hidden," because it is not something that the user is permitted to alter. This is one use of the "hidden" values for the "type" attribute of the <INPUT> tag, described in detail in Chapter 6, "Advanced HTML: Forms, Nested Tables, and Nested Frames." An INPUT with the type "hidden" will not appear as an input field for the user, but it will be included as data to be passed along with the rest of the form data. Of course, in cases where the ID is meaningful to the user, it can be displayed with htp.p. However, displaying text via htp.p does not make it a form element that is passed to a form handler. In this case, use a hidden input to pass the value to the form handler.

For the form in instruct_personal_info, the form handler must update the instructor's record in the database with the values received from the form. In instruct_personal_info, the "p_instructor_id" value is not displayed because it is not meaningful to the user in this case. It is included as a hidden input in the form, specifically so that it can be passed to the form handler. If the p_instructor_id were not included in the form, then the form handler would have all of the new name and contact information for an instructor, but it would not know which instructor's record should be updated with the new data.

Note that the p_instructor_id has to be added to the form. Although it is an IN parameter for the instruct_personal_info form, that does not mean that it will be passed to any forms that instruct_personal_info contains. The p_instructor_id must be added to the form or it will not be passed.

Since the p_instructor_id value is collected in the form, the form handler will receive it and the record with that instructor_id can be updated with the new information.

What happens next? After the form handler procedure finishes its processing, it will typically call the first procedure again, sending any parameters that are needed. The user will see the form they filled out, now refreshed with the new information. This back-and-forth is typical in Web applications. One procedure paints a form. When the user clicks Submit, a second procedure is called that processes the first form's information. After it finishes processing, the second procedure calls the first one again. This can happen repeatedly, until the user clicks on a navigation link to move to another area. This is not the only way to handle navigation in an application, and users will have requirements about what they wish to see. However, what tends to hold true is that separate applications handle form painting and data processing.

FORM ELEMENTS BECOME "IN" PARAMETERS

Here is why it is so important to name your form elements, as recommended in Chapter 6.

Only named form elements are sent to the form handler procedure. If a form element is not given a name, then it will not be sent to the form handler.

The form handler procedure must have an IN parameter that corresponds to each named form element. These IN parameters must have exactly the same names as the form elements. If a form element is named p_first_name, then the form handler procedure must have an IN parameter called p_first_name. The IN parameters must have datatypes that correspond to the type of data being passed in.

In instruct_personal_info, the form elements that have names are:

- p_instructor_id
- p_salutation
- p_first_name
- p_last_name
- p_street_address
- p_zip
- p_phone

To create a form handler procedure called update_instructor, the beginning of this procedure must have an IN parameter for each named form element:

```
CREATE PROCEDURE update_instructor (
    p_instructor_id  IN instructor.instructor_id%TYPE,
    p_salutation     IN instructor.salutation%TYPE,
```

```
          p_first_name       IN instructor.first_name%TYPE,
          p_last_name        IN instructor.last_name%TYPE,
          p_street_address IN instructor.street_address%TYPE,
          p_zip              IN instructor.zip%TYPE,
          p_phone            IN instructor.phone%TYPE)
      AS...
```

BUTTONS DO NOT REQUIRE NAMES

The Submit button is a Form element, but it is not given a name in the sample procedure instruct_personal_info, and it is not one of the IN parameters listed in the form handler. As a rule, the Submit button should not be given a name. If the Submit button is given a name,

```
<INPUT TYPE="submit" NAME="p_submit" VALUE="Save">
```

and then the Submit button is clicked, then an extra name/value pair will be passed to the form handler. In this case, the parameter name would be "p_submit" and the value would be "Save." Because of this additional unexpected parameter, the submission of the form will raise an error, unless the form handler procedure has an additional IN parameter by this name, "p_submit."

The Submit button provides functionality—a way to submit the form—but it is not typically a container for useful information, such as a first name or last name. For this reason, it is unlikely that you would need to pass this additional name/value pair to the form handler procedure. Likewise, buttons of type "reset" and type "button" are typically not given names, unless there is a very specific and compelling reason to do so.

DEFAULT VALUES FOR "IN" PARAMETERS

What if a parameter is missing? Normally, if a PL/SQL procedure is expecting a parameter and it does not receive one, the procedure cannot be displayed, because one of the expected inputs is missing.

There are cases when an expected parameter might not be sent. For example, checkboxes in a form will not pass a value if they are not checked. Imagine a registration form on the Web that displays a checkbox next to the question, "Do you wish to receive junk mail?"

```
<INPUT NAME="p_get_junk_mail" TYPE="checkbox" VALUE="Y">
Do you wish to receive junk mail?
```

If the box is checked, then the p_get_junk_mail parameter will be passed to the form handler with a value of "Y." However, if the box is not checked, p_get_junk_mail will not be passed at all. The form handler will not receive the IN parameter p_get_junk_mail that it is expecting, and the call to the form handler procedure will fail, because of the mismatch between form elements and IN parameters.

To avoid raising an error, the form handler's IN parameter, p_get_junk_mail, can be given a DEFAULT of NULL. If p_get_junk_mail is not sent by the form, then the form handler procedure will assume that the parameter is present with a value of NULL. This ensures that p_junk_mail will be received, with a value of NULL in this case, even if the user does not check the box and the form does not send the parameter. The form handler procedure would need this IN parameter:

```
CREATE OR REPLACE PROCEDURE handle_registration
    (p_get_junk_mail IN VARCHAR2 DEFAULT NULL) IS ...
```

Another strategy is to choose a specific DEFAULT value for the IN parameter. In the case of the junk mail checkbox, if the box is unchecked then the user does not want to receive extra mail. Thus if no value is sent by the form, then a default value of 'N' can be assumed, as shown here:

```
CREATE OR REPLACE PROCEDURE handle_registration (
    p_get_junk_mail IN VARCHAR2 DEFAULT 'N'
    ) IS...
```

Sometimes DEFAULT values are used as a temporary shortcut during development, though this is a problem because they must be removed later. An example of this risky practice is the instruct_personal_info procedure. The procedure expects an IN parameter of p_instructor_id that determines which instructor's information will be displayed. Since there is not a procedure in place yet that calls instruct_personal_info and passes it a specific instructor id, the procedure assumes a default value of 101 if no p_instructor_id is supplied:

```
CREATE OR REPLACE PROCEDURE instruct_personal_info (
    p_instructor_id IN instructor.instructor_id%TYPE  DEFAULT 101
    ) IS...
```

In the case of instruct_personal_info, the DEFAULT is a shortcut that needs to be removed. Although it has been helpful during development to see results in the instruct_personal_info page, it is dangerous to use such shortcuts because it is easy to forget to remove them later.

If DEFAULT values are used for development purposes, be sure to remove them later!

Another way to pass required parameters to a procedure during development is through a querystring, as discussed later in this chapter under the heading, "Passing Parameters in a URL Querystring."

PRESELECT OR PRECHECK A VALUE

The instruct_personal_info procedure displays information for a specific instructor by using textboxes. To display the first name of an instructor in a textbox, simply set the VALUE attribute equal to the value that is retrieved from the database, using concatenation marks.

■ FOR EXAMPLE

```
htp.p('<TD><INPUT TYPE="text" NAME="p_first_name"
VALUE="'||v_first_name||'" SIZE="25"></TD>');
```

What if select lists, radio buttons, and checkboxes are used in a form to display information? For example, an employee record screen might have radio buttons for full-time or part-time, with one of these choices prechecked to indicate the employee's current status.

These inputs—select lists, radio buttons, and checkboxes—do not display the database value directly. Instead, they are controlled by including the keyword SELECTED for a select list, or CHECKED for radio buttons and checkboxes, to preselect or precheck a value. Below are examples of a select list, radio buttons, and checkboxes painted with PL/SQL, with choices preselected.

■ FOR EXAMPLE

```
-- Select List
htp.p('
Show me restaurants in:
<SELECT NAME="p_restaurants">
    <OPTION VALUE="01" SELECTED>Bronx</OPTION>
    <OPTION VALUE="02">Chelsea</OPTION>
    <OPTION VALUE="03">Forest Hills</OPTION>
    <OPTION VALUE="04">Manhattan</OPTION>
    <OPTION VALUE="05">Upper West Side</OPTION>
</SELECT>
');
```

■ FOR EXAMPLE

```
-- Radio Buttons
htp.p('
Employee Status: <BR>
<INPUT NAME="p_status" TYPE="RADIO" VALUE="FT"> Full-Time
<INPUT NAME="p_status" TYPE="RADIO" VALUE="PT" CHECKED> Part-Time
');
```

■ *FOR EXAMPLE*

```
-- Checkboxes
htp.p('
Hobbies (check all that apply): <BR>
<INPUT NAME="p_hobby" TYPE="CHECKBOX" VALUE="01" CHECKED> Karaoke
<INPUT NAME="p_hobby" TYPE="CHECKBOX" VALUE="02" CHECKED> Kayaking
<INPUT NAME="p_hobby" TYPE="CHECKBOX" VALUE="03"> Kazoo Playing
');
```

How do you know which choices need the CHECKED or SELECTED keywords? One customer may be interested in kayaking, whereas another customer is only interested in karaoke. To make sure the appropriate choice is picked, use PL/SQL IF-THEN-ELSE logic. First, use PL/SQL to determine the value that is the "right" answer—the value that should be chosen. This can be done through a trip to the database to retrieve information about a specific record, or through IN parameters that indicate what should be selected or checked.

Then, as each choice is painted to the screen, compare its value with this "right" answer, using IF-THEN-ELSE logic. If the values match, include the word SELECTED for a select list, or CHECKED for radio buttons and checkboxes.

This can be demonstrated by modifying the showzip procedure, created in Chapter 10," Web Toolkit I: HTML and JavaScript with PL/SQL." The showzip procedure is called from the instruct_personal_info procedure. Showzip paints a SELECT list of zipcodes in a popup window, without preselecting any of these zipcodes. Ideally, however, the zipcode for the current instructor should be highlighted when the select list is painted. The original code for showzip from Chapter 10 is below:

■ *FOR EXAMPLE*

```
1   CREATE OR REPLACE PROCEDURE showzip
2   IS
3      CURSOR c_zip IS
4          SELECT city, state, zip
5          FROM zipcode
6          ORDER BY state, city, zip;
7   BEGIN
8   htp.htmlOpen;
9   htp.headOpen;
10  htp.title('Instructor Zipcode');
11  htp.headClose;
12  htp.bodyOpen(cattributes => 'BGCOLOR="#99CCCC"');
13  htp.centerOpen;
14  htp.p('<FORM NAME="zipcode_form" ACTION="" METHOD="post">');
15  htp.p('<SELECT NAME="p_new_zip" SIZE="15">');
16      FOR rec IN c_zip
```

```
17        LOOP
18             htp.p('<OPTION VALUE="'||rec.zip||'">'
19                    ||rec.city||', '||rec.state||'  '||rec.zip||
20              '</OPTION>');
21        END LOOP;
22  htp.p('</SELECT>');
23  htp.p('<BR>');
24  htp.p('<BR>');
25
26  htp.p('<INPUT TYPE="button" VALUE="Select Zipcode">');
27  htp.p('<INPUT TYPE="button" VALUE="Cancel"
    onClick="window.close();">');
28  htp.formClose;
29  htp.centerClose;
30  htp.bodyClose;
31  htp.htmlClose;
32
33  EXCEPTION
34  WHEN OTHERS
35  THEN
36     htp.p('An error occurred: '||SQLERRM||'. Please try again
       later.');
37  END;
```

Here are the steps to take to preselect a zipcode in the showzip procedure.

1. Modify showzip to take a new IN parameter of p_zip. This IN parameter will be the zipcode that should be highlighted.
2. Compare p_zip with the value of each option as it is painted.
3. When p_zip matches the option being painted, include the word SELECTED to highlight that option.

Below is a new version of showzip that incorporates these changes. For development purposes, p_zip is given a DEFAULT value of 10019. Later in this chapter, you will modify the calling procedure, instruct_personal_info, to pass a zipcode to showzip, so that different zipcodes can be highlighted, depending upon what is passed to showzip.

■ FOR EXAMPLE

```
1  CREATE OR REPLACE PROCEDURE showzip
2    (p_zip IN instructor.zip%TYPE DEFAULT '10019')
3  IS
4     CURSOR c_zip IS
5        SELECT city, state, zip
6          FROM zipcode
7         ORDER BY state, city, zip;
```

```
 8   BEGIN
 9     htp.htmlOpen;
10     htp.headOpen;
11     htp.title('Instructor Zipcode');
12     htp.headClose;
13     htp.bodyOpen(cattributes => 'BGCOLOR="#99CCCC"');
14     htp.centerOpen;
15     htp.p('<FORM NAME="zipcode_form" ACTION="instruct_personal_
       info" METHOD=POST>');
16     htp.p('<SELECT NAME="p_new_zip" SIZE=15>');
17        FOR rec IN c_zip LOOP
18        IF rec.zip = p_zip THEN
19           htp.p('<OPTION VALUE="'||rec.zip||'" SELECTED>'
20                    ||rec.city||', '||rec.state||'  '||rec.zip||
21              '</OPTION>');
22        ELSE
23           htp.p('<OPTION VALUE="'||rec.zip||'">'
24                    ||rec.city||', '||rec.state||'  '||rec.zip||
25              '</OPTION>');
26        END IF;
27        END LOOP;
28     htp.p('</SELECT>');
29     htp.p('<BR>');
30     htp.p('<BR>');
31
32     htp.p('<INPUT TYPE="button" VALUE="Select Zipcode" onClick=
       "chooseZip()">');
33     htp.p('<INPUT TYPE="button" VALUE="Cancel" onClick="window.
       close()">');
34     htp.formClose;
35     htp.centerClose;
36     htp.bodyClose;
37     htp.htmlClose;
38
39   EXCEPTION
40   WHEN OTHERS THEN
41      htp.p('An error occurred:  '||SQLERRM||'.  Please try again
        later.');
42   END;
```

PASSING MULTIPLE VALUES IN A PL/SQL TABLE

You may need to pass multiple values for the same parameter. In <SELECT> lists, specifying the keyword MULTIPLE in the <SELECT> tag allows users to select multiple values for the same input, using the Control key. The example below shows the syntax for creating a multiple select list. Here, users are allowed to choose to view restaurant listings for more than one area:

```
Show me restaurants in:<BR>
<SELECT NAME="p_restaurants" MULTIPLE>
   <OPTION VALUE="101">Bronx</OPTION>
   <OPTION VALUE="102">Chelsea</OPTION>
   <OPTION VALUE="103">Forest Hills</OPTION>
   <OPTION VALUE="104">Manhattan</OPTION>
   <OPTION VALUE="105">Upper West Side</OPTION>
</SELECT>
```

This is the same syntax as for a single SELECT list except for the addition of the word MULTIPLE. The resulting select list is shown in Figure 11.1.

It is quite likely that a hungry user would want to search for restaurants in more than one area. When multiple items are selected, multiple values are passed *for the same parameter.* If a user checked the first, third, and fourth options above, then p_restaurants would have three values: Bronx, Forest Hills, and Manhattan.

To hold these multiple values, the form handler must have an IN parameter that is expecting an array of values. With PL/SQL, multiple values can be stored in a PL/SQL table. The IN parameter can have a PL/SQL table type.

For example, if the above SELECT list is in a form with the ACTION="get_restaurants," then the get_restaurants procedure needs an IN parameter named p_restaurants with a datatype of a PL/SQL table.

Oracle has declared several PL/SQL table types in the OWA_UTIL package specification for you to use:

```
TYPE ident_arr IS TABLE OF VARCHAR2(30)
   INDEX BY BINARY_INTEGER;
TYPE num_arr IS TABLE OF NUMBER
 INDEX BY BINARY_INTEGER;
TYPE ip_address IS TABLE OF INTEGER
   INDEX BY BINARY_INTEGER;
```

To refer to these types, use standard PL/SQL package syntax. For example, the declaration section of one of your procedures could contain the following declaration:

```
v_countries OWA_UTIL.ident_arr;
```

Show me restaurants in:

| Bronx |
| Chelsea |
| Forest Hills |
| Manhattan |

Figure 11.1 ■ Select list for choosing restaurants.

If the PL/SQL type declarations provided by Oracle in the OWA_UTIL package specification are not sufficient, such as when you have values that are too long to fit in these predefined types, then you will need to declare additional types in a package specification of your own. The types must be declared in a package specification so that they are available outside of the package. Note that they cannot be declared within the same PL/SQL procedure that is using them because they would be declared too late; the array of values being passed in must be dealt with before the DECLARE section of the procedure is reached.

The values passed in p_restaurants all qualify as VARCHAR2(30), so you can use the datatype OWA_UTIL.IDENT_ARR. The get_restaurants procedure could begin like this:

```
CREATE OR REPLACE PROCEDURE get_restaurants (
    p_restaurants IN OWA_UTIL.IDENT_ARR
    ) IS...
```

Note that you do not need to write `OWA_UTIL.IDENT_ARR%TYPE`. That is because `OWA_UTIL.IDENT_ARR` is itself a type declaration in the `OWA_UTIL` package, so the `%TYPE` is not necessary.

The only values that are sent in p_restaurants are the values that are selected by the user. If the first, third, and fourth options are selected by the user who submits the form, then the PL/SQL table p_restaurants contains the information in Table 11.3.

Notice that the PL/SQL table p_restaurants only has three values stored in it, even though the select list has five options. This is because only three of the five options are selected, and only selected options are passed. Also, notice that the index of the PL/SQL table starts with 1 and increments by 1. Even though options 1, 3, and 4 were selected in our example, the table indices are 1, 2, and 3. This makes it easy to loop through the records in the table without knowing how many there are beforehand, using standard PL/SQL table notation. To retrieve the second value in the list, use p_restaurants(2). To retrieve the index number for the first and last records, use p_restaurants.FIRST and p_restaurants.LAST. The following code would loop through the index numbers of the PL/SQL table, and insert all three table values into the database table REST_REGIONS.

Table 11.3 ■ Data Passed in p_restaurants when Bronx, Forest Hills, and Manhattan Options Selected

PL/SQL Table p_restaurants(index)	Value
p_restaurants(1)	101
p_restaurants(2)	103
p_restaurants(3)	104

■ *FOR EXAMPLE*

```
CREATE OR REPLACE PROCEDURE get_restaurants (
    p_restaurants IN OWA_UTIL.IDENT_ARR
    ) IS
BEGIN
   FOR v_index_number IN p_restaurants.FIRST..p_restaurants.LAST
   LOOP
      INSERT INTO REST_REGIONS (
         region
         )
      VALUES (
         p_restaurants(v_index_number)
         );
   END LOOP;
  COMMIT;
END;
```

**UNIT
11.2**

PASSING NO VALUES IN A PL/SQL TABLE

What happens if someone doesn't select any restaurants at all?

Usually you specify DEFAULT NULL if the user isn't required to supply a parameter. However, specifying DEFAULT NULL for a PL/SQL table parameter will result in an error:

```
PLS-00382: expression is of wrong type
```

There are two workarounds for this problem. The first is to always send a dummy value with the same name as the form element. That way the PL/SQL table will always have at least one value, which can be ignored later. This can be done with a HIDDEN input, created immediately before or after the list. It must be next to the other p_restaurants INPUT:

```
<INPUT TYPE="hidden" NAME="p_restaurants" VALUE="dummy">
```

You can also declare a variable with the type of a PL/SQL table. Declare it in a package specification so that it is easily accessible to other packages/procedures. The syntax is the same as when you declare any other variable—specify the variable name and the datatype:

```
nothungry OWA_UTIL.IDENT_ARR;
```

If this variable is declared in a package specification, such as in a package called "restaurants," other programs could refer to it as restaurants.nothungry, and use it like this:

```
CREATE OR REPLACE PROCEDURE get_restaurants (
  p_restaurants IN OWA_UTIL.IDENT_ARR DEFAULT restaurants.nothungry
) IS...
```

Note that in the example above, nothungry cannot be declared inside the get_restaurants procedure that uses it. The parameter list is read before the DE-CLARE section of get_restaurants, so declaring nothungry in the DECLARE section would be too late.

COMMUNICATING WITH THE USER

Once a form handler has finished processing, how will the user know? How will the user realize when an error occurs during processing?

Notification that a transaction has succeeded should occur only after processing has finished and a commit has been issued. A common mistake is to issue an alert such as "The record is saved," regardless of whether the back-end processing completed and was committed without errors.

Before notifying the user about the status of a transaction, verify that what you will state is true. A message stating that processing completed successfully, followed by an error message, is a serious error that will not inspire trust in the user.

A pop-up JavaScript alert, as described in Chapter 7, "Introduction to JavaScript," is one way to notify the user about how things are going. An alert is informational. It forces the user to click on an "OK" button (or press the Enter key) to make it go away, which might make the reader pay attention to the pop-up message first.

Another way to handle notification is to write an additional message to the next screen. Suppose that the person who fills out the instructor form and clicks "Submit" wants to be returned to the instructor form again, to see the changes reflected on the screen. The way this navigation occurs is for the form handler procedure to call the original form procedure. A message or an error/success code can be passed to the original form procedure, if it has an IN parameter to handle the extra data. The procedure can check this value when painting the form, and display a message as appropriate.

Another consideration is that after calling that procedure, control returns to the form handler. In PL/SQL, if procedure A calls procedure B, when B is finished processing, control passes to A, which continues to the next line after the call to B. In form handlers, the program typically ends after this point, because the call to another procedure happens after all processing is done. However, instead of simply ending the form handler, a line can be printed to the new screen using JavaScript's document.write function. Although the HTML tags are closed, the JavaScript will still execute successfully in most browsers.

Below is a sample form handler, *update_instructor*, to handle data from the form *instructor_personal_form*. It uses a pop-up and the document.write() JavaScript function to notify the user that the record is processed. Also, the EXCEPTION section displays a message to the user if any errors were raised:

```
1    CREATE OR REPLACE PROCEDURE update_instructor
2      (p_instructor_id   IN  instructor.instructor_id%TYPE,
3       p_salutation      IN  instructor.salutation%TYPE,
4       p_first_name      IN  instructor.first_name%TYPE,
5       p_last_name       IN  instructor.last_name%TYPE,
6       p_street_address  IN  instructor.street_address%TYPE,
7       p_zip             IN  instructor.zip%TYPE,
8       p_phone           IN  instructor.phone%TYPE)
10   AS
11   BEGIN
12       -- processing goes here
13       COMMIT;
14
15   -- display an alert
16   htp.p('<HTML>
17          <HEAD><TITLE>Update Instructor Personal
             Info</TITLE></HEAD>
18          <BODY>');
19
20   htp.script('alert("The new information for this instructor
             has been saved successfully!");', 'JavaScript');
21
22   htp.p('</BODY>
23          </HTML>');
24
25   -- call the procedure to repaint the form.
26   instruct_personal_info(p_instructor_id);
27
28   htp.script('document.write("<H3><CENTER><FONT COLOR=RED>The new
     information for this instructor has been successfully saved!
     </FONT></CENTER></H3>");', 'JavaScript');
29
30   EXCEPTION
31   WHEN OTHERS THEN
32       htp.p('An error occurred:  '||SQLERRM||'.  Please try again
           later.');
33   END;
```

The JavaScript alert message shown above must not contain a carriage return. In your code, put the alert message on a single line to avoid carriage returns in the alert message. Alternately, use the JavaScript concatenation symbol, +, to concatenate multiple lines of an alert message.

MULTIPLE FORMS

Forms cannot be placed inside of other forms or overlap with other forms.

However, a page can, and often does, have more than one form. One example of this is when there is a table with many rows, but a user only needs to process one row at a time. A button on the bottom of the screen that processes all rows would not be useful, because the user only needs to process one row, not all of them. One solution is for each row of the table, each item record, to have its own form.

Figure 11.2 is a sample Web page showing the students enrolled in a section. Each student is on a separate row. The last column either contains a final grade, or a button that says, "Calculate Grade" that calls a procedure to calculate the final grade for that student. Grades are calculated for one student at a time, so each student has a separate Submit button. Moreover, each button is in its own form. Each form contains the important pieces of information: the student id number and the section id number. However, the values are different for each form.

Here is the procedure used to create this page. Note that each button is enclosed in FORM tags. Each form has two hidden inputs that hold the section id and student id. As the cursor loops through the records, the student id keeps changing, so each button has a different value for the p_student_id hidden input. The section_id remains the same, but it is included in each form because the form

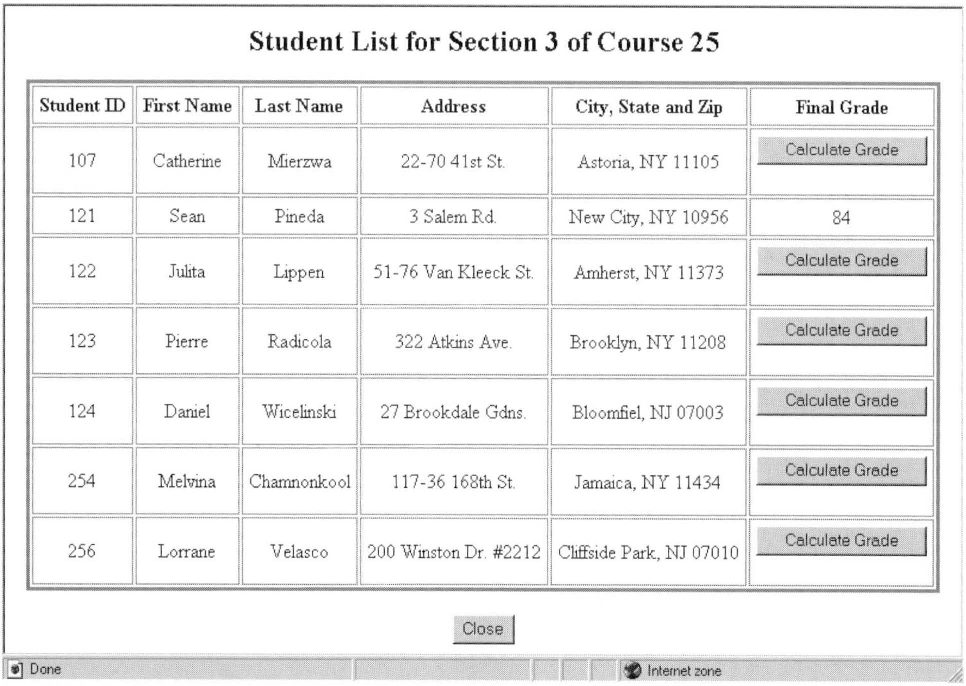

Student List for Section 3 of Course 25

Student ID	First Name	Last Name	Address	City, State and Zip	Final Grade
107	Catherine	Mierzwa	22-70 41st St.	Astoria, NY 11105	Calculate Grade
121	Sean	Pineda	3 Salem Rd.	New City, NY 10956	84
122	Julita	Lippen	51-76 Van Kleeck St.	Amherst, NY 11373	Calculate Grade
123	Pierre	Radicola	322 Atkins Ave.	Brooklyn, NY 11208	Calculate Grade
124	Daniel	Wicelinski	27 Brookdale Gdns.	Bloomfiel, NJ 07003	Calculate Grade
254	Melvina	Chamnonkool	117-36 168th St.	Jamaica, NY 11434	Calculate Grade
256	Lorrane	Velasco	200 Winston Dr. #2212	Cliffside Park, NJ 07010	Calculate Grade

Close

Done — Internet zone

Figure 11.2 ■ Output of procedure student_list as viewed in a Web browser.

handler will need to know both the student's id and the section's id to calculate a grade for the student for this section. For development purposes, a default of 87 was used for the incoming section id.

```
1   CREATE OR REPLACE PROCEDURE student_list
2     (p_section_id IN section.section_id%TYPE DEFAULT 87)
3   IS
4     v_section_no section.section_no%TYPE;
5     v_course_no  course.course_no%TYPE;
6     CURSOR c_students IS
7       SELECT s.student_id, first_name, last_name,
8               street_address, city, state, s.zip,
9               final_grade
10       FROM student s, zipcode z, enrollment e
11      WHERE s.zip        = z.zip
12        AND s.student_id = e.student_id
13        AND section_id   = p_section_id
14     ORDER BY s.student_id;
15
16  BEGIN
17
18     SELECT section_no, course_no
19       INTO v_section_no, v_course_no
20       FROM section
21      WHERE section_id = p_section_id;
22
23  htp.p('<HTML>
24          <HEAD>
25            <TITLE>Instructor Classes/Section Student List</TITLE>
26          </HEAD>
27          <BODY BGCOLOR="#FFFFFF">
28          <CENTER>
29          <H2>Student List for Section '||v_section_no
30                ||' of Course '||v_course_no||'</H2>
31          <TABLE BORDER=3 BORDERCOLOR="#0099CC" CELLPADDING=5>
32            <TR>
33             <TH>Student ID</TH>
34             <TH>First Name</TH>
35             <TH>Last Name</TH>
36             <TH>Address</TH>
37             <TH>City, State and Zip</TH>
38             <TH>Final Grade</TH>
39            </TR>');
40
41     FOR rec IN c_students
42     LOOP
43        htp.p('
44            <TR><TD ALIGN="center">'||rec.student_id||'</TD>
45                <TD ALIGN="center">'||rec.first_name||'</TD>
```

```
46                    <TD ALIGN="center">'||rec.last_name||'</TD>
47                    <TD ALIGN="center">'||rec.street_address||'</TD>
48                    <TD ALIGN="center">'||rec.city||', '||rec.state
49                       ||' '||rec.zip||'</TD>');
50      IF rec.final_grade IS NULL
51      THEN
52         htp.p('<TD ALIGN="center">
53                  <FORM NAME="my_repeating_form"
54                  ACTION="student_list_update" METHOD="POST">
55                    <INPUT TYPE="hidden" NAME="p_student_id"
56                      VALUE="'||rec.student_id||'">
57                    <INPUT TYPE="hidden" NAME="p_section_id"
58                      VALUE="'||p_section_id||'">
59                    <INPUT TYPE="submit"
60                      VALUE="Calculate Grade">
61                  </FORM>
62                  </TD>');
63      ELSE
64         htp.p('<TD ALIGN="center">'||rec.final_grade||'</TD>');
65      END IF;
66         htp.p('</TR>');
67      END LOOP;
68      htp.p('</TABLE>');
69      htp.p('<BR>');
70      htp.p('<INPUT TYPE="button" VALUE="Close"
71             onClick="window.close();">');
72      htp.p('</CENTER>');
73      htp.p('</BODY>');
74      htp.p('</HTML>');
75
76   EXCEPTION
77   WHEN OTHERS THEN
78      htp.p('An error occurred:  '||SQLERRM||'.  Please try again
         later.');
79   END;
```

UNIT 11.2 EXERCISES

a) Change the procedure *instruct_personal_info*. In the FORM tag, change the ACTION to *update_instructor*.

b) Create the procedure *update_instructor*, to update the instructor record in the database based on the information passed in from the form. Then return the user to the instruct_personal_ info page by including this line to call the *instruct_personal_info* procedure:

```
instruct_personal_info(p_instructor_id);
```

Test to see that the update is changing the data in the database. If you enter a new zipcode, use one of the zipcodes listed in the pop-up window.

c) Change and recompile the procedure *showzip* as shown in this section, under the heading "Preselect or Precheck a Value." To test the procedure, specify a DEFAULT value of 10019. Later, in the exercises for Unit 11.3 of this chapter, you will revise instruct_personal_info to pass the p_zip parameter that showzip needs.

d) Create the procedure *student_list* shown in Unit 11.2, under the heading "Multiple Forms." To test the procedure, include a DEFAULT value of 87 for the IN parameter to test the procedure. Then remove this DEFAULT value. Later in this chapter you will create a procedure to call student_list and pass the parameter it needs, and learn another way to supply IN parameters during development.

UNIT 11.2 EXERCISE ANSWERS

a) Change the procedure *instruct_personal_info*. In the FORM tag, change the ACTION to *update_instructor*.

Answer:

```
htp.p('<FORM ACTION="update_instructor" METHOD="get"
NAME="instructor_personal_form">');
```

b) Create the procedure *update_instructor* to update the instructor record in the database based on the information passed in from the form. Then return the user to the instruct_personal_info page by including this line to call the *instruct_personal_info* procedure:

```
instruct_personal_info(p_instructor_id);
```

Test to see that the update is changing the data in the database. If you enter a new zipcode, use one of the zipcodes listed in the pop-up window.

Answer:

```
CREATE OR REPLACE PROCEDURE update_instructor
    (p_instructor_id   IN instructor.instructor_id%TYPE,
     p_salutation      IN instructor.salutation%TYPE,
     p_first_name      IN instructor.first_name%TYPE,
     p_last_name       IN instructor.last_name%TYPE,
     p_street_address  IN instructor.street_address%TYPE,
     p_zip             IN instructor.zip%TYPE,
     p_phone           IN instructor.phone%TYPE)

IS

BEGIN

    UPDATE instructor
       SET salutation        = p_salutation,
           first_name        = p_first_name,
           last_name         = p_last_name,
           street_address    = p_street_address,
           zip               = p_zip,
           phone             = p_phone
     WHERE instructor_id     = p_instructor_id;

    COMMIT;
    htp.p('<HTML>
        <HEAD><TITLE>Update Instructor Personal Info</TITLE></HEAD>
        <BODY>');
    htp.script('alert("The new information for this instructor
             has been saved successfully!");', 'JavaScript');
    htp.p('</BODY>
        </HTML>');

    instruct_personal_info(p_instructor_id);

    htp.script('document.write("<H3><CENTER><FONT COLOR=RED>The new
    information for this instructor has been successfully
    saved!</FONT></CENTER></H3>");', 'JavaScript');

EXCEPTION
WHEN OTHERS THEN
    htp.p('An error occurred:  '||SQLERRM||'.  Please try again
    later.');
END;
```

c) Change and recompile the procedure *showzip* as shown in this unit, under the heading "Preselect or Precheck a Value." To test the procedure, specify a DEFAULT value of 10019. Later, in the exercises for Unit 11.3, you will revise instruct_personal_info to pass the p_zip parameter that showzip needs.

Answer:

```
1   CREATE OR REPLACE PROCEDURE showzip
2       (p_zip IN instructor.zip%TYPE DEFAULT '10019')
3   IS
4       CURSOR c_zip IS
5           SELECT city, state, zip
6             FROM zipcode
7           ORDER BY state, city, zip;
8   BEGIN
9   htp.htmlOpen;
10  htp.headOpen;
11  htp.title('Instructor Zipcode');
12  htp.headClose;
13  htp.bodyOpen(cattributes => 'BGCOLOR="#99CCCC"');
14  htp.centerOpen;
15  htp.p('<FORM NAME="zipcode_form" ACTION="instruct_personal_
    info" METHOD=POST>');
16  htp.p('<SELECT NAME="p_new_zip" SIZE=15>');
17      FOR rec IN c_zip LOOP
18      IF rec.zip = p_zip THEN
19          htp.p('<OPTION VALUE="'||rec.zip||'" SELECTED>'
20                  ||rec.city||', '||rec.state||'  '||rec.zip||
21              '</OPTION>');
22      ELSE
23          htp.p('<OPTION VALUE="'||rec.zip||'">'
24                  ||rec.city||', '||rec.state||'  '||rec.zip||
25              '</OPTION>');
26      END IF;
27      END LOOP;
28  htp.p('</SELECT>');
29  htp.p('<BR>');
30  htp.p('<BR>');
31
32  htp.p('<INPUT TYPE="button" VALUE="Select Zipcode" onClick=
    "chooseZip()">');
33  htp.p('<INPUT TYPE="button" VALUE="Cancel" onClick=
    "window.close()">');
34  htp.formClose;
35  htp.centerClose;
36  htp.bodyClose;
37  htp.htmlClose;
38
39  EXCEPTION
```

```
40   WHEN OTHERS THEN
41      htp.p('An error occurred:  '||SQLERRM||'.  Please try again
         later.');
42   END;
```

d) Create the procedure *student_list* shown in this unit, under the heading "Multiple Forms." To test the procedure, include a DEFAULT value of 87 for the IN parameter to test the procedure. Then remove this DEFAULT value. Later in this chapter you will create a procedure to call student_list and pass the parameter it needs, and learn another way to supply IN parameters during development.

Answer:

```
1    CREATE OR REPLACE PROCEDURE student_list
2       (p_section_id IN section.section_id%TYPE DEFAULT 87)
3    IS
4       v_section_no section.section_no%TYPE;
5       v_course_no  course.course_no%TYPE;
6       CURSOR c_students IS
7          SELECT s.student_id, first_name, last_name,
8                 street_address, city, state, s.zip,
9                 final_grade
10           FROM student s, zipcode z, enrollment e
11          WHERE s.zip        = z.zip
12            AND s.student_id = e.student_id
13            AND section_id   = p_section_id
14         ORDER BY s.student_id;
15
16   BEGIN
17
18      SELECT section_no, course_no
19        INTO v_section_no, v_course_no
20        FROM section
21       WHERE section_id = p_section_id;
22
23   htp.p('<HTML>
24          <HEAD>
25            <TITLE>Instructor Classes/Section Student List</TITLE>
26          </HEAD>
27          <BODY BGCOLOR="#FFFFFF">
28          <CENTER>
29          <H2>Student List for Section '||v_section_no
30                ||' of Course '||v_course_no||'</H2>
31          <TABLE BORDER=3 BORDERCOLOR="#0099CC" CELLPADDING=5>
32            <TR>
33             <TH>Student ID</TH>
34             <TH>First Name</TH>
35             <TH>Last Name</TH>
36             <TH>Address</TH>
```

```
37              <TH>City, State and Zip</TH>
38              <TH>Final Grade</TH>
39          </TR>');
40
41      FOR rec IN c_students
42      LOOP
43          htp.p('
44              <TR><TD ALIGN="center">'||rec.student_id||'</TD>
45                  <TD ALIGN="center">'||rec.first_name||'</TD>
46                  <TD ALIGN="center">'||rec.last_name||'</TD>
47                  <TD ALIGN="center">'||rec.street_address||'</TD>
48                  <TD ALIGN="center">'||rec.city||', '||rec.state
49                      ||' '||rec.zip||'</TD>');
50      IF rec.final_grade IS NULL
51      THEN
52          htp.p('<TD ALIGN="center">
53                  <FORM NAME="my_repeating_form"
54                  ACTION="student_list_update" METHOD="POST">
55                      <INPUT TYPE="hidden" NAME="p_student_id"
56                      VALUE="'||rec.student_id||'">
57                      <INPUT TYPE="hidden" NAME="p_section_id"
58                      VALUE="'||p_section_id||'">
59                      <INPUT TYPE="submit"
60                      VALUE="Calculate Grade">
61                  </FORM>
62                  </TD>');
63      ELSE
64          htp.p('<TD ALIGN="center">'||rec.final_grade||'</TD>');
65      END IF;
66          htp.p('</TR>');
67      END LOOP;
68      htp.p('</TABLE>');
69      htp.p('<BR>');
70      htp.p('<INPUT TYPE="button" VALUE="Close"
71              onClick="window.close();">');
72      htp.p('</CENTER>');
73      htp.p('</BODY>');
74      htp.p('</HTML>');
75
76  EXCEPTION
77  WHEN OTHERS THEN
78      htp.p('An error occurred: '||SQLERRM||'. Please try again
        later.');
79  END;
```

UNIT 11.3

PASSING PARAMETERS WITHOUT SUBMITTING FORMS

Forms are perhaps the most common way of sending data from one page to another on the Web. However, there are other ways that information is passed from one page to another. This section guides you through passing parameters in a URL, in PL/SQL itself, and within JavaScript.

PASSING PARAMETERS IN PL/SQL CALLS

In PL/SQL, parameters can be passed when a procedure or function is called. The procedure being called must have IN parameters that can receive the data. This holds true regardless of whether a PL/SQL procedure contains Web Toolkit functionality.

Suppose a procedure starts like this.

■ FOR EXAMPLE

```
CREATE OR REPLACE PROCEDURE subway
    (p_line       IN   VARCHAR2,
     p_passengers IN   NUMBER)
AS...
```

The procedure *subway* can be called in the following ways:

```
subway('Central', 256);
subway(p_passengers => 256, p_line => 'Central');
```

However, the next procedure call would be incorrect and raise an error, since the value 'Central' cannot be converted into a number field.

```
subway(256,'Central');
```

One difference between passing parameters in PL/SQL, and passing values in an HTML form, is the parameter names. In an HTML form, each form element being passed must have a name, and the parameter in the processing procedure must have exactly the same name. PL/SQL is not so picky; as long as the data being passed is of the same datatype as the parameter that receives it, that is okay. This is why PL/SQL procedures can be called by listing values in parentheses, separated by commas, without any mention of their names, unless you want to explicitly include that information with =>. Otherwise, the values passed in are assigned to the parameters in the order in which they are received. It is important to pass parameters in PL/SQL in the order that the called procedure lists its IN parameters, if you do not choose to use => to specify which parameters have which values.

PASSING PARAMETERS IN A URL QUERYSTRING

Querystrings are a familiar sight for users of the Web. A querystring is a sequence of name/value pairs that appear at the end of a URL. Querystrings can be used to pass values to a PL/SQL procedure. The name/value pairs are added after a question mark, with an ampersand (&) separating each name/value pair. The syntax at the end of the URL is:

```
URL?name1=value1&name2=value2&name3=value3&name4=value4
```

Here is an example of a querystring that passes one parameter (on a single line in the browser):

```
http://server4.virgil.edu/pls/any/instruct_personal_info?
p_instructor_id=101
```

If three parameters are passed, the URL might look like this:

```
http://server4.virgil.edu/pls/any/instruct_personal_info?
p_instructor_id=101&p_user=Administrator&p_new=No
```

To see information for another instructor using your instruct_personal_info procedure, add a querystring to the end of the URL. Try calling the procedure for instructor 102:

```
http://server4.virgil.edu/pls/any/instruct_personal_info?
p_instructor_id=102
```

 Instead of using DEFAULT values for IN parameters while your Web application is still in development, pass values for any required parameters in the URL. In the address bar of the browser, type the querystring at the end of the URL to supply any required parameters.

You may have used METHOD=GET in the FORM tag. Doing this will display the querystring in the URL. This can also be a helpful debugging technique when you want to see the information that was passed in the form in the URL.

QUERYSTRINGS IN LINKS

Links indicate where the browser should go if a link is clicked. A link to another page can include a querystring. Recall that one page can call another using a "relative URL" that does not include the entire string beginning with http.

■ FOR EXAMPLE

```
htp.p('<A HREF="instruct_personal_info?p_instructor_id=109">
Chow, Rick</A>');
```

When a user clicks on the link <u>Chow, Rick</u> the browser calls the procedure instruct_personal_info page, and this instruct_personal_info procedure is passed the p_instructor_id value of 109.

In a PL/SQL procedure, the value for p_instructor_id will most likely come from a variable. If the instructor ID is being held in a variable called v_instructor, that variable can be added to the link by concatenating the variable name with the URL in the link:

```
htp.p('<A HREF="instruct_personal_info?p_instructor_id='||
v_instructor||'">
Chow, Rick</A>');
```

The instructor_list_info procedure in Chapter 10, "Web Toolkit I: HTML and JavaScript with PL/SQL," provides a list of instructors. Each instructor should have a link beside their name that calls the *instruct_personal_info* page and passes the instructor's ID. What changes need to be made to the existing procedure?

First, here is the existing procedure created in Chapter 10.

```
CREATE OR REPLACE PROCEDURE instructor_list_info
AS
    CURSOR get_instructor IS
        SELECT first_name, last_name, instructor_id
        FROM instructor
        ORDER BY last_name, first_name;
BEGIN
htp.p('<HTML>');
htp.p('<HEAD>');
htp.p('<TITLE>Instructor Maintenance Web Site</TITLE>');
htp.p('</HEAD>');
htp.p('<BODY BgColor="#99CCCC">');
htp.p('<CENTER>');
```

```
htp.p('<H2>List of Instructors</H2>');
htp.p('<TABLE ALIGN="center" BORDER="3" BORDERCOLOR="midnight blue"
        CELLPADDING="5" WIDTH="100%">');
htp.p('<TR>');
htp.p('<TH ALIGN="center">Instructor Names</TH>');
htp.p('</TR>');
FOR rec IN get_instructor
LOOP
    htp.p('<TR>');
    htp.p('<TD><FONT FACE="Arial">'
          ||rec.last_name||','||rec.first_name||'</FONT></TD>');
    htp.p('</TR>');
END LOOP;
htp.p('</TABLE>');
htp.p('</CENTER>');
htp.p('</BODY>');
EXCEPTION
WHEN OTHERS
THEN
    htp.p('An error occurred:  '||SQLERRM||'.  Please try again
    later.');
END;
```

What needs to be added is a link where the instructor's name is displayed. Since there needs to be one link for each instructor, the link should be painted inside of the cursor FOR loop. The instructor_id is selected in the cursor, so it will be available for each iteration of the loop. The code within the loop can be changed as follows:

```
FOR rec IN get_instructor
LOOP
    htp.p('<TR>');
    htp.p('<TD><FONT FACE="Arial">
      <A HREF="instruct_personal_info?p_instructor_id='
      ||rec.instructor_id||'">'
      ||rec.last_name||','||rec.first_name||'</A></FONT>
      < /TD>');
    htp.p('</TR>');
END LOOP;
```

QUERYSTRINGS IN FRAMESETS

URLs are in frameset documents, and there are cases in which querystrings must be used to pass parameters from the frameset document to each frame within the frameset. When a frameset document is called, if a parameter is passed to it, the frameset will not do much with the parameter. All that the frameset does is divide the screen into frames, and dictate the contents of each frame. The frameset does not paint anything to the screen; it is the frames within the frameset that display something to the screen. Therefore, the parameter that is passed to the frameset is probably intended not for the frameset, but for one or more of the frames within the frameset.

The way for the frameset to pass parameters to its frames is, again, through name/value pairs appended to the end of a URL. Each frame has an attribute SRC which is equal to a page or URL that should be called to fill that frame. The querystring can be appended to this SRC attribute value.

■ FOR EXAMPLE

```
CREATE OR REPLACE PROCEDURE my_frame(p_id IN VARCHAR2)IS
BEGIN
htp.p('
<HTML>
  <HEAD>
    <TITLE>My Frameset</TITLE>
  </HEAD>
  <FRAMESET COLS="150,*">
    <FRAME NAME="left_frame"
          SRC="left_nav_bar">
    <FRAME NAME="main_frame" SRC="emp?p_id='||p_id||'">
  </FRAMESET>
</HTML>');
END;
```

QUERYSTRINGS IN JAVASCRIPT CODE

When a URL is used in JavaScript, the URL can have a querystring appended to it as well.

One way URLs appear in JavaScript code is when JavaScript is used to change the location of the browser window. In the JavaScript DOM, one of the properties of the window object is its location. The location refers to the current URL of the window, and it can be read with window.location. Not only can JavaScript read this property, it can also change it. By setting window.location to a new value, JavaScript forces the browser to call and display a new page. The value can be a full URL or a relative path, as in the JavaScript code examples below:

```
window.location="http://www.bbc.co.uk";
window.location="instruct_personal_info";
```

In PL/SQL, the second example could be generated with the following code:

```
htp.p('<SCRIPT LANGUAGE="JavaScript">
     window.location="instruct_personal_info";
   </SCRIPT>
  ');
```

What if you want to send instruct_personal_info the ID of a specific instructor, so that you can view the instructor's information? If the instructor being displayed were always instructor 101, it could be done as follows:

```
htp.p('<SCRIPT LANGUAGE="JavaScript">
      window.location="instruct_personal_info?p_instructor_id=101";
     </SCRIPT>
    ');
```

What if you want to pass a p_instructor_ id of 101 as well as a p_session_id of 572? This could be accomplished by using the ampersand to separate name/value pairs in the querystring, as follows:

```
htp.p('<SCRIPT LANGUAGE="JavaScript">        window.location=
"instruct_personal_info?p_instructor_id=101&p_session_id=572";
        </SCRIPT>
       ');
```

FINDING QUERYSTRING VALUES IN JAVASCRIPT

The problem with the above example is that the instructor id of 101 should not be "hard-coded" into the string. The call to instruct_personal_info should be able to work for any instructor's ID.

If there is a PL/SQL variable v_instructor_id that currently holds the correct instructor ID, the instructor's ID could be sent by concatenating it to the end of the string with PL/SQL's concatenation mark.

```
htp.p('<SCRIPT LANGUAGE="JavaScript">   window.location=
"instruct_personal_info?p_instructor_id='||v_instructor_id||'";
       </SCRIPT>
     ');
```

Suppose that there are two parameters to pass, p_instructor_id and p_session_id, and there is a corresponding variable for each parameter: v_instructor_id and v_session_id. Both of these variables could be concatenated into the string.

```
htp.p('<SCRIPT LANGUAGE="JavaScript">   window.location=
"instruct_personal_info?p_instructor_id='||v_instructor_id||
'&p_session_id='||v_session_id||'";
       </SCRIPT>
     ');
```

However, there may not be a PL/SQL variable that the JavaScript function can use. The JavaScript function may be read and loaded by the browser earlier in the PL/SQL procedure than when the v_instructor_id value is determined.

Remember that form element values are easily accessible in JavaScript. When working with JavaScript, always consider whether the DOM can help you retrieve the information that you need. The DOM "sees" each form in a document and the current value of each form element, including form elements of type "hidden." Suppose that the current document contains a form, instructor_form, and the form contains a hidden form element called "p_instructor_id." The value of this input can be "seen" without passing it to the JavaScript function or using PL/SQL variables. The JavaScript DOM can access this value with this syntax:

```
document.instructor_form.p_instructor_id.value
```

Use JavaScript's concatenation symbol, the "+" sign, to append this JavaScript DOM object notation to the end of the string:

```
htp.p('
    <SCRIPT LANGUAGE="JavaScript">
    window.location="instruct_personal_info?p_instructor_id=" +
      document.instructor_form.p_instructor_id.value;
    </SCRIPT>
');
```

Sometimes a value is passed in to a JavaScript function, or stored in a JavaScript variable. If the parameter or variable in JavaScript is called instID, then use JavaScript's concatenation symbol, the "+" sign, to append the JavaScript parameter or variable, instID, to the end of the string:

```
htp.p('
  <SCRIPT LANGUAGE="JavaScript">
  window.location="instruct_personal_info?p_instructor_id=" + instID;
  </SCRIPT>
');
```

If two JavaScript parameters or variables, instID and sessionID, need to be passed, again make use of JavaScript's concatenation symbol to build the querystring.

```
htp.p('
  <SCRIPT LANGUAGE="JavaScript">
  window.location="instruct_personal_info?p_instructor_id=" +
instID + "&p_session_id=" + sessionID;
  </SCRIPT>
');
```

QUERYSTRINGS FOR JAVASCRIPT POP-UP WINDOWS

URLs also appear in the JavaScript command to create a pop-up window, and these URLs may require a querystring as well.

In Chapter 10, "Web Toolkit I: HTML and JavaScript with PL/SQL," you incorporate JavaScript code for a pop-up zipcode window into the PL/SQL procedure instruct_personal_info:

```
htp.p('<TD><INPUT TYPE="button" VALUE="Change Zipcode" onClick=
"javascript:window.open(''showzip'', ''instructor_zip'',
''TOOLBAR=NO, STATUS=yes, MENUBAR=no, SCROLLBARS=auto,
RESIZABLE=yes, WIDTH=640, HEIGHT=480'');"></TD>');
```

The URL for the new window is showzip. The showzip procedure, which will appear in the new pop-up window, is not being passed a parameter. What if you want a zipcode to be preselected in the zipcode list, and you want it to be the zipcode for the current instructor? How would showzip know which option should be preselected?

You can pass a zipcode value to the pop-up window by adding a name/value pair to the URL. The code below sends p_zip=10019 to the showzip procedure:

```
htp.p('<TD><INPUT TYPE="button" VALUE="Change Zipcode" onClick=
"javascript:window.open(''showzip?p_zip=10019'', ''instructor_zip'',
''TOOLBAR=NO, STATUS=yes, MENUBAR=no, SCROLLBARS=auto, RESIZABLE=yes,
WIDTH=640, HEIGHT=480'');"></TD>');
```

Again, you must consider that the value 10019 is probably not something that you want to hard-code into the pop-up window command. If the user happens to be looking at a page for instructor with a different zipcode, then the pop-up window created above would still have the zipcode 10019 preselected.

The answer, again, is to concatenate a value into the querystring. This example gets the value for p_instructor_id from a PL/SQL variable, v_instructor_id:

```
htp.p('<TD><INPUT TYPE="button" VALUE="Change Zipcode"
onClick="javascript:window.open(''showzip?p_zip='||v_zip||''',
''instructor_zip'', ''TOOLBAR=NO, STATUS=yes, MENUBAR=no,
SCROLLBARS=auto, RESIZABLE=yes, WIDTH=640, HEIGHT=480'');"></TD>');
```

What if more than one name/value pair must be passed? Again, you can concatenate the PL/SQL variables to the querystring. Below, the parameters p_zip and p_instructor_id are passed:

```
htp.p('<TD><INPUT TYPE="button" VALUE="Change Zipcode"
onClick="javascript:window.open(''showzip?p_zip='||v_zip||'
&p_instructor_id='||v_instructor_id||''', ''instructor_zip'',
''TOOLBAR=NO, STATUS=yes, MENUBAR=no, SCROLLBARS=auto,
RESIZABLE=yes, WIDTH=640, HEIGHT=480'');"></TD>');
```

MORE ON QUOTES

You may already have noticed that quotes can be tricky to manage.

The line below is a JavaScript call to the JavaScript function get_loan. This call passes three values: fixedrate, 10, and an empty string. The number 10 is not required to be enclosed in single quotes in JavaScript, because it is a number. Here is the JavaScript code:

```
get_loan('fixedrate',10,'');
```

To generate this JavaScript code through PL/SQL and the Web Toolkit, careful attention must be paid to quotes. Wherever a single quote is included as part of the JavaScript syntax, it must be escaped with an additional quote, as shown below.

**UNIT
11.3**

```
htp.p('
  get_loan(''fixedrate'',10,'''');
');
```

Do not be dismayed by the four quotes at the end of the first line; there is a logical explanation. Remember that the call to get_loan is embedded inside of the htp.p procedure call. To PL/SQL, the above statement reads like this:

```
htp.p('xxxxxxxxxxxxxxxxxxxxxxxxx');
```

Any characters enclosed by the single quotes form a literal string that PL/SQL knows should be printed out to an HTML document. PL/SQL is not doing additional work with the code inside of the quotes. If HTML is included inside the quotes, the HTML is not being checked for accuracy. Likewise, the text inside the quotes could be JavaScript with incorrect syntax, and PL/SQL would not recognize the JavaScript syntax errors.

PL/SQL reads the string until it finds another single quote. That way it knows that the literal string has ended. The following lines would raise an error, because PL/SQL would think that it had reached the end of the string, when in fact it had not:

```
htp.p('xxxxxxxxx'xxxxxxxxxxxxxxx');   -- Raises an error!
htp.p('This code won't compile.');   -- Raises an error!
```

When a single quote must be included within the literal string, it can be "escaped" with a second single quote. The two quotes together are regarded as a single literal quote. The following examples are acceptable:

```
htp.p('xxxxxxxxx''xxxxxxxxxxxxxxx');         -- ok
htp.p('This code won''t raise an error.');   -- ok
htp.p('<TITLLLLLE>Aldwin''s Page</TITULLL>'); -- ok,
     --compiles despite HTML error
htp.p(' get_loan(''fixedrate'',10,''''); ');  -- ok
```

Quotes mark the end of literal strings. The strings can be concatenated with PL/SQL variables. Here is an example that should be familiar from the EXCEPTION sections of your PL/SQL procedures. It concatenates a string with a virtual column in Oracle PL/SQL called SQLERRM:

```
htp.p('An error occurred in my_procedure: '||SQLERRM);
```

The call to get_loan can be modified slightly to use variables. Simply replace the literal values with concatenated variables:

```
htp.p('get_loan('''||v_rate_type||''','||v_years||',''');
```

Form elements are another area where quotes can be difficult to interpret. Here is an example of using concatenation to obtain a form element's value from a variable:

```
htp.p('<INPUT TYPE="text" NAME="p_city" VALUE ="'||v_city||'">');
```

The value for the p_city text input comes from the variable, v_city. HTML syntax requires that the VALUE attribute's corresponding text be surrounded by double quotes. Within these double quotes goes the variable v_city, but it must be read as a variable, not the literal characters v_city. The variable is concatenated with the rest of the statement. The single quotes next to the concatenation marks mark the ends of literal strings, and create two literal strings on either side of the v_city variable:

```
<INPUT TYPE="text" NAME="p_city" VALUE ="
    and
">
```

Although additional spaces could make this code more readable, exercise caution. In the example below, the value for the p_city text element is everything within the double quotes after VALUE=. Since extra spaces are added within the double quotes, the extra spaces become part of the value. These extra spaces would be saved to the database if the form element is processed with this value:

```
htp.p('<INPUT TYPE="text" NAME="p_city" VALUE="  '||v_city||'  ">');
```

 Do not add extra spaces in VALUE attributes that you do not want. Be extremely careful when concatenating literal strings with quotes.

To test your understanding of quotes, here again is the call to the instructor_zip pop-up window, first without the querystring added:

```
htp.p('<TD><INPUT TYPE="button" VALUE="Change Zipcode"
onClick="javascript:window.open(''showzip'', ''instructor_zip'',
''TOOLBAR=NO, STATUS=yes, MENUBAR=no, SCROLLBARS=auto,
RESIZABLE=yes, WIDTH=640, HEIGHT=480'');"></TD>');
```

The URL for the new window is:

```
''showzip''
```

UNIT
11.3

The word showzip is being passed as a parameter to JavaScript's window.open function. This value must be enclosed in quotes, since it is non-numeric. Instead of being enclosed in single quotes, the value has two single quotes surrounding it. The second quote is there to "escape" the first quote. If single quotes were used around showzip, then the htp.p procedure would think it had reached the end of the string it is supposed to print, instead of continuing through the rest of the string.

Here is the the same function call with the querystring added:

```
htp.p('<TD><INPUT TYPE="button" VALUE="Change Zipcode" onClick=
"javascript:window.open(''showzip?p_zip='||v_zip||''''', ''instructor_
zip'', ''TOOLBAR=NO, STATUS=yes, MENUBAR=no, SCROLLBARS=auto,
RESIZABLE=yes, WIDTH=640, HEIGHT=480'');"></TD>');
```

Pay particular attention to the three single quotes after the v_zip is concatenated into the statement. Think about exactly what is happening here. The first quote indicates that the literal content of the htp.p statement is resuming. The next two quotes were there before the concatenation was added. They will generate a single quote; the second quote mark is there to "escape" the first.

If v_zip holds the value 08807, then the code above would generate the following in the browser:

```
<TD><INPUT TYPE="button" VALUE="Change Zipcode" onClick=
"javascript:window.open('showzip?p_zip=08807', 'instructor_zip',
'TOOLBAR=NO, STATUS=yes, MENUBAR=no, SCROLLBARS=auto, RESIZABLE=yes,
WIDTH=640, HEIGHT=480');"></TD>
```

 Development software or text editors that use color-coding can be extremely helpful when writing and reading code with many quotes.

USING THE JAVASCRIPT DOM TO PASS VALUES

Frequently, a JavaScript function can navigate the DOM hierarchy to "see" and manipulate parts of a page. If a value is visible to a JavaScript function through the DOM, then it is not necessary to pass the value to the JavaScript function explicitly. The DOM gives a JavaScript function the power to read and manipulate a large amount of data.

For example, the value of the form element p_zip in the form instructor_personal_form has a place in the DOM. In Javascript syntax, the value of p_zip is represented by:

```
window.document.instructor_personal_form.p_zip.value
```

If JavaScript can retrieve the value of p_zip, it can change the value of p_zip. JavaScript uses an equals sign, its assignment operator, to assign a new value. This is done with one line of code. The syntax is as follows:

```
window.document.instructor_personal_form.p_zip.value='10048';
```

Remember to include the "value" attribute to refer to the value of an object. "window.document.instructor_personal_form.p_zip" would only refer to the form element itself, "p_zip," not its value.

The example below, from the section "Querystrings for JavaScript Pop-up Windows," shows how a variable can be concatenated into a JavaScript window.open command:

```
htp.p('<TD><INPUT TYPE="button" VALUE="Change Zipcode" onClick=
"javascript:window.open(''showzip?p_zip='||v_zip||''', ''instructor_
zip'', ''TOOLBAR=NO, STATUS=yes, MENUBAR=no, SCROLLBARS=auto,
RESIZABLE=yes, WIDTH=640, HEIGHT=480'');"></TD>');
```

You can rewrite the call to showzip by getting the value for p_zip from the DOM, instead of the database value in v_zip. The value of the p_zip form element is visible to JavaScript through the DOM. This value can be added to the querystring using JavaScript's concatenation mark, the "+" sign:

```
htp.p('<TD><INPUT TYPE="button" VALUE="Change Zipcode" onClick=
"javascript:window.open(''showzip?p_zip=''+document.instructor_
personal_form.p_zip.value, ''instructor_zip'', ''TOOLBAR=NO,
STATUS=yes, MENUBAR=no, SCROLLBARS=auto, RESIZABLE=yes, WIDTH=640,
HEIGHT=480'');"></TD>');
```

Why use the second example, which requires more typing? In JavaScript, sometimes using the DOM to retrieve a value is more accurate than concatenating the database value. The DOM tracks what a user is doing on the front-end application. The value the DOM sees will always be up-to-the-minute. If a user starts typing in the Zipcode field, JavaScript can see immediately what the user has typed, and JavaScript can work with that value.

Meanwhile, the database only has the last value that was saved to the database. The database value stored in v_zip is passed to the pop-up window every time the button is pressed. That can be very confusing to a user. Suppose the screen displays personal information for an instructor with a zipcode of 07060. If the user clicks the "Change Zipcode" button and goes to the pop-up screen, 07060 is highlighted—so far, so good. But as soon as the user starts changing the value in the zipcode field, the pop-up window will become inaccurate. If a user types over 07060 with 11215 and then clicks "Change Zipcode," the pop-up window still will have 07060 highlighted instead of the new entry, 11215. To a user it might look as though the application is broken.

Within JavaScript, use the DOM when you need to retrieve the most up-to-date value of a form input.

USING THE JAVASCRIPT DOM WITH MULTIPLE WINDOWS

JavaScript's ability to navigate the DOM can be particularly useful when more than one window has been opened within an application. The DOM recognizes all windows opened in a browser session, not just the current window.

In Chapter 7, "Introduction to JavaScript," the instruct_personal_info procedure contains a button that calls showzip, which creates a pop-up window with a list of zipcodes. Earlier in this chapter, you learn how to pass the instructor's current zipcode to showzip, in a name/value pair appended to the end of the URL.

If the user selects a different zipcode from the list in the pop-up window, how will that zipcode be returned to the instructor's personal information page? JavaScript can solve this problem for you through the power of the DOM. Recall that JavaScript, through the DOM, can read—and change—the most recent values of form inputs, and it can do so for multiple windows. In the pop-up window, JavaScript code can do the following:

1. Identify the new zipcode selected by the user in the pop-up window.
2. Reset the value of p_zip in the main window to the new value from the pop-up window.
3. Close the zipcode pop-up window.

The DOM provides an easy way to navigate from a pop-up window to the window that originally opened it. The DOM gives each window an attribute called "opener," which stands for "window that opened the present window":

```
window.opener
```

To refer to the form object p_zip in the original window, the syntax is very similar to that shown earlier. Compare the two examples below:

From the original window:

```
window.document.instructor_personal_form.p_zip.value
```

From the pop-up window:

```
window.opener.document.instructor_personal_form.p_zip.value
```

The new zipcode that is selected in the pop-up window can also be identified using JavaScript. From the pop-up window:

```
document.zipcode_form.p_new_zip.value
```

Here is a JavaScript function called *chooseZip* that accomplishes the above tasks. Note that the statement in the function that begins with "window.opener" should be written on one line when you write the function.

```
htp.script('
  function chooseZip() {
    window.opener.instructor_personal_form.p_zip.value=document.
       zipcode_form.p_new_zip.value;
    window.close();
  }
','JavaScript');
```

For a JavaScript function that is really only four lines long, this is a very powerful piece of code.

Be careful when working with more than one window. If objects have similar names in each window, make sure that you are referring to the one you want.

UNIT 11.3 EXERCISES

a) As shown under the heading "Querystrings in Links," add hyperlinks to the *instructor_list_info* procedure. The instructor's name needs a hyperlink that will call instruct_personal_info. To pass the instructor id to instruct_personal_info, include a querystring with the instructor's p_instructor_id in the link.

b) Create a new procedure called *instructor_list_class*, based on *instructor_list_info*. The screen will look the same as the previous exercise, *instructor_list_info*, so use the previous exercise as a starting point. However, the instructor's name should be hyperlinked to *instruct_classes* instead of *instruct_personal_info*. The *instruct_classes* procedure requires an IN parameter of p_instructor_id, so p_instructor_id should appear at the end of each link in a querystring.

c) Create a procedure called *instruct_classes* that lists the classes an instructor is teaching. It accepts a parameter called p_instructor_id, which is the instructor whose classes should be listed. List the following columns in a table:

```
Course No.              COURSE.course_no
Course Description      COURSE.description
Section ID              SECTION.section_id
Start Date/Time         SECTION.start_date_time
Location                SECTION.location
Roster                  button that says "Student List"
```

In the "Roster" column, the "Student List" button will call the *student_list* procedure in a pop-up window. The *student_list* procedure was created earlier in this chapter, in Exercise 11.2.D. The section_id needs to be passed to the *student_list* procedure. If the instructor is teaching no courses, display a message that the instructor is on sabbatical.

d) Modify the *instruct_personal_info* procedure. First, do some housecleaning and remove the DEFAULT value from the IN parameter. Next, modify the procedure to pass a zipcode to the *showzip* procedure. When the Change Zipcode button is clicked and showzip is called, pass the current zipcode shown on the screen to the showzip procedure. Refer to the code in this unit under the heading, "Using the JavaScript DOM to Pass Values," to find code that can call showzip and pass a parameter to showzip. Check that the correct zipcode is being highlighted in the pop-up window.

e) Enhance the *showzip* procedure begun in Chapter 10, "Web Toolkit I: HTML and JavaScript with PL/SQL." As shown in this chapter in "Using the JavaScript DOM Instead of Passing Parameters," incorporate the function *chooseZip* into the *showzip* procedure. The *chooseZip* function should be called when the button "Select Zipcode" is clicked.

UNIT 11.3 EXERCISE ANSWERS

a) As shown under the heading "Querystrings in Links," add hyperlinks to the *instructor_list_info* procedure. The instructor's name needs a hyperlink that will call instruct_personal_info. To pass the instructor id to instruct_personal_info, include a querystring with the instructor's p_instructor_id in the link.

Answer:

```
CREATE OR REPLACE PROCEDURE instructor_list_info
IS
    CURSOR get_instructor IS
        SELECT first_name, last_name, instructor_id
        FROM instructor
        ORDER BY last_name, first_name;
BEGIN
htp.p('<HTML>');
htp.p('<HEAD>');
htp.p('<TITLE>Instructor Maintenance Web Site</TITLE>');
htp.p('</HEAD>');
htp.p('<BODY BgColor="#99CCCC">');
htp.p('<CENTER>');
htp.p('<H2>List of Instructors</H2>');
htp.p('<TABLE ALIGN="center" BORDER="3" BORDERCOLOR="midnight blue"
        CELLPADDING="5" WIDTH="100%">');
htp.p('<TR>');
htp.p('<TH ALIGN="center">Instructor Names</TH>');
htp.p('</TR>');
FOR rec IN get_instructor
LOOP
    htp.p('<TR>');
    htp.p('<TD><FONT FACE="Arial">
     <A HREF="instruct_personal_info?p_instructor_id='
      ||rec.instructor_id||'">'
      ||rec.last_name||','||rec.first_name||'</A></FONT></TD>');
    htp.p('</TR>');
END LOOP;
```

```
htp.p('</TABLE>');
htp.p('</CENTER>');
htp.p('</BODY>');
EXCEPTION
WHEN OTHERS
THEN
   htp.p('An error occurred:  '||SQLERRM||'.  Please try again
   later.');
END;
```

b) Create a new procedure called *instructor_list_class*, based on *instructor_list_info*. The screen will look the same as the previous exercise, *instructor_list_info*, so use the previous exercise as a starting point. However, the instructor's name should be hyperlinked to *instruct_classes* instead of *instruct_personal_info*. The *instruct_classes* procedure requires an IN parameter of p_instructor_id, so p_instructor_id should appear at the end of each link in a querystring.

**UNIT
11.3**

Answer:

```
1    CREATE OR REPLACE PROCEDURE instructor_list_class
2    IS
3        CURSOR get_instructor IS
4            SELECT first_name, last_name, instructor_id
5            FROM instructor
6            ORDER BY last_name, first_name;
7    BEGIN
8    htp.p('<HTML>');
9    htp.p('<HEAD>');
10   htp.p('<TITLE>Instructor Maintenance Web Site</TITLE>');
11   htp.p('</HEAD>');
12   htp.p('<BODY BgColor="#99CCCC">');
13   htp.p('<CENTER>');
14   htp.p('<H2>List of Instructors</H2>');
15   htp.p('<TABLE ALIGN="center" BORDER="3" BORDERCOLOR="midnight blue"
16          CELLPADDING="5" WIDTH="100%">');
17   htp.p('<TR>');
18   htp.p('<TH ALIGN="center">Instructor Names</TH>');
19   htp.p('</TR>');
20
21   FOR rec IN get_instructor
22   LOOP
23      htp.p('<TR>');
24      htp.p('<TD><FONT FACE="Arial">
25       <A HREF="instruct_classes?p_instructor_id='
26         ||rec.instructor_id||'">'
27         ||rec.last_name||','||rec.first_name||'</A></FONT></TD>');
28      htp.p('</TR>');
29   END LOOP;
30
```

```
31   htp.p('</TABLE>');
32   htp.p('</CENTER>');
33   htp.p('</BODY>');
34   EXCEPTION
35   WHEN OTHERS
36   THEN
37      htp.p('An error occurred:  '||SQLERRM||'.  Please try again
         later.');
38   END;
```

c) Create a procedure called *instruct_classes* that lists the classes an instructor is teaching. It accepts a parameter called p_instructor_id, which is the instructor whose classes should be listed. List the following columns in a table:

```
Course No.            COURSE.course_no
Course Description    COURSE.description
Section ID            SECTION.section_id
Start Date/Time       SECTION.start_date_time
Location              SECTION.location
Roster                button that says "Student List"
```

In the "Roster" column, the "Student List" button will call the *student_list* procedure in a pop-up window. The *student_list* procedure was created earlier in this chapter, in Exercise 11.2.D. The section_id needs to be passed to the *student_list* procedure. If the instructor is teaching no courses, display a message that the instructor is on sabbatical.

Answer:

```
1    CREATE OR REPLACE PROCEDURE instruct_classes
2    (p_instructor_id IN instructor.instructor_id%TYPE)
3    IS
4       v_instructor_name VARCHAR2(60);
5       v_count           INTEGER := 0;
6
7       CURSOR c_courses IS
8          SELECT s.course_no, description, section_id,
9                 TO_CHAR(start_date_time, 'DD-MON-YY') start_date,
10                TO_CHAR(start_date_time, 'HH:MI A.M.') start_time,
11                location
12           FROM course c, section s
13          WHERE c.course_no   = s.course_no
14            AND instructor_id = p_instructor_id
15          ORDER BY s.course_no, section_id;
16
17   BEGIN
18
19      SELECT first_name||' '||last_name
20        INTO v_instructor_name
```

```
21         FROM instructor
22        WHERE instructor_id = p_instructor_id;
23
24      SELECT COUNT(*)
25        INTO v_count
26        FROM course c, section s
27       WHERE c.course_no   = s.course_no
28         AND instructor_id = p_instructor_id
29      ORDER BY s.course_no, section_id;
30
31   htp.p('<HTML>
32          <HEAD><TITLE>Instructor View Classes</TITLE></HEAD>
33          <BODY BGCOLOR="#FFFFFF">
34          <CENTER>');
35
36   IF v_count > 0
37   THEN
38     htp.p('<H1>Classes for '||v_instructor_name||'</H1>
39          <H2>Below is the current list of courses.</H2>
40          <TABLE ALIGN="center" BORDER=3 BORDERCOLOR="#0099CC"
                 CELLPADDING=5 WIDTH="100%">
41          <TR>
42          <TH>Course No.</TH>
43          <TH>Course_Description</TH>
44          <TH>Section ID</TH>
45          <TH>Start_Date/Time</TH>
46          <TH>Location</TH>
47          <TH>Roster</TH>
48          </TR>');
49
50      FOR rec IN c_courses
51      LOOP
52         htp.p('<TR>
53                 <TD ALIGN="center">'||rec.course_no||'</TD>
54                 <TD ALIGN="center">'||rec.description||'</TD>
55                 <TD ALIGN="center">'||rec.section_id||'</TD>
56                 <TD ALIGN="center">'||rec.start_date||'<br>'||
                   rec.start_time||'</TD>
57                 <TD ALIGN="center">'||rec.location||'</TD>
58                 <TD ALIGN="center">'||rec.section_id||'</TD>
59                 <TD><INPUT TYPE="button" VALUE="Student List"
60                 onClick="javascript:window.open(''student_list?
                   p_section_id='||rec.section_id||'''
                   ''student_list'', ''toolbar=no, status=yes,
                   menubar=no, scrollbars=auto, resizable=yes,
                   width=640,height=480''); ">
61                 </TD>
62                 </TR>');
63      END LOOP;
```

**UNIT
11.3**

```
64     htp.p('</TABLE>');
65   ELSE
66     htp.p('<H3>'||v_instructor_name||' is currently on sabbatical.
       </H3>');
67   END IF;
68
69   htp.p('</CENTER></BODY></HTML>');
70
71   EXCEPTION
72   WHEN OTHERS
73   THEN
74     htp.p('An error occurred:  '||SQLERRM||'.  Please try again
       later.');
75   END;
```

d) Modify the *instruct_personal_info* procedure. First, do some housecleaning and re-move the DEFAULT value from the IN parameter. Next, modify the procedure to pass a zipcode to the *showzip* procedure. When the Change Zipcode button is clicked and showzip is called, pass the current zipcode shown on the screen to the showzip procedure. Refer to the code in this unit under the heading, "Using the JavaScript DOM to Pass Values," to find code that can call showzip and pass a parameter to showzip. Check that the correct zipcode is being highlighted in the pop-up window.

Answer:

```
CREATE OR REPLACE PROCEDURE instruct_personal_info
(p_instructor_id IN instructor.instructor_id%TYPE)
AS
   v_instructor_id    instructor.instructor_id%TYPE;
   v_salutation       instructor.salutation%TYPE;
   v_first_name       instructor.first_name%TYPE;
   v_last_name        instructor.last_name%TYPE;
   v_street_address   instructor.street_address%TYPE;
   v_city             zipcode.city%TYPE;
   v_state            zipcode.state%TYPE;
   v_zip              instructor.zip%TYPE;
   v_phone            instructor.phone%TYPE;
BEGIN
   SELECT instructor_id,
          salutation,
          first_name,
          last_name,
          street_address,
          city,
          state,
          i.zip,
          phone
   INTO   v_instructor_id,
```

```
             v_salutation,
             v_first_name,
             v_last_name,
             v_street_address,
             v_city,
             v_state,
             v_zip,
             v_phone
    FROM instructor i, zipcode z
    WHERE i.zip = z.zip
      AND instructor_id = p_instructor_id;
htp.p('<HTML>');
htp.p('<HEAD>');
htp.p('<TITLE>Instructor Personal Info</TITLE>');
htp.p('</HEAD>');
htp.p('<BODY bgColor="#99CCCC">');
htp.p('<CENTER>');
htp.p('<H1>Personal Info For '||v_first_name||' '
||v_last_name||'</H1>');
htp.p('<H2>This Is The Current Information On Record.</H2>');
htp.p('<H3>To Make Changes, Edit The Information And Select
''Save''.</H3>');
htp.p('<FORM ACTION="update_instructor" METHOD="get" NAME=
"instructor_personal_form">');
htp.p('<INPUT TYPE="hidden" NAME="p_instructor_id" VALUE="'||
v_instructor_id||'">');
htp.p('<TABLE >');
htp.p('<TR>');
htp.p('<TD>Salutation:</TD>');
htp.p('<TD><INPUT TYPE="text" NAME="p_salutation" VALUE="'||
v_salutation||'" SIZE="5"></TD>');
htp.p('</TR>');
htp.p('<TR>');
htp.p('<TD>First Name:</TD>');
htp.p('<TD><INPUT TYPE="text" NAME="p_first_name" VALUE="'||
v_first_name||'" SIZE="25"></TD>');
htp.p('</TR>');
htp.p('<TR>');
htp.p('<TD>Last Name:</TD>');
htp.p('<TD><INPUT TYPE="text" NAME="p_last_name" VALUE="'||
v_last_name||'" SIZE="25"></TD>');
htp.p('</TR>');
htp.p('<TR>');
htp.p('<TD>Street Address:</TD>');
htp.p('<TD><INPUT TYPE="text" NAME="p_street_address" VALUE="'||
v_street_address||'"></TD>');
htp.p('</TR>');
htp.p('<TR>');
htp.p('<TD>City:</TD>');
```

```
htp.p('<TD>'||v_city||'</TD>');
htp.p('</TR>');
htp.p('<TR>');
htp.p('<TD>State:</TD>');
htp.p('<TD>'||v_state||'</TD>');
htp.p('</TR>');
htp.p('<TR>');
htp.p('<TD>Zipcode:</TD>');
htp.p('<TD><INPUT TYPE="text" NAME="p_zip" VALUE="'||v_zip||'">
</TD>');
htp.p('<TD><INPUT TYPE="button" VALUE="Change Zipcode"
onClick="javascript:window.open(''showzip?p_zip=''+document.
instructor_personal_form.p_zip.value, ''instructor_zip'',
''TOOLBAR=NO, STATUS=yes, MENUBAR=no, SCROLLBARS=auto,
RESIZABLE=yes, WIDTH=640, HEIGHT=480'');"></TD>');
htp.p('</TR>');
htp.p('<TR>');
htp.p('<TD>Telephone:</TD>');
htp.p('<TD><INPUT TYPE="text" VALUE="'||v_phone||'" NAME="p_phone"
MAXLENGTH="15" SIZE="15"></TD>');
htp.p('</TR>');
htp.p('<TR>');
htp.p('<TD></TD>');
htp.p('<TD ALIGN=left>');
htp.p('<INPUT TYPE="submit" VALUE="SUBMIT">');
htp.p('<INPUT TYPE="reset" VALUE="RESET">');
htp.p('</TD>');
htp.p('</TR>');
htp.p('</TABLE>');
htp.p('</FORM>');
htp.p('</CENTER>');
htp.p('</BODY>');
htp.p('</HTML>');
EXCEPTION
WHEN OTHERS
THEN
    htp.p('An error occurred:  '||SQLERRM||'.  Please try again
    later.');
END instruct_personal_info;
```

e) Enhance the *showzip* procedure begun in Chapter 10, "Web Toolkit I: HTML and JavaScript with PL/SQL." As shown in this chapter in "Using the JavaScript DOM Instead of Passing Parameters," incorporate the function *chooseZip* into the *showzip* procedure. The *chooseZip* function should be called when the button "Select Zipcode" is clicked.

Answer:

```
1   CREATE OR REPLACE PROCEDURE showzip
2     (p_zip IN instructor.zip%TYPE DEFAULT '10019')
3   IS
4     CURSOR c_zip IS
5         SELECT city, state, zip
6           FROM zipcode
7         ORDER BY state, city, zip;
8   BEGIN
9   htp.htmlOpen;
10  htp.headOpen;
11  htp.title('Instructor Zipcode');
12  htp.script('
13     <!--Begin hiding javascript contents from old browsers.
14     function chooseZip() {
15  window.opener.instructor_personal_form.p_zip.value=document.
    zipcode_form.p_new_zip.value;
16     window.close();
17     }
18  //End the hiding here-->', 'JavaScript');
19  htp.headClose;
20  htp.bodyOpen(cattributes => 'BGCOLOR="#99CCCC"');
21  htp.centerOpen;
22  htp.p('<FORM NAME="zipcode_form" ACTION="" METHOD="post">');
23
24  htp.p('<SELECT NAME="p_new_zip" SIZE="15">');
25
26     FOR rec IN c_zip
27     LOOP
28     IF rec.zip = p_zip THEN
29         htp.p('<OPTION VALUE="'||rec.zip||'" SELECTED>'
30                   ||rec.city||', '||rec.state||'  '||rec.zip||
31             '</OPTION>');
32     ELSE
33         htp.p('<OPTION VALUE="'||rec.zip||'">'
34                   ||rec.city||', '||rec.state||'  '||rec.zip||
35             '</OPTION>');
36     END IF;
37     END LOOP;
38  htp.p('</SELECT>');
39  htp.p('<BR>');
40  htp.p('<BR>');
41
42  htp.p('<INPUT TYPE="button" VALUE="Select Zipcode"
    onClick="chooseZip();">');
43  htp.p('<INPUT TYPE="button" VALUE="Cancel" onClick="window.
    close();">');
44  htp.formClose;
```

```
45   htp.centerClose;
46   htp.bodyClose;
47   htp.htmlClose;
48
49   EXCEPTION
50   WHEN OTHERS
51   THEN
52      htp.p('An error occurred:  '||SQLERRM||'.  Please try again
        later.');
53   END;
```

C H A P T E R   1 1

BUILDING THE APP

The answers to these projects can be found at the companion Web site to this book, located at http://www.phptr.com/boardman.

Visit the Web site periodically to share and discuss your answers with other readers.

The Web Toolkit is a set of PL/SQL packages that, when used with the 9iAS server, allows a Web developer to Web-enable a database. Procedures written with Web Toolkit packages are viewable in a browser. Static HTML pages can be created, or dynamic pages can be created that incorporate data from the database at runtime. JavaScript can also be incorporated into the final HTML page served to the client.

You should have the following parts of the application after this chapter:

- instruct_personal_info
- instructor_list_info
- showzip
- instructors_frame
- instructors_left_nav
- update_instructor
- instructor_list_class
- instruct_classes
- student_list

Note: You begin the procedures instruct_personal_info, instructor_list_info, and showzip in Chapter 10, "Web Toolkit I: HTML and JavaScript with PL/SQL."

C H A P T E R   1 2

WORKING WITH PL/SQL SERVER PAGES (PSPs)

Before Oracle 8i Release 2, there was virtually only one way to serve dynamic data directly from the database to the Web using PL/SQL. It was to use the PL/SQL cartridge and associated PL/SQL Web Toolkit provided with the Oracle Application Server. With the advent of Oracle's WebDB, and its Dynamic Pages, developers were then given the ability to create entire Web sites inside an Oracle database. The most recent version of WebDB has been renamed as Portal. And the most recent development in the use of PL/SQL for providing dynamic database content to Web pages is PL/SQL Server Pages (PSPs).

Oracle 9i's iAS (and actually Oracle 8i version 8.1.6 and above) provide the capability to implement PL/SQL Server Pages (PSPs). This is a powerful new feature available for developers. A PL/SQL Server Page, PSP, is a server-side Web page (one that is stored in, loaded, and run from the database server, as opposed to a client-side Web page that runs from a Web browser client) that contains PL/SQL code within predefined tags. When loaded into the database using Oracle's *loadpsp* utility, it becomes a database procedure that runs on the database server to produce and output dynamic content in your Web page/Web application.

 In the 8.1.6 version of the Oracle database, the loadpsp utility has a file load limitation of 32 KB (kilobytes). Attempting to load a file larger than this generates an error.

Oracle's version of a server page technology enables you to distinguish the site design's presentation layer from the application/code-development layer. The benefit of PSPs over the PL/SQL Web Toolkit packaging method is that PSPs can provide a friendlier programming interface for an HTML programmer. They are simply HTML code with PL/SQL code embedded in them. Therefore, PSPs can be edited using a GUI HTML development tool such as FrontPage™ or Dreamweaver™. This way, the presentation design can be initially developed separately from and, therefore, can be distinguished from the application logic/business component design.

Using a tool such as WebAlchemy, a free (as of the writing of this book) program by Alan Hobbs available for download at http://www.users.bigpond.com/ ahobbs/), you can convert HTML into PL/SQL Web Toolkit code. Many critics of server page technologies consider them inefficient since most server page technologies are neither compiled nor cacheable. Fortunately, PSPs can not only be edited in an HTML editor, but the code is stored as compiled PL/SQL code, and is, therefore, cached in the SGA (System Global Area) of an Oracle database when invoked. These added features make PSPs similar to, but better than, Dynamic Pages in WebDB.

This chapter takes you through the use, anatomy, and creation of PSPs. You not only learn to develop PSPs, but you load them into the Oracle database using the loadpsp utility.

UNIT 12.1

WHAT PL/SQL SERVER PAGES ARE

WHAT PSPs ARE

PL/SQL Server Pages (PSPs) are Oracle's PL/SQL scripting (programming/developing) solution for server-side Web application development. They enable PL/SQL programmers to develop Web pages with dynamic content by embedding PL/SQL scripts in HTML pages. After these scripts are loaded into the database, they can then be executed when Web clients request the pages these scripts paint.

PSP pages are HTML pages with embedded PL/SQL scripts that are distinguished from the HTML content. This appearance of separation of application logic (embedded PL/SQL scripts) from the presentation logic (HTML) makes the development and maintenance of PSP pages easy. PSPs can be thought of as the reverse of PL/SQL Web Toolkit pages. A PL/SQL Web Toolkit page is a PL/SQL procedure with HTML code embedded in it. A PSP is an HTML page with PL/SQL code embedded in it.

PSPs are:

- Available in only version 8.1.6 and above of the Oracle database.
- Only used for server-side scripting and, therefore, all load balancing must be performed by the database server.
- Deployed directly into and served from an Oracle 9i (or 8i, v8.1.6 and above) database.
- A way in which Oracle combines third-party Web page design with its current data manipulation and retrieval techniques.

For developers already familiar with PL/SQL, quite possibly the quickest way to create professional-looking Web pages that are integrated with the database is to add PL/SQL to existing HTML pages. You can easily create dynamic Web pages simply by adding some special PL/SQL Server Page (PSP) tags to static HTML pages. This marked-up PSP file is then loaded into the Oracle 9i database so that when a user invokes this page from a browser, the dynamic content for that page is served up and made available from the database.

Another advantage to using PSPs is that they fit well within the lifecycle of a project. A design team can perfect an HTML prototype design, and then hand it off to a programmer to implement. Using the HTML prototype, the programmer can swap out dummy data for actual PL/SQL database calls.

OTHER SERVER TECHNOLOGIES/SCRIPTING SOLUTIONS

It is natural to wonder whether PL/SQL Server Pages follow the same standards as that of other server page technologies. Essentially all server page technologies start out looking like standard HTML and employ a standard scriptlet tag to include a programming or scripting language that generates the dynamic content. OAS employs a server page technology called LiveHTML that uses Perl as its scripting language. However, LiveHTML has been replaced in Oracle 9iAS by PHP. PHP (or *Hypertext Preprocessor*) is an open-source server page technology that uses a scripting language similar to Perl. However, Oracle does not, at the time of this writing, officially support PHP with Oracle 9iAS.

Since any kind of tags can be passed unchanged to the browser through a PL/SQL Server Page, you can embed JavaScript or other client-side script code in a PL/SQL server page the same way you embed JavaScript in an HTML page. You cannot, however, mix PL/SQL Server Pages with other server-side script features, such as server-side include files (*include files* are outlined more fully in the next unit, "Developing PSPs"). It doesn't matter, though; for, in many cases, you can get the same results by using the corresponding PSP features.

Microsoft's server page technology is Active Server Pages (ASP), which is supported by Microsoft's IIS Web Server. ASP uses Visual Basic as its scripting language. PSP uses syntax similar to that of ASP, although the syntax is not identical and you must typically translate from VBScript or JScript to PL/SQL. The best candidates for scripting language migration are pages that use the Active Data Object (ADO) interface to perform database operations. This type of interface is typical in many applications created with Visual Basic. And last, but not least, Java Server Pages (JSP) uses Java as its scripting language. PSP uses the same script tag syntax as JSP, making it easy to switch back and forth.

U N I T   1 2 . 2

WHEN TO USE PSPs

WHEN TO USE PSPs

Your development environment and the skills of your development team will dictate, to a large extent, which project technology (for example, using PSPs vs. using the PL/SQL Web Toolkit) you choose. HTML developers typically prefer using PSPs to writing PL/SQL code with the PL/SQL Web Toolkit. A good rule of thumb is that if you already have applications that were created with the PL/SQL Web Toolkit, keep using them that way and, if you have existing HTML files you'd like to make dynamic, use PSPs. If you are faced with aggressive deadlines and short time periods in which to code, consider the core knowledge base of your development team. If the overall skill set for the team is PL/SQL, and, for example, a third party is producing your presentation HTML layer, then PSPs will most likely prove to be the way to go.

Embedding PL/SQL code in the HTML page that you create allows you to write code quickly and follow a rapid, iterative development process. You maintain central control of the software, with only a Web browser required on the client machine.

HOW TO CHOOSE BETWEEN PSP
AND THE PL/SQL WEB TOOLKIT

When deciding between creating a Web application using PSP and creating a Web application using the PL/SQL Web Toolkit, you can actually produce the same results in different ways:

- Using the PL/SQL Web Toolkit, you can write a stored procedure or a stored package of procedures that produces HTML by calling the HTP, HTF, and OWA_* built-in PL/SQL Web Toolkit packaged procedures and functions.

- Using PSP, you can create an HTML page with embedded PL/SQL code and compile it as a PL/SQL Server Page. You have the option to call procedures from the PL/SQL Web Toolkit, but if you are using PSP, then you are probably not invoking these additional PL/SQL Web Toolkit procedures to generate every line of HTML output. Instead, the PL/SQL code is focused on data handling.

The factors you may find key in choosing between these two methods are:

- What is your starting point?
  - If you have a large body of preexisting PL/SQL code, you may find it easier to produce HTML tags by creating print statements that call the HTP and HTF packages of the PL/SQL Web Toolkit.
  - On the other hand, if you have a large body of preexisting HTML, and you want to include dynamic database content, you may find it more convenient to use PSP.

- What is the quickest and most convenient code-development environment for your group?
  - If most of the development work is done using HTML authoring tools, use PSP.
  - If you use code-writing tools that produce PL/SQL code for you, such as the page-building wizards in WebDB, then using PSP might be less convenient for you.

UNIT 12.3

LOADING PSPs INTO THE DATABASE

LOADING A PSP

The loadpsp utility is a standard utility provided with Oracle versions 8.1.6 and above. To load a PSP file into the database, you use the loadpsp utility from an operating system prompt. It reads in the PSP and translates it into a stored procedure using the attributes provided in the utility directive. Each PSP file corresponds to only one stored procedure in the database. PSP pages are compiled and loaded into the database in one step. An example of the syntax follows:

```
loadpsp -user username/password@service_name file.psp
```

And an example with values is:

```
loadpsp -user web_book/author@web_book_service hello_world.psp
```

In this example, the `hello_world.psp` file is loaded into the `web_book` schema of the database. The *loadpsp* keyword is necessary to invoke the loadpsp utility. The *-user* portion of this command denotes the *user* option to the loadpsp utility, and is always followed by the username and password (and TNSNames service name if you are connecting to a remote database). Hello_world.psp is the name of your PSP file. Additionally, you can also include a path for your PSP file appended to the front of the PSP file name, for example,

```
c:\guest\psp_folder\hello_world.psp
```

*You can load more than one PSP at a time. Keep in mind that PSP files can have no other extension than .psp, and the .psp extension **must** be included in the filename in the loadpsp command.*

REPLACING A PSP

An expanded example of loading a PSP that has already been loaded into the database, but now includes an error page, follows:

```
loadpsp -replace -user username/password@service_name
error_page.psp file.psp
```

And another example with values is:

```
loadpsp -replace -user web_book/author@web_book_service
hello_world_error.psp hello_world.psp
```

You should always use the -replace option. Running the loadpsp utility with the -replace option does not return an error if the procedure does not exist.

MAINTAINING PSP FILES

PSP files can be loaded into the database using the loadpsp utility, but it is a one-way trip. PSP files cannot be retrieved from the database once they have been loaded.

The PSP is loaded to the database as a PL/SQL procedure. As noted elsewhere in this chapter, querying the USER_SOURCE data dictionary view for the procedure will reveal that the PSP has been converted into a PL/SQL procedure that uses the PL/SQL Web Toolkit. So if you have lost the original PSP file that generated this procedure, you can still change and recompile the procedure using Web Toolkit syntax. However, the PSP cannot be reconstructed for you in its original state.

It is important to store and maintain PSP files in a central location. Decide on a storage mechanism before building your PSPs.

CREATING AND LOADING YOUR FIRST PSP

Copy the following code example into a text editor and save it as "hello_world.psp":

```
<%@ page language="PL/SQL"%>
<%@ plsql procedure="hello_world" %>
<%
--------------------------------------------------
-- FILENAME:     hello_world.psp
-- FILEDATE:     02.11.2002
-- CREATED BY:   <Reader, Place Your Name Here>
-- DESCRIPTION:  Simple Page with Message, "Hello World"
-- MODIFIED:
--------------------------------------------------
```

```
%>
<HTML>
<HEAD>
<TITLE>Hello World</TITLE>
</HEAD>
<BODY BGCOLOR="#99CCCC">
<CENTER>
<H1><FONT COLOR="white"><B>HELLO WORLD!</B></FONT></H1>
<H2><FONT COLOR="white"><B>This is my first
PSP!</B></FONT></H2>
</CENTER>
</BODY>
</HTML>
```

**UNIT
12.3**

Now open a DOS window and navigate to the directory where your `hello_world.psp` file is saved. Load your PSP into the Oracle database using the loadpsp utility commands illustrated earlier in this unit. Substitute your user-name, password, and service name for the username, password, and service name values. After successfully loading this PSP, you should receive the following feed-back message:

```
"hello_world.psp": procedure "hello_world" created.
```

Ensure that you are able to successfully view it in your browser. When you enter the URL, be sure to include the name of the server that serves up pages through the 9iAS, followed by /pls/, /<the_name_of_your_DAD>/ (which you should have specified in Chapter 2, "Oracle 9iAS"), followed by "hello_world." The /pls/ and /<thename_of_your_DAD>/ elements will be outlined more fully in Unit 12.1, "Developing PSPs." The syntax you use should be similar to the following:

```
http://my_server/pls/my_dad/hello_world
```

Note carefully, you do not specify the PSP extension after the PSP name. Since this procedure is now inside of the Oracle database, the .psp extension is not needed—it is not part of the procedure name inside the database. Keep in mind that the PSP filename and the procedure name invoked in the browser are two different things. For example, you could call your PSP file hello_world.psp, but call the procedure goodbye_world. Your page should look similar to that shown in Figure 12.1.

*If you run the loadpsp utility on a file more than once, you **MUST** sub-sequently include the -replace option (you can liken this to creating or replacing a stored procedure, because, for all practical purposes, that's exactly what you're doing).*

*Also note that if you include any error pages or include files, the names of the error pages and/or include files **must precede the name of your procedure file.** Otherwise, the load will fail.*

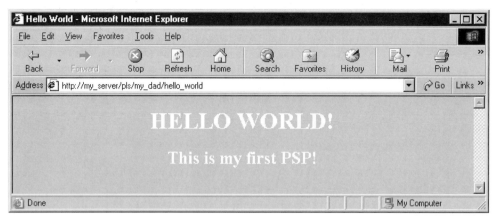

Figure 12.1 ■ The Hello World PSP page displayed in a Web browser.

Note the common and dreaded error:

ORA-01031 insufficient privileges

Though the error message does not explicitly say so, the problem is that upon attempting to load this PSP, the loadpsp utility discovers that the extension, .psp (or any other extension), has been included as part of the PSP name in the procedure directive. For example:

```
<%@ plsql procedure="student_personal_info.psp" %>
```

If you take out the extension and reload your PSP, you should no longer receive this error message.

UNIT 12.4

DEVELOPING PSPs

Whether you start with an existing stored procedure or an existing Web page, you see that with just a few changes and additions, you can create dynamic Web pages that perform database queries and other operations, and display the results from a Web browser. First things first, the file for a PL/SQL server page must have the extension .psp. Table 12.1 provides a summary for the four types of PSP Server Page elements.

PSP DIRECTIVES

A PSP directive is simply a statement that provides the PSP compiler information about the page it is about to load into the database. Here is the syntax for a PSP directive:

```
<%@ directive attribute="value" [ attribute="value" ... ] %>
```

Don't forget the % inside the <, and just before the >. This differentiates a PSP tag from an HTML tag to the compiler.

As Table 12.2 illustrates, there are currently four directives available.

PSP PAGE DIRECTIVES

As Table 12.3 illustrates, the *page* directive can be created with three possible attributes.

This directive is for compatibility with other scripting environments. Here is the syntax for the *page* directive:

```
<%@ page [language="programming language"][contentType="content
type"] [errorPage="error page"] %>
```

Table 12.1 ■ The Four Types of PSP Server Page Elements

PSP Server Page Element	Element Tags	Description
Directives	<%@ %>	Provide header/global information for the current page: the programming language, the name of the procedure, the name and types of parameters, and the name of any include files.
Declaratives	<%! %>	Where all the variables are declared. This is similar to the *declaration* section of a PL/SQL code block.
Scriptlets	<% %>	Any valid PL/SQL code goes here. This is similar to the PL/SQL that is inserted between the BEGIN and END keywords in a PL/SQL code block. Variable declarations can also be placed here. However, this is considered poor style and may inhibit you from easily debugging your procedure.
Expressions	<%= %>	Formats the expression, variable, or literal value for inclusion.

Table 12.2 ■ The Four PSP Directives

Directive Name	Directive Description
Page	Information specific for the page; for example, which programming language is used.
Procedure	The name of the procedure to be created by the PSP. **NOTE:** Do not include any extension, like .psp or otherwise, with the name of your procedure. Not only is an extension not necessary, but, more importantly, if you include one, your PSP will not compile when you attempt to load it into the database. Unit 12.3, "Loading PSPs into the Database," illustrates this point.
Parameter	Name, type, and default value for parameters.
Include	Any include files (such as background image files) to be included.

Table 12.3 ■ Page Directive Attributes

Page Directive Attribute	Attribute Description
Language	The programming language the PSP uses.
ContentType	The type of information (*MIME: Multipurpose Internet MailExtensions* type) it produces. The most common type used is *text/html*. **NOTE:** A detailed explanation of MIME types is beyond the scope of this book. For more information and history about Multipurpose Internet Mail Extensions, you can refer to the following Web site: http://www.rad.com/networks/1995/mime/mime.htm
ErrorPage	The code to run to handle all uncaptured exceptions. This could be an HTML file with a friendly message, renamed to a `.psp` file. Note that you must specify this same file name in the `loadpsp` command that compiles the main PSP file. You must specify exactly the same name in both the `errorPage` directive and in the `loadpsp` command, including any relative pathname such as `../error_include/`.

and a sample page directive is:

```
<%@ page language="PL/SQL" contentType="text/html"
errorPage="error_page.psp" %>
```

The attribute names `contentType` *and* `errorPage` *are case-sensitive.*

Watch your typing! Accidentally inserting a space on either side of your equal signs (=) will cause a compiler error. Type both operands flush against the = operator.

XML, JPEG, GIF, TEXT, OR OTHER DOCUMENT TYPES

The PL/SQL gateway's default behavior for transmitting files is to transmit them as HTML documents, so that the browser renders them according to the HTML tags. If you'd like the browser to interpret the document as XML, plain text (with no formatting), or some other document type, include a `<%@ page content-Type="MIMEtype" %>` directive. Specify `text/html`, `text/xml`, `text/plain`, `image/jpeg`, or some other MIME type that the browser or other client program recognizes. Users may have to configure their browsers to recognize some MIME types. Though typically a PL/SQL Server Page is intended to be displayed in a Web browser, it could also be retrieved and interpreted by a program that can make HTTP requests, like a Perl or Java application.

HANDLING DIFFERENT CHARACTER SETS

The PL/SQL gateway's default behavior for transmitting files is also to transmit files using the character set defined by the Web gateway. If you'd like to convert the data to a different character set for displaying in a browser, include a `<%@ page charset="charset_encoding" %>` directive. Specify UTF-8 (Unicode), Shift_JIS, Big5, or some other encoding that the browser or other client program recognizes. Remember to also configure the character set setting in the database access descriptor (DAD) of the Web gateway. Users may have to select the same encoding in their browsers to see the data displayed properly. For example, your current Web browser may be set up to display Western European (Windows) encoding.

HANDLING ERRORS

Any HTML errors are handled by the Web browser. The PSP loading process does not check for HTML coding errors. If you make a syntax error in the PL/SQL code, the loader stops and you must fix the error before continuing.

Any previous version of the stored procedure can be erased when you attempt to replace it and the script contains a syntax error.

You can include PL/SQL exception-handling code within a PSP file to handle database errors that occur when the script runs and therefore have any unhandled exceptions bring up a special page. The page for unhandled exceptions is another PL/SQL Server Page with the extension `.psp`. The error procedure does not receive any parameters, so to determine the cause of the error, it can call the `SQLCODE` and `SQLERRM` functions. You can also display a standard HTML page without any scripting when an error occurs, but you must still give it the extension `.psp`, and load it into the database as a stored procedure using the loadpsp utility.

When you create such an error page for one of your procedures, you must take care when loading the procedure PSP and its error page PSP into the database. In your loadpsp utility command, you must specify the name of the error page PSP before the name of the procedure PSP the error page is to support. Unit 12.3, "Loading PSPs into the Database," explains how to do this.

PSP PROCEDURE DIRECTIVES

The *procedure* directive can currently be created with only one possible attribute: the name of your procedure. It specifies the name of the stored procedure produced by the PSP file. By default, the name is the filename without the `.psp` extension.

And a sample procedure directive is:

```
<%@ plsql procedure="search_student" %>
```

 There is a new keyword of sorts here: "plsql." It's just hanging out, by itself, or so it would seem. This keyword must appear in both the procedure directive (if specified) and the parameter directive (introduced next), or you will receive a compile error.

PSP PARAMETER DIRECTIVES

The *parameter* directive, like the *page* directive, can currently be created with three possible attributes, as illustrated in Table 12.4.

And a sample parameter directive is:

```
<%@ plsql parameter="p_student_id" type="number" default="null" %>
```

Table 12.4 ■ Parameter Directive Attributes

Parameter Directive Attribute	Attribute Description
parameter name	Name for each parameter expected by the PSP stored procedure.
Type	Data type for the parameter. This is an optional attribute. **HINT:** Varchar2 is the default data type assigned to an input parameter, unless otherwise specified. Therefore, if your input parameter is of any other data type, you should specify it explicitly to avoid any possible compilation or runtime errors.
Default	Default value for the parameter. Like the *type* attribute, the *default* attribute is optional. To specify the default value for a parameter that has a character data type, use single quotes around the value, inside the double quotes required by the directive attribute. For example: `<%@ plsql parameter="p_last_name" type="varchar2" default="'Patel'" %>`

The parameters are passed using name–value pairs, typically from an HTML form. The values for the *default* attribute are substituted directly into a PL/SQL statement, so any strings must be single-quoted, and you can use special values such as `null`. The URL that calls this page would typically look like the following:

```
http://myserver/pls/any/search_student?p_student_id=120
```

Adding another parameter requires adding another parameter directive. Consider the following statements:

```
<%@ plsql parameter="p_student_id" type="number" %>
<%@ plsql parameter="p_first_name" type="varchar2"
default="'Seema'" %>
```

Then the URL that calls this page (from a form, using METHOD="get," remember the "post" method places parameters in the HTTP Header and they will therefore not display as part of the query string in the URL) would look like the following:

```
http://myserver/pls/any/search_student?p_student_id=120&
first_name='Seema'
```

In this URL, the `/pls/` portion indicates that the Apache Web Server is to dispatch this request to the mod_plsql module to process this request. The `/any/` indicates which DAD to use, and the `search_student` part is the procedure being requested. By the time this PSP is invoked through a Web client, it has already been loaded into the Oracle database through the loadpsp utility, so the .psp extension is not needed. It is not part of the procedure name inside the database.

If you are using anchored data types, be careful with the length of those types. The TYPE attribute can currently only handle a maximum of 30 characters, including the %TYPE appendix. For example, the following statement:

```
type="student.student_firstname%TYPE"
```

does not impede your PSP file from compiling as long as there is a column called "student_firstname" in the STUDENT table. The value for the TYPE attribute specified in this example is exactly 30 characters long. However, the following statement:

```
type="student.student_first_name%TYPE"
```

which happens to supply a value to the TYPE attribute that is 31 characters long, raises the following Oracle error message during the execution of the loadpsp command:

```
ORA-06502: PL/SQL: numeric or value error: character
string buffer too small
```

If you avoid creating long table and column names for your database objects, this message should not appear frequently when you are loading your PSPs into the database.

Last but not least, the *include* directive, like the *procedure* directive, can currently be created with only one possible attribute: the file name to be included with your PSP procedure. This file can be composed of any browser-compatible material, for example, HTML, XML, and JavaScript. It specifies the name of a file to be included at a specific point in the PSP file. The file must have an extension other than .psp. It can contain HTML, PSP script elements, or a combination of both. The name resolution and file inclusion happens when the PSP file is loaded into the database as a stored procedure, so any changes to the file after that are not reflected when the stored procedure is run. Substitutions are performed once, at the time of loading/creating, not each time the page is served by the 9iAS.

**UNIT
12.4**

Include a `<%@ include file="`*name_of_include*`" %>` directive at the point where the other file's content should appear. Because the files are processed at the point where you load the stored procedure into the database, the substitution is done only once, not whenever the page is served.

You can use any names and extensions for the included files. If the included files contain PL/SQL scripting code, they do not need their own set of directives to identify the procedure name, character set, and so on. When specifying the names of files to the PSP loader (loadpsp utility), you must include the names of all included files. Specify the names of included files before the names of any .psp files.

You can use this feature to pull in the same content, such as a navigation banner, background image, page footer, toolbar, and so on, into many different files. Or, you can use it as a macro capability to include the same section of script code in more than one place in a page. You must specify exactly the same name in both the include directive and in the loadpsp command, including any relative pathname such as `../include_dir/`. And a sample include directive is:

```
<%@ include file="my_banner.htm" %>
```

The following sample code illustrates creating a PSP that is a simple HTML page with an image file of type GIF.

```
<%@ page contentType="image/gif" %>
<%
---------------------------------------------------------
-- FILENAME:     include_gif.psp
-- FILEDATE:     02.11.2002
-- CREATED BY:   Melanie Caffrey
-- DESCRIPTION:  Simple HTML Page with Image
```

```
-- MODIFIED:
----------------------------------------------------
%>
<HTML>
<HEAD>
<TITLE>Include GIF</TITLE>
</HEAD>
<BODY BGCOLOR="#99CCCC">
<IMG SRC="my_image.gif", ALT="My Image", BORDER=0>
</BODY>
</HTML>
```

Then in the following piece of example code, the PSP just created, include_gif.psp, is *included* as an include file inside another PSP.

```
<%@ page language="PL/SQL"%>
<%@ plsql procedure="splash_page" %>
<%
----------------------------------------------------
-- FILENAME:       splash_page.psp
-- FILEDATE:       02.11.2002
-- CREATED BY:     Melanie Caffrey
-- DESCRIPTION:    Splash Page Using Include Directive
--                 with Include File of Type PSP
-- MODIFIED:
----------------------------------------------------
%>
<HTML>
<HEAD>
<TITLE>Splash Page</TITLE>
</HEAD>
<BODY BGCOLOR="#99CCCC">
<%@ include file="include_gif.psp" %>
</BODY>
</HTML>
```

If you prefer to call a PL/SQL procedure, it might be easier than using an include file. Unlike the case with include files, changes to the called PL/SQL code will be reflected each time the PSP is served. To call a PL/SQL procedure in a PSP, you can use the following syntax:

```
<% student_personal_info; %>
```

PSP DECLARATIONS

A PSP *declaration* is just like the declaration section of a PL/SQL code block. It is the place where you define variables, constants, and cursors. PSP declarations are optional, in that variables, constants, and cursors can also be defined in PSP *scriptlets* (defined next). However, your code will be much more manageable if you remember to include a PSP declaration and define the corresponding PL/SQL elements within it accordingly.

A PSP declarative block comes in especially handy if you wish to use global variables within the script. All the usual PL/SQL syntax is allowed within the block. The delimiters, to an extent, serve as shorthand, allowing you to omit the DE-CLARE keyword. All the declarations are available to the code later on in the file. You can also use explicit DECLARE blocks within the scriptlet `<% %>` delimiters that are explained later. These declarations are only visible to the following BEGIN/END block.

The basic syntax is:

```
<%! variable_namevariable_datatype(variable_datatype_size)
%>
```

So, a declarative statement might look like the following:

```
<%!
student_id NUMBER;
city VARCHAR2(60);
zipcode VARCHAR2(10);
   %>
```

Note the exclamation point within this PSP element!

The order and placement of the PSP directives and declarations is not significant in most cases—only when another file is being included. However, for ease of maintenance, this book recommends that you place the directives and declarations together near the beginning of the file.

PSP SCRIPTLETS

Any PL/SQL or SQL code that one would normally see placed between a BEGIN and END statement in a PL/SQL code block can be embedded inside the *scriptlet* element. The basic syntax of a scriptlet element is:

```
<% PL/SQL script %>
```

This element doesn't require any characters after the first % sign. No @ and no ! are required!

So, deeply embedded within lots of HTML code, a PSP can include PL/SQL code with a scriptlet similar to the following:

```
<% FOR rec IN student_cursor LOOP %>
```

You can include any PL/SQL statements within the delimiters <% %>. The statements can be complete or clauses of a compound statement, such as the IF part of an IF-THEN-ELSE statement.

PSP EXPRESSIONS

Using this element is similar to what you write in PL/SQL when you wish to include an actual database value inside a quoted string that is fed to, for example, the DBMS_OUTPUT.PUT_LINE procedure. (**NOTE:** For more information on the Oracle built-in DBMS_OUTPUT.PUT_LINE procedure, refer to the *Oracle PL/SQL Interactive Workbook* by Ben Rosenzweig and Elena Silvestrova.) For instance, when using the DBMS_OUTPUT.PUT_LINE procedure, you may write a line of code that looks similar to the following:

```
DBMS_OUTPUT.PUT_LINE('The Student ID value for David
Ricciardi is:  '||v_student_id||'.');
```

In this line, the actual database value is included by means of *concatenation*. The actual value for the student ID is contained in the variable v_student_id. It is concatenated into the textual string when it is placed between two sets of double pipe, || ||, delimiters. At runtime, the actual database value contained in v_student_id is placed inside the string and output to the screen by the DBMS_OUTPUT.PUT_LINE procedure. For example, the result of running this line of code may look similar to the following:

```
The Student ID value for David Ricciardi is 123.
```

Similarly, to include a value that depends upon the result of a PL/SQL expression, include the expression within the delimiters <%= %>. Due to the fact that the result is always substituted in the middle of text or tags, it must be a string value or be able to be cast to a string. For any types that cannot be implicitly cast, such as DATE, the value must then be passed to the PL/SQL TO_CHAR function.

The content between the <%= %> delimiters is processed by the HTP.PRN procedure, which trims any leading or trailing whitespace and requires that you quote any literal strings. When values specified in PSP attributes are used for PL/SQL operations, they are passed exactly as you specify them in the PSP file. If PL/SQL requires a single-quoted string, you must specify the string with the single quotes around it—and surround the whole thing with double quotes.

You can also nest single-quoted strings inside single quotes. In this case, you must escape the nested single quotes by specifying the sequence \ '. Thankfully, most characters and character sequences can be included in a PSP file without being changed by the PSP loader.

An example of the general syntax for a PSP expression element is:

```
<%= a PL/SQL expression %>
```

Note the equals (=) sign within this PSP element!

And an example of using the expression element when, for instance, your user is asked to choose a student from a drop-down (HTML SELECT list), is:

```
<% FOR rec IN student_cursor LOOP %>
<OPTION VALUE="<%= rec.student_id %>"><%= rec.last_name
%>, <%= rec.first_name> </OPTION>
<% END LOOP; %>
```

Since the = sign in this element is not part of a name/value pair, it is not necessary to ensure that it is written flush against the value supplied. To make the expression element code clear, this book recommends that you leave a single space between the = sign and the expression value. However, the = sign should be written flush against the % character immediately to its left.

USING COMMENTS IN PSP FILES

To put a comment in the HTML portion of a PL/SQL Server Page for the benefit of people reading the PSP source code, use the syntax:

```
<%-- Comment text for people reading the PSP source code --%>
```

These comments do not appear in the HTML output (source code) from the PSP.

To create a comment that is visible in the HTML output, place the comment in the HTML portion of your PSP and use the regular HTML comment syntax:

```
<!-- Comment text for people reading the HTML source code-->
```

To include a comment inside a PL/SQL block within a PSP, you can use the normal PL/SQL comment syntax.

START CODING PSPs

The following PSP file provides an example of much of what has been discussed in this chapter thus far:

```
1 <%@ page language="PL/SQL" %>
2 <%@ plsql procedure="student_personal_info" %>
3 <%@ plsql parameter="p_first_name" default="null" %>
4 <%@ plsql parameter="p_last_name" default="null" %>
5 <%
6 --------------------------------------------------------
7 -- FILENAME:     student_personal_info.psp
8 -- FILEDATE:     7.15.2001
9 -- CREATED BY:   Melanie Caffrey
10 -- DESCRIPTION:  Student Personal Info
11 -- MODIFIED:
12 -- This PSP is specified as using the PL/SQL language
13 -- in the page directive.
14 -- The name, student_personal_info is provided in the
15 -- procedure directive.
16 -- This procedure takes two input parameters, (PSPs
17 -- do not currently provide the ability for creating
18 -- output parameters), p_first_name and p_last_name.
19 -- The default value for both of these input
20 -- parameters is null.  And, if it isn't obvious by
21 -- now, you see that one can create comments inside
22 -- PSP scriptlet, <% %> tags.
23 -- Below, several variables are declared between PSP
24 -- declarative tags to hold information about the
25 -- particular student your user is editing (updating)
26 -- or entering (inserting).
27 %>
28 <%! v_student_id        student.student_id%TYPE;
29     v_salutation        student.salutation%TYPE;
30     v_first_name        student.first_name%TYPE;
31     v_last_name         student.last_name%TYPE;
32     v_street_address    student.street_address%TYPE;
33     v_city              zipcode.city%TYPE;
34     v_state             zipcode.state%TYPE;
35     v_zip               student.zip%TYPE;
36     v_phone             student.phone%TYPE;
37     v_employer          student.employer%TYPE;
38     v_registration_date
39                         student.registration_date%TYPE;
40     v_count             INTEGER := 0;
```

```
41 %>
42 <%!
43 -- One can also create comments inside of PSP
44 -- declarative, tags.
45 -- The below SELECT statement obtains information
46 -- about the student whose first and last name match
47 -- that of the input parameters. (Later in this
48 -- book, you create PSPs that handle the situation
49 -- where more than one person exists in the
50 -- STUDENT table with the same first name/last name
51 -- combination.)
52 -- The information for that particular student is
53 -- used to populate the variables declared above.
54 %>
55 <%
56   SELECT COUNT(*)
57     INTO v_count
58     FROM student
59    WHERE first_name = p_first_name
60      AND last_name  = p_last_name;
61
62      IF v_count > 0
63      THEN
64
65   SELECT student_id,
66          salutation,
67          first_name,
68          last_name,
69          street_address,
70          city,
71          state,
72          s.zip,
73          phone,
74          employer,
75          registration_date
76     INTO v_student_id,
77          v_salutation,
78          v_first_name,
79          v_last_name,
80          v_street_address,
81          v_city,
82          v_state,
83          v_zip,
84          v_phone,
85          v_employer,
86          v_registration_date
87     FROM student s, zipcode z
88    WHERE first_name = p_first_name
89      AND last_name  = p_last_name
```

```
90      AND s.zip       = z.zip;
91
92    ELSE
93
94        SELECT MAX(student_id) + 1
95           INTO v_student_id
96           FROM student;
97
98      END IF;
99  %>
100
101 <%
102 -- Note the use of the COUNT function used to check
103 -- how many students exist in the STUDENT table with
104 -- the first name and last name entered in the
105 -- p_first_name and p_last_name parameters.
106 -- The v_count variable is initialized to a value of
107 -- zero (0) when it is declared.
108 -- Since the COUNT function always returns some
109 -- value, even if it is zero (0), it provides a way
110 -- to sidestep the formidable NO DATA FOUND error
111 -- message when preparing to perform a SELECT
112 -- statement.
113 -- IF the COUNT function returns a value of zero,
114 -- there is no need to perform the subsequent SELECT
115 -- statement from the STUDENT table, since doing so,
116 -- if the value of v_count is zero, will surely
117 -- result in a NO DATA FOUND message.
118 -- Therefore, it is better to check first, then
119 -- provide an alternative piece of logic in your
120 -- code if no such student exists.
121 -- If no such student exists, then this example
122 -- assumes that both input parameters have been left
123 -- with their default values of null, and therefore,
124 -- the user wishes to create (insert) a new user.
125 -- The ELSE portion of the above conditional
126 -- statement readies the code for such a situation
127 -- by obtaining a new student ID value from the
128 -- database using the MAX function.
129 %>
130 <HTML>
131 <HEAD>
132 <TITLE>Student Personal Info</TITLE>
133 </HEAD>
134 <BODY BGCOLOR="#99CCCC">
135 <%
136 -- Display the student ID, first name and last name
137 -- values for the entered student, if available, as
138 -- a heading.  Otherwise, display a default heading.
```

```
139 %>
140 <% IF v_count > 0
141    THEN
142 %>
143 <H2>Personal Information For Student <%=
144 v_student_id %> - <%= v_first_name %> <%=
145 v_last_name %></H2>
146 <% ELSE %>
147 <H2>Personal Information For New Student</H2>
148 <% END IF; %>
149 <%
150 -- Paint the form using the values from the
151 -- variables populated with the SELECT statement, if
152 -- available.
153 %>
154 <FORM NAME="student_personal_form"
155 ACTION="update_student_info" METHOD="post">
156 <INPUT TYPE="hidden" NAME="p_student_id" VALUE="<%=
157 v_student_id %>">
158 <TABLE>
159 <TR>
160 <TD>Salutation:</TD>
161 <TD><INPUT TYPE="text" NAME="p_salutation"
162 VALUE="<%= v_salutation %>"></TD>
162 </TR>
163 <TR>
164 <TD>First Name:</TD>
165 <TD><INPUT TYPE="text" NAME="p_first_name"
166 VALUE="<%= v_first_name %>"></TD>
167 </TR>
168 <TR>
169 <TD>Last Name:</TD>
170 <TD><INPUT TYPE="text" NAME="p_last_name" VALUE="<%=
171 v_last_name %>"></TD>
172 </TR>
173 <TR>
174 <TD>Street Address:</TD>
175 <TD><INPUT TYPE="text" NAME="p_street_address"
176 VALUE="<%= v_street_address %>"></TD>
177 </TR>
178 <% IF v_count > 0
179    THEN
180 %>
181 <TR>
182 <%
183 -- If your user is editing an existing student's
184 -- personal information, then display city and state
185 -- information for that student, and ensure that the
186 -- button to change zipcode information reads
```

```
187 -- "Change Zipcode."  Otherwise, generically display
188 -- the words "City, State and Zipcode", and create
189 -- the button to change zipcode information with the
190 -- displayed value, "Select City, State and
191 -- Zipcode."
192 %>
193 <TD><%= v_city %>, <%= v_state %> </TD>
194 <TD><INPUT TYPE="text" NAME="p_zip" VALUE="<%= v_zip
195 %>"></TD>
196 <TD><INPUT TYPE="button" VALUE="Change Zipcode"
197 onClick="javascript:void(window.open('
198 student_zipcode?p_student_id=<%= v_student_id
199 %>&p_zip=<%= v_zip %>', 'zipwindow', 'width=740,
200 height=550, scrollbars=yes, resizable=yes'));"></TD>
201 </TR>
202 <% ELSE %>
203 <TR>
204 <TD>City, State and Zipcode</TD>
205 <TD><INPUT TYPE="text" NAME="p_zip" VALUE="<%= v_zip
206 %>"></TD>
207 <TD><INPUT TYPE="button" VALUE="Select City, State
208 and Zipcode"
209 onClick="javascript:void(window.open('
210 student_zipcode?p_student_id=<%= v_student_id
211 %>&p_zip=<%= v_zip %>', 'zipwindow', 'width=740,
212 height=550, scrollbars=yes, resizable=yes'));"></TD>
213 </TR>
214 <% END IF; %>
215 <TR>
216 <TD>Phone:</TD>
217 <TD><INPUT TYPE="text" NAME="p_phone" VALUE="<%=
218 v_phone %>"></TD>
219 </TR>
220 <TR>
221 <TD>Employer:</TD>
222 <TD><INPUT TYPE="text" NAME="p_employer" VALUE="<%=
223 v_employer %>"></TD>
224 </TR>
225 <TR>
226 <TD>Registration Date:</TD>
227 <TD><INPUT TYPE="text" NAME="p_registration_date"
228 VALUE="<%= v_registration_date %>"></TD>
229 </TR>
230 <TR>
231 <TD></TD>
232 <TD ALIGN="left"><INPUT TYPE="submit"
233 VALUE="Submit">    <INPUT TYPE="reset" VALUE="Reset">
234 </TD>
235 </TR>
```

```
236 </TABLE>
237 </BODY>
238 </HTML>
```

The above script at first looks like any other ordinary HTML file. What makes it different from a plain HTML source file is the embedded PSP scripting tags outlined in boldface. Taking a look at each line of this file where boldface exists you can see how PSP enables this HTML static Web form to provide dynamic database content to the user.

The first four lines provide the PSP directives. Every directive but the include directive is represented in this file. Next, the file documentation is enclosed as one long bit of commented text inside a scriptlet tag <% ... %>. A PSP declarative block immediately follows the file documentation and is represented as a list of variable declarations enclosed within the declarative <%! ... %> tags. All of these variables are global to this procedure.

Take careful note of the scriptlet tags and expression tags interspersed throughout the PSP file. Any PL/SQL code can be placed within these tags to query an Oracle database and return dynamic data to each point in the file where this code is called. In other words, the personal information for a fictitious student in the above student_personal_info PSP procedure can be changed dynamically based on the first_name and last_name parameter values entered into the interface for this PSP.

Remember that you can embed other technologies inside a PSP, as evidenced by the inclusion of JavaScript code in this PSP, which can, in turn, call another PSP or a PL/SQL Web Toolkit procedure, as is being done with a call to a procedure named "student_zipcode" from the student_personal_info PSP. To produce an elaborate HTML file, including dynamic content such as JavaScript, you can simplify the source code by implementing it as a PSP. This technique avoids having to deal with nested quotation marks, escape characters, concatenated literals and variables, and indentation of the embedded content. Consider the following JavaScript code from the student_personal_info PSP file:

```
<TD><INPUT TYPE="button" VALUE="Change Zipcode"
onClick="javascript:void(window.open('student_zipcode?p_student_id=
<%= v_student_id %>&p_zip=<%= v_zip %>', 'zipwindow', 'width=740,
height=550, scrollbars=yes, resizable=yes'));"></TD>
```

Since JavaScript allows for mixing of double quotes with single quotes, and vice versa, this code is considerably easier to follow than its PL/SQL Web Toolkit counterpart, which would resemble the following code example:

```
htp.p('<TD><INPUT TYPE="button" VALUE="Change Zipcode"
onClick="javascript:void(window.open(''student_zipcode?p_student_id=
'||v_student_id||'\&p_zip='||v_zip||''', ''zipwindow'', ''width=740,
height=550, scrollbars=yes, resizable=yes''));"></TD>');
```

As you can see, coding this procedure as a PL/SQL Web Toolkit procedure results in lines with doubled single quotes, which makes the embedded JavaScript code harder to read.

DEBUGGING PSP

As you begin developing with PSP, keep these guidelines in mind when you encounter errors or other problems:

- You must have all the PL/SQL syntax and PSP directive syntax right. If you make a mistake here, your file does not compile.
  - Quote your values. You might need to enclose a single-quoted value (needed by PL/SQL) inside double quotes (needed by PSP), as may be the case with specifying values for parameters.
  - Make sure you use semicolons to terminate lines where required.
  - Mistakes in the PSP directives are usually reported through PL/SQL syntax error messages. Ensure that your directives use the right syntax, that directives are closed properly (it's both easy and common to forget a %> tag), and that you are using the right element (expression, declaration, or scriptlet) depending on what should be placed inside it.
  - PSP attribute names are case-sensitive. Most are specified in all lowercase, however, `contentType` and `errorPage` must be specified as mixed-case.
- Run the PSP file by requesting its URL in a Web browser. At this point, you might get an error that the file is not found.
  - Make sure you are requesting the right virtual path, depending on how the Web gateway is configured. Typically, the path includes the hostname, optionally a port number, the schema name, and the name of the stored procedure (remember to not include a .psp extension when you type the name of the stored procedure.)
  - Remember, if you use the `-replace` option when compiling the file, the old version of the stored procedure is erased. So, after a failed compilation, you must fix the error or the page is not available. You should test new scripts in a separate schema until they are ready, then load them into the production schema.
  - If you copied the file from another file, remember to change any procedure name directives in the source file to match the new file name.
  - Once you get one "File Not Found" error, make sure to request the latest version of the page the next time. The error page might be cached by the browser. You might need to press Shift-Reload (or, Ctrl-R) in the browser to fully refresh the page and bypass the browser's cache.

If you are using Internet Explorer, it is a good idea to ensure that the page is fully refreshed with each visit. You can set this option automatically in your browser. Click on the "Tools" menu option and select "Internet Options." Select the "General" tab and click the button that reads "Settings." In the radio button selection that allows you to "Check for newer versions of stored pages," select the option that reads "Every visit to the page."

- When the PSP script is run, and the results come back to the browser, use standard debugging techniques to check for and correct wrong output. The tricky part is to set up the interface between different HTML forms and scripts so that all the right values are passed into your page. The page might return an error because of a parameter mismatch.
  - To see exactly what is being passed to your page, use METHOD= GET in the calling form so that the parameters are visible in the URL.
- Make sure that the form that calls your page passes the correct number of parameters, and that the names specified by the NAME= attributes on the form match the parameter names in the PSP file.

**UNIT
12.4**

If a form includes any hidden input fields, or mistakenly uses the NAME= *attribute on the* Submit *or* Reset *buttons, the PSP file handling that form must declare equivalent parameters.*

- Make sure that the parameters can be cast from string into the correct PL/SQL types. For example, do not include alphabetic characters if the parameter in the PSP file is declared as a NUMBER.
- Make sure that the URL's query string consists of name–value pairs, separated by equals signs (p_student_id=123), and that those name–value pairs in turn are separated with ampersands (p_student_id=123&p_first_name=Mary), especially if you are passing parameters by constructing a hard-coded link to the page.

Try to avoid unnecessary whitespace. Spaces on either side of the equals (=) sign separating a name–value pair can potentially break the query string, particularly when you are using JavaScript. This is why it is good coding practice to always surround the values passed to the HTML VALUE attribute with double quotes, that is, <INPUT TYPE="text"VALUE="My text here">.

- If you are passing a lot of parameter data, such as large strings, you might exceed the volume that can be passed with METHOD=GET. You can switch to METHOD=POST in the calling form without changing your PSP file.

Occasionally, PSP compilation error messages may not provide descriptive information about PL/SQL coding errors. When a PSP is loaded into the database, it is loaded as a PL/SQL Web Toolkit procedure. If the PSP is loaded into the database without compiling successfully, you can view the source code of the PSP through SQL*Plus by using a SELECT statement similar to the following:

```
SELECT line, text
   FROM user_source
 WHERE name = <PSP Name>;
```

Substitute the PSP name in brackets, <>, with your PSP name. Try to compile this procedure again (using the code returned from the above SQL statement because you cannot compile PSPs with SQLPlus.) You may find that you receive more descriptive and helpful error messages about mistakes in your PL/SQL code.

UNIT
12.4

A FEW NOTEWORTHY ITEMS

USING OWA_UTIL.SHOWSOURCE

If you use the OWA_UTIL.SHOWSOURCE utility procedure to view the source code of your PSP procedure once you've loaded it into the database, you will notice something worth mentioning. Your code, once primarily PL/SQL code embedded in HTML tags, is converted by the modplsql module of the Apache Web Server to PL/SQL Web Toolkit commands. In other words, you cannot see PSP directives in the source file of a procedure stored in the database. The only place to see these directives is in the original text file that was used to create the PSP. You learn more about the OWA_UTIL.SHOWSOURCE procedure in Chapter 16, "The OWA_UTIL Package: Dynamic SQL, HTML, Date Utilities, and More."

PACKAGING PSPs

To share procedures, constants, and types across different PL/SQL server pages, you can compile them into a separate package in the database using a normal PL/SQL source code file. Although you can reference packaged procedures, constants, and types from PSP scripts, the PSP scripts can only produce standalone procedures, not packages. There is currently no way to package your PSPs. Each procedure created as a PSP is stored individually in the database.

OUT PARAMETERS

There is currently no way to pass output parameters using PSPs. If you must use output parameters, then you must convert your stored procedure to a PL/SQL Web Toolkit procedure.

UNIT 12.4 EXERCISES

a) Create a PSP that paints a search screen for choosing a student. Name this PSP Search_Student.psp. The PSP should be created with the following requirements.

1. There should be one *text-inputtable* field for last_name and one for first_name. *HINT:* To make this search as useful as possible, it should allow a user to enter a partial search. You'll need a pattern-matching approach in order to be able to accomplish this task. Also, be sure to make the search case-INsensitive.

2. Feel free to retrieve all results when a user simply doesn't enter any data in either of the two text fields. Search_Student.psp should merely be created as a form where you collect any information entered by a user to then be passed to another PSP.

b) Create a PSP called Get_Student.psp. This PSP is an intermediate PSP to be created solely for the purpose of handling the programmatic decision as to whether to invoke Student_Personal_Info.psp (already coded earlier in this chapter) or Student_List.psp (explained shortly).

1. When Search_Student passes the student last_name and first_name parameter information to Get_Student, create a cursor that uses the parameters as its filter (WHERE clause).

2. To handle NULLS, don't use too many IF constructs. Instead, make use of Oracle's NVL function.

3. When looping through the cursor, you might try using a record counter to help you accomplish your decision-branching logic.

4. If you have more than one matching result in your cursor, invoke Student_List. If you have just one matching record, invoke Student_Personal_Info. Otherwise, display a JavaScript alert to your user informing her that no records match her search criteria (this will especially come in handy if anyone has entered something along the lines of !@#$%).

5. *VERY IMPORTANT:* If you create the ALERT, be sure to recall Search_Student so that your user may try again.

c) Create a PSP called Student_List.psp. If more than one record matches your user's search criteria, she should be brought to a page painted by Student_List.

1. Display the search results as a tabled list of students with each name displayed as a hyperlink to the Add/Edit Student screen (the PSP for the Add/Edit Student screen is Student_Personal_Info).
2. Display the names (concatenated last_name, first_name) and sort this list alphabetically by last_name, first_name.

UNIT 12.4 EXERCISE ANSWERS

a) Create a PSP that paints a search screen for choosing a student. Name this PSP Search_Student.psp. The PSP should be created with the following requirements.
1. There should be one *text-inputtable* field for last_name and one for first_name. *HINT:* To make this search as useful as possible, it should allow a user to enter a partial search. You'll need a pattern-matching approach in order to be able to accomplish this task. Also, be sure to make the search case-INsensitive.
2. Feel free to retrieve all results when a user simply doesn't enter any data in either of the two text fields. Search_Student.psp should merely be created as a form where you collect any information entered by a user to then be passed to another PSP.

Answer: The PSP you create should look similar to the following example.

```
 1 <%@ page language="PL/SQL"
 2 errorPage="search_student_error.psp" %>
 3 <%@ plsql procedure="search_student" %>
 4 <%
 5 -----------------------------------------------------------
 6 -- FILENAME: search_student
 7 -- FILEDATE: 02.02.2002
 8 -- CREATED BY: Melanie Caffrey
 9 -- DESCRIPTION: Search Student
10 -- URL: http://localhost/pls/any/search_student
11 -----------------------------------------------------------
12 %>
13<HTML>
14 <HEAD>
```

```
15 <TITLE>Search Student</TITLE>
16 </HEAD>
17 <BODY BGCOLOR="#99CCCC">
18 <P></P>
19 <H2 ALIGN=center>Please enter your Student/Instructor
20 Search criteria.</H2>
21 <P></P>
22 <FORM METHOD="post" ACTION="get_student"
23 NAME="student_search">
24 <TABLE BORDER=0>
25 <TR>
26 <TD ALIGN="right"><FONT FACE="Arial">First
27 Name</FONT></TD>
28 <TD>
29 <INPUT TYPE="text" NAME="p_first_name" SIZE="30" >
30 </TD>
31 </TR>
32 <TR>
33 <TD ALIGN="right"><FONT FACE="Arial">Last
34 Name</FONT></TD>
35 <TD>
36 <INPUT TYPE="text" NAME="p_last_name" SIZE="30" >
37 </TD>
38 </TR>
39 <TR>
40 <TD></TD>
41 <TD ALIGN="left"><INPUT TYPE="submit" VALUE="Search">
42 <INPUT TYPE="reset" VALUE="Reset">
43 </TD>
44 </TR>
45 </TABLE>
46 </FORM>
47 </BODY>
48 </HTML>
```

b) Create a PSP called Get_Student.psp. This PSP is an intermediate PSP to be created solely for the purpose of handling the programmatic decision as to whether to invoke Student_Personal.psp (already coded earlier in this chapter) or Student_List.psp (explained shortly).

1. When Search_Student passes the student last_name and first_name parameter information to Get_Student, create a cursor that uses the parameters as its filter (WHERE clause).
2. To handle NULLS, don't use too many IF constructs. Instead, make use of Oracle's NVL function.
3. When looping through the cursor, you might try using a record counter to help you accomplish your decision-branching logic.

4. If you have more than one matching result in your cursor, invoke Student_List. If you have just one matching record, invoke Student_Personal_Info. Otherwise, display a JavaScript alert to your user informing her that no records match her search criteria (this will especially come in handy if anyone has entered something along the lines of !@#$%).

5. *VERY IMPORTANT:* If you create the ALERT, be sure to recall Search_Student so that your user may try again.

Answer: The PSP you create should look similar to the following example.

```
1 <%@ page language="PL/SQL" %>
2 <%@ plsql procedure="get_student" %>
3 <%@ plsql parameter="p_first_name" default="null" %>
4 <%@ plsql parameter="p_last_name" default="null" %>
5 <%
6  ----------------------------------------------------------
7  -- FILENAME:     get_student.psp
8  -- FILEDATE:     02.02.2002
9  -- CREATED BY:   Melanie Caffrey
10 -- DESCRIPTION:  Get Student
11 -- URL         : http://local_host/pls/any/get_student
12 ----------------------------------------------------------
13 %>
14 <%! CURSOR get_student IS
15     SELECT first_name, last_name
16       FROM student
17     WHERE NVL(UPPER(first_name), 'QQ') LIKE
18           NVL(UPPER('%'||p_first_name||'%'), 'QQ')
19       AND UPPER(last_name)              LIKE
20           NVL(UPPER('%'||p_last_name||'%'),
21           UPPER(last_name));
22
23 v_counter    INTEGER := 0;
24 v_last_name  student.last_name%TYPE;
25 v_first_name student.first_name%TYPE;
26 %>
27 <HTML>
28 <HEAD>
29 <TITLE>Get Student</TITLE>
30 </HEAD>
31 <BODY BGCOLOR="#99CCCC">
32 <% FOR rec IN get_student
33   LOOP
34      v_counter := v_counter + 1;
35      v_last_name := rec.last_name;
36      v_first_name := rec.first_name;
37   END LOOP;
38   IF v_counter > 1
```

```
39    THEN
40       student_list(p_first_name, p_last_name);
41    ELSIF v_counter = 1
42    THEN
43       student_personal_info(v_first_name, v_last_name);
44    ELSE
45 %>
46 <SCRIPT language="JavaScript">
47    alert("Sorry.  No Records Match Your Search
48          Criteria.");
49 </SCRIPT>
50 <%  search_student;
51    END IF;
52 %>
53 </BODY>
54 </HTML>
```

c) Create a PSP called Student_List.psp. If more than one record matches your user's search criteria, she should be brought to a page painted by Student_List.

   1. Display the search results as a tabled list of students with each name displayed as a hyperlink to the Add/Edit Student screen (the PSP for the Add/Edit Student screen is Student_Personal_Info.)

   2. Display the names (concatenated last_name, first_name) and sort this list alphabetically by last_name, first_name.

Answer: The PSP you create should look similar to the following example.

```
1 <%@ page language="PL/SQL" %>
2 <%@ plsql procedure="student_list" %>
3 <%@ plsql parameter="p_first_name" %>
4 <%@ plsql parameter="p_last_name" %>
5 <%
6  --------------------------------------------------------
7  -- FILENAME:    student_list.psp
8  -- FILEDATE:    02.02.2002
9  -- CREATED BY:  Melanie Caffrey
10 -- DESCRIPTION: Student List
11 -- URL        : http://local_host/pls/any/student_list
12 --------------------------------------------------------
13 %>
14 <%! CURSOR get_student IS
15    SELECT first_name, last_name
16      FROM student
17     WHERE NVL(UPPER(first_name), 'QQ') LIKE
18           NVL(UPPER('%'||p_first_name||'%'), 'QQ')
19       AND UPPER(last_name)              LIKE
20           NVL(UPPER('%'||p_last_name||'%'),
21           UPPER(last_name))
```

```
22     ORDER BY last_name, first_name;
23 %>
24 <HTML>
25 <HEAD>
26 <TITLE>Student List</TITLE>
27 </HEAD>
28 <BODY BGCOLOR="#99CCCC">
29 <CENTER>
30 <H2>List of Students</H2>
31 <TABLE BORDER="3" BORDERCOLOR="midnight blue"
32  CELLPADDING="5">
33 <TR>
34 <TH ALIGN=center>Student Names</TH>
35 </TR>
36 <% FOR rec IN get_student
37    LOOP
38 %>
39 <TR>
40 <TD>
41 <A HREF="student_personal_info?p_first_name=<%=
42  rec.first_name %>&p_last_name=<%= rec.last_name %>">
43 <FONT FACE="Arial">
44 <%= rec.last_name||', '||rec.first_name %>
45 </FONT></A>
46 </TD>
47 </TR>
48 <% END LOOP; %>
49 </TABLE>
50 </CENTER>
51 </BODY>
52 </HTML>
```

C H A P T E R   1 2

BUILDING THE APP

An example of what you should be working toward can be seen in the companion Web site for this book, located at http://www.phptr.com/boardman/.

Visit the Web site periodically to share and discuss your answers with other readers.

If you haven't already done so, use the loadpsp utility to load the PSP procedures you create, then ensure that you are able to successfully view them and interact with them from your Web browser. Feel free to experiment with the inclusion of error page PSPs and other types of include files.

After completing this chapter, you should find that you have created the following parts of this book's application:

- student_personal_info (as a PSP)
- search_student
- get_student
- student_list

You find that you can easily mix and match your PL/SQL Web Toolkit procedures and PSPs. Feel free to experiment with converting one or two of your application's PL/SQL Web Toolkit procedures to PSPs. You learn useful tips for code reusability (particularly for insert/update purposes) in Chapter 18, "Web Tips and Techniques."

CHAPTER 13

IMAGES

In the development of your Web application you will often choose to include some graphics on the Web page you develop in order to give your pages a better look and feel. This chapter addresses the use of graphics in PL/SQL applications developed for use with the Oracle 9iAS. The use of graphics in Web design is a large subject. If you wish to use many graphic images on your Web page it would be wise to consult a book on graphics design for the Web.

This chapter introduces the main image file types used in Web applications and gives you the basic information that is required to use these images in a Web page. You learn how to store images in a database table and retrieve them for use in Web pages. The section on the use of images with JavaScript covers image rollovers and an example of an image list and a flip list. In the last section, you build a Web page that makes use of a clickable image map.

There are a number of ways that graphics can be displayed on the Web. Inline images appear in the browser window as the HTML file is displayed. Graphics also can be displayed only when a reader clicks on a link, then these graphics are displayed in a window separate from the Web browser. A graphic can also be tiled as a background pattern by most browsers.

Every graphic that is rendered in the Web page by use of the <IMG> tag is an in-line image. Adding a tag to an HTML page to render an image can be done simply by writing HTML code similar to the following:

```
<IMG SRC="filename.jpg">
<IMG SRC="image.jpg" BORDER=1 WIDTH="150" HEIGHT="60">
```

Some Web designers make the sloppy mistake of using a full-size image and then reducing the display size of the image file through the HTML <IMG> tag's WIDTH and HEIGHT attributes. This results in a large image file being shrunk to display on the Web. Even though the image is not taking up a large amount of screen real estate, the page will take a long time to load because the image file is still as large as ever. It is not worth the trade-off. The solution is to resize the image file using a graphics program. As you learn more about file types you will learn the pros and cons from the choices you need to make in order to display an image on the Web.

Single graphics can serve as links to many HTML documents. These kinds of images are known as *imagemaps, image mapped graphics,* or simply *ismaps.* You can add information within the <BODY> tag at the beginning of the document <BODY BACKGROUND= "imagefile.gif">. This enables a single, small image to

Table 13.1 ■ Common Attributes for the IMG Tag

Attribute	Usage
SRC	The path of the image file that is the source for the image to be displayed.
ALIGN	Left, right, or center will indicate that the image will have text wrapping around it based on the value given to the align tag.
ALT	Text to be displayed when the picture cannot be displayed. This will also appear when the mouse is hovered above the image.
BORDER	A number for the thickness of the border. The value should be 0 for no border, in combination with the HREF tag, you will often see a small blue border if you fail to give this attribute a value of 0.
HEIGHT	Indicates the height of the image to be displayed. This can be different from the image's real height in which case you tell the browser to enlarge or shrink the text. Giving the exact height of the image helps the browser allocate space on the page prior to loading the image.
WIDTH	Operates the same as height only in regard to width.
LOWSRC	This attribute is for a low-resolution image that can be initially displayed while the browser is loading the image for the SRC attribute.

be repeated so that it fills an entire Web page. Some nonstandard images may require a plug-in to display correctly. This can also be handled by indicating the file type. This allows the browser to call the application it has registered to handle the MIME file type. The source of the image then indicates the MIME file type by adding a "TYPE=" parameter to the file name as follows: <IMG SRC= "image. bmp?type=bmp">. This chapter addresses only those image types that do not require a browser plug-in in order to be displayed.

U N I T   1 3 . 1

IMAGE TYPES

There are many things to consider when making use of images in your Web application. The two main things to consider are image quality and download speed. These two considerations work in juxtaposition. In order for the image to be the best quality it will be a large file, but you also want your image files to be the smallest size possible in order to reduce the time it takes for the page to display. In order for an image to be displayed, the entire image file must be downloaded into the browser. The use of images can add to the look and feel of a Web page but if they take a long time to appear, your users will not have the patience to use your application. You need to understand the basic issues around file types and characteristics so you can choose the best file type. There are a number of image-editing programs where you can alter the properties of an image to fit the needs of your Web page.

FORMATS

There are two main types of image formats: bitmap and vector. There are also metafiles for files that are created for specific programs. Most browsers can only display bitmap images. If you have images that are vector type you will have to use an image-editing program to convert them. A full-blown image-editing program such as Adobe's PhotoShop or Macromedia's FireWorks will give you the most options for file conversion. The Microsoft Windows program, Paint (that comes with the Windows operating system), can convert files to and from the basic image file types. Although Paint will allow you to convert your files, it does not have all the compression options in how the files are converted and your image quality may suffer.

The main types of image files that are used on the Web are bitmap or raster graphics. These file types store the image as a series of tiny dots called *pixels*. Each pixel is assigned a color, and when they're viewed all together, they form a picture. Bitmap graphics can be edited by erasing or changing the color of individual pixels. There are many different bitmap file formats: BMP is the Windows standard, GIF and JPG are for the Web, TIFF for print, and PSD for Photoshop.

The other category of image files use vector graphics. Unlike bitmaps, vector graphics are not based on pixel patterns, but instead use mathematical formulas consisting of lines and curves that make shapes. Vector graphics are ideal for illustrations, line art, and type. These files can only be seen in a browser if the appropriate plug-in is installed in the client's computer. Two common browser plug-ins to generate animation in a Web page are Macromedia's Flash and Shockwave. Both of these programs use vector graphic file formats. Since all the common Web browsers do not support the display of vector graphics without a plug-in, you may choose to convert vector graphics to bitmap (rasterized) graphics for display on the Web.

Optimizing a Web graphic file can be tricky. There is a fine line between reducing file size for faster download speeds and maintaining the integrity of the image. Most of the major graphic programs like Fireworks and Image Ready offer a file optimizing toolbar with preview capabilities.

Older browsers could only render images that were in the GIF file format. Once the JPEG format was developed, browsers were improved to display both image types. Additional file formats will gain popularity as browsers support them. It also depends on the availability of plug-in applications for browsers. It is not wise to make use of plug-ins unless your application depends on them. In most cases, if a plug-in is used, the first page of the application will have a hyperlink to download and install the plug-in application. It is also customary to have an alternative site that does not require the plug-in.

THE GIF IMAGE FORMAT

CompuServe Information Service originated the Graphic Interchange Format (GIF) (pronounced "jif") in the 1980s as a format that would minimize image file size to allow images to be transmitted quickly across data networks. The GIF file format became very popular. In the early 1990s the original designers of the World Wide Web adopted the GIF format because it was efficient and it had gained widespread familiarity. Initially, the majority of images on the Web were of the GIF format. The GIF format incorporates a compression schema to keep file sizes small. GIF files are limited to 8-bit (which corresponds to 256 or fewer colors) color palettes. The "8-bit" refers to the number of memory bits assigned to each pixel in a GIF image. Each digital bit can only be a "1" or a "0". The 8 bits of memory allocated to each pixel means there can only be 256 (2 to the eighth power) possible unique combinations of 0s and 1s. "Indexed colors" reside in the 256-color index palette from which each image draws its color. The GIF format is generally used for page design elements and the JPEG format, described below, is used for photographs. GIFs are better suited for graphics with areas of solid or flat colors such as illustrations and logos. Other advantages to the GIF format are that it lets you create transparencies and animations. Animated GIFs are similar to the JavaScript rollover method (explained later in this chapter) in that they are images with multiple frames. JPEGs indicate every pixel, whereas GIFs indicate the color and how many times it should be repeated.

Table 13.2 ■ Major Image File Types

Bitmap (Raster) Images	Metafile Images	Vector Images
BMP (Windows/OS2 bitmaps)	AI (Adobe Illustrator)	CLT (CGM Metafile)
DIB (Windows Bitmap)	CDR (CorelDRAW 3-7)	CGM (CGM Metafile)
GIF (Compuserve)	CLP (Windows Clipboard)	GCA (IBM GOCA)
ICA (IBM IOCA)	CMX (Corel Metafile Exchange)	GEM (Gem Metafile)
ICO (Windows Icon)	DRW (Micrografx Draw)	HGL (HP Plotter 7475a)
IFF (Amiga ILBM)	EMF (Enhanced Windows Metafile)	P10 (Tektronix Plot 10*)
IMG (Gem Paint)	EPS (Encapsulated Postscript)	PGL (HP Plotter 7475a)
JPG (JPEG)	IGF (Inset Graphics)	PIC (Lotus PIC)
JPEG (JPG)	PCL (HP LaserJet II)	PLT (HP Plotter 7475a)
KFX (KOFAX Group 4)	PICT (Macintosh Resource Format PICT)	TXT (ASCII Text)
MAC (MacPaint)	PCT (Macintosh PICT1, PICT2)	
MSP (Microsoft Paint)	PIX (Inset PIX)	
PCD (Kodak Photo CD)	PS (Postscript Level 2)	
PCX (PC Paintbrush)	WMF (Windows Metafile)	
PGM (Portable Bitmap)	WPG (WordPerfect)	
PNG (Portable Network Graphics)		
PNM (Portable Bitmap)		
PPM (Portable Bitmap)		
PSD (Photoshop)		
RAS (Sun Raster)		
RGB (Silicon Graphics RGB)		
RLC (Image Systems)		
RLE (Windows Bitmap)		
SBP (IBM Storyboard PIC*)		
SGI (Silicon Graphics RGB)		
SUN (Sun Raster)		
TIF (Tagged Image File) or TIFF		
XBM (X-Windows Bitmap)		
XPM (X-Windows Pixelmap)		
XWD (X-Windows Dump)		

THE JPEG IMAGE FORMAT

The second image format used widely on the Web is the JPEG format (pronounced "jay-peg"). JPEG stands for Joint Photographic Experts Group, the original name of the committee that wrote the standard. On the Windows operating system, these files will have the JPG extension. The JPEG standardized image compression mechanism was designed especially for images of photographic quality. JPEG compression is 24-bit, which means files can contain up to 16.7 million colors and they will also have a larger file size than their 8-bit counterpart,

GIFs. As a result, JPEGs are ideal for photographs, drawings, and any image with complex or subtle color gradations. JPEG is designed for compressing either full-color or gray-scale digital images of "natural," real-world scenes. It does not work very well on nonrealistic images, such as cartoons or line drawings. You would never want to make a two-color black and white JPEG. It tends to introduce blur or ugly artifacts around the edges.

Image-editing programs make use of certain image-compressing algorithms in order to generate the desired file format. The JPEG file format has a specific algorithm that is used when compressing an image into the JPEG format. Regular JPEG is "lossy," meaning that the image you get out of decompression isn't quite identical to what you originally put in. It throws away information in order to compress the graphic. The JPEG algorithm achieves much of its compression by exploiting the known limitations of the human eye; in particular, the fact that small color details aren't perceived as well by the human eye as small details of light and dark. Thus, JPEG is intended for compressing images that will be looked at by humans (as opposed to ones that would be machine-analyzed).

GIF does significantly better on images with only a few distinct colors, such as line drawings and simple cartoons. Not only is GIF lossless (not lossy) for such images, but it also often compresses them more than JPEG can. For example, large areas of pixels that are all exactly the same color are compressed very efficiently by GIF. JPEG cannot squeeze such data as much as GIF does without introducing visible defects. JPEG has a hard time with very sharp edges: a row of pure black pixels adjacent to a row of pure white pixels, for example. Sharp edges tend to come out blurred unless you use a very high quality setting. Plain black-and-white (two-level) images should never be converted to JPEG; they violate all of the conditions just mentioned. You need at least 16 gray levels before JPEG is useful for grayscale images. It should also be noted that GIF is lossless for grayscale images of up to 256 levels, while JPEG is not.

RESOLUTION

Resolution is a measure of the number of pixels that make up a digital image. The higher the resolution, the better your image will look and print. Lower resolutions often result in grainy prints. However, a higher resolution (more pixels) means a larger file size. The resolution of the picture also determines the size of the image.

A 15-inch monitor typically is set to a resolution of 800 pixels horizontally by 600 pixels vertically. This setting will result in an image with dimensions of 800 pixels by 600 pixels to fill the screen. On a larger monitor with the same 800-by-600-pixel setting, the same image (with 800-by-600-pixel dimensions) would still fill the screen, but each pixel would appear larger. Changing the setting of this larger monitor to 1024-by-768 pixels would display the image at a smaller size, occupying only part of the screen. When preparing an image for view only in a Web browser display (meaning you do not intend your user to print the image), pixel dimensions become especially important. Because your image may be viewed on a 15-inch monitor, you may want to limit the size of your image to 800-by-600 pixels to allow room for the Web browser window controls. You can find your settings by going to the Control Panel, going to the Display settings, going to the Settings tab, and looking at the section called Screen Area. There will be a slide bar there where you can adjust the resolution.

MONITOR VS. PRINTER RESOLUTION

The number of pixels displayed per unit of printed length in an image is measured in pixels per inch (ppi). The number of pixels or dots displayed per unit of length on the monitor is measured in dots per inch (dpi). A dot and a pixel are interchangeable. Monitor resolution depends on the size of the monitor plus its pixel setting. Newer monitors often have a resolution of about 96 dpi, while older monitors generally have a resolution of 72 dpi. It is important to understand monitor resolution in order to realize why the display size of an image onscreen can differ from its printed size. Image pixels are translated directly into monitor pixels/dots. This means that when the image resolution is higher than the monitor resolution, the image appears larger onscreen than its specified print dimensions. For example, when you display a 1-by-1 inch, 144-ppi image on a 72-dpi monitor, it appears in a 2-by-2-inch area onscreen. Because the monitor can display only 72 pixels per inch, it needs 2 inches to display the 144 pixels that make up one edge of the image. The exercises for this section will show you how you can find out the ppi of your image. Image-editing programs will allow you to save your file with a lower ppi.

Printers generally have a much higher resolution than monitors. Most desktop laser printers can print at a resolution of 600 ppi, and high quality printers have a resolution of 1200 dpi or higher. Inkjet printers produce a spray of ink, not actual dots. For this reason it is not technically correct to assign these printers a ppi measurement. However, most inkjet printers have an approximate resolution of 300 to 600 ppi and can still produce good results when printing images of up to 150 ppi.

If you want images to be available for printing, it is a good idea to have a link on the page where the user can download the file to their hard drive and then print it locally. The reason is that an image file that you intend to print will need a much higher resolution than an image that is displayed on a Web page. If you place print-quality images on your Web page, then the page will take a very long time to display, and the image quality will be wasted since the high quality cannot be seen on a computer monitor. You can use a lower quality image for the Web page, and provide a link to a higher quality image that users can download and print.

File size is proportional to the pixel dimensions of the image. Images with more pixels may produce more detail at a given printed size, but they require more disk space to store and may be slower and require more time to display on the Web. For instance, a 1-by-1-inch, 200-ppi image contains four times as many pixels as a 1-by-1-inch, 100-ppi image and therefore is four times the file size. Image resolution thus becomes a compromise between image quality (capturing all the data you need) and file size (hard disk space and download time required).

Another factor that affects file size is file format—due to varying compression methods used by GIF, JPEG, and PNG file formats, file sizes can vary considerably for the same pixel dimensions. Similarly, color bit-depth and the number of layers and channels in an image also affect file size. These factors can be controlled only in more advanced image-editing programs.

IMAGE-EDITING PROGRAMS

The two most popular programs for image editing (at the time of this writing) are Adobe's PhotoShop and Macromedia's Fireworks. PhotoShop has a special windowpane called "Save For Web," which will allow you to convert any file type that PhotoShop can read to a GIF or a JPEG. The program will show you how the image will look on the Web, as well as file size, and it will tell you how long it will take a client to download the file at a 28.8Kbps (Kilobytes per second) modem connection speed. The conversions to both JPEG and GIF have numerous options that allow you to trade off image size for quality. There is a preview pane allowing you to see how the file would appear with the given setting before you convert the file.

Fireworks' output options are not for the faint of heart. You can specify every conceivable parameter: extensions, HTML and spacer style, empty cell color and contents, and slice naming convention, not to mention the various optimization settings for GIF, PNG, and JPEG file formats. Like PhotoShop, the program offers a selective JPEG compression that compacts only selected portions of your image, creating a nice compromise between image quality and file size. With selective JPG compression you can specify different compression levels for different image areas. This lets focal points remain crisp and clear, while less important image areas, such as backgrounds, are compressed more. In addition, files may be saved in a variety of other formats. Fortunately, Fireworks includes an export Wizard that automatically selects the best format for the document for viewing on the Web (as well as other presentation mediums) and lets you preview and edit the results.

A complete image-editing program such as PhotoShop will use a process called *dithering* to convert an image from one with 16 million colors to a GIF with only 256 colors. This process involves juxtaposing pixels of different colors into a fine dot pattern to make it seem as if a wider range of intermediate colors are present in the image.

A useful property of JPEG is that adjusting compression parameters can vary the degree of lossiness. This means that the image-maker can trade off file size against output image quality. You can make extremely small files if you don't mind poor quality; if you aren't happy with the output quality at the default compression setting, you can jack up the quality until you are satisfied, and accept lesser compression (larger file size).

Media Tags

There are two HTML tags available that allow a browser to load an image or media file other than those that are native to the browser. The <EMBED> tag placed around the name of a file indicates that a plug-in helper application (such as Apple Quicktime) is necessary in order for the browser to handle the file. The <EMBED> tag includes an attribute called PLUGINSPAGE to indicate where the helper application is available for download. Some browsers can make use of this attribute to download the helper application and render the object. Other attributes are available depending upon the file type.

There is also a tag called <OBJECT>, which works much the same way as the <EMBED> tag. The basic rule of thumb is that the <EMBED> tag is for Navigator-compatible browsers, and the <OBJECT> tag is for Explorer-compatible browsers. Generally, these tags are used in a nested fashion to cover all possibilities.

Here is an example of an Apple QuickTime Movie file being rendered inside an HTML page using the <EMBED> tag (note that there are many parameters that can be used for this type of file):

```
<EMBED SRC ="sample.mov"
PLUGINSPAGE="http://www.apple.com/quicktime/download/"
WIDTH="250" HEIGHT="100" CONTROLLER=true
LOOP=false AUTOPLAY=true CACHE=true>
</EMBED>
```

Here is an example of a Macromedia Flash file being rendered inside an HTML page with <EMBED> and <OBJECT>:

```
<OBJECT CLASSID="clsid:D27CDB6E-AE6D-11cf-96B8-
444553540000" CODEBASE="http://download.macromedia.com/
pub/shockwave/cabs/flash/swflash.cab#version=5,0,0,0"
WIDTH="32" HEIGHT="32">
   <PARAM NAME=movie VALUE=" moviename.swf ">
   <PARAM NAME=quality VALUE=high>
   <EMBED SRC=" moviename.swf " QUALITY=high PLUGINSPACE=
"http://www.macromedia.com/shockwave/download/index.cgi?
P1_Prod_Version=ShockwaveFlash" TYPE="application/
x-shockwave-flash" WIDTH="32" HEIGHT="32">
</EMBED>      </OBJECT>
```

It is important to note that with file types such as Flash and Real Audio, the Web server also has to be set up to serve the file correctly. The example above also makes use of a nested OBJECT and

EMBED tag pair so it can be properly rendered in both Navigator-compatible browsers, and Internet Explorer–compatible browsers. If you want to make use of these tags, you can get more details on usage by consulting the documentation for the plug-in that you are using.

UNIT 13.1 EXERCISES

ADDING IMAGES TO YOUR SPLASH PAGE

Modify your splash page by first adding a small image that is tiled for the background and then add one image to the foreground of your splash page. The first step will be to find an image to be used as your background. A background image needs to be soft so that text that is placed on top of it can easily be read. You do not want the background image to dominate the layout. A small image will repeat like a set of bricks and a large image may be broken. It is best to use a soft pattern when choosing a background image. It is important to make sure your Web page does not seem too busy or it will be difficult for the reader.

a) Go to your search engine of choice, such as http://www.google.com, and search for free images. You will find many sites where you can download copyright-free images. Look for two types of images. The first one should be a small soft image that you can tile for the background and the second one can be anything you like. Before you download an image, check its file type and resolution by making a right-click above the image and choosing the properties selection. You will see a dialog box similar to the one shown in Figures 13.1 and 13.2.

The property box in Figure 13.1 displays the dimensions for how the file is displayed on the Web browser. This means if the <IMG> tag WIDTH and HEIGHT attributes force a particular width and height, that is what you will see as the dimensions in the property box. The property box shown in Figure 13.2 is what you will see if you check the properties of an image file on your hard drive using Windows Explorer. This shows you more properties. The dimensions for the file are the true dimensions of the image. Viewing the dimensions of your image file provides some key details about the image you have chosen. The *type*

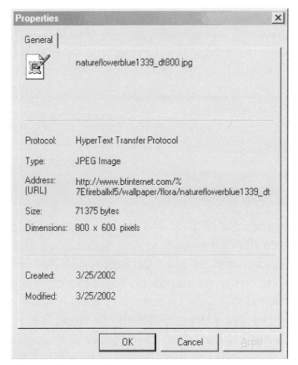

Figure 13.1 ■ **Web image properties.**

will indicate whether it is JPEG or GIF, and the *address* will tell you the exact address for the image file. Remember that an HTML page may indicate an image from a source that is either on the same server, but in a different directory from the HTML file itself, or on an entirely different server. It is not a wise idea to indicate your source image on a server you do not control. If the image is moved or deleted, your Web page will either not display properly or not display at all.

   b) Make sure you have chosen a file that meets the needs of your Web page. If you have a good image-editing program, you can convert the file to meet your needs. If you do not, then make sure it is the correct size and type for your needs. Now it is time to save the image file so you can use it. Right-click on the image file again and choose the "Save Picture As" option. You will then be prompted for a file location.

   c) You are now ready to modify your splash page. Create a directory on the computer that is running the Oracle 9*i*AS called

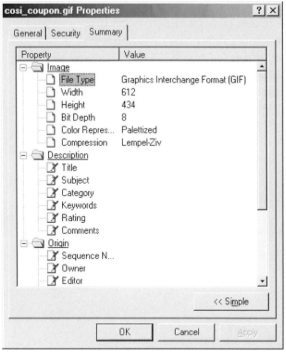

Figure 13.2 ■ Windows Explorer image properties.

images under the directory <OracleHome>/Apache/Apache/ htdocs and upload your two files to this directory. Then create a new version of your splash.psp page to incorporate the background and the image. It should look something like this:

```
<%@ page language="PL/SQL" %>
<%@ plsql procedure="splash" %>
<HTML>
<HEAD>
<TITLE>Splash Page</TITLE>
</HEAD>
<BODY BACKGROUND="/images/imagefile1.jpg">
<CENTER>
<H1>Welcome to the University Maintenance Application</H1>
<IMG SRC="/images/imagefile2.jpg" BORDER="0" WIDTH="200" HEIGHT="150">
</CENTER>
</BODY>
</HTML>
```

There are a few things to which you should pay close attention. The first is that the source for the image begins with the directory that the file resides in. Since the directory begins with a backslash '/', the server knows to start from the docroot and drill down the directories. This is a directory on the server, not a subdirectory of the current directory. Also note that in the previous incarnation of this file, a BGCOLOR attribute was specified in the <BODY> tag. This has been taken out since the background image has precedence and will therefore prevent the background color from being seen.

UNIT 13.2

STORING AND RETRIEVING IMAGES IN THE DATABASE

The process of uploading and downloading files to the database via the Web is dependent on a few key configuration settings for the DAD as well as the proper table in the database to store the files. There are many pros and cons associated with making a decision about saving files in the database or on the file system. Storing your image in the database will mean that you can back up your entire Web site all at once since the procedure that generates the Web pages and the image files are both in the database.

SETTING UP THE DATABASE FOR FILE STORAGE

In order to store files in the database that the Oracle 9iAS can retrieve and understand, you must create a database table to store the images. This is known as the document storage table. One document storage table can be set up for each DAD. The document storage table must have a column that can accept a binary file type. The datatype that can hold binary files is either Long Raw or BLOB (Binary Large Object). The 9iAS Web Listener will expect your table to have a few key columns. Create the following tables in your schema with the following code:

```
CREATE TABLE documents (
        NAME VARCHAR2(256) NOT NULL,
        MIME_TYPE VARCHAR2(128) NULL,
        DOC_SIZE NUMBER NULL,
        DAD_CHARSET VARCHAR2(128) NULL,
        LAST_UPDATED DATE NULL,
        CONTENT_TYPE VARCHAR2(128) NULL,
        CONTENT LONG RAW NULL,
        BLOB_CONTENT BLOB);
```

The document storage table definition is not flexible. It must be identical to the table defined above. The content_type column is used to track which content column the document is stored in. When a document is uploaded, the PL/SQL Gateway will set the value of this column to be the type name. For example, if a document was uploaded into the BLOB content column, then the CONTENT_ TYPE column for the document will be set to the string 'BLOB.' There is a document path parameter when configuring the DAD and this specifies the path element to immediately follow the DAD name in the URL to access a document. For example, if the document access path is docs, then the URL to access a document named domes.jpg would look like (the dad being used here is named demo2, the file name has a number prior to the name of the file; this was generated in the code that will be explained in a few pages):

http://MyServer/pls/demo2/docs/?p_file= F18015/8546_ domes.jpg

 Note that Oracle documentation claims that the ?p_file= is not required in the URL, but this is not the case. In a future release, this bug may be fixed. In this way, the 'docs' notation only helps to abbreviate the need to type the name of the procedure used by the DAD for file download.

Another URL format can also be used to call the procedure to download the file. Assuming the procedure is named FileDownload.download, the URL would be

http://MyServer/pls/demo2/FileDownload.download?p_file= imagefile2.jpg

You can use these URLs as an image source when calling an image in the IMG tag. For example, if you upload the two images that you use in your splash page in Section 16.1, you can now modify your PSP to call the image from the database. You have to check the document's table to be sure you have the correct name for the file. The upload procedure will add more details to the name of the file. If the file did have the name imagefile2.jpg, then your image source that was originally:

<IMG SRC="/images/imagefile2.jpg" BORDER="0" WIDTH="200" HEIGHT="150">

would become:

<IMG SRC="http://MyServer/pls/demo2/FileDownload.download?p_file= imagefile2.jpg" BORDER="0" WIDTH="200" HEIGHT="150">

The document access procedure, FileDownload.download, calls the Oracle-supplied package `wpg_docload.download_file(filename)` to download a file. It knows the filename based on the URL specification. For example, this can be used by an application to implement file-level access controls and versioning.

Now go to the configuration page on the computer that is running your Oracle 9iAS: http://<ServerNAme>:<port>/pls/admin_/gateway.htm. You learned about the configuration page in Chapter 2, "Oracle 9iAS."

CONFIGURE THE DAD TO UPLOAD
AND DOWNLOAD FILES

Go to the configuration for the DAD that will be used when uploading and downloading documents to the server and enter the following parameters. Note that up until now these items were empty. It is important that you configure the DAD correctly since the Web listener relies on the DAD being configured properly in order to accomplish its work effectively.

Document Table	documents
Document Access Procedure	FileTransfer.download
Extensions to be uploaded as LONG RAW	*

Note that you can also use BLOB and this will enable you to make use of Oracle Ultra Search. (Oracle Ultra Search is a turn-key solution that can search across multiple Oracle databases, IMAP mail servers, and files on disk. Ultra Search enables a 'Portal'-based search.) The files are uploaded into the document table. A primary key is passed to the PL/SQL upload handler routine so that it can retrieve the appropriate row of the table.

To send files from a client machine to a database you need to create an HTML page that contains a form tag whose ENCTYPE attribute is set to multipart/form-data and whose ACTION attribute is set to the PL/SQL procedure that has been specified as the document access procedure in the configuration of the DAD. The form must have an INPUT element whose TYPE and NAME attributes are set to "file." By having an input TYPE="file," the user is able to browse and select files from the file system. The submit in the form will perform the following:

- The browser will upload the file specified by the user, as well as other data, to the server.
- The mod_plsql module will store the file contents in the database in the table specfied in the DAD configuration.

■ *FOR EXAMPLE*

```
<FORM ACTION="FileAccess.upload" METHOD="POST"
      ENCTYPE="multipart/form-data">
<INPUT TYPE="FILE" NAME="name">
<INPUT TYPE="submit" VALUE="Submit">
</FORM>
```

If you want the form to submit multiple files at once, then the Oracle-supplied package OWA contains a type, owa.vc_arr, that must be used. Once the files have been sent to the database you can download them, delete them from the database, and read and write their attributes. In order to download the file from the database, you must create a procedure that calls the Oracle-supplied procedure WPG_DOCLOAD.DOWNLOAD_FILE(File_name) to process the download. The way this occurs is that the mod_plsql module looks for the filename in the document table. There must be a unique row in the document table whose NAME column matches the filename. The mod_plsql module generates an HTTP header with the correct mimetype, which it has gathered from the mime_type column in the document table. The contents of the document are sent as the body of the HTTP response. The listener does the actual upload or download. You simply initialize the process by providing the file to be uploaded. The actual download is handled by the mod_plsql gateway based on the settings in your DAD. The code in the procedure simply initializes the process by specifying which file to get.

UNIT 13.2 EXERCISES

CREATE A WEB PAGE TO UPLOAD AND DOWNLOAD FILES

Once you have created the document table and configured the DAD, you are ready to create a Web utility page to upload your files. Note that you can use this as a means to store other binary-type files but you will not be able to view them in your browser. Run the following code in your SQL*Plus session to create the FileAccess package. The start page for this will be the FileAccess.Frameset procedure. This package incorporates everything that is discusssed in this section up to this point.

```
CREATE OR REPLACE PACKAGE  FILEACCESS IS
PROCEDURE frameset;
 PROCEDURE top;
 PROCEDURE empty;
 PROCEDURE upload_file;
 PROCEDURE upload(name IN owa.vc_arr);
 PROCEDURE download_file;
 PROCEDURE download(p_file IN VARCHAR2);
 PROCEDURE erase_file;
 PROCEDURE erase(p_file IN owa.vc_arr);
END;
/


CREATE OR REPLACE PACKAGE BODY FileAccess IS
PROCEDURE frameset IS
BEGIN
 htp.P('
 <HTML>
    <FRAMESET ROWS="25%,*">
      <FRAME SRC="FileAccess.top" NAME="top_frame">
        <FRAMESET COLS="30%,*">
          <FRAME SRC="FileAccess.empty" NAME="left_frame">
          <FRAME SRC="FileAccess.empty" NAME="right_frame">
        </FRAMESET>
```

```
      </FRAMESET>
</HTML>');
EXCEPTION
  WHEN OTHERS THEN
       htp.p(sqlerrm);
  RETURN;
END frameset;
```

```
PROCEDURE top IS
BEGIN
HTP.P('
<HTML><BODY>
<CENTER><FONT  Size="+2">File Upload/Download Utility for
</FONT><BR>');
htp.p(owa_util.Get_Cgi_Env('HTTP_HOST')||' using the DAD: ');
htp.p(owa_util.Get_Cgi_Env('DAD_NAME'));
htp.p('</CENTER><BR>
<TABLE  BORDER="0" WIDTH="100%" >
  <TD ALIGN=CENTER><A HREF="FileAccess.upload_file"
      TARGET="left_frame">Upload Files</A></TD>
  <TD ALIGN=CENTER><A HREF="FileAccess.download_file"
      TARGET="left_frame">Download Files</A></TD>
  <TD  ALIGN=CENTER><A HREF="FileAccess.erase_file"
      TARGET="right_frame">Remove Files</A></TD>
</TR>  </TABLE> </BODY> </HTML>');
EXCEPTION
  WHEN OTHERS THEN
   htp.p(sqlerrm);
  RETURN;
END top;


PROCEDURE empty IS
BEGIN
 htp.p('<HTML>
        <BODY>
        </BODY>
        <HTML>');
EXCEPTION
  WHEN OTHERS THEN
   htp.p(sqlerrm);
  RETURN;
END empty;


PROCEDURE upload_file IS
 BEGIN
 htp.p('<HTML><BODY>
<CENTER><FONT  Size="+1">
 Upload a file into the Database
<FORM ACTION="FileAccess.upload"
```

```
        METHOD="POST" ENCTYPE="multipart/form-data">
      <INPUT TYPE="FILE" NAME="name">
      <INPUT TYPE="submit" VALUE="Submit">
</FORM></BODY> </HTML> ');
 EXCEPTION
  WHEN OTHERS THEN
      htp.p(sqlerrm);
  RETURN;
 END upload_file;


 PROCEDURE upload(name IN owa.vc_arr) IS
 BEGIN
  htp.p('<HTML><BODY> The File has been renamed '||name(1)
        ||' and has been uploaded into the database </BODY> </HTML>');
 EXCEPTION
  WHEN NO_DATA_FOUND THEN
   NULL;
  WHEN OTHERS THEN
   htp.p(sqlerrm);
  RETURN;
 END upload;


 PROCEDURE download_file IS
 CURSOR c_docs IS
  SELECT name FROM documents;
 BEGIN
  htp.p('<HTML> <BODY>');
  FOR rec IN c_docs LOOP
   htp.anchor2(curl => 'FileAccess.download?p_file='||rec.name,
               ctext => rec.name, ctarget => 'right_frame');
   htp.br;
  END LOOP;
  htp.p('</HTML> </BODY>');
 EXCEPTION
  WHEN OTHERS THEN
   htp.p(sqlerrm);
  RETURN;
 END download_file;


 PROCEDURE download(p_file IN VARCHAR2) IS
 BEGIN
  wpg_docload.download_file(p_file);
 EXCEPTION
  WHEN OTHERS THEN
   htp.p(sqlerrm);
  RETURN;
 END download;


PROCEDURE erase_file IS
```

```
CURSOR c_file IS
 SELECT name, mime_type, doc_size, dad_charset, last_updated,
 content_type
FROM documents;
BEGIN
Htp.p('<H3>Select the file(s) you wish to remove then submit</H3>
    <FORM ACTION="FileAccess.erase" METHOD="POST">
    <TABLE BORDER=1>');
 FOR r_file IN c_file LOOP
   htp.tableRowOpen;
   htp.tableData(htf.formCheckbox(cname => 'p_file',
                 cvalue => r_file.name));
   htp.tableData(r_file.name);
   htp.tableData(r_file.mime_type);
   htp.tableData(r_file.doc_size);
   htp.tableData(r_file.dad_charset);
   htp.tableData(r_file.last_updated);
   htp.tableData(r_file.content_type);
   htp.tableRowClose;
 END LOOP;
 htp.p('</TABLE><INPUT TYPE="submit" VALUE="Submit"></FORM>');
EXCEPTION
   WHEN OTHERS THEN
    htp.p(sqlerrm);
   RETURN;
END erase_file;

PROCEDURE erase(p_file IN owa.vc_arr) IS
i BINARY_INTEGER := 0;
BEGIN
 LOOP
 i := i +1 ;
 htp.p('The File: '||p_file(i)||' has been removed');
 htp.br;
 DELETE FROM documents WHERE name = p_file(i);
 END LOOP;
EXCEPTION
   WHEN NO_DATA_FOUND THEN
    NULL;
   WHEN OTHERS THEN
    htp.p(sqlerrm);
   RETURN;
END erase;
END FileAccess;
/
```

UNIT 13.3

JAVASCRIPT AND IMAGES

There are many ways that JavaScript can manipulate images. This section covers the popular use of Rollover buttons and an image list.

JAVASCRIPT ROLLOVER

A JavaScript Rollover refers to what happens when you move or "roll" the mouse over a specific area on a page. One of the most common kinds of rollover is a clickable button that changes its appearance when the mouse is moved over it. In reality, one image is being swapped very quickly for another image. This is a popular element in Web pages because it focuses attention on the spot where the user has placed the mouse. When the image changes it also gives the user a sense that this button will cause an event to occur. Without this functionality in place, clickable buttons that do not change their appearance when the mouse is moved over them can be confusing to users when there are many graphic elements on a page and some are just for design and some act as buttons. The rollover helps emphasize the buttons that actually work.

What makes a rollover possible is JavaScript. JavaScript uses its DOM, or Document Object Model, that encompasses all of the elements on a Web page. Images and their sources are visible to the DOM. Additionally, JavaScript uses event handlers that respond to actions on a Web page. An *event handler* is JavaScript that sits inside an HTML tag. It responds to an event on a Web page. It does not require the <SCRIPT> tags. When the event specified in the event handler occurs, the JavaScript is executed. Usually, the JavaScript just calls a separate JavaScript function, for the sake of readability, reusability, and ease of use. A commonly used event handler is the onClick event. It can be implemented in the following manner:

```
<INPUT TYPE="button" VALUE="Click Here" onClick="alert('Hello!');">
```

An event handler can also call a JavaScript function loaded earlier in the page. Here is an example of a call to a JavaScript function called MyFunction:

```
<INPUT TYPE="button" VALUE="Click Here for List"
onClick="MyFunction();">
```

The Event Handlers that are relevant for a Rollover button are:

> **onMouseOver**—when a mouse is passed over a specified area/object

> **onMouseOut**—when the mouse leaves a specified area/object

"ON" AND "OFF" IMAGES

To make a button change when the mouse passes over it, two images are needed. The first image that is needed is called the "Off" image. This is the image that will be seen when the mouse is not over the image. The "On" image is the version of the image that is seen when the mouse is passed over the button. Generally, these images are reverses of each other, or at least of different enough colors to provide a contrast.

TIP: The "on" and "off" images should be exactly the same size, in order for them to be displayed properly in the browser when one image is swapped for another.

Create three sets of images to be used as On and Off images for your top navigation bar. This can be done in a program such as Paint. Think about the choice of making them either a GIF or a JPEG.

For example, Figures 13.3 and 13.4 are two images for the Student Navigation bar:

Student

Figure 13.3 ■ Off image: Student_off.gif.

Student

Figure 13.4 ■ On image: Student_on.gif.

Next look at the code that you develop for the Top Navigation bar in the file top_menu.psp:

```
<A HREF="students_frame" TARGET="main">
<FONT FACE="Arial">Students</FONT></A>
```

The first step is to make the hyperlink a clickable image instead of just being the word "Students," with a hyperlink. This is done as follows:

```
<A HREF="students_frame" TARGET="main">
<IMG SRC="Student_off.gif" BORDER="0" NAME="student _button">
</A>
```

Be sure to give the IMAGE a NAME attribute. This name will be useful in the JavaScript. Also note that the border is set to zero to avoid a blue outline around the clickable image.

Now put everything together:

```
<A HREF="students_frame" TARGET="main"
onMouseOver="document.student_button.src='student_on.gif'"
onMouseOut="document.student_button.src='student_off.gif'">
<IMG SRC="Student_off.gif" BORDER="0" NAME="student_
button">
</A>
```

UNIT 13.3 EXERCISES

UPDATE YOUR MENU PAGE WITH ROLLOVERS

Complete this exercise by creating a JavaScript Rollover, similar to the one you create for the Students hyperlink, for the Instructors and Classes hyperlink. The first step is to create four more images, two pairs of ON and OFF images for both the Instructors and Classes hyperlinks. Your final result may look as follows:

```
<%@ page language="PL/SQL" %>
<%@ plsql procedure="top_menu" %>
<HTML>
<HEAD>
<TITLE>University Maintenance Website
</TITLE>
</HEAD>
<BODY BGCOLOR="#99CCFF">
<P ALIGN="center">
<FONT FACE="Arial" SIZE="5" >University Maintenance Website</FONT></P>
<TABLE BORDER="0" WIDTH="100%">
<TR>
<TD ALIGN="center">
<A HREF="students_frame" TARGET="main"
onMouseOver="document.student_button.src='/images/student_on.gif'"
onMouseOut="document.student_button.src='/images/student_off.gif'">
```

```
<IMG SRC="/images/Student_off.gif" BORDER="0"
NAME="student_button"></A></TD>
<TD ALIGN="center">
<A HREF="instructors_frame" TARGET="main"
onMouseOver="document.instructor_button.src='/images/instructor_on.
gif'"
onMouseOut="document.instructor_button.src='/images/instructor_off.
gif'">
<IMG SRC="/images/instructor_off.gif" BORDER="0"
 NAME="instructor_button"></A></TD>
<TD ALIGN="center">
<A HREF="classes_frame" TARGET="main"
onMouseOver="document.classes_button.src='/images/classes_on.gif'"
onMouseOut="document.classes_button.src='/images/classes_off.gif'">
<IMG SRC="/images/classes_off.gif" BORDER="0"
NAME="classes_button"></A></TD>
</TR>
</TABLE>
</BODY>
</HTML>
```

JAVASCRIPT IMAGE LIST

There are many ways that you can make use of JavaScript to manipulate images on your Web pages. Here are two examples of popular methods to view many photos on one Web page by only seeing one image at a time. These are both examples that you can add to your splash page of the application you are creating by working through this book. These will help make your splash page more dramatic. In the first example you need a set of image files that are completely different (different in height and width?) and store them in the images directory on your application server. You can also store them in the database. In this case, the initial array of images will be drawn from the database. To do this, you need to change the elements in the fotoArray array (outlined below) so that instead of having the first element be images/photo_1.jpg, it will be :

```
http://MyServer/pls/any/FileDownload.download?p_file=
F26702/photo_1.jpg
```

This page also assumes that you have two triangular images that are used as buttons for navigation. One file is called back_button1.gif and the other one is called forward_button1.gif. There are three arrays that are created in the beginning of the JavaScript function in the example below. The fotoArray array holds a list of all the images that will be shown, the txt array holds all the text that will be displayed as the images are rotated, and finally the clr array holds the list of colors. The key variable here is the arryPostion, which is the variable that holds the current position in the array. This is used to increment the array position and it is referenced in the imageFlip function (outlined below) to determine which element in the three arrays is to be displayed.

```
<HTML>
<HEAD>
<TITLE>PHOTOS</TITLE>
<script language="JavaScript">
// make the arrays
fotoArry = new Array('/images/photo_1.jpg', '/images/photo_2.jpg',
'/images/photo_3.jpg',
'/images/photo_4.jpg');
txt = new Array('text1', 'text2', 'text3', 'text4');
clr = new Array('maroon', 'lightblue', 'khaki');
// arryPostion will point to successive images in the fotoArry array
arryPostion = 0;
function imageFlip(where) {
 if (where == "back") {
   arryPostion= arryPostion - 1
 } else if (where == "go") {
   arryPostion = arryPostion + 1
 } else {
   chgPos = 0;
 }
 // increment the pointer
if(arryPostion == fotoArry.length) {
   arryPostion = 0;
 } else if (arryPostion < 0) {
   arryPostion = fotoArry.length-1;
 } else {
   //arryPostion++;
 }
 // change the image, background color, and text
 document.bgColor = clr[arryPostion];
 document.images['aImagem'].src = fotoArry[arryPostion];
 document.forms[0].foto_txt.value = txt[arryPostion];
}
</SCRIPT>
</HEAD>
<BODY onLoad="imageFlip('load');">
<TABLE border="0" width="100%" bgcolor="#000000">
  <tr>
    <TD align="center"><FONT face="Arial"
        size="6" color="#FF0000">Our</FONT>
    <FONT face="Arial" size="6" color="#FFFFFF">
University</FONT></TD>
  </TR>
</TABLE>
```

```
<p align="center"><font face="Arial" color="#FFFFFF">
   SomeWhere  - in the USA<br>
 This year</font></p>
<form>
  <div ><center><table>
    <tr align="center">
      <td><table bgcolor="#000000">
        <tr>
           <p>
          <CENTER>
            <input type="text" name="foto_txt" value size="80">
          </CENTER>
          <img name="aImagem" src="/images/photo_1.jpg"
            border="4" height="410" width="599">
    </tr>
    <tr align="center">
      <td align="center"> 
      <a href="javascript:imageFlip('back');">
      <img src="/images/back_button1.gif" width="41" height="28"
       alt="Back" border="0"></a>
      <a href="javascript:imageFlip('go');">
      <img src="/images/forward_button1.gif" width="41"
      height="28" alt="Go" border="0">
      </a>
      <br>
      <a href="javascript:window.close();">Close</a> </td>
    </tr>
  </table>
  </center></div>
</form>
</body>
</html>
```

FLIP BOOK

A JavaScript Flip book runs through many images one after another without the need for user input. This is done with a slight modification to the previous JavaScript function to create the image list. In the flip book the image navigation buttons have been removed from the HTML and the JavaScript imageFlip function has been simplified so it no longer has an input of "back" to get the previous image or "go" to get the next image. It adds the line `setTimeout('image-Flip()', 2000);` to the end of the imageFlip fuction. This additional code causes the imageFlip function to continue to run again and again, cycling through the three arrays, to automatically rotate images, image text, and background color. Note that an HTML form is used so that the JavaScript function has "form" elements to reference and change. The form is not being submitted.

```
<HTML>
<HEAD>
<TITLE>PHOTOS</TITLE>
<SCRIPT language="JavaScript">
// make the arrays
fotoArry = new Array('/images/photo_1.jpg', '/images/photo_2.jpg',
'/images/photo_3.jpg', '/images/photo_4.jpg');
txt = new Array('This is the first photo', 'This is the second photo',
'This is the third photo', 'This is the fourth photo');
clr = new Array('blue', 'pink', 'yellow');
// arryPostion will point to successive images in the fotoArry
array
arryPostion = 0;
function imageFlip() {
// increment the pointer
  if(arryPostion == fotoArry.length-1) {
    arryPostion = 0;
  } else {
    arryPostion++;
  }
 // change the image, background color, and text
 document.bgColor = clr[arryPostion];
 document.images['aImagem'].src = fotoArry[arryPostion];
 document.forms[0].foto_txt.value = txt[arryPostion];
 setTimeout('imageFlip()', 2000);
}
</script>
</head>
<body onLoad="imageFlip('load');">
<table border="0" width="100%" bgcolor="#000000">
  <tr>
    <td align="center"><font face="Arial" size="6"
     color="#FF0000">Our</font><font
     face="Arial" size="6" color="#FFFFFF"> University</font></td>
  </tr>
</table>
<p align="center"><font face="Arial" color="#FFFFFF">
SomeWhere  - in the USA<br>
 This year</font></p>
<form>
  <div align="center"><center><table>
    <tr align="center">
      <td><table bgcolor="#000000">
        <tr>
            <p>
          <CENTER>
            <input type="text" name="foto_txt" value size="80">
          </CENTER>
```

```
            <img name="aImagem" src="/images/photo_1.jpg" border="4"
            height="410" width="599">
      </tr>
      <tr align="center">
        <a href="javascript:window.close();">Close</a> </td>
      </tr>
    </table>
    </center></div>
</form>
</body>
</html>
```

UNIT 13.4

IMAGE MAPS

An image map is a picture that has clickable regions: when the user clicks a region, the appropriate hyperlink is invoked. There are two kinds of clickable image maps. One is called *server-side* because the logic to determine what action is to be performed based on where the user clicks is done on the server. The other type is called *client-side,* because the logic is done entirely on the client. This section covers both types. You will have to choose which one makes more sense for the given usage. Generally, client-side image maps are used more frequently because the logic is done on the "client" side and there is no need for network traffic. When you want a different result for every point that a user could click then you must use a server-side image map. You will learn the details of both and realize when each would be more beneficial.

SERVER-SIDE IMAGE MAPS

In a server-side image map the image displayed on the client (the HTML file) is a form input of the type IMAGE. This means that when the user clicks on the image the form is submitted. The x and y coordinates where the user clicked are received as IN parameters by the form handler procedure. Note that you do not need a Submit button for this type of form. The <INPUT> tag with TYPE="image" is the only required input element in the form. As you learned in Chapter 5, "Advanced HTML: Forms, Nested Tables, and Nested Frames," this input type creates an image field on which the user can click and cause the form to be submitted immediately. The coordinates of the selected point are measured in pixels, and returned (along with other contents of the form) in two named value pairs. The x coordinate is submitted under the name of the field with ".x" appended, and the y coordinate with ".y" appended. Any VALUE attribute is ignored. The image input syntax is as follows:

```
<INPUT TYPE="image" NAME="p_image" SRC="/images/picture1.jpg">
```

The type here is "image." The name is required, as this will be the name of the parameter that is being sent to the action of the form.

There are a number of elements of the OWA_IMAGE package for generating this HTML. The example above can be generated by the use of the Oracle-supplied HTP.formImage procedure. The syntax for this procedure is as follows:

```
htp.formImage ( cname in varchar2
                csrc in varchar2
                calign in varchar2 DEFAULT NULL
                cattributes in varchar2 DEFAULT NULL);
```

The parameters for this procedure are detailed in Table 13.3.

Here is an example (only the first two parameters are passed in here):

```
htp.formImage('v_image','/images/location.gif');
```

generates the following HTML:

```
<INPUT TYPE="image" NAME="p_image" SRC="/images/location.gif">
```

An HTML form needs a form handler procedure that can be used as the action of the form. This procedure must be able to accept what is sent by the image-input item. The IN parameter for the image supplied to the form handler procedure must have the same name as the image input, and a datatype of OWA_IMAGE.POINT, which is supplied by Oracle. This data type contains both the x and y values of a coordinate, so there will only be one IN parameter for the image.

There are two more functions in the OWA_IMAGE package that can extract the x or y coordinate from an OWA_IMAGE.POINT data type. These are the functions, OWA_IMAGE.GET_X, for the x coordinate, and OWA_IMAGE.GET_Y, for the y coordinate.

Using the OWA_IMAGE.GET_X and OWA_IMAGE.GET_Y functions, the form handler procedure will be able to access the coordinates the user clicked, and be able to work with these numbers. Figure 13.5 is a very simple example using the image of a floor in a university with eight different rooms. When the user clicks anywhere on the image, a new page displays, showing the x and y coordinates

Table 13.3 ■ Parameters for the htp.formImage Procedure

Parameter	Usage
CNAME	The VALUE for the NAME attribute, the name of the parameter to be submitted.
CSRC	The value for the SRC attribute, which specifies the image file.
CALIGN	The value for the ALIGN attribute, which is optional.
CATTRIBUTES	Any other attributes to be included as-is in the tag.

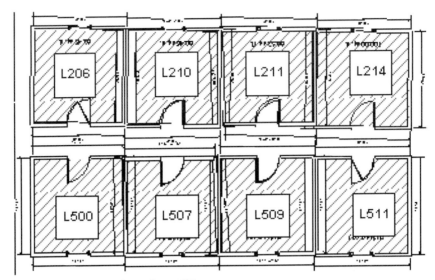

Figure 13.5 ■ The location.gif image.

where the user clicked. There are two procedures in the sample package below called find_coords. The first one is display_image. It makes use of the procedure htp.formImage to create the image input. The next procedure, show_cords, is the action of the display_image procedure. This means that the IN parameter named for the image must be of owa_image.Point data type. The show_coords procedure uses the functions owa_image.Get_X and owa_image.Get_Y to determine the *x* and *y* coordinates, and then displays them on a new Web page. You can use this package to create a development page to assist you in creating the client-side image map procedure later in this chapter.

```
CREATE OR REPLACE Package find_coords
AS
  PROCEDURE  display_image;
  PROCEDURE  show_coords (p_image    IN  owa_image.Point);
END find_coords;
/
CREATE OR REPLACE PACKAGE BODY find_coords    AS
PROCEDURE display_image    IS
BEGIN
   htp.headOpen;
   htp.title('Display the Image');
   htp.headClose;
   htp.p('<BODY bgcolor="khaki">');
   htp.header(1,'Find the Coordinates');
   htp.p('Click on the image and you will see the x,y
         coordinates on the next page');
   htp.formOpen('find_coords.show_coords');
```

```
    htp.formImage('p_image','/images/location.gif');
    htp.formClose;
    htp.p('</BODY>');
    htp.p('</HTML>');
EXCEPTION
    WHEN OTHERS THEN
        htp.p('An error occurred: '||SQLERRM||'. Please try again
        later.');
END display_image;
Procedure show_coords
    (p_image IN owa_image.Point)
IS
    x_in NUMBER(4) := owa_image.Get_X(v_image);
    y_in NUMBER(4) := owa_image.Get_Y(v_image);
BEGIN
    htp.headOpen;
    htp.title('Find Your coordinates');
    htp.headClose;
    htp.p('<BODY bgcolor="khaki">');
    htp.header(1,'These are the Coordinates you clicked on:');
    htp.p('<P>
            You have selected '||x_in||' as your X coordinate </p>');
    htp.p('<P>
            You have selected '||Y_in||' as your Y coordinate </p>');
    htp.p('</BODY>');
    htp.p('</HTML>');
EXCEPTION
    WHEN OTHERS THEN
        htp.p('An error occurred: '||SQLERRM||'. Please try again
        later.');
END ;
END find_coords;
/
```

The display_image procedure creates an HTML file as follows:

```
<HTML>
<HEAD>
<TITLE>Display the Image</TITLE>
</HEAD>
<BODY bgcolor="khaki">
<H1>Find the Coordinates</H1>
Click on the image and you will see the x,y
coordinates on the next page
<FORM ACTION="find_coords.show_coords" METHOD="POST">
<INPUT TYPE="image" NAME="p_image" SRC="/images/location.gif">
</BODY>
</HTML>
```

CLIENT-SIDE IMAGE MAPS

There are two steps involved in creating a client side image map in HTML.

1. Set up an image map.
2. Show an image and use the image map.

You can think of the initial image map as being similar to a JavaScript function that is defined in the beginning of an HTML file, then used later.

CREATE THE IMAGE MAP

The first tag in an image map is the <MAP> tag. This tag must have a name attribute or it cannot be referenced later on in the file. The image map contains a number of areas that are each a hyperlink. Each area uses an <AREA> tag. Each <AREA> tag must have a SHAPE attribute to indicate the shape of the area and an HREF attribute to indicate the hyperlink to where clicking on the map will direct the user. The various types of shapes have different sets of coordinates used to define the shape. The coordinates used to define an image map's shape are supplied in the value for the COORDS attribute. Figure 13.6 is a simple example of four rectangular shapes in a map. The shape that is called "default" indicates the hyperlink for any area of the image that is not covered by one of the shapes. The coordinates used here are meaningless and are just used to complete the example.

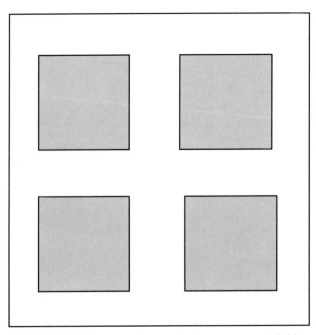

Figure 13.6 ■ **Sample image for image map MyMap.**

```
<map name="MyMap">
<area shape="rect" href="first.htm" coords="20,20,70,60">
<area shape="rect" href="second.htm" coords="90,20,140,60">
<area shape="rect" href="third.htm" coords="20,80,70,120">
<area shape="rect" href="fourth.htm" coords="90,80,140,120">
<area shape="default" href="default.htm">
</map>
```

SHAPES

Table 13.4 shows the various shapes and how they are used.

LINKING TO YOUR IMAGE MAP
FROM YOUR HTML DOCUMENT

Image maps help <img> tags target multiple URLs through a single <a href> tag. Take a look at the following HTML syntax for calling a client-side image map:

```
<IMG SRC="/images/MyImage.gif" ISMAP USEMAP="#MyMap">
```

To make this link look around for a client-side map, just add the usemap= "#MyMap " modifier to its <img> tag. This means you must have defined an image map with the

Table 13.4 ■ Image Map Shapes

Shape	Required Coordinates	Example
Rectangle	shape="rect" coords="X1,Y1 X2,Y2" Defines the top left corner and the bottom right corner	
Circle	shape='circle' coords=' x,y, r' Defined by center coordinate (x,y) and radius (r)	
Oval	shape='oval' coords='x,y x,y' Defined by tangential rectangle surrounding oval; top left corner (x,y) and bottom right corner (x,y)	
Polygon	shape='poly' coords=' x1,y1 x2,y2 ... xN,yN ' Defined by contiguous line segments, conventionally in clockwise rotation	
Point	shape='point' coords='x,y' Defines a single point (x,y)	

name MyMap earlier on in the HTML file. Note that the code for usemap="#MyMap" starts with a hash mark ("#"). As the HTML 1.0 specification decrees, anything following a hash mark in a URL describes a specific anchor point within a file. So if your IMG tag is pointing to #MyMap, then it is pointing to a map within the current file. The result is a link to a client-side image map within your HTML file. You can just think of it as a pointer, though, because the browser does not ask the server for an extra file.

IMAGE MAPS IN PL/SQL

The method to generate this in PL/SQL, using the supplied Oracle packages within the Oracle Web Toolkit, is to take the following steps:

1. Name the map.
2. Divide it into clickable areas.
3. Specify the image to be used.

Using PL/SQL, you make use of the HTP.mapOpen and HTP.mapClose procedures to open and close the map definition. You use the HTP.AREA procedure to define the areas within the map. Then, when you display the image, you make use of the HTP.IMG2 procedure to create the HTML <IMG> tag with the corresponding image map.

The IS MAP that is generated in the IMG tag indicates that this image is going to use an image map, the USEMAP= determines the name of the image map to be used. The image map must have been previously defined in the HTML for the page or the image map will not function.

At runtime:

1. Click on the image.
2. The browser processes the coordinates.

Table 13.5 ■ Parameters for the htp.formImage Procedure

Procedure	Resulting HTML	Purpose
htp.mapOpen('map1');	<MAP NAME="map1" >	Name the map
htp.area ('0,0,50,50', rect, 'www.prenhall.com');	<AREA SHAPE="rect" COORDS="0,0,50,50"	Specify the regions
	HREF="www.prenhall.com">	
htp.mapClose;	</MAP>	Close the map
htp.img2('MyImage.gif', cismap=>'1', cusemap=>'#map1');	<IMG SRC="MyImage.gif" ISMAP USEMAP="#map1">	Specify the image and link to the region

Unit 13.4 Exercises

Create the *CLASS_LOCATION PSP*

Create a PSP file that displays an image with a corresponding image map. The purpose of this page is to assign or update the meeting location for a specific section of a course. The top of the page should display all the section details—course number, course description, instructor first and last name, section number, start_date_time, and location. Use the same image that is used in the find_coords procedure outlined earlier in this chapter. This image is available on the companion Web site at http://www.phptr.com/boardman. Clicking one of the classrooms should result in a call to the class_location_update procedure. This should all be accomplished using a clickable image map. Use the procedures in the HTP Oracle-supplied package: htp.mapOpen, htp.area, htp.mapClose, and htp.img2 . Each classroom should be created as a square region with a hyperlink to the class_location_update procedure, passing the room number as a parameter. You will still need to use the find_coords page you created earlier in this chapter in order to determine the coordinates for each of the classrooms. When a user clicks on one of the classrooms in the image, the class_location_update procedure should update the location for the class and then call the procedure, class_location again, so the new value for the location can be seen and validated by the user.

A possible solution to this exercise is as follows:

```
<%@ page language="PL/SQL" %>
<%@ plsql procedure="class_location" %>
<%@ plsql parameter="p_section_id"    type="SECTION.section_id%TYPE"
default="NULL" %>
<%! v_course_no            COURSE.course_no%TYPE;
    v_description          COURSE.description%TYPE;
    v_ifirst_name          INSTRUCTOR.first_name%TYPE;
    v_ilast_name           INSTRUCTOR.last_name%TYPE;
    v_section_no           SECTION.section_no%TYPE;
    v_start_date_time      VARCHAR2(50);
    v_location             SECTION.location%TYPE;
%>
<%  SELECT s.course_no,
           c.description,
           i.first_name,
           i.last_name,
```

```
                  s.section_no,
                  TO_CHAR(s.start_date_time,'Mon-DD-YYYY HH:MIAM'),
                  s.location
        INTO v_course_no,
             v_description,
             v_ifirst_name,
             v_ilast_name,
             v_section_no,
             v_start_date_time,
             v_location
        FROM section s,
             course c,
             instructor i
        WHERE s.section_id   = p_section_id
        AND   s.course_no     = c.course_no
        AND   s.instructor_id= i.instructor_id;
%>
<HTML>
<HEAD>
<TITLE>Class Location Information</TITLE>
</HEAD>
<BODY >
<P ALIGN="CENTER">
<STRONG>
<EM>
<FONT SIZE="+2" COLOR="BLUE">Class Location Information for Section
<%= v_section_no %><BR>
</FONT>
</EM>
</STRONG>
</P>
<P>
<TABLE BORDER="2" ALIGN="CENTER" CELLSPACING="0" CELLPADDING="0"
BGCOLOR="WHITE">
  <TR>
    <TD ALIGN="CENTER"><B><I>Course<BR>No</I></B></TD>
    <TD WIDTH="30%" ALIGN="CENTER"><B><I>Course</I></B></TD>
    <TD WIDTH="20%" ALIGN="CENTER"><B><I>Instructor<BR>Name
    </I></B></TD>
    <TD ALIGN="CENTER"><B><I>Section<BR>No</I></B></TD>
    <TD WIDTH="30%" ALIGN="CENTER"><B><I>StartDate<BR>and<BR>
    Time</I></B></TD>
    <TD ALIGN="CENTER"><FONTCOLOR="MAROON"><B><I>Location</I></B></
    FONT></TD>
  </TR>
  <TR>
    <TD ALIGN="CENTER"><%= v_course_no %></TD>
    <TD ALIGN="CENTER"><%= v_description %></TD>
```

```
    <TD ALIGN="CENTER"><%= v_ifirst_name || ' ' || v_ilast_name
    %></TD>
    <TD ALIGN="CENTER"><%= v_section_no %></TD>
    <TD ALIGN="CENTER"><%= v_start_date_time %></TD>
    <TD ALIGN="CENTER"><%= v_location %></TD>
  </TR>
</TABLE>
<% htp.mapOpen('location_map');
    htp.area('14 ,12 ,84 ,86
    ','RECT','class_location_update?p_section_id='
            ||p_section_id||'&p_location=L206');
    htp.area('89 ,15 ,158,86
    ','RECT','class_location_update?p_section_id='
            ||p_section_id||'&p_location=L210');
    htp.area('163,17 ,230,85
    ','RECT','class_location_update?p_section_id='
            ||p_section_id||'&p_location=L211');
    htp.area('236,19 ,303,88
    ','RECT','class_location_update?p_section_id='
            ||p_section_id||'&p_location=L214');
    htp.area('16 ,112,84
    ,180','RECT','class_location_update?p_section_id='
            ||p_section_id||'&p_location=L500');
    htp.area('88
    ,114,156,182','RECT','class_location_update?p_section_id='
            ||p_section_id||'&p_location=L507');
  htp.area('161,113,229,180','RECT','class_location_update?
  p_section_id='
                ||p_section_id||'&p_location=L509');
    htp.area('236,115,303,183','RECT','class_location_update?
    p_section_id='
                ||p_section_id||'&p_location=L511');
  htp.mapClose;
%>
<BR>
<BR>
<CENTER>
<% htp.img2('/images/location.gif',cismap=>'1',cusemap=>'#location_
map'); %>
</CENTER>
</BODY>
</HTML>
```

This produces the following HTML file (for section 101).

```
<HTML>
<HEAD>
<TITLE>Class Location Information</TITLE>
</HEAD>
```

```
<BODY>
<P ALIGN="CENTER">
<STRONG>
<EM>
<FONT SIZE="+2" COLOR="BLUE">Class Location Information for Section
2<BR>
</FONT>
</EM>
</STRONG>
</P>
<P>
<TABLE BORDER="2" ALIGN="CENTER" CELLSPACING="0" CELLPADDING="0"
BGCOLOR="WHITE">
  <TR>
    <TD ALIGN="CENTER"><B><I>Course<BR>No</I></B></TD>
    <TD WIDTH="30%" ALIGN="CENTER"><B><I>Course</I></B></TD>
    <TD WIDTH="20%" ALIGN="CENTER"><B><I>Instructor<BR>
    Name</I></B></TD>
    <TD ALIGN="CENTER"><B><I>Section<BR>No</I></B></TD>
    <TD WIDTH="30%" ALIGN="CENTER"><B><I>Start Date<BR>and<BR>
    Time</I></B></TD>
    <TD ALIGN="CENTER"><FONTCOLOR="MAROON"><B><I>Location
    </I></B></FONT></TD>
  </TR>
  <TR>
    <TD ALIGN="CENTER">240</TD>
    <TD ALIGN="CENTER">Intro to the Basic Language</TD>
    <TD ALIGN="CENTER">Tom Wojick</TD>
    <TD ALIGN="CENTER">2</TD>
    <TD ALIGN="CENTER">May-24-1999 09:30AM</TD>
    <TD ALIGN="CENTER">L509</TD>
  </TR>
</TABLE>
<MAP NAME="location_map">
<AREA SHAPE="RECT" COORDS="14 ,12 ,84 ,86 "
HREF="class_location_update?p_section_id=102&p_location=L206">
<AREA SHAPE="RECT" COORDS="89 ,15 ,158,86 "
HREF="class_location_update?p_section_id=102&p_location=L210">
<AREA SHAPE="RECT" COORDS="163,17 ,230,85 "
HREF="class_location_update?p_section_id=102&p_location=L211">
<AREA SHAPE="RECT" COORDS="236,19 ,303,88 "
HREF="class_location_update?p_section_id=102&p_location=L214">
<AREA SHAPE="RECT" COORDS="16 ,112,84 ,180"
HREF="class_location_update?p_section_id=102&p_location=L500">
<AREA SHAPE="RECT" COORDS="88 ,114,156,182"
HREF="class_location_update?p_section_id=102&p_location=L507">
<AREA SHAPE="RECT" COORDS="161,113,229,180"
HREF="class_location_update?p_section_id=102&p_location=L509">
<AREA SHAPE="RECT" COORDS="236,115,303,183"
```

```
HREF="class_location_update?p_section_id=102&p_location=L511">
</MAP>
<BR>
<BR>
<CENTER>
<IMG SRC="/images/location.gif" ISMAP USEMAP="#location_map">
</CENTER>
</BODY>
</HTML>
```

CREATE THE **CLASS_LOCATION_UPDATE** PROCEDURE

Using the image map defined in the classlocation procedure, the class_location_update procedure receives a location and a sectionIN as IN parameters to be used to update the classroom location for a section of a course.

A possible solution is as follows:

```
CREATE OR REPLACE PROCEDURE CLASS_LOCATION_UPDATE
  (p_location  IN  section.location%TYPE,
   p_section_id  IN  section.section_id%TYPE)
IS
BEGIN
  UPDATE section
     SET location = p_location
   WHERE section_id = p_section_id;
  COMMIT;
  htp.script('alert("Update successful.")');
  class_location(p_section_id);
EXCEPTION
  WHEN OTHERS
  THEN
    htp.script('alert("Update failed'||SQLERRM||'"');
END;
```

CHAPTER 13

BUILDING THE APP

The answers to these projects can be found at the companion Web site to this book, located at http://www.phptr.com/boardman.

Visit the Web site periodically to share and discuss your answers with other readers.

In this chapter you learned a number of methods to use images in your Web pages. You can use any one of these methods to enhance your splash page. Additionally, you created a clickable image map in the following PSP:

- Class_Location.psp

Now take a look at the companion Web site. The specification for the complete application has a number of new Web pages that will make use of what you learned in this chapter to round out the application. The full source code to the complete application is also available at the companion Web site.

C H A P T E R   1 4

JAVASCRIPT FORM VALIDATION

HTML forms help make a Web site more interactive by allowing the user to input information that can be processed by a server-side script. Usually, the data is input into a database. Since the data is entered by a Web site user, the data will not always be complete nor of the correct datatype. Problems with the data will be uncovered only upon an attempt to insert into or update current values in the database. This wastes valuable time, network bandwidth, and database resources. Validating the data on the front-end as much as possible before sending it to the back-end will aid in the performance of your Web site as well as the efficient use of system resources. JavaScript enables a Web application developer to "clean up" the data on the front-end, before it reaches the back-end database. Validation simply means checking that data is entered in all required fields, that no illegal characters have been entered, and that the datatype is correct for each field, among other possible checks.

U N I T   1 4 . 1

FORM VALIDATION USING JAVASCRIPT

As you learned in Chapter 7, "Introduction to JavaScript," JavaScript is loaded into the browser with the HTML document. Thus, JavaScript form validation executes completely on the front-end, or client. There are situations where some back-end validation is necessary, for example, a class registration application would first check that a student has taken any prerequisites for a class before allowing that student to register for a class. This would have to be done on the back-end since data from the database is necessary. The majority of form validation, however, can be accomplished with JavaScript on the front-end.

What can you accomplish with JavaScript form validation? Since JavaScript can read the values of each form input through the DOM, here are some examples of what you can verify with JavaScript form validation:

- Check whether each field has been filled in with data
- Check whether a credit card number has 16 digits
- Check whether an expiration date field is filled in when a credit card number field is filled in
- Check whether a Social Security Number is 10 digits
- Check whether a U.S. zipcode field contains five digits, or five digits plus four digits
- Check that a phone number field does not contain any letters

Here are some examples of what JavaScript validation cannot accomplish, because it runs on the front-end:

- Check whether a Social Security Number already exists in the database
- Check whether a zipcode exists in the database
- Check a database table to see whether a phone number's area code is valid for the state the user provided

Thus JavaScript is a popular preliminary method for cleaning up data that is entered by users, though it is not a substitute for back-end validation.

Use radio buttons, drop-down select lists, and checkboxes where appropriate to limit users' choices to valid ones. Drop-down select lists can be painted with database values from a lookup table, ensuring that the user will choose a value that is valid in the database.

STEPS IN JAVASCRIPT FORM VALIDATION

What occurs with JavaScript form validation? Many different concepts that you learn in Chapter 7 are employed in validating a form:

- An event handler is triggered, for example, onClick invokes JavaScript.
- The event handler calls a JavaScript function.
- The JavaScript function references the form's fields using the DOM hierarchy.
- The function tests the values of the form fields to see if they meet validation requirements.
- If one of the fields fails a test, then a message is displayed to the user. The submit is not initiated and focus is returned to the form.
- If all tests succeed, the form is submitted.

There are different variations on form validation. The specifications for this book's application require that validation be done upon submission. Other applications validate each form field as it is input and the user moves out of that field (onBlur). It is a matter of personal choice and/or project requirements as to which style you should implement.

FRONT-END VALIDATION VS. BACK-END VALIDATION

As mentioned above, JavaScript code runs completely on the client because it is loaded into the browser along with the HTML document. You can validate the form data on the client before sending it to the back-end to be processed. If you do not validate the data on the client and there is invalid data, the following is a typical scenario of what happens when the 'Submit' button is clicked by the user. This scenario is also reviewed in Chapter 7, "Introduction to JavaScript":

1. The data is sent via the network to the database (back-end).
2. An insert/update of the data is attempted. This causes processes in the database to be initiated, rows locked for update, rollback segment space allocated, etc.
3. An Oracle error message is generated upon attempting to insert/ update invalid data.

4. This error message is captured and code is executed to handle it.

5. An HTML error message page is generated.

6. This HTML page is served by the Web server to the client via the network.

Compare this to what happens when JavaScript validation is in place. When the 'Submit' button is clicked by the user:

1. A JavaScript function is called. The function is already loaded into the browser.

2. The data in the form is validated by the JavaScript function.

3. If the data is invalid, then a JavaScript message in the form of a pop-up alert is displayed to the user. The user clicks 'OK' on the message.

4. The user may be returned to a form element with invalid data using the element's focus(); method.

5. The user corrects the form data and tries to submit the form again.

There are no trips to the back-end and no processes are initiated on the Web server or database server. Since everything takes place on the client the response time is very fast.

The gains in performance become even more significant the more users the site has. Front-end form validation is an important component of Web site development.

A FIRST FORM VALIDATION

Validate the Student_Personal_Info form. The Application specifications indicate that every field in this form is required. Write a JavaScript function that will check each field in the form for user input. If every form field has data, then submit the form. If any field is empty, then display a message to the user specifying which fields must be completed, put the cursor in the first field that is empty, and do not submit the form.

Note: The form in the example below is not formatted within a table like the other forms in this book's application in order to concentrate on the JavaScript code.

Look at the form that is being validated. The Student_Personal_Info form has six text fields and one select list. Since all of the fields are required, check that the user has input some data into the text fields. Since the select list defaults to the option 'Please Select a Zipcode' with a value of –1, then check that the selected option does not equal to –1. If at least one form element fails a validation test, display a message to the user and give focus to the first form element that failed.

■ *FOR EXAMPLE*

```
<HTML>
<HEAD>
<SCRIPT LANGUAGE="JavaScript1.3">
function ckFrm(frm) {
//This is the main validation function
//Declare variables used for building the
//error message and for giving focus to the
//first element which fails
nme = "";
msg = "You must enter a value into the following field(s):\n\n";
fcs = "-1";
//first, loop over each element in the form
for (var i=0; i < frm.elements.length; i++) {
//For each element, test whether it is a text field and
//has no data.  If yes, it fails.  Start building
//the error message.  Also, get the array number of the
//first element to fail and assign it to fcs.
//This will be used when setting focus.
//Since the first element to fail should be given
//focus, then this will be assigned only on the first
//element to fail.
  if (frm.elements[i].type == "text" && frm.elements[i].value == "") {
     nme = mapName(frm.elements[i].name);
     msg +=  nme + "\n";
     if (fcs == "-1") {
       fcs = i;
     }
  }
//This block of code deals with validating
//a Select list.  This is covered in more
//detail in the next sub-section.
//If not a text field, test to if a select list.
//If yes, test if the selected option equals to -1.
//If yes, it fails.  Build on the error message.  Same
//as above for giving focus.
  if (frm.elements[i].type ==  "select-one") {
     if (frm.elements[i].options[frm.elements[i].selectedIndex].
     value == -1) {
       nme = mapName(frm.elements[i].name);
       msg +=  nme + "\n";
     if (fcs == "-1") {
       fcs = i;
     }
     }
  }
}
//END For loop
```

```
}
//If the message variable, nme, has not been set,
//then no element failed.  Submit the form.
//Otherwise, an element did fail.  Display the
//error message and give focus to the first
//element that failed.
if (nme == "") {
  frm.submit();
} else {
  alert(msg);
  frm.elements[fcs].focus();
}
//END ckFrm function
}
//This function is called from within the
//ckFrm function.
//It's purpose is to map the actual form name of an
//element to a user-friendly name to be displayed
//in the error message.  For example, 'Salutation' is
//displayed in place of the variable 'p_salutation'.
//The '\t' at the beginning of each display name
//is a tab character.
function mapName (nm) {
 switch (nm) {
    case "p_salutation":
      return "\tSalutation";
    case "p_fname":
      return "\tFirst Name";
    case "p_lname":
      return "\tLast Name";
    case "p_street_address":
      return "\tStreet Address";
    case "p_zip":
      return "\tZipcode";
    case "p_phone":
      return "\tPhone Number";
    case "p_employer":
      return "\tEmployer";
    default:
      return "";
}
}
</SCRIPT>
</HEAD>
<BODY>
<FORM ACTION="update_student" METHOD="post" NAME="student_personal_
form">
Salutation: <INPUT TYPE="text" NAME="p_salutation" VALUE="" SIZE="5">
<BR>
```

```
First Name: <INPUT TYPE="text" NAME="p_fname" VALUE="" SIZE="25"><BR>
Last Name: <INPUT TYPE="text" NAME="p_lname" VALUE="" SIZE="25"><BR>
Address: <INPUT TYPE="text" NAME="p_street_address" VALUE=""
SIZE="50"><BR>
Zipcode: <SELECT NAME="p_zip">
<OPTION VALUE="-1" SELECTED>Please Select a
Zipcode</OPTION>
<OPTION VALUE="10015">10015</OPTION>
<OPTION VALUE="10016">10016</OPTION>
<OPTION VALUE="10017">10017</OPTION>
<OPTION VALUE="10018">10018</OPTION>
</SELECT><BR>
Phone Number:<INPUT TYPE="text" VALUE="" NAME="p_phone" MAXLENGTH="15"
SIZE="15"><BR>
Employer:<INPUT TYPE="text" VALUE="" NAME="p_employer" MAXLENGTH="50"
SIZE="25"><BR>
<INPUT TYPE="hidden" VALUE="" NAME="p_id">
<INPUT TYPE="reset" VALUE="Reset">
<INPUT TYPE="button" VALUE="Submit" onClick="ckFrm(this.form);">
</FORM>
</BODY>
</HTML>
```

VALIDATION WITH SELECT LISTS

Why does the select list have "Please Select a Zipcode" as its first option rather than a zipcode?

When the form is being used for new data input, this option allows you to verify that a user has actually selected a zipcode. When the form first loads into the browser with no data, then "Please Select a Zipcode" is displayed since it is the first option. The value for this option is "–1." If the value of the Select list is "–1", then you know that the user did not change the Select list. Without this option the first zipcode would be displayed, and you could not tell whether the user selected it or not. It also presents a more professional user interface to display "Please Select a Zipcode."

■ FOR EXAMPLE

```
//If not a text field, test to if a select list.
//If yes, test if the selected option equals to -1.
//If yes, it fails.  Build on the error message.  Same
//as above for giving focus.
  if (frm.elements[i].type ==  "select-one") {
    if (frm.elements[i].options[frm.elements[i].selectedIndex].
    value == -1) {
      nme = mapName(frm.elements[i].name);
      msg +=  nme + "\n";
```

```
if (fcs == "-1") {
  fcs = i;
}
}
}
```

The other options in the select list do not need validation since they have been selected from the database.

SUBMIT BUTTON VS. JAVASCRIPT BUTTON

Two types of buttons can be used in JavaScript validation: INPUT TYPE="submit" or INPUT TYPE="button" (Table 14.1).

Either one works fine, though each has its own requirements. It is a matter of personal preference as to which one you use. They differ in one significant way: The submit button initiates the form submittal process, whereas the JavaScript button does not. This is the source of the slight coding differences between the two choices.

BUTTON METHOD

Since this method does not initiate the form submittal process, then JavaScript must be used to submit the form once it passes the validation tests. Clicking the button simply executes the JavaScript specified in the event handler.

Table 14.1 ■ Button Vs. Submit Method

	Button Method	Submit Method
Button type	button	submit
JavaScript event	onClick	onSubmit
Location of JS event	<INPUT>	<FORM>
Sample	<INPUT type="button" onClick="ckFrm (this.form);">	<FORM onSubmit="return ckFrm(this);">
Form submitted via submit(); in Javascript?	yes	no
Form submitted via HTML submit button?	no	yes
How is submit prevented?	By not reaching the submit(); in the JavaScript code	By returning false to FORM tag's event the handler

First, create the JavaScript button:

```
<INPUT TYPE="button" VALUE="Button" onClick="ckFrm(this.form);">
```

This creates a JavaScript button that calls a JavaScript function when clicked. Within the JavaScript function ckForm, check the data. If all the validation tests succeed, then submit the form:

```
frm.submit();
```

If the form fails the validation tests, then simply display a message to the user using a JavaScript alert. You can also give focus to the form element by using the element's focus(); method to move the cursor to that form element.

The keyword 'this' in the event handler is being used to pass a reference to the form's object to the function. Knowing the name of the form is not necessary. The argument 'frm' is used in place of the form name. If nothing was passed in the event handler to the function, then the submit statement would be constructed as below, drilling down the DOM hierarchy and using the form's name:

```
document.formName.submit();
```

If using the Button method with a single line text input field, then a user may be able to submit the form by hitting the Enter key while focus is on the text input field, thereby bypassing your JavaScript form validation. This is because the HTML standards as set forth by W3.org specify that a browser should submit a form in this restricted situation. As a best practice, where you have only one single line input field use the Submit method, discussed in detail below.

SUBMIT METHOD

With this method, when the user clicks the Submit button, it initiates the form submit process. The form submit process must be stopped if the form fails validation.

First, create the submit button *without an event handler:*

```
<INPUT TYPE="submit" VALUE="Submit">
```

Second, in the <FORM> tag add the event handler:

```
<FORM ACTION="update_student" METHOD="post" NAME="student_
personal_form" onSubmit="return ckFrm(this);">
```

Adding this event handler captures the submit event and calls the function ckFrm. The submit process is deferred while the JavaScript specified in the submit event handler is executed. The JavaScript function will validate the form data and return either a true or a false value.

The *return* is necessary in the form handler because the JavaScript function should return either a true or false value that determines whether the form submission should resume. The returned value tells the form whether it should

1. continue with the submit if "true" is returned; or
2. cancel the submit if "false" is returned.

In the JavaScript function, use:

```
return true;
```

or

```
return false;
```

In other words, to compare this with the Button method, replace the code *frm.submit();* with the code *return true;*. Additionally, add the code *return false;* after the alert and focus commands if validation fails.

■ FOR EXAMPLE

```
<SCRIPT LANGUAGE="JavaScript1.3">
function ckFrm(frm) {
...
if (nme == "") {
  return true;
} else {
  alert(msg);
  frm.elements[fcs].focus();
  return false;
}
//END ckFrm function
}
</SCRIPT>
```

Be careful not to confuse the two methods. If the Submit button has an "onClick" event handler that calls JavaScript validation, the form data may be found invalid, but the form would be submitted anyway.

It is good to check your assumptions about data validation against any existing data. If you develop forms for an existing database, it is possible that form validation may require cleaning up of existing data. If the database contains a value of "Mr." for a title, but your form validation does not allow periods in that field, then any user updating that record will be required to clean up that value before the form will be successfully submitted.

UNIT 14.2

UNIT
14.2

REGULAR EXPRESSIONS IN FORM VALIDATION

The JavaScript validation script discussed in Unit 14.1 tests only for an empty value in the case of text fields. This is not a very stringent form validation. A space in the text field would be enough to pass this script's validation test. Stricter validation is usually more desirable so that as much validation is done on the front-end as possible. Other things that could be checked are:

1. Whether a field exceeds its maximum length.
2. Whether only numbers were entered into the Phone Number field.
3. Whether only text was entered in the First Name and Last Name fields.

Writing the code to test for the length is possible with the JavaScript introduced so far in this book. However, to check if only numbers or text was input into a field requires the use of regular expressions.

Regular expressions is a way to perform pattern matching on a string using patterns that you create. If the pattern is found, true is returned; if not, false is returned. For example, you can test whether a string contains only lowercase letters, only uppercase letters, lowercase and uppercase letters, or numbers. You can also test whether a string contains a more specific pattern. For example, imagine that one of the columns in a table is a serial code. Serial codes (such as used for products) have a series of subcodes. The format for the serial code could be NNNMMYYLL, where NNN is the product code, MMYY is the month and year fabricated, and LL is the identification of the plant where fabricated. An example of a serial code would look like this: 512070218. If you need only those serial codes of products made at a specific plant or within a certain time period, then that can be tested using regular expressions. If the pattern is found in the correct position within the serial code, then true is returned.

The concept of regular expressions is not unique to JavaScript. Other programming languages also implement it: C++, PERL, TCL, and AWK, among others. If you have worked with UNIX, then you will recognize regular expressions from using the tool GREP, an acronym for *Global Regular Expression Print.*

Note: Regular expressions are not available in JavaScript 1.1 and earlier.

JAVASCRIPT REGULAR EXPRESSION SYNTAX

Regular expressions in JavaScript are objects. There are three steps to implementing regular expressions in JavaScript:

1. Formulating the pattern.
2. Creating the regular expression object.
3. Comparing a string against the regular expression object using the regular expression methods.

The syntax covered here is sufficient for the majority of form validations. For complete syntax details, please refer to the Netscape JavaScript documentation.

CREATING A REGULAR EXPRESSION

When creating a regular expression in JavaScript an object is created that holds the pattern. This object also has properties and methods used in string evaluation and manipulation. There are two methods for creating a regular expression object. The first method is to initialize an object:

```
myPattern = /testPattern/
```

The second method is to use the RegExp's constructor function. To learn more about the constructor function, please refer to Netscape's JavaScript documentation. For purposes of this discussion, it is enough to know that this is another way to create a regular expression object.

```
myPattern = new RegExp("testPattern")
```

The difference between the two is that the constructor function is compiled at runtime (just before use) while the object initializer method is compiled when the script is evaluated. Use the constructor function only if the regular expression pattern will change, or is not known at the time of evaluation. For this chapter the object initializer method is used.

The syntax for the object initialized method is similar to the syntax for declaring and initializing a variable. The forward slashes in the syntax tell JavaScript that this is a regular expression pattern. The pattern is created as an object and assigned to the variable *myPattern.*

The newly created regular expression object, *myPattern,* can now be compared against a string using regular expression object methods.

When creating a regular expression, there are two optional flags that you can add to indicate a global or case-insensitive search. Use "g" for the global flag (during search and replacement of a substring) and "i" for a case-insensitive search. They can be used alone or together. The syntax is:

```
pattern = /testPattern/[g|i|gi]
```

or

```
pattern = new RegExp("testPattern", ['g'|'i'|'gi'])
```

First, let's look at how to write a pattern.

WRITING PATTERNS

The pattern is what will be tested against the string. Patterns can be constructed of two different types of characters:

- Simple or literal characters
- Meta or symbolic characters

A simple character in a pattern will match that exact character in a string. What you see is what you get. For example, to test whether the Phone field contained a hyphen, the pattern can be created like this:

```
pattern = /-/
```

or, to test whether the Salutation field contains the string "Mr," the pattern can be created as follows:

```
pattern = /Mr/
```

Using the hyphen pattern on the string "(212) 555 5555" would not match anything in the string and false would be returned. However, true would be returned on the string "212-555-5555." In the Salutation field regular expression, the pattern would match "Mr" but not "mr". The case-insensitive flag was not used when the pattern was initialized, so case is significant. These are straightforward examples but not the most useful regular expressions.

What if you wanted to test whether the user entered any nonalphabet characters in the first or last name field? To do this you would need to use meta or special characters along with the simple characters.

Meta characters are characters that have a special meaning. For instance, the escape character is a backslash, "\". By combining simple and meta characters you are able to create complex patterns. For example, enclosing simple characters within brackets creates a character set pattern:

/[lmnop]/

Any one of the characters within brackets will be matched.

Tables 14.2 to 14.5 list the most commonly used metacharacters. For a complete list, please refer to the JavaScript documentation on the Netscape Web site.

UNIT
14.2

Table 14.2 ■ Single Character Meta Characters

Character	Meaning
[xyz]	Defines a character set that matches any one of the enclosed characters. May use a hyphen to specify a range of characters. [abcd] is the same as [a-d]. Matches the "a" in "almost" and the "c" in "itch."
[^xyz]	Defines a negated or complemented character set that matches anything that is not enclosed in the brackets. May use a hyphen to specify a range of characters. [^abcd] is the same as [^a-d]. Matches the "r" in "car" but matches nothing in "bad."
\d	Matches a digit character. Same as [0–9]. /\d/ or /[0–9]/ matches "3" in "Apt. 3B."
\D	Matches any nondigit character. Same as [^0–9]. /\D/ or /[^0–9]/ matches "A" in "Apt. 3B."
\s	Matches a single whitespace character that includes a space, tab, form feed, or line feed. Same as [\f\n\r\t\v].
\S	Matches a single character other than whitespace. Same as [^ \f\n\r\t\v].
\w	Matches any alphanumeric character plus the underscore. Same as [A–Za-z0–9_]. /\w/ matches "a" in "apt" and "3" in "#3B."
\W	Matches any nonword character. Same as [^A–Za-z0–9_]. /\W/ or /[^$A–Za-z0–9_]/ matches "#" in "#3B."

Table 14.3 ■ Escape Meta Characters

Character	Meaning
\	The backslash means either of the following: 1) Placing a backslash in front of a literal character causes it to be treated as a special character and not interpreted literally. For example, /d/ matches the character 'd'. By placing a backslash in front of d, /\d/, the character becomes special to mean that it should be used to match a digit character. Or 2) Conversely, it causes a special character to be interpreted literally. For example, $ is a special character that matches the end of input or line. By preceding it with a backslash it will be interpreted literally as a dollar sign: /\$/ matches the "$" in "$500."

METHODS USED WITH REGULAR EXPRESSION PATTERNS

After the regular expression pattern and object has been created, the final step is to use it.

The RegExp object has two methods for using regular expressions:

- exec
- test

The difference between these two methods is that "exec" returns an array with information about the search if a match was found. If no match was found, null is returned, which is converted into false. The method "test" returns either true

Table 14.4 ■ Anchor Meta Characters

Character	Meaning
^	Matches beginning of input or line. /^B/ matches "B" in "Building 3B" but does not match in "building 3B ."
$	Matches end of input or line. /y$/ matches "y" in "New York City" but does not match in "xyz."
\b	Matches a word boundary, such as a space or a newline character (different from [\b], which matches a backspace). /\bS/ matches "S" in "Sixth Avenue"; /h\b/ matches "h" in "Sixth Avenue."
\B	Matches a non-word boundary. For example, /\w\Bf/ matches 'of' in "coffee."

Table 14.5 ■ Quantifier Meta Characters

Character	Meaning
*	Matches the preceding character 0 or more times.
	For example, /of*/ matches "off" in "coffee" and "o" in "computer," but nothing in "taffy."
+	Matches the preceding character 1 or more times. Same as {1,}.
	/e+/ matches "e" in "wed" and all the es in "weeds" or "weeeeeds."
?	Matches the preceding character 0 or 1 time.
	For example, /e?le?/ matches the 'el' in "angel" and the 'le' in "angle."
.	(The decimal point) matches any single character except the newline character.
	/.n/ matches "an" (man), "an" (an), and "an" (island) in "no man is an island," but not "no."
(x)	Matches "x" and remembers the match.
	/(New)/ matches and remembers "New" in "New York City." The matched substring can be recalled from the resulting array's elements [1], ..., [n], or from the predefined RegExp object's properties $1, ..., $9.
x|y	Matches either "x" or "y."
	For example, /Mr|Mrs/ matches "Mr" in "Mr. Smith" and "Mrs" in "Mrs. Smith."
{n}	Where *n* is a positive integer. Matches exactly *n* occurrences of the preceding character.
	/a{2}/ doesn't match the "a" in "anteater" but does match the first two occurrences of "a" in "aardvark."
{n,}	Where *n* is a positive integer. Matches at least *n* occurrences of the preceding character.
	/o{2,}/ doesn't match the "o" in "echo" but matches all of the o's in "echoo" and "echoooooo."
{n,m}	Where *n* and *m* are positive integers. Matches at least *n* and at most *m* occurrences of the preceding character.
	/o{1,3}/ matches nothing in "ech," the "o" in "echo," the first two o's in "echoo," and the first three o's in "echoooo."

**UNIT
14.2**

or false. If you want to know whether a pattern is in a string, then use "test." It's performance is faster than "exec."

The String object also has four methods, which are used with regular expressions:

- match
- search
- replace
- split

The method *match* returns an array of information like the *exec* method. However, an array of information is returned whether or not a match was found. The *search* method returns the index of the matched string if found; if not found, it returns −1. As with the exec and test methods, use the search method instead of the match method if you only need to know whether a pattern is in a string. The performance is faster with the search method.

The *replace* and *split* methods use regular expressions to find a string and then perform an action upon it. Replace finds a substring within a string and switches it with a replacement substring. Split looks for a substring and splits the string into an array composed of the substrings.

■ FOR EXAMPLE

```
<SCRIPT LANGUAGE="JavaScript1.2">
ID = "One-Two-Three";
spltId = ID.split("-");
leng = spltId.length
for (var i = 0; i < leng; i++) {
alert(spltId[i])
}
</SCRIPT>
```

The script above takes the string ID and splits it at the hyphens and creates an array. The number of elements in the array is set to the variable leng. Using this count the script loops through each of the elements in the array and displays each one in an alert.

■ FOR EXAMPLE

```
<SCRIPT LANGUAGE="JavaScript1.2">
txt = "A well-written sql Select statement is as important..."
pattern = /sql/;
txtR = txt.replace(pattern, "SQL");
alert(txtR);
</SCRIPT>
```

The script above replaces the text "sql" with uppercase "SQL" by using a regular expression to search for the substring. When the substring is found, it is replaced with the replacement string.

SOME FIRST REGULAR EXPRESSIONS

Perhaps it is easier to understand regular expressions by working with examples. For this reason the examples below are structured to allow you to easily type them into a .htm document and view the results. To view in your browser, type the code into a .htm document. Make sure you place it between <SCRIPT> tags.

1a)

```
pattern = /sql/;
result = pattern.test("SQL");
alert(result);
```

Returns false—sql does not match SQL. Case is significant.

1b)

```
pattern = /sql/i;
result = pattern.test("SQL");
alert(result);
```

Returns true—case-insensitive flag used.

1c)

```
pattern = /SQL/;
result = pattern.test("SQL");
alert(result);
```

Returns true—since case-insensitive flag not used, then case is significant.

2a)

```
pattern = /[lmnop]/;
result = pattern.test("Some text");
alert(result);
```

Returns true—matches any character in the pattern: Matches *o* in *Some*.

2b)

```
pattern = /[l-p]/;
result = pattern.test("Some text");
alert(result);
```

Returns true—same as #2a. May use a hyphen to define character set.

3a)

```
pattern = /[^aeiou]/;
result = pattern.test("ou");
alert(result);
```

Returns false—looking for any character that is not in pattern.

3b)

```
pattern = /[^aeiou]/;
result = pattern.test("you");
alert(result);
```

Returns true—looking for any character not in pattern. Matches *y* in *you*.

4a)

```
pattern = /\d/;
result = pattern.test("Apartment Number 3B");
alert(result);
```

Returns true—\d is a metacharacter for any digit. Matches *3* in *3B*.

4b)

```
pattern = /[0-9]/;
result = pattern.test("Apartment Number 3B");
alert(result);
```

Returns true—character set of all digits. Matches *3* in *3B*.

5a)

```
pattern = /[A-Za-z0-9_]/;
result = pattern.test("Brooklyn NY 11215");
alert(result);
```

Returns true—character set looking for upper- and lowercase alphabet characters, any digit, or an underscore. Matches *B* in *Brooklyn*.

5b)

```
pattern = /\w/;
result = pattern.test("Brooklyn NY 11215");
alert(result);
```

Returns true—metacharacter same as 5a. Matches *B* in *Brooklyn*.

Query: What is returned if the pattern is changed to [^A–Za-z0–9_], that is, to look for anything that is not an alphanumeric character or an underscore? True is returned because a space is found. To return false, the space metacharacter has to be added to the pattern:

```
[^A-Za-z0-9_\s]
```

6)

```
Create your own Regular Expression patterns and test
against different strings.
```

UNIT 14.2 EXERCISE

JAVASCRIPT FORM VALIDATION USING REGULAR EXPRESSIONS

Take the same form as validated in the beginning of this chapter, Student_Personal_Info, and validate it using regular expressions. Only allow alphanumeric characters, spaces, and periods. For instance, the '#' symbol before an apartment number in the address field would not be allowed. If a user enters only a space or spaces into a field, or if a user enters nothing into a field, then do not submit the form.

UNIT 14.2 EXERCISE ANSWER

Your HTML/JavaScript code should be similar to the following example:

```
<HTML>
<HEAD>
<SCRIPT LANGUAGE="JavaScript1.3">
function ckFrm(frm) {
//initialize counter to 0
z = 0;
//create the Regular Expression patterns
var pattern = /[^a-zA-Z0-9\s\.]/;
var pattern2 =  /^\s+$/;
//Get the number of elements in the form and set it to a variable
frmLgth = frm.elements.length;
//Now loop through  the fields in the form.
```

```
//If you come across a 'text' field, then test the value of the
field against the Regular Expression pattern.
    while(z < frmLgth) {
            propty= frm.elements[z].type;
                if (propty == 'text') {
                    var Val = frm.elements[z].value;
                    var testfirst = pattern.test(Val);
                    var testsecond = pattern2.test(Val);
                    if (testfirst || testsecond || Val == "") {
                            alert('Please fill in every field with
                            alphanumeric characters only.');
                                    frm.elements[z].select();
                                    return false;
                        } else {
                            z++
                        }
                } else if (propty == "select-one") {
                    if (frm.elements[z].options[frm.elements[z].
                    selectedIndex].value == -1) {
                        alert("Select a Zipcode!!!!");
                    return false;
                    } else {
                        z++
                    }
                } else {
                    z++
            }
    }


    return true;



}

</SCRIPT>
</HEAD>
<BODY>
<H2>Personal Information for Instructor 101</H2>
<FONT SIZE="+1">
<FORM ACTION="update_student.html" METHOD="post" NAME="student_
personal_form"  onSubmit="return ckFrm(this);">
Salutation: <INPUT TYPE="text" NAME="p_salutation" VALUE="" SIZE="5">
<BR>
First Name: <INPUT TYPE="text" NAME="p_fname" VALUE="" SIZE="25">
<BR>
Last Name: <INPUT TYPE="text" NAME="p_lname" VALUE="" SIZE="25"><BR>
Address: <INPUT TYPE="text" NAME="p_street_address" VALUE=""
SIZE="50"><BR>
```

```
Zipcode: <SELECT NAME="p_zip">
<OPTION VALUE="-1">Please Select a
Zipcode</OPTION>
<OPTION VALUE="10015">10015</OPTION>
<OPTION VALUE="10016">10016</OPTION>
<OPTION VALUE="10017">10017</OPTION>
<OPTION VALUE="10018">10018</OPTION>
</SELECT><BR>
Phone Number:<INPUT TYPE="text" VALUE="" NAME="p_phone"
MAXLENGTH="15" SIZE="15"><BR>
Employer:<INPUT TYPE="text" VALUE="" NAME="p_employer"
MAXLENGTH="50" SIZE="25"><BR>
<INPUT TYPE="hidden" VALUE="" NAME="p_id">
<INPUT TYPE="reset" VALUE="Reset">
<INPUT TYPE="submit" VALUE="Submit">
</FORM>

</BODY>
</HTML>
```

C H A P T E R   1 4

BUILDING THE APP

The answers to these projects can be found at the companion Web site to this book, located at http://www.phptr.com/boardman/.

Visit the Web site periodically to share and discuss your answers with other readers.

In this chapter you learned many concepts that you should keep in mind when you read the subsequent chapters. These concepts include:

- The benefits of JavaScript form validation
- How to implement JavaScript form validation in an HTML page
- The JavaScript code differences when using a submit or JavaScript button
- How to create regular expressions in JavaScript and use them in form validation

You should have the following parts of the application after this chapter: all of the forms with JavaScript validation.

C H A P T E R   1 5

MAINTAINING STATE WITH COOKIES AND TABLES

CHAPTER OBJECTIVES

After this lab, you will learn about:

- ✔ Using Cookies to Maintain State
- ✔ The Web Toolkit and Cookies
- ✔ JavaScript and Cookies
- ✔ Storing State in Database Tables

Cookies are one way for an application developer to handle the challenge of preserving state on the Web. State refers to information about the current session—the current state of affairs. Applications that maintain information about the user's experience are described as stateful, whereas protocols like HTTP are by their nature stateless. Each HTTP request from a browser is a separate transaction with a server.

Cookies allow a developer to get around the stateless nature of the HTTP protocol. Cookies and how they work are explored in this chapter. Cookies can be read and manipulated through the components provided in Oracle's Web Toolkit package OWA_COOKIE. They can also be read and set through the JavaScript DOM.

When used in conjunction with tables, cookies can become a useful tool for tracking user requests and application information. Finally, this chapter shows how cookies can work together with database tables to create lasting records of user activity and interests.

UNIT 15.1

USING COOKIES
TO MAINTAIN STATE

MAINTAINING STATE IN A WEB APPLICATION

It can be difficult to grasp that each request is unrelated when surfing the Web. What happens when a browser requests a Web page or resource from a site? In short:

- Browser identifies the server that has the resource
- Browser requests the resource from the server
- Server returns the resource to the browser for rendering

Although each request is separate, Web browsers create the feeling of a user session by placing each request for a page into a larger context; thus a Web browsing session can unfold like a story, with you as the protagonist and the sequence of pages you travel through as the plot. Browsers keep track of each page request, and provide "Previous" and "Next" buttons that reinforce the impression that each request is part of a larger session. However, this impression is the work of the browser. From the server's point of view, the server is handling separate page requests without being able to recognize that the same user is making them.

In a Web application, it is often necessary to maintain information about users from one page request to the next. For example, if a site's splash page requires a user to provide a name and password to access a site, how does each subsequent page know whether the user already logged in successfully? If a user clicks a link to add an item to a shopping cart, how does the server know whose shopping cart to fill? How can an application identify and track its users?

Even if users do not provide a name and password to identify them, a Web site might want to assign an id number to a visitor and track their activity as they travel through the site. For this to work, a number such as a "session id" must be accessible throughout the application. Applications that maintain a shopping cart for visitors must know which visitor is on each page. The shopping cart items might be stored in the database, but they must still be linked to the user by a session id or user name.

Some state information can be passed in parameters, as shown throughout Chapter 11, "Web Toolkit II: Frames, Forms, Parameters." Including name/value pairs at the end of URLs in links is one way to share information from one page to another; clicking on a specific instructor's name in a list can take you to a page with personal details about that instructor because the instructor_id is passed as a parameter from one page to the next. Forms also pass information to the programs/procedures specified in their ACTION attributes, through inputs like text boxes, text areas, checkboxes, and radio buttons, as well as through hidden inputs.

However, parameter passing can become cumbersome when information is needed across an entire Web site. Consider the above example of a Web site that has a login screen. Once a user has logged in, their user id can be passed from one page to the next throughout the site. However, each page must be written to handle this additional parameter.

How else can this state information about the user be maintained? Another way is to use cookies.

WHAT IS A COOKIE?

A *cookie* is a text string. The string contains a name and a value. You can think of it as a name–value pair, or as a variable—a holder of information.

Cookies are stored and managed by the browser. It is logical to have browsers manage cookie information. Browsers are already keeping track of the previous and next sites that a user has visited. A cookie is simply another piece of information about the user's browsing experience that the browser manages. The advantage of cookies is that they outlast a single request to a Web server.

Cookies are sent to a user's browser by servers. When a server responds to a browser's request by delivering a page to the browser, this response can include a request to set a cookie. If the user's browser is configured to accept cookies, the browser then stores the cookie information, which is tagged as coming from a specific server. A communication between a browser and a server that wants to set a cookie looks like this:

- Browser identifies the server that has the resource.
- Browser requests the resource from the server.
- Server returns the resource to the browser for rendering. Included in the resource may be a request to the browser to set a new cookie.
- Browser stores any cookies received and renders the page.
- End of communication.

The next time a user requests a resource from the same server, how does the server see the cookie information? The browser returns the cookie to the server that sent it. Now, when a user requests a resource through the browser, the entire communication looks like this:

- Browser identifies the server that has the resource.
- Browser checks for any existing cookies from the server.
- Browser requests the resource from the server. The request includes any cookie information previously placed by that server.
- Server receives the cookies along with the request. The cookie information can be used to assemble the resource for the browser.
- Server returns the resource to the browser for rendering. Included in the response may be a request to the browser to set a new cookie.
- Browser stores any cookies received and renders the page.
- End of communication.

WHAT A COOKIE LOOKS LIKE

A cookie is simply a string of text.

■ FOR EXAMPLE

```
.mysite.org TRUE / FALSE 1047428811 SITESERVER_ID=6e9151adb730a62
```

This cryptic string, stored in a single line by the browser, is really just a way of storing a variable called SITESERVER ID with a value of 6e9151adb730a62 for the site mysite.org.

Breaking this cookie into parts, you will see that the parts correspond to the parameters you need to supply when you send cookies of your own (Table 15.1).

Expiration dates are in seconds—the number of seconds since January 1, 1970. To translate this into a readable date, simply divide the number of seconds by 86,400 to know how many days the number represents: in other words, 60 (seconds) × 60 (minutes) × 24 (hours). Once you have the number of days, add the days to January 1, 1970. Ex: `SELECT TO_DATE('01-JAN-1970')+ROUND(1047428811/ 86400) from dual;`

COOKIE STORAGE

Cookies are stored in two ways. They can be held by the browser temporarily, and then vanish when the user exits the browser program. This short-term cookie is a *session-level* cookie. Session-level cookies can be used to:

- Store a session id for a user until the browser is closed
- Store other data that is temporary until the browser is closed

- Maintain a shopping cart until the browser is closed
- Track activity in a single browser session until the browser is closed

The other type of cookie is a *persistent cookie*. The browser places persistent cookies directly into your machine's file system. As with other files saved to your file system, they remain on the computer even after the browser programs have been closed and the computer is turned off. It is persistent cookies that enable a Web site to do the following:

- Greet you by name when you return to a site the next day using the same computer
- Tell you how many times the browser on that specific computer has visited a site overall
- Provide you with a list of stores near you based on a zipcode you provided the previous visit

Table 15.1 ■ Parts of a Cookie

Cookie Part	Description	Example
Domain	The domain that set the cookie. This is the domain that will have access to the cookie later.	.mysite.org
T/F Flag	A TRUE/FALSE value indicating whether all machines within the domain can access the cookie later. This value is set automatically by the browser unless a value is provided when the cookie is set.	TRUE
Path	The path within the domain that the cookie is valid for. If / is specified, then all directories in the domain can access the cookie. Otherwise, the default is the current directory and any of its subdirectories.	/
Secure	A TRUE/FALSE value indicating whether a secure protocol such as HTTPS is needed to access the cookie. The word secure must be added to specify that HTTPS is needed.	secure
Expires	Whether this cookie part is present determines how the cookie will be stored. This cookie part represents the UNIX time when the cookie will expire. UNIX time is defined as the number of seconds since January 1, 1970, 00:00:00 GMT (Greenwich Mean Time).	1047428811
Name	The name of the cookie	SITESERVER_ID
Value	The value of the cookie	6e9151adb730a62

When a server sends a cookie, it specifies an expiration date for the cookie. The expiration date determines whether a cookie is a session-level or persistent cookie.

If cookies are sent with no expiration date specified, then they are session-level cookies. They are held in the browser's memory until the browser application is closed.

If cookies are sent with an expiration date, then they are stored in the computer's file system. Most browsers will store up to 20 cookies per site.

The way to locate persistent cookies that have been placed on your file system varies, since different versions of browsers store cookies differently on different versions of operating systems. You can always do a search for *cookie*.* in your file system to locate cookie-related files or directories. Here are some additional guidelines:

> *In IE for Windows:* Each Windows user will have a directory created in the same volume as the operating system. For example: "C:\Documents and Settings\YourUserName\Cookies." "YourUserName" should be replaced with your user name for the machine. If you are using an older version of Windows that does not require a login, look in the directory Windows for a subdirectory called Cookies. There are multiple files stored here.
>
> *In Netscape for Windows:* Look for a single file called cookies.txt, usually stored in: ProgramFiles/Netscape/Users/YourUserName/cookies.txt. "YourUserName" should be replaced with your user name for the machine. The location of cookies.txt will depend on the installation of Netscape on your computer.

HOW COOKIES ARE SENT

Cookies are sent in the HTTP header. Cookies are not part of HTML; they are part of the HTTP protocol. Recall from Chapter 1, "Introduction to Oracle Web Applications," that HTTP is the protocol of the World Wide Web. Requests for Web pages, as well as the Web pages that are returned, are sent with HTTP headers that can contain cookies.

Within the HTTP header, the cookie specification looks something like this:

```
Set-Cookie: name=<value> expires=<expires> path=<path>
domain=<domain> [secure]
```

NOTE: Since servers send cookies in the HTTP header, you will not see cookies or cookie values if you view the source of an HTML page in the browser.

HTTP HEADERS AND ENVIRONMENT VARIABLES

Normally you do not see the HTTP header in the browser. As explained in Chapter 1, "Introduction to Oracle Web Applications," the HTTP header is the behind-the-scenes means by which a browser communicates with a Web server, and vice versa. It is through this header that HTTP requests and responses are made.

Some of the most common environment variables that can be part of the HTTP header are:

- SERVER_SOFTWARE—The name and version number of the server software
- SERVER_PROTOCOL—The HTTP version number, e.g., HTTP/1.1
- SERVER_NAME—The server's host name
- SERVER_PORT—The port number the server is using, e.g., 80
- REQUEST_METHOD—The request method, e.g., GET, HEAD, or POST
- QUERY_STRING—The query string of the URL, i.e., the part following the "?" (if present)

The HTTP header begins with an instruction to open the header. Another instruction closes the header. Note that this header is not the same as the HTML header created by the <HEAD> tag.

To respond to a client's request for a page, the PL/SQL agent in the Application Server automatically creates an HTTP header. It indicates that the contents have a MIME type (Multipurpose Internet Mail Extension) of "text/html," and closes the HTTP header. Then it takes the HTML output from your procedures, and sends it with this HTTP header.

To perform certain tasks, such as creating a cookie or activating a content handler on the user's browser, we must interrupt this normal flow of events. This is done with the OWA_UTIL procedures that change the default HTTP header. Unlike the htp procedures, these OWA_UTIL procedures do not generate HTML. Instead they create text within the HTTP header that contains special instructions that cause the browser to act in a particular way. Other parts of the OWA_UTIL package are covered in more detail in Chapter 16, "The OWA_UTIL Package: Dynamic SQL, HTML, Date Utilities, and More."

HOW COOKIES ARE RETURNED

How does a server "read" the cookie later on? Browsers transmit cookie data along with requests for new pages from the same source. Again, this is done in the HTTP header of the request, not in the HTML page itself.

First the browser has to identify the server that has the resource the user wants.

Then the browser checks all of its existing cookies, both session-level and persistent cookies, to see whether any of them are from that site. If it finds any cookies from that site, it bundles them up and includes them in the HTTP header of the request for the new page. The browser does this for every new request, regardless of whether the server actually requires the cookie information to serve up that particular page; the cookies are always along for the ride with each new request.

Since the cookie arrives at the server as part of the page request, the server can use the cookie when putting together the page for the user. If the cookie contains a user's id, then the user's name can be retrieved from a database and built into the page. If the cookie contains a zipcode, a page can be built containing regional information. The server is supplied with the cookie information before the user even sees the resulting page to view, and the server can tailor a page to a specific user.

It is important to note that the browser only returns cookies to the site that has placed them. For example, imagine that you went thumbtack shopping and provided your personal information to a Web site that sold thumbtacks when placing your order. The thumbtack site placed several persistent cookies on your computer. You then visit a completely different site that sells refrigerator magnets. Would the magnet site be sent the cookies placed by the thumbtack site? No—recall that each cookie contains the name of the site that placed the cookie, and the browser only sends cookies back to the site that placed them.

Realize, however, that a single page may be composed of material from several different sites. A page for Thumbtack World could contain advertisements from Refrigerator Magnet Land. The advertisements might be pictures whose source attribute is a URL on Refrigerator Magnet Land's server. So the browser requests resources from two different company's servers in order to build the page. In this case, the browser would send Thumbtack World its own cookies, and also send Refrigerator Magnet Land its own cookies, based on the user's visit to a single page.

BROWSER SETTINGS FOR COOKIES

Browsers offer users some options with regard to cookies. Most browsers allow users to completely turn off cookie functionality. If you do this, some sites may not display properly, or they may demand that you configure your browser to accept cookies before visiting their sites. If your application requires cookies, your only recourse is to tell users to accept cookies.

Your browser may offer users the option of being warned about cookies before accepting them. For each cookie sent by a server, the browser will display a pop-up window telling the user that the server is attempting to send a cookie, and asking whether or not it should accept the cookie. The message may not use the word "cookie," but instead refer to a "piece of temporary information" that a server wants to store on your computer. If you choose this setting in your browser, you will see many pop-up windows as you browse through the Web that prompt you as to whether or not to accept cookies, and you will gain an understanding of when servers are sending cookies to your browser.

However, more commonly, users set their browsers to accept all cookies, and many cookies are accepted by browsers automatically, unbeknownst to the users.

Browsers provide options to warn users before accepting a cookie, but how about returning cookies to servers that were already placed? This activity—returning cookies to servers with new requests—is even more automatic than the browser's acceptance of cookies in the first place. Browsers that give users the option of being warned when a cookie is being sent may not provide an option to be warned when existing cookies are sent back to a server. If any cookies already exist, they will be returned to the servers that sent them, whenever new pages are requested from those same servers. Usually it is only by disabling cookies completely, or by deleting existing cookies, that this activity can be halted. However, browsers are responding to users' distrust of cookies by offering more elaborate levels of cookie settings.

PROBLEMS WITH COOKIES

There are technical as well as philosophical problems with cookies.

Persistent cookies, which are stored on the file system, have numerous limitations. Perhaps the most problematic aspect of persistent cookies is that they assume use of the same physical computer, which is not always an accurate assumption. If you let a friend named Daniel Shultz use your computer to purchase something from one of your favorite sites, and then you visit that site later, you could be greeted cheerily with the words, "Welcome Back, Daniel Shultz!" Most sites recognize that such a greeting can be inaccurate, and so they also include an existential disclaimer such as this: "If you are not Daniel Shultz, click here." While some systems require a user login and store cookies separately for each user, that type of configuration cannot be relied upon.

Moreover, because persistent cookies are stored in a file system, they are gone if the user deletes the cookie files or if the hard drive is cleaned and the software reinstalled.

For these reasons, persistent cookies are best used to provide features that are nice but not absolutely necessary to the function of the site. For example, having your zipcode preloaded into a restaurant locator is convenient, but it is easily added or changed if the zipcode is inaccurate or missing. Likewise, if you are presented with options based on what Daniel Shultz likes to view because he visited the site last, you can always tell the site that you are someone else.

Other problems with cookies are less technical than ethical. Many users find cookies problematic and do not appreciate having their system compromised without their knowledge. When you visit an outside site, it can place a cookie file on your computer's file system, such as the innocuous-looking string of text in the section "What a Cookie Looks Like" in this unit. The fact of an outside site placing a file on a user's personal computer without the user's explicit permission is disconcerting to many people. Moreover, visiting a site that greets you by name when you have not logged in or identified yourself in any way can be unsettling. The convenience of having a site tailored to your preferences or needs wars with a need for privacy.

Since cookies allow a site to identify a user from one request to the next, and throughout each request during a visit, the site can deduce information about the user's likes and dislikes and compile a profile of that user's interests. If the user has provided name and/or address information previously, then the site may be able to tie that together. Even with session-level cookies, a single visitor's activity can be tracked by assigning them a session ID number, and then recognizing each subsequent request by the Session ID that is sent along with each subsequent request of the same site. This is valuable information that helps the site find out how effective it is and which of its links are used the most. This is also valuable information for any advertisers that want to place an ad on that site. It is much more useful to know which route a user took to access a page on a Web site than it is to know simply the total number of requests for each page. However, it is an invasion of the user's privacy. The user is not anonymously browsing a site, but rather browsing a site with each request noted and possibly tracked in a database. If a persistent cookie is used, or if the user logs in or purchases something, then the user's identity is known and linked to the previous activity.

As mentioned earlier in this chapter, the fact of each site being associated with different cookies can be an illusion when it comes to advertising. Suppose that a site contains an advertisement that is a clickable image. The IMG SRC can be a URL for a completely different server. That server returns a resource to the browser, and it can place its own cookies when it returns the advertisement. If another site uses the same advertiser, that advertiser can be returned its cookie, and recognize that the same person is visiting both sites.

UNIT 15.1 EXERCISES

15.1.1 LOCATE YOUR COOKIES

Locate cookies stored on your computer. Experiment with deleting cookies and observe how that changes the behavior of sites you visit regularly.

15.1.2 EXPERIMENT WITH BROWSER SETTINGS FOR COOKIES

Change the settings for cookies on your browser. Experiment with different cookie settings and observe how that changes the behavior of sites you visit regularly.

U N I T   1 5 . 2

THE WEB TOOLKIT AND COOKIES

THREE COOKIE ACTIONS

As a Web developer, there are three main actions you need to know in order to work with cookies; in fact, you will probably only use the first two:

1. send—Send a cookie, or reset the value of an existing cookie
2. get—Get, or read, the value of an existing cookie
3. delete—Delete an expired cookie by setting its expiration date to the past. (This option is not often done and may not be handled as expected by the browser.)

OWA_COOKIE PACKAGE

Oracle provides a package, OWA_COOKIE, with procedures that allow you to perform each of these actions (Table 15.2). Other elements in the OWA_COOKIE package, such as the OWA_COOKIE type, provide additional built-in support for cookies.

HTTP HEADER

Cookies are sent (and removed) in the HTTP header.

To send and remove cookies, use the following syntax to open and then later close this HTTP header:

1. OWA_UTIL.mime_header(bclose_header=>FALSE);
2. Use OWA_COOKIE.send or OWA_COOKIE.remove here
3. OWA_UTIL.http_header_close;

Table 15.2 ■ OWA_COOKIE Procedures

Procedure	Description
OWA_COOKIE.send(name, value, expires, path, domain, secure)	OWA_COOKIE.send('USER_TYPE','Student', NULL,'/',NULL,NULL); **Name** is the name you give your cookie, which you use when you are referring to the cookie later. **Value** is a text string you set for the value of the cookie. **Expires** is an Oracle DATE type expiration date for the cookie. This is a date in Oracle DATE format, not seconds as in the previous UNIX example. If expires is null, then the expiration is the end of the "current session," i.e., when the user closes the browser window. Cookies that only last for the length of the session are sometimes referred to as "session cookies"—they are stored in the browser temporarily and are deleted when the browser is closed. These session cookies are not stored on the file system. **Path** is used to specify a path that the cookies are valid for on your server. Specify / so that any branch of your "root" URL directory tree can get the cookie. In other words, you would indicate that requests for resources in other paths off your main site should also be sent the cookie. If you have several directories in your site, such as products.thumbtackworld.com/news and products.thumbtackworld.com/contact _us, specify / to allow the browser to send the cookie with requests for either page. By default, the path is the same directory as the current document. **Domain** is used similarly to specify a domain that a cookie is valid for on the server. By default, the domain is the current domain, so you can specify NULL. If you have several machines in your domain, such as orders.thumbtackworld. com and products.thumbtackworld.com, you can specify a domain of .thumbtackworld.com to encompass both domains. You cannot choose a different domain, however. **Secure** means the cookie can only be passed over an SSL (Secure Socket Layer) connection. You can only send cookies from within the HTTP header. Use this procedure between OWA_UTIL.mime_header and OWA_UTIL.http_header_close.
OWA_COOKIE.cookie	Record type for a cookie. A PL/SQL variable declared with a type of OWA_COOKIE.cookie holds the results of a call to the procedure, OWA_COOKIE.get. Example: DECLARE v_cookie OWA_COOKIE.cookie;

(continued)

Table 15.2 ■ *continued*

Procedure	Description

OWA_COOKIE.cookie (cont.)	BEGIN
	  v_cookie := OWA_COOKIE.get('COUNTER');
	
	END;

	There are two additional characteristics of a variable declared with the datatype OWA_COOKIE.cookie: **NUM_VALS**: returns the number of values stored in the array. **VALS(n)**: returns the nth value stored in the array. Since the HTTP specification allows multiple values for the same cookie name, the cookie value must be retrieved using this notation. The OWA_COOKIE data type is a PL/SQL record.
OWA_COOKIE.vc_arr	Array to hold multiple values of type VARCHAR2(4096). It is provided as a datatype to use when declaring variables to hold results of retrieving all cookies.
OWA_COOKIE.get(name)	Gets a cookie with the specified name. The result of this goes into a variable of type OWA_COOKIE.COOKIE.
	Examples:
	v_cookie := OWA_COOKIE.GET('LOGIN_NAME');
	Check that a cookie was found for the v_cookie variable by using num_vals:
	IF (v_cookie.Num_Vals != 0) THEN ...
	You cannot refer to the value of v_cookie directly. Instead use Vals(1):
	v_cookie.Vals(1) Since the HTTP specification allows multiple values for the same cookie name, the cookie value must be retrieved using this notation. The OWA_COOKIE data type is a PL/SQL record.
OWA_COOKIE.get_all()	Retrieves all cookies that the server has access to in the order they were sent by the browser.
OWA_COOKIE.remove(name, value, path)	Example: OWA_COOKIE.REMOVE('USER_ID', v_cookie_user_type.vals(1));
	Name is the name of the cookie you want to remove. **Value** is the value for the cookie. **Path** is optional.
	You can only remove cookies from within the HTTP header. Use this procedure between OWA_UTIL.mime_header and OWA_UTIL.http_header_close.

UNIT
15.2

■ FOR EXAMPLE

```
[procedure text goes here - no HTML generated]
OWA_UTIL.mime_header(bclose_header=>FALSE);
OWA_COOKIE.send('SESSION_ID', 572, sysdate+365);
OWA_UTIL.http_header_close;
[generate any HTML here, after closing http header]
```

 The HTTP header must be opened and closed before any htp proce-dures or functions are executed; that is, before any HTML is generated by the PL/SQL procedure. If not, then the cookie will not be sent/re-moved.

The OWA_UTIL.mime_header procedure actually takes several parameters (Table 15.3):

```
OWA_UTIL.mime_header(ccontent_type, bclose_header, ccharset);
```

If you just want to read or "get" the value of a cookie, you do not need to worry about the HTTP header. It is not necessary to put the OWA_COOKIE.get proce-dure inside of an HTTP header.

COOKIE RECIPES

The best way to manage cookies is to write small procedures and functions that work with cookies. Whenever possible, create modular code that can be reused.

The next sections contain short procedures and functions to set a cookie, read a cookie value, read all cookie values, and check for a cookie. Once these are created, you can use these procedures and functions as needed throughout your site.

Table 15.3 ■ OWA_UTIL.mime_header parameters

Parameter	Default Value	Description
ccontent_type	'text/html'	The MIME type for the document being sent. Has a default value of 'text/html,' which is fine.
bclose_header	TRUE	A Boolean value. TRUE means the header will be closed immediately. When you specify FALSE, the HTTP header remains open until you explicitly close it with OWA_UTIL.http_header_close. Close the HTTP after your cookie send/remove commands.
ccharset	NULL	Character set. Optional.

SET A COOKIE: OWA_COOKIE.SEND

The following code sets a cookie for whatever name and value are passed in. The expiration date is optional. If it is supplied, the cookie will be set as a persistent cookie by the browser, with the expiration date supplied. If no expiration date is supplied, then the default value of NULL will be used, making it a session-level cookie. Session-level cookies cease to exist when the browser is closed.

■ *FOR EXAMPLE*

```
CREATE OR REPLACE PROCEDURE set_cookie
     (p_cookie_name   IN VARCHAR2,
      p_cookie_value IN VARCHAR2,
      p_expires       IN DATE DEFAULT NULL)
  IS
BEGIN
   OWA_UTIL.mime_header(bclose_header=>FALSE);
   OWA_COOKIE.SEND(p_cookie_name,
                    p_cookie_value,
                    p_expires);
   OWA_UTIL.http_header_close;
END;
```

Now any time that you need to set a cookie, call this procedure from PL/SQL— but only call it before any HTML has been generated by your PL/SQL procedure.

```
set_cookie('SESSION_ID','572');
```

To set a persistent cookie, supply an expiration date. The following call sets the cookie to expire in 5 days:

```
set_cookie('SESSION_ID','572',sysdate+5);
```

CHANGE A COOKIE VALUE: OWA_COOKIE.SEND

To change a cookie value, use the same code that you would use to set the cookie. The name you supply should be the name of the cookie you want to change. Provide this name and the new value.

A cookie value can only be set from within the HTTP header, even if you are changing the value of an existing cookie. Again, the HTTP header must be opened and closed before any HTML is generated.

READ A COOKIE VALUE: OWA_COOKIE.GET

The next function retrieves the value of a cookie with the name passed in. If no values are found, then the function returns a NULL value.

In the example below, note that a variable v_cookie is declared. This declaration is necessary because OWA_COOKIE.get is used to retrieve cookie values, and a container must exist to hold these returned values. The resulting cookie information must be stored in a variable of type OWA_COOKIE.cookie.

The OWA_COOKIE.cookie datatype is an array datatype. Any variable of type OWA_COOKIE.cookie has three characteristics.

NAME: The name of the cookie in the array.

NUM_VALS: The number of values stored in the array.

VALS(n): The *n*th value stored in the array. Unlike JavaScript arrays, this array starts with 1.

The syntax for these is demonstrated in the get_cookie function, below. This function is reusable. It has an IN parameter of a cookie name. The function checks for the existence of a cookie with the name that is passed in. If a cookie exists with that name, the procedure returns the cookie value. Otherwise, it returns a NULL value.

■ FOR EXAMPLE

```
CREATE OR REPLACE FUNCTION get_cookie
   (p_cookie_name IN VARCHAR2)
 RETURN VARCHAR2
 IS
    v_cookie     OWA_COOKIE.cookie;
 BEGIN
   v_cookie := OWA_COOKIE.GET(p_cookie_name);
   IF v_cookie.num_vals != 0 THEN
      RETURN v_cookie.vals(1);
   ELSE
      RETURN NULL;
   END IF;
END;
```

READ ALL COOKIE VALUES: OWA_COOKIE.GET_ALL

The OWA_COOKIE.get_all function retrieves all cookies. It has three out parameters. Two of them are arrays to hold the names and values of the cookies, since more than one cookie may be returned:

- NAMES: The name of each cookie in the array.
- VALS: The values of each cookie stored in the array.
- NUM_VALS: The total number of values stored in the array. This is an integer, not an array.

The syntax for using these parameters is demonstrated in the get_all_cookies procedure, below. It does not have an IN parameter of a cookie name, because it is retrieving all cookies, not a specific one. Arrays of type OWA_COOKIE.vc_arr are declared to hold the names and values of the cookies.

This procedure paints all cookie names and values to the screen, if any are found. Note that the step where cookie values are displayed to the screen is not typical cookie processing; normally, users would not see cookie values on the screen. Instead, cookie values would be used for other processing.

■ FOR EXAMPLE

```
CREATE OR REPLACE PROCEDURE get_all_cookies
  IS
     v_cookie_names   OWA_COOKIE.vc_arr;
     v_cookie_values OWA_COOKIE.vc_arr;
     v_cookie_count   INTEGER;
  BEGIN
    OWA_COOKIE.get_all(v_cookie_names,
                        v_cookie_values,
                        v_cookie_count);
    htp.p('<HTML><BODY>');
    FOR num IN 1..v_cookie_count LOOP
       htp.p('Cookie #'||num||': Name='||
             v_cookie_names(num)||', Value='||
             v_cookie_values(num)||'<BR>');
    END LOOP;
    htp.p('</BODY></HTML>');
    EXCEPTION
       WHEN OTHERS THEN
       htp.p('Error in get_all_cookies: '||SQLERRM);
  END;
```

CHECK WHETHER A COOKIE EXISTS

Sometimes it is enough to know whether a cookie exists or not, without retrieving its value. The following function checks for the existence of a cookie with the name passed in. The function returns a TRUE value if cookie values are found. It returns FALSE if there are no values stored for the cookie.

■ *FOR EXAMPLE*

```
CREATE OR REPLACE FUNCTION cookie_exists
    (p_cookie_name IN VARCHAR2)
 RETURN BOOLEAN
 IS
   v_cookie OWA_COOKIE.COOKIE;
BEGIN
   v_cookie := OWA_COOKIE.GET(p_cookie_name);
   IF v_cookie.num_vals != 0 THEN
       RETURN TRUE;
   ELSE
       RETURN FALSE;
   END IF;
END;
```

UNIT 15.2 EXERCISES

15.2.1 COMPILE THE PROCEDURES

Compile the procedures/functions from this chapter:

- set_cookie
- get_cookie
- get_all_cookies
- cookie_exists

15.2.2 COLLECT INFORMATION FOR A COOKIE

Create a procedure called *visitor_name* that displays a form asking for the user's name. The action of the form should be a procedure called *process_visitor_name*.

15.2.3 SET A COOKIE

Create the procedure *process_visitor_name*, the action of the form in *visitor_name*. Set a cookie called VISITOR that stores the visitor name passed in. To set the cookie, utilize the set_cookie procedure from this chapter. Then paint a page with a hyperlink to the *main_frame* procedure.

15.2.4 CHECK FOR THE EXISTENCE OF A COOKIE

Change the *main_frame* procedure to check for the existence of the VISITOR cookie. Use the *cookie_exists* function to check for the VISITOR cookie. If the cookie value returned is not null, display the name. Otherwise, call *visitor_name*.

15.2.5 RETRIEVE AND DISPLAY A COOKIE VALUE

Change the *top_frame* procedure to retrieve the value of the VISITOR cookie. Use the *get_cookie* function to retrieve the value of the VISITOR cookie. After the words "University Maintenance Website," display the words "for" and the visitor's name. Underneath, in smaller letters, include the message, "If you are not <visitor name>, click here." Make the word "here" a hyperlink to the *visitor_name* page.

15.2.6 RETRIEVE AND DISPLAY A COOKIE VALUE

Change the *process_visitor_name* procedure to set a persistent cookie by giving the cookie an expiration date. Make sure that the visitor name is displayed on subsequent pages by reading the cookie. Close and reopen the browser—it should still display the visitor's name.

Unit 15.2 Exercise Answers

15.2.1 Answer

Compile the procedures/functions from this chapter:
- set_cookie
- get_cookie
- get_all_cookies
- cookie_exists

Answer:

```
CREATE OR REPLACE PROCEDURE set_cookie
     (p_cookie_name   IN VARCHAR2,
      p_cookie_value  IN VARCHAR2,
      p_expires       IN DATE DEFAULT NULL)
  IS
BEGIN
  OWA_UTIL.mime_header(bclose_header=>FALSE);
  OWA_COOKIE.SEND(p_cookie_name,
                  p_cookie_value,
                  p_expires);
  OWA_UTIL.http_header_close;
END;

CREATE OR REPLACE FUNCTION get_cookie
   (p_cookie_name IN VARCHAR2)
  RETURN VARCHAR2
  IS
     v_cookie     OWA_COOKIE.cookie;
  BEGIN
    v_cookie := OWA_COOKIE.GET(p_cookie_name);
    IF v_cookie.num_vals != 0 THEN
       RETURN v_cookie.vals(1);
    ELSE
       RETURN NULL;
    END IF;
END;

CREATE OR REPLACE PROCEDURE get_all_cookies
  IS
     v_cookie_names   OWA_COOKIE.vc_arr;
     v_cookie_values  OWA_COOKIE.vc_arr;
     v_cookie_count   INTEGER;
  BEGIN
    OWA_COOKIE.get_all(v_cookie_names,
                       v_cookie_values,
```

```
                              v_cookie_count);
     htp.p('<HTML><BODY>');
     FOR num IN 1..v_cookie_count LOOP
        htp.p('Cookie #'||num||': Name='||
               v_cookie_names(num)||', Value='||
               v_cookie_values(num)||'<BR>');
     END LOOP;
     htp.p('</BODY></HTML>');
     EXCEPTION
        WHEN OTHERS THEN
        htp.p('Error in get_all_cookies: '||SQLERRM);
END;

CREATE OR REPLACE FUNCTION cookie_exists
     (p_cookie_name IN VARCHAR2)
 RETURN BOOLEAN
 IS
   v_cookie OWA_COOKIE.COOKIE;
BEGIN
   v_cookie := OWA_COOKIE.GET(p_cookie_name);
   IF v_cookie.num_vals != 0 THEN
        RETURN TRUE;
   ELSE
        RETURN FALSE;
   END IF;
END;
```

15.2.2 ANSWER

Create a procedure called *visitor_name* that displays a form asking for the user's name. The action of the form should be a procedure called *process_visitor_name*.

Answer:

```
CREATE OR REPLACE PROCEDURE VISITOR_NAME
    IS
BEGIN
htp.p('<HTML>
        <HEAD><TITLE>Name, Please</TITLE></HEAD>
        <BODY>
        <H1>What is Your Name?</H1>
        <FORM NAME="visitor_name_form"
              ACTION="process_visitor_name"
              METHOD="POST">
        <INPUT NAME="p_visitor_name" TYPE="text" >
        <INPUT TYPE="submit" VALUE="Save">
        </FORM>
        </BODY>
        </HTML>');
```

```
EXCEPTION
    WHEN OTHERS THEN
        htp.p('An error occurred in VISITOR_NAME: '
            ||SQLERRM);
END;
```

15.2.3 ANSWER

Create the procedure *process_visitor_name*, the action of the form in *visitor_name*. Set a cookie called VISITOR that stores the visitor name passed in. To set the cookie, utilize the set_cookie procedure from this chapter. Then paint a page with a hyperlink to the *main_frame* procedure.

Answer:

```
CREATE OR REPLACE PROCEDURE PROCESS_VISITOR_NAME
    (p_visitor_name IN VARCHAR2)
    IS
BEGIN
    set_cookie('VISITOR',p_visitor_name);
    htp.p('<HTML>
            <HEAD><TITLE>Thank You</TITLE></HEAD>
            <BODY>
            Click <A HREF="main_frame">here</A> to
            enter the application.
            </BODY>
            </HTML>');
EXCEPTION
    WHEN OTHERS THEN
        htp.p('An error occurred in
        PROCESS_VISITOR_NAME: '||SQLERRM);
END;
```

15.2.4 ANSWER

Change the *main_frame* procedure to check for the existence of the VISITOR cookie. Use the *cookie_exists* function to check for the VISITOR cookie. If the cookie value returned is not null, display the name. Otherwise, call *visitor_name*.

Answer:

```
CREATE OR REPLACE PROCEDURE MAIN_FRAME AS
    v_val VARCHAR2(100);
BEGIN
IF cookie_exists('VISITOR') THEN
htp.p('
<HTML>
<HEAD>
```

```
<TITLE>University Maintenance Website
</TITLE>
</HEAD>
<FRAMESET ROWS="133,*">
  <FRAME NAME="top" SCROLLING="no" NORESIZE
        TARGET="main" SRC="top_menu">
  <FRAME NAME="main" SRC="splash" TARGET="main">
  <NOFRAMES>
    <BODY>
    <P>This page uses frames, but your browser doesn''t
support them. </P>
    </BODY>
    </NOFRAMES>
</FRAMESET>
</HTML>
');
ELSE
  htp.script('document.location="visitor_name";');
END IF;
END;
```

15.2.5 ANSWER

Change the *top_frame* procedure to retrieve the value of the VISITOR cookie. Use the *get_cookie* function to retrieve the value of the VISITOR cookie. After the words "University Maintenance Website," display the words "for" and the visitor's name. Underneath, in smaller letters, include the message, "If you are not <visitor name>, click here." Make the word "here" a hyperlink to the *visitor_name* page.

Answer:

```
CREATE OR REPLACE PROCEDURE TOP_MENU AS
    v_visitor   VARCHAR2(100);
BEGIN
    v_visitor := get_cookie('VISITOR');
    htp.p('
<HTML>
<HEAD>
<TITLE>University Maintenance Website
</TITLE>
</HEAD>
<BODY BGCOLOR="#99CCFF">
');
    htp.p('
<P ALIGN="center">
<FONT FACE="Arial" SIZE=5 >University Maintenance Website for
'||v_visitor||'</FONT></P>
<P ALIGN="right">If you are not '||v_visitor||', click <A
HREF="visitor_name" TARGET="_top">here</A></P>
```

```
');

htp.p('
<TABLE BORDER="0" WIDTH="100%">
<TR>
<TD ALIGN="center"><A HREF="students_frame" TARGET="main"><FONT
FACE="Arial">Students</FONT></A></TD>
<TD ALIGN="center"><A HREF="instructors_frame"
TARGET="main"><FONT FACE="Arial">Instructors</FONT></A></TD>
<TD ALIGN="center"><A HREF="classes_frame" TARGET="main"><FONT
face="Arial">Classes</FONT></A></TD>
</TR>
</TABLE>
</BODY>
</HTML>
');
END;
```

15.2.6 ANSWER

Change the *process_visitor_name* procedure to set a persistent cookie by giving
the cookie an expiration date. Make sure that the visitor name is displayed on
subsequent pages by reading the cookie. Close and reopen the browser; it
should still display the visitor's name.

Answer:

```
CREATE OR REPLACE PROCEDURE PROCESS_VISITOR_NAME
    (p_visitor_name IN VARCHAR2)
    IS
BEGIN
    set_cookie('VISITOR',
               p_visitor_name,
               sysdate+5);
    htp.p('<HTML>
           <HEAD><TITLE>Thank You</TITLE></HEAD>
           <BODY>
           Click <A HREF="main_frame">here</A> to
           enter the application.
           </BODY>
           </HTML>');
EXCEPTION
    WHEN OTHERS THEN
          htp.p('An error occurred in
          PROCESS_VISITOR_NAME: '||SQLERRM);
END;
```

UNIT 15.3

JAVASCRIPT AND COOKIES

DOCUMENT.COOKIE

Cookies can also be created, sent, and read with JavaScript. Cookies are supported starting with JavaScript 1.0 as part of the Document Object Model. They are a property of the document object.

■ FOR EXAMPLE

```
document.cookie
```

READING DOCUMENT.COOKIE

Below is an alert that will show all cookies that have been created for the current page. If you want to check the values of the cookies you created via the Web Toolkit, simply read document.cookie:

■ FOR EXAMPLE

```
htp.p('<SCRIPT>alert(document.cookie);</SCRIPT>');
```

Reading the document.cookie object returns all of the name/value pairs stored in all cookies for the page. The information is returned in a long string of name/value pairs, separated by semicolons. The other attributes of the cookies, such as path and expires, are not shown.

Here is sample output you would see in an alert using the example above.

■ FOR EXAMPLE

```
SESSIONID=101; FAVORITE=Shortbread; ZIP=10003
```

For cookie debugging purposes, it can be handy to use an alert to display all existing cookie values for your site.

As of JavaScript 1.5 there are no built-in JavaScript methods provided for setting, retrieving, and deleting specific cookies, unlike the PL/SQL Web Toolkit built-in packages discussed previously in Unit 15.2, "The Web Toolkit and Cookies."

To find a specific cookie value, you must parse the string that contains all cookies using JavaScript text functions. First, find the position of the cookie name that you are interested in, using indexOf. JavaScript's indexOf function is similar to the Oracle SQL function INSTR—indexOf can search the string for the word "FAVORITE" and return a number, which corresponds to the position of the word "FAVORITE" in the string. If "FAVORITE" is not found in the string, a value of –1 is returned. The first parameter passed to indexOf is the value to search for, such as "FAVORITE". The second, optional parameter passed to indexOf is the position at which to start searching. This second parameter lets you find the position of one occurrence of "FAVORITE," and then look after that position to see if there is a second occurrence.

Cookie values start after the cookie name and the equals sign, and end with a semicolon. In the string above, the cookie value is between "FAVORITE=" and a semicolon.

The example below is an example of parsing a cookie string, such as the one shown above, for the value of the cookie named "FAVORITE." The code uses JavaScript's indexOf function to search for the position of "FAVORITE" in a cookie string. If "FAVORITE" is found, then add 9 to its position to isolate the part of the string beginning after "FAVORITE=" (9 characters long) and ending at the position of the next semicolon.

■ *FOR EXAMPLE*

```
htp.p('
<SCRIPT LANGUAGE="JavaScript">
if (document.cookie.length>0){
    start = document.cookie.indexOf("FAVORITE");
    if (start != -1){
        start += 9;
        end = document.cookie.indexOf(";",start);
        if (end==-1){
            end=document.cookie.length;
        }
        thecookie=document.cookie.substring(start,end);
      alert(unescape(thecookie));
    }
    else{
```

```
        alert("No favorite cookie found.");
      }
   }
   else{
     alert("No cookies found.");
   }
   </SCRIPT>
   ');
```

DOCUMENT.COOKIE SYNTAX

To set a cookie, use the assignment operator (=) to assign a new value to document.cookie. When setting a cookie through JavaScript, it is entirely up to you to write the correct cookie syntax. You are creating a literal string that will serve as a cookie. If the syntax is not correct, then the cookie will not be understood by the browser. Moreover, if your values might contain any spaces, semi-colons, or commas, you will need to use the JavaScript function escape() on the values, and unescape() when you read them later. Table 15.4 shows the parts of a cookie string:

Table 15.4 ■ Parts of a Cookie String

Cookie Part	Description	Example
Name	The name of the cookie.	Visitor
Expires	The expiration date of the cookie. If this is not specified then the cookie will not be stored after the user exits the browser. Use GMT format for the date: DAY, DD-MMM-YYYY HH:MI:SS GMT	Fri, 02-Jan-1970 00:00:00 GMT Sat, 01-Jan 2000 17:00:00 GMT
Domain	Set the domain to ensure that several servers for the same site all receive the cookie. Ex. orders. thumbtackworld.com and products.thumbtackworld.com	.thumbtackworld.com
Path	The path within the domain that the cookie is valid for. If / is specified, then all directories in the domain can access the cookie.	/
Secure	If the word "secure" is included then the cookie is only transmitted when the browser connects to the server using a secure protocol such as HTTPS.	secure

You do not need to provide all of these cookie attributes when setting a cookie through JavaScript.

CREATING AN EXPIRATION DATE IN JAVASCRIPT

To work with dates in JavaScript, you will need to familiarize yourself with JavaScript functions, objects, and methods created to support dates. As explained in Chapter 7, "Introduction to JavaScript," JavaScript is a loosely typed language, so you cannot declare a variable with the datatype DATE. However, you can create a Date object, and special date methods and functions exist to work with dates.

To get you started, below are some lines of JavaScript code that can be used to create a date in JavaScript, and set it to a number of months in the future. This is useful for creating expiration dates to be used in cookies.

■ *FOR EXAMPLE*

```
var expDate = new Date();
  //set expDate to 12 months in the future using JS date functions
expDate.setMonth(expDate.getMonth() + 12);
  //set expDate to 10 days in the future
expDate.setTime(expdate.getTime() + 10*24*60*60*1000);
```

CHANGING DOCUMENT.COOKIE

Below are several examples of setting cookies. These make use of the code that creates the expDate variable in "Creating an Expiration Date in JavaScript." Also note the toGMTString JavaScript date function, which converts the date to a string in GMT format.

■ *FOR EXAMPLE*

```
document.cookie="visitor=Ned";
document.cookie="visitor=Ned; expires=" + expDate.toGMTString(); +
"; path=/";
document.cookie="visitor=Ned; expires=" + expDate.toGMTString(); +
"; domain=.thumbtackworld.com; path=/; secure";
```

JAVASCRIPT COOKIE BEHAVIOR

Cookies set through JavaScript from the client will behave the same way as a cookie set on the server through a language such as PL/SQL; the next time that a page is requested from the same site, the browser will find the cookie and transmit it in the HTTP header with the request for the new page.

JavaScript code does not set the cookie directly. Instead, it communicates to the browser that a cookie should be set. The browser still handles the cookie request.

JavaScript can see your site's cookies on the client. It is possible that JavaScript can see cookies on the client that have not been sent back to the server—particularly if cookies have just been set using JavaScript. In such cases, different cookies will be seen by document.cookie and the OWA_COOKIE package. When the browser initiates a call to the server for an additional resource, the browser will transmit the new cookies to the server.

**UNIT
15.3**

UNIT 15.4

STORING STATE
IN DATABASE TABLES

TRACK PAGE VISITS

Cookies are useful for storing small pieces of data. Using cookies in conjunction with database tables makes cookies much more useful. Information stored in the database will be held there permanently. You can analyze the statistics that accumulate in database tables.

Statistics about Web traffic are frequently a requirement for a Web application. This is the kind of information that you would want to hold in a database table, so that you can query the table later and collect more and more information over time.

In Unit 15.2, you create a cookie called VISITOR that holds the name the user provided. Since the user's name is captured in a cookie, each request can be identified as coming from a specific user. The user's activity—the pages the user visits—can be tracked in a database table.

First, create a table that will hold information about which pages are visited. Include the visitor name, since that can be retrieved from the VISITOR cookie. Also include the page requested.

Other potentially valuable pieces of information can be collected easily. Each request comes from an IP address, and since the IP address is included in the HTTP header, it can be retrieved. Also, the browser type can be an interesting statistic to collect, particularly if you want to be sure that you are supporting all of your users. Finally, it is useful to collect a timestamp.

Here is a sample table for holding general statistics.

■ *FOR EXAMPLE*

```
CREATE TABLE page_visit
   (visitor    VARCHAR2(200),
    ip_address VARCHAR2(20),
    browser    VARCHAR2(200),
    page       VARCHAR2(200),
    timestamp  DATE);
```

Instead of asking the user for a first name, you can assign them a visitor ID code. This can be a unique identifier for the visitor, and you could use a sequence to help generate this ID code for any user that does not have one already. Many sites track users this way because it does not alert the user's attention to the fact that their requests for pages are monitored.

Now create a procedure that populates the page_visit table. One piece of information, the page name, will be passed as an IN parameter, p_page. Values for the other columns in the table can be obtained programmatically. The cookie value for the VISITOR cookie can be obtained by using the get_cookie procedure, created earlier in this chapter. The IP address and the browser are available by using the OWA_UTIL.get_cgi_env procedure, as described in Chapter 16, "The OWA_UTIL Package: Dynamic SQL, HTML, Date Utilities, and More." The timestamp is available through the Oracle pseudocolumn, sysdate.

■ *FOR EXAMPLE*

```
CREATE OR REPLACE PROCEDURE track_page_visit
      (p_page IN VARCHAR2)
   AS
BEGIN
  INSERT INTO page_visit
   (visitor,
    ip_address,
    browser,
    page,
    timestamp)
  VALUES
   (get_cookie('VISITOR'),
    OWA_UTIL.GET_CGI_ENV('REMOTE_ADDR'),
    OWA_UTIL.GET_CGI_ENV('HTTP_USER_AGENT'),
    p_page,
    sysdate);
END;
```

Finally, insert the call for this procedure into any page where you want to track information. Here is a sample call.

■ *FOR EXAMPLE*

```
track_page_visit(OWA_UTIL.GET_PROCEDURE);
```

The function OWA_UTIL.get_procedure used above to pass the procedure name is described in Chapter 16. It retrieves the name of the current procedure. It could not be placed directly in the track_page_visit procedure, because the procedure name would always come up as track_page_visit.

Using this Oracle-supplied package, sometimes called a "built-in" package, offers advantages over a hard-coded procedure name. If a procedure name were hard-coded in the call to track_page_visit, then this call would need to be changed for each procedure, to hard-code a different procedure name. Also, using the owa_util.get_procedure retrieves the correct procedure name, without typos. The above line can be copied into any procedure without changing it each time. Since this call must be included in every page that you want to track, coding the call in this manner not only promotes code reusability, but also provides you with a time savings that is a distinct advantage.

TRACK CONTENT

A shopping site might find it useful to know that a visitor looked at a page called show_product, but it would be more interesting to know which product was being viewed. Likewise, knowing that a user visited the instruct_personal_info page is helpful, but it might also be interesting to know which instructor's information was viewed.

In order to do this, you create a new table called instructor_visit. It is similar to the page_visit table, except for the addition of two columns to hold the instructor's id and name.

■ *FOR EXAMPLE*

```
CREATE TABLE instructor_visit
   (visitor          VARCHAR2(200),
    ip_address       VARCHAR2(200),
    browser          VARCHAR2(200),
    page             VARCHAR2(200),
    instructor_id    NUMBER,
    instructor_name  VARCHAR2(200),
    timestamp        DATE);
```

Then, create a procedure called track_instructor_visit, based upon track_page_visit. It must include the two additional IN parameters that hold the values for populating instructor_id and instructor_name.

■ *FOR EXAMPLE*

```
CREATE OR REPLACE PROCEDURE track_instructor_visit
     (p_page IN VARCHAR2,
      p_instructor_id IN NUMBER,
      p_instructor_name IN VARCHAR2)
  AS
BEGIN
 INSERT INTO instructor_visit
  (visitor,
   ip_address,
   browser,
   page,
   instructor_id,
   instructor_name,
   timestamp)
 VALUES
  (get_cookie('VISITOR'),
   OWA_UTIL.GET_CGI_ENV('REMOTE_ADDR'),
   OWA_UTIL.GET_CGI_ENV('HTTP_USER_AGENT'),
   p_page,
   p_instructor_id,
   p_instructor_name,
   sysdate);
END;
```

Finally, insert the call for this procedure into any page where you want to track students' visited information. Here is a sample call.

■ *FOR EXAMPLE*

```
track_instructor_visit
   (OWA_UTIL.GET_PROCEDURE,
    v_instructor_id,
    v_first_name||' '||v_last_name);
```

Here is the sample call embedded into the instruct_personal_info procedure.

■ *FOR EXAMPLE*

```
CREATE OR REPLACE PROCEDURE instruct_personal_info
(p_instructor_id IN instructor.instructor_id%TYPE)
AS
    v_instructor_id     instructor.instructor_id%TYPE;
    v_salutation        instructor.salutation%TYPE;
    v_first_name        instructor.first_name%TYPE;
    v_last_name         instructor.last_name%TYPE;
    v_street_address    instructor.street_address%TYPE;
```

```
        v_city              zipcode.city%TYPE;
        v_state             zipcode.state%TYPE;
        v_zip               instructor.zip%TYPE;
        v_phone             instructor.phone%TYPE;
    BEGIN

        SELECT instructor_id,
               salutation,
               first_name,
               last_name,
               street_address,
               city,
               state,
               i.zip,
               phone
          INTO v_instructor_id,
               v_salutation,
               v_first_name,
               v_last_name,
               v_street_address,
               v_city,
               v_state,
               v_zip,
               v_phone
          FROM instructor i, zipcode z
         WHERE i.zip        = z.zip
           AND instructor_id = p_instructor_id;

    track_instructor_visit
       (OWA_UTIL.GET_PROCEDURE,
        v_instructor_id,
        v_first_name||' '||v_last_name);


    htp.p('<HTML>');

    <rest of procedure>
```

Note that the call to track_instructor_visit is made when the instructor's ID, first name, and last name are known. If the call were made before the SELECT statement, then v_instructor_id, v_first_name, and v_last_name would be null, and there would be no information to pass to the track_instructor_visit procedure for the instructor's name and ID.

In similar fashion, a news site could track exactly which articles are being rendered in the browser. For a retail application, a table called window_shopping could track each product that a user views, along with a user id from a cookie. An analysis of the data stored in window_shopping would tell a site which items generate any interest. If a user clicks that they are interested in an item, a table called shopping_cart could keep track of every item that a user was interested in by getting the visitor's id from a cookie and storing the visitor's id with the item they are interested in. When the user wants to see all of the items they have put into their shopping cart, a query to the shopping_cart table for the user identified by a cookie would produce the results.

UNIT 15.4 EXERCISES

15.4.1 CREATE TABLES TO HOLD STATISTICS

Create database tables called PAGE_VISIT and INSTRUCTOR_VISIT, as shown in this unit.

15.4.2 COMPILE THE PROCEDURES THAT POPULATE THE TABLES

Compile the procedures *track_page_visit* and *track_instructor_visit,* as shown in this unit.

15.4.3 TRACK VISITS BY CALLING THE PROCEDURES

Add a call to *track_page_visit* to any procedures in your application for which you want to track visitors.

15.4.4 DISPLAY COLLECTED STATISTICS

Create a procedure *show_page_visits* that queries the PAGE_VISIT database table and paints the results in an HTML table. The page should display the following information:

- Visitor
- IP Address
- Browser
- Page
- TO_CHAR(timestamp, 'DD-Mon-YYYY HH:MI AM')

15.4.5 TRACK VISITS TO SPECIFIC INSTRUCTOR RECORDS

Add a call to *track_instructor_visit* to the instruct_personal_info procedure. Pass the procedure name, instructor id, and instructor name, as shown in this unit.

15.4.6 DISPLAY INSTRUCTOR STATISTICS

Write a procedure *show_instructor_visits* that queries the IN-STRUCTOR_VISIT database table and paints the results in an HTML table. The page should display the following information:

- Instructor ID
- Instructor name
- Visitor
- Number of visits

UNIT 15.4 EXERCISE ANSWERS

15.4.1 ANSWER

Create database tables called PAGE_VISIT and INSTRUCTOR_VISIT, as shown in this unit.

Answer:

```
CREATE TABLE page_visit
  (visitor    VARCHAR2(200),
   ip_address VARCHAR2(20),
   browser    VARCHAR2(200),
   page       VARCHAR2(200),
   timestamp  DATE);

CREATE TABLE instructor_visit
  (visitor         VARCHAR2(200),
   ip_address      VARCHAR2(200),
   browser         VARCHAR2(200),
   page            VARCHAR2(200),
   instructor_id   NUMBER,
   instructor_name VARCHAR2(200),
   timestamp       DATE);
```

Compile the procedures track_page_visit and track_instructor_visit, as shown in this unit.

Answer:

```
CREATE OR REPLACE PROCEDURE track_page_visit
     (p_page IN VARCHAR2)
  AS
BEGIN
 INSERT INTO page_visit
  (visitor,
   ip_address,
   browser,
   page,
   timestamp)
 VALUES
  (get_cookie('VISITOR'),
   OWA_UTIL.GET_CGI_ENV('REMOTE_ADDR'),
   OWA_UTIL.GET_CGI_ENV('HTTP_USER_AGENT'),
   p_page,
   sysdate);
END;

CREATE OR REPLACE PROCEDURE track_instructor_visit
     (p_page IN VARCHAR2,
      p_instructor_id IN NUMBER,
      p_instructor_name IN VARCHAR2)
  AS
BEGIN
 INSERT INTO instructor_visit
  (visitor,
   ip_address,
   browser,
   page,
   instructor_id,
   instructor_name,
   timestamp)
 VALUES
  (get_cookie('VISITOR'),
   OWA_UTIL.GET_CGI_ENV('REMOTE_ADDR'),
   OWA_UTIL.GET_CGI_ENV('HTTP_USER_AGENT'),
   p_page,
   p_instructor_id,
   p_instructor_name,
   sysdate);
END;
```

**UNIT
15.4**

15.4.3 ANSWER

Add a call to *track_page_visit* to any procedures in your application for which you want to track visitors.

Answer: Add the following call within the body of any PL/SQL procedure:

```
track_page_visit(OWA_UTIL.GET_PROCEDURE);
```

15.4.4 ANSWER

Create a procedure show_page_visits that queries the PAGE_VISIT database table and paints the results in an HTML table. The page should display the following information:

- Visitor
- IP address
- Browser
- Page
- TO_CHAR(timestamp, 'DD-Mon-YYYY HH:MI AM')

Answer:

```
CREATE OR REPLACE PROCEDURE SHOW_PAGE_VISITS AS
   CURSOR c_visits IS
      SELECT * FROM PAGE_VISIT;
BEGIN
    htp.p('<HTML>
       <HEAD><TITLE>Page Visits</TITLE></HEAD>
       <BODY>
       <TABLE BORDER="2" CELLPADDING="5">
         <TR><TH>Visitor</TH>
             <TH>IP Address</TH>
             <TH>Browser</TH>
             <TH>Page</TH>
             <TH>Timestamp</TH>
         </TR>');
    FOR rec IN c_visits LOOP
       htp.p('<TR><TD>'||rec.visitor||'</TD>
                 <TD>'||rec.ip_address||'</TD>
                 <TD>'||rec.browser||'</TD>
                 <TD>'||rec.page||'</TD>
                 <TD>'||TO_CHAR(rec.timestamp, 'DD-Mon-YYYY HH:MI
                 AM')|| '</TD>
             </TR>');
    END LOOP;
    htp.p('</TABLE>
       </BODY>
```

```
          </HTML>');
EXCEPTION
   WHEN OTHERS THEN
      htp.p('Error in SHOW_PAGE_VISITS: '||SQLERRM);
END;
```

15.4.5 ANSWER

Add a call to track_instructor_visit to the instruct_personal_info procedure. Pass the procedure name, instructor id, and instructor name, as shown in this unit.

Answer:

```
CREATE OR REPLACE PROCEDURE instruct_personal_info
(p_instructor_id IN instructor.instructor_id%TYPE)
AS
   v_instructor_id     instructor.instructor_id%TYPE;
   v_salutation        instructor.salutation%TYPE;
   v_first_name        instructor.first_name%TYPE;
   v_last_name         instructor.last_name%TYPE;
   v_street_address    instructor.street_address%TYPE;
   v_city              zipcode.city%TYPE;
   v_state             zipcode.state%TYPE;
   v_zip               instructor.zip%TYPE;
   v_phone             instructor.phone%TYPE;
BEGIN

   SELECT instructor_id,
          salutation,
          first_name,
          last_name,
          street_address,
          city,
          state,
          i.zip,
          phone
   INTO   v_instructor_id,
          v_salutation,
          v_first_name,
          v_last_name,
          v_street_address,
          v_city,
          v_state,
          v_zip,
          v_phone
   FROM instructor i, zipcode z
   WHERE i.zip = z.zip
    AND instructor_id = p_instructor_id;
```

```
track_instructor_visit
   (OWA_UTIL.GET_PROCEDURE,
    v_instructor_id,
    v_first_name||' '||v_last_name);

htp.p('<HTML>');

<rest of procedure>
```

15.4.6 ANSWER

Write a procedure show_instructor_visits that queries the INSTRUCTOR_VISIT database table and paints the results in an HTML table. The page should display the following information:

- Instructor ID
- Instructor name
- Visitor
- Number of visits

Answer:

```
CREATE OR REPLACE PROCEDURE SHOW_INSTRUCTOR_VISITS
  AS
    CURSOR c_visits IS
       SELECT instructor_id,
              instructor_name,
              visitor,
              count(*)   thecount
         FROM INSTRUCTOR_VISIT
      GROUP BY instructor_id,
              instructor_name,
              visitor;
BEGIN
    htp.p('<HTML>
       <HEAD>
       <TITLE>Instructor Page Visits</TITLE>
       </HEAD>
       <BODY>
       <TABLE BORDER="2" CELLPADDING="5">
         <TR><TH>Instructor ID</TH>
             <TH>Instructor Name</TH>
             <TH>Visitor</TH>
             <TH># of Visits</TH>
         </TR>');
    FOR rec IN c_visits LOOP
       htp.p('<TR><TD>'||rec.instructor_id||'</TD>
              <TD>'||rec.instructor_name||'</TD>
              <TD>'||rec.visitor||'</TD>
```

```
                        <TD>'||rec.thecount||'</TD>
                    </TR>');
       END LOOP;
       htp.p('</TABLE>
           </BODY>
           </HTML>');
   EXCEPTION
      WHEN OTHERS THEN
         htp.p('Error in SHOW_INSTRUCTOR_VISITS: '||SQLERRM);
   END;
```

SECTION III

TAPAS

C H A P T E R   1 6

THE OWA_UTIL PACKAGE: DYNAMIC SQL, HTML, DATE UTILITIES, AND MORE

CHAPTER OBJECTIVES

Oracle provides built-in PL/SQL packages to enhance, speed up, maintain, or debug your Web-based applications. A "built-in" package is one that is written for you and compiled into the Oracle database. These are powerful packages that can be used to support and enhance iAS applications. They accomplish specific tasks for you and are easy to use. A familiarity with them will help you do some things you can't do without them, and keeps you from writing code that is already written for you. This chapter provides a brief overview of the Oracle OWA_UTIL built-in packages with utilities, which can be subdivided into the following categories:

This chapter outlines some of the many built-in PL/SQL packages that Oracle provides to assist developers by providing them with a toolkit they can use to develop technical solutions quickly and easily. These packages are handy for those repetitive tasks in which nothing would be gained by using the precious time and resources of the development team in creating certain programmatic solutions from scratch for such tasks such as authenticating requests. Some of the built-in PL/SQL packages, such as HTP, HTF, OWA_COOKIE (discussed in Chapter 15, "Maintaining State with Cookies and Tables"), and OWA_UTIL, were designed specifically to be used in conjunction with the *i*AS to generate Web pages using PL/SQL. However, most of the built-ins have broader uses.

This book does not cover every Oracle built-in package available. Such coverage is beyond the scope of this book. Instead, the built-in packages that the authors of this book deem to be the most relevant for Web development are outlined. Furthermore, two important built-in packages, OWA_COOKIE and OWA_IMAGE, are illustrated in Chapter 15, "Maintaining State with Cookies and Tables," and Chapter 13, "Images," respectively.

Lastly, Oracle has a built-in package called simply OWA. This package contains a set of procedures called only by the Oracle PL/SQL Agent. None of the subprograms in this package should be called directly from programmer-developed PL/SQL.

All of these packages are not part of the Oracle iAS, but are part of the Oracle database. This means they can be used with or apart from the iAS.

For more information about the packages discussed in this book, you can read Oracle's online documentation located at their primary site, http://docs.oracle.com, and/or on Technet, http://technet.oracle.com. The latter site requires you to register with Technet and sign on using a username/password. There is no fee to become a registered Technet user.

Also be sure to take a look at the package headers of the packages themselves. Often the package headers contain inline documentation. You can read these package headers using the ALL_SOURCE data dictionary view.

UNIT 16.1

DYNAMIC SQL UTILITIES

UNIT OBJECTIVES

After this unit, you will know how to:

✔ Send a Dynamically Generated Query
✔ Generate an HTML Table from the Output of a SQL Query
✔ View the Contents of a Database Table in the Browser

SEND A DYNAMICALLY GENERATED QUERY

Most SQL statements in your PL/SQL will be known ahead of time. However, there are situations when you do not know the exact syntax of the query you will need at runtime; for example, a WHERE clause might depend on a sort order selected by a user, or different queries may be run depending on what the user requests to see. Dynamic SQL refers to SQL that is built and run when it is called. The SQL can be built as required, which is why it is called "Dynamic SQL." The way Dynamic SQL works is to have placeholders, called "bind variables," that can be replaced with actual values at runtime.

Use the *owa_util.bind_variable* function when you want to retrieve a set of data using SQL, but want to substitute one or more values in your SQL at runtime. The *owa_util.bind_variables* function takes an SQL query, binds variables to it, and stores the output in an opened cursor. This function is then normally used as a parameter to a procedure that takes a dynamically generated query as an IN parameter. You can specify up to 25 bind variable name/value pairs. The syntax for owa_util.bind_variables is as follows:

```
owa_util.bind_variables (
  theQuery     IN VARCHAR2 DEFAULT NULL,
  bv1name      IN VARCHAR2 DEFAULT NULL,
  bv1value     IN VARCHAR2 DEFAULT NULL,
```

```
. . .
bv25name        IN VARCHAR2 DEFAULT NULL,
bv25value       IN VARCHAR2 DEFAULT NULL)
RETURN INTEGER;
```

The *theQuery* parameter is a string variable, possibly with bind variables, to be used to contain an SQL query statement. The statement must be a SELECT statement. The *bv1name* and *bv1value* parameters are to be used for the name and value, respectively, of a bind variable. The return value is an integer that is a unique identifier for the opened cursor.

To illustrate an example of owa_util.bind_variables, consider the following incomplete PL/SQL package, `current_semester`. This package is expanded upon in subsequent sections of this chapter. The code for owa_util.bind_variables is highlighted in bold.

■ FOR EXAMPLE

```
1   CREATE OR REPLACE PACKAGE current_semester AS
2   PROCEDURE enter_course;
3   PROCEDURE get_enrollments (p_course IN
4                             course.course_no%TYPE);
5   END current_semester;
6   /
7   CREATE OR REPLACE PACKAGE BODY current_semester AS
8   PROCEDURE enter_course
9   IS
10  BEGIN
11     htp.htmlOpen;
12     htp.headOpen;
13     htp.title('Enter a Course');
14     htp.headClose;
15     htp.bodyOpen(cattributes => 'BGCOLOR="#99CCCC"');
16   htp.centerOpen;
17   htp.header(1, 'Enter a Course Number');
18   htp.header(2, 'You will receive the current
19                 enrollment information for this
20                 course.');
21   htp.p('<FORM NAME="course_form"
22         ACTION="current_semester.get_enrollments"
23         METHOD="post">');
24   htp.tableOpen();
25   htp.tableRowOpen();
26   htp.p('<TD><FONT FACE="arial"><B>Course Number:
27         </B></FONT></TD>');
28   htp.tableData(htf.formText('p_course', NULL,
29                             NULL, 'Enter a Course
30                             Number.'));
31   htp.tableRowClose;
```

```
32    htp.tableRowOpen();
33    htp.p('<TD ALIGN=left>');
34    htp.formSubmit;
35    htp.formReset('Reset');
36    htp.p('</TD>');
37    htp.tableRowClose;
38    htp.tableClose;
39    htp.formClose;
40    htp.centerClose;
41    htp.bodyClose;
42    htp.htmlClose;
43  EXCEPTION
44  WHEN OTHERS
45  THEN
46    htp.p('An error occurred:  '||SQLERRM||'.  Please
47            contact Technical Support.');
48  END enter_course;
49  PROCEDURE get_enrollments (p_course IN
50                              course.course_no%TYPE)
51  IS
52    v_query        VARCHAR2(1024);
53    v_cursor_id    INTEGER;
54    v_description course.description%TYPE;
55  BEGIN
56      SELECT description
57        INTO v_description
58        FROM course
59       WHERE course_no = p_course;
60      htp.htmlOpen;
61      htp.headOpen;
62      htp.title('Dynamic SQL Utilities');
63      htp.headClose;
64      htp.bodyOpen(cattributes => 'BGCOLOR="#99CCCC"');
65      htp.centerOpen;
66      htp.line;
67      htp.header(1,'Current Enrollments');
68      htp.header(2, p_course||'  '||v_description);
69      htp.line;
70      v_query :=
71        'SELECT first_name, last_name, section_no ' ||
72        '  FROM section s, enrollment e, student st' ||
73        ' WHERE s.section_id  = e.section_id ' ||
74        '    AND st.student_id = e.student_id ' ||
75        '    AND s.course_no   = :bvcourse  ' ||
76        'ORDER BY section_no, last_name, first_name';
77      v_cursor_id :=
78      owa_util.bind_variables(v_query,
79                              'bvcourse', p_course);
80      htp.centerClose;
```

```
81      htp.bodyClose;
82      htp.htmlClose;
83   EXCEPTION
84   WHEN OTHERS
85   THEN
86     htp.p('An error occurred:  '||SQLERRM||'.  Please
87          contact Technical Support.');
88   END get_enrollments;
89   END current_semester;
90   /
```

GENERATE AN HTML TABLE FROM THE OUTPUT OF A SQL QUERY

The *owa_util.cellsprint* procedure generates an HTML table from the output of a SQL query. SQL column values are mapped to HTML table data items, and SQL rows to HTML table rows. The code to begin and end the HTML table is not included in the owa_util.cellsprint procedure. You must write this code separately.

There are currently nine versions of this procedure. The first parameter is always a query string, or an integer that represents a cursor opened with owa_util.bind_ variables, above. This procedure is overloaded. An "overloaded" procedure is a procedure where the appropriate choice will be called, based on the input the user supplies.

- For the first version, you perform the query and pass the number of columns that the index table should consist of, as well as an array containing the result set of your query to owa_util.cellsprint, and owa_util.cellsprint formats the output in HTML.
- The second and third versions display rows (up to a specified maximum) returned by the query. The second version takes a query string and the third takes an integer value that is a unique cursor identifier. Use these to limit the number of results a user sees.
- The fourth and fifth versions exclude a specified number of rows from the HTML table. Again, one takes a query string and the other takes an integer value that is a unique cursor identifier. Use these to scroll through result sets by saving the last row seen in a hidden form element and providing the user with Previous and Next buttons.
- The sixth through ninth versions are essentially the same as the first four versions. The only difference is they return a row count output parameter.

The syntax for all nine versions of owa_util.cellsprint is as follows:

```
owa_util.cellsprint(
   p_colCnt          IN INTEGER,
   p_resultTbl       IN VC_ARR,
   p_format_numbers IN VARCHAR2 DEFAULT NULL);
```

```
owa_util.cellsprint(
   p_theQuery        IN VARCHAR2,
   p_max_rows        IN NUMBER DEFAULT 100,
   p_format_numbers  IN VARCHAR2 DEFAULT NULL);

owa_util.cellsprint(
   p_theCursor       IN INTEGER,
   p_max_rows        IN NUMBER DEFAULT 100,
   p_format_numbers  IN VARCHAR2 DEFAULT NULL);

owa_util.cellsprint(
   p_theQuery        IN VARCHAR2,
   p_max_rows        IN NUMBER DEFAULT 100,
   p_format_numbers  IN VARCHAR2 DEFAULT NULL,
   p_skip_rec        IN NUMBER DEFAULT 0,
   p_more_data       OUT BOOLEAN);

owa_util.cellsprint(
   p_theCursor       IN INTEGER,
   p_max_rows        IN NUMBER DEFAULT 100,
   p_format_numbers  IN VARCHAR2 DEFAULT NULL,
   p_skip_rec        IN NUMBER DEFAULT 0,
   p_more_data       OUT BOOLEAN);

owa_util.cellsprint(
   p_theQuery        IN VARCHAR2,
   p_max_rows        IN NUMBER DEFAULT 100,
   p_format_numbers  IN VARCHAR2 DEFAULT NULL,
   p_reccnt          OUT NUMBER);

owa_util.cellsprint(
   p_theCursor       IN INTEGER,
   p_max_rows        IN NUMBER DEFAULT 100,
   p_format_numbers  IN VARCHAR2 DEFAULT NULL,
   p_reccnt          OUT NUMBER);

owa_util.cellsprint(
   p_theQuery        IN VARCHAR2,
   p_max_rows        IN NUMBER DEFAULT 100,
   p_format_numbers  IN VARCHAR2 DEFAULT NULL,
   p_skip_rec        IN NUMBER DEFAULT 0,
   p_more_data       OUT BOOLEAN,
   p_reccnt          OUT NUMBER);

owa_util.cellsprint(
   p_theCursor       IN INTEGER,
   p_max_rows        IN NUMBER DEFAULT 100,
   p_format_numbers  IN VARCHAR2 DEFAULT NULL,
   p_skip_rec        IN NUMBER DEFAULT 0,
```

```
p_more_data        OUT BOOLEAN,
p_reccnt           OUT NUMBER);
```

- *p_colCnt*—The number of columns that the resulting index table should consist of.
- *p_resultTbl*—The index table to contain the result of the query. Each entry in the query corresponds to one column value; therefore, later corresponding to one HTML table data item.
- *p_format_numbers*—When the value of this parameter is not NULL, number fields are right-justified and rounded to two decimal places.
- *p_theQuery*—An SQL SELECT statement.
- *p_max_rows*—The maximum number of rows you'd like printed.
- *p_theCursor*—A unique cursor ID. This can be the return value from the owa_util.bind_variables function.
- *p_skip_rec*—The number of rows you'd like to skip before displaying results in the HTML table.
- *p_more_data*—This value is set to TRUE if there are more rows in the query or cursor. Otherwise, it is set to FALSE. Use this to determine whether to provide the user with a "Next" button.
- *p_reccnt*—The number of rows returned by the query, excluding skipped rows (if any).

An example of owa_util.cellsprint is illustrated in this expanded version of the current_semester package, started earlier. The owa_util.cellsprint addition is outlined in boldface. Since the only parameter supplied is the integer corresponding to a unique cursor ID, and no OUT parameters are expected, you can conclude that the third version of owa_util.cellsprint, listed above, is used to create the HTML table.

■ FOR EXAMPLE

```
1    CREATE OR REPLACE PACKAGE current_semester AS
2    PROCEDURE enter_course;
3    PROCEDURE get_enrollments (p_course IN
4                                  course.course_no%TYPE);
5    END current_semester;
6    /
7    CREATE OR REPLACE PACKAGE BODY current_semester AS
8    PROCEDURE enter_course
9    IS
10   BEGIN
11      htp.htmlOpen;
12      htp.headOpen;
13      htp.title('Enter a Course');
14      htp.headClose;
15      htp.bodyOpen(cattributes => 'BGCOLOR="#99CCCC"');
```

```
16      htp.centerOpen;
17      htp.header(1, 'Enter a Course Number');
18      htp.header(2, 'You will receive the current
19                   enrollment information for this
20                   course.');
21      htp.p('<FORM NAME="course_form"
22             ACTION="current_semester.get_enrollments"
23             METHOD="post">');
24      htp.tableOpen();
25      htp.tableRowOpen();
26      htp.p('<TD><FONT FACE="arial"><B>Course Number:
27             </B></FONT></TD>');
28      htp.tableData(htf.formText('p_course', NULL,
29                                 NULL, 'Enter a Course
30                                 Number.'));
31      htp.tableRowClose;
32      htp.tableRowOpen();
33      htp.p('<TD ALIGN=left>');
34      htp.formSubmit;
35      htp.formReset('Reset');
36      htp.p('</TD>');
37      htp.tableRowClose;
38      htp.tableClose;
39      htp.formClose;
40      htp.centerClose;
41      htp.bodyClose;
42      htp.htmlClose;
43   EXCEPTION
44   WHEN OTHERS
45   THEN
46   htp.p('An error occurred:  '||SQLERRM||'.  Please
47          contact Technical Support.');
48   END enter_course;
49   PROCEDURE get_enrollments (p_course IN
50                                 course.course_no%TYPE)
51   IS
52     v_query        VARCHAR2(1024);
53     v_cursor_id    INTEGER;
54     v_description  course.description%TYPE;
55   BEGIN
56      SELECT description
57        INTO v_description
58        FROM course
59       WHERE course_no = p_course;
60      htp.htmlOpen;
61      htp.headOpen;
62      htp.title('Dynamic SQL Utilities');
63      htp.headClose;
64      htp.bodyOpen(cattributes => 'BGCOLOR="#99CCCC"');
```

```
65       htp.centerOpen;
66       htp.line;
67       htp.header(1,'Current Enrollments');
68       htp.header(2, p_course||' '||v_description);
69       htp.line;
70       v_query :=
71         'SELECT first_name, last_name, section_no' ||
72         '  FROM section s, enrollment e, student st' ||
73         ' WHERE s.section_id  = e.section_id ' ||
74         '   AND st.student_id = e.student_id ' ||
75         '   AND s.course_no   = :bvcourse ' ||
76         'ORDER BY section_no, last_name, first_name';
77       v_cursor_id :=
78         owa_util.bind_variables(v_query,
79                                 'bvcourse', p_course);
80       htp.tableOpen(cborder => 'BORDER=1');
81       owa_util.cellsprint(v_cursor_id);
82       htp.tableClose;
83       htp.centerClose;
84       htp.bodyClose;
85       htp.htmlClose;
86    EXCEPTION
87    WHEN OTHERS
88    THEN
89       htp.p('An error occurred:  '||SQLERRM||'.  Please
90             contact Technical Support.');
91    END get_enrollments;
92    END current_semester;
93    /
```

Copy this code example into the text editor of your choice. Save it as `current_semester.sql` and compile it using SQL*Plus. After invoking this procedure in your Web browser, entering a course number in the course entry form, and submitting the form, the result of this action should look similar to that shown in Figure 16.1.

VIEW THE CONTENTS OF A DATABASE TABLE IN THE BROWSER

Use this function to see what is stored in a database table. The *owa_util.tablePrint* function generates either preformatted tables or HTML tables from database tables. Whether this function is successful in generating each type of table (preformatted or HTML) is dependent on the user's browser. The majority of browsers display HTML tables, but if you have trouble displaying an HTML table, generate a preformatted table that uses <PRE> tags instead, as explained in this section.

You can view all columns or specify the ones you wish to see, and you can include WHERE and ORDER BY clauses. RAW columns are supported. LONG RAW

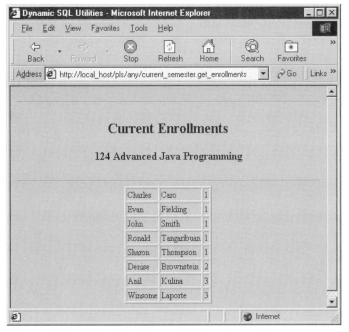

Figure 16.1 ■ The list of enrolled students for course number 124.

columns are not supported, and references to such columns cause the result "Not Printable" to print. The syntax for owa_util.tablePrint is as follows:

```
owa_util.tablePrint(
    ctable        IN VARCHAR2,
    cattributes   IN VARCHAR2 DEFAULT NULL,
    ntable_type   IN INTEGER DEFAULT HTML_TABLE
    ccolumns      IN VARCHAR2 DEFAULT '*'
    cclauses      IN VARCHAR2 DEFAULT NULL
    ccol_aliases  IN VARCHAR2 DEFAULT NULL
    nrow_min      IN NUMBER DEFAULT 0
    nrow_max      IN NUMBER DEFAULT NULL) RETURN BOOLEAN;
```

- *ctable*—The database table to be printed from.
- *cattributes*—Other attributes to be included, as is, in the <PRE> or <TABLE> tags, depending on which table type you choose.
- *ntable_type*—The table type you choose to use. Specify "OWA_UTIL.PRE_TABLE" to generate the table using the <PRE> tag or "OWA_UTIL.HTML_TABLE" to generate the table using the <TABLE> tags. Note that "PRE_TABLE" and "HTML_TABLE" are OWA_UTIL datatypes.
- *ccolumns*—A comma-delimited list of columns from *ctable* to ultimately include in the table you generate. If no columns are specified, then the default value, '*', determines that all columns will be returned.

- *cclauses*—WHERE or ORDER BY clauses that let you specify which rows to retrieve from *ctable,* and how to order them.
- *ccol_aliases*—A comma-delimited list of headings for the generated table.
- *nrow_min*—Specifies the minimum number of rows to be printed.
- *nrow_max*—Specifies the maximum number of rows to be printed.

Note that in this function, cattributes is the second, rather than the last, parameter.

This function generates a preformatted or HTML table and returns a value of TRUE if there are more rows beyond the *nrow_max* requested. Otherwise, it returns a value of FALSE. You can use this return value to decide whether to provide a user with a "Next" button to see more results.

An example of owa_util.tablePrint is illustrated in the following example PL/SQL package, *print_tables.* The code for owa_util.tablePrint is highlighted in bold.

■ *FOR EXAMPLE*

```
1    CREATE OR REPLACE PACKAGE print_tables AS
2      PROCEDURE print_courses;
3      PROCEDURE print_instructors;
4    END print_tables;
5    /
6    CREATE OR REPLACE PACKAGE BODY print_tables AS
7    PROCEDURE print_courses IS
8       more_rows BOOLEAN;
9    BEGIN
10      more_rows := owa_util.tablePrint
11         ('course', 'BORDER="1"', OWA_UTIL.PRE_TABLE,
12          'course_no, description',
13          'WHERE UPPER(description) LIKE
14           UPPER(''Intro%'') ORDER BY course_no',
15          'Course Number, Description');
16   END print_courses;
17   PROCEDURE print_instructors IS
18      more_rows BOOLEAN;
19   BEGIN
20      more_rows := owa_util.tablePrint
21         ('instructor', 'BORDER', OWA_UTIL.HTML_TABLE,
22          'first_name, last_name',
23          'WHERE zip IS NOT NULL ORDER BY last_name,
```

```
24                  first_name',
25                  'First Name, Last Name');
26   END print_instructors;
27 END print_tables;
28 /
```

Copy this code example into the text editor of your choice. Save it as `print_tables.sql` and compile it using SQL*Plus. Invoke each procedure in your Web browser. The result of invoking `print_tables.print_courses` should look similar to that shown in Figure 16.2.

Right-click on the Web page that is generated from running print_tables.print_courses. Select "View Source" from the pop-up Edit menu. The result of viewing the source code for this Web page should look similar to the following:

```
<PRE>
---------------------------------------------------
| Course Number |           Description         |
---------------------------------------------------
| 20            | Intro to Computers            |
| 25            | Intro to Programming          |
| 120           | Intro to Java Programming     |
| 130           | Intro to Unix                 |
| 204           | Intro to SQL                  |
| 230           | Intro to Internet             |
| 240           | Intro to the Basic Language   |
---------------------------------------------------
</PRE>
```

The result of invoking `print_tables.print_instructors` should look similar to that shown in Figure 16.3.

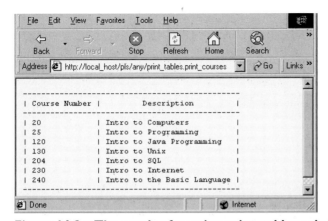

Figure 16.2 ■ The result of running print_tables.print_courses.

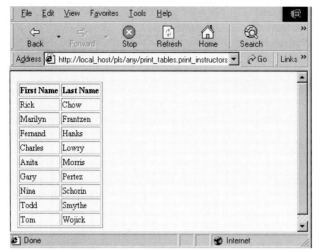

Figure 16.3 ■ **The result of running print_tables.print_instructors.**

Right-click on the Web page that is generated from running print_tables.print_instructors. Select "View Source" from the pop-up Edit menu. The result of viewing the source code for this Web page should look similar to the following:

```
<TABLE  BORDER>
<TR>
<TH>First Name</TH>
<TH>Last Name</TH>
</TR>
<TR>
<TD ALIGN="LEFT">Rick</TD>
<TD ALIGN="LEFT">Chow</TD>
</TR>
<TR>
<TD ALIGN="LEFT">Marilyn</TD>
<TD ALIGN="LEFT">Frantzen</TD>
</TR>
<TR>
<TD ALIGN="LEFT">Fernand</TD>
<TD ALIGN="LEFT">Hanks</TD>
</TR>
<TR>
<TD ALIGN="LEFT">Charles</TD>
<TD ALIGN="LEFT">Lowry</TD>
</TR>
<TR>
<TD ALIGN="LEFT">Anita</TD>
<TD ALIGN="LEFT">Morris</TD>
</TR>
<TR>
```

```
<TD ALIGN="LEFT">Gary</TD>
<TD ALIGN="LEFT">Pertez</TD>
</TR>
<TR>
<TD ALIGN="LEFT">Nina</TD>
<TD ALIGN="LEFT">Schorin</TD>
</TR>
<TR>
<TD ALIGN="LEFT">Todd</TD>
<TD ALIGN="LEFT">Smythe</TD>
</TR>
<TR>
<TD ALIGN="LEFT">Tom</TD>
<TD ALIGN="LEFT">Wojick</TD>
</TR>
</TABLE>
```

UNIT 16.2

HTML UTILITIES

UNIT OBJECTIVES

After this unit, you will know how to:

✔ Generate an HTML Select List from a SQL Query
✔ Generate a Signature Line on an HTML Document
✔ View the Source Code of a Procedure, Function, or Package in the Browser
✔ Print Out the HTML Output of a Procedure in SQL*Plus, SQL*DBA, or Oracle Server Manager

---

GENERATE AN HTML SELECT LIST FROM A SQL QUERY

The *owa_util.listprint* procedure generates an HTML selection list form element from the output of a SQL query. The columns in the output of the query are handled as follows:

- The first column specifies the values to be used in the SELECT list. These values are supplied to the VALUE attribute of the OPTION tag.
- The second column specifies the displayed values; those that the user sees.
- The third column specifies whether or not the returned row is marked as SELECTED in the OPTION tag. The row is selected if the value is not NULL.

Two versions of this procedure exist. The first version uses a hard-coded SQL query, and the second version contains a dynamic query prepared with the owa_util.bind_variables function. The syntax for owa_util.listprint is as follows:

```
owa_util.listprint(
   p_theQuery IN VARCHAR2,
   p_cname    IN VARCHAR2,
   p_nsize    IN NUMBER,
   p_multiple IN BOOLEAN DEFAULT FALSE);
owa_util.listprint(
   p_theCursor IN INTEGER,
   p_cname     IN VARCHAR2,
   p_nsize     IN NUMBER,
   p_multiple  IN BOOLEAN DEFAULT FALSE);
```

- *p_theQuery*—An SQL SELECT statement.
- *p_cname*—The name of the HTML select list form element.
- *p_nsize*—The size of the select list form element (which controls how many items the user can see without having to scroll.)
- *p_multiple*—Specifies whether multiple selection is permitted.
- *p_theCursor*—A unique cursor ID. This can be the return value from the owa_util.bind_variables function.

An example of owa_util.listprint is illustrated in the following example PL/SQL procedure, *student_fill_out_form*. This procedure allows a user to choose an introductory course from a drop-down select list. The code for owa_util.listprint is highlighted in bold.

■ FOR EXAMPLE

```
1    CREATE OR REPLACE PROCEDURE student_fill_out_form
2    AS
3    BEGIN
4    htp.htmlOpen;
5    htp.headOpen;
6    htp.title('HTML Utilities:  Student Fill Out Form');
7    htp.headClose;
8    htp.bodyOpen(cattributes => 'BGCOLOR="#99CCCC"');
9    htp.centerOpen;
10   htp.line;
11   htp.header(2, 'Student Enrollment Fill Out Form');
12   htp.header(3, 'At a minimum, please enter your first
13                  and last name.  If you are enrolling
14                  this semester, please choose your
15                  course from the drop-down list
16                  below.');
17   htp.line;
18   htp.p('<FORM NAME="student_fill_out_form" ACTION=""
19          METHOD="post">');
20   htp.tableOpen();
```

```
21  htp.tableRowOpen();
22  htp.tableData('First Name:');
23  htp.tableData(htf.formText('p_first_name'));
24  htp.tableRowClose;
25  htp.tableRowOpen();
26  htp.tableData('Last Name:');
27  htp.tableData(htf.formText('p_last_name'));
28  htp.tableRowClose;
29  htp.tableRowOpen();
30  htp.tableData('Telephone:');
31  htp.tableData(htf.formText('p_phone'));
32  htp.tableRowClose;
33  htp.tableRowOpen();
34  htp.tableData('Email Address:');
35  htp.tableData(htf.formText('p_email'));
36  htp.tableRowClose;
37  htp.tableRowOpen();
38  htp.tableData('Selected Course');
39  htp.p('<TD>');
40  owa_util.listprint(
41      'SELECT course_no, description,'
42  ||  '    NULL'
43  ||  '  FROM course'
44  || ' WHERE UPPER(description) LIKE '
45  ||  '        UPPER(''Intro%'')'
46  || 'UNION '
47  || 'SELECT TO_NUMBER(-1), ''Please Select a '
48  || 'Course'', ''SELECTED'''
49  ||  '  FROM dual '
50  || 'ORDER BY 1 '
51    ,'p_course', 1, FALSE);
52  htp.p('</TD>');
53  htp.tableRowClose;
54  htp.tableRowOpen();
55  htp.tableData();
56  htp.p('<TD ALIGN=left>');
57  htp.formSubmit;
58  htp.formReset;
59  htp.p('</TD>');
60  htp.tableRowClose;
61  htp.tableClose;
62  htp.formClose;
63  htp.centerClose;
64  htp.bodyClose;
65  htp.htmlClose;
66  EXCEPTION
67  WHEN OTHERS
68  THEN
```

```
69  htp.p('An error occurred:  '||SQLERRM||'.  Please
70        contact Technical Support.');
71 END student_fill_out_form;
72 /
```

Copy this code example into the text editor of your choice. Save it as `student_fill_out_form.sql` and compile it using SQL*Plus. Invoke it in your Web browser. The result of invoking `student_fill_out_form` should look similar to that shown in Figure 16.4.

Right-click on the Web page that is generated from running student_fill_out_form. Select "View Source" from the pop-up Edit menu. The result of viewing the HTML select list form element source code for this Web page should look similar to the following:

```
<SELECT NAME="p_course" SIZE="1">
<OPTION SELECTED value="-1">Please Select a Course
<OPTION value="20">Intro to Computers
<OPTION value="230">Intro to Internet
<OPTION value="120">Intro to Java Programming
<OPTION value="25">Intro to Programming
<OPTION value="204">Intro to SQL
<OPTION value="130">Intro to Unix
```

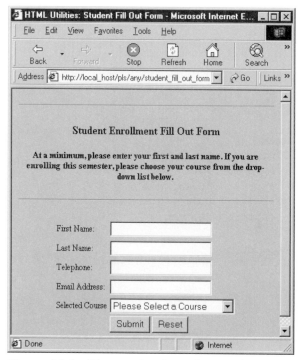

Figure 16.4 ■ **The result of running student_fill_out_form.**

```
<OPTION value="240">Intro to the Basic Language
</SELECT>
```

GENERATE A SIGNATURE LINE ON AN HTML DOCUMENT

Use this procedure to paint a Web Toolkit signature and timestamp, usually at the very bottom of a page. You can also use it in development to easily view source code. The *owa_util.signature* procedure generates an HTML horizontal rule line followed by a signature line on an HTML document. If a parameter is supplied to this procedure, the procedure also generates a hypertext link to view the PL/SQL source code for that procedure. The link invokes the *owa_util.showsource* procedure (explained shortly). The syntax for owa_util.signature is as follows:

```
owa_util.signature;
owa_util.signature (cname IN VARCHAR2);
```

The parameter, *cname*, refers to the function or procedure whose source you would like to show. An example of owa_util.signature is illustrated in a slightly altered version of student_fill_out_form, started earlier. The owa_util.signature additions are outlined in boldface.

■ FOR EXAMPLE

```
 1   CREATE OR REPLACE PROCEDURE student_fill_out_form
 2   AS
 3   BEGIN
 4   htp.htmlOpen;
 5   htp.headOpen;
 6   htp.title('HTML Utilities:  Student Fill Out Form');
 7   htp.headClose;
 8   htp.bodyOpen(cattributes => 'BGCOLOR="#99CCCC"');
 9   htp.centerOpen;
10   htp.line;
11   htp.header(2, 'Student Enrollment Fill Out Form');
12   htp.header(3, 'At a minimum, please enter your first
13                  and last name.  If you are enrolling
14                  this semester, please choose your
15                  course from the drop-down list
16                  below.');
17   htp.line;
18   htp.p('<FORM NAME="student_fill_out_form" ACTION=""
19          METHOD="post">');
20   htp.tableOpen();
21   htp.tableRowOpen();
22   htp.tableData('First Name:');
23   htp.tableData(htf.formText('p_first_name'));
24   htp.tableRowClose;
```

```
25   htp.tableRowOpen();
26   htp.tableData('Last Name:');
27   htp.tableData(htf.formText('p_last_name'));
28   htp.tableRowClose;
29   htp.tableRowOpen();
30   htp.tableData('Selected Course');
31   htp.p('<TD>');
32   owa_util.listprint(
33     'SELECT course_no, description,'
34     || '    NULL'
35     || '  FROM course'
36     || ' WHERE UPPER(description) LIKE '
37     || '        UPPER(''Intro%'')'
38     || 'UNION '
39     || 'SELECT TO_NUMBER(-1), ''Please Select a '
40     || 'Course'', ''SELECTED'''
41     || '   FROM dual '
42     || 'ORDER BY 1 '
43      ,'p_course', 1, FALSE);
44   htp.p('</TD>');
45   htp.tableRowClose;
46   htp.tableRowOpen();
47   htp.tableData();
48   htp.p('<TD ALIGN=left>');
49   htp.formSubmit;
50   htp.formReset;
51   htp.p('</TD>');
52   htp.tableRowClose;
53   htp.tableClose;
54   htp.formClose;
55   owa_util.signature;
56   owa_util.signature('student_fill_out_form');
57   htp.centerClose;
58   htp.bodyClose;
59   htp.htmlClose;
60   EXCEPTION
61   WHEN OTHERS
62   THEN
63   htp.p('An error occurred:  '||SQLERRM||'.  Please
64          contact Technical Support.');
65   END student_fill_out_form;
66   /
```

Copy this code example into the text editor of your choice. Save it as `student_fill_out_form.sql` and compile it using SQL*Plus. Invoke it in your Web browser. The result of invoking this newest version of `student_fill_out_form` should look similar to that shown in Figure 16.5.

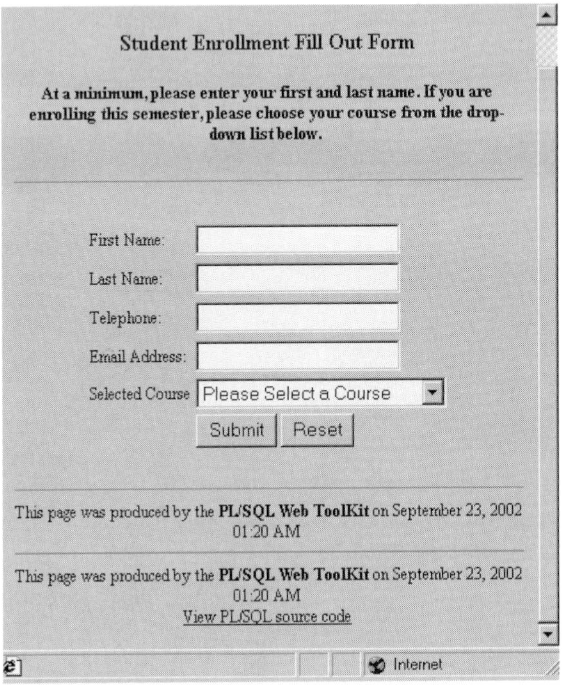

Figure 16.5 ∎ The result of running student_fill_out_form with owa_util.signature lines.

Notice that two signature lines now appear on `student_fill_out_form`. The first signature line simply displays the following information:

This page was produced by the **PL/SQL Web ToolKit** on April 07, 2002 01:09 PM

Whereas, the second signature line displays the following:

This page was produced by the **PL/SQL Web ToolKit** on April 07, 2002 01:09 PM
<u>View PL/SQL source code</u>

The second signature line was created by passing a procedure name, `student_fill_out_form`, as a parameter to the owa_util.signature procedure. The second line is a hypertext link to view the source code for `student_fill_out_form`. If you click this hypertext link, you should see a result that looks similar to that shown in Figure 16.6.

Note the URL address line in this figure, particularly after the last forward slash, /, character. Here you see how the hypertext link invokes the *owa_util.showsource* procedure (explained in the following section).

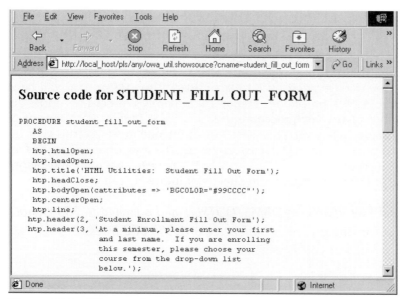

Figure 16.6 ■ The result of clicking the <u>View PL/SQL source code</u> hypertext link in student_fill_out_form.

VIEW THE SOURCE CODE OF A PROCEDURE, FUNCTION, OR PACKAGE IN THE BROWSER

The *owa_util.showsource* procedure prints the source of the specified package, function, or procedure. If the specified procedure or function belongs to a package, the source code for the entire package is displayed. Use this procedure to view source code easily. The syntax for owa_util.showsource is as follows:

```
owa_util.showsource (cname IN VARCHAR2);
```

The parameter, *cname*, refers to the function, procedure, or package whose source you'd like to show.

You can use owa_util.showsource directly in the browser to view source code. This can be a handy way to debug code. Simply call owa_util.showsource?cname=student_fill_out_form at the end of the URL. For example: http://www.domain.org/pls/any/owa_util.showsource?cname= student_fill_out_form

PRINT OUT THE HTML OUTPUT OF A PROCEDURE IN SQL*PLUS, SQL*DBA, OR ORACLE SERVER MANAGER

Use the owa_util.showpage procedure when you are in SQL*Plus, SQL*DBA, or Oracle Server Manager, and would like an idea of the HTML that will be generated from a PL/SQL procedure. The *owa_util.showpage* procedure prints out the HTML output of the last procedure executed in SQL*Plus, SQL*DBA, or Oracle Server Manager. Whatever procedure you print out must use the HTP or HTF packages to generate the HTML page involved. The owa_util.showpage procedure must be issued after the PL/SQL procedure has been executed and before any other HTP or HTF subprograms are directly or indirectly called.

This procedure uses DBMS_OUTPUT and is limited to 255 characters per line and an overall buffer size of 1,000,000 bytes.

The syntax for owa_util.showpage is as follows:

```
owa_util.showpage;
```

Invoking the owa_util.showpage procedure in SQL*Plus after executing the student_fill_out_form yields a result similar to the following:

■ FOR EXAMPLE

```
SQL> set serveroutput on size 1000000
SQL> execute student_fill_out_form

PL/SQL procedure successfully completed.

SQL> execute owa_util.showpage
<HTML>
<HEAD>
<TITLE>HTML Utilities:  Student Fill Out
Form</TITLE>
</HEAD>
<BODY BGCOLOR="#99CCCC">
<CENTER>
<HR>
<H2>Student
Enrollment Fill Out Form</H2>
<H3>At a minimum, please enter your first and last name.  If you
are enrolling this semester, please choose your course from the
drop-down list below.</H3>
<HR>
```

```
<FORM NAME="student_fill_out_form" ACTION=""
METHOD="post">
<TABLE >
<TR>
<TD>First Name:</TD>

<TD><INPUT TYPE="text" NAME="p_first_name"></TD>
</TR>
<TR>
<TD>Last
Name:</TD>
<TD><INPUT TYPE="text"
NAME="p_last_name"></TD>
</TR>
<TR>
<TD>Selected Course</TD>
<TD>
<SELECT
NAME="p_course" SIZE="1">
<OPTION value="">
<OPTION value="20">Intro to Comp
uters
<OPTION value="230">Intro to Internet
<OPTION value="120">Intro to Java
Programming
<OPTION value="25">Intro to Programming
<OPTION SELECTED
value="204">Intro to SQL
<OPTION value="130">Intro to Unix
<OPTION
value="240">Intro to the Basic Language
<
/SELECT>
</TD>
</TR>
<TR>
<TD></TD>
<TD ALIGN=left>
<INPUT TYPE="submit"
VALUE="Submit">
<INPUT TYPE="reset"
VALUE="Reset">
</TD>
</TR>
</TABLE>
</FORM>
<HR>
This page was produced by the
```

```
<B>PL/SQL Web ToolKit</B> on April      07, 2002 02:59 PM<BR>
</CEN
```

```
PL/SQL procedure successfully completed.
```

The student_fill_out_form procedure is altered in this example to exclude the owa_util.signature line with a parameter. If an owa_util.signature line is included with a parameter in the procedure you execute just before executing owa_util.showpage, then you receive the following PL/SQL error:

```
ORA-06502: PL/SQL: numeric or value error.
```

UNIT 16.3

DATE UTILITIES

UNIT OBJECTIVES

After this unit, you will know how to:

✔ Create a Calendar in HTML
✔ Generate Three HTML Form Elements that Allow a User to Select a Day, Month, and Year

---

CREATE A CALENDAR IN HTML

The *owa_util.calendarprint* procedure generates a calendar in the form of an HTML table with a visible border. Each date in the calendar can contain any number of hypertext links. Your query should be designed as follows:

- The first column should be a DATE. This is necessary to correlate the output of the query with the calendar output automatically generated by the procedure.

- The second column should contain any text you'd like printed for that date.

- The third column specifies the destination for automatically generated links. Each item in the second column then becomes a hypertext link to the destination specified in the third column. If this column is omitted, the items in the second column are then displayed as simple text, not hypertext links.

- The query must be sorted by the first column, the DATE, using an ORDER BY clause.

There are two versions to this procedure. The first version uses a hard-coded SQL query, and the second version contains a dynamic query prepared with the owa_util.bind_variables function. The syntax for owa_util.calendarprint is as follows:

```
owa_util.calendarprint(
    p_query    IN VARCHAR2,
    p_mf_only IN VARCHAR2 DEFAULT 'N');

owa_util.calendarprint(
    p_cursor  IN INTEGER,
    p_mf_only IN VARCHAR2 DEFAULT 'N');
```

- *p_query*—An SQL SELECT statement.
- *p_mf_only*—If this parameter is set to "N" (the default value), then the generated calendar includes Sunday through Saturday. Otherwise, it includes Monday through Friday only.
- *p_cursor*—A unique cursor ID. This can be the return value from the owa_util.bind_variables function.

An example of owa_util.calendarprint is illustrated in a very simple package, list_enrollments, listed below. The code for owa_util.calendarprint is highlighted in boldface.

■ FOR EXAMPLE

```
1   CREATE OR REPLACE PACKAGE list_enrollments
2   AS
3   PROCEDURE students_and_dates;
4   PROCEDURE student_info;
5   END list_enrollments;
6   /
7   CREATE OR REPLACE PACKAGE BODY list_enrollments
8   AS
9   PROCEDURE students_and_dates
10  IS
11  BEGIN
12  htp.htmlOpen;
13  htp.headOpen;
14  htp.title('Date Utilities:  Students and Dates');
15  htp.headClose;
16  htp.bodyOpen(cattributes => 'BGCOLOR="#99CCCC"');
17  htp.centerOpen;
18  htp.line;
19  htp.header(2, 'Alphabetic Enrollments');
20  htp.header(3, 'This page displays those enrolled
21             students whose last name begins with
22             the letter ''A''.');
23  htp.line;
24  owa_util.calendarprint(
```

```
25  'SELECT DISTINCT enroll_date,
26  ||   last_name||'', ''||first_name , '
27  ||   ' ''list_enrollments.student_info'' '
28  ||   '  FROM enrollment e, student s '
29  ||   ' WHERE last_name LIKE (''A%'') '
30  ||   '   AND enroll_date IS NOT NULL '
31  ||   '   AND e.student_id = s.student_id '
32  ||   'ORDER BY enroll_date '
33  );
34  owa_util.signature(
35              'list_enrollments.students_and_dates');
36  htp.centerClose;
37  htp.bodyClose;
38  htp.htmlClose;
39  EXCEPTION
40  WHEN OTHERS
41  THEN
42  htp.p('An error occurred:  '||SQLERRM||'.  Please
43          contact Technical Support.');
44  END students_and_dates;
45  PROCEDURE student_info
46  IS
47  CURSOR get_info IS
48  SELECT DISTINCT last_name, first_name
49    FROM student s, enrollment e
50   WHERE last_name LIKE ('A%')
51     AND enroll_date IS NOT NULL
52     AND e.student_id = s.student_id
53  ORDER BY last_name, first_name;
54  BEGIN
55  htp.htmlOpen;
56  htp.headOpen;
57  htp.title('Date Utilities:  Student Info');
58  htp.headClose;
59  htp.bodyOpen(cattributes => 'BGCOLOR="#99CCCC"');
60  htp.centerOpen;
61  htp.line;
62  htp.header(2, 'Students Whose Last Names Begin With
63            ''A''.');
64  htp.line;
65  htp.tableOpen();
66  FOR rec_info IN get_info
67  LOOP
68  htp.tableRowOpen();
69  htp.tableData(rec_info.last_name||',
70                '||rec_info.first_name);
71  htp.tableRowClose;
72  END LOOP;
73  htp.tableClose;
```

```
74   owa_util.signature('list_enrollments.student_info');
75   htp.centerClose;
76   htp.bodyClose;
77   htp.htmlClose;
78   EXCEPTION
79   WHEN OTHERS
80   THEN
81   htp.p('An error occurred:  '||SQLERRM||'.  Please
82          contact Technical Support.');
83   END student_info;
84   END list_enrollments;
85   /
```

Copy this code example into the text editor of your choice. Save it as `list_enrollments.sql` and compile it using SQL*Plus. Invoke it in your Web browser. The result of invoking `list_enrollments.students_and_dates` should look similar to that shown in Figure 16.7.

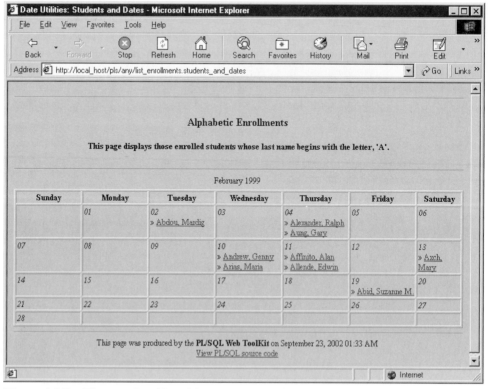

Figure 16.7 ■ The result of invoking list_enrollments.students_and_dates.

GENERATE THREE HTML FORM ELEMENTS THAT ALLOW A USER TO SELECT A DAY, MONTH, AND YEAR

The *owa_util.choose_date* procedure displays a date in HTML as three form elements that allow the user to select the day, the month, and the year. Instead of creating your own form inputs, you can use this procedure to allow the user to input a date.

The form handler procedure must have an IN parameter with the datatype *owa_util.dateType* to receive the values. The datatype, owa_util.dateType, is an array and is defined as follows:

```
TYPE dateType IS TABLE OF VARCHAR2(10) INDEX BY BINARY_INTEGER
```

The *owa_util.todate* function can then be used to convert an item of this type to the type DATE, which is understood and validated by the database. There is no space or underscore in the function name—the correct syntax is owa_util.todate.

The syntax for owa_util.choose_date is as follows:

```
owa_util.choose_date(
    p_name IN VARCHAR2,
    p_date IN DATE DEFAULT SYSDATE);
```

p_name specifies the name of the form elements, and *p_date* indicates the initial date that is selected when the HTML page is displayed. Note that the range of years that are supplied is five years before and five years after the date passed in as *p_date*. Also note that since the date range is from 1 to 31, the inputs allow a user to select an incorrect date, such as April 31st—however, the owa_util.todate function corrects such an inaccurate date. For example, February 30th would be replaced with the highest possible date, either February 28th or February 29th depending on the year.

An example of owa_util.choose_date is illustrated in the small package, enroll_dates, listed below. The code for owa_util.choose_date is highlighted in boldface:

■ FOR EXAMPLE

```
1  CREATE OR REPLACE PACKAGE enroll_dates AS
2  PROCEDURE choose_enroll_date;
3  PROCEDURE display_enroll_date(p_date IN
4                              OWA_UTIL.dateType);
5  END enroll_dates;
6  /
7  CREATE OR REPLACE PACKAGE BODY enroll_dates AS
```

**UNIT
16.3**

```
 8     -- Main entry procedure.
 9      PROCEDURE choose_enroll_date IS
10      BEGIN
11         htp.htmlOpen;
12         htp.headOpen;
13         htp.title('Date Utilities:  Choose Enroll
14                    Date');
15         htp.headClose;
16         htp.bodyOpen(cattributes =>
17                      'BGCOLOR="#99CCCC"');
18         htp.centerOpen;
19         htp.line;
20         htp.header(2, 'Choose Your Enrollment Date.');
21         htp.header(3, 'Enter a year, month, and day
22                       below, and then press
23                       Submit:');
24         htp.line;
25         htp.formOpen(curl =>
26                 'enroll_dates.display_enroll_date');
27         owa_util.choose_date(p_name => 'p_date');
28         htp.formSubmit;
29         htp.formReset;
30         htp.formClose;
31         owa_util.signature(
32                  'enroll_dates.choose_enroll_date');
33         htp.centerClose;
34         htp.bodyClose;
35         htp.htmlClose;
36    END choose_enroll_date;
37    -- Receives the date selected.
38  PROCEDURE display_enroll_date(p_date IN
39                                 OWA_UTIL.dateType) IS
40    BEGIN
41      htp.htmlOpen;
42      htp.headOpen;
43      htp.title('Date Utilities:  Display Enroll
44                Date');
45      htp.headClose;
46      htp.bodyOpen(cattributes =>
47                   'BGCOLOR="#99CCCC"');
48      htp.centerOpen;
49      htp.line;
50      htp.header(2, 'You have selected ');
51      htp.header(3, TO_CHAR(OWA_UTIL.todate(p_date),
52                   'MONTH DD, YYYY'));
53      htp.line;
54      owa_util.signature(
55                  'enroll_dates.display_enroll_date');
```

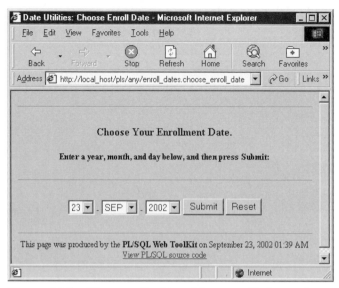

Figure 16.8 ■ The result of invoking enroll_dates.choose_enroll_dates.

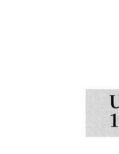

```
56        htp.centerClose;
57        htp.bodyClose;
58        htp.htmlClose;
59     END display_enroll_date;
60   END enroll_dates;
61 /
```

Copy this code example into the text editor of your choice. Save it as enroll_dates.sql and compile it using SQL*Plus. Invoke it in your Web browser. The result of invoking enroll_dates.choose_enroll_date should look similar to that shown in Figure 16.8.

Right-click on the Web page that is generated from running enroll_dates.choose_enroll_date. Select "View Source" from the pop-up Edit menu. The result of viewing the HTML select list form element source code for this Web page should look similar to the following:

```
<SELECT NAME="p_date" SIZE="1">
<OPTION value="01">1
<OPTION value="02">2
<OPTION value="03">3
<OPTION value="04">4
<OPTION value="05">5
<OPTION value="06">6
<OPTION SELECTED value="07">7
<OPTION value="08">8
<OPTION value="09">9
```

```
<OPTION value="10">10
<OPTION value="11">11
<OPTION value="12">12
<OPTION value="13">13
<OPTION value="14">14
<OPTION value="15">15
<OPTION value="16">16
<OPTION value="17">17
<OPTION value="18">18
<OPTION value="19">19
<OPTION value="20">20
<OPTION value="21">21
<OPTION value="22">22
<OPTION value="23">23
<OPTION value="24">24
<OPTION value="25">25
<OPTION value="26">26
<OPTION value="27">27
<OPTION value="28">28
<OPTION value="29">29
<OPTION value="30">30
<OPTION value="31">31
</SELECT>
-
<SELECT NAME="p_date" SIZE="1">
<OPTION value="01">JAN
<OPTION value="02">FEB
<OPTION value="03">MAR
<OPTION SELECTED value="04">APR
<OPTION value="05">MAY
<OPTION value="06">JUN
<OPTION value="07">JUL
<OPTION value="08">AUG
<OPTION value="09">SEP
<OPTION value="10">OCT
<OPTION value="11">NOV
<OPTION value="12">DEC
</SELECT>
-
<SELECT NAME="p_date" SIZE="1">
<OPTION value="1997">1997
<OPTION value="1998">1998
<OPTION value="1999">1999
<OPTION value="2000">2000
<OPTION value="2001">2001
<OPTION SELECTED value="2002">2002
<OPTION value="2003">2003
<OPTION value="2004">2004
<OPTION value="2005">2005
```

```
<OPTION value="2006">2006
<OPTION value="2007">2007
</SELECT>
```

 NOTE: Remember to place the resulting Select Lists inside <FORM> </FORM> tags if you wish to submit this data to a processing procedure.

U N I T   1 6 . 4

MISCELLANEOUS UTILITIES

UNIT OBJECTIVES

After this unit, you will know how to:

✔ Return the Value of a CGI Environment Variable
✔ Return Names and Values of All CGI Environment Variables for a Particular PL/SQL Procedure
✔ Return the Full Virtual Path of the PL/SQL Agent that is Handling an HTTP Request
✔ Return the Name of a Procedure that is Being Invoked by the PL/SQL Gateway
✔ Return Information about the Calling PL/SQL Code Unit to the Called PL/SQL Code Unit

---

RETURN THE VALUE OF A CGI ENVIRONMENT VARIABLE

The *owa_util.get_cgi_env* function returns the value of a specified CGI environment variable. If the variable is not defined, the function returns a NULL value. Although the WRB (Web Request Broker) is not operated through the CGI (Common Gateway Interface), many WRB cartridges, including the PL/SQL Gateway, can make use of CGI environment variables. The syntax for owa_util.get_cgi_env is as follows:

```
owa_util.get_cgi_env(param_name IN VARCHAR2) RETURN VARCHAR2;
```

param_name is the name of the CGI environment variable, and it is case-insensitive. The parameters in Table 16.1 may be obtained using the owa_util.get_cgi_env function and, depending on the operating system, additional parameters may be available.

Table 16.1 ■ CGI Environment Variable Parameters

CGI Environment Variable	Description	Example
GATEWAY_INTERFACE	The name and version of the gateway being used. The gateway interface name and version are separated by a forward slash with no spaces.	CGI/1.1
HTTP_USER_AGENT	The name of the client program making the request. This variable tells you which browser and operating system the user is using.	Mozilla/4.0 (compatible; MSIE 5.5; MSN 2.0; Windows 95)
PATH_INFO	Extra path information as it was passed to the server in the URL. For 9iAS, this is the name of the (packaged) procedure that was called.	/enroll_dates.choose_enroll_date
PATH_TRANSLATED	Extra path information in the query URL, translated into a final, usable form for the Web server. It contains the physical path name, obtained in the PATH_INFO environment variable, after the document root has been prepended to it.	/local/host/enroll_dates. choose_enroll_date (This example assumes that the document root is /local/web.)
REMOTE_ADDR	The IP address of the client that made the request.	111.22.333.44
REMOTE_HOST	The name or IP address of the remote computer that made the request.	webdevbook_server (**NOTE:** This variable will only be set if the remote machine is registered in the DNS [many personal computers are not], and hostname lookup is enabled in the server.)
SCRIPT_NAME	The name of the script involved. For 9iAS, this is the PL/SQL agent name.	/pls/webdevbook_dad
SERVER_NAME	The domain name of the computer that is running the server software (i.e., the domain name of the Web server).	webdevbook_server

(continued)

Table 16.1 ■ continued

CGI Environment Variable	Description	Example
SERVER_PORT	The TCP port number on which the server that invoked the CGI application is operating. 80 is the default HTTP port number.	80
SERVER_PROTOCOL	The name and version of the protocol the server is using. The protocol name and version are separated by a forward slash with no spaces.	HTTP/1.1
SERVER_SOFTWARE	The name of the server handling the request (i.e., the Web server software in use).	Oracle HTTP Server Powered by Apache/ 1.3.12 (Win32) ApacheJServ/1.1 mod_ssl/2.6.4 OpenSSL/0.9.5a mod_perl/1.24

UNIT 16.4

owa_util.get_cgi_env can get the values for all CGI environment variables except QUERY_STRING, because the PL/SQL Gateway parses the value of QUERY_STRING to determine the parameters to pass to the stored procedure.

An example of owa_util.get_cgi_env is illustrated with a slight change to the procedure, `student_fill_out_form`. The additional code using owa_util.get_cgi_env is highlighted in boldface.

■ FOR EXAMPLE

```
 1  CREATE OR REPLACE PROCEDURE student_fill_out_form
 2  AS
 3  v_http_user_agent VARCHAR2(110);
 4  BEGIN
 5  htp.htmlOpen;
 6  htp.headOpen;
 7  htp.title('HTML Utilities:  Student Fill Out Form');
 8  htp.headClose;
 9  htp.bodyOpen(cattributes => 'BGCOLOR="#99CCCC"');
10  htp.centerOpen;
11  htp.line;
12  htp.header(2, 'Student Enrollment Fill Out Form');
```

```
13  htp.header(3, 'At a minimum, please enter your first
14                  and last name.  If you are enrolling
15                  this semester, please choose your
16                  course from the drop-down list
17                  below.');
18  htp.line;
19  v_http_user_agent := owa_util.get_cgi_env(
20                           'HTTP_USER_AGENT');
21  htp.p(v_http_user_agent);
22  htp.line;
23  htp.p('<FORM NAME="student_fill_out_form" ACTION=""
24       METHOD="post">');
25  htp.tableOpen();
26  htp.tableRowOpen();
27  htp.tableData('First Name:');
28  htp.tableData(htf.formText('p_first_name'));
29  htp.tableRowClose;
30  htp.tableRowOpen();
31  htp.tableData('Last Name:');
32  htp.tableData(htf.formText('p_last_name'));
33  htp.tableRowClose;
34  htp.tableRowOpen();
35  htp.tableData('Selected Course');
36  htp.p('<TD>');
37  owa_util.listprint(
38     'SELECT course_no, description,'
39  || '    NULL'
40  || '  FROM course'
41  || ' WHERE UPPER(description) LIKE '
42  || '        UPPER(''Intro%'')'
43  || 'UNION '
44  || 'SELECT TO_NUMBER(-1), ''Please Select a '
45  || 'Course'', ''SELECTED'''
46  || '  FROM dual '
47  || 'ORDER BY 1 '
48    ,'p_course', 1, FALSE);
49  htp.p('</TD>');
50  htp.tableRowClose;
51  htp.tableRowOpen();
52  htp.tableData();
53  htp.p('<TD ALIGN=left>');
54  htp.formSubmit;
55  htp.formReset;
56  htp.p('</TD>');
57  htp.tableRowClose;
58  htp.tableClose;
59  htp.formClose;
60  owa_util.signature('student_fill_out_form');
61  htp.centerClose;
```

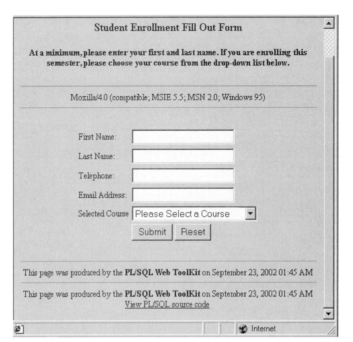

Figure 16.9 ■ The result of running student_fill_out_form with output from owa_util.get_cgi_env.

```
62   htp.bodyClose;
63   htp.htmlClose;
64   EXCEPTION
65   WHEN OTHERS
66   THEN
67   htp.p('An error occurred:  '||SQLERRM||'.  Please
68        contact Technical Support.');
69   END student_fill_out_form;
70 /
```

Copy this code example into the text editor of your choice. Save it as student_fill_out_form.sql and compile it using SQL*Plus. Invoke it in your Web browser. The result of invoking this newest version of student_fill_out_form should look similar to that shown in Figure 16.9.

RETURN NAMES AND VALUES OF ALL CGI ENVIRONMENT VARIABLES FOR A PARTICULAR PL/SQL PROCEDURE

The *owa_util.print_cgi_env* procedure generates all the CGI environment variables and their values made available by the PL/SQL agent to a PL/SQL procedure. The syntax for owa_util.print_cgi_env is as follows:

```
owa_util.print_cgi_env;
```

This procedure can also be called directly from the browser to view all available environment variables.

This procedure receives no parameters and generates a list in the following output:

```
cgi_env_var_name = value\n
```

That is the name of the environment variable followed by its value and a *newline* character, otherwise known as a carriage return. An example of owa_util. print_cgi_env is illustrated with the small procedure, all_environment_ variables, listed below. The code outlining owa_util.print_cgi_env is high-lighted in boldface.

■ *FOR EXAMPLE*

```
 1   CREATE OR REPLACE PROCEDURE
 2     all_environment_variables
 3   AS
 4   BEGIN
 5   htp.htmlOpen;
 6   htp.headOpen;
 7   htp.title('Miscellaneous Utilities:  All Environment
 8             Variables');
 9   htp.headClose;
10   htp.bodyOpen(cattributes => 'BGCOLOR="#99CCCC"');
11   htp.centerOpen;
12   htp.line;
13   htp.header(2, 'All Environment Variables');
14   htp.line;
15   owa_util.print_cgi_env;
16   owa_util.signature('all_environment_variables');
17   htp.centerClose;
18   htp.bodyClose;
19   htp.htmlClose;
20   EXCEPTION
21   WHEN OTHERS
22   THEN
23   htp.p('An error occurred:  '||SQLERRM||'.  Please
24          contact Technical Support.');
25   END all_environment_variables;
26   /
```

Copy this code example into the text editor of your choice. Save it as all_envi-ronment_variables.sql and compile it using SQL*Plus. Invoke it in your Web browser. The result of invoking this procedure should look similar to that shown in Figure 16.10.

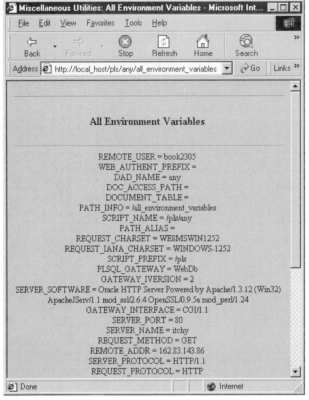

Figure 16.10 ■ The result of running all_environment_variables with output from owa_util.print_cgi_env.

RETURN THE FULL VIRTUAL PATH OF THE PL/SQL AGENT THAT IS HANDLING AN HTTP REQUEST

The *owa_util.get_owa_service_path* function returns the name of the full, currently active virtual path of the PL/SQL Gateway that is handling the request. The syntax for owa_util.get_owa_service_path is as follows:

```
owa_util.get_owa_service_path RETURN VARCHAR2;
```

This procedure receives no parameters. An example of owa_util.get_owa_service_path is illustrated with the small procedure, print_owa_service_path, listed below. The code outlining owa_util.get_owa_service_path is highlighted in boldface.

■ FOR EXAMPLE

```
1   CREATE OR REPLACE PROCEDURE print_owa_service_path
2   AS
3   BEGIN
```

```
 4   htp.htmlOpen;
 5   htp.headOpen;
 6   htp.title('Miscellaneous Utilities:  Print OWA
 7             Service Path');
 8   htp.headClose;
 9   htp.bodyOpen(cattributes => 'BGCOLOR="#99CCCC"');
10   htp.centerOpen;
11   htp.line;
12   htp.header(2, 'Print OWA Service Path');
13   htp.line;
14   htp.p(owa_util.get_owa_service_path);
15   htp.line;
16   htp.centerClose;
17   htp.bodyClose;
18   htp.htmlClose;
19   EXCEPTION
20   WHEN OTHERS
21   THEN
22   htp.p('An error occurred:  '||SQLERRM||'.  Please
23          contact Technical Support.');
24   END print_owa_service_path;
25   /
```

Copy this code example into the text editor of your choice. Save it as `print_owa_service_path.sql` and compile it using SQL*Plus. Invoke it in your Web browser. The result of invoking this procedure should look similar to that shown in Figure 16.11.

Other, more common uses for owa_util.get_owa_service_path are as an appendix to package/procedure names invoked, for example, in HTML form actions and in JavaScript.

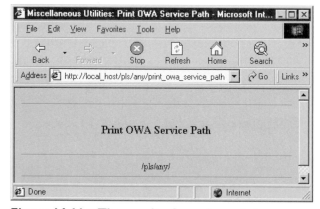

Figure 16.11 ■ **The result of running print_owa_service_path with output from owa_util.get_owa_service_path.**

■ *FOR EXAMPLE*

```
1   htp.p('<FORM NAME="course_form"
2   ACTION="
3   '||owa_util.get_owa_service_path||'
4   current_semester.get_enrollments" METHOD="post">');
```

```
1   htp.p('<TD><INPUT TYPE="button" NAME="student_list"
2   VALUE="Student List" onClick="javascript:window.open(
3   '''||owa_util.get_owa_service_path||'
4   instructor.student_list?p_section_id='
5   ||r_courses.section_id||''', ''student_list'',
6   ''toolbar=no, status=yes, menubar=no,
7   scrollbars=auto, resizable=yes, width=640,
8   height=480''); ">');
```

UNIT
16.4

Be aware that owa_util.get_owa_service_path only retrieves the virtual path of the PL/SQL cartridge that is handling the request. It does not return both the server name/path AND this virtual path. This is yet another reason why it is always a good idea to structure your code to be amenable to the use of relative pathnames whenever possible.

RETURN THE NAME OF A PROCEDURE THAT IS BEING INVOKED BY THE PL/SQL GATEWAY

The *owa_util.get_procedure* function returns the name of the procedure that is being invoked by the PL/SQL agent. The syntax for owa_util.get_procedure is as follows:

```
owa_util.get_procedure RETURN VARCHAR2;
```

This procedure receives no parameters and returns the name of a procedure, including the package name if the procedure is defined in a package. An example of owa_util.get_procedure is illustrated with a small change to the procedure, print_owa_service_path. The additional code outlining owa_util.get_procedure is highlighted in boldface.

■ *FOR EXAMPLE*

```
1   CREATE OR REPLACE PROCEDURE print_owa_service_path
2   AS
3   BEGIN
4   htp.htmlOpen;
5   htp.headOpen;
6   htp.title('Miscellaneous Utilities:  Print OWA
7           Service Path');
8   htp.headClose;
9   htp.bodyOpen(cattributes => 'BGCOLOR="#99CCCC"');
```

```
10   htp.centerOpen;
11   htp.line;
12   htp.header(2, 'Print OWA Service Path');
13   htp.line;
14   htp.p(owa_util.get_owa_service_path);
16   owa_util.signature(owa_util.get_procedure);
17   htp.centerClose;
18   htp.bodyClose;
19   htp.htmlClose;
20   EXCEPTION
21   WHEN OTHERS
22   THEN
23   htp.p('An error occurred:  '||SQLERRM||'.  Please
24           contact Technical Support.');
25   END print_owa_service_path;
26   /
```

Notice that the only difference between the owa_util.signature line in the example above and that used in earlier examples in this chapter is that the parameter fed to owa_util.signature is a call to owa_util.get_procedure. By using owa_util.get_ procedure, you never have to worry about memorizing or mistyping the current procedure name for which you'd like to provide a link that displays the procedure source code. Copy this code example into the text editor of your choice. Save it as `print_owa_service_path.sql` and compile it using SQL*Plus. Invoke it in your Web browser. The result of invoking this newest version of `print_owa_service_ path.sql` should give you a result similar to the one you would receive if you were to include this same call to owa_util.signature as:

```
owa_util.signature('print_owa_service_path');
```

RETURN INFORMATION ABOUT THE CALLING PL/SQL CODE UNIT TO THE CALLED PL/SQL CODE UNIT

The *owa_util.who_called_me* procedure returns information (in the form of output parameters) about the PL/SQL code unit that invoked it. If you are interested in gaining information about Web traffic hits on your pages and you'd like to track user visits to your site, then owa_util.who_called_me can be a very useful method for doing so. The syntax for owa_util.who_called_me is as follows:

```
owa_util.who_called_me(
    owner    OUT VARCHAR2,
    name     OUT VARCHAR2,
    lineno   OUT NUMBER,
    caller_t OUT VARCHAR2);
```

- *owner*—The owner of the program unit.
- *name*—The name of the program unit. This is the name of the pack- age, if the calling program unit is contained within a package, and the

name of the function or procedure if the calling program unit is a standalone function or procedure. If the calling program unit is part of an anonymous block, the value for this parameter is NULL.

- *lineno*—The line number within the program unit where the call was made.

- *caller_t*—The type of program unit that made the call. Possible types are package body, anonymous block function, and procedure. The function and procedure types are returned only for standalone functions and procedures.

You can develop a generic procedure that you call from each procedure. Including owa_util.who_called_me in the generic procedure will tell you which procedure called the generic procedure. An example of owa_util.who_called_me is illustrated in the two following example PL/SQL procedures: *generic_get_who* and *print_get_who*. *generic_get_who* contains the call to owa_util.who_called_me. *print_get_who* places the call to the generic procedure, *generic_get_who*. The code for both calls to *generic_get_who* and *owa_util.who_called_me* are highlighted in boldface.

UNIT 16.4

■ *FOR EXAMPLE*

```
1   CREATE OR REPLACE PROCEDURE print_get_who
2   AS
3   BEGIN
4   htp.htmlOpen;
5   htp.headOpen;
6   htp.title('Miscellaneous Utilities:  Print Get
7            Who');
8   htp.headClose;
9   htp.bodyOpen(cattributes => 'BGCOLOR="#99CCCC"');
10  htp.centerOpen;
11  htp.line;
12  htp.header(2, 'Who Called Me?');
13  htp.line;
14  htp.line;
15  generic_get_who;
16  htp.line;
17  owa_util.signature(owa_util.get_procedure);
18  htp.centerClose;
19  htp.bodyClose;
20  htp.htmlClose;
21  EXCEPTION
22  WHEN OTHERS
23  THEN
24     htp.p('An error occurred:  '||SQLERRM||'.  Please
25            contact Technical Support.');
26  END print_get_who;
27  /
```

```
 1   CREATE OR REPLACE PROCEDURE generic_get_who
 2   AS
 3     v_owner        VARCHAR2(20);
 4     v_name         VARCHAR2(40);
 5     v_lineno       NUMBER;
 6     v_caller_t     VARCHAR2(30);
 7   BEGIN
 8      htp.htmlOpen;
 9      htp.headOpen;
10      htp.title('Miscellaneous SQL Utilities');
11      htp.headClose;
12      htp.bodyOpen(cattributes => 'BGCOLOR="#99CCCC"');
13      htp.centerOpen;
14      owa_util.who_called_me(v_owner, v_name, v_lineno,
15                             v_caller_t);
16      htp.tableOpen;
17      htp.tableOpen();
18      htp.tableRowOpen();
19      htp.p('<TD><FONT FACE="arial"><B>Owner of Program
20            Unit:  </B></FONT></TD>');
21      htp.tableData(v_owner);
22      htp.tableRowClose;
23      htp.tableRowOpen();
24      htp.p('<TD><FONT FACE="arial"><B>Name of Program
25            Unit:  </B></FONT></TD>');
26      htp.tableData(v_name);
27      htp.tableRowClose;
28      htp.tableRowOpen();
29      htp.p('<TD><FONT FACE="arial"><B>Line Number
30            Within the Program Unit:
31            </B></FONT></TD>');
32      htp.tableData(v_lineno);
33      htp.tableRowClose;
34      htp.tableRowOpen();
35      htp.p('<TD><FONT FACE="arial"><B>Type of Program
36            Unit:  </B></FONT></TD>');
37      htp.tableData(v_caller_t);
38      htp.tableRowClose;
39      htp.tableClose;
40      htp.centerClose;
41      htp.bodyClose;
42      htp.htmlClose;
43   EXCEPTION
44   WHEN OTHERS
45   THEN
46      htp.p('An error occurred:  '||SQLERRM||'.  Please
47            contact Technical Support.');
48   END generic_get_who;
49   /
```

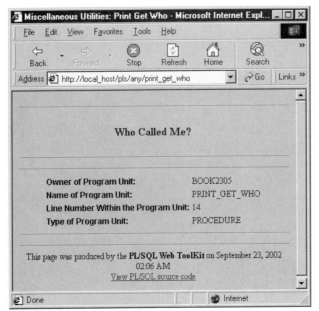

Figure 16.12 ■ **The result of running print_get_who with output from owa_util.who_called_me.**

Copy these code examples into the text editor of your choice. Save each procedure as two separate files, `print_get_who.sql` and `generic_get_who.sql`, respectively. Compile them using SQL*Plus. Invoke `print_get_who` in your Web browser. The result of invoking this procedure should look similar to that shown in Figure 16.12.

C H A P T E R 1 6

BUILDING THE APP

The inclusion of many of these owa_util.* built-in functions/procedures can be found in the completed example application at the companion Web site for this book, located at http://www.phptr.com/boardman/.

Visit the Web site periodically to share and discuss your answers with other readers.

To reduce the coding required for repetitive and often necessary tasks such as obtaining information about CGI environment variables, printing the source of a specified procedure, or creating a calendar in HTML, to name a few, Oracle provides several useful PL/SQL built-in utilities. Many of these utilities are included in the OWA_UTIL package and can be included in your Web page procedures to assist in debugging, enhancing, or maintaining your Web pages. Subsequent chapters introduce and explain some of the other PL/SQL built-in packaged procedures/functions (like OWA_COOKIE, OWA_IMAGE, OWA_SEC, OWA_CACHE, and more) available to further assist you in enhancing your Web sites/pages.

Take a moment to include a call to owa_util.signature(owa_util.get_procedure) in every packaged procedure or standalone procedure you have created thus far. Remember, your PSPs are standalone procedures. Therefore, include them when considering which procedures you need to add this line of code to. You are also encouraged to add functionality for any of the other utilities you learned about in this chapter to your existing procedures as well.

C H A P T E R   1 7

TROUBLESHOOTING

Troubleshooting is one of the most valuable skills for a programmer, yet perhaps the last skill to be learned in many cases. Knowing how to find and fix a problem with code is best learned from experience. There are some tips, however, which will help in this learning process, and some common pitfalls that can be avoided with a little warning.

By now you should have successfully called a PL/SQL procedure from the browser, and viewed the HTML/JavaScript output successfully. If you need to review 9iAS configuration and URL syntax, refer to Chapters 1–3, as well as Chapter 10, "Web Toolkit I: HTML and JavaScript with PL/SQL." This chapter discusses how to solve problems beyond the basics discussed in the aforementioned chapters.

When developing with 9iAS, be sure that it is configured to display error messages. The default configuration for 9iAS is to display a user-friendly, nonspecific error message when an error occurs in the application. The user-friendly message is a "404 Page cannot be found" message. This is not useful for a programmer in development mode. The application server can be configured to display useful error messages instead of the generic 404 error. For details on how to do this please refer to Chapter 2, "Oracle 9iAS." Once the application moves out of development mode, then the application server should be configured to display the user-friendly message.

This chapter presents some general advice on how to code and debug code. The focus, however, is on Web Toolkit procedures rather than PL/SQL Server Pages (PSPs). PSPs present unique coding considerations. Please refer to Chapter 12, "Working with PL/SQL Server Pages (PSPs)," for details on coding and debugging a PSP.

UNIT 17.1

USE GOOD CODING AND DEBUGGING PRACTICES

APPROACH TO CODING

Coding is a process with a beginning, middle, and end. An application is not coded in one sitting and then compiled. It is an iterative process in which smaller components of the larger whole are built first. These components are added to and integrated within the application. Think of coding an application as building it layer by layer. Experienced programmers develop an approach to coding that incorporates testing and debugging at each step.

CODE PIECE BY PIECE

A good general rule to follow when coding is to develop the code piece by piece. In other words, start from a basic code structure and build on the code one piece at a time, compiling and testing the code at each stage. By doing this it is much easier to pinpoint the origin of an error message.

As an example, the *instructor_list_info* procedure, created in Exercise 11.3, is created piece by piece until finished. First, begin with the outline needed for a PL/SQL procedure. NULL is a placeholder.

■ *FOR EXAMPLE*

```
CREATE OR REPLACE PROCEDURE instructor_list_info
IS

BEGIN
  NULL;
EXCEPTION
WHEN OTHERS
```

```
THEN
    htp.p('An error occurred:  '||SQLERRM||'.  Please try again
    later.');
END instructor_list_info;
/
```

Save this procedure as a .sql file and compile it. It should compile with no errors. This creates the basis for the procedure. Although the procedure doesn't do anything at this point, it provides a basis to which more complex code can be added. Next, add the HTML code.

In many cases, a Web application developer is given the HTML code from a Web designer. In this situation it is advisable to use htp.p or PSPs rather than attempting to convert the HTML into Web Toolkit procedures such as htp.form().

■ FOR EXAMPLE

```
CREATE OR REPLACE PROCEDURE instructor_list_class
IS

BEGIN
htp.p('<HTML>');
htp.p('<HEAD>');
htp.p('<TITLE>Instructor Maintenance Web Site</TITLE>');
htp.p('</HEAD>');
htp.p('<BODY BgColor="#99CCCC">');
htp.p('<CENTER>');
htp.p('<H2>List of Instructors</H2>');
htp.p('<TABLE ALIGN="center" BORDER="3" BORDERCOLOR="midnight blue"
        CELLPADDING="5" WIDTH="100%">');
htp.p('<TR>');
htp.p('<TH ALIGN="center">Instructor Names</TH>');
htp.p('</TR>');
htp.p('<TR>');
htp.p('<TD><FONT FACE="Arial"><A HREF="">
Last Name 1, First Name</A></FONT></TD>');
htp.p('</TR>');
htp.p('<TR>');
htp.p('<TD><FONT FACE="Arial"><A HREF="">
Last Name 2, First Name</A></FONT></TD>');
htp.p('</TR>');
htp.p('<TR>');
htp.p('<TD><FONT FACE="Arial"><A HREF="">
Last Name 3, First Name</A></FONT></TD>');
htp.p('</TR>');

htp.p('</TABLE>');
htp.p('</CENTER>');
```

```
htp.p('</BODY>');
htp.p('</HTML>');
EXCEPTION
WHEN OTHERS
THEN
   htp.p('An error occurred:  '||SQLERRM||'.  Please try again
   later.');
END instructor_list_class;
/
```

Compile the procedure again until it compiles with no errors. It is now viewable in a Web browser. Open up a Web browser and view the procedure. Notice that "dummy" data is put in the place of data to be selected from the database, that is, "Last Name 1, First Name," et al. for the instructor's name.

Now we are ready to add PL/SQL code to select data from the database. For this page, the first name, last name, and instructor ID is needed. The first name and last name columns are used for display, and the instructor ID is used to create the hyperlink to the classes page.

It is good practice to write SQL statements in SQL*Plus first and confirm that the result set is the desired data.

■ FOR EXAMPLE

```
SQL>   SELECT first_name, last_name, instructor_id
  2        FROM instructor
  3   ORDER BY last_name, first_name;

FIRST_NAME        LAST_NAME         INSTRUCTOR_ID
---------------   ---------------   -------------
Rick              Chow                        109
Marilyn           Frantzen                    107
Fernand           Hanks                       101
Charles           Lowry                       108
Anita             Morris                      105
Gary              Pertez                      104
Nina              Schorin                     103
Todd              Smythe                      106
Irene             Willig                      110
Tom               Wojick                      102

10 rows selected.
```

In this case, the Select statement is straightforward. When the Select statement is more complex, or when looping through multiple Select statements, then it is more important to confirm the result sets being returned.

Place the Select statement above in a cursor and compile the procedure.

■ *FOR EXAMPLE*

```
CREATE OR REPLACE PROCEDURE instructor_list_class
IS
    CURSOR get_instructor IS
        SELECT first_name, last_name, instructor_id
          FROM instructor
      ORDER BY last_name, first_name;

BEGIN
htp.p('<HTML>');
htp.p('<HEAD>');
htp.p('<TITLE>Instructor Maintenance Web Site</TITLE>');
htp.p('</HEAD>');
htp.p('<BODY BgColor="#99CCCC">');
htp.p('<CENTER>');
htp.p('<H2>List of Instructors</H2>');
htp.p('<TABLE ALIGN="center" BORDER="3" BORDERCOLOR="midnight blue"
      CELLPADDING="5" WIDTH="100%">');
htp.p('<TR>');
htp.p('<TH ALIGN="center">Instructor Names</TH>');
htp.p('</TR>');
htp.p('<TR>');
htp.p('<TD><FONT FACE="Arial"><A HREF="">
Last Name 1, First Name</A></FONT></TD>');
htp.p('</TR>');
htp.p('<TR>');
htp.p('<TD><FONT FACE="Arial"><A HREF="">
Last Name 2, First Name</A></FONT></TD>');
htp.p('</TR>');
htp.p('<TR>');
htp.p('<TD><FONT FACE="Arial"><A HREF="">
Last Name 3, First Name</A></FONT></TD>');
htp.p('</TR>');
htp.p('</TABLE>');
htp.p('</CENTER>');
htp.p('</BODY>');
htp.p('</HTML>');

EXCEPTION
WHEN OTHERS
THEN
   htp.p('An error occurred:  '||SQLERRM||'.  Please try again
   later.');
END instructor_list_class;
/
```

Finally, take the data in the cursor and use it to display the instructor's first and last name as a hyperlink. The hyperlink calls instruct_classes and passes the instructor ID to it, which displays classes taught by that instructor. A loop statement is used to loop over the data and create the table rows.

■ FOR EXAMPLE

```
CREATE OR REPLACE PROCEDURE instructor_list_class
IS
    CURSOR get_instructor IS
        SELECT first_name, last_name, instructor_id
        FROM instructor
        ORDER BY last_name, first_name;
BEGIN
htp.p('<HTML>');
htp.p('<HEAD>');
htp.p('<TITLE>Instructor Maintenance Web Site</TITLE>');
htp.p('</HEAD>');
htp.p('<BODY BgColor="#99CCCC">');
htp.p('<CENTER>');
htp.p('<H2>List of Instructors</H2>');
htp.p('<TABLE ALIGN="center" BORDER="3" BORDERCOLOR="midnight blue"
        CELLPADDING="5" WIDTH="100%">');
htp.p('<TR>');
htp.p('<TH ALIGN="center">Instructor Names</TH>');
htp.p('</TR>');
FOR rec IN get_instructor
LOOP
htp.p('<TR>');
htp.p('<TD><FONT FACE="Arial">
<A HREF="instruct_classes?p_instructor_id='
   ||rec.instructor_id||'">'
   ||rec.last_name||', '||rec.first_name||'
</A></FONT></TD>');
htp.p('</TR>');
END LOOP;
htp.p('</TABLE>');
htp.p('</CENTER>');
htp.p('</BODY>');
EXCEPTION
WHEN OTHERS
THEN
   htp.p('An error occurred:  '||SQLERRM||'.  Please try again
   later.');
END instructor_list_class;
/
```

Notice that before adding the Loop statement there were three rows with dummy data. Those three rows are replaced with one row and PL/SQL variables.

 This procedure will compile with no errors even if the procedure "instruct_ classes" does not exist. This is contrary to PL/SQL procedures that do not contain Web Toolkit procedures. A call in a procedure to another procedure or package that does not exist or is invalid will cause that procedure to fail upon compiling. In this case, the procedure will compile because the nonexistent or invalid procedure reference is part of the string that prints out to the HTML page and not part of a PL/SQL statement outside of the Toolkit procedure htp.p(). An error will be generated only upon clicking that hyperlink once the HTML document has loaded into the Web browser.

TAKE A BREAK

If there is a bug in your code and you are having a difficult time finding the source of the problem, it is a good practice to get up from your computer and take a break. Sometimes the source of the problem is something very simple, which a fresh mind and pair of eyes will easily find. Many times the problem is something as simple as a misspelled variable name or a missing semi-colon.

When debugging, look at all of the code with a critical eye; don't quickly pass over a block of code assuming that it is bug-free. Stepping away for a moment can help clear away preconceptions so that you can look at code clearly again.

UNIT 17.2

DISTINGUISH ERROR MESSAGES

PL/SQL VS. JAVASCRIPT VS. HTML ERRORS

When something goes wrong, the first step is to identify which type of error you are seeing. The error could result from PL/SQL code, or from JavaScript, or from HTML code. It might even result from these errors working together.

You have two kinds of source code to look at:

1. Source code for the PL/SQL procedure
2. Source code for the HTML page (generated by the PL/SQL procedure)

Line numbers are different in the PL/SQL and in the HTML source code. Keep this in mind when you see an error message. PL/SQL error messages give line numbers that correspond to the PL/SQL procedure. JavaScript errors are generated by the browser, and if a line number is given in the error message, it corresponds to a line in the HTML page source.

IDENTIFYING PL/SQL ERRORS

PL/SQL code may generate errors at two points. Typically, PL/SQL compilation errors are encountered first, because the first step in creating a Web Toolkit page is to compile a PL/SQL procedure. When the procedure is being compiled with the CREATE OR REPLACE command, it will not compile if it has invalid PL/SQL syntax.

A procedure that compiles with errors will be invalid, and will not be accessible through a browser. If a procedure is not accessible through a browser, it is a good idea to check that the procedure is compiled. Although the procedure itself might not have been changed, it might be dependent upon another object that did change, such as a table that had columns added to it or a package of constants used by the procedure. In that case, simply recompile the procedure.

Recall that if there are errors in the HTML and JavaScript, such as missing closing tags or a misspelled attribute name, those HTML and JavaScript errors will not raise an error at the time the PL/SQL procedure is compiled. Within the PL/SQL procedure, the HTML and JavaScript are simply literal strings, included in htp or htf procedures. Only PL/SQL syntax is checked.

As you know from working with PL/SQL, even if a PL/SQL procedure compiles, it may not work the way you expect. You can also experience PL/SQL errors when the procedure is called by the browser. In generating the page, there might be a PL/SQL error, such as no data being found, or a variable being populated with a value that is too large or of the wrong datatype. PL/SQL programs should always include an EXCEPTION section that catches these errors. The error message can be shown on the screen by using htp.p, as shown in earlier chapters.

Tips on dealing with specific PL/SQL error messages can be found in this chapter in Unit 17.3, "Find and Debug PL/SQL Errors."

IDENTIFYING JAVASCRIPT ERRORS

The next errors you might encounter are JavaScript errors, since the browser provides clear error messages when there is a JavaScript error.

Once PL/SQL generates a page, the page is sent to the browser. The browser reads the page and tries to render it on the screen. This is when the JavaScript is first read for accuracy. If there are problems with the JavaScript syntax, such as missing closing curly braces, then an error message will be raised as the page is loaded.

JavaScript errors can also be raised in response to events on the screen. Suppose that a button on a screen has an "onClick" event handler associated with it. The event handler calls a JavaScript function, called "validateForm," which the programmer created earlier in the HTML page. If validateForm is expecting an input parameter, and that parameter is not sent in the function call, then an error could be raised at that point. Likewise, the information sent to the function may not be what is expected; it could be a variable that happens to be NULL, or a DOM element that is not specified correctly. So when the JavaScript function works with this parameter, it may not find what it expects and an error may be raised.

Debugging JavaScript and PL/SQL is similar in this way. With PL/SQL, first the code is checked for syntax at the time the PL/SQL code is compiled. Then when it is run, real data is used and unforeseen errors can occur. Likewise, when the HTML page containing JavaScript functions is loaded, any JavaScript functions are checked for accurate syntax as the page is initially rendered by the browser. Then, when JavaScript functions are called, they are basically being "run" and further errors can occur.

Remember that the line numbers you see in a JavaScript error message refer to lines in the HTML page's source code, not lines in the PL/SQL procedure. The browser works with the HTML page source code. The browser never sees the PL/SQL code; the browser has no way to tell what the line numbers are in the original PL/SQL procedure that generated the page. An HTML listing of 20 students might have been generated by a PL/SQL loop, but the browser never knows this; the browser receives a document with a list of 20 students, and renders it. The browser only receives the output from the procedure after it has run.

Tips on debugging JavaScript can be found in this chapter, in Unit 17.4, "Find and Debug JavaScript Errors."

IDENTIFYING HTML ERRORS

Browsers do not display error messages when they render invalid HTML.

Browsers can be very forgiving. In fact, poorly written HTML is very common, because browsers tend to compensate for coders' mistakes. Browsers will try to display what they receive, and have been coded to work around programmers' mistakes as much as possible. If there are invalid tags, or attributes that are incorrect, the browser tries to fill in the gaps and display what it can, ignoring what it cannot understand. A page that includes no <HTML> tags will still be rendered in the browser, even though it is terrible form to leave them out.

You will know that you have an HTML error because the page simply does not display the way you want; for example, a table might be off-kilter.

Another way to identify an HTML error is by process of elimination; if you are not dealing with a PL/SQL error, and a JavaScript error is not raised, then look at the HTML code.

Tips on common HTML errors can be found in this chapter in Unit 17.5, "Find and Debug HTML Errors."

UNIT 17.3

FIND AND DEBUG PL/SQL ERRORS

HOW TO FIND AND DEBUG PL/SQL ERRORS

PL/SQL errors can occur either during compilation, or when viewing the output from a successfully compiled PL/SQL procedure or package in a Web browser. Errors on compile always result in an error message, so you have immediate feedback. Errors when viewing the output from your code in a Web browser can result in one of two types of errors:

1. An explicit error message.
2. No error message is generated but the code does not do what it is supposed to do.

This second type of error can be more elusive to pinpoint and debug.

ERRORS ON COMPILE

Compilation errors always generate an error message. A procedure/package will not compile if the correct syntax and keywords are not used, for instance.

When you encounter a compilation error and you are using a development tool, it may take you directly to the source of the error. If you are compiling in SQL*Plus, you may see an error message such as this:

```
Warning: Procedure created with compilation errors.
```

To find out where and what the errors are, type show errors at the SQL*Plus prompt, or use this shorthand:

```
sho err
```

You will see a list of errors and their line numbers. The error code should be looked up in Oracle's documentation. The line number corresponds to line numbers in the PL/SQL procedure. To view the entire procedure with line numbers, simply type the letter l. To see the text of a specific line, just type letter l followed by the desired line number. The example below displays line 14. Remember to use the letter l, not a number 1.

```
l 14
```

Below are some of the most common errors that will generate a compilation error.

SYNTACTICAL ERRORS

Syntactical errors are things like missing semi-colons or keywords. Another common error is to misspell PL/SQL keywords. These mistakes are easy to make and hard to find.

Below are some examples of the error messages generated for selected syntactical errors.

SINGLE QUOTE QUAGMIRE   The single quote below is not correctly escaped:

```
...htp.p('<TH ALIGN="center">Instructor's Names</TH>');
```

Produces this error message:

```
SQL> sho errors
Errors for PROCEDURE INSTRUCTOR_LIST_CLASS:
LINE/COL ERROR
-------- ----------------------------------------------------
18/38    PLS-00103: Encountered the symbol "S" when
         expecting one of the following:
         . ( ) , * @ % & | = - + < / > at in is mod not
         range rem => .. <an exponent (**)> <> or != or ~=
         >= <= <> and or like as between from using ||
SQL>
```

This is the corrected code:

```
...htp.p('<TH ALIGN="center">Instructor''s Names</TH>');
```

MISSING PL/SQL KEYWORDS—END LOOP   The keywords "END LOOP" are missing.

```
...
FOR rec IN get_instructor
LOOP
htp.p('<TR>');
```

```
htp.p('<TD><FONT FACE="Arial">
<A HREF="instruct_classes?p_instructor_id='
  ||rec.instructor_id||'">'
  ||rec.last_name||', '||rec.first_name||'
</A></FONT></TD>');
htp.p('</TR>');
htp.p('</TABLE>');
htp.p('</CENTER>');
htp.p('</BODY>');
EXCEPTION
...
```

Produces this error message:

```
SQL> sho errors
Errors for PROCEDURE INSTRUCTOR_LIST_CLASS:
LINE/COL ERROR
-------- -----------------------------------------------------
32/1     PLS-00103: Encountered the symbol "EXCEPTION" when
         expecting one of the following:
         begin case declare end exit for goto if loop mod
         null pragma raise return select update while with
         <an identifier> <a double-quoted delimited-
         identifier> <a bind variable> <<close current
         delete fetch lock insert open rollback
         savepoint set sql execute commit forall merge
         <a single-quoted SQL string> pipe
37/0     PLS-00103: Encountered the symbol "end-of-file"
         when expecting one of the following:
LINE/COL ERROR
-------- -----------------------------------------------------
         begin function package pragma procedure form
SQL>
```

MISSING PL/SQL KEYWORDS—CREATE OR REPLACE   A common mistake often occurs when converting a PSP page into a PL/SQL procedure. Since a PSP page is converted into a PL/SQL procedure when stored in the database, it is easy enough to copy that code into a text editor and save it with a .sql extension. Be careful when doing this. The PL/SQL keywords "CREATE OR REPLACE" are missing. The code as stored in the database begins like this:

```
PROCEDURE instructor_list_class
```

This will not compile and produces this error message:

```
PROCEDURE instructor_list_class
*
ERROR at line 1:
ORA-00900: invalid SQL statement
```

This is the corrected code:

```
CREATE OR REPLACE PROCEDURE INSTRUCTOR_LIST_CLASS
   ...
```

MISSING ENDING SEMI-COLON The ending semi-colon has been left off in this example.

```
htp.p('<H2>List of Instructors</H2>')
htp.p('<TABLE>');
```

Produces this error message:

```
SQL> sho errors
Errors for PROCEDURE INSTRUCTOR_LIST_CLASS:
LINE/COL ERROR
-------- -------------------------------------------------
19/1     PLS-00103: Encountered the symbol "HTP" when
         expecting one of the following:
         := . ( % ;
         The symbol ":=" was substituted for "HTP" to
         continue.
```

CALLING AN INVALID OR NONEXISTENT PROCEDURE OR PACKAGE

Calling an invalid or nonexistent procedure from within a procedure generates an error message when compiling. In Exercise 11.2.1, the instructor information is updated and the instructor personal information is displayed with the update information as well as a confirmation message.

■ *FOR EXAMPLE*

```
...
htp.p('<HTML>
  <HEAD><TITLE>Update Instructor Personal Info</TITLE></HEAD>
  <BODY>');
htp.script('alert("The new information for this instructor
  has been saved successfully!");', 'JavaScript');
htp.p('</BODY>
  </HTML>');

instruct_personal_info(p_instructor_id);

htp.script('document.write("<H3><CENTER><FONT COLOR=RED>The new
  information for this instructor has been successfully
  saved!</FONT></CENTER></H3>");', 'JavaScript');
```

```
EXCEPTION
WHEN OTHERS THEN
   htp.p('An error occurred:  '||SQLERRM||'.  Please try again
   later.');
END update_instructor;
```

If the procedure "instruct_personal_info" were invalid or did not exist, then the following error message would be generated when attempting to compile this procedure:

UNIT 17.3

```
SQL> sho errors
Errors for PROCEDURE update_instructor:
LINE/COL ERROR
-------- ----------------------------------------------------------
33/1     PLS-00201: identifier 'INSTRUCT_PERSONAL_INFO' must
         be declared
33/1     PL/SQL: Statement ignored
SQL>
```

ERRORS WHEN VIEWING (OR EXECUTING) A PROCEDURE VIA A WEB BROWSER

Even though a procedure/package successfully compiles, there still may be problems with the code. Compiling is only the first hurdle to overcome. Compiling treats the procedure as isolated and singular, whereas viewing that same procedure in the Web browser requires that it be integrated within the Web application and the other procedures with which it must function. There are many parts that must work together: HTML, JavaScript, and PL/SQL, in more than one procedure. Plus, procedures can call other procedures and pass parameters to them. The HTML form elements must be coordinated with the IN parameters of the called procedure.

As stated earlier in this unit, there are two types of errors when viewing or executing a procedure via the Web browser:

1. An explicit error message.
2. Code logic mistakes where no error message is generated, that is, the code does not do what it is supposed to do.

EXPLICIT ERROR MESSAGES

Below are some common explicit error messages generated when viewing a procedure through a Web browser. These errors often occur when the user clicks on a hyperlink, which calls another procedure and passes parameters to it.

FORM PARAMETER MISMATCH   The form parameter mismatch error message appears like this:

```
ORA-06550: line 7, column 2:
PLS-00306: wrong number or types of arguments in call to 'MY_PROCEDURE'
ORA-06550: line 7, column 2:
PL/SQL: Statement ignored

  DAD name: any
  PROCEDURE  : MY_PROCEDURE
  USER       : SMORSE
  URL        : http://your_server/pls/any/MY_PROCEDURE
  PARAMETERS :
  ============
  ID:
   1
```

A form parameter mismatch error occurs when the values submitted in a form to the processing procedure do not match exactly in number and name. The processing procedure must have IN parameters that correspond to each incoming name/value pair. The name of the form element must also match the name of the corresponding IN parameter of the processing procedure.

A common mistake is to name the submit or reset button. In most cases the buttons hold no significance worth passing to the processing procedure, but it has been named by accident (or not accidentally but explicitly by an HTML editing program). If there is no corresponding IN parameter to handle the incoming button data, then an error occurs. To correct, simply remove the NAME attribute from the button tag.

In the example above, a name/value pair of 'ID=1' is being passed to MY_PROCEDURE that has not been declared as an IN parameter in that procedure. To correct this error, either do not pass ID to MY_PROCEDURE, or declare ID as an IN parameter in MY_PROCEDURE.

CODE LOGIC ERRORS

Code logic errors are errors that cause the application to behave in ways that are not intended. These errors can include faulty IF clause tests, variables not being set or set with the wrong value, and mishandling of loops, among others. These types of errors are harder to debug. Here are some tips on how to approach debugging this type of error.

DISPLAY DEBUGGING MESSAGES   There are two ways to display debugging messages in the HTML document:

1. Display SQLERRM error messages.
2. Display variables using htp.p/htp.script or <%= variable %>.

These allow you to see what's happening on the back end. SQLERRM is a function that returns the error message associated with the Oracle error. Use

SQLERRM in the EXCEPTION clause of a Web Toolkit procedure, or in the error page associated with a PSP. Since SQLERRM is a function, then an expression directive must be used in a PSP error page, that is, <%= SQLERRM %>.

For Web Toolkit procedures, htp.p and htp.script can be used to display variables that are not meant for display, such as primary keys. For PSP pages, display variables using the expression directive: <%= variable %>. A coder can confirm whether the variable is being set, and if so, whether it's being set with the correct value.

Variables used specifically for debugging can be set at different levels of the code to confirm that that block of code is being accessed. This is especially useful in verifying tests used in IF statements.

HANDLE LOOPS PROPERLY   Loops are an important tool in the creation of Web pages using data from a database. They allow the Web developer to loop over selected database rows and dynamically create drop-down lists or tables for the display of that information. Loops, however, present special problems, and a Web developer should be prepared to deal with them. The worst mistake that can be made with loops is the infinite loop.

Infinite loops occur when the loop's exit condition never equals true. This means that the loop keeps repeating forever. This can create grave performance problems on the database server, causing a large percentage of the memory resources to be utilized by the infinite loop. There should be an exit condition for the loop always.

There are other situations that you should consider, too, when writing loops. Your code should be able to handle the situations where no rows are returned, exactly one row is returned, or more than one row is returned. Take the example of a search page. If only one row is returned by the search, then the details of that search result should be displayed. If no rows are found, then a message should be displayed to the user. If more than one record matches the search, then an intermediate page that lists a column of the result set as a hyperlink should be displayed, similar to the page you create in Chapter 12, "Working with PL/SQL Server Pages (PSPs)." Only in the case of more than one row being returned should the loop logic ever be employed.

RUN CURSORS AS SQL IN PL/SQL   It is good practice to always check result sets of SQL statements in a tool such as SQL*Plus. This allows you to verify the result set being returned before using it in a procedure. Take the example of a nested loop where you want to create a table that lists every course in the COURSE table, and for each course you want to list its sections. This action requires a nested loop. The outer loop loops over each course and the inner loop loops over the sections for the current course in the outer loop. If either loop's result sets returns the wrong or undesired data, then the resulting table will not be accurate. For example, if the outer loop cursor contains duplicate course rows, then the number of duplicate rows in the outer loop will be multiplied by the number of sections. This can result in a very large and meaningless table. To correct, check the join clause, among others, of the outer loop.

DATA MANIPULATION LANGUAGE

Data Manipulation Language (DML) commands within PL/SQL procedures can present problems of their own. When inserting/updating the database with user input, the data should be validated to account for table column definitions, check constraints, and integrity constraints. Validation can be done on the front-end using JavaScript and HTML form elements, or on the back-end using PL/SQL. Use front-end and back-end validation to ensure that "clean" data is being used in the DML statement. It is important that the data used in a DML command does not cause an error.

INSERT/UPDATE CONSIDERATIONS   The length and type of data being inserted/updated should match the datatype column definition. If a column is defined as a Number, then do not try to insert text into that column. JavaScript validation can be helpful here; for example, it can validate that a "Quantity" field contains numbers only so that no errors are caused by attempting to insert a character into a number field in the database.

Also, be aware of the length allowed by a column. A column defined as VarChar2(10) will not allow a string that is 11 characters long; an error will occur. Integrity constraints also must be considered. If you try to insert a foreign key that does not exist in the primary key table, then an integrity constraint error message will be generated. This type of error is usually avoided by controlling that column's data with a drop-down list. For example, in the instructor's address form, the zipcode is a drop-down list. The user is not allowed to select a zipcode for insertion into the instructor table that does not already exist in the zipcode table.

If a column is defined as NOT NULL, then make sure a value is provided for it when inserting a new record. JavaScript validation can help with this by checking that required fields are filled in by the user.

Remember that primary key values should never be updateable in a form.

DELETE CONSIDERATIONS   When deleting data, it is important to know whether Delete Cascade has been defined as part of the foreign key. If so, then you only need to issue the Delete command on the parent table. Delete Cascade will cause the foreign key rows to be deleted, too. If not, then you have to first delete the child rows before deleting the rows in the parent table.

Rather than deleting the record, you might include a Status column that lets you flag the record as inactive. The application can be coded to only retrieve active records for a user.

COMMITS AND ROLLBACKS   Always issue a commit after a DML command. Failure to issue a commit often results in the user not being able to view a new record just added, or to see updates. Since the DML was not committed, then the application will not be able to see the changed data.

GRANT PERMISSIONS

If you are running your own procedures, you will have access to them. Procedures and packages that you create will be part of your own schema, so you have permission to run them. If you try to run another user's code, however, you may have a problem. Your user ID must either have DBA-level privileges to run any procedure—which certainly most users will not have—or you must have been granted permission to execute the procedure. Likewise, if you want other users to view your pages, you will need to grant them permission to execute these procedures.

If a user Carl tried to access a procedure owned by Mary, and Mary has not granted him access to it, he would see an error. Depending on the configuration of the server, it could be a cryptic "Page Not Found" or "Request Failed" error. If the server is configured to show more developer-friendly error messages, he might see the following error in the browser.

■ FOR EXAMPLE

```
ORA-06550: line 7, column 2:
PLS-00201: identifier 'MARY.INSTRUCT_PERSONAL_INFO' must be declared
ORA-06550: line 7, column 2:
PL/SQL: Statement ignored
   DAD name: any
   PROCEDURE   : mary.instruct_personal_info
   USER        : carl
   URL         :
http://server4:80/pls/any/mary.instruct_personal_info
   PARAMETERS :
   ============
```

If Mary wants to grant Carl permission to execute the procedure instruct_personal_info, the syntax is:

```
grant execute on instruct_personal_info to carl;
```

After Mary issues this command, the user Carl is permitted to run the procedure instruct_personal_info.

How can you verify which objects the user Carl can access? One way is to check Oracle's Data Dictionary. The Data Dictionary view user_objects includes the objects that Carl owns. The view all_objects includes the objects Carl owns, as well as the objects that Carl has been granted access to by other users. Issue a DESCRIBE command on this view to see what information is available.

■ *FOR EXAMPLE*

```
SQL> describe all_objects;
Name                             Null?     Type
-------------------------------- --------- ----
OWNER                            NOT NULL  VARCHAR2(30)
OBJECT_NAME                      NOT NULL  VARCHAR2(30)
SUBOBJECT_NAME                             VARCHAR2(30)
OBJECT_ID                        NOT NULL  NUMBER
DATA_OBJECT_ID                             NUMBER
OBJECT_TYPE                                VARCHAR2(18)
CREATED                          NOT NULL  DATE
LAST_DDL_TIME                    NOT NULL  DATE
TIMESTAMP                                  VARCHAR2(19)
STATUS                                     VARCHAR2(7)
TEMPORARY                                  VARCHAR2(1)
GENERATED                                  VARCHAR2(1)
SECONDARY                                  VARCHAR2(1)
```

Using the columns in this view, you can find out which objects you can access. If you are logged in as Carl, you could see all of the procedures accessible by Carl, as well as those owned by other users who have granted him privileges on these objects. The following list shows that Mary owns the procedure instruct_ personal_info, but it appears here because Carl can access it.

■ *FOR EXAMPLE*

```
SQL> SELECT owner, object_type, object_name
  2    FROM all_objects
  3    WHERE object_type in ('PROCEDURE','PACKAGE')
  4    ORDER BY owner, object_type, object_name;
```

OWNER	OBJECT_TYPE	OBJECT_NAME
CARL	PACKAGE	RESTAURANTS
CARL	PROCEDURE	GET_RESTAURANTS
CARL	PROCEDURE	VIEW_RESTAURANTS
MARY	PROCEDURE	INSTRUCT_PERSONAL_INFO
MARY	PROCEDURE	INSTRUCTOR_LIST_INFO
MARY	PROCEDURE	STUDENT_LIST

PREFIX WITH SCHEMA NAME

There is another reason you might see a "Page Not Found" error. Suppose Carl wants to run Mary's procedure student_list, and he attempts to access the following URL:

```
http://www.server4.virgil.edu/pls/any/student_list
```

Carl would receive an error message saying that the page is not found, or that the request failed.

■ *FOR EXAMPLE*

```
ORA-06550: line 7, column 2:
PLS-00201: identifier 'STUDENT_LIST' must be declared
ORA-06550: line 7, column 2:
PL/SQL: Statement ignored
  DAD name: any
  PROCEDURE  : student_list
  USER       : carl
  URL        : http://server4:80/pls/any/student_list
  PARAMETERS :
  ============
```

Yet, Carl double-checks the spelling, and knows that he typed in the name "student_list" correctly. Carl has also verified that Mary has granted him execute privileges on this procedure. Why isn't he seeing the page?

The reason is that Carl does not own a procedure called student_list. Even though the user Mary has granted Carl execute privileges on this procedure, Carl cannot run it without specifying the owner:

```
http://www.server4.virgil.edu/pls/any/mary.student_list
```

Prefixing the owner of the object in every URL can be cumbersome. How can Carl be allowed to use the first URL above? A solution is to create a synonym for the object mary.student_list. This may be done two ways. Carl could create a synonym, within his own schema, that lets him refer to mary.student_list as simply student_list. This would be a private synonym, available only to Carl; other users would have to create the same synonym for themselves:

```
create synonym student_list for mary.student_list;
```

Also, Mary could create a public synonym for mary.student_list, so that any user granted access to mary.student_list could refer to it as either mary.student_list, or simply student_list:

```
create public synonym student_list for student_list;
```

Public synonyms are useful for a procedure that is used to enter a site, such as a splash page. If Carl's site has a procedure called "home" that everyone will access, it would be a good idea to create a public synonym for home, so that users can refer to it as home instead of carl.home. The initial URL for a Web site should be as simple as possible, since it may need to be typed in the first time a user visits it.

UNIT 17.4

FIND AND DEBUG
JAVASCRIPT ERRORS

CONFIGURE YOUR BROWSER
TO SHOW JAVASCRIPT ERRORS

Set your browser's preferences to alert you when there is a JavaScript error. You may have seen alert windows pop up as you browse through other sites on the Web, or as you have worked on your own JavaScript code. Refer to Chapter 7, "Introduction to JavaScript," for instructions on how to set your browser preferences to give you more information about JavaScript errors.

MAKE USE OF JAVASCRIPT ALERTS

JavaScript alerts are a handy way to find out the value of an object or parameter or to see what the value of a form object is. Once you have found out what you need to know, delete any extra alerts from your code.

Figure 17.1 is an example of an alert generated by the browser when a JavaScript error is encountered.

In this example, the error was raised because JavaScript did not find a value for the object, document.instructor_personal_form.P_zip.value. The procedure that generated this error is the instruct_personal_info procedure, from Chapter 11, "Web Toolkit II: Frames, Forms, and Parameters"—with a mistake added.

To debug this, you can use a series of alerts to find out which part of the object is invalid:

```
htp.script('alert(document.instructor_personal_form)');
htp.script('alert(document.instructor_personal_form.P_zip)');
htp.script('alert(document.instructor_personal_form.p_zip)');
htp.script('alert(document.instructor_personal_form.p_zip.value)');
```

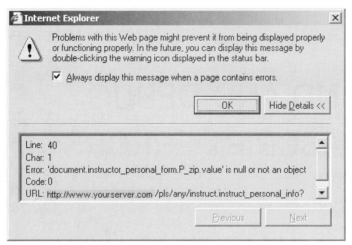

Figure 17.1 ■ Sample JavaScript error message.

Figure 17.2 ■ Alert that indicates the presence of an object.

Figure 17.3 ■ Alert that indicates an object is undefined and does not exist.

Figure 17.4 ■ Alert verifying that document.instructor_personal_form.p_zip exists.

Figure 17.5 ■ **Alert showing value of document.instructor_personal_ form.p_zip.value.**

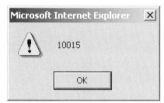

Figure 17.6 ■ **Alert showing value of JavaScript variable theZip.**

Figure 17.7 ■ **Alert showing value of JavaScript variable theZip plus an identifier.**

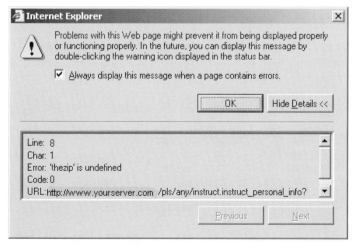

Figure 17.8 ■ **JavaScript error generated by a reference to an undefined JavaScript variable.**

The first alert should display document.instructor_personal_form. Since this is simply an object, there is no value to display, so the alert in Figure 17.2 appears.

The second alert should show document.instructor_personal_form.P_zip. This is not a valid object, so the alert in Figure 17.3 appears that indicates the object is invalid.

The third alert should display document.instructor_personal_form.p_zip. The difference between this alert and the alert for Figure 17.2 is that p_zip is not capitalized. Remember, JavaScript is case-sensitive. When p_zip is used instead of P_zip, the form object was found, as shown in Figure 17.4.

The final alert shows document.instructor_personal_form.p_zip.value. This alert should display the actual value of the form element, as shown in Figure 17.5. In this case, the value is 10015, but if it were NULL, or perhaps something unexpected like a person's name, then that would be useful to know.

JavaScript alerts can also show you the value of any JavaScript variables. Suppose the function, checkZipcode, creates a JavaScript variable called theZip, and assigns the value of document.instructor_personal_form.p_zip.value to theZip:

```
htp.script('

function checkZipcode(){
theZip = document.instructor_personal_form.p_zip.value;
alert(theZip);
}

');
```

A simple call to this function would be written as follows:

```
htp.script('checkZipcode();');
```

The alert in the checkZipcode function shows the actual value of theZip, if any (Figure 17.6). This lets you check whether the value was assigned correctly to the variable.

You could provide explanatory text in the alert if you wish:

```
alert("theZip is: " + theZip);
```

The above code would generate the alert in Figure 17.7.

Suppose the alert were changed to refer to a variable that doesn't exist (Figure 17.8):

```
alert(thezip);
```

The changed alert would raise an error, because the variable thezip does not actually exist—its correct name is theZip, not thezip.

From these examples, you can infer some ways to use JavaScript alerts in debugging:

1. Verify that an object exists
2. Try out different JavaScript syntax to identify an object
3. Find out the current value of a form object
4. Check the value of a JavaScript variable
5. Check that a JavaScript variable name is recognized

Remember to remove any alerts added for debugging purposes!

WORK WITH LOCAL HTML SOURCE CODE

If you are working intensively on a few lines of JavaScript code to get them right, you might not want to take the time to recompile the PL/SQL procedure with each change to the JavaScript code.

A shortcut is to work with an HTML file locally. When you view the page source in a browser, save the page source as a local file with the extension .htm on your computer. Then you can open this local file in your browser. You can make changes to this local file using Notepad, and then view the local file again in your browser. This way you do not have to recompile the PL/SQL procedure each time.

However, once the JavaScript is in good working condition, you must copy it back into the PL/SQL procedure. The new JavaScript code must be copied and pasted back into the PL/SQL, and the PL/SQL must be recompiled. Otherwise, the PL/SQL procedure will not contain the new improvements.

Because the JavaScript code must be copied back into the PL/SQL procedure, it can be easy to miss something. Therefore, this trick is best used for getting one specific JavaScript function working, or a few isolated lines of JavaScript code working. That way, the changed code is easily identified and copied back into the PL/SQL procedure.

WATCH LINE BREAKS IN JAVASCRIPT

Line breaks in HTML and PL/SQL are usually a matter of style and do not affect the processing of the code. However, in JavaScript, line breaks in the wrong places can cause your JavaScript code to fail. JavaScript recognizes that it has reached the end of a statement when it sees one of two things: a semicolon or a line break. If each JavaScript command is on its own line, semicolons are not strictly necessary; however, semicolons add to the clarity of the code, and it is good practice to include them.

This causes problems when you have a very long JavaScript statement that you want to be read as one statement. It is tempting to include a line break somewhere in the window.open command, because it tends to be long. However, the line break can raise an error if JavaScript reads the line break as the end of the command when the command continues onto the next line. Here is the window.open command in the event handler from the instruct_personal_info procedure in Chapter 10, "Web Toolkit I: HTML and JavaScript with PL/SQL." Here, the line in bold was split into two lines:

```
htp.p('<TD>
<INPUT TYPE="BUTTON" VALUE="Change Zipcode"
 onClick="javascript:window.open(''showzip'', ''instructor_zip'',
 ''TOOLBAR=no, STATUS=yes, MENUBAR=no,
SCROLLBARS=auto, RESIZABLE=yes, WIDTH=640, HEIGHT=480'');">
</TD>');
```

Focus on the section in bold text. The parameter supplying the characteristics of the window is:

```
''TOOLBAR=NO, STATUS=yes, MENUBAR=no,
SCROLLBARS=auto, RESIZABLE=yes, WIDTH=640, HEIGHT=480''
```

If this line break is left in place so that there is a line break after MENUBAR=no and SCROLLBARS=auto is the start of the next line, then a JavaScript error will be raised, as shown in Figure 17.9.

The error, "Unterminated string constant," indicates that a string was left unfinished. To find out exactly where the problem is, go to the line number that is specified in the JavaScript error message in the HTML page source. In this exam-

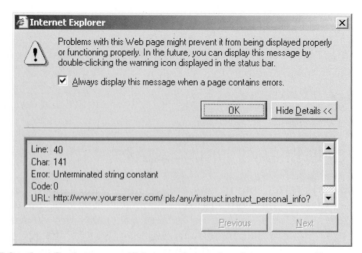

Figure 17.9 ■ JavaScript error "Unterminated string constant" caused by line breaks.

ple, line number 40 is specified. Remember, this refers to line number 40 in the HTML page source and not the PL/SQL procedure.

This is the line referred to by the JavaScript error. Note that the following text is on one line in the HTML source code:

```
onClick="javascript:window.open(''showzip'', ''instructor_zip'',
''TOOLBAR=NO, STATUS=yes, MENUBAR=no,
```

The "string" that is "unterminated" is at the end of the line, which was reached with:

```
''TOOLBAR=NO, STATUS=yes, MENUBAR=no,
```

JavaScript considers the line break to be the end of the command. Then it tries to make sense of the partial window.open command. The line break occurs before the quotes are closed and the window.open command is thus made incomplete.

UNIT
17.4

If you see the "Unterminated string constant" error, put your entire JavaScript command on a single line and try again.

WATCH FOR ILLEGAL CHARACTERS WHEN REUSING CODE

Snippets of JavaScript are often reused. Be careful when cutting and pasting JavaScript. Illegal characters can sometimes be carried over, and render the script unusable.

In order to see this, you need to open the code in a plain text editor, such as Notepad, and look for invalid characters, usually shown as a solid block. Delete these characters; JavaScript should only contain plain text.

UNDERSTAND CONCATENATION MARKS

There are different concatenation symbols in JavaScript and PL/SQL. It is important to understand when to use each.

In PL/SQL, the concatenation mark is two vertical pipes: | |

In JavaScript, the concatenation mark is the plus sign: +

The following is a sample line of code that uses PL/SQL concatenation:

```
htp.p('<INPUT NAME="p_first_name" TYPE="text"
VALUE="'||v_first_name||'">');
```

The following is a sample line of code that uses JavaScript concatenation:

```
htp.p('
<SCRIPT LANGUAGE="JavaScript">
alert("The first name is " +
document.student_form.p_first_name);
</SCRIPT>
');
```

The JavaScript sample does not concatenate a PL/SQL variable for the first name. Instead, JavaScript makes use of the document object model (DOM) to retrieve the first name. JavaScript validation should always make use of the DOM when checking values, not PL/SQL. The DOM is more powerful than PL/SQL in this case; JavaScript can see the up-to-the-moment value that the user has entered. On the other hand, the PL/SQL code has already finished running by the time the user is seeing a page in the browser, and the original value for first name that PL/SQL retrieved from the database may have been changed by the user. JavaScript should read the most current values available from the DOM.

In the rare cases when you might want to concatenate PL/SQL within JavaScript, you can make use of the PL/SQL concatenation mark. The literal string being printed by the htp.p command would be interrupted to concatenate a PL/SQL variable.

```
htp.p('
<SCRIPT LANGUAGE="JavaScript">
alert("The original value for first name was '||v_first_name||'");
</SCRIPT>
');
```

DISTINGUISH BACK-END FROM FRONT-END

JavaScript's strength is that it can view the entire DOM, and read to it and write to it.

However, JavaScript's limitation is that it cannot access the back-end database.

This can be inconvenient for form validation. JavaScript performs sophisticated form validation, and prevents unnecessary trips to the database by doing so. When validating a form with a first and last name, JavaScript can ensure that values for both fields are entered, that these values only contain letters, and that each value's length is longer than one letter, for example.

However, JavaScript cannot go to the database to check whether there is already an entry with a similar first name and last name. That back-end validation must be performed by PL/SQL, in the form handler procedure.

To get around this limitation, some programmers select values from the database and store arrays of values within JavaScript variables, using the concatenation syntax above. However, this can slow down the rendering of the page in the browser when working with large numbers of values, such as every first and last name stored in a database. More likely, you will need to employ both front-end and back-end validation in your applications.

**UNIT
17.4**

UNIT 17.5

FIND AND DEBUG
HTML ERRORS

VIEW SOURCE CODE

HTML errors are easiest to figure out by looking at the source code that the browser received. This source code is all that the browser has to work with, so it is the place to look for errors.

Commercial software can check HTML for you. Also try the HTML validator at http://www.w3c.org.

PLACE FORM ELEMENTS IN FORMS

If a form button does not appear on a page, check whether it was placed within a form. Some browsers will not display a button that is outside of a form. The form may be very small and only include the button, but it must be present. Even if the button has a JavaScript event attached to it, and does not necessarily need to be in a form, you should still include it within a form to ensure that it is displayed correctly.

NO NESTED FORMS

Nested forms are not permitted in HTML, as emphasized in Chapter 11, "Web Toolkit II: Frames, Forms, and Parameters." Functionality will be badly affected if you do not adhere to this standard.

It might happen that a page contains several forms, and the forms need to include some of the same form elements. Thus, it might seem like the forms "overlap" in some way, and need to be nested. However, this is not the case. If several forms need the same elements, simply repeat the form elements in each form.

These elements can be inputs with TYPE="hidden" so that they are included in each form without being displayed on the screen multiple times.

HTML VISIBLE ON PAGE

You might find that HTML tags are displaying on the page along with your content. In the middle of your Web page, if you see

```
FONT FACE="Helvetica">
```

or other HTML that should not be displayed in the browser window, find the first place in the page that you see HTML. Then look at the HTML source code, and find the part of the code that corresponds to where the problem starts. Once there, look for missing brackets around the tags.

When HTML is visible in a Web browser, this usually happens when either the < or the > character is missing from an HTML tag. These marks tell the browser when a tag begins and ends, so a browser will be thrown off without these marks. One missing < or > can affect many subsequent lines of code.

USE QUOTES WITH FORM ELEMENT VALUES

Always enclose the VALUE attribute of a form input in double quotes. For example:

```
-- INCORRECT
htp.p('<TD>
<INPUT TYPE="text" NAME="p_first_name"
VALUE='||v_first_name||' SIZE="25">
</TD>');

-- CORRECT
htp.p('<TD>
<INPUT TYPE="text" NAME="p_first_name"
VALUE="'||v_first_name||'" SIZE="25">
</TD>');
```

Double quotes are needed in case there is a space within the value. As long as the value does not contain a space in the middle of it, you do not notice a problem. For example, if the first name is Lori, the form displays "Lori," the submitted form saves Lori, and you therefore do not realize the error. However, if the first name is Lori Jill, only "Lori" is displayed on the form. Everything after the space in the middle of the name is ignored.

Moreover, if the user saves the information in the form, the value "Lori" is saved, not "Lori Jill". The correct information that was loaded into the database previously would be lost, overwritten with bad data, due to an error in coding the application.

Always use double quotes around the value attribute to avoid the kind of error described above.

AVOID EXTRA SPACES IN FORM ELEMENT VALUES

Another similar problem can occur when extra spaces are added by accident around the value attribute of a form input.

Look at the examples below. In the first example, spaces are added in the value attribute. This may make the code easier to read, and it is tempting to add these spaces. The problem is that the spaces within the double quotes are part of the value of this form element. In the first example, the first name includes a space at either end of the value attribute. The second example is correct:

```
-- INCORRECT
htp.p('<TD>
<INPUT TYPE="text" NAME="p_first_name"
VALUE=" '||v_first_name||' " SIZE="25">
</TD>');
```

```
-- CORRECT
htp.p('<TD>
<INPUT TYPE="text" NAME="p_first_name"
VALUE="'||v_first_name||'" SIZE="25">
</TD>');
```

What will happen to Lori Jill if the extra spaces are included within the double quotes? In the first example above, if the user saves the record, the name is saved in the database as `'Lori Jill'`, with spaces around the name. If the record is updated a second time, additional spaces are saved around the value. So the database would have `'Lori Jill'`, or 'space-space-Lori-space-Jill-space-space'. Each time the record is modified, the name would be saved with additional spaces around it. Such an error might not be obvious when the record is viewed in a browser. Remember that HTML compresses multiple space—you must use   to display more than one nonbreaking space. So it might not be apparent that extra spaces are being added around the value each time the record is saved. Querying the database directly would reveal that extra spaces were added erroneously.

To avoid this type of error, never include extra spaces as part of the VALUE of an INPUT in a form.

USE BORDERS TO DEBUG TABLES

The easiest way to determine what is happening with tables is to make use of two table attributes: BORDER and BORDERCOLOR. The values can be reset to their original values once the tables have been modified to your satisfaction.

BORDER lets you make a border visible. Set BORDER equal to a number. The number determines the thickness of the border.

BORDERCOLOR lets you specify the color of the border. You can use a color name or hexadecimal color notation, though for debugging purposes, values such as "red," "blue," "green," and "yellow" stand out and contrast well with each other.

Together, these two attributes can help make sense of complicated nested tables. Add these attributes to each TABLE in your HTML, and you will immediately see where tables begin and end, and how many rows and columns they contain. Use a different BORDERCOLOR for each table so that you can distinguish between them. For example:

```
<TABLE BORDER="3" BORDERCOLOR="red">
<TR>
  <TD>
   <TABLE BORDER="3" BORDERCOLOR="yellow">
 . . .
```

This trick will almost certainly clash with your current design, but it will help you quickly pinpoint what is happening with your tables. Once you have reformatted the tables, remember to change or remove these attributes and return your page to its original color palette.

CHECK ATTRIBUTE SPELLINGS

If an HTML attribute is misspelled or malformed, then the browser will not recognize anything after the malformed/misspelled attribute.

The danger here is that the HTML will not produce an error message for invalid HTML. Therefore, the effects of this error vary, depending on which attribute is misspelled, and where it is placed in the tag.

As a general rule, check the spelling and syntax of your HTML if it is not behaving the way you expect.

Here is one example. Suppose you have a form tag that includes an "onSubmit" event handler that validates the form elements, but it has a misspelled attribute before the form handler:

```
<FORM ACTION="update_student" NAME="student_personal_form"
METHODDD="post" onSubmit="return ckFrm(this);">
```

The attribute METHOD is misspelled. As mentioned earlier in this chapter, browsers attempt to work with what they are given, and tolerate some mistakes. Here, the browser will recognize the opening FORM tag, the ACTION attribute, and the NAME attribute. The METHODDD attribute would not be recognized, so the browser would stop reading what is in the tag. Everything that comes after the misspelled METHODDD attribute, including the onSubmit form handler, would be ignored. As a result, form validation would be skipped.

How would this appear in a browser? In this case, the form would be created, with the name "student_personal_form" and the action "update_student." The method would not be known, so the default of GET would be used. Since the onSubmit form handler comes after the misspelled attribute, it is ignored, and the form would be submitted without calling the ckFrm JavaScript function. Since the JavaScript form validation is in the ckFrm function, and it would not be called, erroneous data could be entered in the form.

If the first attribute, ACTION, had been misspelled, then none of the attributes in the <FORM> tag would have been recognized. The browser would render the form in the browser, and it would appear to be in good working order. However, nothing would happen if the user tried to submit the form.

Check the spelling of tags and attributes in your HTML.

WEB TIPS
AND TECHNIQUES

<table>
<tr><td colspan="2" align="center">CHAPTER OBJECTIVES</td></tr>
<tr><td colspan="2">After this chapter, you will know how to:</td></tr>
<tr><td>✔ Add Functionality to Forms</td><td>Page 631</td></tr>
<tr><td>✔ Use Stylesheets</td><td>Page 640</td></tr>
<tr><td>✔ Store Images for Performance</td><td>Page 649</td></tr>
<tr><td>✔ Use Dynamic SQL</td><td>Page 653</td></tr>
<tr><td>✔ Write and Reuse Modular Components</td><td>Page 658</td></tr>
</table>

This chapter offers some additional tips and techniques to enhance your Web site that builds on the information learned throughout this book.

Unit 18.1, "Add Functionality to Forms," covers some additional form functionality you might need, such as creating read-only form inputs, and incorporating search functionality directly in your pages.

Unit 18.2, "Use Stylesheets," provides an overview of this popular mechanism for controlling the look and feel of a Web site.

Unit 18.3, "Store Images for Performance," extends the discussion of image handling begun in Chapter 13, "Images." It shows how to store images externally to the database, while storing references to those images within the database.

Unit 18.4, "Use Dynamic SQL," introduces Native Dynamic SQL and offers sample syntax for using it on the Web.

Unit 18.5, "Write and Reuse Modular Components," provides sample PSP code for handling an insert and an update with shared code. Guidelines for using packages and modularizing code are offered, in preparation for topics discussed in Chapter 20, "Web Application Architecture."

U N I T   1 8 . 1

ADD FUNCTIONALITY
TO FORMS

USE DYNAMIC DROP-DOWNS TO SEARCH

Drop-downs are useful tools for allowing users to quickly search for the record they would like to see, without going to a separate search screen. A drop-down can be placed at the top of a detail-level screen to allow a user to select a new record to view and refresh the screen based upon that value. Implementing this functionality requires an understanding of JavaScript events and creating multiple forms on the same page.

One of the JavaScript events described in Chapter 7, "Introduction to JavaScript," is onChange. When a drop-down selection box changes, an onChange event handler can respond to this action. The example below shows an onChange event handler attached to a SELECT tag. When the user chooses a new selection, the form "document.course_list_form" is submitted.

■ *FOR EXAMPLE*

```
htp.p('<SELECT NAME="p_course_no"
       onChange="javascript: alert("You changed the drop-down!");
                 document.course_list_form.submit();">
    ');
```

Imagine a screen that allows users to update course information, as shown in Figure 18.1. Instead of giving users a search screen to choose the course they want to update, you can include the search mechanism right on the same screen. A separate form at the top of the screen could contain a drop-down that lists all courses. When the user chooses a course from the drop-down, the screen refreshes with the information for the newly selected course.

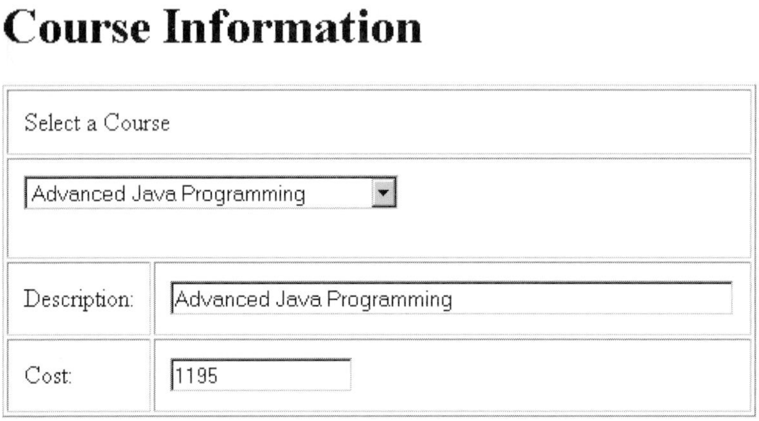

Course Information

Figure 18.1 ■ Screen for updating course information that includes a drop-down for searches.

Implementing this functionality requires two forms. Create a sample procedure called view_course that contains the following forms:

- course_list_form that contains a drop-down list for selecting a course
- course_info_form that lets users update course information for a specific course_no

The actions of each form are different. The course_info_form is submitted to update the course information, so it has a form handler that can process the course information. But what is the action of the course_list_form? It is the view_course procedure itself. This form exists to allow users to choose a new course to see in view_course. So course_list_form will call view_course again, but it will pass in a new course_no to display. This will have the effect of refreshing the screen with information for the newly selected course.

How about the first time the user comes to the screen? Since the user is not going through a search screen, a course_no is not being passed in on the first visit. To handle that situation, the procedure view_course must check the value of course_no. If none is found, then the procedure must select one. The procedure opens the same cursor that is used to paint the drop-down select list of courses. It selects the first record and stores its course_no. This course_no will be SELECTED in the drop-down in course_list_form, and this course_no's detail information will be updateable in the course_info_form.

Note that the parameter p_course_no exists in both forms. The two forms are completely separate. If the first form is submitted, it does not pass any of the inputs in the second form. The reverse is also true. So the second form contains a hidden input with the course_no. Otherwise, when the second form is submitted, the course_no would be unknown.

■ FOR EXAMPLE

```
1   CREATE OR REPLACE PROCEDURE view_course
2      (p_course_no IN COURSE.course_no%TYPE   DEFAULT NULL)
3   AS
4    v_course_no    COURSE.course_no%TYPE;
5    v_description COURSE.description%TYPE;
6    rec_course     COURSE%ROWTYPE;
7
8    CURSOR c_courses IS
9      SELECT course_no, description
10       FROM course
11      ORDER BY description;
12  BEGIN
13     -- Determine course selected for display
14     IF p_course_no IS NOT NULL THEN
15        v_course_no := p_course_no;
16     ELSE
17        OPEN c_courses;
18        FETCH c_courses INTO v_course_no, v_description;
19        CLOSE c_courses;
20     END IF;
21
22  htp.p('<HTML>
23         <HEAD><TITLE>Course Information</TITLE></HEAD>
24         <BODY>
25         <H1>Course Information</H1>
26         <TABLE BORDER="1" WIDTH="75%" CELLPADDING="10">
27         <TR>
28         <TD COLSPAN="2">Select a Course</TD>
29         </TR>');
30  -- Paint form for selecting a new course using a drop-down
31  htp.p('<TR>');
32  htp.p('<TD COLSPAN="2">');
33  htp.p('<FORM NAME="course_list_form" ACTION="view_course"
34         METHOD="GET">');
35  htp.p('<SELECT NAME="p_course_no"
36    onChange="javascript:document.course_list_form.submit();">');
37
38  FOR rec IN c_courses LOOP
39      IF rec.course_no = v_course_no THEN
40        htp.p('<OPTION VALUE="'||rec.course_no||'" SELECTED>'
41          ||rec.description||'</OPTION>');
42      ELSE
43        htp.p('<OPTION VALUE="'||rec.course_no||'">'
44          ||rec.description||'</OPTION>');
45      END IF;
46  END LOOP;
```

```
47
48   htp.p('</SELECT>');
49   htp.p('</FORM>');
50   htp.p('</TD>');
51   htp.p('</TR>');
52
53      -- Display course name and cost
54      SELECT *
55        INTO rec_course
56        FROM course
57       WHERE course_no = v_course_no;
58
59      htp.p('<FORM NAME="course_info_form" ACTION="">');
60         -- The course_no must be stored in the second form also
61      htp.p('<INPUT TYPE="hidden" NAME="p_course_no"
62                     VALUE="'||v_course_no||'">');
63
64   htp.p('<TR><TD>Description:</TD>
65         <TD><INPUT TYPE="text" NAME="p_description" SIZE="50"
66                    VALUE="'||rec_course.description||'"></TD>
67         </TR>');
68   htp.p('<TR><TD>Cost:</TD>
69         <TD><INPUT TYPE="text" NAME="p_cost" SIZE="15"
70                    VALUE="'||rec_course.cost||'"></TD>
71         </TR>');
72   htp.p('</FORM>');
73   htp.p('</TABLE>
74         </BODY>
75         </HTML>');
76   EXCEPTION
77     WHEN OTHERS THEN
78        htp.p('An error occurred in view_course: '||SQLERRM);
79   END;
```

MULTIPLE SELECTS

Sometimes two drop-downs are needed to retrieve the record for the user. If a user wishes to look up section information, this would be very difficult using the section number alone. Sections are numbered starting with 1 for each course, so they are not unique, and a long list with many 1s, 2s, and 3s would be unhelpful for the user. There is a numeric primary key for each record, called section_id, but that is likewise meaningless to the user. The user needs to know both the course number and the section number.

One approach is to allow the user to choose from a list of courses, and then choose from the sections available for that course. This requires two drop-downs. Imagine a drop-down menu for courses next to a drop-down menu for sections, as shown in Figure 18.2. When a course is selected in the first drop-down, the

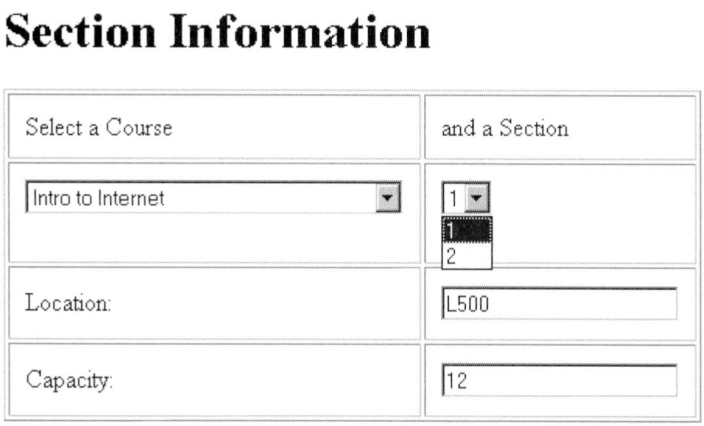

Section Information

Select a Course	and a Section
Intro to Internet ▼	1 ▼ 1 2
Location:	L500
Capacity:	12

Figure 18.2 ■ Screen for updating section information including multiple drop-downs for searching.

screen refreshes to show the appropriate sections in the second drop-down box. The rest of the screen is devoted to detailed information for the chosen section. If the section changes, the screen is refreshed so that the bottom of the screen contains section information for the correct section.

Implementing this functionality requires three forms. Create a sample procedure called view_section that contains the following forms:

- course_list_form that contains a drop-down list for selecting a course
- section_list_form that contains a drop-down list for selecting a section; the drop-down list will only contain sections for the course selected in course_list_form
- section_info_form that allows users to update section information for a specific section_id

What are the actions of each form? The course_list_form will call view_section to refresh the screen. The section_list_form will also call view_section to refresh the screen. The user can change either the course or the section, and changing either one will have an effect on what is displayed. The section_info_form simply has a form handler to process changes to section detail information.

With the addition of the section_list_form, an additional IN parameter is needed. The previous procedure, view_course, has one IN parameter: p_course_no. On this page, however, users can select a specific course_no, and they can also select a specific section_id. Both of these must be IN parameters so that the correct choices can be selected, and the correct section's detail information displayed.

Since two IN parameters are needed, the view_section procedure must check both of them to see if there is a NULL value. If the course_no is not passed in, then the procedure can use the cursor for painting the courses drop-down list to determine the course that should be selected. If the section_id is not passed in, then one must be determined, based on the course_no that is selected for the first drop-down.

Look at the cursor that retrieves sections for the section drop-down box, c_sections. This is a parameterized cursor. It takes an IN parameter, pi_course_no, and uses the course_no to limit the sections that are selected from the database. The only sections that should be displayed in the section drop-down are sections for the course selected in the first drop-down; the second drop-down depends on the value selected in the first one.

■ FOR EXAMPLE

```
1   CREATE OR REPLACE PROCEDURE view_section
2      (p_course_no IN COURSE.course_no%TYPE     DEFAULT NULL,
3       p_section_id IN SECTION.section_id%TYPE DEFAULT NULL)
4   AS
5   v_course_no    COURSE.course_no%TYPE;
6   v_description COURSE.description%TYPE;
7   v_section_id   SECTION.section_id%TYPE;
8   v_section_no   SECTION.section_no%TYPE;
9   rec_section    SECTION%ROWTYPE;
10
11    CURSOR c_courses IS
12     SELECT course_no, description
13       FROM course
14      ORDER BY description;
15
16    CURSOR c_sections(pi_course_no NUMBER) IS
17     SELECT section_id, section_no
18       FROM section
19      WHERE course_no = pi_course_no
20      ORDER BY section_no;
21
22  BEGIN
23
24    IF p_course_no IS NOT NULL THEN
25       v_course_no := p_course_no;
26    ELSE
27       OPEN c_courses;
28       FETCH c_courses INTO v_course_no, v_description;
29       CLOSE c_courses;
30    END IF;
31
32    IF p_section_id IS NOT NULL THEN
33       v_section_id := p_section_id;
34    ELSE
35       OPEN c_sections(v_course_no);
```

```
36        FETCH c_sections INTO v_section_id, v_section_no;
37        CLOSE c_sections;
38    END IF;
39
40  htp.p('<HTML>
41        <HEAD><TITLE>Section Information</TITLE></HEAD>
42        <BODY>
43        <H1>Section Information</H1>
44        <TABLE BORDER="1" CELLPADDING="10">
45        <TR>
46        <TD>Select a Course</TD>
47        <TD>and a Section</TD>
48        </TR>');
49
50  htp.p('<TR>');
51  htp.p('<TD>');
52  htp.p('<FORM NAME="course_list_form" ACTION="view_section"
53              METHOD="GET">');
54  htp.p('<SELECT NAME="p_course_no"
55    onChange="javascript:document.course_list_form.submit();">');
56
57    FOR rec IN c_courses LOOP
58      IF rec.course_no = v_course_no THEN
59        htp.p('<OPTION VALUE="'||rec.course_no||'" SELECTED>'
60          ||rec.description||'</OPTION>');
61      ELSE
62        htp.p('<OPTION VALUE="'||rec.course_no||'">'
63          ||rec.description||'</OPTION>');
64      END IF;
65    END LOOP;
66
67  htp.p('</SELECT>');
68  htp.p('</FORM>');
69  htp.p('</TD>');
70
71  htp.p('<TD>');
72  IF v_section_id IS NULL THEN
73    htp.p('No sections yet.');
74  ELSE
75   htp.p('<FORM NAME="section_list_form" ACTION="view_section"
76           METHOD="GET">');
77   htp.p('<INPUT TYPE="hidden" NAME="p_course_no"
78               VALUE="'||v_course_no||'">');
79   htp.p('<SELECT NAME="p_section_id"
80    onChange="javascript:document.section_list_form.submit();">');
81
82    FOR rec IN c_sections(v_course_no) LOOP
83      IF rec.section_id = v_section_id THEN
84        htp.p('<OPTION VALUE="'||rec.section_id||'" SELECTED>'
```

```
 85                          ||rec.section_no||'</OPTION>');
 86         ELSE
 87           htp.p('<OPTION VALUE="'||rec.section_id||'">'
 88                          ||rec.section_no||'</OPTION>');
 89         END IF;
 90      END LOOP;
 91
 92      htp.p('</SELECT>');
 93      htp.p('</FORM>');
 94    END IF;
 95    htp.p('</TD>');
 96    htp.p('</TR>');
 97
 98    IF v_section_id IS NOT NULL THEN
 99
100       SELECT *
101         INTO rec_section
102         FROM section
103        WHERE section_id = v_section_id;
104
105       htp.p('<FORM NAME="section_details" ACTION="">');
106       htp.p('<INPUT TYPE="hidden" NAME="p_section_id"
107                     VALUE="'||v_section_id||'">');
108       htp.p('<TR><TD>Location:</TD>
109             <TD><INPUT TYPE="text" NAME="p_location"
110                        VALUE="'||rec_section.location||'"></TD>
111           </TR>');
112       htp.p('<TR><TD>Capacity:</TD>
113             <TD><INPUT TYPE="text" NAME="p_capacity"
114                        VALUE="'||rec_section.capacity||'"></TD>
115           </TR>');
116       htp.p('</FORM>');
117    END IF;
118    htp.p('</TABLE>
119           </BODY>
120           </HTML>');
121    EXCEPTION
122      WHEN OTHERS THEN
123          htp.p('An error occurred in view_section: '||SQLERRM);
124    END;
```

CREATE READ-ONLY TEXT BOXES

If you want to show the user information that is display only, you can paint it to the screen using the htp.p command. However, displayed text is not part of the DOM. On the other hand, form elements are very easy to manipulate using JavaScript.

The solution may be to create an inactive, or "grayed-out," text box. This might happen where you want to display a value in a text box, but update that value dynamically on the front end, depending on what a user clicks or enters elsewhere on the page.

The keyword READONLY can be added to an input to make it nonupdateable:

```
<INPUT NAME="p_state" TYPE="text" VALUE="Tennessee" READONLY>
```

While this book focuses on Internet Explorer, it is important here to note one discrepancy between IE and earlier versions of Netscape. Prior to Version 6.2, Netscape does not understand the READONLY keyword. This difference could have the serious consequence of allowing a user to update a field that you intend to be display only.

To create a text field that is not modifiable in either browser, add JavaScript.

```
<INPUT NAME="p_state" TYPE="text" VALUE="Tennessee" READONLY
onFocus="this.blur();">
```

Note that a read-only field does not look any different from a regular text input. Text inputs do not have attributes such as background color. To give them a different appearance, make use of the additional formatting features available with stylesheets, introduced in this chapter in Unit 18.2, "Use Stylesheets."

UNIT 18.2

USE STYLESHEETS

ADVANTAGES OF USING STYLES

The terms stylesheets and cascading style sheets (CSS) simply refer to a way to declare how you want to display something in an HTML document. Stylesheets let you create a set of properties and apply that set of properties as needed, throughout your document or across many different documents in a site.

Why are stylesheets increasingly popular? Stylesheets allow you to:

- Enforce a consistent look and feel across an application
- Avoid retyping formatting tags and attributes
- Change the appearance of a site with less effort
- Choose from more formatting options
- Link content (tags) with display (formatting)
- Manipulate appearance through JavaScript

The power of styles is that they are reused. One style can affect many different elements in a site. You can avoid spelling out sets of formatting tags that you use repeatedly on a site, such as <FONT>, <B>, and <I>, by creating a style that accomplishes the same formatting. After declaring the style once, you can apply it to many different tags, and even across many different documents.

You can also link styles with specific tags, so that all occurrences of a tag have the same style. For example, by declaring a style for the <UL>, <OL>, and <LI> tags for a page, you can give each ordered and unordered list on the page the same look and feel. Again, this can be done across different documents as well.

By centralizing the style specifications for your site into stylesheets, you can change the look and feel of a site easily. Each page in a site could refer to the same stylesheet. If a stylesheet specifies that all H1 headings will be displayed in red, then all pages that are linked to that stylesheet will all have <H1> tags with red text. If the site is redesigned, and blue headings are called for, then changing the style in one place—the stylesheet—causes the entire site to have a new look.

Stylesheets have more display options than HTML. HTML does let you control display to some extent; you can make text bold, choose font colors, and so forth. Stylesheets provide this and more. Text formatting options that have become standard in word processing programs, such as right-alignment of a paragraph and choice of specific point sizes for text, are available with styles.

The HTML specification recommends that developers switch to using stylesheets instead of using the HTML formatting tags. This is why so many tags and attributes are marked in the HTML specification as "deprecated." While deprecated tags and attributes are still supported, using them is not encouraged. Stylesheets are taking the place of HTML tags and attributes for creating the aesthetic of a page. The CSS specification is being enhanced to provide even more display options, whereas the same type of display work is not being done in HTML.

Because styles are part of the DOM, they can be manipulated through JavaScript. An element's style could be read and changed by JavaScript, depending upon the browser's support of styles for that element.

Different browsers, and different versions of browsers, offer varying levels of support for styles. Verify that styles display as expected in each browser version you must support.

STYLE SYNTAX

A style declaration is comprised of a name/value pair. You will notice that the style names do not correspond exactly to HTML tags. Most style names use dashes between words. For example, while HTML uses <B> to denote bold text, a style declaration for bolding text is:

```
font-weight: bold
```

Support for stylesheets varies from browser to browser, and from version to version. Table 18.1 shows examples of some of the most commonly used and supported style declarations, and the result.

To create a style declaration with multiple properties, list the name/value pairs separated by semicolons.

■ FOR EXAMPLE

```
font-size: 20pt; color: red; background-color: yellow;
font-weight: bold; font-family: Garamond, Arial
```

Table 18.1 ■ A Few Style Declarations

Style Declaration	Result
font-size: 20pt	Font size is 20 point
color: red	Color is red
color: #FF0000	Color is red
background-color: #FF0000	Background color is red
background-image: newbg.jpg	The image newbg.jpg is used as a background image
font-weight: bold	Text is bolded
font-style: italic	Text is italicized
background-color: yellow	Background is yellow; makes text look highlighted
text-decoration: line-through	Text has a line through it; makes text look crossed-out like a strike-through option
text-transform: lowercase	Text is transformed to lowercase
text-align: right	Right-aligns text
text-indent: 10%	Indents first line of text by 10%
text-indent: 10	Indents first line of text by 10 pixels
cursor: wait	On mouseover, cursor rendered as an hourglass (only in some browsers)

How you apply these styles depends on where you define the style. There are three ways to use styles:

1. In-Line Styles (also called Local Styles)—tag level
2. Global Styles—document level
3. Linked Styles—multiple documents

IN-LINE STYLES

In-line styles, or local styles, are limited to a single tag. Since they are tag level, these styles are not reused. Their main advantage is the additional formatting options they offer.

To specify an in-line style, simply place a STYLE attribute directly within an HTML tag, and define styles there.

■ FOR EXAMPLE

```
<H1 STYLE="font-size: 20pt; color: red; background-color:
yellow; font-weight: bold; font-family: Garamond,
Arial">Important Phone Numbers</H1>
```

Compare this with the HTML version that doesn't use styles:

```
<H1><B><FONT FACE="Garamond, Arial" COLOR="red">Important
Phone Numbers</FONT></B></H1>
```

Specifying background color lets you display text as if it is highlighted; this is something that cannot be done with text except through styles. Also, the text size cannot be specified with a point value in HTML.

Realize that styles can be applied to form elements as well. The following will give a text input a gray background, as shown in Figure 18.3. This is useful formatting for any read-only text fields you create.

```
Tennessee
```

Figure 18.3 ■ Grayed-out textbox using styles.

■ FOR EXAMPLE

```
<INPUT NAME="p_state" TYPE="text" VALUE="Tennessee" READONLY
    onFocus="this.blur();"
    STYLE="background-color: gray">
```

The additional formatting options are useful, but they could also be cumbersome to retype for every header in the document. How can you apply a style to all H1 tags at once? The answer is to use Global Styles.

GLOBAL STYLES

Global styles apply to an entire HTML document.

Global styles are defined within the <HEAD> section of an HTML document (or at least before the <BODY> begins). Define global styles within <STYLE> and </STYLE> tags.

The global styles are listed within the <STYLE> tags. Each style is a rule comprised of two parts: the selector and the declaration.

```
selector{declaration}
```

The declaration goes after the selector name, within curly brackets.

The selector can be an HTML tag or a name supplied by the user.

SELECTOR IS AN HTML TAG

If the selector is an HTML tag, then the style will be applied automatically to all instances of that tag in the document. You are choosing the look and feel of a specific tag throughout your document.

```
<STYLE>
H1{font-size: 20pt; color: red; background-color: yellow;
font-weight: bold; font-family: Garamond, Arial}
</STYLE>
```

To apply the style from the previous section to all H1 headers throughout the document, look at the following example.

■ *FOR EXAMPLE*

```
<HTML>
<HEAD>
<STYLE>
H1{font-size: 20pt; color: red; background-color: yellow;
font-weight: bold; font-family: Garamond, Arial}
</STYLE>
</HEAD>
<BODY>
<H1>Important Phone Numbers</H1>
<P>Important Phone Numbers go here.</P>
<H1>Important Email Addresses</H1>
<P>Important Email Addresses go here.</P>
</BODY>
</HTML>
```

The <H1> tags within the document are plain, and do not appear to have any formatting tags. However, they will both be displayed according to the style rule that is declared for H1 tags. This is powerful functionality.

SELECTOR IS USER-DEFINED CLASS

Instead of linking a style rule to a specific tag, a user can create a style and give it a name. The style will not be automatically picked up by any HTML tag. However, the style will be visible to all tags within the document. Any tag that wants to make use of the style can refer to the style directly by name.

A selector named by the developer must begin with a period.

```
<STYLE>
.footnote{font-size: 8 pt; color: black; font-style: italic;
font-family: Garamond, Arial}
</STYLE>
```

To reference a style for a tag, use the CLASS attribute within an HTML tag.

■ *FOR EXAMPLE*

```
<HTML>
<HEAD>
<STYLE>
H1{font-size: 20pt; color: red; background-color: yellow; font-weight:
bold; font-family: Garamond, Arial}
.disclaimer{font-size: 8pt; color: black; font-style: italic;
font-family: Garamond, Arial}
</STYLE>
</HEAD>
<BODY>
<H1>Important Phone Numbers</H1>
<P>Important Phone Numbers go here.</P>
<H1>Important Email Addresses</H1>
<P>Important Email Addresses go here.</P>
<P CLASS="disclaimer">Contact information may change at any time
without warning, especially when it is really important.</P>
</BODY>
</HTML>
```

If you find yourself cutting and pasting the <STYLE> section of your document into other documents, you need to make use of Linked Styles.

LINKED STYLES

Linked stylesheets can apply to many different documents.

Style rules are stored in an external, plain-text document with an extension ".css". Many different HTML pages can refer to the same stylesheet document. Think of many HTML pages that all source the same JavaScript file; this is the same concept.

Below are the contents of a sample stylesheet document called stylin.css. Note that the document contains the style rules only. It does not contain any HTML tags like <STYLE>.

■ *FOR EXAMPLE*

```
H1{font-size: 20pt; color: red; background-color: yellow; font-weight:
bold; font-family: Garamond, Arial}
.disclaimer{font-size: 8pt; color: black; font-style: italic;
font-family: Garamond, Arial}
```

A style rule can be specified for multiple tags at once, such as H1, H2, and H3. Also note that line breaks between styles can be used if desired—it is a matter of, well, style. Here is another example of a stylesheet document.

■ FOR EXAMPLE

```
H1,H2,H3{font-size: 20pt; color: red; background-color:
yellow; font-weight: bold; font-family: Garamond, Arial}
.disclaimer{
font-size: 8pt;
color: black;
font-style: italic;
font-family: Garamond, Arial
}
```

How can pages make use of this stylesheet file? Multiple pages can refer to the stylesheet by "linking" to the stylin.css document. This is done by including a <LINK> tag within the <HEAD> tag of the document. <LINK> has three attributes to specify when linking to a stylesheet:

- REL—relationship of linked document to this page: stylesheet
- HREF—name of stylesheet, specified by using a relative or absolute path. This file will have a .css extension.
- TYPE—MIME type of the document: text/css

■ FOR EXAMPLE

```
        <HTML>
<HEAD>
<LINK REL="stylesheet" HREF="stylin.css" TYPE="text/css">
</HEAD>
<BODY>
<H1>Important Phone Numbers</H1>
<P>Important Phone Numbers go here.</P>
<H1>Important Email Addresses</H1>
<P>Important Email Addresses go here.</P>
<P CLASS="disclaimer">Contact information may change at any time
without warning, especially when it is really important.</P>
</BODY>
</HTML>
```

Note that the BODY of this page looks the same as the BODY in the "Global Styles" example. The difference between the two HTML pages is in the HEAD tag. In the Global Styles example, the style rules are listed in the <HEAD> tag. In this example, the <LINK> tag tells the browser where to find style rules for this document.

If the stylesheet is stored in another directory from the page, specify a path as well.

<SPAN> AND <DIV> TAGS

<SPAN> and <DIV> allow you to demarcate text, and then apply a style to that text.

- <SPAN> is traditionally used for in-line text
- <DIV> is traditionally used for larger sections, or divisions, of a page

These tags are helpful when you want to apply a style to a section of text that is not neatly enclosed within a tag. The following example will place a line through the text "20%."

```
<P>We're taking <SPAN STYLE="text-decoration: line-
through">20% </SPAN> 30% off!!</P>
```

INTEGRATION WITH THE WEB TOOLKIT

The HTML document that contains stylesheet references can be embedded within htp.p commands just as any other HTML is.

The stylesheet document remains the same. It should be written in plain text, through a tool like Notepad, and uploaded to the server.

■ FOR EXAMPLE

```
H1{font-size: 20pt; color: red; background-color: yellow; font-weight:
bold; font-family: Garamond, Arial}
.disclaimer{font-size: 8pt; color: black; font-style: italic;
font-family: Garamond, Arial}
```

The Web page generated by PL/SQL can still be generated with htp.p.

■ FOR EXAMPLE

```
htp.p('
<HTML>
<HEAD>
<LINK REL="stylesheet" HREF="stylin.css" TYPE="text/css">
</HEAD>
<BODY>
<H1>Important Phone Numbers</H1>
<P>Important Phone Numbers go here.</P>
```

```
<H1>Important Email Addresses</H1>
<P>Important Email Addresses go here.</P>
<P CLASS="disclaimer">Contact information may change at any time
without warning, especially when it is really important.</P>
</BODY>
</HTML>
');
```

UNIT 18.3

STORE IMAGES FOR PERFORMANCE

INTERNAL OR EXTERNAL STORAGE

In Chapter 13, "Images," you learn how to manipulate and store images in an Oracle database. Due to the potential size of Oracle images, they are often stored in what is referred to as a *LOB*. *LOB* is an Oracle datatype as well as an acronym for *large object.* Oracle considers a large object to be an item that may potentially contain large amounts of text or binary data. Oracle supports two major types of LOBs: internal LOBs and external LOBs.

The distinction between the two is based on whether the datatype is stored internally or externally with respect to the Oracle database. An internal LOB is one that is stored inside the database files. Though you do not create an image with a LOB datatype in Chapter 13, "Images," you do learn how to load, and consequently store, an image in a database. Some of the benefits of storing LOBs internally are:

- Operations on internal LOBs participate fully in transactions.
- You can make changes to an internal LOB and then roll back or commit those changes.
- Internal LOBs get backed up with the database.
- You can use normal database recovery operations to restore them.

CHOOSING EXTERNAL LOB FILES

An external LOB is one that is stored in a file outside of Oracle. A database table stores only a reference to the external file in a column of type *BFILE*. The *BFILE* type is an external LOB type; it is really just a pointer to an operating system file.

The actual LOB data is stored in an external file, not within the database. *BFILE* is the only external LOB type that Oracle supports.

Unlike internal LOBs, BFILEs are read only. You cannot create them using Oracle. They must be obtained from some other source. Also, unlike internal LOBs, BFILEs do not participate in transactions. The BFILE type can be useful if you are dealing with files that are normally accessed by external programs and that only occasionally need to be retrieved through the database. If you have a set of GIF files supporting a Web site, you may want to store them as BFILEs. This way, you eliminate the overhead of loading them all into the database.

MAP THE PHYSICAL DIRECTORY

Typically, a BFILE is a file stored on disk, but it could also be stored on a CD-ROM, a network drive, or any other external media devices connected to an Oracle server. Before you can use BFILEs, you need to create a *DIRECTORY* object. The *DIRECTORY* object is used as an alias for the physical operating system directory that contains the BFILE object. It maps a physical directory to a virtual one defined within the database. An example of creating directory objects follows.

■ FOR EXAMPLE

```
CREATE DIRECTORY TEAK_ALIAS
    AS 'E:\DEV\CLIENT_WEB_APP\TEAKUS_FILES';
```

The above statement associates an alias, TEAK_ALIAS, with the path e:\dev\client_web_app\teakus_files.

You must have the CREATE ANY DIRECTORY system privilege in order to create a directory object. Also, creating a directory object in Oracle does not create the directory at the operating-system level. You must create the corresponding operating system directory yourself.

For users to be able to use your directory, you must grant them read access to the directory. The following grant statement gives the user LORI read access to the TEAK_ALIAS directory.

```
GRANT READ ON DIRECTORY TEAK_ALIAS TO LORI;
```

If you create a directory, you automatically have read privileges on it. There is no need to grant these privileges to yourself.

CREATE TABLE WITH BFILE COLUMN

It is also important to note that having read access to a directory in Oracle does not mean that you have automatic access to the underlying operating system file. Therefore, the Oracle software must be given access to the directory at the operating-system level. To create a table that uses BFILE columns, your CREATE TABLE statement could look similar to the following.

■ *FOR EXAMPLE*

```
CREATE TABLE WEB_DATA
(  IMAGE_ID    INTEGER,
   IMAGE_NAME  VARCHAR2(40),
   IMAGE_DATA  BFILE);
```

INSERT POINTERS WITH BFILENAME FUNCTION

With a directory object created, as well as a table defined with a column of type BFILE, you can use the BFILENAME function to insert a value into a table's BFILE column. This function maps a physical file to a table's BFILE column. The value stored in the BFILE column will be a pointer to the physical file. Sometimes this value is called a BFILE locator. The BFILENAME function takes two parameters:

```
FUNCTION BFILENAME(directory_alias IN VARCHAR2,
              filename IN VARCHAR2)
     RETURN BFILE;
```

The directory_alias passed in must be a directory object that has already been created through the CREATE DIRECTORY command. The filename passed in must be a file in the physical directory indicated by the directory_alias parameter. For example, the following statement inserts the file Em_and_Christopher.gif into the WEB_DATA table.

■ *FOR EXAMPLE*

```
INSERT INTO WEB_DATA (IMAGE_ID,
                 IMAGE_NAME,
                 IMAGE_DATA)
        VALUES (1,
            'The Eckhardt Children',
            BFILENAME('TEAK_ALIAS',
                 'EM_AND_CHRISTOPHER.GIF')
            );
```

Remember that the contents of a BFILE are not stored in the database. Only the file name and directory alias are recorded there. For the data to be accessible to applications, the file must remain available on disk.

READ EXTERNAL FILE DATA

The following procedure provides an example for how to read data from a BFILE by using the built-in PL/SQL package, DBMS_LOB.

■ *FOR EXAMPLE*

```
CREATE OR REPLACE PROCEDURE read_bfile_images IS
    file_loc       BFILE := BFILENAME('TEAK_ALIAS',
                                        'COCO_AND_HARRY.GIF');
    tot_amount     INTEGER := 40000;
    start_position INTEGER := 1;
    buffer_amount  RAW(40000);
BEGIN
    -- Select the BFILE LOB.
    SELECT image_data
      INTO file_loc
      FROM web_data
     WHERE image_id = 3;
    -- Open the BFILE.
    DBMS_LOB.OPEN(file_loc, DBMS_LOB.LOB_READONLY);
    -- Read the image data.
    DBMS_LOB.READ(file_loc, tot_amount, start_position,
                  buffer_amount);
    -- Close the BFILE.
    DBMS_LOB.CLOSE(file_loc);
END;
```

The maximum amount of data you can store in a LOB is 4GB. If you'd like to read an entire GIF, for instance, into the variable file_loc, then simply ensure that the tot_amount and buffer_amount variables have been declared with large enough values to hold the entire contents of your retrieved image file. Once you've read your image file into your procedural variable, you can then use this variable in your application, perhaps to display an image in a Web page. If you have many image files to display in your Web application's pages, the advantage of using BFILES is that your overhead can be noticeably decreased by storing and obtaining your image data from operating system files rather than having the Oracle server do the work of storing and subsequently reading extensive binary data from the database. In this way, your application's overall performance can be significantly increased.

UNIT 18.4

USE DYNAMIC SQL

WHAT IS DYNAMIC SQL?

Dynamic SQL allows you to construct a string and then run it as an SQL statement at runtime. It is useful when you do not know exactly what your SQL statement is going to look like. This might happen on the Web because you will run a different SQL depending on what a user submits in a FORM.

You can construct queries that have different conditions or different ORDER BY clauses. You can even decide to query completely different tables. You could also add optimizer hints to your query at runtime.

Along with SELECT queries, Dynamic SQL can be used to execute DDL within PL/SQL. Normally, you are not permitted to execute DDL such as a GRANT or CREATE TABLE or DROP SYNONYM statement. However, you can create a dynamic SQL statement that contains these commands, and execute it successfully. Thus, Dynamic SQL provides some functionality that is not available any other way.

Dynamic SQL also helps you avoid hard-coding. If the user can choose from among four different sort options for a list of students, you could create four different cursors with four different ORDER BY clauses. Dynamic SQL lets one query do the work of four. The ORDER BY clause could be changed based on what the user submits.

Oracle offers two ways to use Dynamic SQL. Native Dynamic SQL is available starting with Oracle 8*i*, and is the easiest method to use. It is intended to be a new alternative to the DBMS_SQL package offered by Oracle. Please refer to Oracle Documentation for details on the few cases when you might need to use DBMS_SQL. This unit focuses on Native Dynamic SQL.

SYNTAX

BUILD A STATEMENT STRING

Construct a VARCHAR2 string that will hold the SQL statement you wish to run. The example below is concatenated over several lines, though this is not required.

```
v_mystring  VARCHAR2(100) := 'SELECT first_name, last_name '
                          ||' FROM STUDENT';
```

To choose a value that will be provided at runtime, place a colon before the host variable used to pass the runtime value.

```
v_mystring  VARCHAR2(100) := 'SELECT first_name, last_name '
                          ||' FROM STUDENT '
                          ||' WHERE student_id = :the_id ';
```

You can add to this string throughout your code, up until the time you decide to execute it.

Do not include a final semicolon inside this SQL statement string!

EXECUTE THE STRING

To execute the string, use the keywords EXECUTE IMMEDIATE. If the string is a query that is returning values, you must include an INTO clause, the way you would for a SQL SELECT statement inside PL/SQL.

This string:

```
v_mystring  VARCHAR2(100) := 'SELECT first_name, last_name '
                          ||' FROM STUDENT';
```

Can be executed with EXECUTE IMMEDIATE:

```
EXECUTE IMMEDIATE v_mystring
INTO v_variable1, v_variable2;
```

However, the next string requires an additional value at runtime, as indicated by the colon.

```
v_mystring  VARCHAR2(100) := 'SELECT first_name, last_name '
                          ||' FROM STUDENT '
                          ||' WHERE student_id = :the_id ';
```

UNIT
18.4

To execute this statement, include a USING clause. USING lets you replace part of the string with a variable.

```
EXECUTE IMMEDIATE v_mystring
INTO v_variable1, v_variable2
USING 101;
```

If there are several values that need to be supplied at runtime, supply them all in the USING clause, in the order they are required, separated by commas.

SELECT A RECORDSET

If you wish to retrieve a recordset, then you must declare a REF CURSOR type, and then declare a cursor of that type, to hold the recordset returned by the query.

■ FOR EXAMPLE

```
TYPE t_cursor IS REF CURSOR;
c_cursor t_cursor;
```

The example below illustrates how to retrieve a recordset that is then used to paint the page shown in Figure 18.4. This procedure paints a list of students. The screen allows users to choose different sort options for data. The ORDER BY clause of the query is constructed using the column name that is passed in.

Sort By:

○ First Name
○ Last Name
⊙ Employer

Lorraine	Harty	A.D. Tihany, Intnl
Adele	Rothstein	A.H.R.B.
Kate	Page	A.H.R.B.
Anil	Kulina	ARFBO
Winsome	Laporte	ARFBO
Julius	Kwong	Adler & Shaykin
Fred	Crocitto	Albert Hildegard Co.
J.	Landry	Albert Hildegard Co.
Laetia	Enison	Albert Hildegard Co.

Figure 18.4 ■ List using Native Dynamic SQL to sort records.

To allow users to pick another sort order, a radio button is used. The onClick event can be used for the radio buttons to refresh the page with the new sort order as soon as a radio button is clicked.

■ FOR EXAMPLE

```
1   CREATE OR REPLACE PROCEDURE get_students (
2        p_column IN VARCHAR2 DEFAULT 'last_name')
3   IS
4        TYPE t_cursor IS REF CURSOR;
5        c_cursor t_cursor;
6        r_student STUDENT%ROWTYPE;
7        v_select_statement VARCHAR2(250);
8        v_checked VARCHAR2(9);
9
10  BEGIN
11       v_select_statement := ' SELECT * '
12       ||' FROM STUDENT '
13       ||' ORDER BY '||p_column;
14
15       htp.p('<HTML><BODY>');
16       htp.p('Sort By: <BR>');
17       htp.p('<FORM NAME="column_form" ACTION="get_students">');
18       IF p_column='first_name'
19           THEN v_checked := ' CHECKED ';
20           ELSE v_checked := NULL;
21       END IF;
22       htp.p('<INPUT NAME="p_column" TYPE="radio" VALUE="first_name"
23                        ||v_checked||'onClick="this.form.submit();">
24               First Name<BR>');
25       IF p_column='last_name'
26           THEN v_checked := ' CHECKED ';
27           ELSE v_checked := NULL;
28       END IF;
29       htp.p('<INPUT NAME="p_column" TYPE="radio" VALUE="last_name"'
30                        ||v_checked||'onClick="this.form.submit();">
31               Last Name<BR>');
32       IF p_column='employer'
33           THEN v_checked := ' CHECKED ';
34           ELSE v_checked := NULL;
35       END IF;
36       htp.p('<INPUT NAME="p_column" TYPE="radio" VALUE="employer"'
37                        ||v_checked||'onClick="this.form.submit();">
38                 Employer<BR>');
39       htp.p('</FORM>');
40
41       htp.p('<TABLE BORDER="1">');
42
```

```
43      OPEN c_cursor FOR v_select_statement;
44
45         LOOP
46         FETCH c_cursor INTO r_student;
47         EXIT WHEN c_cursor%NOTFOUND;
48         htp.p('
49           <TR>
50           <TD>'||r_student.first_name||'</TD>
51           <TD>'||r_student.last_name||'</TD>
52           <TD>'||r_student.employer||'</TD>
53           </TR>
54           ');
55         END LOOP;
56
57      CLOSE c_cursor;
58      htp.p('</TABLE>');
59      htp.p('</BODY></HTML>');
60   EXCEPTION
61      WHEN OTHERS THEN
62      htp.p('Error in get_students: '||SQLERRM);
63   END;
```

BEWARE OF INVALID SQL

Because it is constructed at runtime, the SQL string itself is not compiled and checked for errors. So if you have a reference to a table or column that does not exist, or if you have typos like SELCET, the PL/SQL procedure will compile successfully. However, when the program is run, the SQL statement is assembled and executed, and a PL/SQL error will be raised at that point.

To help debug this problem, always use a PL/SQL variable to hold the SQL statement you wish to run. Then it is very easy to use htp.p to print the SQL statement to the screen, where it can be checked for errors, or even cut-and-pasted into a SQL*Plus session and tested.

UNIT 18.5

WRITE AND REUSE MODULAR COMPONENTS

REUSE CODE FOR INSERT AND UPDATE

In Chapter 12, "Working with PL/SQL Server Pages (PSPs)," you created a PSP, student_personal_info.psp, that allows a user to edit an existing student, based on the values of first name and last name parameters input into another PSP, search_student.psp. When a first name/last name combination for a student yields a matching result from the database, then the resulting form painted by the procedure, student_personal_info.psp, displays the personal information for that student. If the submitted values yield no matching result from the database, then the form that is painted by student_personal_info.psp is a generic input form, ready for a new student to be inserted into the database.

In the interest of brevity, this example excludes the possibility of a user not entering any values at all, or the user entering a first name/last name combination that yields more than one matching result from the database. In both instances, the user is brought to another Web page painted by the PSP, student_list.psp, where she is prompted to choose one student from a list of possible students in the result set.

The fact that you create the PSP student_personal_info.psp in such a way as to be able to either display a blank input form, or display an editable form populated with information from the database for a single student, makes your PSP *reusable*. You could create two PSPs: one for adding a student and another for editing an existing student. However, the hallmark of good database and Web application design is to reuse as much code as possible, thereby streamlining your coding approach, scaling down the number and types of programs you need to keep track of, and making your entire application more manageable.

In this chapter, you complete the entire process for adding/editing a student by creating the PSP update_student.psp. Though this PSP is titled "update_student," it is a multipurpose (i.e., reusable) procedure in that it can be used to either add a new student or edit an existing student. This PSP is the ACTION of the PSP student_personal_info. Please refer to Chapter 12, "Working with PL/SQL Server Pages (PSPs)," for an example of the student_personal_info procedure. An example of the update_student procedure you can use as the ACTION of your student_personal_info procedure follows:

■ FOR EXAMPLE

```
1   <%@ page language="PL/SQL" %>
2   <%@ plsql procedure="update_student" %>
3   <%@ plsql parameter="p_student_id" type="number"
4       default="null" %>
5   <%@ plsql parameter="p_salutation" default="null" %>
6   <%@ plsql parameter="p_first_name" default="null" %>
7   <%@ plsql parameter="p_last_name" default="null" %>
8   <%@ plsql parameter="p_street_address" default="null" %>
9   <%@ plsql parameter="p_phone" default="null" %>
10  <%@ plsql parameter="p_employer" default="null" %>
11  <%@ plsql parameter="p_registration_date" type="date"
12      default="null" %>
13  <%@ plsql parameter="p_zip" default="null" %>
14  <%
15  ---------------------------------------------------------
16  -- FILENAME:    update_student.psp
17  -- FILEDATE:    02.02.2002
18  -- CREATED BY:  Melanie Caffrey
19  -- DESCRIPTION: Update Student
20  -- URL:         http://local_host/pls/any/update_student
21  ---------------------------------------------------------
21  %>
22  <%! v_count INTEGER := 0;
23  %>
24  <% SELECT COUNT(*)
25       INTO v_count
26       FROM student
27      WHERE student_id = p_student_id;
28  <%
29  -- If the value passed in for p_student_id matches one
30  -- already stored in the database, (i.e., the value of
31  -- v_count is greater than 0), then the information for
32  -- the student whose student ID value matches the
33  -- p_student_id value is updated.
34  %>
35    IF v_count > 0
36    THEN
37    UPDATE student
38       SET salutation = p_salutation,
```

```
39              first_name = p_first_name,
40               last_name = p_last_name,
41          street_address = p_street_address,
42                   phone = p_phone,
43                employer = p_employer,
44       registration_date = p_registration_date,
45                     zip = p_zip
46       WHERE student_id = p_student_id;
47
48     COMMIT;
49 %>
50 <%
51 -- A JavaScript alert informs the user that, not only
52 -- does this student exist in the database, but that
53 -- this student's information has now been successfully
54 -- updated with the values passed in from the
55 -- student_personal_info procedure's form.
56 %>
57 <SCRIPT LANGUAGE="JavaScript">
58   alert("This student has been updated.");
59 </SCRIPT>
60 <%
61 -- Another call to student_personal_info then redisplays
62 -- the newly updated values for this student, just after
63 -- the update and the informational JavaScript alert, so
64 -- that the user may double-check her work immediately,
65 -- without having to re-query.
66 %>
67 <% student_personal_info(p_student_id);
68 <%
69 -- Otherwise, if the student ID passed in does not match
70 -- that of any student in the database, then the student
71 -- information in the student_personal_info procedure's
72 -- form is for that of a new student.  Therefore, the
73 -- DML action to be taken is an insert statement,
74 -- instead of an update statement.
75 %>
76   ELSE
77      INSERT INTO student (student_id,
78                            salutation,
79                            first_name,
80                            last_name,
81                            street_address,
82                            phone,
83                            employer,
84                            registration_date,
85                            zip,
86                            created_by,
87                            created_date,
```

```
88                          modified_by,
89                          modified_date)
90              VALUES (p_student_id,
91                          p_salutation,
92                          p_first_name,
93                          p_last_name,
94                          p_street_address,
95                          p_phone,
96                          p_employer,
97                          NVL(p_registration_date,
98                              SYSDATE),
99                          p_zip,
100                         USER,
101                         SYSDATE,
102                         USER,
103                         SYSDATE);
104
105     COMMIT;
106 %>
107 <%
108 -- Notice that the message displayed in this JavaScript
109 -- alert, following a successful insert statement, is
110 -- slightly different from the one displayed in the
111 -- JavaScript alert that immediately follows a
112 -- successful update statement.
113 %>
114 <SCRIPT LANGUAGE="JavaScript">
115  alert("This new student has been added.");
116 </SCRIPT>
117 <%
118 -- Here again, you should always redisplay the form so
119 -- that the user may double-check her work.
120 %>
121 <% student_personal_info(p_student_id);
122   END IF;
123 %>
```

By the same token, the PSP that is used to invoke a JavaScript pop-up window, allowing a user to choose a zipcode value for the student she is editing, should also be reusable. If the student being edited exists in the database, then that student's zipcode value should be preselected in the zipcode JavaScript pop-up window when the pop-up is invoked. Otherwise, no zipcode value should be preselected.

■ FOR EXAMPLE

```
1 <%@ page language="PL/SQL" %>
2 <%@ plsql procedure="student_zipcode" %>
3 <%@ plsql parameter="p_student_id" type="number"
4     default="null" %>
```

```
 5 <%
 6 ----------------------------------------------------------
 7 -- FILENAME:    student_zipcode.psp
 8 -- FILEDATE:    02.02.2002
 9 -- CREATED BY:  Melanie Caffrey
10 -- DESCRIPTION: Change Zipcode (and City and State)
11 -- URL:         http://local_host/pls/any/student_zipcode
12 ----------------------------------------------------------
13 %>
14 <%! CURSOR c_zip
15     IS
16         SELECT city, state, zip
17           FROM zipcode
18         ORDER BY state, city, zip;
19
20     v_count INTEGER := 0;
21     v_zip zipcode.zip%TYPE := NULL;
22 %>
23
24 <% SELECT COUNT(*)
25      INTO v_count
26      FROM student
27     WHERE student_id = p_student_id;
28
29    IF v_count > 0
30    THEN
31      SELECT zip
32        INTO v_zip
33        FROM student
34       WHERE student_id = p_student_id;
35    END IF;
36 %>
37
38 <HTML>
39 <HEAD>
40 <TITLE>Student Zipcodes</TITLE>
41 <SCRIPT LANGUAGE="JavaScript">
42 function chooseZip() {
43 window.opener.student_personal_form.p_zip.value=
44 document.zip_form.p_newzip.value;
45 window.close();
46 }
47 </SCRIPT>
48 <%
49 -- Remember that the code for this JavaScript function
50 -- MUST be written on one line.  Otherwise, your
51 -- function call with fail.
52 %>
53 </HEAD>
```

```
54 <BODY BGCOLOR="pink">
55 <H2>List of Available Zipcodes With Associated
56     City/State Values</H2>
57 <FORM NAME="zip_form" ACTION="">
58 <CENTER><TABLE BORDER="1" BORDERCOLOR="forest green"
59           CELLPADDING=5>
60 <TR>
61 <TH ALIGN="center">City, State and Zipcode</TH>
62 </TR>
63 <TR>
64 <TD ALIGN="left"><SELECT SIZE="20" SCROLLBARS="yes"
65  NAME="p_newzip">
66 <% FOR rec IN c_ZIP
67    LOOP
68        IF rec.zip = v_zip
69        THEN
70 %>
71 <OPTION VALUE="<%= rec.zip %>" SELECTED><%= rec.city %>,
72 <%= rec.state %> <%= rec.zip %>
73 </OPTION>
74 <%     ELSE %>
75 <OPTION VALUE="<%= rec.zip %>"><%= rec.city %>,
76 <%= rec.state %> <%= rec.zip %>
77 </OPTION>
78 <%     END IF;
79    END LOOP;
80 %>
81 </SELECT>
82 </TD>
83 </TR>
84 </TABLE></CENTER>
85 <BR>
86 <CENTER><INPUT TYPE="button" VALUE="Select Zipcode"
87 onclick="javascript:chooseZip();">  
87 <INPUT TYPE="button" VALUE="Close"
88 onClick="window.close();"></CENTER>
89 </FORM>
90 </BODY>
91 </HTML>
```

ORGANIZE PL/SQL CODE INTO PACKAGES

PL/SQL packages are reviewed in detail in Chapter 9, "PL/SQL Review." There are a number of advantages to using packages with Web Toolkit code.

- Organization
- Security
- Combining frequently used code

Packages are an excellent way to organize code. Related procedures and functions can be grouped together under a short, informative name.

Using packages also allows you to take advantage of security features. Packages allow you to determine what is public and what is private. By declaring something in the package specification, it becomes public. Something that is declared only in the package body is private, and can only be accessed by other procedures/functions in the same package body.

Any procedures, variables, cursors, or other objects you want to access directly from the URL must be public, that is, declared in the package specification. This includes URLs that HTML must access directly, such as the FORM tag's ACTION attribute value and procedures specified as the source code for a FRAME.

Anything that is private cannot be called directly through a URL. This is a helpful security precaution on the Web. The code that calculates a salary bonus could be a private function called by a form handler.

Package specifications are a place to store variables for look and feel on the Web. If the value of background color is always taken from a package variable, instead of being hard-coded, then the application can be redesigned with less pain. You can change the value of your background color variable in the package specification once, and affect the whole application.

**UNIT
18.5**

Cursors can be declared in a package and then used throughout the application. A cursor that will be used by multiple procedures to build your site is a good candidate. Instead of cutting and pasting the same cursor in multiple procedures, declare it in one place, in the package specification. You could declare a cursor in the package specification to select students who list an employer.

■ FOR EXAMPLE

```
CURSOR c_students IS
   SELECT *
     FROM student
    WHERE employer IS NOT NULL
    ORDER BY last_name, first_name;
```

This cursor is used in procedures the same way that it would be if it were declared locally. The only difference is that the package name must prefix the cursor name. If the cursor above were declared in the package specification called IN-STRUCT, it could be used in a procedure like this.

■ FOR EXAMPLE

```
CREATE OR REPLACE PROCEDURE GET_EMPLOYED_STUDENTS AS
BEGIN
htp.p('<HTML>
```

```
      <HEAD><TITLE>Employed Students</TITLE></HEAD>
      <BODY>');
 FOR rec IN INSTRUCT.c_students LOOP
   htp.p(rec.last_name||', '||rec.first_name||' -- '||rec.em-
ployer);
 END LOOP;
htp.p('</BODY>
      </HTML>');
END;
```

A cursor declared in the package specification is easier to maintain. If the requirements change and the cursor should be limited to students who are registered in one class, the cursor can be changed in one place, and affect the rest of the application that calls it. This kind of modularity is ideal in any application.

As covered in Chapter 11, "Web Toolkit II: Frames, Forms, and Parameters," multiple selections for the same parameter are sent as a PL/SQL table, and Oracle provides PL/SQL types in OWA_UTIL to assist with this situation. However, a PL/SQL table cannot be declared as an IN parameter with the keywords NOT NULL because a PL/SQL table cannot be NULL. Instead, declare a variable with the type of a PL/SQL table. Declare it in a package specification so that it is easily accessible by other packages/procedures. To review, the syntax is:

```
   nothungry OWA_UTIL.IDENT_ARR;
```

If this is declared in a package specification, such as a package called "restaurants," other programs could use it like this:

```
   PROCEDURE do_search (p_restaurants IN OWA_UTIL.IDENT_ARR
                        DEFAULT restaurants.nothungry) IS...
```

CODE STANDARDS

Coding standards can be enforced by using packages. Frequently used code should be placed in a package. A good convention is to give the package a name ending in "_UTIL," indicating that the contents are "utilities," much like Oracle does with the OWA_UTIL package, explored in detail in Chapter 16, "The OWA_UTIL Package: Dynamic SQL, HTML, Date Utilities, and More." Programs contained in your utility package should handle specific jobs well and be reusable.

Setting aside commonly used code into an easily identifiable package encourages programmers to check whether there is existing code that they can call, instead of reinventing it. Anything that promotes reusing code is a good idea. The programs in a utility package can also communicate coding standards by example. The programs should reflect the best coding practices on the project, since they will be used by many different programs.

STANDARDIZE HEADERS AND FOOTERS

Headers and footers are easily standardized on Web pages, just as they are in print media. A typical Web application might have standard procedures to paint headers and footers.

A standard header on the Web might:

- Set a background color and standard font
- Paint a logo for the application and/or the organization
- Set the window's title
- Paint standard navigational links

A standard footer on the Web might contain such elements as:

- The current date and time
- A copyright symbol and a department or company name
- A link for email feedback
- Audit information from the database for the current record

Displaying the date and time, which is easily done by selecting and formatting the "SYSDATE" pseudo column in Oracle, is a quick way to give an application a professional and up-to-date appearance.

The advantages of creating standard code to paint a header and footer are clear. The code is modular; the statements that create the header and footer on each page are isolated and can be reused. The code is stored in one place and can easily be changed. Each page that calls these header and footer procedures will have a unified look and feel, which is a goal for any well-designed application. If a logo is changed, it is very easy to update the code in one place, the procedure that paints the header, and affect the rest of the application.

First, create a procedure that can paint a header page for you.

■ FOR EXAMPLE

```
CREATE OR REPLACE PROCEDURE paint_header AS
BEGIN
htp.p('<HTML>
       <HEAD>
       <TITLE>University Maintenance Website </TITLE>
       </HEAD>
       <BODY BGCOLOR="#99CCCC">
       <FONT FACE= "'||instruct.v_font||'">
```

```
        ');
EXCEPTION
  WHEN OTHERS THEN
      htp.p('An error occurred in paint_header: '||SQLERRM);
END;
```

Now create a procedure to paint a page footer. Note that the closing </FONT>, </BODY>, and </HTML> tags are placed in the footer procedure since it will close out the page.

■ FOR EXAMPLE

```
CREATE OR REPLACE PROCEDURE paint_footer AS
BEGIN
htp.p('<HR>
        <I><CENTER>University Maintenance Website '
        ||TO_CHAR(sysdate,'MM/DD/YYYY HH24:MI')||'</CENTER></I>
        </FONT>
        </BODY>
        </HTML>
     ');
EXCEPTION
  WHEN OTHERS THEN
     htp.p('An error occurred in paint_footer: '||SQLERRM);
END;
```

This procedure makes use of the variable, *v_font*, declared in the package specification for the `instruct` package defined in Chapter 9, "PL/SQL Review." If the font needs to be changed in the application, then the value assigned to *v_font* can be changed in the package specification. The background color is hard-coded in paint_header, but it could also be defined in the package specification instead, and referenced here.

For more on designing the architecture of your Web application, please refer to Chapter 20, "Web Application Architecture." This chapter provides more guidance on how to structure a Web application for maximum reusability.

C H A P T E R   1 9

ADDITIONAL WEB TOOLKIT UTILITIES AND PL/SQL BUILT-INS

CHAPTER OBJECTIVES

In this chapter you learn about:

This chapter continues the book's ongoing illustration of some of the many PL/SQL built-in functions and utilities that can be used to speed up and enhance your Web-based applications. It is important to remember that many of the PL/SQL packages introduced in this chapter (except for OWA_SEC, OWA_OPT_LOCK, and OWA_PATTERN) are part of the Oracle database—not the Oracle iAS—and therefore can be used with or apart from the iAS. These packages are part of your Web development "toolkit" that provides you with the built-in assistance you need to develop technical solutions quickly and troubleshoot problems efficiently.

UNIT 19.1

SENDING ELECTRONIC MAIL FROM AN ORACLE DATABASE

If you'd like to send email from PL/SQL applications and from an Oracle database, you can use the UTL_SMTP package. This package follows the Simple Mail Transfer Protocol (SMTP) standards. *SMTP* is the Internet's standard protocol for email. SMTP serves as an Application Programmer Interface (API) to SMTP mail systems. Since Oracle's UTL_SMTP package uses SMTP standards, you are given the ability to call its functions or procedures to send email directly from the database. You can use PL/SQL to construct your email message text, and easily incorporate information retrieved from the database. You will need to know the name or IP address of the SMTP mail server used by the sender, as well as the email addresses for the sender and recipient(s).

    UTL_SMTP does not receive mail. It only sends mail.

To send email with the UTL_SMTP package, you must perform the following steps:

1. Open an SMTP connection to an SMTP mail server.
   (UTL_SMTP.open_connection)
2. Perform initial handshaking with the SMTP server after connecting.
   (UTL_SMTP.helo)
3. Identify the domain/host of the sender. (UTL_SMTP.mail)
4. Identify the domain/host of the recipient. (UTL_SMTP.rcpt)
5. Open the body of the mail transmission using standard syntax.
   (UTL_SMTP.data)
6. Write the mail message. (UTL_SMTP.data)
7. Close the connection. (UTL_SMTP.quit)

The following example provides you with a very simple starting point for learning how to send email from the database.

```
1  CREATE OR REPLACE PROCEDURE send_mail_tamra
2  IS
3  -- Declare a variable for a carriage return and a line feed.
4  -- Conveniently name it "crlf."
5    crlf VARCHAR2(2):= CHR(13) || CHR(10);
6
7    mailhost VARCHAR2(30) := '111.22.33.444';
8
9    -- utl_smtp.connection is a record type, illustrated below:
10   --TYPE connection IS RECORD (
11   --host                 VARCHAR2(255),     -- remote host name
12   --port                 PLS_INTEGER,       -- remote port number
13   --tx_timeout           PLS_INTEGER,       -- Transfer time-out
     --                                        (in
14   --                                        seconds)
15   --private_tcp_con   utl_tcp.connection,  -- private, for
     --                                        implementation
16   --                                        use
17   --private_state        PLS_INTEGER       -- private, for
     --                                        implementation
18   --                                        use
19   --);
20   mail_conn utl_smtp.connection;
21
22   -- Declare a variable to hold the contents of your mail message.
23   message VARCHAR2(1000);
24 BEGIN
25   -- The variable mailhost holds the contents of the remote host
26   -- name or IP address. (See above declaration.)
27   -- 25 is the port number of the remote SMTP server.  This is a
28   -- default value.
29   mail_conn := utl_smtp.open_connection(mailhost, 25);
30
31   -- Perform initial handshaking with SMTP server after connecting.
32   utl_smtp.helo(mail_conn, mailhost);
33
34   -- The sender must be a valid email address.
35   utl_smtp.mail(mail_conn, 'don_and_fran@newton_solutions.com');
36
37   -- The recipient must also be a valid email address.
38   utl_smtp.rcpt(mail_conn, 'lori_and_chris@columbia.edu');
39
40   -- You can even add HTML tags inside your message body.
41   message := '<FONT COLOR=TEAL> <H1> Tamra, <H1></FONT> <BR>'||
```

```
42              '<H3><FONT COLOR=BLUE> This message has been sent
                to you
43              using the UTL_SMTP package.  </FONT><BR>'||
44              '<FONT COLOR=RED>Note the fact that I am using HTML
                to send
45              you this message.  </FONT><BR>'||
46              '<FONT COLOR=PURPLE>I hope the readers will enjoy
                using
47              this package as much as you do.  </FONT><BR>'||
48              '<FONT COLOR=MAROON>Oh, and please let me know if you
49              received this correctly. </FONT></H3>';
50
51    -- Specifies the body of an email message.
52    utl_smtp.data(mail_conn,
53                    'MIME-Version: 1.0' || crlf ||
54                    'Content-type: text/html' || crlf ||
55                    'Date: ' || TO_CHAR( SYSDATE, 'dd Mon yy
                    hh24:mi:ss' )
56                    || crlf ||
57                    'From: ' || 'Frances and Donald' || ' <' ||
58                    'don_and_fran@newton_solutions.com' ||'>' ||
                    crlf ||
59                    'Subject: ' || 'Let''s See If This Works' ||
                    crlf ||
60                    'To: ' ||'Tamra Newton' || ' <' ||
61                    'lori_and_chris@columbia.edu'
62                    ||'>' || crlf || message );
63
64    -- Terminates an SMTP session and disconnects from the server.
65    utl_smtp.quit(mail_conn);
66 EXCEPTION
67 WHEN OTHERS THEN
68 DBMS_OUTPUT.PUT_LINE('Send Mail Error: ' || SUBSTR(SQLERRM,1,100));
69 END;
```

This example provides a basic sample of what UTL_SMTP can do for you. There are many other procedures and functions in the UTL_SMTP package that have not been included here because they are not necessary for the purposes of this illustration. For a more extensive overview of UTL_SMTP, please consult your Oracle software documentation. All Oracle documentation can be downloaded from http://docs.oracle.com.

UNIT 19.2

READING OTHER WEB SITES

Oracle provides an interesting package that allows PL/SQL to read Web pages like a text-only browser. This package is *UTL_HTTP*. UTL_HTTP reads HTML into a PL/SQL table or a VARCHAR2 variable. You are then free to analyze the resulting HTML source code.

A natural question is: Why would anyone be interested in analyzing the HTML of someone else's Web site? There are numerous reasons. You might want to read a document, then, after having analyzed its contents, isolate the data you find most relevant, then load it into your database. You might also wish to read a document from your own site and save the text in the database. This saved text could serve as an audit trail of how the document source code changes over time.

There are two things to consider when using UTL_HTTP. If you have trouble connecting to a site using UTL_HTTP, then see whether a browser has the same difficulty connecting to the site. Place a browser on the same machine/node (as the database server), and then try to connect using the browser. If you cannot connect to the Web site using a browser, then you cannot connect to the Web site using UTL_HTTP.

 UTL_HTTP does not accept cookies. So make sure you turn cookies off in the browser you are using for testing.

UTL_HTTP FUNCTIONS

The two UTL_HTTP functions are REQUEST and REQUEST_PIECES. Table 19.1 illustrates the difference between the two.

Table 19.1 ■ UTL_HTTP Functions

Function	Return Value
REQUEST	4,000-character string
REQUEST_PIECES	VARCHAR2 PL/SQL table (array) of 2,000-byte pieces

If the page you are reading is longer than 4,000 characters, REQUEST truncates the results. Therefore, you could potentially miss some of the important contents of the document. Since most documents are longer than 4,000 bytes, this book recommends you use REQUEST_PIECES.

In order to use REQUEST_PIECES, you must first define a PL/SQL table in which to receive the result.

■ FOR EXAMPLE

```
v_html_table utl_http.html_pieces;
```

HTML_PIECES is a table type defined in the UTL_HTTP package. It is defined as follows:

```
TYPE html_pieces IS TABLE OF VARCHAR2(2000) INDEX BY BINARY_INTEGER;
```

And an example of making a procedural call that would populate this v_html_table PL/SQL table with HTML source code is:

```
v_html_table := utl_http.request_pieces
('http://www.some_web_site.com');
```

The REQUEST_PIECES function accepts several input parameters. However, only the first parameter, the URL, is mandatory (as illustrated in the above example). The other input parameters are optional and are described briefly in Table 19.2.

Despite its drawbacks, however ...

UTL_HTTP.REQUEST can be used fairly easily. Consider the following example syntax:

```
SELECT UTL_HTTP.REQUEST('www.some_web_site.com')
  FROM dual;
```

Table 19.2 ■ REQUEST_PIECES Parameters

Parameter	Description
MAX_PIECES	**(Optional)** Used to specify the maximum number of pieces (array records) REQUEST_PIECES returns before truncating the page. The default is 32K (approximately 17 pieces or array records). This parameter only needs to be specified if the document storage exceeds this amount.
PROXY	**(Optional)** Used to tell UTL_HTTP the IP address or domain of your proxy server. The default is NULL, which indicates none is required.
WALLET_PATH	**(Optional)** Specifies a client-side wallet, which contains the list of trusted certificate authorities required for HTTPS requests. Non-HTTPS requests do not require an Oracle wallet.
WALLET_PASSWORD	**(Optional)** Specifies the password required to open the wallet.

Note that the pieces retrieved from the REQUEST_PIECES function are put together in byte order, one after another. Every array element is a full 2,000 bytes (though not quite 2K) long, except the last one. REQUEST_PIECES does NOT return the document with clean line breaks. Lines in the document are put together to a maximum length of 2,000 bytes, one at a time (including new line characters), with the next piece picking up immediately where the previous piece left off. An example of how UTL_HTTP can be used to read a document from a Web site, which could either be displayed in a table data cell or a frame, or printed using SQL*Plus, follows:

```
CREATE OR REPLACE PROCEDURE utl_http_example
(ip_url IN VARCHAR2 DEFAULT 'http://www.Some_Web_Site.com')
IS
   v_html_table utl_http.html_pieces;
BEGIN
   htp.header(1, 'Begin Retrieving and Printing '||ip_url);
   v_html_table := utl_http.request_pieces(ip_url);
   -- "Count" is an attribute of the table type that holds the
   -- number of pieces retrieved.
   FOR i IN 1 .. v_html_table.count
   LOOP
      htp.p(v_html_table(i));
   END LOOP;
   htp.header(1, 'Completed Retrieving and Printing '||ip_url);
END;
```

UTL_HTTP EXCEPTIONS

There are two exceptions you should declare when using the UTL_HTTP function. If you do not declare these exceptions, it is then possible that you will receive an ORA-06510 error indicating a PL/SQL unhandled user-defined exception has occurred each time any other error has occurred. The two exceptions that should be declared are:

```
DECLARE
    init_failed     EXCEPTION;
    request_failed EXCEPTION;
```

The init_failed exception occurs when initialization of the HTTP callout subsystem fails. This means that an environmental failure, such as lack of available memory, has occurred. When the HTTP call fails, the request_failed exception takes place. The HTTP call fails when the HTTP *daemon* (background process) fails or if the URL argument cannot be interpreted as a URL because it either has non-HTTP syntax or is NULL. You will receive a request_failed error if the site doesn't respond, or the site is down.

ADDITIONAL USES OF UTL_HTTP

There are numerous other possible uses of UTL_HTTP. For instance, you can track stock prices, use UTL_HTTP as a cyber robot (collecting URL and keyword information) to gather information about your competitors, create semistatic Web pages (like creating a static home page from data like weekly financial news or weather information), call other CGI programs, read templates, and perform load testing.

If the Course Cost value in your application's COURSE table fluctuates from semester to semester, for example, and you would like to keep a historical record of those fluctuating cost values, you could obtain and retain such information in a database table or an operating system file. If, for instance, you have created a Web page called *course_info*, accessible by students and instructors, that displays course cost information, the HTML source code for the portion of the page that displays the course cost value might look like the following:

```
<TABLE BORDER="1">
<TR>
<TH>Course Description</TH>
<TH>Course Cost</TH>
</TR>
<TR>
<TD ALIGN="LEFT">Intro to SQL</TD>
<TD ALIGN="LEFT">1200</TD>
</TR>
</TABLE>
```

With UTL_HTTP, you can retrieve the HTML from the table in this page by coding a statement similar to the following, passing in the Course Number value of 204:

```
v_html_table := utl_http.request_pieces
('http://local_host/pls/any/course_info?p_course_no=204');
```

After execution, the results of the query are placed into the PL/SQL table, v_html_table. These results can then be parsed to extract key information like the following:

```
start_pos := INSTR(v_html_table(i), '<TABLE>');
end_pos   := INSTR(v_html_table(i), '</TABLE>', start_pos+1);
key_info  := SUBSTR(v_html_table(i), start_pos, end_pos - start_pos);
```

The value from the key_info variable can then be used to perform other tasks stored in the database or written to a file. You can even break down the key_information variable further, to meet your individual needs.

UNIT 19.3

ENCRYPTING SENSITIVE DATA

It is vital to keep your data confidential and secure. The obvious example is passwords; they should not be accessible to just anyone. Though HTML provides the password input type to hide manually typed passwords, until recently, Oracle did not provide any built-in functionality of its own to hide sensitive data. Though Oracle passwords have always been encrypted, occasionally an overcurious observer can see things he or she isn't supposed to see.

Due to these types of circumstances, you may choose to *obfuscate*, or scramble, the data as it is stored. This way, no one is able to tell what it truly means just by merely querying the database using a simple SELECT statement. Oracle's answer to a method for encrypting and decrypting data is provided with the DBMS_OBFUSCATION_TOOLKIT package. This package makes use of the Data Encryption Standard (DES), developed by IBM around 1974 and adopted as a U.S. national standard in 1977. Encrypted data can be stored in the database just as passwords are.

The DBMS_OBFUSCATION_TOOLKIT package is often referred to as simply DBMS_OBFUSCATE. However, always use the full name in your code.

The DBMS_OBFUSCATION_TOOLKIT package contains two broad kinds of routines, as well as some supporting objects in the package header. The two kinds of routines include those procedures and functions used to *encrypt* (encode) data, and those procedures and functions used to *decrypt* (decode) data. For instance, the unencrypted (raw) value of a variable could be "STUDENT4," but after this value has been encrypted, the new encrypted value might look more like "Qpr~Uv_t," thereby hiding it. The decryption process would then restore "Qpr~Uv_t" to its original value of "STUDENT4."

The procedures and functions in this package are further subdivided by data type. One set of procedures and functions operates on raw, unformatted data, and another set operates on regular character data.

DESENCRYPT AND DESDECRYPT

The character version of the DesEncrypt procedure has three parameters: *input_string* and *key_string* are input parameters, and *encrypted_string* is an output parameter. The function version accepts only the first two values and returns the encrypted value as the function return value. All are of data type VARCHAR2, and all must have lengths that are multiples of eight characters. If any one of them is not a multiple of eight characters, then the function (or procedure) returns the following error message:

```
ORA-28232: invalid input length for obfuscation toolkit
```

The *input string* is the piece of data to be encoded: a Social Security number, a password, or any other piece of data requiring encryption. The data type of the input string must be character (or raw, for the raw routines). If you need to encode an input string of another data type, make sure you convert it to character data first.

The *key* is a text value used to encode the input string. Different keys (i.e., different text values) applied to the same input string produce different encoded results.

Once data has been encoded, it is extremely important not to lose the key that was used to encode it. While it IS possible to break encoded values without a key, this is very difficult and, the longer the key value is, the harder it is to break its encoded string.

Keys must be greater than or equal to eight characters.

Some versions of Oracle will not allow you to call the DesEncrypt function using positional notation. Therefore, in some instances, you'll have to use named notation instead.

The following example encrypts the string "MATTHEW2" using a key string (or password) of "MICHAEL3," and places the resulting encrypted string into the *v_encrypted* variable. This example uses named notation.

```
dbms_obfuscation_toolkit.desencrypt(
    input_string      ==> 'MATTHEW2'
    key_string        ==> 'MICHAEL3'
    encrypted_string  ==> v_encrypted
);
```

And, by the same token, the next bit of code decrypts the string currently in the v_encrypted variable using the key string denoted by *v_key,* and finally places the decrypted value into the text variable named *v_decrypted.*

```
dbms_obfuscation_toolkit.desdecrypt(
    input_string      ==> v_encrypted
    key_string        ==> v_key
    decrypted_string  ==> v_decrypted
);
```

DES3ENCRYPT AND DES3DECRYPT

The DES has proven to be easier to break over time, with the availability of increased computing power that can churn through possible keys. In response, a more powerful standard called Triple DES (also called 3DES or DES3) has been developed, based on the same DES algorithm but using a longer key length.

Des3Encrypt and Des3Decrypt are a little more complicated than their DesEncrypt and DesDecrypt counterparts because they have more rules attached to them. The Des3 modules are more secure because they require longer keys, which must be precisely 128 or 192 bytes in length. Why did Oracle choose the values of 128 and 192? Because both numbers are multiples of 64 and use 2 ($64 \times 2 = 128$) or 3 ($64 \times 3 = 192$) 64-byte keys to encrypt the data. You can control whether 128 or 192 bytes are used by using an extra parameter called "which." The *which* parameter can have only one of two values: 0 (defined for the TwoKey-Mode package variable) and 1 (defined for the ThreeKeyMode package variable.) Thus, if you use 0, the key must be 128 characters long. And if you use 1, the key must be 192 characters long. The example below provides the syntax for the Des3Encrypt procedure:

```
dbms_obfuscation_toolkit.des3encrypt(
    input_string      ==> v_text
    key_string        ==> v_key_192
    encrypted_string  ==> v_encrypted
    which             ==> 1
);
```

And the next example provides the syntax for the Des3Decrypt procedure:

```
dbms_obfuscation_toolkit.des3decrypt(
    input_string      ==> v_encrypted
    key_string        ==> v_key_192
    encrypted_string  ==> v_decrypted
    which             ==> 1
);
```

The following sample procedure illustrates both encryption and decryption using the DBMS_OBFUSCATION_TOOLKIT package.

```
1 CREATE OR REPLACE PROCEDURE obfuscation_test
2 (ip_key    VARCHAR2 DEFAULT 'MARY_JUR',
```

```
3   ip_key_128 VARCHAR2 DEFAULT  NULL,
4   ip_key_192 VARCHAR2 DEFAULT  NULL,
5   ip_text    VARCHAR2 DEFAULT 'MIKE_LIN')
6 IS
7     v_decrypted VARCHAR2(1000);
8     v_encrypted VARCHAR2(1000);
9     v_key_128   VARCHAR2(128) := RPAD(NVL(ip_key_128, ip_key), 128);
10    v_key_192   VARCHAR2(192) := RPAD(NVL(ip_key_192, ip_key), 192);
11 BEGIN
12    htp.header(1, 'Test Encryption and Decryption');
13    htp.tableOpen('Border=1');
14    htp.tableRowOpen;
15    htp.tableHeader('Unencrypted starting text');
16    htp.tableData(ip_text);
17    htp.tableRowClose;
18
19     BEGIN
20        -- Encrypt your text string.
21        dbms_obfuscation_toolkit.desencrypt
22           (input_string      => ip_text,
23            key_string        => ip_key,
24            encrypted_string => v_encrypted);
25        htp.tableRowOpen;
26        htp.tableHeader('Encrypted text with the key '||ip_key);
27        htp.tableData(v_encrypted);
28        htp.tableRowclose;
29
30        -- Then, decrypt it.
31        dbms_obfuscation_toolkit.desdecrypt
32           (input_string      => v_encrypted,
33            key_string        => ip_key,
34            decrypted_string => v_decrypted);
35        htp.tableRowOpen;
36        htp.tableHeader('Decrypted text with the key '||ip_key);
37        htp.tableData(v_decrypted);
38        htp.tableRowclose;
39     EXCEPTION
40     WHEN OTHERS
41     THEN
42        htp.header(3, 'The following error has occurred:
          '||SQLERRM);
43     END;
44
45 ----------------------------------------------------------------
46 -- Obfuscate using mode value 0 (128 length key value)
47 ----------------------------------------------------------------
48     BEGIN
49        dbms_obfuscation_toolkit.des3encrypt
```

```
50          (input_string     => ip_text,
51           key_string       => v_key_128,
52           encrypted_string => v_encrypted,
53           which            => dbms_obfuscation_toolkit.
                                  TwoKeyMode);
54      htp.tableRowOpen;
55      htp.tableHeader('Encrypted text with the 128-byte key
56                      '||v_key_128);
57      htp.tableData(v_encrypted);
58      htp.tableRowclose;
59
60      dbms_obfuscation_toolkit.des3decrypt
61          (input_string     => v_encrypted,
62           key_string       => v_key_128,
63           decrypted_string => v_decrypted,
64           which            => dbms_obfuscation_toolkit.
                                  TwoKeyMode);
65      htp.tableRowOpen;
66      htp.tableHeader('Decrypted text with the 128-byte key
67                      '||v_key_128);
68      htp.tableData(v_decrypted);
69      htp.tableRowclose;
70    EXCEPTION
71    WHEN OTHERS
72    THEN
73       htp.header(3, 'The following error has occurred:
         '||SQLERRM);
74    END;
75
76  ------------------------------------------------------------------
77  -- Obfuscate using mode value 0 (192 length key value)
78  ------------------------------------------------------------------
79    BEGIN
80      dbms_obfuscation_toolkit.des3encrypt
81          (input_string     => ip_text,
82           key_string       => v_key_192,
83           encrypted_string => v_encrypted,
84           which            => dbms_obfuscation_toolkit.
                                  ThreeKeyMode);
85      htp.tableRowOpen;
86      htp.tableHeader('Encrypted text with the 192-byte key
87                      '||v_key_192);
88      htp.tableData(v_encrypted);
89      htp.tableRowclose;
90
91      dbms_obfuscation_toolkit.des3decrypt
92          (input_string     => v_encrypted,
93           key_string       => v_key_192,
94           decrypted_string => v_decrypted,
```

```
95          which            => dbms_obfuscation_toolkit.
                                ThreeKeyMode);
96      htp.tableRowOpen;
97      htp.tableHeader('Decrypted text with the 192-byte key
98                    '||v_key_192);
99      htp.tableData(v_decrypted);
100     htp.tableRowclose;
101     EXCEPTION
102     WHEN OTHERS
103     THEN
104     htp.header(3, 'The following error has occurred:
        '||SQLERRM);
105   END;
106 END;
```

UNIT 19.4

SECURITY AND AUTHENTICATION

CUSTOM AUTHENTICATION

Custom authentication is for applications that want to control the access within the application itself, as well as for applications that do not have a separate schema for every user who uses the application. Users are authenticated at the Application level and not within the Database level. Acceptable user IDs and passwords can be stored in a table, or the authentication code can contain the acceptable user IDs and passwords.

Custom authentication needs a static database username/password to be stored in the configuration of the DAD, and cannot be combined with the dynamic username/password authentication (such as the "any DAD" created in Chapter 2, "Oracle 9iAS").

When a DAD is configured with the schema name, user, and password, procedures are executed without asking the client to log on with an Oracle database user and password. In this case, an application developer may want to perform other methods of authentication, such as limiting access to a certain range of IP addresses. The Oracle-supplied package OWA_SEC is a utility that provides security to the procedures accessed via the MOD_PLSQL module of the Oracle 9iAS. When a Web client attempts to access a PL/SQL procedure, the utility OWA_SEC can be used to access the client's authentication information and perform an authorization check before allowing access to the procedure. You can either use the utility within the authorization callback procedure or the execution procedure itself, depending on how the DAD is configured.

The OWA_SEC package must be called by a procedure that is performing authentication. If OWA_SEC is called outside of performing authentication, the return value will be NULL.

Also, the authentication mode must be configured correctly in the DAD to use OWA_SEC, as explained in more detail in the next section, "DAD Authentication Modes."

The OWA_SEC package is a set of procedures that allow you to access the username, password, IP address, and hostname from the client that is making a request to the MOD_PLSQL module. In order to make them work, you need to use the OWA_SEC.SET_AUTHORIZATION.

DAD AUTHENTICATION MODES

You can enable different authentication modes using the Authentication Mode parameter on the Gateway Configuration pages for the DAD (see Chapter 2, "Oracle 9iAS," for more details). The Oracle 9iAS module MOD_PLSQL uses the username/password provided in the DAD to log into the database. Once the login is complete, authentication control is passed to the procedures and packages that are being called from the client's browser. These packages have functions that act as PL/SQL hooks that are then called. There are various methods to implement these functions. The return value of the callback function determines if the authentication succeeded or failed. If the function returns TRUE, authentication succeeded. If it returns FALSE, authentication failed and code in the procedure is not executed.

The default mode of authentication is the **Basic Mode**. The authentication used in this mode requires users to supply Oracle database usernames and passwords. No authentication functions are called in this mode. The database username and password can be defined in the DAD, in which case users are allowed to call procedures without supplying a name and password. If they are not specified in the DAD configuration (as in the ANY DAD created in Chapter 2, "Oracle 9iAS"), a logon dialog box will appear asking for an Oracle database username and password for a realm with the name of the DAD being used.

The **Global OWA** authentication mode makes use of a procedure in the schema where the PL/SQL Web Toolkit has been installed. This is usually the SYS schema. In order to implement this mode, the OWA_SEC procedure in the SYS schema will have to be modified.

The **Custom OWA** mode makes use of a procedure in the user's schema to determine authentication. Using this mode requires a customized version of OWA_CUSTOM to be compiled in the user's schema. If an authentication procedure is not found in the user's schema, it will look in the schema that owns the OWA_CUSTOM package, usually the SYS schema.

The **Per Package** mode will make use of packages and procedures in the user's schema. Each package will need to have a function named Authenticate that returns a Boolean value. This is the function that will be used for authenticating the user. It will make use of the procedures and functions in the OWA_SEC package in order to process the authentication.

The **Single Sign-On** mode will make use of a logon server. This is generally used for Oracle Portal 3.0 and above.

OWA_SEC PACKAGE COMPONENTS

The OWA_SEC package contains four functions and one procedure that can be used in OWA authentication. These are detailed in Table 19.3.

OWA_SEC IN THE PER PACKAGE MODE

Per Package authentication mode is used when the authentication takes place within a specified package or in an anonymous authorize function.

Table 19.3 ■ OWA_SEC Package Components

Object	Parameters	Usage
Get_Client_Hostname (Function)	Return: varchar2	This function returns the hostname of the client.
Get_Client_Ip (Function)	Return: owa_util.ip_address	This function returns the IP address of the client in the datatype of four rows in a PL/SQL table. There are four rows, corresponding to the four elements of an IP address.
Get_Password (Function)	Return: varchar2	This function returns the password the user used to log on, but only if a custom authentication mode was configured for the DAD in use.
Get_user_id (Function)	Return varchar2	This function returns the username that was used to log on.
Set_Authorization (procedure)	Return varchar2	This procedure is used with the OWA_CUSTOM package to set the mode of authentication.
Set_Protection_Realm	IN Parameter VARCHAR2	This procedure is to be used in the Authenticate function. It will set a realm to the procedure that has been called. Each realm can have a separate set of users and passwords. When this procedure is called it will ask the user for a username and password for the new realm.

Each package in the DAD that the user calls must have a function called AUTHO-RIZE. Within this function, you must include logic that determines whether the username and password supplied by the user are valid, and returns a false or true Boolean value accordingly. The Authorize function must be called by any procedure in the package that is being executed, in order to authenticate the user properly. Depending on the value returned by the Authorize function, you can continue executing the procedure or halt execution of the procedure.

If you configure the DAD for Per Package authentication mode, and you call a procedure that is part of a package that does not have an authorize function, you will get the following error message:

```
Custom Authentication Failure. [authorize] oerr = 6550
ORA-06550: line 7, column 6:
PLS-00201: identifier 'AUTHORIZE' must be declared
ORA-06550: line 7, column 2:
PL/SQL: Statement ignored
```

Any package that has code that the user wishes to execute will need to have a function with the name "Authorize." This function must be called at the beginning of each procedure.

**UNIT
19.4**

■ *FOR EXAMPLE*

```
CREATE OR REPLACE PACKAGE authen_test IS
    FUNCTION authorize RETURN BOOLEAN;
    PROCEDURE Hello_world;
END;
/
```

The package body is created as follows:

```
CREATE OR REPLACE PACKAGE BODY authen_test IS
FUNCTION authorize RETURN BOOLEAN IS
   v_user       VARCHAR2(10);
   v_password   VARCHAR2(10);
BEGIN
   owa_sec.set_protection_realm('The Realm of Testing');
   v_user := UPPER(owa_sec.get_user_id);
   v_password  := UPPER(owa_sec.get_password);
   IF v_user = 'PREN' AND v_password = 'HALL' THEN
      RETURN TRUE;
   ELSE
      RETURN FALSE;
   END IF;
END authorize;

PROCEDURE hello_world IS
```

```
      v_status BOOLEAN;
BEGIN
   v_status := authorize;
   IF v_status = TRUE THEN
     htp.p('<HTML><BODY>');
     htp.p('Hello World, You have been authorized to use the
     application');
   ELSE
      NULL;
   END IF;
END hello_world;
END authen_test;
```

In the package Authen_Test there are two objects. One is the function, Authorize, and the other is the procedure, Hello_World. The function, Authorize, starts off by calling the Oracle-supplied function, Set_Protection_Realm, within the OWA_SEC package. This procedure takes the name of the realm being set as an IN parameter. When this function is called, it will cause a logon dialog box to appear to the client, and will ask for the username and password for the realm that was just set. In this case, the realm is "The Realm of Testing." The username that was just entered, as well as the password that was passed in, will be captured into the function variables v_user and v_password. This is done by use of the Oracle-supplied functions Get_User_ID and Get_Password in the OWA_SEC package. The Authorize function returns a Boolean value, meaning it will be true if the user passes the authentication test and false if the user fails the test.

In this simple example, the required username and password are hard-coded. The username must be PREN and the password must be HALL in order for the Authorize function to return a value of true. The Authorize function could have performed a more elaborate test instead. If the allowable users and their passwords were stored in a table, then the function could have checked for a valid user and password in this table.

Once you have configured a DAD for Per Package authentication mode, you can test the procedure Hello_World in the Authen_Test package. Name your DAD PPTEST and enter the following URL in your browser:

```
http://server_name/pls/pptest/authen_test.hello_world
```

CUSTOM AND GLOBAL OWA AUTHENTICATION

The Custom OWA authentication and the Global OWA authentication are very similar modes. Both modes of authentication make use of a package, OWA_CUSTOM, which must be customized by the application developer. In the Custom OWA authentication mode, a version of OWA_CUSTOM must be copied from the SYS schema to the DAD user's schema, configured in the DAD. The Global OWA mode uses the OWA_CUSTOM package already located in the SYS schema, otherwise the two methods are identical. In both cases, the OWA_CUSTOM package will execute prior to the execution of any procedure or package. Unlike with Per Package authentication mode, each package will not require its own Authorize function, because the authorization will automatically be directed to an Authorize procedure located within the OWA_CUSTOM package.

The programmer is responsible for customizing the Authorize function. As with the Per Package authentication mode, it will be necessary for the programmer to include logic within the Authorize function to determine whether the user passes authentication. The Boolean value passed back by the Authorize function determines whether the user passes authentication or not.

CUSTOM AND GLOBAL OWA CONFIGURATION

The following steps involve logging on to the database as the DBA. It is important that you do not follow these steps if you do not have DBA experience.

The Custom OWA and the Global OWA authentication methods require the same initial setup. The Custom OWA needs a few additional steps as well. The original code for the SYS.OWA_CUSTOM on your database is as follows:

```
CREATE OR REPLACE
package owa_custom is
    -- If your timezone is not in the list of standard timezones,
    -- then use dbms_server_gmtdiff to give the number of hours
    -- that your database server is ahead (or negative if behind)
    -- Greenwich Mean Time
    dbms_server_timezone constant varchar2(3) := 'PST';
    dbms_server_gmtdiff  constant number       := NULL;
/**********************************************************************/
/*  Global PLSQL Agent Authorization callback function -            */
/*     it is used when PLSQL Agent's authorization scheme is set to  */
/*       GLOBAL or CUSTOM when there is no overriding OWA_CUSTOM package */
/**********************************************************************/
    function authorize return boolean;

end;
/


CREATE OR REPLACE
package body owa_custom is
    /**********************************************************************/
    /*  Global PLSQL Agent Authorization callback function -            */
    /*     It is used when PLSQL Agent's authorization scheme is set to  */
    /*     GLOBAL or CUSTOM when there is no overriding OWA_CUSTOM package.*/
    /*     This is a default implementation. User should modify.         */
    /**********************************************************************/
```

```
function authorize return boolean is
begin
   owa_sec.set_protection_realm('To-be-defined realm');
   return FALSE;
end;
begin /* OWA_CUSTOM package customization */
   /*******************************************************************/
   /* Set the PL/SQL Agent's authorization scheme --                  */
   /*   This should be modified to reflect the authorization needs of */
   /*   your PLSQL Agent                                              */
   /*******************************************************************/
   owa_sec.set_authorization(OWA_SEC.NO_CHECK);
end;
/
```

**UNIT
19.4**

The OWA_CUSTOM procedure will be as in the example above in the SYS schema. In order to make use of the Global OWA or the Custom OWA authentication mode, you must change the lines in the initialization part of the package body, so that the line below:

```
owa_sec.set_authorization(OWA_SEC.NO_CHECK);
```

will become:

```
owa_sec.set_authorization(OWA_SEC.CUSTOM);
```

This can only be done when logged in as SYS, since SYS is the owner of the OWA_SEC package. Once this has been accomplished, you can customize the OWA_SEC.Authorize function. If you are using the Custom OWA authentication mode, log in again as the user, such as STUDENT. In the user's schema you need to create a customized version of OWA_CUSTOM. If you are using the Global OWA method, then you only change the OWA_CUSTOM package in the SYS schema. A test page called Owa_Test.First_Page is created for the purpose of testing. Then a customized version of the OWA_CUSTOM package must be compiled (in the user's schema for Custom OWA mode and in the SYS schema for Global OWA mode).

■ FOR EXAMPLE

```
CREATE OR REPLACE PACKAGE owa_test IS
 PROCEDURE first_page;
END;
/

CREATE OR REPLACE PACKAGE BODY owa_test IS
PROCEDURE first_page IS
BEGIN
 htp.p('<HTML><BODY>');
 htp.p('You are allowed in this realm');
```

```
      http.p('</HTML></BODY>');
   END;
   END;
   /
   CREATE or REPLACE package body OWA_CUSTOM IS
   FUNCTION authorize RETURN BOOLEAN IS
       v_user        VARCHAR2(10);
       v_password  VARCHAR2(10);
   BEGIN
       owa_sec.set_protection_realm('The OWA Testing Realm');
       v_user := UPPER(owa_sec.get_user_id);
       v_password  := UPPER(owa_sec.get_password);
       IF v_user = 'PREN' AND v_password = 'HALL' THEN
          RETURN TRUE;
       ELSE
          RETURN FALSE;
       END IF;
   END authorize;

   BEGIN
    owa_sec.set_authorization(OWA_SEC.CUSTOM);
   END;
   /
```

In the Custom OWA or Global OWA modes, other objects in the OWA_SEC package can be used to retrieve useful information for authentication. OWA_SEC.GET_CLIENT_HOSTNAME can be used to get the hostname for use in the authentication test. Similarly, OWA_SEC.CLIENT_IP_ADDRESS can be used to create an authentication test based on the client's IP address. When using OWA_SEC.CLIENT_IP_ADDRESS, there are a few key points that must be kept in mind. An IP address such as 111.22.33.44 is composed of four sets of numbers. OWA_SEC.CLIENT_IP_ADDRESS will return the IP address in the form of a PL/SQL table. The OWA_UTIL package has a datatype OWA_UTIL.IP_ADDRESS that can be used to hold the value returned by OWA_SEC.CLIENT_IP_ADDRESS. The return value will place each of the four sets of numbers in a row of the PL/SQL table. This allows you to focus easily on a specific component or components of an IP address.

■ *FOR EXAMPLE*

```
CREATE OR REPLACE  package owa_custom is
   function authorize return boolean;
end;
/

CREATE or REPLACE package body OWA_CUSTOM IS
FUNCTION authorize RETURN BOOLEAN IS
   v_user        VARCHAR2(10);
   v_password  VARCHAR2(10);
```

```
v_ip             OWA_UTIL.IP_ADDRESS;
I                NUMBER := 0;
BEGIN
   owa_sec.set_protection_realm('The OWA Testing Realm');
   v_user       := UPPER(owa_sec.get_user_id);
   v_password   := UPPER(owa_sec.get_password);
   v_ip         := owa_sec.get_client_ip;
   IF v_user = 'PREN' AND v_password = 'HALL'
  -- change the next line so the 192 is the beginning of your
  -- IP address
  AND v_ip(1) = 192 THEN
      RETURN TRUE;
   ELSE
      RETURN FALSE;
   END IF;
END authorize;

BEGIN
   owa_sec.set_authorization(OWA_SEC.CUSTOM);
END;
/
```

This example only allows a client with an IP address beginning with 192 to execute any procedure on the given DAD. Additionally, the user must enter the correct username and password when the prompt appears. Be sure to change the IP address to the first three numbers of the IP address of your client test PC.

Create the package OWA_TEST so that you have a simple procedure you can test the authentication mode with. The code for the package is as follows:

```
CREATE OR REPLACE PACKAGE BODY OWA_TEST   IS
PROCEDURE first_page IS
BEGIN
  htp.p('<HTML><BODY>');
  htp.p('You are allowed in this realm');
  htp.p('</HTML></BODY>');
END;

END;
```

Run the procedure from a Web browser using the DAD you have configured for Global OWA authentication mode. If the DAD is named OWA_TEST, then the URL would be

```
http://server_name/pls/owa_test/hello_world
```

The function OWA_SEC.Get_Client_Hostname will return NULL if the configuration of the DAD is not correct. It also relies on DNS lookup to resolve the hostname of the client. If this is not configured properly the hostname returned will always be NULL. It is also possible to get the client IP address in a format of 123.45.67.89 by using the function OWA_UTIL.GET_CGI_ENV(REMOTE_ADDR), which is not dependent on being part of an authentication method in order to function.

ADDITIONAL CUSTOM OWA CONFIGURATION

There are a few additional steps that are required for the Custom OWA configuration. You must first start with the configuration steps that were just mentioned for the Global OWA, but then you must continue with the following steps. In order to continue, you will need to make some modifications to the PL/SQL Web Toolkit procedures owned by SYS. The source SQL files can be found in your Oracle Home with the path $ORACLE_HOME/Apache/modplsql/owa/. The file you will need to modify for this configuration is privowa.sql. Edit the file privowa.sql, and alter the following line (near line 116):

```
auth_scheme := OWA_SEC.NO_CHECK;
```

to

```
auth_scheme := OWA_SEC.CUSTOM;
```

The next step is to log in to the database as user SYS and run the file privowa.sql. Then log in to the database as the schema owner that is used to log on in your DAD that has Custom OWA set as the authentication mode. The OWA_CUSTOM package must be compiled.

**UNIT
19.4**

UNIT 19.5

READ-CONSISTENT UPDATES

DATA CONSISTENCY

When generating Web pages with PL/SQL you cannot use the traditional database locking schemes because HTTP is a stateless protocol. Think about this example. You go to update the information for the instructor, Nina Schorin. You get to the Web page to view her personal information. But then you run out of the room and come back. In this time, another user on another computer updates the zipcode for Nina Schorin. Now you go and try to update her street address, but you just had the old zipcode in your form. The question is: Which version of the zipcode should be saved?

To handle this situation, Oracle provides a PL/SQL package called OWA_OPT_
LOCK that lets you utilize "optimistic locking." Again, since HTTP is a stateless protocol, the row being updated is not actually locked in the database, which is why the locking is "optimistic"—it is not really locking anything at all. Instead, this package provides two methods for determining whether the data was changed by another user since it was painted to your screen.

The first method is to use the OWA_OPT_LOCK procedure to perform a row checksum at the time the screen is painted, and again as the data is being saved. The two checksums can be compared to see if data was changed in the interim. The alternate option would be to capture the current values of the record and place them in hidden form fields in the HTML page. Then, when the form is submitted with the updates, the procedure can make a check first to see if the values stored in the database still match the values captured in the hidden fields. If either method shows that the values do not match, the procedure could abort the update and notify the user that the data has changed since the data was last viewed.

KEEPING A COPY OF THE DATA

This method makes use of the OWA_OPT_LOCK.STORE_VALUES procedure to generate hidden values of the record at the time a SELECT statement is issued. This procedure takes in three IN parameters:

1. p_owner—the owner of the table
2. p_tname—the name of the table
3. p_rowid—the rowid for the record that required locking

The following example generates a Web page that displays the first name and last name of the instructor with an ID value of 103. These values are available for update. All values of the instructor record are stored in hidden form fields.

■ *FOR EXAMPLE*

```
CREATE OR REPLACE PROCEDURE show_inst_store IS
  v_first_name         instructor.first_name%TYPE;
  v_last_name          instructor.last_name%TYPE;
  v_curr_inst          instructor%ROWTYPE;
  v_curr_inst_rowid    ROWID;
BEGIN
  SELECT *
  INTO   v_curr_inst
  FROM   instructor
  WHERE  instructor_id = 103;
  SELECT rowid
  INTO   v_curr_inst_rowid
  FROM   instructor
  WHERE  instructor_id = 103;

  htp.p('<HTML><BODY>');
  htp.FormOpen('modify_inst_store');
  owa_opt_lock.store_values(USER,'instructor',v_curr_inst_rowid);
  htp.TableOpen;
  htp.TableRowOpen;
  htp.FormHidden('p_id',v_curr_inst.instructor_id);
  htp.TableData('Instructor First Name: ');
  htp.TableData(htf.FormText('p_fname','40',
                '40',v_curr_inst.first_name));
  htp.TableRowClose;
  htp.TableRowOpen;
  htp.TableData('Instructor Last Name: ');
  htp.TableData(htf.FormText('p_lname','40',
                '40',v_curr_inst.last_name));
  htp.TableRowClose;
  htp.TableClose;
  htp.FormSubmit;
  htp.FormReset;
  htp.FormClose;
  htp.p('</HTML></BODY>');
END;
```

The above example generates the following Web page:

```
<HTML><BODY>
<FORM ACTION="modify_inst_store" METHOD="POST">
<INPUT TYPE="hidden" NAME="old_instructor" VALUE="Alyce">
<INPUT TYPE="hidden" NAME="old_instructor" VALUE="instructor">
<INPUT TYPE="hidden" NAME="old_instructor" VALUE="AAAIb-
dAABAAAPrfAAC">
<INPUT TYPE="hidden" NAME="old_instructor" VALUE="103">
<INPUT TYPE="hidden" NAME="old_instructor" VALUE="Ms.">
<INPUT TYPE="hidden" NAME="old_instructor" VALUE="Nina">
<INPUT TYPE="hidden" NAME="old_instructor" VALUE="Schorin">
<INPUT TYPE="hidden" NAME="old_instructor" VALUE="210 West
101st Street">
<INPUT TYPE="hidden" NAME="old_instructor" VALUE="10025">
<INPUT TYPE="hidden" NAME="old_instructor" VALUE="2125551212">
<INPUT TYPE="hidden" NAME="old_instructor" VALUE="ESILVEST">
<INPUT TYPE="hidden" NAME="old_instructor" VALUE="02-JAN-99">
<INPUT TYPE="hidden" NAME="old_instructor" VALUE="ESILVEST">
<INPUT TYPE="hidden" NAME="old_instructor" VALUE="02-JAN-99">
<INPUT TYPE="hidden" NAME="old_instructor" VALUE="">
<TABLE >
<TR>
<INPUT TYPE="hidden" NAME="p_id" VALUE="103">
<TD>Instructor First Name: </TD>
<TD><INPUT TYPE="text" NAME="p_fname" SIZE="40" MAXLENGTH="40"
VALUE="Nina"></TD>
</TR>
<TR>
<TD>Instructor Last Name: </TD>
<TD><INPUT TYPE="text" NAME="p_lname" SIZE="40" MAXLENGTH="40"
VALUE="Schorin"></TD>
</TR>
</TABLE>
<INPUT TYPE="submit" VALUE="Submit">
<INPUT TYPE="reset" VALUE="Reset">
</FORM>
</HTML></BODY>
```

The old values of the instructor record are all hidden values of the same name, old_instructor. (**NOTE:** The OWA_OPT_LOCK.STORE_VALUES procedure will create the name with "old_" and then the table name). This form will be submitted to a procedure that must take in all the hidden fields as a PL/SQL table by the name *old_instructor*. The OWA_OPT_LOCK package contains a datatype that can be used to hold a VARCHAR2 PL/SQL table. It is called OWA_OPT_LOCK.VCARRAY. The OWA_OPT_LOCK package contains a function that will verify whether the data has changed. This Boolean function is VERIFY_VALUES. The IN parameter is a PL/SQL table where the first three rows are as follows:

1. The owner of the table
2. The table name
3. The ROWID of the row to be verified

These are in the same order as the output from the STORE_VALUES procedure. So if the old_instructor PL/SQL table from the prior example is submitted to the VERIFY_VALUES function, the return value shows whether the values have been updated. The update procedure would look similar to the following:

```
CREATE OR REPLACE PROCEDURE modify_inst_store
   (old_instructor    owa_opt_lock.vcArray,
    p_id              instructor.instructor_id%TYPE,
    p_fname           instructor.first_name%TYPE,
    p_lname           instructor.last_name%TYPE)    IS
    curr_rowid        ROWID;
BEGIN
    curr_rowid := owa_opt_lock.get_rowid(old_instructor);

    IF (owa_opt_lock.verify_values(old_instructor)) THEN
      UPDATE instructor
        SET first_name    = p_fname,
            last_name     =  p_lname
       WHERE instructor_id = p_id;
      COMMIT;
    ELSE
      htp.p('You cannot update this record because it has
            changed since your query.');
    END IF;
    show_inst_store;
END;
/
```

VERIFY UPDATES WITH A CHECKSUM

The OWA_OPT_LOCK package has a second method for performing a check on data changes before making an update. The concept is the same as in the hidden form field example but the method is very different. To see whether the data changed since it was painted to the screen, this option makes use of a checksum. A checksum is a number calculated from all the bytes stored in the block with a particular ROWID. When data is updated, a checksum performed for the same ROWID will produce a different result. To use this method, calculate the checksum for the ROWID being changed, and store both the ROWID and checksum values in hidden form fields. When these values are sent to the update procedure, calculate the checksum again for the same ROWID, and compare it with the checksum value passed in. If there is no difference, you can proceed with the update. Otherwise, alert the user to the problem.

The procedure CHECKSUM in the OWA_OPT_LOCK package returns a number that is the checksum on the row of data in question. The IN parameters are:

> p_owner—The owner of the table
>
> p_tname—The name of the table
>
> p_rowid—The ROWID of the row under examination

■ FOR EXAMPLE

```
CREATE OR REPLACE PROCEDURE show_inst IS
   v_first_name        instructor.first_name%TYPE;
   v_last_name         instructor.last_name%TYPE;
   v_curr_inst         instructor%rowtype;
   v_curr_inst_rowid   ROWID;
BEGIN
   SELECT *
   INTO   v_curr_inst
   FROM   instructor
   WHERE  instructor_id = 103;
   SELECT rowid
   INTO   v_curr_inst_rowid
   FROM   instructor
   WHERE  instructor_id = 103;

   htp.p('<HTML><BODY>');
   htp.FormOpen('modify_inst');
   htp.FormHidden('p_checksum',
           owa_opt_lock.checksum(USER,'instructor',v_curr_inst_
           rowid));
   htp.FormHidden('p_rowid', v_curr_inst_rowid);
   htp.TableOpen;
   htp.TableRowOpen;
   htp.FormHidden('p_id',v_curr_inst.instructor_id);
   htp.TableData('Instructor First Name: ');
   htp.TableData(htf.FormText('p_fname','40',
                 '40', v_curr_inst.first_name));
   htp.TableRowClose;
   htp.TableRowOpen;
   htp.TableData('Instructor Last Name: ');
   htp.TableData(htf.FormText('p_lname','40',
                 '40',v_curr_inst.last_name));
   htp.TableRowClose;
   htp.TableClose;
   htp.FormSubmit;
   htp.FormReset;
   htp.FormClose;
   htp.p('</HTML></BODY>');
END;
```

The HTML page that is generated should look similar to the following:

```
<HTML><BODY>
<FORM ACTION="modify_inst" METHOD="POST">
<INPUT TYPE="hidden" NAME="p_checksum" VALUE="7897">
<INPUT TYPE="hidden" NAME="p_rowid" VALUE="AAAIbdAABAAAPrfAAC">
<TABLE>
<TR>
<INPUT TYPE="hidden" NAME="p_id" VALUE="103">
<TD>Instructor First Name: </TD>
<TD><INPUT TYPE="text" NAME="p_fname" SIZE="40" MAXLENGTH="40"
VALUE="Nina"></TD>
</TR>
<TR>
<TD>Instructor Last Name: </TD>
<TD><INPUT TYPE="text" NAME="p_lname" SIZE="40" MAXLENGTH="40"
VALUE="Schorin"></TD>
</TR>
</TABLE>
<INPUT TYPE="submit" VALUE="Submit">
<INPUT TYPE="reset" VALUE="Reset">
</FORM>
</HTML></BODY>
```

The update procedure will perform the checksum again and match it with the new checksum. If they are the same the update will be permitted.

```
CREATE OR REPLACE PROCEDURE modify_inst
  (p_checksum IN NUMBER,
   p_rowid    IN rowid,
   p_id       IN instructor.instructor_id%TYPE,
   p_fname    IN instructor.first_name%TYPE,
   p_lname    IN instructor.last_name%TYPE) IS
BEGIN
   IF p_checksum = owa_opt_lock.checksum(
               User, 'INSTRUCTOR', p_rowid)
   THEN
     UPDATE instructor
        SET first_name    = p_fname,
            last_name     = p_lname
      WHERE instructor_id = p_id;
      COMMIT;
   ELSE
      htp.p('You cannot update this record because it has
            changed since your query.');
   END IF;
 show_inst;
 END;
 /
```

If you receive an ORA-00900 error (invalid SQL statement error) with owa_opt_lock.checksum, this is most likely due to a privilege problem. The OWA_OPT_LOCK package resides in the SYS schema (owner of the PL/SQL Web Toolkit). In order to perform the checksum, the schema owner must have privileges to perform a SELECT statement on the table being used. If the toolkit owner has insufficient privileges on this table, the checksum cannot be calculated.

UNIT 19.6

SEARCHING AND REPLACING TEXT

REGULAR EXPRESSIONS

Though PL/SQL's INSTR and SUBSTR functions perform efficient text manipulation, the OWA_PATTERN package provides procedures and functions that perform more complex text manipulation than is possible with their PL/SQL predecessors. Regular expressions make this sophistication possible. A *regular expression* is a string/pattern of characters used to find matches within another string of characters. Chances are you have used a simple regular expression to perform wildcard file searches using commands such as `ls *.txt`, `dir *.txt`, and Oracle's LIKE statement with the wildcard character, %. Additionally, you learned about JavaScript regular expressions in Chapter 14, "JavaScript Form Validation." In these searches, instead of looking for a specific file, you are looking for any file that matches the *.txt* extension. In this case, the regular expression translates to the sentence "Any string of characters that ends in *.txt.*"

You can use regular expressions to create more sophisticated patterns. For example, suppose you want to take some action if any date appears within a string; you do not know its value ahead of time, but instead are only interested in knowing whether it is present. The following test using the INSTR function is not very effective.

■ FOR EXAMPLE

```
IF INSTR (date_string, '09/15/2003')
   OR INSTR (some_string, '09/16/2003')
   OR INSTR (some_string, '09/17/2003')
   OR INSTR (some_string, '09/18/2003') ...
```

What you'd like to achieve is a pattern consisting of three sets of two digits separated by slashes (this book's example assumes the date is always MM-DD-YY.) A regular expression is a compact description that can be used to describe these patterns.

The first part of how a regular expression works defines the different types of characters that can be matched, such as digits, letters, or whitespace characters (new-line characters and tabs). These characters are sometimes referred to as *wild-card tokens* or *atoms,* and they form the basic building blocks on which the expressions are based. The wildcard tokens that can be used in OWA_PATTERN are illustrated in Table 19.4.

The next part of how a regular expression works defines how many characters must appear to constitute a match. For example, you may want to return a match only if there are exactly two consecutive digits. The characters in this set are called the *quantifiers*; the possibilities for them are shown in Table 19.5.

Any of the wildcard tokens, except &, can have its meaning extended by any of the quantifiers. You can also apply these quantifiers to literals.

Table 19.4 ■ Regular Expression Wildcard Tokens

Wildcard Tokens	Matches (Description)
^	Either a new-line character or the beginning of the target string.
$	Either a new-line character or the end of the target string.
\n	A new-line character.
.	Any character except a new-line character.
\t	A tab.
\d	Any digit (0 ... 9).
\D	Any nondigit.
\w	Any alphanumeric character (0 ... 9, a ... z, A ... Z).
\W	Any nonalphanumeric character.
\s	Any whitespace character (space, tab, or new-line).
\S	Any nonwhitespace character.
\b	Word boundary (between \w and \W).
\x*nn*	Character having the hexadecimal value *nn* (i.e., \x20 is a space).
nnn	Character having the octal value *nnn* (i.e., \040 is a space).
c	Any character matching *c* (as long as *c* is not W, s, S, b, or x).
&	This wildcard token applies only to the OWA_PATTERN. CHANGE function (described later in this unit). This token ensures that the string matching the regular expression is included in the string that replaces it. It is different from the other tokens in that it specifies how the target string is to be changed, rather than how it is to be matched.

Table 19.5 ▪ Regular Expression Quantifiers

Quantifiers	Description
?	Exactly 0 or 1 occurrence of a wildcard token.
*	Zero or more occurrences of a wildcard token.
+	One or more occurrences of a wildcard token.
{n}	Exactly *n* occurrences of a wildcard token.
{n,}	At least *n* occurrences of a wildcard token.
{n,m}	At least *n*, but not more than *m*, occurrences of a wildcard token.

Finally, in addition to target strings and regular expression parts, the OWA_PATTERN functions and procedures contain a set of *flags* that are used to control the behavior of the search. Unlike the wildcard tokens and quantifiers, these flags are passed as a separate parameter to control how the various OWA_TEXT procedures behave. The two available flags are shown in Table 19.6.

There are additional special characters that remember the portions of the original string that was matched. The first special character, the ampersand (&) (noted in Table 19.4), can be used during the replace phase of a search and replace operation. The & represents the original pattern found in a match; including it in a replace string recreates the original string of characters that matched the pattern. The second set of special characters is a pair of parentheses. When a portion of a match string is enclosed in parentheses, the subsequent replace operation can remember each parenthesized match. These remembered strings are called *back references* and are stored in an array.

You must supply a regular expression to each function in OWA_PATTERN so that it knows which pattern to search for. Initially, the pattern is stored as a simple VARCHAR2 string. In order to use the expression, however, OWA_PATTERN transforms it into a more useful format. This process converts the regular expression from a VARCHAR2 string into a PL/SQL array, using the following declaration:

```
TYPE pattern IS TABLE OF VARCHAR2(4) INDEX BY BINARY_INTEGER;
```

UNIT 19.6

Table 19.6 ▪ Flags Available in OWA_PATTERN

Quantifiers	Description
i	The search is case-insensitive.
g	Used in the OWA_PATTERN.CHANGE procedure to specify a global search and replace.

Pattern datatypes are initialized by calling a procedure. The procedure used to initialize a pattern is called GET_PAT. This procedure has two parameters. The first is a VARCHAR2 string called "arg" that holds the regular expression to be parsed. The second is a pattern datatype (declared as an IN OUT mode parameter) to hold the resultant parsed pattern.

In addition to GET_PAT, the OWA_PATTERN package contains three other basic functions: MATCH, AMATCH, and CHANGE. In an attempt to match the enormous flexibility of Perl, each function has several overloaded versions that derive from the data structures found in OWA_TEXT. For example, the MATCH function can search either a simple VARCHAR2 string or the more complex OWA_TEXT. MULTI_LINE data structure.

The OWA_TEXT package is not discussed in this book. For a discussion on OWA_TEXT, please consult your Oracle software documentation.

The procedures and functions for this package are outlined in Table 19.7.

The following example, based on the CHANGE procedure, allows you to test the effect of various regular expressions in search and replace operations.

The example procedure, Test_Owa_Pattern, builds an HTML table that is divided into two columns. The first column contains a data entry form with the fields necessary to test the CHANGE procedure. The second column displays the results of the CHANGE procedure when it is executed with the Test_Owa_Pattern procedure's parameters.

This procedure preserves the values entered when the user submits the form. This is accomplished by setting the form's ACTION attribute back to the Test_Owa_

Table 19.7 ■ OWA_PATTERN Procedures and Functions

Procedure/Function	Description
AMATCH	Returns the position of the end of the first regular expression pattern found within a string of text.
CHANGE	Replaces the matched regular expression pattern with a new string of characters.
GET_PAT	Initializes a pattern datatype.
MATCH	Returns a Boolean value indicating whether a regular expression pattern was found inside a text string.

Pattern procedure. When the form is submitted, the procedure reconstructs the form using the input from the previous screen:

```
CREATE OR REPLACE PROCEDURE test_owa_pattern (
    p_line_test   IN OUT VARCHAR2,
    p_from_string IN VARCHAR2 DEFAULT NULL,
    p_to_string   IN VARCHAR2 DEFAULT '<B>&</B>',
    p_flags       IN VARCHAR2 DEFAULT NULL
    )
IS
BEGIN
    htp.p ('<HTML><TITLE>Test OWA_PATTERN</TITLE><BODY>');
    htp.p ('<TABLE BORDER=1><TR><TD>');   -- Used to format the
                                                   results.
    htp.p ('<FORM ACTION="test_owa_pattern"');
    htp.p ('Line:<TEXTAREA NAME=p_line_test>' ||
            p_line_test ||
            '</TEXTAREA><BR>');
    htp.p ('From:<INPUT NAME=p_from_string VALUE="' ||
            p_from_string ||
            '"><BR>');
    htp.p ('To:<INPUT NAME=p_to_string VALUE="' ||
            p_to_string ||
            '"><BR>');
    htp.p ('Flags:<INPUT NAME=p_flags VALUE="' ||
            p_flags ||
            '"><BR>');
    htp.p ('<INPUT TYPE="submit">');
    htp.p ('</FORM></TD><TD>');   -- The results are printed in the
    --                                second column.
    -- Call the change procedure.
    OWA_PATTERN.change (p_line_test, p_from_string, p_to_string,
    p_flags);
    htp.p (p_line_test);
    htp.p ('</TD></TR></HTML>');
END;
```

Though there are four overloaded versions of the OWA_PATTERN.CHANGE function, this version of the CHANGE function returns the number of substitutions made. After the function exits, the p_line_test parameter is updated with the results of the search and replace. Note that the p_to_string parameter's default value uses the assertion character, &. This way, the original value is preserved so that the user may be able to make a visual comparison between the old values and the new values, as a result of the search and replace action, once the Web page is redisplayed.

This discussion on the OWA_PATTERN package is meant to be a brief, introductory overview. For a more extensive discussion on the over 14 overloaded versions of all of OWA_PATTERN's functions and procedures, consult your Oracle software documentation.

 Please visit this book's companion Web site for practice questions and examples provided to further your understanding of the utilities introduced in this chapter. The companion Web site for this book is located at http://www.phptr.com/boardman.

**UNIT
19.6**

C H A P T E R   2 0

WEB APPLICATION ARCHITECTURE

Up to this point, the focus of this book has been on how to create a Web page using PL/SQL, HTML, and JavaScript. The overall architecture of a Web application has not been considered beyond how one Web page relates or communicates with another Web page. For example, this book covers in detail the situation where a Web page with a form must call and pass parameters to a processing procedure. Furthermore, in Chapter 4, "Web Application Design," you learn about things to consider when designing the graphic user interface.

This chapter changes focus and discusses some of the considerations you should take into account when designing a Web application. More questions should be raised than are answered. Coding an application is but one part of a larger process of designing and implementing an application. This chapter attempts to introduce some of the other parts of this process. Note: The term "architecture," as used here, is used in a broad sense and encompasses issues that may not strictly be considered architecture.

UNIT 20.1

DESIGNING CODE STRUCTURES

REUSING CODE

You should be thinking as you design your code architecture of how to avoid code duplication. A good example of code reuse is discussed in Chapter 18, "Web Tips and Techniques." The HTML form code for inserting and updating a student, as well as the JavaScript form validation code, is exactly the same. For insert, the form is empty and the student ID is unknown, while for update, the form fields are prepopulated for the selected student. If the form needs to be changed, then only one procedure has to be changed, in only one place. Whereas, if two separate procedures were created (one for insert and one for update), then the form would have to be revised in two procedures. This increases the chances that something will be done incorrectly when revising the code. Moreover, with each change it is increasingly likely that the two procedures would become inconsistent and handle processing differently.

Other ways to reuse code are by using global variables and constants and templates.

GLOBAL VARIABLES AND CONSTANTS

Global variables and constants can have many uses. Well-designed applications make use of global variables and constants where applicable. A good example of their usefulness is how they can make your Web site more portable when moving from one environment to another. For example, portal Web sites incorporate content from different sources. A Human Resources Portal could reference .pdf forms that are physically located on another Web server. Thus, when creating links to these .pdf forms an absolute path would have to be used instead of the preferred relative path. In other words, if the Human Resources Portal's URL is http://myDomain1/HRSite and the .pdf's URL is http://yourDomain2/pdfForms, then using a relative path reference will not work; that is, <A HREF="/pdfForms/

FormOne.pdf">. The browser will look in the root directory on myDomain1 and not on yourDomain2. Instead, the full, absolute path must be used.

There are potential problems with using the absolute path. If the .pdf forms are moved to another Web server and their subsequent URL is http://theirDomain3/HRForms, all of the links in your Web site that link to any of these forms are now broken. You would then have to search and correct every .pdf link on your Web site. This can be tedious and prone to error.

To avoid this situation use a global constant. Set a global constant with the domain and directory of the .pdf form's Web server. First, create the global constant in a Package header. Then reference it from a procedure.

■ FOR EXAMPLE

```
CREATE OR REPLACE PACKAGE global_constants AS
    /* Declare externally visible constant. */
    url CONSTANT VARCHAR2(30) := 'http://yourDomain2/pdfForms/';
    END;
/
CREATE OR REPLACE PROCEDURE call_global_con
IS
BEGIN
    htp.p('An example of using this is:
    <A HREF="'||global_constants.url||'Form1.pdf">Form 1</A>');
EXCEPTION
    WHEN OTHERS THEN
        htp.p('An error occurred in call_global_con: '||SQLERRM);
END;
/
```

If the .pdf forms are moved to another Web server, then the domain and directory need only be changed in one place.

TEMPLATES

You should carefully look over your Web site for repeating elements that exist on most, if not all, of the Web pages. These repeating elements can be placed in their own procedures/components and included within a template. Not doing this means that the same code will be duplicated many times.

A template is a way of creating a display structure for a Web site. This helps enforce a consistent look and feel, and it makes maintenance and display changes easier to implement. Often there is a main template, and it is broken down into smaller templates, or components. Take, as an example, a typical e-newspaper site. A typical e-newspaper Web site has a top navigation bar, a left navigation bar, a story area, and space for a logo and advertisements. Figure 20.1 shows a screen shot for an imaginary e-newspaper Web site.

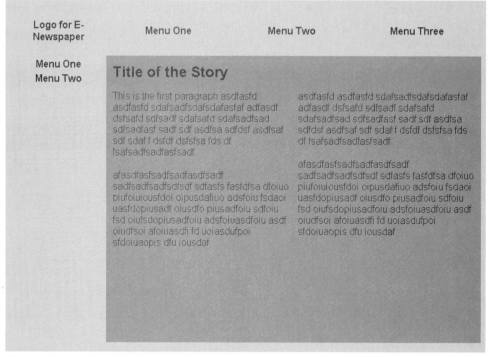

Figure 20.1 ■ Imaginary e-newspaper Web site.

Although this book's application is created using frames, this example uses the nested tables layout that you learn about in Unit 6.2. The majority of Internet sites today do not use frames. However, intranet Web sites do use frames, especially for the type of application created in this book.

Breaking this Web site down to its base components, the Web page looks as it does in Figure 20.2.

Each of these repeating areas becomes a component within the main template. A call to each component is placed in its appropriate location within the template. First, look at the procedure without any components.

■ *FOR EXAMPLE*

```
CREATE OR REPLACE PROCEDURE main_template
AS
BEGIN
htp.p('
<HTML>
<HEAD>
```

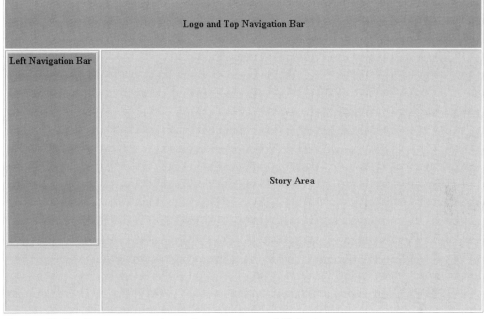

Figure 20.2 ■ **Deconstruction of e-newspaper Web site.**

```
<TITLE>E-Newspaper</TITLE>
</HEAD>
<BODY BGCOLOR="#99CCCC">
<TABLE BORDER="0" WIDTH="100%" HEIGHT="542" BGCOLOR="#99CCCC">
<!--Begin Top Nav Bar-->
  <TR>
    <TD WIDTH="20%" ALIGN="center" HEIGHT="53"><B><FONT
    FACE="Arial">Logo for E-Newspaper</FONT><B></TD>
    <TD WIDTH="80%" ALIGN="center" HEIGHT="53">
      <TABLE BORDER="0" WIDTH="100%">
       <TR>
        <TD WIDTH="33%" ALIGN="center"><FONT FACE="Arial"><B>Menu
        One</B></FONT></TD>
        <TD WIDTH="33%" ALIGN="center"><FONT FACE="Arial"><B>Menu
        Two</B></FONT></TD>
        <TD WIDTH="34%" ALIGN="center"><FONT FACE="Arial"><B>Menu
        Three</B></FONT></TD>
       </TR>
      </TABLE>
    </TD>
  </TR>
<!--End Top Nav Bar-->
  <TR>
    <TD WIDTH="20%" ALIGN="center" HEIGHT="277" VALIGN="top">
<!--Begin Left Nav Bar-->
```

```
    <TABLE BORDER="0" WIDTH="100%">
     <TR>
       <TD ALIGN="center"><FONT FACE="Arial"><B>Menu One</B></FONT>
       </TD>
     </TR>
     <TR>
       <TD ALIGN="center"><FONT FACE="Arial"><B>Menu Two</B></FONT>
       </TD>
     </TR>
    </TABLE>
<!--End Left Nav Bar-->
    </TD>
    <TD ALIGN="left" BGCOLOR="#0099CC" VALIGN="top">
<!--Begin Story Area-->
    <TABLE BORDER="0" WIDTH="100%" CELLSPACING="5" CELLPADDING="5">
     <TR>
       <TD WIDTH="100%" COLSPAN="2"><FONT FACE="Arial"><BIG><BIG>
       <B>Title of the Story</B></BIG></BIG></FONT></TD>
     </TR>
     <TR>
       <TD WIDTH="50%"><FONT FACE="Arial">This is the first para-
       graph asdfasfd asdfasfd
       sdafsadfsdafsdafasfaf adfasdf dsfsafd sdfsadf sdafsafd
       sdafsadfsad sdfsadfasf sadf
         sdf asdfsa sdfdsf asdfsaf sdf sdaf  f dsfdf dsfsfsa fds df
       fsafsadfsadfasfsadf.</FONT><P><FONT FACE="Arial">afasdfasf-
       sadfsadfasdfsadf
       sadfsadfsadfsdfsdf sdfasfs fasfdfsa dfoiuo piufoiuiousfdoi
       oipusdafiuo adsfoiu
       fsdaoi uasfdopiusadf oiusdfo piusadfoiu sdfoiu fsd oiufs-
       dopiusadfoiu adsfoiuasdfoiu asdf
       oiudfsoi afoiuasdfi fd uoiasdufpoi sfdoiuaopis dfu ious-
       daf</FONT></TD>
       <TD width="50%" valign="top" align="left"><FONT FACE="Arial">
       asdfasfd asdfasfd
       sdafsadfsdafsdafasfaf adfasdf dsfsafd sdfsadf sdafsafd
       sdafsadfsad sdfsadfasf sadf
         sdf asdfsa sdfdsf asdfsaf sdf sdaf  f dsfdf dsfsfsa fds df
       fsafsadfsadfasfsadf.</FONT><P><FONT FACE="Arial">afasdfasf-
       sadfsadfasdfsadf
       sadfsadfsadfsdfsdf sdfasfs fasfdfsa dfoiuo piufoiuiousfdoi
       oipusdafiuo adsfoiu
       fsdaoi uasfdopiusadf oiusdfo piusadfoiu sdfoiu fsd oiufs-
       dopiusadfoiu adsfoiuasdfoiu asdf
       oiudfsoi afoiuasdfi fd uoiasdufpoi sfdoiuaopis dfu ious-
       daf</FONT></TD>
     </TR>
    </TABLE>
```

```
<!--End Story Area-->
    </TD>
  </TR>
</TABLE>
</BODY>
</HTML>
');
EXCEPTION
WHEN OTHERS
THEN
   htp.p('An error occurred:  '||SQLERRM||'.  Please try again
   later.');
END;
/
```

Now, take out the top navigation bar, left navigation bar, and main area and put them into their own procedures.

■ *FOR EXAMPLE*

```
CREATE OR REPLACE PROCEDURE top_component AS
BEGIN
htp.p('
    <TR>
     <TD WIDTH="20%" ALIGN="center" HEIGHT="53"><B><FONT
FACE="Arial">Logo for E-Newspaper</FONT><B></TD>
     <TD WIDTH="80%" ALIGN="center" HEIGHT="53">
       <TABLE BORDER="0" WIDTH="100%">
        <TR>
         <TD WIDTH="33%" ALIGN="center"><FONT FACE="Arial"><B>Menu
         One</B></FONT></TD>
         <TD WIDTH="33%" ALIGN="center"><FONT FACE="Arial"><B>Menu
         Two</B></FONT></TD>
         <TD WIDTH="34%" ALIGN="center"><FONT FACE="Arial"><B>Menu
         Three</B></FONT></TD>
        </TR>
       </TABLE>
     </TD>
  </TR>
  ');
EXCEPTION
WHEN OTHERS
THEN
   htp.p('An error occurred:  '||SQLERRM||'.  Please try again
   later.');
END;
/
```

```
CREATE OR REPLACE PROCEDURE left_component AS
BEGIN
htp.p('
  <TABLE BORDER="0" WIDTH="100%">
     <TR>
        <TD ALIGN="center"><FONT FACE="Arial"><B>Menu One</B></FONT>
</TD>
     </TR>
     <TR>
        <TD ALIGN="center"><FONT FACE="Arial"><B>Menu Two</B></FONT>
</TD>
     </TR>
   </TABLE>
  ');
EXCEPTION
WHEN OTHERS
THEN
   htp.p('An error occurred:  '||SQLERRM||'.  Please try again
   later.');
END;
/

CREATE OR REPLACE PROCEDURE story_component AS
BEGIN
htp.p('
 <TABLE BORDER="0" WIDTH="100%" CELLSPACING="5" CELLPADDING="5">
     <TR>
        <TD WIDTH="100%" COLSPAN="2"><FONT FACE="Arial"><BIG><BIG>
        <B>Title of the Story</B></BIG></BIG></FONT></TD>
     </TR>
     <TR>
        <TD WIDTH="50%"><FONT FACE="Arial">This is the first para-
        graph asdfasfd asdfasfd
        sdafsadfsdafsdafasfaf adfasdf dsfsafd sdfsadf sdafsafd
        sdafsadfsad sdfsadfasf sadf
          sdf asdfsa sdfdsf asdfsaf sdf sdaf  f dsfdf dsfsfsa fds df
        fsafsadfsadfasfsadf.</FONT><P><FONT FACE="Arial">afasdfasf-
        sadfsadfasdfsadf
        sadfsadfsadfsdfsdf sdfasfs fasfdfsa dfoiuo piufoiuiousfdoi
        oipusdafiuo adsfoiu
        fsdaoi uasfdopiusadf oiusdfo piusadfoiu sdfoiu fsd oiufs-
        dopiusadfoiu adsfoiuasdfoiu asdf
        oiudfsoi afoiuasdfi fd uoiasdufpoi sfdoiuaopis dfu ious-
        daf</FONT></TD>
        <TD width="50%" valign="top" align="left"><FONT FACE="Arial">
        asdfasfd asdfasfd
        sdafsadfsdafsdafasfaf adfasdf dsfsafd sdfsadf sdafsafd
        sdafsadfsad sdfsadfasf sadf
          sdf asdfsa sdfdsf asdfsaf sdf sdaf  f dsfdf dsfsfsa fds df
```

```
        fsafsadfsadfasfsadf.</FONT><P><FONT FACE="Arial">afasdfasf-
        sadfsadfasdfsadf
        sadfsadfsadfsdfsdf sdfasfs fasfdfsa dfoiuo piufoiuiousfdoi
        oipusdafiuo adsfoiu
        fsdaoi uasfdopiusadf oiusdfo piusadfoiu sdfoiu fsd oiufs-
        dopiusadfoiu adsfoiuasdfoiu asdf
        oiudfsoi afoiuasdfi fd uoiasdufpoi sfdoiuaopis dfu ious-
        daf</FONT></TD>
      </TR>
    </TABLE>
');
EXCEPTION
WHEN OTHERS
THEN
    htp.p('An error occurred:  '||SQLERRM||'.  Please try again
    later.');
END;
/
```

The main template now contains little more than procedure calls to the components. A holding structure for the other templates has been left in the main_template. This gives you more freedom to customize the individual components. Dummy data has been inserted in the story component for now. PL/SQL code to retrieve real data from the database would replace the dummy data.

■ FOR EXAMPLE

```
CREATE OR REPLACE PROCEDURE main_template
AS
BEGIN
htp.p('
<HTML>
<HEAD>
<TITLE>E-Newspaper</TITLE>
</HEAD>
<BODY BGCOLOR="#99CCCC">
<TABLE BORDER="0" WIDTH="100%" HEIGHT="542" BGCOLOR="#99CCCC">
');
top_component;
htp.p('
  <TR>
    <TD WIDTH="20%" ALIGN="center" HEIGHT="277" VALIGN="top">
');
left_component;
htp.p('
    </TD>
    <TD ALIGN="left" BGCOLOR="#0099CC" VALIGN="top">
');
```

```
story_component;
htp.p('
     </TD>
   </TR>
</TABLE>
</BODY>
</HTML>
');
EXCEPTION
WHEN OTHERS
THEN
   htp.p('An error occurred:  '||SQLERRM||'.  Please try again
   later.');
END;
/
```

UNIT 20.2

DESIGNING FOR PERFORMANCE

PERFORMANCE ISSUES

When the Internet was in its infancy, Web pages were comprised mainly of static HTML files stored on a server. When a request came in for a particular page, the Web server would locate the page and send it to the calling browser. This was adequate to meet the expectations of users at that time in terms of content and performance.

Then the Internet experienced explosive growth in the number of users, and users' expectations of the Internet also grew. Static HTML files no longer were sufficient to meet the needs of Web sites and users. For example, users demanded pages with personalized features for shopping, or pages with fresh content that take too long to maintain if static pages are used. So, technology grew and expanded to meet these new expectations. Today, many Web pages are dynamic, just like the Web Toolkit/PSP pages created in this book.

GENERATING A DYNAMIC WEB PAGE

Dynamic Web page generation allows Web developers to create and manage Web sites that would have been impossible before. The procedures created in this book that select data from the database and combine it with HTML and JavaScript are examples of dynamic Web pages. In other words, the content and the presentation are separate. The application server assembles the content and HTML at the time that a request comes in from a Web browser. This separation of content and presentation allow the Web site administrators to more easily maintain the Web site, change the content frequently, and change the look and feel of the Web site.

Dynamic Web pages, however, use a lot of resources and can adversely affect the performance of a Web site. To create one dynamic Web page, a series of actions must be accomplished before the user can view the final Web page. A typical scenario of what happens when a user types in a URL for a Web-enabled PL/SQL procedure, such as http://www.server4.virgil.edu/pls/any/my_procedure, is as follows:

1. Web browser sends URL to DNS server.
2. DNS server converts URL to IP address and sends it back to Web browser.
3. Using the IP address, the Web browser sends the request to the Oracle HTTP server.
4. The HTTP server directs the request to the PL/SQL module since the address path contains "pls."
5. The PL/SQL module parses the request and extracts parameter/header information. The PL/SQL module then queries the database using the database access descriptor (DAD) in the address path.
6. The database executes the PL/SQL procedure, assembles the HTML page, and sends it back to the HTTP server.
7. The HTTP server sends it back to the requesting Web browser.
8. The Web browser receives the HTML pages and begins requests for static embedded files.

The steps detailed above must all occur in order to generate one Web page. This is a high-level look at how a dynamic Web page is created. Each step above could be deconstructed into many more steps. For example, step 5 could be broken down to show all of the steps in querying a database, such as the processes invoked and the memory allocated for various purposes (rollback, etc.). Imagine the overhead cost and use of system resources for a Web site with a 100, 500, or 1,000 hits per hour ratio.

Internet users are notorious for their impatience. If the wait is too long for a page to display, then the user will simply go to another site or page. So, what can be done to help increase performance of Web sites with dynamic page generation?

One solution is a distributed environment that balances the load between servers. This requires the purchase of additional hardware and maintenance, which can become expensive. Another solution is caching.

CACHING

Caching has existed since the early days of the Internet. Caching refers to saving, or caching, a resource. Pages that are cached do not need to be retrieved again. Two early caching solutions are browser caching and proxy caching.

Every Web browser has the functionality to cache Web pages. The cached pages are stored on the user's hard drive. When a user tells the browser to request a resource, such as a page or an image within a page, the browser can first check its cache to see if it already has the resource stored there. If it has the resource in its cache, it can display it quickly, without initiating a new request for it from the server. To the user, the first time a resource is accessed, it would be rendered slowly, but the second time, it would be rendered much more quickly. This is the advantage of browser caching. However, the disadvantage would be when a user does not see the most current version of a resource because it has been updated since the browser cached it. The user's browser settings for caching are important here. Users can turn off caching in the browser, or specify that the cached version should be ignored after a certain period of time.

Proxy caching involves storing the cached pages on a proxy server that sits in between a large number of users and the Internet. The proxy server receives requests for resources from browsers. If the resource being requested is cached in the proxy server, then the proxy server can respond to the browser's request and send the resource. If the browser is requesting a resource that has not been cached by the proxy server, then the proxy server must pass the request for the resource on to the server. Most corporations, as well as most ISPs, have proxies. Some companies will encourage their programmers to quickly visit all of the most important pages in a site when a site is revised—this way, the proxy server caches these pages, and outside visitors to the site will see the pages more quickly. The advantage of proxy servers is that pages that are frequently requested by users are cached in the proxy server, which reduces demands on the main server and speeds the response to the user. The Web developer, however, has little control over these caching solutions, which do not provide adequate solutions to the problem.

Oracle 9iAS Web Cache is a caching solution that acts as a reverse proxy cache. It sits in front of a Web server and stores frequently accessed Web pages. This allows content generation and content delivery to be separated. The application server and database are freed up to generate content (content generation), and the Web Cache takes on the role of serving the content to requesting Web browsers as much as possible (content delivery.)

Web Caching works as follows:

1. A request is received by the Web Cache. Heretofore, the request went directly to the HTTP server.
2. Web Cache checks for whether it has a cached copy of the requested page. If so, then this is called a cache hit. Web Cache serves a copy of the cached page to the Web browser. If not, then this is called a cache miss and the request is sent to the HTTP server.
3. Steps 4, 5, and 6 in the above list are now performed, that is, the request is sent through the PL/SQL gateway/module to the database. The procedure is executed and the HTML page is assembled and sent back to the application and HTTP server. The HTTP server then sends it to Web Cache.
4. Having been previously configured to know which pages are to be cached, Web Cache recognizes this page as one that is to be cached and checks for a cached copy. If no cached copy is found, Web cache caches a copy of the page and sends the page on to the Web browser.
5. The next time this page is requested, Web Cache returns a copy of the cache instead of allowing a new copy to be generated.

Web Cache allows you to determine which pages should be cached. What happens, however, when the content of a cache page changes? Web Cache allows manual invalidation of the cache copy, which can be cumbersome for sites that change content frequently. The cache copy of a page also can be cleared programmatically. Thus, when the content of a page changes, then the code can clear the cache for that content. This prevents large numbers of cache pages being cleared at once.

Another option is to set the cache copy to expire after a predetermined amount of time. This allows you to get the benefits of caching and keep the content fresh without manually invalidating each cache copy. For a site such as an e-newspaper site, the cache could be set to expire every day, or sooner if news is updated more frequently.

What can be cached with Web Cache?

- Static and dynamic HTML
- Image files and other static files
- Personalized page assembly
- Components of a Web page

To get an idea of how a caching strategy can be implemented in a Web site, take the imaginary e-newspaper Web site in Unit 20.1 as an example. There are four separate procedures: main_template, top_component, left_component, and story_component. Each of the three components called from within main_template can be cached and each of them can have different cache clearing rules. The top component may contain the logo and top navigation menu. This may change only two or three times a year. The left component would contain the left navigation menu and may change more frequently, say once a month. And the story component would contain the story. This component would change the most frequently, perhaps once or more times per day.

Thus, the top and left components could be set up for the cache to be cleared either manually or programmatically. The story component could be set up for the cache to be cleared either programmatically or at a specified time interval, say every 4 hours. In the real world, the caching strategy would be more complex than this example. The top, left, and story components could include within themselves other components with their own caching rules.

Caching is a broad and complex subject. This discussion of caching is meant only as an introduction to the subject matter. The caching possibilities for different Web sites will differ depending on the technology available. A caching strategy, however, is necessary for any dynamic Web site. Since implementing a caching strategy has an affect on the design and architecture of a Web site, then it should be considered from the outset and not as an afterthought.

UNIT 20.3

OVERVIEW OF ARCHITECTURE CONSIDERATIONS

UNIT
20.3

GENERAL CONSIDERATIONS

All Web sites have base technology requirements and resources/skill sets requirements in common. The minimum technology required for a Web site is a Web server, users who have access to a Web browser, and the Internet or intranet to connect the two. The minimum skill set for the resources, or coders, is knowledge of HTML. This is all that is required for a Web site with static HTML pages.

Fewer and fewer Web sites today are comprised of purely static HTML pages. Such a Web site is limited in what it can offer to a user. A Web user now expects much more from a Web site, and technology has developed to try and meet these expectations. The technology required for a particular Web site depends on what the Web site is intended to do, or its purpose.

PURPOSE AND CONTENT OF THE WEB SITE

The first thing to consider when planning a Web site is its purpose. This can usually be found in the business specifications, usually produced by a business analyst. The customer and the business analyst work together to create the specifications for the site.

The purpose of the Web site will have some bearing on the architecture. For example, an electronic newspaper Web site will have constantly changing content, and this content will most likely be produced by the customer. So not only will an application be needed to display the content, but an application for the customer to enter the stories into the database will be needed. The site will have to have a mechanism to display stories that are current and ignore stories that are old or have not yet been approved for "publication" to the Web site.

Whereas a Web site for a personnel department may have pages that rarely change and serve only to download forms saved as .pdf files or Word documents. Thus, this site could be static HTML pages with some mechanism for uploading .pdf files to the Web server. This site would also be an Intranet site available to employees of a certain department behind a firewall. The electronic newspaper site would be an Internet site accessible to anyone with a computer and access to the Internet.

Internet applications present greater security risks due to the greater number of people who can access them. If a site is to allow a user to perform DML actions on its underlying database, then security should be incorporated into the design from the very earliest stages, especially if the data being inserted or updated is sensitive or confidential.

TECHNOLOGY AND RESOURCES AVAILABLE

The second thing to consider when designing a Web site is the technology available. The phrase "technology available" does not refer to what is available on the market, but rather what technology you have at your disposal. Designing a Web application with the most cutting-edge technology is very different from designing a Web application and working within the limitations of the technology of your company or client. Oftentimes the greatest architecture challenges arise from trying to get older technology to do things that newer technology easily accomplishes. On the other hand, using new technology simply for the sake of it adds additional challenges and hurdles that may not be necessary.

Another important consideration is the number and qualifications of the resources available to code the application. If the resources are Java developers, then you would not design the application to be created using Web Toolkit. If, on the other hand, the resources were PL/SQL developers, then you would have to further consider the skill set of the resources to determine whether PSPs or Web Toolkit procedures should be used.

TIMELINE

Another factor that affects the architectural design is the timeline for finishing the project. The timeline is tightly intertwined with the previously discussed factors, purpose/content of the Web site, and technology/resources available. If the date for finishing a project is firmly fixed, the other two factors must be adjusted if the project has slipped, that is, more resources must be added to the project, or the scope and functionality of the application must be cut back. In this way the timeline can affect the design.

MAINTENANCE AND FUTURE ENHANCEMENTS

The design should also keep in mind maintenance of the application and future enhancements. While meeting the requirements for the present application is important, it is just as important to design an application that is easy to maintain and lays the groundwork for future enhancements. A customer will usually specify in the business specifications that the design of the site should allow for some kind of future enhancement, such as adaptability to wireless news feeds.

WEB-SPECIFIC CONSIDERATIONS

Web application design and architecture differs from traditional client/server application design and architecture, such as Developer2000 applications, and requires a different perspective.

WEB APPS VS. CLIENT/SERVER APPS

With traditional client/server applications, the developer has more control over the client side of the application. The developer can access every part of the client-side application and effect changes wherever they are desired. This is because the client-side application has to be installed on the user's computer with the user's permission. There are no security issues here. This is analogous to installing a word processing program on your computer.

Furthermore, a client/server application is self-contained; it is used only for the purposes of the application. A Web browser, on the other hand, plays the role of host or intermediary to a Web application. It serves other purposes for the user, and users have the option of configuring many browser settings that are outside of the application's control. The browser software was not created by a Web developer specifically for your application. To give unlimited control of and access to a Web browser to a Web developer would present serious security and privacy issues for the user.

On the other hand, a Web application is easier to maintain in that changes to the Web application need to be deployed only on the server side. Since the client side of a Web application is a browser, then there is nothing to deploy here. With a traditional client/server application, changes or enhancements to the application can require that each client-side installation of the application be upgraded. Not only can this be a tedious and protracted task, but it can be expensive, too.

LIMITATIONS OF WEB APP BROWSERS

There are other limitations with Web browsers besides security issues. These limitations make it more difficult or problematic to develop a Web application. For instance, with most traditional client/server applications, you can control the appearance and text of pop-up messages. If you want the buttons on a confirmation message to say Yes and No, then this is possible.

Achieving the same result with a Web application is more problematic. First, JavaScript does not currently allow a confirmation message to be fully customized. The buttons are OK and Cancel, even though the confirmation message can be customized. VBScript does allow the buttons to be customized, but it is not widely supported by most browsers.

You could create your own pop-up window using JavaScript, that is, window.open, but then you lose the modal functionality of a built-in JavaScript "confirm" message. This means that the main window cannot be accessed until the user clicks either OK or Cancel on the confirm message window. To achieve this same functionality with your own pop-up window would require a lot of coding and testing effort. And in the end it still would not function as well as the built-in JavaScript confirm message.

**UNIT
20.3**

DIFFERENT WEB APP BROWSERS

Another difficulty that can arise is with the different Web browsers that a user may be using. There's Internet Explorer, Netscape, AOL, WebTV Web browsers, among others, not to mention the Macintosh versions. The same Web page can display differently in each of these Web browsers. Therefore, it should be decided from the outset which browsers are to be supported by the Web site. This should also include which versions for each browser are to be supported.

Netscape and Internet Explorer handle tables and form elements in slightly different manners from each other. Extensive testing must be done in both browsers for a Web site that supports both. Other elements of a Web page may be supported in one browser and not in the other. For example, the HTML tag <IFRAME> is supported by the latest versions of Internet Explorer but not by Netscape. So a page using IFRAMES will display properly only in the latest versions of Internet Explorer.

The same is true for JavaScript. Older browser versions do not support all the functionality offered in the latest version of JavaScript. If you use any of the newest JavaScript functionality, then your JavaScript code will not function properly, if at all, in older browser versions. For example, the strictly equality operators === and !== are not available in JavaScript versions earlier than 1.2. JavaScript 1.5 has a function operator that allows you to define an anonymous function within an expression. If a browser that does not support JavaScript 1.5 encounters the function operator in your JavaScript code, then it will fail.

Visit the companion Web site for practice questions on this chapter. The companion Web site for this book can be found at http://www. phptr.com/boardman.

A P P E N D I X   A

STUDENT DATABASE SCHEMA

TABLE AND COLUMN DESCRIPTIONS

COURSE: Information for a course

Column Name	Null	Type	Comments
COURSE_NO	NOT NULL	NUMBER(8, 0)	The unique course number
DESCRIPTION	NULL	VARCHAR2(50)	The full name for this course
COST	NULL	NUMBER(9,2)	The dollar amount charged for enrollment in this course
PREREQUISITE	NULL	NUMBER(8, 0)	The ID number of the course that must be taken as a prerequisite to this course
CREATED_BY	NOT NULL	VARCHAR2(30)	Audit column—indicates user who inserted data
CREATED_DATE	NOT NULL	DATE	Audit column—indicates date of insert
MODIFIED_BY	NOT NULL	VARCHAR2(30)	Audit column—indicates who made last update
MODIFIED_DATE	NOT NULL	DATE	Audit column—date of last update

SECTION: Information for an individual section (class) of a particular course

Column Name	Null	Type	Comments
SECTION_ID	NOT NULL	NUMBER(8,0)	The unique ID for a section
COURSE_NO	NOT NULL	NUMBER(8,0)	The course number for which this is a section
SECTION_NO	NOT NULL	NUMBER(3)	The individual section number within this course
START_DATE_TIME	NULL	DATE	The date and time on which this section meets
LOCATION	NULL	VARCHAR2(50)	The meeting room for the section
INSTRUCTOR_ID	NOT NULL	NUMBER(8,0)	The ID number of the instructor who teaches this section
CAPACITY	NULL	NUMBER(3,0)	The maximum number of students allowed in this section
CREATED_BY	NOT NULL	VARCHAR2(30)	Audit column—indicates user who inserted data
CREATED_DATE	NOT NULL	DATE	Audit column—indicates date of insert
MODIFIED_BY	NOT NULL	VARCHAR2(30)	Audit column—indicates who made last update
MODIFIED_DATE	NOT NULL	DATE	Audit column—date of last update

STUDENT: Profile information for a student

Column Name	Null	Type	Comments
STUDENT_ID	NOT NULL	NUMBER(8,0)	The unique ID for a student
SALUTATION	NULL	VARCHAR2(5)	This student's title (Ms., Mr., Dr., etc.)
FIRST_NAME	NULL	VARCHAR2(25)	This student's first name
LAST_NAME	NOT NULL	VARCHAR2(25)	This student's last name
STREET_ADDRESS	NULL	VARCHAR2(50)	This student's street address
ZIP	NOT NULL	VARCHAR2(5)	The postal zipcode for this student

PHONE	NULL	VARCHAR2(15)	The phone number for this student, including area code
EMPLOYER	NULL	VARCHAR2(50)	The name of the company where this student is employed
REGISTRATION_DATE	NOT NULL	DATE	The date this student registered in the program
CREATED_BY	NOT NULL	VARCHAR2(30)	Audit column—indicates user who inserted data
CREATED_DATE	NOT NULL	DATE	Audit column—indicates date of insert
MODIFIED_BY	NOT NULL	VARCHAR2(30)	Audit column—indicates who made last update
MODIFIED_DATE	NOT NULL	DATE	Audit column—date of last update

ENROLLMENT: Information for a student registered for a particular section of a particular course (class)

Column Name	Null	Type	Comments
STUDENT_ID	NOT NULL	NUMBER(8,0)	The ID for a student
SECTION_ID	NOT NULL	NUMBER(8,0)	The ID for a section
ENROLL_DATE	NOT NULL	DATE	The date this student registered for this section
FINAL_GRADE	NULL	NUMBER(3,0)	The final grade given to this student for all work in this section (class)
CREATED_BY	NOT NULL	VARCHAR2(30)	Audit column—indicates user who inserted data
CREATED_DATE	NOT NULL	DATE	Audit column—indicates date of insert
MODIFIED_BY	NOT NULL	VARCHAR2(30)	Audit column—indicates who made last update
MODIFIED_DATE	NOT NULL	DATE	Audit column—date of last update

INSTRUCTOR: Profile information for an instructor

Column Name	Null	Type	Comments
INSTRUCTOR_ID	NOT NULL	NUMBER(8)	The unique ID for an instructor
SALUTATION	NULL	VARCHAR2(5)	This instructor's title (Mr., Ms., Dr., Rev., etc.)
FIRST_NAME	NULL	VARCHAR2(25)	This instructor's first name
LAST_NAME	NULL	VARCHAR2(25)	This instructor's last name
STREET_ADDRESS	NULL	VARCHAR2(50)	This instructor's street address
ZIP	NULL	VARCHAR2(5)	The postal zipcode for this instructor
PHONE	NULL	VARCHAR2(15)	The phone number for this instructor, including area code
CREATED_BY	NOT NULL	VARCHAR2(30)	Audit column—indicates user who inserted data
CREATED_DATE	NOT NULL	DATE	Audit column—indicates date of insert
MODIFIED_BY	NOT NULL	VARCHAR2(30)	Audit column—indicates who made last update
MODIFIED_DATE	NOT NULL	DATE	Audit column—date of last update

ZIPCODE: City, state, and zipcode information

Column Name	Null	Type	Comments
ZIP	NOT NULL	VARCHAR2(5)	The zipcode number, unique for a city and state
CITY	NULL	VARCHAR2(25)	The city name for this zipcode
STATE	NULL	VARCHAR2(2)	The postal abbreviation for the U.S. state
CREATED_BY	NOT NULL	VARCHAR2(30)	Audit column—indicates user who inserted data
CREATED_DATE	NOT NULL	DATE	Audit column—indicates date of insert
MODIFIED_BY	NOT NULL	VARCHAR2(30)	Audit column—indicates who made last update
MODIFIED_DATE	NOT NULL	DATE	Audit column—date of last update

GRADE_TYPE: Lookup table of a grade type (code) and its description

Column Name	Null	Type	Comments
GRADE_TYPE_CODE	NOT NULL	CHAR(2)	The unique code that identifies a category of grade (e.g., MT, HW)
DESCRIPTION	NOT NULL	VARCHAR2(50)	The description for this code (e.g., Midterm, Homework)
CREATED_BY	NOT NULL	VARCHAR2(30)	Audit column—indicates user who inserted data
CREATED_DATE	NOT NULL	DATE	Audit column—indicates date of insert
MODIFIED_BY	NOT NULL	VARCHAR2(30)	Audit column—indicates who made last update
MODIFIED_DATE	NOT NULL	DATE	Audit column—date of last update

GRADE_TYPE_WEIGHT: Information on how the final grade for a particular section is computed; for example, the midterm constitutes 50%, the quiz 10%, and the final examination 40% of the final grade

Column Name	Null	Type	Comments
SECTION_ID	NOT NULL	NUMBER(8)	The ID for a section
GRADE_TYPE_CODE	NOT NULL	CHAR(2)	The code which identifies a category of grade
NUMBER_PER_SECTION	NOT NULL	NUMBER(3)	How many of these grade types can be used in this section (i.e., there may be three quizzes)
PERCENT_OF_FINAL_GRADE	NOT NULL	NUMBER(3)	The percentage this category of grade contributes to the final grade
DROP_LOWEST	NOT NULL	CHAR(1)	Is the lowest grade in this type removed when determining the final grade? (Y/N)
CREATED_BY	NOT NULL	VARCHAR2(30)	Audit column—indicates user who inserted data
CREATED_DATE	NOT NULL	DATE	Audit column—indicates date of insert
MODIFIED_BY	NOT NULL	VARCHAR2(30)	Audit column—indicates who made last update
MODIFIED_DATE	NOT NULL	DATE	Audit column—date of last update

GRADE:The individual grades a student received for a particular section (class)

Column Name	Null	Type	Comments
STUDENT_ID	NOT NULL	NUMBER(8)	The ID for a student
SECTION_ID	NOT NULL	NUMBER(8)	The ID for a section
GRADE_TYPE_CODE	NOT NULL	CHAR(2)	The code that identifies a category of grade
GRADE_CODE_ OCCURRENCE	NOT NULL	NUMBER(38)	The sequence number of one grade type for one section. For example, there could be multiple assignments numbered 1, 2, 3, etc.
NUMERIC_GRADE	NOT NULL	NUMBER(3)	Numeric grade value (e.g., 70, 75)
COMMENTS	NULL	VARCHAR2(2000)	Instructor's comments on this grade
CREATED_BY	NOT NULL	VARCHAR2(30)	Audit column—indicates user who inserted data
CREATED_DATE	NOT NULL	DATE	Audit column—indicates date of insert
MODIFIED_BY	NOT NULL	VARCHAR2(30)	Audit column—indicates who made last update
MODIFIED_DATE	NOT NULL	DATE	Audit column—date of last update

GRADE_CONVERSION: Converts a number grade to a letter grade

Column Name	Null	Type	Comments
LETTER_GRADE	NOT NULL	VARCHAR(2)	The unique grade as a letter (A, A–, B, B+, etc.)
GRADE_POINT	NOT NULL	NUMBER(3,2)	The number grade on a scale from 0 (F) to 4 (A)
MAX_GRADE	NOT NULL	NUMBER(3)	The highest grade number that corresponds to this letter grade
MIN_GRADE	NOT NULL	NUMBER(3)	The lowest grade number that corresponds to this letter grade
CREATED_BY	NOT NULL	VARCHAR2(30)	Audit column—indicates user who inserted data
CREATED_DATE	NOT NULL	DATE	Audit column—indicates date of insert
MODIFIED_BY	NOT NULL	VARCHAR2(30)	Audit column—indicates who last made update
MODIFIED_DATE	NOT NULL	DATE	Audit column—date of last update

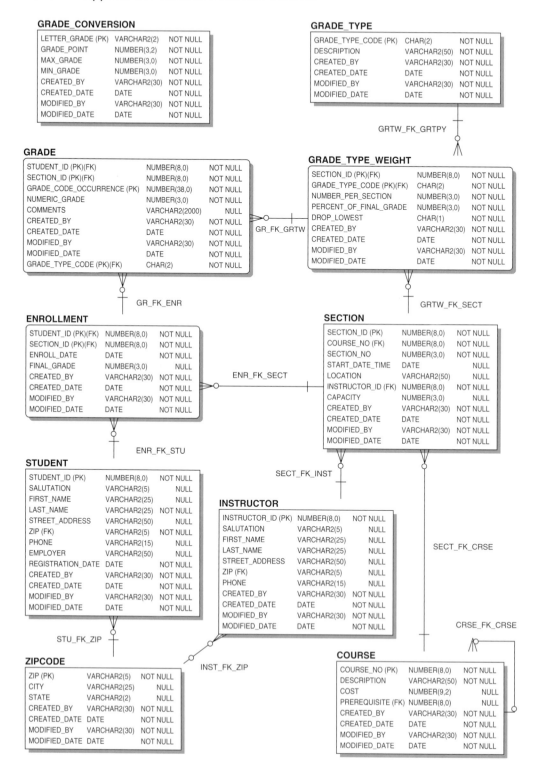

GRADE_CONVERSION

LETTER_GRADE (PK)	VARCHAR2(2)	NOT NULL
GRADE_POINT	NUMBER(3,2)	NOT NULL
MAX_GRADE	NUMBER(3,0)	NOT NULL
MIN_GRADE	NUMBER(3,0)	NOT NULL
CREATED_BY	VARCHAR2(30)	NOT NULL
CREATED_DATE	DATE	NOT NULL
MODIFIED_BY	VARCHAR2(30)	NOT NULL
MODIFIED_DATE	DATE	NOT NULL

GRADE_TYPE

GRADE_TYPE_CODE (PK)	CHAR(2)	NOT NULL
DESCRIPTION	VARCHAR2(50)	NOT NULL
CREATED_BY	VARCHAR2(30)	NOT NULL
CREATED_DATE	DATE	NOT NULL
MODIFIED_BY	VARCHAR2(30)	NOT NULL
MODIFIED_DATE	DATE	NOT NULL

GRTW_FK_GRTPY

GRADE

STUDENT_ID (PK)(FK)	NUMBER(8,0)	NOT NULL
SECTION_ID (PK)(FK)	NUMBER(8,0)	NOT NULL
GRADE_CODE_OCCURRENCE (PK)	NUMBER(38,0)	NOT NULL
NUMERIC_GRADE	NUMBER(3,0)	NOT NULL
COMMENTS	VARCHAR2(2000)	NULL
CREATED_BY	VARCHAR2(30)	NOT NULL
CREATED_DATE	DATE	NOT NULL
MODIFIED_BY	VARCHAR2(30)	NOT NULL
MODIFIED_DATE	DATE	NOT NULL
GRADE_TYPE_CODE (PK)(FK)	CHAR(2)	NOT NULL

GR_FK_GRTW

GRADE_TYPE_WEIGHT

SECTION_ID (PK)(FK)	NUMBER(8,0)	NOT NULL
GRADE_TYPE_CODE (PK)(FK)	CHAR(2)	NOT NULL
NUMBER_PER_SECTION	NUMBER(3,0)	NOT NULL
PERCENT_OF_FINAL_GRADE	NUMBER(3,0)	NOT NULL
DROP_LOWEST	CHAR(1)	NOT NULL
CREATED_BY	VARCHAR2(30)	NOT NULL
CREATED_DATE	DATE	NOT NULL
MODIFIED_BY	VARCHAR2(30)	NOT NULL
MODIFIED_DATE	DATE	NOT NULL

GR_FK_ENR

GRTW_FK_SECT

ENROLLMENT

STUDENT_ID (PK)(FK)	NUMBER(8,0)	NOT NULL
SECTION_ID (PK)(FK)	NUMBER(8,0)	NOT NULL
ENROLL_DATE	DATE	NOT NULL
FINAL_GRADE	NUMBER(3,0)	NULL
CREATED_BY	VARCHAR2(30)	NOT NULL
CREATED_DATE	DATE	NOT NULL
MODIFIED_BY	VARCHAR2(30)	NOT NULL
MODIFIED_DATE	DATE	NOT NULL

ENR_FK_SECT

SECTION

SECTION_ID (PK)	NUMBER(8,0)	NOT NULL
COURSE_NO (FK)	NUMBER(8,0)	NOT NULL
SECTION_NO	NUMBER(3,0)	NOT NULL
START_DATE_TIME	DATE	NULL
LOCATION	VARCHAR2(50)	NULL
INSTRUCTOR_ID (FK)	NUMBER(8,0)	NOT NULL
CAPACITY	NUMBER(3,0)	NULL
CREATED_BY	VARCHAR2(30)	NOT NULL
CREATED_DATE	DATE	NOT NULL
MODIFIED_BY	VARCHAR2(30)	NOT NULL
MODIFIED_DATE	DATE	NOT NULL

ENR_FK_STU

SECT_FK_INST

STUDENT

STUDENT_ID (PK)	NUMBER(8,0)	NOT NULL
SALUTATION	VARCHAR2(5)	NULL
FIRST_NAME	VARCHAR2(25)	NULL
LAST_NAME	VARCHAR2(25)	NOT NULL
STREET_ADDRESS	VARCHAR2(50)	NULL
ZIP (FK)	VARCHAR2(5)	NOT NULL
PHONE	VARCHAR2(15)	NULL
EMPLOYER	VARCHAR2(50)	NULL
REGISTRATION_DATE	DATE	NOT NULL
CREATED_BY	VARCHAR2(30)	NOT NULL
CREATED_DATE	DATE	NOT NULL
MODIFIED_BY	VARCHAR2(30)	NOT NULL
MODIFIED_DATE	DATE	NOT NULL

INSTRUCTOR

INSTRUCTOR_ID (PK)	NUMBER(8,0)	NOT NULL
SALUTATION	VARCHAR2(5)	NULL
FIRST_NAME	VARCHAR2(25)	NULL
LAST_NAME	VARCHAR2(25)	NULL
STREET_ADDRESS	VARCHAR2(50)	NULL
ZIP (FK)	VARCHAR2(5)	NULL
PHONE	VARCHAR2(15)	NULL
CREATED_BY	VARCHAR2(30)	NOT NULL
CREATED_DATE	DATE	NOT NULL
MODIFIED_BY	VARCHAR2(30)	NOT NULL
MODIFIED_DATE	DATE	NOT NULL

SECT_FK_CRSE

CRSE_FK_CRSE

STU_FK_ZIP

INST_FK_ZIP

ZIPCODE

ZIP (PK)	VARCHAR2(5)	NOT NULL
CITY	VARCHAR2(25)	NULL
STATE	VARCHAR2(2)	NULL
CREATED_BY	VARCHAR2(30)	NOT NULL
CREATED_DATE	DATE	NOT NULL
MODIFIED_BY	VARCHAR2(30)	NOT NULL
MODIFIED_DATE	DATE	NOT NULL

COURSE

COURSE_NO (PK)	NUMBER(8,0)	NOT NULL
DESCRIPTION	VARCHAR2(50)	NOT NULL
COST	NUMBER(9,2)	NULL
PREREQUISITE (FK)	NUMBER(8,0)	NULL
CREATED_BY	VARCHAR2(30)	NOT NULL
CREATED_DATE	DATE	NOT NULL
MODIFIED_BY	VARCHAR2(30)	NOT NULL
MODIFIED_DATE	DATE	NOT NULL

A P P E N D I X   B

PL/SQL FORMATTING GUIDE

PL/SQL CODE NAMING CONVENTIONS AND FORMATTING GUIDELINES

CASE

PL/SQL, like SQL, is case-insensitive. The general guidelines here are as follows:

- Use uppercase for keywords (BEGIN, EXCEPTION, END, IF THEN ELSE, LOOP, END LOOP, etc.), datatypes (VARCHAR2, NUMBER), built-in functions (LEAST, SUBSTR, etc.), and user-defined subroutines (procedures, functions, packages).
- Use lowercase for variable names as well as column and table names in SQL.

WHITE SPACE

White space (extra lines and spaces) is as important in PL/SQL as it is in SQL. It is a main factor in providing readability. In other words, you can reveal the logical structure of the program by using indentation in your code. Here are some suggestions:

- Put spaces on both sides of an equality sign or comparison operator.
- Line up structure words on the left (DECLARE, BEGIN, EXCEPTION, and END, IF and END IF, LOOP and END LOOP, etc.). In addition, indent three spaces (use the spacebar, not the tab key) for structures within structures.
- Put blank lines between major sections to separate them from each other.
- Put different logical parts of the same structure on a separate lines even if the structure is short. For example, IF and THEN are placed on one line, while ELSE and END IF are placed on separate lines.

NAMING CONVENTIONS

To ensure against conflicts with keywords and column/table names, it is helpful to use the following prefixes:

- `v_variable_name`
- `con_constant_name`
- `i_in_parameter_name, o_out_parameter_name, io_in_out_parameter_name`
- `c_cursor_name` or `name_cur`
- `rc_reference_cursor_name`
- `r_record_name` or `name_rec`

  `FOR r_stud IN c_stud LOOP...`

  `FOR stud_rec IN stud_cur LOOP`
- `type_name, name_type` (for user-defined types)
- `t_table, name_tab` (for PL/SQL tables)
- `rec_record_name, name_rec` (for record variables)
- `e_exception_name` (for user-defined exceptions)

The name of a package should be the name of the larger context of the actions performed by the procedures and functions contained within the package.

The name of a procedure should be the action description that is performed by the procedure. The name of a function should be the description of the return variable.

■ FOR EXAMPLE

```
PACKAGE student_admin
   -- admin suffix may be used for administration.

   PROCEDURE remove_student
      (i_student_id IN student.studid%TYPE);

   FUNCTION student_enroll_count
      (i_student_id student.studid%TYPE)
   RETURN INTEGER;
```

COMMENTS

Comments in PL/SQL are as important as in SQL. They should explain the main sections of the program and any major nontrivial logic steps.

Use single-line comments "--" instead of the multiline "/*" comments. While PL/SQL treats these comments in the same way, it will be easier for you to debug the code once it is completed because you cannot embed multiline comments within multiline comments. In other words, you are able to comment out portions of code that contain single-line comments, and you are unable to comment out portions of code that contain multiline comments.

OTHER SUGGESTIONS

- For SQL statements embedded in PL/SQL, use the same formatting guidelines to determine how the statements should appear in a block.
- Provide a comment header that explains the intent of the block, lists the creation date and author's name, and have a line for each revision with the author's name, date, and the description of the revision.

■ FOR EXAMPLE

The following example shows the aforementioned suggestions. Notice that it also uses a monospaced font (Courier) that makes the formatting easier. Proportional spaced fonts can hide spaces and make lining up clauses difficult. Most text and programming editors by default use a monospace font.

```
REM *********************************************************
REM * filename: coursediscount01.sql              version: 1
REM * purpose:  To give discounts to courses that have at
REM *           least one section with an enrollment of more
REM *           than 10 students.
REM * args:     none
REM *
REM * created by:  s.tashi        date: January 1, 2000
REM * modified by: y.sonam        date: February 1, 2000
REM * description: Fixed cursor, added indentation and
REM *              comments.
REM *********************************************************
DECLARE
   -- C_DISCOUNT_COURSE finds a list of courses that have
   -- at least one section with an enrollment of at least 10
   -- students.
   CURSOR c_discount_course IS
      SELECT DISTINCT course_no
        FROM section sect
       WHERE 10 <= (SELECT COUNT(*)
                      FROM enrollment enr
                     WHERE enr.section_id = sect.section_id
                   );

   -- discount rate for courses that cost more than $2000.00
   con_discount_2000 CONSTANT NUMBER := .90;
```

```
    -- discount rate for courses that cost between $1001.00
    -- and $2000.00
    con_discount_other CONSTANT NUMBER := .95;

    v_current_course_cost course.cost%TYPE;
    v_discount_all NUMBER;
    e_update_is_problematic EXCEPTION;
BEGIN
    -- For courses to be discounted, determine the current
    -- and new cost values
    FOR r_discount_course in c_discount_course LOOP
        SELECT cost
          INTO v_current_course_cost
          FROM course
         WHERE course_no = r_discount_course.course_no;

        IF v_current_course_cost > 2000 THEN
           v_discount_all := con_discount_2000;
        ELSE
           IF v_current_course_cost > 1000 THEN
              v_discount_all :=  con_discount_other;
           ELSE
              v_discount_all := 1;
           END IF;
        END IF;

        BEGIN
           UPDATE course
              SET cost = cost * v_discount_all
            WHERE course_no = r_discount_course.course_no;
        EXCEPTION
           WHEN OTHERS THEN
              RAISE e_update_is_problematic;
        END;    -- end of sub-block to update record
    END LOOP; -- end of main LOOP

    COMMIT;

EXCEPTION
    WHEN e_update_is_problematic THEN
        -- Undo all transactions in this run of the program
        ROLLBACK;
        DBMS_OUTPUT.PUT_LINE
            ('There was a problem updating a course cost.');
    WHEN OTHERS THEN
        NULL;
END;
/
```

A P P E N D I X   C

HTML FORMATTING GUIDE

HTML CODE NAMING CONVENTIONS AND FORMATTING GUIDELINES

CASE

HTML, like PL/SQL, is case-insensitive. The guideline here is to use upper case for tags and tag attributes and use lower case for tag attribute values.

WHITE SPACE AND QUOTES

White space (extra lines and spaces) is as important in HTML as it is in PL/SQL. It provides the main readability factor. Put double quotes around all attribute values, whether the value contains a space or not.

Suggestion: Line up opening and closing tags (<HTML>, <BODY>, etc.) on the left. Indent 3 spaces (use the spacebar, not the tab key) for structures within structures, such as table rows within a table and table cells within table rows. Put each part of the structure on a new line.

NAMING CONVENTIONS

In the context of this book naming in HTML has a twofold purpose: 1) names of form elements become IN parameters in the processing procedure and 2) names of form elements, forms, images, and so on are used by JavaScript to access those objects. Thus, names of form elements must be the same as the IN parameters for a processing procedure and follow the PL/SQL naming standards for naming parameters.

```
p_parameter_name
formName_form
```

It is recommended that buttons not be named unless absolutely necessary.

COMMENTS

Comments are equally as important in HTML as in PL/SQL. Comments should explain the main sections of the program and any major logic that is involved.

■ FOR EXAMPLE

The following example shows the suggestions above. Notice that it also uses a monospaced font (Courier) which makes the formatting easier. Proportional spaced fonts can hide spaces and make lining up clauses difficult. Most text and programming editors by default use monospace font.

```
<HTML>
<HEAD>
<TITLE>E-Newspaper</TITLE>
</HEAD>
<BODY BGCOLOR="#99CCCC">
<TABLE BORDER="0" WIDTH="100%" HEIGHT="542"
BGCOLOR="#99CCCC">
<!--Begin Top Nav Bar—>
  <TR>
    <TD WIDTH="20%" ALIGN="center" HEIGHT="53"><B><FONT
    FACE="Arial">Logo for E-Newspaper</FONT><B></TD>
    <TD WIDTH="80%" ALIGN="center" HEIGHT="53">
      <TABLE BORDER="0" WIDTH="100%">
       <TR>
        <TD WIDTH="33%" ALIGN="center"><FONT
        FACE="Arial"><B>Menu One</B></FONT></TD>
        <TD WIDTH="33%" ALIGN="center"><FONT
        FACE="Arial"><B>Menu Two</B></FONT></TD>
        <TD WIDTH="34%" ALIGN="center"><FONT
        FACE="Arial"><B>Menu Three</B></FONT></TD>
       </TR>
      </TABLE>
    </TD>
  </TR>
<!--End Top Nav Bar-->
  <TR>
    <TD WIDTH="20%" ALIGN="center" HEIGHT="277"
    VALIGN="top">
<!--Begin Left Nav Bar-->
      <TABLE BORDER="0" WIDTH="100%">
       <TR>
        <TD ALIGN="center"><FONT FACE="Arial"><B>Menu
        One</B></FONT></TD>
       </TR>
       <TR>
        <TD ALIGN="center"><FONT FACE="Arial"><B>Menu
        Two</B></FONT></TD>
```

```
        </TR>
      </TABLE>
<!--End Left Nav Bar-->
      </TD>
      <TD ALIGN="left" BGCOLOR="#0099CC" VALIGN="top">
<!--Begin Story Area-->
        <TABLE BORDER="0" WIDTH="100%" CELLSPACING="5"
        CELLPADDING="5">
        <TR>
          <TD WIDTH="100%" COLSPAN="2"><FONT
          FACE="Arial"><BIG><BIG><B>Title of the
          Story</B></BIG></BIG></FONT></TD>
        </TR>
        <TR>
          <TD WIDTH="50%"><FONT FACE="Arial">This is the
          first paragraph asdfasfd asdfasfd</FONT>
          </TD>
        </TR>
      </TABLE>
<!--End Story Area-->
      </TD>
    </TR>
  </TABLE>
  </BODY>
  </HTML>
```

INDEX

741

informIT

YOUR GUIDE TO IT REFERENCE

Articles

Keep your edge with thousands of free articles, in-depth features, interviews, and IT reference recommendations – all written by experts you know and trust.

Online Books

Answers in an instant from **InformIT Online Book's** 600+ fully searchable on line books. Sign up now and get your first 14 days **free**.

POWERED BY

Safari

Catalog

Review online sample chapters, author biographies and customer rankings and choose exactly the right book from a selection of over 5,000 titles.

Prentice Hall PTR   InformIT   InformIT Online Books   Financial Times Prentice Hall   ft.com   PTG Interactive   Reuters

PRENTICE HALL PTR

TOMORROW'S SOLUTIONS FOR TODAY'S PROFESSIONALS

Prentice Hall **Professional Technical Reference**

Browse | Book Series | What's New | User Groups | Alliances | Special Sales | Contact Us

Search | Help | Home

Quick Search

PTR Favorites

Find a Bookstore

Book Series

Special Interests

Newsletters

Press Room

International

Best Sellers

Solutions Beyond the Book

Shopping Bag

Keep Up to Date with

PH PTR Online

We strive to stay on the cutting edge of what's happening in professional computer science and engineering. Here's a bit of what y...

What ... PHPTR? We don't just publish books for the professional community, we're a part of it. Check out our convention schedule, keep up with your favorite authors, and get the latest reviews and press releases on topics of interest to you.

Special interest areas offering our latest books, book series, features of the month, related links, and other useful information to help you get the job done.

User Groups Prentice Hall Professional Technical Reference's User Group Program helps volunteer, not-for-profit user groups provide their members with training and information about cutting-edge technology.

Companion Websites Our Companion Websites provide valuable solutions beyond the book. Here you can download the source code, get updates and corrections, chat with other users and the author about the book, or discover links to other websites on this topic.

Need to find a bookstore? Chances are, there's a bookseller near you that carries a broad selection of PTR titles. Locate a Magnet bookstore near you at www.phptr.com.

Subscribe today! **Join PHPTR's monthly email newsletter!** Want to be kept up-to-date on your area of interest? Choose a targeted category on our website, and we'll keep you informed of the latest PHPTR products, author events, reviews and conferences in your interest area.

Visit our mailroom to subscribe today! **http://www.phptr.com/mail_lists**